CD START INSTRUCTIONS

1 Place the CD-ROM in your CD-ROM drive.

2 Launch your Web browser. *See below if you do not have a Web browser.

3 From your Web browser, select Open File from the File menu. Select the CD-ROM (usually drive D for PCs and the Desktop for Macs), then select the file called Welcome.htm.

* We have included the Microsoft Web browser Internet Explorer on this CD in case you do not have a browser or would like to upgrade or change your browser. Please review the CD-ROM appendix of this book for more information on this software as well as other software on this CD.

MINIMUM SYSTEM REQUIREMENTS

Designed to work on both Macintosh and Windows operating systems

Macintosh

Computer: 68030
Memory: 8MB of RAM
Platform: System 7.0 or higher
Software: Web browser
Hardware: 2X CD-ROM Drive

Windows

Computer: 386 IBM PC-compatible
Memory: 8MB of RAM
Platform: Windows 3.1, NT or 95
Software: Web browser
Hardware: 2X CD-ROM Drive

Senior *Net's*

Official Guide to the Web

Senior *Net's*

Official Guide to the Web

Eugenia Johnson

and

Kathleen McFadden

Lycos Press
An imprint of Macmillan Computer Publishing USA
Emeryville, California

Publisher	**Joe Wikert**
Associate Publisher	**Juliet Langley**
Publishing Director	**Cheryl Applewood**
Acquisitions Editor	**Kenyon Brown**
Development Editor	**Katharine English**
Copy Editor	**Katharine English**
Production Editors	**Barbara Dahl and Edith Rex**
Proofreader	**Jeff Barash**
Cover Illustration, Design	**Bay Graphics**
Book Design and Layout	**Bruce Lundquist**
Software Specialist	**Stephen DeLacy**

Lycos Press books are developed as a joint effort of Lycos and Que. They are published by Macmillan Computer Publishing USA, a Simon & Schuster Company.

Lycos ™ is a trademark of Carnegie Mellon University.

Lycos Press imprint books are produced on a Macintosh computer system with the following applications: FrameMaker®, Microsoft® Word, QuarkXPress®, Adobe Illustrator®, Adobe Photoshop®, Adobe Streamline™, MacLink®Plus, Aldus® FreeHand™, Collage Plus™.

Lycos Press, an imprint of
Macmillan Computer Publishing USA
5903 Christie Avenue
Emeryville, CA 94608
http://www.mcp.com/lycos

ISBN 0-78971-069-2

Manufactured in the United States of America

10 9 8 7 6 5 4 3 2

This book is dedicated to Katharine, without whose continued encouragement and persistent flogging it would never have seen the light of day.

—*Eugenia "Tin Lizzie" Johnson*

This book is gratefully dedicated to Steve Ellis, "a fellow of infinite jest, of most excellent fancy," who makes life so much more interesting.

—*Kathleen McFadden*

Foreword   xiii

Preface   xv

Acknowledgments   xvii

About Lycos, Inc.   xix

CHAPTER 1: THE BIG BUY   1

Drivin' Miss Ruby   1

Shoppin' Around   1

The Biggest Honker on the Block   1

A Little Techno-Babble   3

Hard as a Rock   3

The Dark Side   4

Zipidee-Doo-Dah   4

Rev Up the Throttle   5

Gather Together   5

Wishbooks and Dreams   5

Buried Alive   6

Those Wonderful Mags   6

Read On, MacDuff   7

Goodies Galore   7

Getting Hooked Up
(Or Just Getting Hooked)   8

The Muscle Tussle   8

Roils and Coils and Wriggly Things   8

Disorderly Disarray   9

At the End of the Tunnel   9

Changing and Rearranging   9

Bytes and Sites for Neophytes   10

Books for Beginners   10

More Sites to Excite or Incite   11

CHAPTER 2: NEW COMPUTERS, NEW CONNECTIONS   15

Let's Get Going   15

Modems, Shmodems
(And Getting a Little Damp)   15

Streaking Along   15

Dialing in and Getting On With It   16

It's Your Purse!   16

Use It or Lose It!   17

So Dive In!   17

Just for Starters: The Big Boys   17

Hooking Up Can Be Hard to Do   18

The Other Guys   18

Some National Internet Service Providers
(ISPs)   18

More Help Is on the Way!   21

Going, Going, Gone   21

Not Quite!   21

There's More to Come   22

PPP   22

The New P.O.   22

Browsin' an' Carousin'   23

Digging Around   23

Download, Download, Download!   24

Additional Online Help   24

Duh!   25

More Internet Access Providers   25

When You're Looking for Something More,
Let Your Keyboard Do the Walking   26

The Chatting Masses   26

Palaver and Prattle   26

Yakkity-Yak   27

It Takes a Global Village   28

Lurk, Don't Lurch   28

Do Yak Back   28

Mind Your Manners   28

A Few BBSs and Chat Resources   29

For the Totally Confused   30

The Whole Enchilada   30

The Search Is On   30

If You Crave a Little Extra...   33

Tools for Fools   33

Browsers   33

Goodies Galore   34

So Join Us   34

CHAPTER 3: SIMPLY SENIOR   37

In the Beginning   37

Partnerships   37

And Grants   38

Learning   38

Let There Be Light!   39

SeniorNet on AOL   39

SeniorNet on the World Wide Web   43

Become a Member   46

SeniorNetters' Own Web Sites   46

Strength in Numbers   47

Hats Off!   48

Make a Wave!   48

Stand Up and Be Counted!   48

Move It and Shake It   49

Open Sesame   49

Simply Senior Web Sites   50

CHAPTER 4: A TOUCH OF CLASS   59

Architecture   59

It's Greek to Me   59

City Lights   60

Art on the Web   68

Virtual Collections   68

Galleries and Museums   72

Not Least   77

CHAPTER 5: THE WELL OF CIVILIZATION   79

History   79

Reminiscences   79

The Big One   80

And Recollections   80

And Then There's Harry   80

Best History Sites   82

Literature   90

A Little Light Reading   90

For Your Review   93

Poetry   93

A Little Help From Your Friends   96

Museums   96

Philosophy and Religion   102

A Selection of Philosophy Sites   102

And Now for a Look at Religion   106

CHAPTER 6: BANKROLLS AND BUCKS   113

Money Is the Root   113
   In the Pot   113
   The Color of Money   113
   The Rules of the Road   114
   Plastic Pockets   114
   Banking and Personal Finance Resources on the WWW   115

Investor Wake-Up Call   119
   Heaps upon Heaps   119
   Investing and Investments Online   120

The Right Stuff   122
   Glass Slippers Do Break   122
   Insurance-Related Sites   123

CHAPTER 7: HOME IS WHERE THE HEART IS   127

What Now?   127
   Smaller and Smaller   127
   Three Times Is the Charm   127

Don't Trip over the Sill   127
   Buying   128
   Selling   133

New Escapades   137

CHAPTER 8: ENTREPRENEURIAL YOU   139

A Diller, A Dollar   139
   I'll Have Mine with Catsup...This Year   140
   Giggles and Gaggles   140

The Belly of the Ball   140
And Pull Out a Plum   140
For Sheer Chutzpah   141
Balloons and Whistles   141
Becoming a Postretirement Entrepreneur   141

Let the Fresh Air In   153
   Just For You   153
   Water Your Garden and Watch It Grow   153
   Worry Warts   153
   Opportunities—Small Businesses and Franchises   153

Home Bodies   154
   The High Hurdles   155
   Take a Break   155

CHAPTER 9: YOU'RE NEVER TOO OLD TO LEARN   159

The Mind Is a Terrible Thing to Waste   159
   The Games Have Got It   160
   Jack Be Nimble   160

A Bigger Game   161
   Learning Resources Worldwide   162

CHAPTER 10: GOOFING OFF (OR JUST PLAIN HAVING FUN)   173

Tomes and Opuses—Turn the Page Slowly   173
   Books on the Web   173

A Little Toe Tapping, Maestro   177

Cooking, Crafting, and Living   178

Marvelous Martha   178

Sweet Peas   179

It's *Not* a Good Thing?   179

Martha Stewart Disease   179

Domestic Domination   180

Martha Notwithstanding...   180

NetFood: Cooking In and Dining Out   180

Diggin' in The Dirt   187

Gardening Sites   187

The Virtual Hobbyist   189

Hobbies Galore   190

Hollywood, Here I Come   195

Movie Webbing   196

The Blues You Can Use   198

Music Sites   200

Our Best Friends   206

Dog Daze   206

Making Rounds   207

A Member of the Family   208

Pet Stuff   208

CHAPTER 11: BIG BROTHER ... WATCHING OVER YOU?   211

Executive Branch   212

The President and Vice President   212

The President's Cabinet   212

Packing a Heater   213

And Now for Something Completely Different...   214

Selected Cabinet Agencies   215

Taxed to the Max   216

On With the Cabinets   220

Judicial Branch   221

Legislative Branch—Senate and House of Representatives   221

In a Class by Themselves—Independent Federal Agencies   222

Federal Documents and Other Info Sources   224

State and Tribal Government Sites   225

Individual State Pages   225

Multistate Resources   227

Tribal Government Sites   228

CHAPTER 12: TO YOUR HEALTH!   231

Snare the Care   231

Doctor, Doctor!   232

In Search of the Country Doc   233

Where Is SuperDoc?   233

Well, Well, Well!   235

But What if I'm Really Sick?   240

Medical Centers and Hospitals   245

Professional Home Care, Hospice, and Family Caregivers   247

A Selection of Medical Reference Materials   247

CHAPTER 13: MEET THE MEDIA   251

All for One and One for All   251

Magazines   252

Newspapers and Wire Services 256

Your Quick Link List to Favorite U.S. Papers Online 258

Your Quick Link List to Other Favorite English Language Papers Online 259

Radio and Television 259

CHAPTER 14: ROADS LESS TRAVELED 265

Written in the Stars, or ...? 265

Conspiracies, Crimes, Hoaxes, and Inquiring Minds 265

I See a Tall, Dark, Handsome Future in Your Man ..., er ... 268

Your House or Mine? 268

Deal the Cards! 268

Tough Tarot 269

Provinces of the Mind and States of Consciousness 271

Spiritual, Mystical, and Other Soulful Matters 273

UFOs, Their Drivers, and Other Mysterious Creatures 277

Drop in Any Time 277

CHAPTER 15: THE WONDERS OF SCIENCE 283

Probing the Red Planet 283

Once a Dunce 284

Flub-a-Dub-Dub 284

The Brew of Champions 284

Wars WITH the Stars 285

Them Bones 285

Pulling the Plug 285

The Many Facets of Science 286

Cosmic Wonders 286

Helpful Sites for the Amateur Sky Gazer 288

Archaeology and Paleontology 289

General Science and Ecology 290

CHAPTER 16: SHOP 'TIL YOU DROP 299

The Cart before the Horse 299

Piling down the Aisle 299

End Shopping Pain 300

Hello!, Noah 300

Keep 'Em Rollin' 300

A Shopper's Dream 300

Hassle-Free 300

Whee! It's Free! 302

Stuff for Free 302

Enough Already! 304

Voice Mail from Hell 304

Be a Bulldog 304

Lots Better Than the Mall 305

Major Retailers and Catalogers 305

Online Shopping Malls and Catalog Shopping Outlets 308

Specialty Shops 310

CHAPTER 17: CITIZENRY AND COMMUNITY, ISSUES AND AFFAIRS   317

What's Wrong with This Picture?   317

Uncle Sam Wants You!   317

Back to Basics   318

What's the Answer?   319

Hot-Button Issues   320

Something Borrowed, Something Blue   320

Capital Punishment   321

The Communications Decency Act   322

Making Your Voice Heard and Your Efforts Count   324

Animal Rights   324

Child Advocacy   325

Civil Liberties and Civic Responsibility   326

The Environment   327

Humanitarian Organizations   328

Specifically for Seniors   329

CHAPTER 18: TAKE ME OUT TO THE BALL GAME   333

Couch Potatoes au Gratin   333

Geronimo!   333

The Sport of Kings   333

The Handicap   334

Place Your Bets!   334

Older and Bolder   336

Baseball   336

Basketball   337

Bowling   337

Climbing and Spelunking   337

Cycling   338

Football   339

Golf   340

Hockey   340

Martial Arts   341

Running, Walking, and Hiking   342

Skiing   342

Soccer   343

Tennis   344

Vehicular Sports   344

Water Sports   345

Sports Miscellany   346

General Sports and Gambling Sites   347

The Gaming Arcade   348

Online Parlor Games   348

CHAPTER 19: RAMBLING, TOURING, AND TREKKING   355

On the Road Again   355

Burma Shave   355

No-Man's Land   356

The Facilities   356

It Was a Funnel Story   356

Over Hill, Over Dale   357

A Few Freebies (Or Nearly Freebies)   357

Move Over Kathy Lee!   357

Your Call!   358

You Can Take It with You   358

Roll With It!   358

Destination: Fun, Adventure, Romance… Whatever   359

General Travel Sites   359

Island Destinations   361

North American Destinations   362

Where in the World?   364

This Ain't No Stagecoach   366

Livin' on the Road   367

CHAPTER 20: UP CLOSE AND PERSONAL   371

Lizzie's Tips for Long Distance Grandparenting   371

Clean Up Your Act!   373

Bag the Nag   373

On the Wavelength   374

The Slippery Side   374

Nuclear Grandparenting   374

An Oscar Winner   375

Parenting, Grandparenting, and Great-Grandparenting   375

In the Mood   376

Tie the Knot Tighter   376

Magic Fingers   376

Ways to Keep Your Love Alive   376

Two Hearts Beating as One   376

Relationships Sites   377

Just Away   379

Grief and Trauma Support Services   379

A Cappella   380

Seniors' Home Pages and Profiles   380

Appendix A: Tips for Using Lycos to Search the Web   386

Appendix B: Using the CD-ROM   390

Credits   394

Index   396

It is with pleasure that we at SeniorNet International join with Lycos Press to produce this book.

If you are already online you know what an exciting new world it is, where you can travel, who you can meet, what you can learn. If you are just beginning, you are entering a new age of telecommunications which, you will soon learn, is changing our world.

SeniorNet, a ten-year-old nonprofit international organization, is dedicated to introducing the rich benefits of computer and online technology into the expanded lives of older adults. SeniorNet accomplishes this with two related programs: first, through over one hundred Learning Centers across the country, where hundreds of senior volunteers teach thousands of older adults how to use computers and online services; and second, through noncommercial sites on America Online and the World Wide Web, where SeniorNet provides communities for older adults built around education, social and intellectual engagement, and the exciting avenues for support that new technology offers. And from this education through technology comes enhancement of confidence and personal growth.

A shorter way of saying most of this is our concise statement of purpose: SeniorNet's mission is to provide older adults education for and access to digital technology to enhance their lives and enable them to share their knowledge and wisdom.

We want you to join in our community of SeniorNet, and in the larger global community of computer-using seniors who will be the most useful, provocative, and influential technocrats in our population.

Best wishes and best of luck.

—Peter T. Esty
President, SeniorNet

Shortly after starting my online "Tin Lizzie" column for Lycos, I joined SeniorNet as a paid member. As time went on and the column began to express more and more senior interests, I decided to attend the convention held last year in Saint Louis, Missouri.

There were about 450 members in attendance, along with many presenters from large corporations. This was an incredibly well organized event, and I learned a great deal about the SeniorNet Learning centers, their partnerships with companies, and all the volunteers who aid in teaching us older folks how to use a computer.

I learned something else, too: that most of my counterparts were not really all that well acquainted with the total experience of the World Wide Web, and that most confined themselves to the more restricted environment of America Online. Many of them had never even been on the Internet.

Surfing the Web was second nature to me by that time, as I was leading readers to interesting Web sites via my Lizzie columns every week. It occurred to me then how much these people were missing by not familiarizing themselves more fully with the Internet, living a little more dangerously, and getting away from the cocoon of AOL.

On my way back home, the idea came to me that I could do a book that would tell SeniorNetters how to go about breaking the barrier and really get online! Shortly before that, SeniorNet had also designed a Web page for the Internet and was offering it to those who wanted a bit more than the commercial carriers could provide. With that in mind, I proceeded to map it out and give directions.

The SeniorNet online site is a wonderful way to meet people with ideas, those who think about issues, and who are living life to the fullest. If you haven't visited yet, get on board. You are missing the time of your life.

It is my hope that the instructions and tips provided in this book will enhance your Internet experience, not only to make it easier to understand how to get online and use the technology, but to fully experience the revolution going on out there before our very eyes.

—Eugenia "Tin Lizzie" Johnson

My deepest thanks to Kathleen McFadden, my co-author, who really pulled me out of the soup. Thanks to Ralph Fiske, my neighbor, whose optimistic nature and spirituality has sustained me through thick and thin. And to Gregory Dougherty and Steve Glenski, who kept me laughing and entertained. Thanks to Lois Daniel, who understood and lent support. To Janet Landis and Maxine Collister who pulled me out of the house for fun and games. Thanks to Overton Durrett and Lydia Carson for keeping me sane during some trying times while this book was being written. Thanks also to Kenyon Brown, Lycos Press Acquisitions Editor, who really believed in this project; to the unseen editorial and production staff at Lycos Press, toiling behind the scenes to make deadline. And to all those friends and family who were patient with me when I went underground. —EJ

Hearty thanks to Katharine English for the opportunities, encouragement, and praise. To Sean McFadden for his inestimable contributions to this book and unflagging good humor. To Ian Ellis for his valuable technical support. To Nuke Ellis for his emotional support. And to the staff at Lycos Press for their professionalism, guidance, and timely answers to questions. —KM

In the brief time since the world has had point-and-click access to the multigraphic, multimedia World Wide Web, the number of people going on-line has exploded to 30 million at last count, all roaming about the tens of millions of places to visit in cyberspace.

As the Web makes its way into our everyday lives, the kinds of people logging on are changing. Today, there are as many Webmasters as novices, or newbies, and all are struggling to get the most from the vast wells of information scattered about the Web. Even well-prepared surfers stumble aimlessly through cyberspace using hit-or-miss methods in search of useful information, with few results, little substance, and a lot of frustration.

In 1994, the Lycos technology was created by a scientist at Carnegie Mellon University to help those on the Web regain control of the Web. The company's powerful technology is the bedrock underlying a family of guides that untangle the Web, offering a simple and intuitive interface for all types of Web surfers, from GenXers to seniors, from Net vets to newbies.

Lycos (http://www.lycos.com) is a premium navigation tool for cyberspace, providing not only searches but also unique editorial content and Web reviews that all draw on the company's extensive catalog of over 60 million (and growing) Web sites.

Lycos designed its home base on the premise that people want to experience the Web in three fundamentally different ways: They want to search for specific subjects or destinations, they want to browse interesting categories, or they want recommendations on sites that have been reviewed for the quality of their content and graphics. Traditionally, Internet companies have provided part of this solution, but none has offered a finding tool that accommodates all degrees and types of curiosity. Lycos has.

Lycos utilizes its CentiSpeed spider technology as the foundation for finding and cataloging the vast variety of content on the World Wide Web. CentiSpeed processes a search faster than earlier technologies, featuring Virtual Memory Control, User-Level Handling, and Algorithmic Word Compaction. This advanced technology allows the engine to execute more than 4,000 queries per second. CentiSpeed provides faster search results and unparalleled power to search the most comprehensive catalog of the World Wide Web. Lycos uses statistical word calculations and avoids full-word indexing, which helps provide the most relevant search results available on the Web.

In mid 1995, Lycos acquired Point Communications, widely recognized by Web veterans for its collection of critical reviews of the Web. Now an integrated part of the Lycos service, Point continues to provide thousands of in-depth site reviews and a thorough rating of the top Web sites throughout the world. The reviews are conducted by professional reviewers and editors who rate sites according to content, presentation, and overall experience on a scale of 1 to 50. Reviews are presented as comprehensive abstracts that truly provide the user with subjective critiques widely heralded for their accuracy and perceptiveness. In addition, Point's top five percent ratings for Web sites receive a special "Top 5% Badge" icon, the Web's equivalent to the famed consumer "Good Housekeeping Seal."

And for Web browsers who don't need a touring list of well-reviewed sites but who may not be destination-specific, Lycos offers its Sites by Subject. Organizing thousands of Web sites into subject categories, Lycos Sites by Subject gives the cybersurfer at-a-glance Web browsing, including sports, entertainment, social issues, and children's sites. A compilation of the most popular sites on the Internet by the Lycos standard—those with the greatest number of links from other sites—the directory provides Web travelers with a more organized approach to finding worthwhile places to visit on the Web.

Lycos was originally developed at Carnegie Mellon University by Dr. Michael "Fuzzy" Mauldin, who holds a Ph.D. in conceptual information retrieval. Now chief scientist at the company, Dr. Mauldin continues to expand the unique exploration and indexing technology. Utilizing this technology, Lycos strives to deliver a family of guides to the Internet that are unparalleled for their accuracy, relevance, and comprehensiveness. Lycos is one of the most frequently visited sites on the Web and is one of the leading sites for advertisers.

The Lycos database is constantly being refined by dozens of software robots, or agents, called "spiders." These spiders roam the Web endlessly, finding and downloading Web pages. Once a page is found, the spiders create abstracts which consist of the title, headings and subheading, 100 most weighty words, first 20 lines, size in bytes, and number of words. Heuristic (self-teaching) software looks at where the words appear in the document, their proximity to other words, frequency, and site popularity to determine relevance.

Lycos eliminates extraneous words like "the," "a," "and," "or," and "it" that add no value and slow down finding capabilities. The resulting abstracts are merged, older versions discarded, and a new, up-to-date database is distributed to all Lycos servers and licensees. This process is repeated continuously, resulting in a depth and comprehensiveness that makes Lycos a top information guide company.

Online providers or software makers can license Lycos—the spider, search engine, catalog, directory, and Point reviews—to make them available to users.

Lycos, Inc., an Internet exploration company, was founded specifically to find, index, and filter information on the Internet and World Wide Web. CMG Information Services, Inc. (NASDAQ: CMGI) is a majority shareholder in Lycos, Inc. through its strategic investment and development business unit, CMG@Ventures. CMGI is a leading provider of direct marketing services investing in and integrating advanced Internet, interactive media, and database management technologies.

Chapter 1
THE BIG BUY

DRIVIN' MISS RUBY

ZIPIDEE-DOO-DAH

REV UP THE THROTTLE

THOSE WONDERFUL MAGS

GETTING HOOKED UP
(OR JUST GETTING HOOKED)

BYTES AND SITES FOR NEOPHYTES

Seniors aren't much different from their junior counterparts when it comes to impulse buying. I remember particularly the day I bought my first computer. Now remember—steady, sane, and senior!

I headed out to the mall with my friend Janet, and found myself drifting aimlessly down the aisles of a large department store, fingering garments that were on sale. I quickly grew discouraged, as I was so pudgy and shapeless that any garment I bought would look like the last tattered tent from a week spent at Boy Scout camp. No, it wasn't clothes, but something more solid I needed to satisfy my shopping penchant that day.

Leaving Janet and her tidy figure to try on clothes, I beat a hasty retreat to the lower level where all the appliances sat tucked in their cozy niches waiting for the appearance of my plastic—and LO! There it was, sleek and sassy, smiling at me, the Macintosh that shares my office with me today. Of course, I immediately called a salesperson to talk me out of it, as I had only gone down to "browse."

You know how the story ends—Ruby Perl (my computer) came home with me that very day, and since then, we have developed a very close relationship. And although things have worked out swell for us, this is really the worst possible way to buy your computer. I had given no thought to how I would use Ruby, and what components she possessed that would best suit my work style. For I *had* no style at that point.

DRIVIN' MISS RUBY

Even though Ruby Perl and I cohabitate successfully, we have made a lot of modifications and upgrades because of the need to keep up with the amazing changes taking place in the Computer Universe. We have a lot more than the original 4 megabytes of RAM we started with—up to 32 at last count. And the original hard drive is assisted by a 1 gigabyte outboard drive that now does most of the work. Add some pretty killer speakers and a CD-ROM drive to the mix, and I can groove to the glorious sounds of Aretha or Puccini, serenading my daily forays onto the Internet.

SHOPPIN' AROUND

When I first took Ruby Perl home, I knew nothing of bytes and megabytes, drives or RAM, even from a short distance away; what's more, I certainly did not know how I would put all those bytes and RAM to use. This purchase could have been a disaster, or at the very least, a major disappointment, because I had not shopped around to look at other models, nor had I talked to friends who owned computers, nor done any research using the trade magazines.

There are many ways to purchase a computer, from brightly lit mega computer stores with well-informed sales staffs, to refreshed and returned models, used but refurbished for resale. The prices will be lower on rebuilt models, but keep in mind that an older computer will not always be up-to-date with the latest technological developments, if that matters to you. Catalogs and mail order services are good resources, some offering blowout deals. Their customer service personnel are quick and savvy, and delivery is often overnight.

THE BIGGEST HONKER ON THE BLOCK

In this day and age of spectacular change, it is a good idea to purchase the biggest honker your purse will allow, because you will need all the juice you can get before you know it. Eight megabytes of RAM used to be adequate, even considered pretty beefed up, but now it's stretching it a little for frequent World Wide Web use—even though it is plenty just for the Internet, or posting to an electronic bulletin board service ("BBS"). Today, with the huge increase in

INTRODUCING TIN LIZZIE

Tin Lizzie, like many others, was born by accident. While I was buzzing along writing descriptive text for the Lycos Web directory, I received a call from an editor asking if I had ever thought of writing a column—a column that would be directed to Seniors, an audience of "Internauts" the editor felt was growing all the time. I was so surprised that, without having time to think, I immediately answered, "Yes." And then I panicked!

I was certainly no authority on the World Wide Web; I was no techie, no wire-head. I was just an ordinary oldster who happened to enjoy surfing! "But that's perfect," my editor replied. "That's just what we want!"

The next step was to develop a persona for the column that ultimately became an extension of myself. That part was easy, because the name "Tin Lizzie" seemed to me to represent a lot of things "senior."

First, it reminded me of the olden days and those innovative, chugging cars. Second, even in third gear it would be hard to pull a steep hill with so few cylinders pumping, which is me in "QuickTime"—I'm there; it just takes me a little longer. And third (and perhaps most important), those cars made a lot of noise. That seemed to me as apt a description of a Senior as I could find.

Feeling very comfortable with the identity I had created, I began at once to metamorphose into Lizzie, and she became an important part of my being. I spoke with her voice and she echoed my ideas and opinions. We made a lot of noise together without really trying, sounding off about issues we felt were important to all ages, as well as sharing a bit of nostalgia with those who could remember the old days.

When I decided to do this book, it was only natural that I would speak as Lizzie, and that she and I would write this to all Seniors, in one voice: sharing a little sentiment, sounding off on issues we consider elemental to our well-being, ladling out a few pithy observations, and doling out large helpings of computer tips and surfing advice. We both hope you really enjoy it.

Yours in schizophrenia,
Eugenia L. Johnson, a.k.a. Tin Lizzie

graphics being displayed, and the multiplicity of sites to visit, you will be pushing your computer to the max with only eight megabytes, and you could end up with screen freezes, and system crashes if your use is heavy.

My recommendation is that you purchase a system with no less than 16 megabytes of RAM, or get a good used system cheaply enough so that it does not tear your wallet to shreds to upgrade to more memory. RAM fluctuates greatly in price, and is currently much cheaper than it used to be. You need enough RAM to run your applications (check the documentation to see what each manufacturer recommends), your browser, and still have a little runnin' room to spare.

Make sure the hard drive has enough storage capacity for your needs. In today's world, 1 gigabyte would be a comfortable standard unless you are into graphics or movies. But again, you can always purchase a used or refurbed system with low storage,

Lizzie's Tips

Before you start tinkering too much, if you are a beginner, READ the manual that comes packed with your computer. Browse over the complicated parts, but more importantly, pay attention to the basics, like how to turn your computer on and off. There really is a right and a wrong way to do this. Do it wrong and you could mess something up. On the other hand, these days, you practically have to set your computer on fire to do permanent damage. Hardware has come a long way, and it can *go* a long way, and even take a beating or two from fumbling fingers. Nevertheless, read my lips: Read the manual!

and plug in an outboard (external) drive that has a lot of storage, just as Ruby Perl and I did.

A LITTLE TECHNO-BABBLE

Bytes, megabytes, and gigabytes: What's a byte? It's a unit of measurement, a standard in the world of computing used to measure the size of memory, storage, and the size of software applications.: One byte is equal to one letter of the English language. A megabyte is equal to 1000 bytes. A typical hard drive used to have about 200 to 500 megabytes of storage space for applications and documents (and in the old days, even 4MB was considered a serious machine). But in this age of high tech, it is common to see hard drives with a gig (short for gigabyte) or more. A floppy disk (a removable storage medium) has 800 to 1400 kilobytes. And a CD-ROM disk typically holds around 600 megabytes.

To keep this simple: 8 bits equal a byte; 1024 bytes equal a kilobyte; 1024 kilobytes equal a megabyte; 1023 megabytes equal a gigabyte. So there!

RAM is the acronym for "random access memory." RAM measures the amount, in megabytes, of space you have available to run your computer's applications. This includes your machine's operating system, the software which runs your computer (in a nutshell, the thing that makes it tick). It used to be that DOS (the original operating system for personal computers) was the only game in town. But today, you can choose from Windows 3.xx, Windows 95, Unix, or my favorite system, the Mac OS.

Before you can run a program, create a new file, edit a report, or change anything on a document, your computer must read it into memory. Your document exists at that time, only in memory, or RAM, until you save it on your hard drive, floppy disk, or external drive. The more RAM that you have, the more programs you can operate, and the more you can do with your computer.

HARD AS A ROCK

The hard drive is the fixed disk inside your computer where you store all the things that you want to save from memory (RAM). It goes without saying that the larger the drive, the more storage you will have. Your hard drive is really like a library, storing your files safely so that you can get to them later when you need them.

Most of us take the monitor that comes with the deal when we purchase a computer at a mega store. But if we are buying separate pieces, we can choose which monitor we need. Monitors come from 12" to over 20", with the 14-inchers usually a part of the bundle. If you work on multiple projects or do a lot of work with graphics, a larger monitor is just the thing for you.

As for color, you don't *have* to get a color monitor if text and line art are your primary metier; they often look much crisper on a grayscale monitor, anyway. Personally, I think color is more fun (and you

Lizzie's Tips

Oh my gosh! My computer has died, everything is black! I've killed it!

Almost everyone has had this experience. It might be something as simple as your power source, so check all the cords and connections to look for a loose one. First, turn off your computer according to the manual's guidelines; don't unplug any cords, just make sure that they are plugged in good and tight and then restart your computer according to the manual. Very often, this can solve the problem. If it doesn't, check your manual again in the "trouble-shooting" section for more advice. If all else fails, don't hesitate to call the manufacturer's "help" or technical support line. Never, ever, be afraid to ask for guidance.

will surely miss the fun of the WWW if you're working in grayscale), but anyone on a budget who's looking at a used computer system having only a grayscale monitor shouldn't despair (you can always upgrade later). And these days, almost all new computers come bundled with color monitors, so if you're looking at a new system, you needn't worry.

If you're buying your monitor separately, before you plunk down any money, be sure that the monitor is compatible with your computer. Monitors are like stereo speakers: You really need to try them out. Look for a sharp screen image that is easy on your eyes. Make sure the screen is big enough so that you are not constantly scrolling. Make sure the images aren't distorted, and that the screen doesn't flicker. Test it to see if the controls are easy to use, and, if the monitor is color, that the screen displays colors with relative accuracy—that is, that hue, saturation, and

lightness seem balanced. If you're unsure, ask your sales rep to help.

Monitors do produce electromagnetic emissions called ELF and VLF (extremely low frequency and very low frequency) radiation. Some research has stated that these emissions may increase your risk of cancer. There is no conclusive evidence for this, however, and no level of exposure has been determined to be "safe," so the U.S. Government does not regulate monitors for emission safety. If this is a serious concern, you can buy an energy saving monitor, whose screen will dim when usage is low, reducing the power consumption and thus emissions. In particular, look at those made by Apple, NEC, Sony, and Radius.

THE DARK SIDE

Some folks believe that a screen saver will protect their screen when the monitor is left on for long periods of time. My Mac Guru, George, says, "Not so." When you operate a screen saver, you are still running an application, and like anything else, when it's used over long periods of time you risk a screen burn—an "etching" of an image in your screen. Just turn the monitor off—which automatically darkens your screen—and you will protect it completely.

Checking with the folks at Apple, I found that no one there uses screen savers at all! But for sheer fun, a screen saver provides relief from the monotony of a long project and gives chuckles if you are running one of the kooky and outrageous ones.

ZIPIDEE-DOO-DAH

A modem lets computers exchange information through the telephone lines. You use the same lines for modem calls that you do for voice calls. You'll need a modem before you can access the Internet or the World Wide Web.

The speed of your modem bears a direct relation to the quality of your experience on the Internet, as its speed is in direct ratio to how fast you'll be able to retrieve—or "download"—pages, or "sites," when you are surfin' the Web. A slow modem can be very tedious and make you tear your hair. So, go for the fastest modem out there. At the time of this writing, the most popular is the 28,800 bps (bauds per second, the rate at which information is transferred from one computer to another), made by all manufacturers of quality modems, and available in every computer store or catalog.

Don't forget, we're out here to enjoy this new technology—maybe even become expert in its use, or start a new career. So get the best and most efficient equipment you can afford and get out there!

REV UP THE THROTTLE

For those burning to get started and who have not yet purchased a system, call your public library and get a list of computer user groups in your area. Attend a meeting and mosey around. These folks can be your greatest resource in picking up information on equipment, where to buy it, and in providing advice for getting peak performance from your existing programs. Computer nerds love to help the novice, and many user groups will have classes tailored to your specific system.

GATHER TOGETHER

Becoming a member of a user group was one of the first things I did, and even now, several years later, I get excited when I know that my Mac User Group ("MUG") meeting is just a few days away. It's a chance to meet the real experts, review programs, and get inexpensive disks and CD-ROMs containing little tricks and discounted programs. Nothing is as much fun as thronging with others that are bitten

 Lizzie's Tips
The ongoing debate about when to turn off your computer occupies many people. Some turn the switch on and off every time they quit using their machine, even for short periods of time. Others leave it on all day and switch it off at night. I leave my computer on during the day, turning it off at night to save energy. You can turn off your screen separately when leaving it for long periods to protect it from the inevitable burn, and leave the system running, if you like. Color monitors, unlike the grayscale ones, can take many hours of use without showing any signs of burn.

with the bug as badly as you are. It is a social evening and a chance to brush up on techniques, and learn about the latest techno stuff. Some groups even have a Seniors' subgroup.

WISHBOOKS AND DREAMS

And then there are the catalogs. Most computer users are deluged with them, and are only too happy to lighten some of the load. Computer magazines such as *Macworld* and *PC World* can be picked up at large newsstands and bookstores everywhere, and offer many insights into new products, reviews of software, hardware, and commentary on the computer user's world. These magazines make fascinating reading, and will be of great help once you get over being confused.

Catalogs and direct order can be a lot of fun to use. I find myself pouring over them and dreaming about a glamorous new system (don't tell Ruby Perl!) or educating myself on new software. They are a good reference to keep track of new products and prices, as they fluctuate often, and to generally get

Lizzie's Tips

When dialing in to the Internet with your modem, make sure that no one picks up the telephone using another extension. If they do, they'll get a big surprise: a loud, unpleasant, hissing noise (the sound of computers talking!). Their pick-up may even disconnect you.

If you have call waiting, be sure to turn off this feature, as it will also disconnect you when a call comes in. Your access provider can give you a code to use when you are on-line that will disable call waiting, but the most common code is ***70**, which you'll insert in your communication software's modem configurations where prompted. Double-check this code with your provider before you enter it.

Lizzie's Tips

Did we forget the mouse? Many computers come with built-in software complete with exercises and drills to help you get more proficient with the mouse. You will need a mouse pad, easily picked up at any computer store, and then practice, practice, practice, until you are as expert as your 12-year-old grandchild. Don't let her put you down and make fun of your progress. Slower makes for fewer mistakes, right?

For those already over the hurdle, with your system in place and modem connected, take a peek at the sites I have included at the end of this section next time you connect to the Internet.

THOSE WONDERFUL MAGS

PC Magazine
http://www.ziff.com/~pcmag/

This is one of the most popular computer magazines out there. The online copy is actually an electronic version of the same magazine you can get in print. There are features on software and hardware, reviews of products, editorials that take up current computing issues, and even back issues for you to research.

better acquainted with your system and the peripherals that are available. Some people are so addicted, they never throw catalogs away. I keep mine in a box ("just for catalogs"), and try to thin them out occasionally, keeping the most current ones as they come in. You can never tell when you might need something in a hurry, especially when you aren't equal to driving miles to the mega store.

BURIED ALIVE

Of course, once you have purchased your computer you will have more catalogs and special offers than you can imagine. You have gotten on the mailing lists! Your mail carrier may even change his or her route just to avoid you. A few online catalogs await you at the end of this section, both for serious browsing, or just to keep handy in the "reading room."

Now that all that grisly stuff is done, clutch your computer manual tightly to your chest and Let the Games Begin!

Macworld

http://www.macworld.com

This magazine for Mac users offers colorful graphics, information on new products, reviews of software and hardware, and industry commentary. There is a wealth of information to be found, and besides, it's a lot of fun to read. Be sure to make a spot somewhere on your hard drive for saving copies of articles. You won't want to throw them away.

MacUser

http://www.zdnet.com/macuser/

This magazine, also geared for the Mac user, runs the gamut of all the news that's fit to print about Apple's famous computer, software, and OS; with reviews of new products and an interesting mailbag.

READ ON, MACDUFF

Introduction to PC Hardware

http://pclt.cis.yale.edu/pclt/pchw/
platypus.htm

Those folks contemplating buying a new PC would do well to read this comprehensive article that clears up the gobbledygook of terms, and explains clearly what the optimum in PC hardware should be for today's user.

Macintosh Tips and First Aid

http://pclt.cis.yale.edu/pclt/pchw/platypus.htm

If you're scared to death you have done irreparable harm to your Macintosh, or just curious in case you might, this is the hotspot of info, loaded with tips and advice on how to treat your ailing Apple.

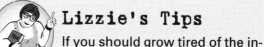

Lizzie's Tips

If you should grow tired of the influx of mailed material, special offers, unsolicited newsletters, and catalogs, write with your request for removal to: Mail Preference Service, 11 W. 42nd St., P.O. Box 3861, New York, NY 10163-3861, and your name will be removed from many mailing lists.

Power Computing

http://www.powercc.com

If you are savvy enough, you can tailor-make your dream computer with the varied options featured on this site. Included are outboard drives and modems for your review, as well as monitors, with service and support resources included.

GOODIES GALORE

MacWarehouse

http://www.warehouse.com

This is an extensive catalog primarily for Mac users. Comes complete with every possible piece of equipment you can think of, including a large inventory of software both for office and home use. The staff knows its stuff, and delivery is timed for the next day.

Club Mac

http://www.club-mac.com

Another bright array of Mac goodies. Keep it in your "reading room" for inspiration, and maybe find just the thing you have been looking for.

Directware

http://www.directware.com/E-Store/about/
index.html/

PC users can pull up a shopping cart and browse through most of the prominent PC manufacturers' products and fill in the gaps with Packard Bell, IBM, Adobe, Hewlett Packard, and then some. Specials and promotions will catch your eye, and technical support is available. Ask for a free catalog.

Lizzie's Tips

What is an icon? You hear this word bandied about a lot in computer realms. An icon is a graphic representation or colorful picture of any program, document, printer, or anything else you may work with. Most applications already come with their own identifying icons so that they are easily recognized when you need to use them, but you can also design your own or download many examples from the Web. Some people even collect them.

For the catalogs PC Connection and/or MacConnection, call 1-800-800-3333 and ask that a catalog be sent to you. This is another company that offers extensive product lines, good tech help, and overnight service on your orders.

GETTING HOOKED UP (OR JUST GETTING HOOKED)

One of the things I learned about buying a computer on impulse is that nothing quite fits into place the way it does when you buy a car. With a car, following dealer prep, you just drive it away. The afternoon I bought Ruby Perl, I looked into the back seat of my car and saw a box big enough to hide a body in. The burly guys at the store had just plopped that box on the seat without working up a bead of sweat. But there I stood alone, in my middle sixties, on the street of a changing neighborhood, gazing with a sinking heart at my new computer; it was hidden away in a box that could have been a grand piano, for all the ease it would take me to move it.

THE MUSCLE TUSSLE

One of the prerequisites for getting on in years is the need to stockpile all the hardbodies the neighborhood can offer up, so that plenty of muscle is always available when you need it. This particular afternoon, a single call brought forth one of the gorgeous ones, larded with impressive pectorals and wearing his usual brilliant smile. A minor hoist, and in moments Ruby Perl was gently resting at my doorstep.

After unpacking and getting all the cords and manuals sorted out, I directed the gorgeous strongman politely to put the hardware on a sofa table so I could set it up. He looked at me in shock. "You're not going to try to use it here?" he asked incredulously. It made sense to me. It wasn't taking up too much room, it fit quietly and unobtrusively into the decor, and I planned to pull up a little folding chair stacked in the corner. "It will work just fine," I said in ignorant bliss.

ROILS AND COILS AND WRIGGLY THINGS

If you find yourself surrounded by piles of writhing cords, don't panic. Each port on the back of your computer's main box will have a little picture that matches up to the end of a cord, with its corresponding little picture. (Proper computer people would call these icons.) Turn to your manual and follow the instructions telling you which cords plug in where; going slowly through this step by step, you will have it all done right.

Lizzie Sez

Don't forget to take the time to wander off into the trivial and aimless. It can lighten the load of the heavy-duty moments in life.

Once you have gotten each cord in its proper port, you can then plug into your power source, preferably using a surge protector.

DISORDERLY DISARRAY

In a matter of weeks, books and papers were strewn all over the dining room, and my back and shoulders felt as though they were in a cast. The public rooms of the house had become trashed. Ruby Perl had taken over. I hadn't expected to spend such long hours hunkered down over the computer, much less try to do anything very fancy. After all, I led an active life in the outside world, away from this computer stuff. I didn't know that I would become an addict. I needed to think this through—and fast—before I was plugged into a back brace.

AT THE END OF THE TUNNEL

Then I thought of a solution: I could always use the back bedroom, make a little office for myself, get the front of the house back in civilized order, and best of all, be comfortable.

And so, the twin bed my son spent his teenage years wallowing on was shuffled out to another growing boy. The trophies and pictures and baseball cards were packed away. Old clothes left behind were donated to charity. As my project began to grow and take shape, I slowed down and began to dawdle, postponing my office transformation while feeling a sense of sadness and loss. A dear friend dropped by to see how things were going and looked at me out of wise eyes and chuckled, "Well, I see that you are having a little trouble dismantling the 'shrine'."

CHANGING AND REARRANGING

That comment hit its mark, and I realized something that, of course, I had known all along: Life is nothing but change, and it is how flexible you can be with those changes that determines the richness of the life

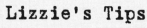

Lizzie's Tips

Surge protectors are good friends, helping to keep your work-in-progress (not to mention your hardware) from being blasted by a brown-out or a lightning bolt, and keeping your total system safe from a total blowout. Your computer is worth it! Get a surge protector! They range in price from the very cheap, about $5.95 at any hardware store, to hundreds of dollars. Most of us aren't running graphics studios, so we can get good results with surge protectors costing from $19.95 to forty dollars (I don't recommend you go the total cheapie route). Be sure your protector has enough receptacles for all your plugs, and get one that will also accommodate your phone jack.

you live. So, thinking lovingly of my son, I set about the rearrangement of the back bedroom with gusto—for me!

An office of my own, with no stale memories, only the anticipation that something creative and exciting was opening up for my enrichment and enjoyment. For the "genie" is out of the bottle, and the would-be computer nerd is loose upon the land. Better yet, I was out of the generational straightjacket that had me fearful of trying things technical, being too adventurous; I now was ready to immerse myself in something I would never have had time for until I creeped into these senior years.

Lizzie Sez

Never miss a chance to have someone scratch your back and shoulders.

Now, with a comfortable chair, spacious computer desk, surrounded by my computer manuals and Ruby Perl—I'm wired!—jamming in the back room to Fleetwood Mac for inspiration. I'm regressing a little to my teenage years (or maybe those were my daughter's teenage years)—so look out world!

The Web sites below should be of help to anyone just starting out. They are full of information and ideas; give a click and check them out.

BYTES AND SITES FOR NEOPHYTES

Cyberian Outpost
http://www.cybout.com/cyberian.html

The Cyberians advertise that they are the cool place to shop for Mac and PC stuff, and indeed, there is a lot to see, with good bargains and shopping even for the kids. Stop in and browse through this jazzy site and sample the wares. You may find something tantalizing.

Mac OS Software and Hardware Guide
http://www.macsoftware.apple.com/

These folks brag that they offer lists of the hottest software and hardware products available in retail stores, in catalogs, and online. Good software for home and office, accounting programs, and much more is available. Some shareware and freeware is to be found here, too. Definitely worth a peek for the Mac user.

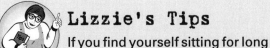
Lizzie's Tips

If you find yourself sitting for long periods of time and the chair you have is not ergonomically designed, put a small footstool by your feet to use as a perch. This gives you a chance to change your position by raising and lowering your feet when your legs get tired.

Works like a charm. Even a cardboard box will do the job. Get a really good chair if you can afford one, though.

Windows News and Reviews
http://www.netcenter.com/netcentr/news/hardware.html

This PC magazine lists many categories of software and hardware, along with reviews. If you are more than a novice, you might find some interesting facts about the hardware you plan to purchase.

BOOKS FOR BEGINNERS

IDG Books Worldwide
http://www.idgbooks.com

IDG has a large roster of books, from humurous and, wry, to educational. These are the folks that publish the big *Dummies* series.

Ziff/Davis Press
http://guide-p.infoseek.com/Titles?qt=Ziff%2FDavis&col=WW&sv=N2&lk=no frames

This huge publisher has a large catalog of computer books and software sites to interest all but the most jaded. Awaiting you are beautifully presented books about the Internet, your computer, and many technical manuals to get you out of trouble.

Lizzie's Tips

As you set up your computer in its proper receptacle in the desk, notice how much space you have on either side of the hard drive. What a wonderful place for dictionaries and those books you need for quick and easy reference. Before you stash them there, be sure you leave at least 2" of clear space on either side of the hard drive. This space is necessary for your computer's fans to work efficiently, and to keep your system from overheating.

Peachpit Press
http:www.peachpit.com

This prestigious publisher prints beautifully formatted computer help books both for the Mac and PC user, with offerings for the beginner, along with more complicated books for the advanced programmer.

Lycos Press
http://www.tenderbuttons.com/lycos/000.html

Shameless self-promotion? Well, maybe a little. But I wouldn't dream of leading you astray. In addition to the book you now hold in your hand, check LP's roster of other tantalizing selections, from serious tomes that cover all things Webby from soup to nuts, to Net collections for game-lovers, and the best advice around for getting the most from Internet travel resources.

MORE SITES TO EXCITE OR INCITE

MacLinq
http:www.maclinq.com

Adobe Systems
http:www.adobe.com/

Eudora
http://www.qualcomm.com/quest/
QuestMain.html

Lizzie's Tips

Backing up your system—that is, making a spare copy of it—is crucial, as it is the only thing you have to "fall back on" if the worst possible thing happens—a system crash! Look upon it as insurance against disaster. Back up! Back-up your whole system by inserting a clean, formatted disk into your hard drive and following the instructions in your manual. You'll need a lot of disks to complete the task; use multiple floppies, a separate hard drive, or portable drives like Zip, EZ135, or Jazz. Ask your local computer guru, or browse the catalogs to determine what method is best for you.

Once you've selected a back-up method, copy the work you want to save permanently. Do it with disks if you have to, but a portable, outboard drive will do all the work for you.

The worst scenario I know is losing a long, important document near a deadline, and having to completely rewrite it from memory. Use the pull-down menu provided by the program you are using (or the keyboard shortcuts, if you know them) to save your work, and do it often.

Of course, you are already saving your work from memory to hard drive as you go, so if you save often, you generally won't lose it before you have the chance to back it up. But backing up your system copies more than just your documents: It saves a copy of everything on your computer, *including* your operating system.

HotJava

http://java.sun.com

Internet Phone

http://www.vocaltec.com

The program that some say could one day could crush the phone companies.

RealAudio

http://www.realaudio.com

Webspace

http://www.cts.com/~template

Many refer to this as the best 3-D browser available.

Chapter 2
NEW COMPUTERS, NEW CONNECTIONS

LET'S GET GOING

HOOKING UP CAN BE HARD TO DO

MORE HELP IS ON THE WAY!

THERE'S MORE TO COME

THE CHATTING MASSES

MIND YOUR MANNERS

FOR THE TOTALLY CONFUSED

THE SEARCH IS ON

SO JOIN US

There's not much out there that is more exciting than fiddling with your newly purchased computer. Well, all right: a few things.

LET'S GET GOING

Getting acquainted with the new kid is just as rewarding for the old hand as it is for the novice. After familiarizing yourself with your system's peculiarities and quirks, it's time to get that modem hooked up to an access provider so you can start surfin' the Web, and find out what everyone is so excited about.

MODEMS, SHMODEMS (AND GETTING A LITTLE DAMP)

A modem comes bundled with almost every state-of-the-art computer these days, either built into the system internally, or packed into the box with all the rest of your goodies. Usually included in your bundle is a disk for one of the large commercial services, such as CompuServe, Prodigy, or America Online (AOL).

America Online is everywhere! And due in part to their extensive advertising campaigns, they claim to have some 16 million subscribers. Connecting to a service like AOL is an easy way to begin to familiarize yourself with the vast array of material available to you in cyberspace. It's easy to connect, using a disk and easy-to-follow instructions that carry you from place to place in the enormous empire of media information.

Even though the commercial services offer easy online access, chat areas where you can visit with friends, and resources for research in many areas (including software collections), they are really just

Lizzie Sez
Get organized! If you don't know where to start, no one else will, so begin at the beginning.

Lizzie's Tips
With so much marketing hype, the large commercial services can weigh you down with loads of their software disks sent in the mail, included with computer magazines, and along with almost every gadget you buy these days. Don't throw them out! These are real nuggets and can be used over again.

Simply unlock and erase the disk, then re-initialize it for your personal use. Watch your collection grow! Some people I know haven't bought disks in years!

a pale imitation of the real thing, often using proxied pages (stored copies) of sites from the World Wide Web, and sometimes blocking access to sites you might want to visit, such as the Netscape Navigator home page. And very often, you are limited to use of the browser provided by your commercial provider, generally less advanced and with fewer bells and whistles than those you'll find on browsers like Netscape Navigator and Internet Explorer.

To experience the full impact of the delirious Web, you'll do well to sign on with an independent Internet service provider (an "ISP"), who will give you direct access to the Internet via a dial-up account. More about how to do this as we move ahead.

STREAKING ALONG

Along with the keyboard, mouse, manuals, and cords packed in my bundle with Ruby Perl, there was a modem—streaking along at the unspeakably slow speed of 2400bps, just barely enough to carry the freight to a local bulletin board (or "BBS").

This small modem was powerful enough, though, to hook up to the local number accessing America Online. I knew nothing about baud rates, so I muddled along in my ignorance with a modem that

Lizzie's Tips

One of the best things about being on the Internet is the fabulous opportunity to grab software. So much is available for download that it's hard to keep up with it all. Some of this loot is absolutely free (called, appropriately, "freeware"), with the developer asking only for an e-mail note or a postcard stating how you liked the program. Other applications, called shareware, will require you to send the developer a fee if you like the program and plan to continue using it. And please: Send in the fee if you use the program, as it keeps these bright folks rolling out more fodder for our troughs. What's wrong with a little motivation?

would never be able to really get out there on the Internet, but would do fine for connecting to these large commercial companies and the local numbers they provide.

It is important to have a modem that has a fast baud rate, preferably 28,800 (faster speeds are in the offing), in order to access the World Wide Web. The faster the baud rate, the faster the Web site will load. You don't want to wait an eternity for a Web page to deliver its goodies to your desktop. This is especially important when loading graphics, which are denser than text and longer-loading to begin with. Most computers now have built-in (or bundled) modems, and the standard is now 28,800 bps. If you must purchase one separately, they are much less expensive than they used to be. See Chapter 1 if you need to review more on modems.

DIALING IN AND GETTING ON WITH IT

After connecting to a commercial provider using the disk they provide—which is surprisingly easy—follow the explicit instructions on your monitor screen, and spend some time sorting out your password and local access numbers. Take the time to browse through the online help documentation in case you should need it (most commercial providers permit you to browse their help sections at no charge, i.e., your time spent in these areas will not count against your free sign-up hours, nor your monthly allotment).

Besides many special interest groups, software larders, and news, America Online has a special site dedicated to SeniorNet users that includes topics in which we are especially interested (see Chapter 3). This area also has reduced rates for us at certain times on designated days. As Martha Stewart would say, "That's a good thing."

Now, you are all set to explore the rich motherlode of soap operas, financial news, and the denizens of Senior Netizens.

IT'S YOUR PURSE!

The charge for commercial services like AOL is typically about $9.95 a month, which includes your first five hours of time spent online. You are wooed initially with an offer of from five to fifteen hours of free time if you take the plunge. After you've used up your free time (and your first five hours on the pay clock), the real costs begin. For each additional hour over the initial five hours you'll be assessed an additional charge from $1.95 to $2.95 per hour. These costs change from service to service, and may change again with renewed marketing onslaughts.

Note: As of this writing, AOL had announced plans to initiate a lower cost, flat rate pricing plan for unlimited monthly use. Details were not available at press time, but be sure to check with AOL about plan options before signing on.

It doesn't take an Einstein to figure that in no time at all your bill could ricochet into another orbit. But, I urge you to take advantage of these initial ex-

Lizzie Sez

Always keep your mind open to new ideas; you never know when something brilliant may come along and change your life.

ploratory forays, using the free hours to develop competence with the ins and outs of e-mail, lurking in chat rooms, finding research sources, and just having fun.

USE IT OR LOSE IT!

Initial free hours from services like AOL can be a bonanza to you as you dive right into the Internet, discovering its mindblowing resources and the many areas of interest that pertain particularly to you. Check out the software archives for freeware and shareware. Visit the virtual newsstands for up-to-the minute information on a global scale. Zap friends and family with zany e-mail. Bust loose on the Web browser and get a taste of the excitement as you break into another dimension of fun and frivolity, serious science, illuminating information, or the weird and provocative.

SO DIVE IN!

Joining the hordes and connecting to one of the commercial servers is really the best and quickest way to teach yourself to get comfortable with the technology of the Internet. Before you have gone through your free hours, you'll have a pretty good idea of what is available and what interests you. You'll also have developed some skills in mastering the technology. Before long, you may be the guru on your block, called upon to look up Web pages for your favorite college student, looking up some statutes for the lawyer around the corner, or just sharing tips with your friends as you help them get connected.

Lizzie's Tips

"HONEY PLUM"

My granddaughter, a college student, was over with her roommate the night I hooked up to America Online. She immediately signed on as a second user with the moniker "Honey Plum." She found the chat lounges right away, and was soon engaged in conversations with all these guys who saw that sexy handle and zeroed in on her like flies to a road apple. My moniker, "Lavinia," was a dead giveaway of old and infirm, and I couldn't dredge up one single soul who was willing to spend any time chatting with me. So there I was in the kitchen, innocently preparing a light repast for these growing girls, enjoying the sounds of hilarity and mirth coming from my office, all the while unconscious of the time whizzing by as they played and chatted with their anonymous conquests. Needless to say, my AOL bill took a heavy hit for that night, but it surely brings to mind, YOU MUST MIND THE TIME!

JUST FOR STARTERS: THE BIG BOYS

CompuServe
http://world.compuserve.com/

Prodigy
http://www.prodigy.com/

America Online
http://www.aol.com/

HOOKING UP CAN BE HARD TO DO

As would be the case with any good, red-blooded, obsessive-compulsive, addictive personality, a few hours or so online did not sate my newbie hunger to surf the Internet. Quite the contrary: That small taste of magical wonders merely whetted my appetite for more.

It was not long before my hours spent on America Online were racking up and my plastic was wilting. Obviously, this information junkie and born-again Web addict was not going to be able to feed the habit this way (unless I wanted to dabble awhile in bankruptcy as I went).

THE OTHER GUYS

A little research turned up some independent Internet service providers (ISPs) that bill a flat monthly rate for hours spent online, often for an unlimited period of time. Check your yellow pages, computer stores, or the user group with whom you are affiliated to track them down. Some business news sections in your daily paper will have listings or advertisements for such services, or a friendly call to the computer departments of your local college or university will bring forth the right results. Not-for-profit servers operating from community colleges, libraries, and public radio and television stations, often have substantially lower rates but may have restrictions on hours of usage. It does make sense, though, to get the best rates for yo' mon', hon'.

Several companies were available in my Metro area, and within a day I had received a disk containing all that I needed to hookup online, along with complete instructions.

Getting online with your own independent ISP is really a thrill. There is so much more latitude, more challenge, and best of all, so much more freedom from the button-down feeling of the commercial servers. This is really much more fun.

SOME NATIONAL INTERNET SERVICE PROVIDERS (ISPs)

ANS CO+RE Systems Inc.
http://www.ans.net/
ANS CO+RE Systems Inc. is a national Internet service provider offering high-speed connections and dedicated Internet access to businesses and individuals. Review services and prices at this promotional site.

BBN Planet
http://www.BBN.com/
"We helped build the Internet" is one of the many bona fides claimed by Internetworking broker and managed access provider BBN Planet. The company whose clients include the likes of Harvard University, the U.S. Senate and Silicon Graphics offers Internet access, site maintenance and network infrastructure development for businesses and organizations worldwide.

CERFnet
http://www.cerf.net/
This promotional site is the home of CERFnet, an Internet access provider for businesses. Visitors to its home page can read about the company, review its services, and find out about its special projects.

CNS, Inc
gopher://cscns.com:70/1
National Internet service provider, Internet Express, introduces its services and connection options via info provided in this gopher menu. Visitors can plug into game servers and link to selected business clients.

CommerceNet Directories of Products & Services
http://www.commerce.net/directories/news/inet.prov.dir.html
Visitors shopping for an Internet provider or consultant on the national or regional level will find an index of com-

panies here. The site also includes information on how to be listed.

CRL Network Services
http://www.crl.com/

CRL Network Services is a nationwide, business-oriented Internet service provider based in San Francisco, Calif. This page provides details about the company's products and services, technical support information, employment opportunities, and a list of CRL's dialup locations.

EarthLink Network
http://www.earthlink.net/

The EarthLink Network provides full Internet access to users across the United States and Canada. In addition to dialup services, EarthLink offers Web storage space for businesses and individuals, as well as domain name registration.

Flightpath Communications
http://www.flightpath.com/

The Flightpath Communications site caters low-cost Internet services to small businesses, nonprofits and individuals. Commercial transactions and application kits are among the page's offerings.

FreeMark Communications
http://www.freemark.com/

FreeMark Mail offers free e-mail service to all PC users in the continental United States, with the fees for the service picked up by "discreetly placed" advertisements. Check out a demo at the FreeMark home page.

GES Internet
http://www.jvnc.net/

Global Enterprise Services provides Internet access and network services to commercial, academic, and government organizations worldwide. This site provides links to company directories, client lists and more.

IBM Internet Connection
http://www.ibm.net/

Visitors to this corporate site will find IBM's collection of links to corporate news, customer service information, computer resources, and an index of IBM servers worldwide. Includes information about Big Blue's Global Network dialup Internet access service, plus an online help desk. In English and Japanese.

I-Link
http://www.i-link.net/

This United States-based Internet access provider offering nationwide dialup services details its products and pricing. Register for a free trial run, or become a subscriber online.

InfiNet
http://www.infi.net/

Internet access provider InfiNet is owned by newspaper publishing heavy hitters, Gannett Co. Inc. and Knight-Ridder Inc. and, not surprisingly, specializes in bringing newspapers online. The site includes service descriptions, a 411 directory, and an electronic newsstand.

INFO.Net
http://www.info.net/

INFO.Net, part of the Infonet Services Corporation, is a provider of Internet access. This site presents corporate information and details on products and services, as well as tools and resources.

Intercon: Internet Information and Resources
http://www.intercon.net/

Intercon is a nationwide Internet access provider offering Web starting points and basic guides to the Internet at its home page. The site offers a listing of what's new on the Internet, as well as links to downloadable software.

LDS iAmerica
http://www.iamerica.net/

Internet service provider LDS iAmerica, an affiliate of Long Distance Savers Inc., pitches its access options in the local Texas and Oklahoma area and in the rest of the continental United States. The page includes links to customer pages and technical support.

MCI
http://www.mci.com/

Telecommunications giant MCI, providing long distance, wireless, local access, paging and Internet services, offers this corporate home page. Visitors can learn about its latest connectivity promotions and find detailed information about its products for business and home.

MSN
http://www.msn.com/

Microsoft Corporation, having conquered operating systems, moves on to the Internet with the Microsoft Network, an online service and Web exploration starting point that can be customized with sports scores, stock quotes, comics…whatever content the customer prefers. Includes information about Microsoft's products and services.

NETCOM
http://www.netcom.com/

NETCOM On-line Communication Services Inc. is a national provider of Internet access. At the NETCOM site learn about products and services, subscribe electronically, and download the company's custom interface, NetCruiser.

Network-USA's ISP Catalog
http://www.netusa.net/ISP/

This Internet access provider catalog indexes countries, complete with links to individual area codes, allowing users to find available Internet services in any desired region. Internet service providers can add themselves to the list via e-mail.

The NFIC MultiHost Server
http://www.nfic.com/Multi/Host

The New Frontiers Information Corporation MultiHost Server provides a demonstration of the firm's services here. Includes answers to Frequently Asked Questions, tech specifications, and pricing info.

Pilot Network Services Inc.
http://www.pilot.net/

Pilot Network Services Inc., headquartered in San Francisco with offices in Los Angeles, Chicago, and New York, provides secure Internet services for commercial use. Visitors to its home page can learn more about the company and its services.

Pronet Global Interactive Business Centre
http://www.pronett.com/

British Columbia-based Pronet Enterprises Ltd. provides Internet access and Web page development for businesses around the world. This commercial page contains pricing and contact information for the company.

PSINet
http://www.psi.net/

PSINet, a major mainstream commercial Internet access provider, provides an overview of the company, descriptions of services, and pricing information. Includes an analysis of the company's stock performance, corporate services, and a listing of international and domestic business affiliates.

Random Access
http://www.randomc.com/

An Internet access provider posts its services and rates here along with a catalog of hardware. The page also contains links to the server's user pages.

Real/Time Communications
http://www.realtime.net/

Real/Time Communications provides Internet access to individuals and business users, supporting terminal-based access and SLIP/PPP accounts attached directly to the global network. Contact and account information are provided, as well as a help desk.

Source Internet Services, North America
http://www.sisna.com/

Source Internet Services offers Internet access and Web page development services nationwide. Review SIS product offerings and connectivity options at this promotional site.

SprintLink

http://www.sprintlink.net/

Information on SprintLink, the wide area network service of the major U.S. telecommunications company, Sprint Corporation, is available at this site. Visitors will find its customer handbook, contact information, and links to the main Sprint home page. Includes index of Internet-related career opportunities.

U.S. Internet

http://www.usit.net/usit.html

U.S. Internet is a full-service Internet provider. Includes information about the company, a description of services, and pricing.

U.S. Internet Service Providers List

http://www.primus.com/staff/peggy/
provider.html

Provided by Primus Consulting, this page contains a list of Internet access providers in the United States. Pointers to other lists of providers, some including access providers from around the world, are also featured.

USA.NET

http://www.usa.net/

USA.NET offers Web hosting services which include domain registration, Web site design, and other commercial presence options. The Internet service provider serves up company info, along with a newsstand and gloss of Web resources.

UUNET Technologies

http://www.uu.net/

UUNET Technologies, a commercial Internet service provider, promotes itself and its products here. The company describes the services it markets to the business community and offers a corporate profile.

West Coast Online Inc.

http://www.wco.com/

The home page of this Internet access provider explains the company's business and personal service offerings. The company's online newspaper, available here, provides coverage of telecommunication and technology is-

sues. Site includes links to the Jumbo Software Archive and similar resources.

WinNET Communications Inc.

http://www.win.net/

WinNET hawks its international Internet access services through this corporate home page. The site explains who WinNET is, describes its services, and includes links to customer Web sites.

MORE HELP IS ON THE WAY!

There are many books written these days that tell all about getting on the Internet, and that provide CD-ROMs containing software, enabling you to do the deed with ease. In fact, there are so many, and changing every day, it's best to find a good computer bookstore and browse to your heart's content to find one that looks right for you. One comes immediately to mind: *Internet in a Box,* published by Hayden Books, for both PCs and Macs. This book explains everything and comes complete with a disk providing all you need to start surfin'.

GOING, GOING, GONE

Forgetting that these instructions are often written by computer geniuses and not regular folks like you and me, I thought to myself how easy this looked. I had a brand new modem capable of handling the massive tracks I expected to lay on the Net, and it was officially hook-up time.

NOT QUITE!

Stepping off with confidence, I read through the modem manual that told me which wires and plugs went into what ports, and into the telephone and computer. Before long, cords were everywhere, plugged into anything, yet nothing would work.

Hours later, having tried to follow the manual to the best of my limited ability, reading the diagrams

Lizzie's Tips

When hooking up your modem, if you can do away with your old answering machine and use an alternate method to collect messages (like your phone company's voicemail system), do so. It makes the hook-up much less complicated and leaves less to go wrong when Murphy's Law asserts itself.

until I reached a volcanic level of self-destruction, I lay on the floor sighing with frustration and fatigue. It was good I had thought to have a friend nearby who coaxed me to keep on trying. Too weak to argue and numb with exhaustion, I finally got it right!

I know what you're thinking: How can anybody be so dumb? Well, here I am. Bronze me! But seriously: These days, modems and modem connections are pretty foolproof. And if you get stuck and start scratchin' your head, help is usually just a phone call away.

THERE'S MORE TO COME

Installing and configuring the software which permits entrance to the realms of the Internet is your next step, and can prove to be another challenge. Approach this slowly, carefully, and calmly. If you need tech support, they can be on the line at the touch of your dialpad, walking you through every detail. These people are great, usually well informed about your system, and are trained to answer your questions.

And don't forget, your ISP should have provided you with complete instructions in written form, as well as software in its welcome packet. Follow it to the letter and you're home free. Even I can do this!

PPP

All computers use a PPP, or Point to Point Protocol, which allows the use of TCP/IP (Transmission Control Protocol/Internet Protocol) applications over asynchronous serial lines. (Don't panic, it's only techno-talk.) Without the PPP and TCP/IP there would be no way to make a connection to the Internet. A little bit like a conveyor belt at the post office, TCP/IP packages and addresses information, and then ensures that it arrives safely at the right destination. With this technology, you can use telnet, e-mail, FTP, gopher, and you can access the World Wide Web, directly from your computer. Getting confusing already, eh?

THE NEW P.O.

E-mail is the most widely used feature on the Internet, allowing you to exchange electronic mail with people all over the world. You must have an e-mail program installed on your computer to send and receive mail. Eudora is a very popular program available for both Mac and PC, in freeware and commercial versions. Commercial service providers like AOL have their own built-in e-mailers, and if you sign up with an ISP, they will provide you with e-mail software in a "getting started" package.

Electronic messages move so much faster than the old post office system, now known in these digital times as "snail mail." E-mail can travel around the world in only minutes. A message can contain a few lines, or many paragraphs, and unlike the P.O., you aren't charged by weight! Most ISPs don't charge you additional fees for sending and receiving e-mail, no matter how many miles it travels. Sure beats those long distance tabs when you have a lot of friends and family around the world.

BROWSIN' AN' CAROUSIN'

Almost all the software you will need is included on introductory disks from access servers, and on CD-ROMs from the basic books you may buy. But if you plan to be a Web junkie, the browser is the most important piece you'll get, as this is the interface which you'll use to view sites on the World Wide Web. The browser allows you to connect to one of the millions of addresses out in cyberland that you have chosen. Many companies will provide you with a copy of Netscape Navigator, but there are others. To help you get started, you'll find a copy of Microsoft's Internet Explorer on the CD-ROM which accompanies this book.

The World Wide Web is a graphical, simple-to-use system that is a part of the Internet. This is where you'll find all the good stuff. The Web consists of an enormous collection of documents—called "sites," or "pages"—that are stored on computers around the world. There is an unimaginable amount of information contained on these pages, many with gorgeous graphics, sound, and even mini-movies. Your browser acts as transportation to and from these different pages or sites.

HTML, or Hypertext Markup Language, is the programming language used to create pages on the Web, and to create links from one page to another (those links are called "hyperlinks," and you'll recognize them on Web pages because they'll appear as underlined, colored text; click on one and see what happens!). HTML also defines how text and graphics will appear on each page.

A URL, short for Uniform Resource Locator, is the original location ("address") for each page on the Web. Inserting these addresses into your browser's "Open," "Netsite," or "Go to" window will deliver pages from individual Web sites to your computer (you don't actually "visit" the Web sites yourself; instead, the text and graphics appearing on

Lizzie's Tips

When you find a Web site that you like a lot and want to revisit, use the "Bookmark" or "Favorites" feature of your browser's menu. While the page is displayed in your browser window, pull down on the "bookmark" or "favorites" menu and select the "add" feature. This automatically marks and saves the URL in a bookmark or favorites file. Next time you want to visit that site, you can do so without having to remember the address, simply by recalling it from your cache of bookmarks.

those pages are delivered to you via your browser). Almost all Web addresses start with "http://," the acronym for "hypertext transfer protocol," the HTML system which enables your browser to transfer Web pages from host computers to your desktop.

Understanding how this whole gigantic and mysterious thing works should make it little easier to get out there and grapple with it, taming the bear. Even though I am far from being a "techno-nerd," I find the way the Internet is set up extremely interesting.

DIGGING AROUND

Gopher is also an Internet tool, used for accessing information (usually text-only files, but often graphics or software, too) stored by universities, government agencies, companies, or even private individuals. These sites are often called "gopher holes," a term which comes from the first gopher site ever established, hosted at the University of Minnesota, and named after their mascot (you guessed it, a gopher). You'll need gopher software to access these sites, such as TurboGopher for the Macintosh (although many gopher holes have companion sites on the World Wide Web, which you can access via your

Lizzie's Tips

Keep it simple. If you are a beginner, just use the tools provided by your ISP's starter disk. When you have gained some expertise, it won't be so confusing to get into more depth. You'll know all the terms then, and you'll have more confidence.

browser). Use the program provided by your ISP, or follow the instructions for accessing gopher sites provided by your commercial service provider.

If you find yourself blocked attempting to enter a gopher hole, don't panic. These sites sometimes have limited access and can only accommodate limited numbers of people. Try again later during off-peak hours: late nights and weekends.

A FEW POPULAR GOPHER SITES

World Health Organization
gopher.who.ch

Library of Congress
gopher.loc.gov

United Nations
gopher.undp.org

University of Minnesota
gopher.tc.umn.edu

This spot contains a huge index of other gopher sites.

DOWNLOAD, DOWNLOAD, DOWNLOAD!

Almost anything and everything you can think of is available on the Internet for downloading, from great literary texts, government reports, wild and crazy sound files, to satellite images. FTP, or File Transfer Protocol, makes it possible for you to access these files

and use them on your home computer, no matter what your platform (and no matter what the platform of the host computer). Be sure your ISP provides you with a good FTP program (for Mac users, try Fetch); if you're sticking with a commercial provider like AOL, they'll have built-in download programs.

If you plan to download many items (and once you've started, it will be hard to stop!), be sure you have a good compression and decompression application for converting software and other files. These programs compress files (and decompress them once they've been received by you) so that the time it takes to transfer, or download, them is minimized.

For Mac users, nothing beats StuffIt Expander and DropStuff, freeware and shareware applications, respectively (there's also a swell commercial version that does it all, called StuffIt Deluxe; check with your software vendor to obtain a copy). Both of these applications are available for download in AOL's Macintosh software forum, and on Macintosh software download sites like the Info-Mac Archives (**http://neptune.dcez.com/mac/infomac.html**).

PC users will want to obtain copies of PKZip and PKUnzip, two tried-and-true compression/decompression utilities that no software junkie should be without.

Again, if you're unsure about where to obtain any of these compression utilities, check with the tech support people from your ISP, or consult the software archives housed by your commercial service provider.

ADDITIONAL ONLINE HELP

Guide to Slip and PPP
http://www.charm.net/ppp.html

This site gives instructions on how to use Internet dial-up tools, and offers explanations of how they work, with pointers on where to find installation and configuration details.

Guide to Network Resource Tools
http://www.earn.net/gnrt/notice.html

This is as good as going to college. Every tool for the PC or Mac to enhance your enjoyment of the cyberspace world is here, discussed and explained in detail. Part the clouds of confusion, step right in, and ease your pain.

DUH!

If you jump into this on your own and start to get discouraged, don't despair. Remember that the computer know-it-all's who write the "How-To" manuals can forget that the average reader could be a rank beginner; "beginner" stuff may left by the wayside in favor of "short-cuts" or more complex information, often leaving you at the post in total confusion, wondering what steps have been left out.

Get a buddy to sit by your side, preferably one who has gone through this before and can lead you out of the swampland—one tough enough to watch a grown man cry, and sensitive enough to fill the role of psychic counselor.

At one point, I had my modem working from the printer port, as it refused to do anything from the more logical modem port. This caused no real trouble as the printer happily ground away from the modem port, and the modem from the printer port, but the whole thing disturbed my orderly mind. In a day or so, frazzled but determined, I was properly hooked up and ready to roll onto the Internet. Any 12-year-old could have done this in 20 minutes…but never mind that. The real secret here is: None of this stuff is really all that hard. It just seems that way when it's still new and different. Once you familiarize yourself with your tools (both hard and soft) and the terminology, you'll be clicking your tongue over your initial bafflement.

With all your communication software properly installed, and your modem firmly connected to the cyberworld, take pride in your accomplishment. Don your suit, jump in, and dial up! Let's go surfin'.

Lizzie's Tips

It's always best to keep your hard drive less than full. Maintaining twenty percent free space is a good rule of thumb. When you do this, you're less apt to suffer a dreaded system crash.

MORE INTERNET ACCESS PROVIDERS

Welcome to Delphi Internet
http://www.delphi.com/dir-html/benefits/register.htm

This access server offers good deals for new sign-ups, with expert tech help and conversation as part of the package. Find out how to construct your own home page on the Web.

Primenet
http://www.primenet.com/

This national Internet access server offers excellent tech help with all the tools you need to get on board, complete with pointers to Web sites galore.

Internet Access Providers List
http://www.umd.umich.edu/~clp.i-access.html

For a complete list of public Internet access providers, sorted by the area codes they service, this index gives full details and information, along with telephone numbers and Internet mailing addresses. For those in remote areas or far from major metropolitan areas, this could be the perfect answer for finding the very best provider close to home.

The Unnamed List of Access Providers
http://www.resnet.cornell.edu/IAP/INAccess.html

If you are having trouble finding a provider near you from the list above, check this site. Providers are listed by regions, both national and international, and the list is constantly updated.

Lizzie's Tips

If you get befuddled, it is still best to let your access provider's technical crew lead you through. They know the configurations for every modem and operating system out there, and they can help you with everything you need. Your new partner in this venture is your ISP, providing you not only with a gateway to the Internet, but the know-how you need to get there with ease. They can continue to give you ongoing tech support should you need it, and can usually send you written instructions upon request. Once you have passed that first connection hurdle, the rest is a cakewalk.

WHEN YOU'RE LOOKING FOR SOMETHING MORE, LET YOUR KEYBOARD DO THE WALKING

Internet White Pages
http://home.mcom.com/home/internet-white-pages.html

Just like that old phone book at home, the Internet White Pages contains thousands of listings of individuals; but unlike that paper phone book, this one lists not phone numbers and street addresses, but e-mail addresses. This is the easy way to locate that special person you'd like to write to.

Worldwide Yellow Pages
http://www.yellow.com/

Like the yellow pages of your phone book, this is the electronic version, listing nearly all businesses with a presence on the Internet.

THE CHATTING MASSES

Bulletin Boards (BBSs) and "chat" services proliferate in every city, and on the Web as well. Even with a slow modem connecting only to a local number,

it's easy to join a group of people who enjoy posting messages to each other on a BBS, or indulging in a real-time chat session, where each sentence posted by the participants appears on your screen as if by magic, while it's being written somewhere else at that very moment—perhaps even miles away. These online chats are truly "live" discussions, connecting people who might otherwise never meet, and all without the bother of long distance phone charges!

Some people go completely nuts and become addicted to this form of communication. Often, some brave soul has set up a system in his basement, providing a server that you can access to "talk" to newly made friends in cyberspace. For local bulletin boards (not quite the same thing as live chat), you'll be given a phone number for dial-in through your modem, and the next thing you know, you are transported into a virtual posting area (much like that cork-style bulletin board that may be hanging on your kitchen or office wall), where all kinds of people are yakking about their favorite subjects.

PALAVER AND PRATTLE

Most BBSs let you use their services free of charge, while some charge a yearly fee. Many BBBs provide games, and some even have chat lounges available for live discussions. Still others provide limited use of the Internet for exchanging e-mail.

All you need to connect to a local BBS is a basic communications program, usually bundled with your modem or computer (Macintosh Performas come bundled with a terrific program called Clarisworks, which includes communication software, a word processor, spread sheet, and even a drawing program). Follow the instructions provided by your host BBS to activate your connection. Once you've done that, you will post and communicate using simple lines of text, but no pictures (for that, you'll need to visit the World Wide Web).

Your public library should have a list of local bulletin boards, including telephone numbers and any charges for dialing in (keep in mind that a lot of community bulletin boards are free!). Or you can pick up one of the local computer newspapers at your newsstand or bookstore, and check the BBS listings there.

You might also want to check with your library to see whether your community has a "freenet." A freenet is a bulletin board system and ISP that posts community information, local business and political news, current events, school calendars, and usually offers basic access to the Internet at no charge (or at substantially reduced rates). Generally these freenets are manned by volunteers. Some are supported by local community colleges.

YAKKITY-YAK

Then there's Usenet. Usenet is short for "Users Network," and is the largest discussion forum in the world, consisting of thousands of discussions (called newsgroups), on any subject you can think of. Each group takes up a particular topic, such as basketball, chemistry, UFOs, travel, a foreign language, history of the Civil War, a special hobby…phew! The possibilities are endless.

Newsgroup participants will post notes to their group's forum in much the same way you would post to your local BBS. An "article" (or, as with a BBS, a "posting") is the message a person sends to his or her newsgroup. It can be a few lines, or the length of a full book. The "thread" in a newsgroup is the subject of the original article, and includes all replies to the original article. Threads can contain questions and answers from other readers, and can continue for weeks, months…even years.

The name of a newsgroup reveals the kind of information the group discusses, usually consisting of two or more words or abbreviations separated by periods, such as "rec.sport.basketball.pro," or

Lizzie Sez

Be forgiving of others when they make mistakes, but more importantly, be forgiving of yourself when you make one.

"alt.ufo.reports." The first part of the newsgroup name reveals the general Usenet area of interest— for example, "rec" stands for recreation, and "alt" stands for alternative. The group "rec.sport.basketball.pro" will appeal to those persons interested in discussing professional basketball; while the second group will appeal to those interested in UFO sightings and reports.

You must subscribe to a newsgroup if you want to read and post to it on a regular basis. When you subscribe, a program called a "newsreader" will keep track of which articles you have or have not read. (There are many newsreaders available for both PC and Macintosh users. Your ISP should provide you with one, along with instructions for its use, when you sign up for dial-up access.) Every day there are new articles posted, and you can choose which ones you wish to read, much like your morning newspaper.

Reply to a newsgroup article only if you have something pertinent to add. "Oh, Golly," just takes up space and does not really contribute anything very valuable to the discussion. Make sure you include a quote from the original article so other readers can identify the article you are referring to. If you want to keep your response private, send an e-mail to the author of the article.

Some newsgroups are moderated. This means that someone checks to see if the material being submitted is appropriate for the particular group, and ensures that the article or post meets the group's guidelines, before it is actually posted. In an unmoderated group, all messages are posted automatically.

If you want to practice sending an article to a newsgroup, send your message or article to "alt.test.newsgroup."

IT TAKES A GLOBAL VILLAGE

If you prefer the ease of your e-mail box over the posting functions of a newsreader, you might want to think about subscribing to a mailing list. Hundreds of mailing lists discuss topics of interest with people all over the world. These groups use e-mail to communicate with each other. Mailing lists are similar to newsgroups, but are often even more topically specific, and your messages are delivered straight into the mailbox on your computer.

In order to participate in a mailing list, you must subscribe to it. Most lists are free of charge, and you can unsubscribe at any time. Some lists come in the form of a digest where messages are grouped together and sent as one message. For a whole host of available mailing lists, take a look at the Web site **http://www.neosoft.com/internet/paml**, or go to the "news.answers" newsgroup and look for messages with the subject line, "Publicy Accessible Mailing Lists."

LURK, DON'T LURCH

For newsgroups and mailing lists, it is a good idea to read over messages for at least a week before jumping in with your own posting. This way, you can learn the drill. There are certain rules of etiquette (called "Netiquette") that you must observe, and each group will have its own peculiar style, tone, and point of view. It's important to understand each group's method and style before you lurch in and make a silly comment, or before you incite someone's ire. Standing in the sidelines and observing for a bit (known in Internet parlance as "lurking") is a good idea.

DO YAK BACK

Like the hubbub and conversation of cocktail lounges and smoky bars? There's no cover charge in these virtual lounges. IRC, or Internet Relay Chat, lets you communicate instantly with people around the globe without the horror of long distance telephone charges, allowing the unbridled addict a means to yak with folks all over the place. Similar to chatting on the telephone, IRC allows you to talk to one or more people by typing on the keyboard of your computer. When you type text, it appears immediately on the screen, so that everyone involved in the conversation can see it. Like newsgroups and mailing lists, chat areas—grouped by "channel"— usually focus on specific topics, and everyone uses a handle or nickname. With anonymity a factor here, never assume that folks are who they say they are.

You'll need special software in order to access IRC channels, and it's a good idea to locate a book- or Web-based tutorial on how to use IRC. Unlike the easy-to-use chat rooms on AOL, for example, IRC requires a bit more technical fiddling and expertise. But don't let this put you off giving it a try: IRC is much more freewheeling than most chat rooms sponsored by commercial service providers, and you're much more likely to hook up with an international audience there. For introductions to IRC and to sample some IRC software, visit mIRC at **http://www.geocities.com/SiliconValley/park/6000/index.html**, or Global Chat at **http://prospero.com/globalchat**.

MIND YOUR MANNERS

"Netiquette" is the term used to describe good manners on the Internet. Here are a few tips so that you won't breach the code!

1 Read the FAQ (pronounced "FACK," and short for "Frequently Asked Questions") that pertains

to the group you have joined. This will keep you up-to-date on questions that have already been asked so that you don't make the mistake of asking them over and over again. The newsgroup "news.answers" provides a list of many FAQs from different newsgroups so that you can learn about a lot of topics in a short time.

2 Choose your words carefully, remembering that thousands of people around the world will be reading your posting. You don't want it to be misinterpreted. Sarcasm is especially difficult to get across in a written message, and may offend some readers, so be careful! Be sure that you are clear and concise, and that your spelling and grammar errors are kept to a minimum.

3 Pick an interesting subject heading, as this is the first introduction to your article, and it should identify your topic clearly.

4 Be certain your posting goes to the appropriate group. Posting to many inappropriate groups is called "spamming," and is very annoying to those who have little interest in your topic—or even worse, if you are advertising a commercial product. This is frowned on severely.

Most Netiquette applies to all functions on the Internet, including e-mail. However, there are a couple of no-no's in particular to avoid when you are writing to a friend, or posting to a newsgroup or mailing list:

- To "flame" someone is to write an angry or insulting message. This is easy to do when you're posting anonymously, but it's considered bad form and bad taste. Think calmly before you respond to someone out of anger, even if you feel that the person's post warrants an angry response. A flamewar is an argument that continues between two or more list or group participants for a period of time, and if it gets out of hand, can result in ter-

mination of participants' subscriptions. Avoid engaging in such activity.

- A message written in all capital letters is called shouting. These messages are hard to read, and are just pain annoying, having much the same effect as raising your voice in a crowd. Always use upper and lower case letters when you are writing a message or posting.

Many people who are online a lot and who participate in a goodly number of newsgroups, mailing lists, and chat channels, use abbreviations to avoid so much typing. Here are just a few acronyms to get you started:

- LOL = lauging out loud
- MOTOS = member of opposite sex
- SO = significant other
- FYI = for your information
- IMO = in my opinion
- IMHO = in my humble opinion

It may take a little time to familiarize yourself with the many abbreviations true devotees use, but soon you'll have the hang of it, feeling like an old hand in no time at all.

A FEW BBSs AND CHAT RESOURCES

Channel 1 BBS
http:www.channel1.com/
This bulletin board/chat forum offers all kinds of meat and potatoes stuff, from financial market summaries to evaluations of software programs. There are 600 message boards, and the subscriber gets 30 minutes a day free chat time.

Quantum Net
http://www.quantum.net/

Discussion areas here cover every topic you can imagine: from hobbies and computers, to medicine and politics. Comes complete with a shareware library as well. Jump on board.

Rockpile BBS
http://rockpile.com/

This bulletin board is for the Mac freak who can't get enough info, or who can never be done talking about it. There are fonts, games, graphics, general information files, and Newton applications.

Sorcery BBS

Here there are massive amounts of shareware and images for the game lover, coupled with message boards. Sorcery will give you 25 free minutes of use a day before charges kick in.

   And for those who become BBS junkies, the World Wide Web BBS list (**http://dkeep.com/sbi.html**) is just the thing to sate your appetite. Gorge yourself on all that anonymous glory, lurk in those lairs, and post to the world.

FOR THE TOTALLY CONFUSED

Glossary of Internet Terms
http://www.matisse.net/files/clossary/html

The Internet is chock full of hundreds of confusing terms. Use this comprehensive glossary to uncover the meaning of those you do not know.

The Internet Classroom
http:uu-gna.mit.edu:8001/uu-gna/text/internet/notes

You can experience hands-on learning about the Internet and the Web, available in tutorials, FTP, Usenet, and mail. Try out the homework. No one fails this class.

THE WHOLE ENCHILADA

Planet Earth
http://www.nosc.mil/planet_earth/internet.html

Planet Earth takes you on a tutorial of the whole Internet and its quirks. This is a complete guide to Cyberspace which includes a video for beginners, book lists, and directory services. This site is loaded with information from shopping and points of interest, to network information and references. To tighten up your understanding and your skills, this site should not be missed.

THE SEARCH IS ON

Internet search engines do a lot of work for you. Lost, need a site title, FTP address, or a URL? These little babies reach their long tentacles out through the vast, dark corridors of cyberspace, and bring to you in minutes the site you sought, maybe even hundreds of them.

   There are several ways that a search engine finds pages on the Web: One way is to use automated "robots" or "spiders" that travel around the Web looking for new sites. Then the robots or spiders "bring them home" to a database which search engine administrators house and maintain on a giant computer. Other engines and directories will ask people to submit information about sites they have created, and build their databases in this way (this is more true of smaller, highly specialized search and database services than it is of the large commercial search services).

To do a search using Lycos, you'll have to first visit the home page: **http://www.lycos.com** (see Figure 2.1). Start your search by entering a phrase that best describes the information you're looking for. Avoid using prepositions (of, with, for, to) and articles (a, an, the); like most engines, Lycos will ignore these words.

When your search is complete, a lot of Web pages listings will be returned to you (in groupings of 10) that contain the word or words you specified. Lycos will display the results of your search in order of relevancy to your subject matter.

You can also narrow your search by performing a "customized" query. Select the "custom search" link to the right of the Lycos search box (see Figure 2.2), and you'll be presented with a number of options which will help you to refine your results. You may get less information returned to you, but chances are that it will be a better fit.

A custom search permits you to use connector words ("and," "or"), and to "match" as many as seven terms in your search string. For example, if you choose to use the "or" option (which is also the default setting on the standard Lycos search), documents returned to you will contain any one of the words you entered as your search phrase, but not necessarily all of them together. If you chose to

search for "University of Mississippi Alumni," you could find that you have thousands (perhaps even millions) of Web sites returned to you, all of which would contain at least one of the words, "university," "Mississippi," or "alumni." Wow! That could mean clawing your way through millions of sites before you reached the one you really wanted.

You can narrow the results by entering the search phrase "university mississippi alumni," and choosing the search option "match all terms (AND)" (see Figure 2.3), to ensure that every document returned to you will contain all three words, thereby enhancing the probability that the sites you get will have something to do with alumni matters at Ole Miss.

You can also use the custom search options to change the number of sites displayed on each results page from the default setting of 10, to 20, 30, or even 40 per page; to define the strength of the match to your query words ("loose," "fair," "good," "close," or "strong"); and to change the kind of information you receive about each Web site. For example, "standard results" will return the name of the Web site, its URL, and the text of the first three paragraphs on its opening page. "Detailed results" will return a lot more text from the site's opening page, and "summary results" will get you the bare bones: the site name and URL.

Figure 2.1
The Lycos search engine gateway

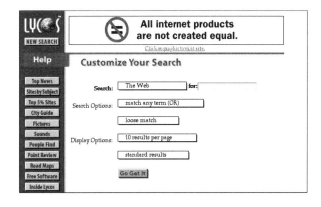

Figure 2.2
The Lycos "custom search" feature allows you to conduct more specific searches.

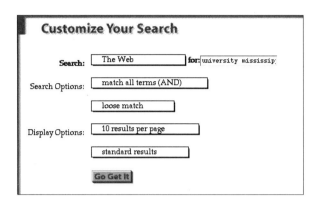

Figure 2.3

Selecting the "match all terms" option in a Lycos custom search is one way to increase the relevance of sites retrieved for you.

Which one you use will depend greatly on your individual searching style, how well you know your subject, and how much time you have to spare.

There are other good engines and directories out there in addition to Lycos. The list below includes some that are currently available. Find a favorite, or use them all, as I often do.

Top 5% of All Web Sites
http://point.lycos.com/categories/

This site, sponsored by Lycos, contains a comprehensive directory of sites which Lycos writers and editors have rated as being among the top five percent of all sites on the Web. These sites are rated and reviewed according to content, presentation, and experience. Selections here are among the most visited and most interesting sites you will find.

The Net Search Directory
http://home.netscape.com/home/internet-search.html

This is a listing of major search engines and their directories. Click on the one of your choice and see miles of info, just by selecting the search button and entering your query. Includes Infoseek, Magellan, Alta Vista, and Lycos. Net Search can also be found on the tool bar of Netscape Navigator. One click and you're there.

Beaucoup Search Engines
http://www.beaucoup.com/engines.html

Over 500 search engines are listed here, including the most familiar, but how about "Tribal Voice" and "Link-Monster"? Subscribe to the free newsletter *SearchZine*.

search.com
http//:www.search.com

This was one of the first meta-search engines on the Net, containing all the biggies—Lycos, Yahoo!, Excite, and more—but home to many obscure, lesser-known searchable databases geared to specialized topics. You can also do your searching directly from this site, courtesy of Alta Vista. A service of c|net.

Internet Sleuth
http://www.isleuth.com/

This search engine will query other popular search engines with your questions, all at the same time. A time saver for you. This little zinger also has many categories for you to browse.

Sherlock and the Search
http://www.intermediacy.com/sherlock/

This witty site is packed with innovative ideas, and shows how Sherlock Holmes can doff his deerstalker and gather Internet information. Every two weeks he delivers "The Tip of The Fortnight," one that is certain to be very worthwhile to you.

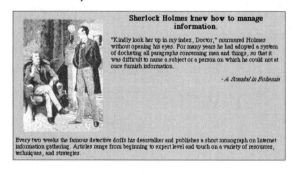

IF YOU CRAVE A LITTLE EXTRA...

The Virtual Library
http://www.virtuallibrary.com/

These Netizens specialize in information management, classifying books and periodicals, reports, and heaps of other reference material for your retrieval.

TOOLS FOR FOOLS

Res-Links
http://www.cam.org/~intsci/

This is your all-in-one resource page for utilities, tools, catalogs, archives, and libraries. You could spend hours here doin' your thang.

Apple
http://www.apple.com/

All the news that fit to print concerning the Mac, complete with technology, online resources, customer support, and product information. The site comes complete with a search tool so you find out the particulars about your favorite Macintosh toy.

Microsoft
http://www.microsoft.com/

This is a complete inventory of products from this super large company. Browsers, viewers, add-ins, Web authoring tools, and entertainment packs are all available. Upgrade your system with free software for Windows 95, Microsoft Office, and Encarta.

BROWSERS

Internet Explorer
http://www.microsoft.com/ie/ie.htm

This is the download site for Microsoft's browser, Internet Explorer. There has been a lot of excitement awaiting its coming on the scene, and the graphics are great (and don't forget to check the CD-ROM accompanying this book; we've already supplied you with a copy).

Lizzie Sez

Not all Internet users have bleary, red, sunken eyes because we are crazed with an insatiable appetite for information, staying up all night lusting for more. Only some of us.

Netscape
http://home.netscape.com/

This is the big momma of Internet browsers, still a favorite among many Web developers. Netscape has a lot of features that make Web life easy, like a built in e-mailer, bookmarks, and convenient helper applications. The site provides purchase and download information, and other software relevant to the Internet. Visit the Netscape General Store for T-shirts and other goodies.

Webreference.com
http://www.webreference.com/browsers.html

Everything you ever wanted to know about current Web browsers is right here. A complete list of browsers and helper apps with collections and comparisons.

The Anonymizer
http://www.anonymizer.com/

If you're concerned about logging onto sites and getting caught in their data banks, drop into the Anonymizer and see how you can protect your privacy while you surf.

GOODIES GALORE

Some of the sites I've already mentioned will offer software to be downloaded, such as Apple and Microsoft, MacWorld and PCWorld, but here are two more important software sites that have large archives of wonderful additions for your hard drive.

So Much Software, So Little Time
http://www.clicked.com/shareware/

There is a ton of good material here for the PC user: graphics, Internet stuff, communication software, and utilities. Give it a good browse and fill your coffers.

Shareware.Com
http://www.shareware.com/
Developed for the PC and Mac user alike, this site offers new arrivals and most popular selections, along with old favorites for your downloads. A very popular place, and one you may want to visit often in your quest for the latest upgrade. Hosted by c|net.

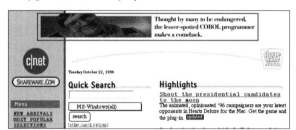

SO JOIN US

One of my e-mail pals, Toni, says jokingly that her husband of 85 is contemplating a divorce, naming her computer as co-respondent. I hope that it doesn't come to that for you, but I am in trouble with most of my friends who can never reach me when they call, and my children who have finally forced me to put in a second telephone line so that the horrible frustration of trying to communicate with MOTHER can be put to rest.

But if you can't reach me, and I forget to return your calls, you always know where to find me. I'm

Lizzie's Tips
How to download: It's simple. Just click on the underlined, hyperlinked word or phrase that has already been identified as downloadable, and wait, following along with the dialog box that tells you the status (and progress) of your download. And lo! There it is on your desktop (or in your designated download folder) for you to unstuff or unzip and pack away where you want it (Netscape will unzip/unstuff files for you automatically).

in the back room, groovin' with Ruby Perl and surfin' the Web. These days, it's best to send me an e-mail. Olé!

And so, gentle reader, I leave this chapter with a little challenge for you: One of the advantages of being Seniors is that we've been out here hiding in the bushes for a number of years, watching as our world has slowly turned, yet swiftly changed. And among the most rapid changes we've seen: computer technology. Don't you think it's high time we showed 'em just how expert we can get?

C'mon in, all you gray panthers. The surfin's just fine.

Chapter 3
SIMPLY SENIOR

IN THE BEGINNING

PARTNERSHIPS

AND GRANTS

LEARNING

LET THERE BE LIGHT!

STRENGTH IN NUMBERS

Sometimes, wondrous things just happen, with no rhyme or reason or explanation. And it was just such a wondrous thing that occurred when Mary Furlong began a research project at The University of San Francisco in 1986, and had a far-reaching idea—an idea that started by saying, "yes," older folks *will* welcome computer technology, use it, enjoy it, and enhance their lives with it. With no defined goals or blueprints, Mary sought funding and bought inexpensive computers at toy stores, setting them up in church basements, Senior centers, and nursing homes. The response was overwhelming.

Taking a page from her grandmother's book, Furlong had recognized immediately how important it was for Seniors to have community. Many Seniors feel left out of the fast-paced society in which we live, and do not see their value in a fast-moving world. Furlong knew it was imperative to change this, by trying to link the 35 million adults over age 55 into a caring and sharing community. And so, SeniorNet was born.

IN THE BEGINNING

Today SeniorNet is more "simply Senior" than any other organization out there; it gathered momentum from founder Mary Furlong, who consistently challenged the prevailing notion a decade or so ago that Seniors did *not* need to use computer technology to enhance their lives. Strapping on her sword and shield, Furlong, full of energy and zeal—and using the back seat of her car as an office—gathered 20 people together to begin SeniorNet as a non-profit organization dedicated to teaching oldsters all they need to begin taking advantage of computers and new online technologies.

From that small beginning has grown an international organization with 20,000 dedicated members, 100 learning centers, 1500 volunteers, and an extensive online community. This early vision has touched the lives of 85,000 older people from age 55 to 102.

"I've got my world right in front of me. I can contact anyone and get all the information I need. I can go online and laugh with anyone, anytime."
    —E.B. Clark, Seattle, WA

Along with that vision has come a new image of aging, and the knowledge that older adults do have a great deal to contribute to our understanding of the world, giving credibility to the importance of how and why this technology should be used. And with all this, a huge community of members and volunteers has developed, celebrating the achievement.

Furlong says, "SeniorNet's focus and mission is always on the people—using the technology to support their work and the work of others."

"Continued learning is the only real fountain of youth. My computer—I couldn't live without it!"
    —Matt Lehmann, Cupertino, CA

PARTNERSHIPS

Combining all this talent with corporations that believed in the mission was the next step. Bell Atlantic, one of the partners in the SeniorNet endeavor, has been an avid supporter since the crystallization of the original idea, embracing the notion of involved Seniors, and helping to dispel the myth that folks over 55 are unwilling (or unable) to embrace opportunities presented by the new technologies that computers have brought into their lives.

"SeniorNet members have always provided kind, uncritical, patient consultation and training, both online and at the sites, making it possible for newcomers to join the community at any level of expertise."
    —Joan Elswitt, Warrenton, VA

Sponsoring ten SeniorNet Learning Centers, Bell Atlantic has discovered that Seniors are eager to get on the Internet to pursue a wide range of interests, from leisure and learning, to community involvement. And more importantly, Seniors are quick to realize the potential of Internet access, e-mail, wireless phones, and video-on-demand services, and how these advances can enhance the quality of their lives.

Raymond W. Smith, Chairman & CEO of Bell Atlantic has said, "What we find so attractive about SeniorNet is that its fundamental purpose, to bolster lifelong learning and create new communities unrestricted by geography, is consistent with our business goals—building 'virtual' communities, expanding educational opportunities, and giving people the flexibility to work, shop, or bank at home. That's the business we're in, and why we are working so closely with SeniorNet. After all, our business is really not about linking technologies; rather, it's about making connections between people."

> "You'll find SeniorNet an invigorating, challenging group of people, with an astonishing range of interests."
>
> —Dick Behan, Flagstaff, AZ

AND GRANTS

There from the launch of SeniorNet was the Markle Foundation in New York City. From 1986 through 1996, Markle supported the purpose and evolution of SeniorNet with a series of grants totaling over $6,000,000. SeniorNet reports that IBM has consistently provided generous grants, making it possible to expand the Learning Center program into many new communities, and to provide better support to volunteers and members of existing centers.

IBM has been and continues to be the largest sponsor of Learning Centers. Their retirees have served as coordinators and instructors in many of the centers already established.

IBM is also funding a new program for Learning Centers called "IBM Champions." These "Champions" have been selected from the many outstanding retirees who volunteer at the centers. Working in two important areas, Champions participate in the start-up process of new centers and provide follow-up support to ensure that each new center gets off to a successful start. Others develop hands-on computer courses.

LEARNING

SeniorNet Learning Centers are also sponsored by local organizations that are interested in enhancing the lives of older adults in their communities. Besides the regional Bell operating companies, IBM, and others, many health care providers, educational institutions, computer companies, and financial services offer their support to the Centers.

Centers usually offer hands-on computer classes in the basics of hardware operation, word processing, and how-to's for getting online. Larger Centers sometimes offer classes designed to enhance Seniors' employment situations, or that will provide instruction in necessary skills for those seeking new employment. Some even sponsor Job Placement Bureaus.

Other SeniorNet funders include: AcerComputer, Adobe Corp., American Express, Apple Computer, Inc., AT&T, Bell Atlantic, Bell South, Goldsmith Foundation, Intel, Kaiser, Microsoft, NYNEX Corporation, Pacific Bell, Pacific Telesis Group, Retirement Research Foundation, Searle Pharmaceuticals, Southcentral Bell, Southwestern Bell, Sprint, and Sybase U.S. West.

"At the start of every class, we ask, 'Why are you taking the class?' The answer is often, 'I want to keep up with my grandkids.' They want to be able to do the same thing the kids are doing, to interact with them. If they're distant from them they also talk about [being] online as a way of communicating with their families—especially their grandchildren."

—Phil Carnahan,
San Jose Learning Center

LET THERE BE LIGHT!

Today, ten years after its founding, SeniorNet has come a long way, with Learning Centers established all over the land, funders and corporate friends as partners, and thousands of active members volunteering, learning, and forming online communities.

Besides attracting the always active online groups to chat areas and bulletin boards on SeniorNet's area on America Online, SeniorNet has established its own Web site on the Internet, using the same combination of friendship and caring that has been its watchword for the past ten years. Let's take a look at these great resources.

SENIORNET ON AOL

America Online has had an established relationship with SeniorNet since 1991.

Once online, Seniors can choose areas of interest in which to participate (see Figure 3.1). The most popular areas are (you guessed it) the chat forums. On AOL, there are several areas where you are invited to sit down and read the messages, enjoy a visit with friends, or perhaps a virtual cup of coffee. The "Coffee and Danish" forum is home to the Peaceful Valley Cafe, where regulars drop in daily to share the news in their lives: a new grandchild, freshly harvested veggies from the garden, or even a new joke.

Sometimes it's congratulations, other times it's commiseration, but all enjoy wishing each other a good day and swapping stories.

SeniorNet's real-time chat room on AOL is active twenty-four hours a day. There may be a few scheduled events, but most of the time, folks just drop in and visit with whomever is there at the time. The conversation is usually just a few friends engaging in small-talk, making new friends, and passing the time.

AOL SENIOR NETIZENS FIND SUPPORT

One SeniorNetter's son gave her a computer to help make up for the debilitating effects of Parkinson's disease. Homebound most of the time, she still has daily access to friends all over the country through the forums at SeniorNet AOL.

One day, her online friends began to notice that her chat in the live area had become nonsensical, but she was able to tell her friends that she was in trouble. Calling 911 for her, they were able to get her the help she needed. She recovered and is back online with her old community and says, "I'm an old lady except when I am online; then I'm a 37-year-old, blue-eyed blond, ready to roll."

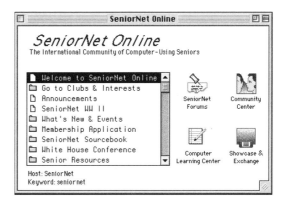

Figure 3.1
SeniorNet's main gateway on AOL offers a world of options to users.

A LEARNING CENTER NEAR YOU

Almost every state in the Union has a Learning Center, and some have several. Check the list below to find a Center near you; give them a call, and find out how you can participate in the fun, excitement, and community.

If there is not one near you and you would like to be a leader in developing one, call the SeniorNet main office in San Francisco 415-352-1210 (or e-mail LCoutreach@AOL.com).

Alabama
Birmingham, 202-599-8719
Huntsville, 205-880-7080

California
Bakersfield, 815-0322-9695 and 815-834-6951
Culver City, 310-253-6700
Fullerton, 714-449-7061
Orinda, 510-254-5939
San Francisco, 415-771-7950 and
415-922-7249
San Jose, 408-448-6400
San Mateo, 415-377-4735
Santa Cruz, 408-429-3506

Connecticut
Groton, 860-441-6785
Manchester, 860-647-3211
Norwalk, 203-847-3115

Florida
Boynton Beach, 407-737-7733 ext 4195
Fort Meyers, 813-334-5949
Orlando, 407-245-0921
St. Petersburg, 813-974-2403
Sunrise, 305-742-2299
Tampa, 813-974-5263
Winter Park, 407-647-6366

Georgia
Atlanta, 770-564-4680
Fulton County, 404-351-3889
Gwinnett County, 770-564-4680

Lawerenceville/Smyrna, 770-801-5320
Savannah, 912-651-7559

Hawaii
Hilo, 808-933-3555
Honolulu/Oahu, 808-845-9296
Kahului/Maui, 808-242-1216
Kokua Outpost, 808-528-4839

Illinois
Chicago, 312-747-0189
Cicero, 708-863-3552
Northfield, 708-446-8765
Palatine, 708-358-9962
Peoria, 309-691-4896
Skokie, 708-675-2200 ext 287
Springfield, 217-525-5699

Indiana
Indianapolis, 317-849-1099

Kansas
Overland Park, 913-469-8500 ext 3844

Kentucky
Lexington, 606-255-2527
Louisville, 502-459-0660

Louisiana
Baton Rouge, 504-923-8000

Maryland
Camp Springs, 301-248-6546

Minnesota
Minneapolis, 612-288-9048

Missouri
St. Louis, 314-993-0006

Nebraska
Omaha, 402-552-2209

Nevada
Las Vegas, 702-363-2626

New Jersey
Brick, 908-840-9400
Eatontown, 908-542-1326
Ewing, 609-883-1009
Tenafly, 201-569-7900
West Orange, 201-736-3200, ext 256

New York
New York City:
Forest Hills (Queens), 718-699-1010
Hudson Guild (Manhattan, Chelsea),
212-924-6710
Kingsbridge Heights (Bronx), 718-884-0700
Stanley Isaacs Neighborhood Center
(Manhattan, Upper East Side),
212-360-7620
Staten Island, 718-981-1500
University Settlement (Manhattan, Lower
East Side), 212-463-8217
Other New York Learning Centers:
Endicott, 607-754-0127
Kingston, 914-331-0902

North Carolina
Charlotte, 704-522-6222
Greensboro, 910-378-0766
Raleigh, 919-954-3105
Wilmington 910-452-6400

Ohio
Akron, 216-867-2150
Columbus, 614-228-8888
Toledo, 419-865-4415
Toledo South, 419-385-2595

Oklahoma
Oklahoma City, 405-728-1230

Oregon
Eugene, 503-345-9441

Pennsylvania
Philadelphia, 215-276-6148

Tennessee
Knoxville, 423-690-0444
Nashville, 615-327-4551

Texas
Dallas, 214-768-4332
Nacogdoches, 409-564-2411
Waco, 817-666-6154

Vermont
Essex (Burlington Area), 802-878-9530

Virginia
Springfield, 703-922-2474

Washington D.C.
Mazza Gallerie, 202-232-5892

Washington
Seattle, 206-232-5892

Wisconsin
Appleton, 414-735-4864

Lizzie's Tips

Finding other Seniors on AOL is easy. Simply log on to your AOL account, and enter the keyword "Senior-Net." As if by magic, the SeniorNet gateway will appear on your screen, placing you in the middle of good conversation, lively news, and access to folks around the world who are as active and curious as you are.

Another SeniorNetter, confined at home while caring for her elderly mother, says this of the Alzheimer/Dementia Forum on SeniorNet on America Online: "I found this message board on AOL about a year ago, and have been posting messages of my own ever since. It is my lifeline to sanity."

The Alzheimer's Caregiver's Forum contains messages posted to give support, understanding, and advice to others in similar situations, which bolster them and give new vigor and added faith to their lives.

Members of support groups on SeniorNet Online have done remarkable things in their forums. One such group, posting in the wake of the deadly Northridge earthquake in Southern California stayed online in the search for their friends, keeping the group advised of others' whereabouts, and offering them comfort and support in the face of this disaster. A typical message: "Polly's house is damaged, computers and TVs are damaged. Larry has a badly cut foot that required 20 stitches. They do not have water or power. Keep thinking of us."

Another bunch of posters kept track of their entire group, making sure all were accounted for and safe. SeniorNetters who are regular posters know that their online communications can be a valuable source of information and a great comfort in times of sorrow.

LET'S PARTY!

And then there are the bashes! A bash is an event that brings two or more SeniorNetters together, be it for a simple breakfast or a huge gathering of 200 (see Figure 3.2). An enterprising group from one of the SeniorNet forums forged an alliance with Elderhostel, a senior organization devoted to lifelong learning, and hosted a gathering in San Diego at the Center for Studies of the Future. One SeniorNetter says, "The greatest treat was meeting with computer friends and enthusiasts from all over the U.S., and having a lot of fun."

At any given time, picnics, lunches, and weekends are being planned online in the "Gatherings and Events" folder on SeniorNet Online.

KEEPING IN TOUCH WITH FAMILY

Developing a relationship with grandchildren you may see only a couple of times a year can be a stilted and difficult ordeal. To make it easier and more enriching, a SeniorNetter, Mike Moldevan, began to write to his grandchildren from his computer, telling them about all the little things that were happening

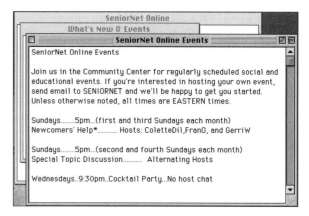

Figure 3.2

In addition to real-time "bashes" and get-togethers, SeniorNet on AOL hosts a variety of online events, bringing together Seniors from around the world for regular "cocktail parties" and topical discussions.

in his world. He wrote simple and colorful stories, just the kind children like, about spiders' webs, taking walks, and the neighbor's dog.

As the number of stories grew and were successful with his own grandchildren, Mike created "A Grandfather's Notebook: Ideas and Stories to Encourage Grandparent-Grandchild Interaction, Communications and Well-Being," as a way to help other grandparents develop and deepen lasting relationships with their grandchildren. Many of these stories can be downloaded from the SeniorNet site on AOL.

> "Ask any SeniorNet member what they value about their SeniorNet experience, and you will invariably hear that SeniorNet has brought to them the sense of belonging to a community. Whether it is on or offline, in a forum or a Learning Center, the camaraderie, understanding, and friendship members give and get is the essence of SeniorNet."
>
> —From SeniorNet Online

SENIORNET ON THE WORLD WIDE WEB

SeniorNet
http://www.seniornet.org

With its usual compassion, humor, and outreach, this successful international organization composed of 22,000 dues-paying Seniors states its mission to make today's computer technology accessible to the over-55 crowd through teaching, information, and building community. With access to 100 physical sites worldwide, Seniors can learn the latest in computer technology. This Web site contains reflections of the varied interests of the participants along with a host of interactive activities and Senior-oriented news (see Figure 3.3).

Figure 3.3
The SeniorNet home page

MAKING CONNECTIONS

In addition to a strong presence on AOL, you are invited to drop into SeniorNet's online WWW community. Here's where you will find some of the most stimulating conversation and commentary on the Web. Look into the RoundTable discussions, where you can post your own opinions on contemporary issues and topics, or offer your observations on the opinions of others. Numerous "cyberhosts," guide you through the RoundTables, introducing you to the forums, and generally sticking with you to answer questions until you are sure of yourself. Take a moment to introduce yourself. They will take good care of you as you embark on this adventure.

> "... bobbing on a sailboat in France ... at the moment."

ROUNDTABLES

You will find plenty of interesting topics and easy discussion in the topical folders of the RoundTables (see Figure 3.4). There are many talented (and opinionated) people dropping in. Take the time to go to

Figure 3.4
SeniorNet's RoundTable discussion area

"How to Use the RoundTables" tour, an online help file which shows you how to maneuver through RoundTable postings without tripping. "Folders" are used to organize the conferences, like a directory. Each folder contains discussions, and other subfolders, so that you can see where you are and never get lost.

Take a few minutes to peruse the RoundTable posting forums to find an area that particularly interests you. Some of the topics up for discussion are: Art, Gardening, Computer Help, Travel, and Person-to-Person. You'll find opinions galore—there are no shrinking violets here. Let's tip-toe inside and see what's happening in a few of these forums.

- **Introductions** Getting acquainted with new friends on SeniorNet is easy. Stop by the Introductions forum to find other newbies like yourself, or welcome greetings from an old pro. One member writes in the Introduction forum that she is posting from New Zealand, and says, "Am thoroughly enjoying the Internet and have joined

a group here in Auckland and find them a super bunch of people."

- **Books and Literature** Bibliophiles will delight at the opportunity to discuss their favorite novels, mysteries, and works of non-fiction. One regular visitor to the online Book Club writes, "A book is a kind of food for people to eat, so that they will grow up healthy and strong"; while another posts, "The first Emperor of China killed many intellectuals and burned many books…, because they were afraid books would open peoples' hearts and make them clever." Member Joan Pearson talks about what she has learned from reading *Snow Falling on Cedars*, a work of fiction that has much to teach us, she says, about our everyday lives.

- **Religion** In *Life After Death*, an area of the Religion forum, a discussion stems from a member's thoughts on psychic research. The poster comments, "Most of the messages from the 'other side' seem relatively trivial. One would think the dead would have more important things to say to us."

- **SeniorNet Cafe** You'll find cheerful and friendly people offering easy conversation in the SeniorNet Cafe. Drop in and add your brand of spice, grab a virtual cappuccino, and settle in for lively discussion. The Cafe is open for postings from folks wishing one another good tidings, telling the news of their days, swapping recipes, planning bashes, and generally sharing good fellowship. You get the feeling, right at first, that these people are very good friends. Some even include pictures, and exchange much warmth as they detail their lives to each other, like chit chat over the garden fence. This is a good place to come for a lift, and to meet some great folks.

Thanksgiving, 1996:
"Teresa!! Canned gravy???!!! Just give me the drippings from our big bird and five minutes...I'll make you the best turkey gravy you've ever tasted. A true Louisiana native can look out over a field of rice and tell you how much gravy you need to cover it!

- **The Parlor** If you are a real freak for live chat and like that feeling of immediacy, take a seat in the "Parlor," spread your skirts, and gossip away. This is a favorite spot to park for awhile, and is just the place for an immediate answer to a question, a little advice, or the latest dish on a favorite subject.

"When I have time, I drop in to read the postings. I can't help laughing when I read them. People ask me why I am so happy and I tell them it is because I have been watching some wonderful happy people talking, and their talking made me laugh."

JOIN THE DEBATE

But most fun of all is "Squabble," where Netters enter into the most spirited discussions by posting their opinions on various topics that are currently up for debate (see Figure 3.5).

An issue posed recently in a "Censoring the Wild Web" Squabble forum was whether the Communications Decency Act, passed as part of the huge telecommunications bill, was a swipe at the First Amendment. Fifty-eight Netters chose to respond with their own arguments, opinions, and insights:

- "I grew up in England at a time when *Lady Chatterley's Lover* was banned as obscene, & of course all we kids wanted to read it. A court case freed it and when we read it we thought it pretty tame. It's all in the mind of the beholder, don't you see. So refuse to behold and everything should be okay."

- "Give people the education to make the decision themselves; if they make a decision that doesn't fit with what you think they should make; so be it—they take the consequences of their action."

- "The Web should not be censored. It should be labeled, preferably by the Web site owners."

I stepped into the "I Now Pronounce You...?" Squabble to find the topic to be the appropriateness of same-sex marriages, with these additional questions posed: "Is this a federal or state issue?"; and "What are the possible outcomes of legalizing same-sex marriage?" Here are a few of the postings in reply.

- One member suggested that "...false assumptions about homosexuals casts a thick cloud over our moral fitness" to judge the issue at all.

- Another urged 'Netters to locate a tape of the ABC "Turning Point" program on same-sex marriages. " It was so well done; sensitive and fair and answered so many of the questions that were

Figure 3.5
The Squabble forums change and rearrange from week to week, and run the gamut from heated political and social debates, to thoughtful discussions of Senior-oriented issues.

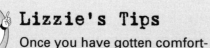

Lizzie's Tips

Once you have gotten comfortable, learned where everything is, become acquainted with other Netters and know the drill, you'll want to make postings of your own. The best way to learn how the discussion is going, who the folks are, and what their general opinions are, is to "lurk" for a while (see Chapter 2).

To post a message, click on the button provided for you on your screen marked "Post a Message," or scroll down to the message form at the end of each discussion. If you are shy, or you want to change the message you have posted, these kind folks will give you another chance. Change it to something more glamorous and exciting, but don't give up; you'll miss the fun.

asked in the earlier parts of this discussion—about why homosexuals want to get married and what it means emotionally and socially."

• And another responded, "I wish that all homophobics could have seen it [ABC's "Turning Point"]. The subject was treated with sensitivity and joy. And as the families found out, much to their surprise…it wasn't the tragedy they first imagined it would be…."

There were 127 postings just on this issue alone. Don't hesitate to put your toe in the water. Your opinion is awaited, and valued. Involvement is the name of this game, and you will be busy as a bee, trying to keep up with all these active minds, well-read peers, and humor junkies.

And of course, keeping it interesting all the time are changing topics inviting different ideas. Everything is in constant motion—always.

Lizzie Sez

Is the magic in the modem? As of publication, six SeniorNet couples found romance in the SeniorNet forums and have married.

"When I was a child, I dreamed of Ali Baba and his cave. It took me 50 years to find the magic word that would open the doors and reveal the treasure. SeniorNet is the 'open sesame' I have been searching for!"

BECOME A MEMBER

For all this and Heaven, too, fill out the membership form, a small questionnaire about your computer, and $35 in tax deductible dues. The quarterly newsletter, *Newsline,* comes with the deal, containing hardware and software reviews, and lots of news about what's happenin' at SeniorNet Centers around the country, along with all the dish on plans for the annual convention. What more could you ask?

For more information, call or write SeniorNet headquarters directly: SeniorNet, 1 Kearney Street, 3rd Floor, San Francisco, CA 94108, 415-352-1210 or 1-800-747-6848.

SENIORNETTERS' OWN WEB SITES

Not to be outdone by the whippersnappers, some Seniors have gotten so expert that they have their own Web pages posted on the Internet. Expressing their own brand of flair and expertise, these Seniors have become well-versed in this new technology, and have designed some beautiful and interesting Web sites for our pleasure. To view SeniorNetters' sites (they're growing all the time), or to add some favorite sites you have stumbled onto, duck into the folder on SeniorNet Online titled "Online Destinations" and get a quick fix. Here are some favorites.

Floral Design Newsletter
http://members.aol.com/ikenobo

This site, from member Jackie Nunes, shows one of her beautiful flower arrangements and publicizes her free on-line newsletter about floral design. Tips are offered for flower arrangements and preservation. The newsletter is free upon request.

If you are interested in receiving a free flower arranging newsletter sent via e-mail, please contact me: Ikenobo@aol.com

Waterfalls Online
http://www.btnet.com/infoman/ waterfallsonline

Carlo J. Flores, also a SeniorNetter, has made it his life's work to create an archive of the world's most beautiful waterfalls, and has compiled information about them to share with children (of all ages). CJ's notorious waterfall safaris and expeditions have taken him all over the world. He says that he will even answer e-mail while on safari.

Computer Related Stress
http://webz.com/stress

Al Berger reveals potential risks to computer users due to repetitive motions while at the keyboard. Al has created a nonprofit organization, "Public Awareness...Repetitive

Public Awareness...
Repetitive Strain Injury
109 Minna #323
San Francisco, CA 94105
Phone: 415-243-4122
Fax: 415-243-3971
Send us E-mail! stress1212@aol.com

Why didn't somebody tell me these things are dangerous?

If this is you, we are too late. But you can help some one else who is getting involved with the computer. There is nothing wrong with that, but the person must know, as you now know, some risks are all too prevalent.

Strain Injury," along with this Web site that links to support groups in the field. Book lists related to repetitive strain injury are provided.

John R Dye's Home Page
http://www.cco.net/~johnrd/

John R. Dye treats the viewer to an interactive map of his hometown, Olympia, Washington. Click on the map to find your way around this lovely northwestern city.

Herbert's Midi Music Page
http://www.ccnet.com/~herbca/

You be the triangle and I'll be the drums as we boogie on down to Herbert's Midi Music Page. Another talented SeniorNetter, Herb Harari, has created this wonderful musical site full of traditional jazz, Dixieland, roaring twenties, boogie woogie, blues, barrelhouse, and lots of other "good ole music." Most of the songs are compositions on Herb's Roland JV-30 keyboard, but some samples have been downloaded from other sites. Learn more about digital music from Herb's online resources. Be sure to download the Crescendo plug-in (located on Herb's front door) for full benefits!

Pat Scott's Irish Recipe Page
http://www.why.net/home/exuian/irishcook/ index.html

Hailing from Ontario, active Roundtabler Pat Scott shares several Irish recipes with personalized backgrounds for each. Traditional items such as breads, cakes, and biscuits, form the backbone of Ireland's culinary heritage, and grace the well-appointed tea table. Try out the Irish Soda Bread, brown bread, and dark spicy treacle bread. You're in for some yummy treats.

STRENGTH IN NUMBERS

As long as memory holds, Senior citizens in America have been relegated to the back seat, the end of the line, or...put out to pasture, if you will. The long and short of it is that younger people in modern society have viewed us as -unproductive, except for babysitting, keeping the lawn tamed, or just puttering about while we nurse our various physical complaints.

Marketing moguls often see only the image of "Granny Grunt," so products are rarely targeted in our direction. Advertising is geared mostly toward the "young and the restless." Many movies produced are admittedly targeted toward the teen-age boy, said to make up the largest movie-going audience, while television shows made in America showcase the beautiful and hard-bodied, living fast-paced lives of glamour and crime. Even sitcoms characterize us as mentally unstable, completely whacko, or physically feeble.

HATS OFF!

Thanks to Angela Landsbury, a charming Senior sleuth; Dick Van Dyke, rakish and devil-may-care as a physician cum detective; and Cosby, our favorite funny man, seniors are regaining a small toehold in the media, where formerly age was meant to be respected, not reviled. The Brits have got it right: People seem real in their dramas and soaps, and if Senior, then they are portrayed as normal folk who happen to be over 55 years old. Who could ask for a more reckless and handsome Senior than Lovejoy, the adventurous and slippery art connoisseur? Or Inspector Morse, the opera-loving, pint-drinking, Oxford policeman (see Figure 3.6)? And let's not forget Hilda Ogden, perhaps England's most famous (and loved) soap star, and not a day less than 60.

Are the David Nivens and Cary Grants of this world lost to us forever? Not by a long shot!

MAKE A WAVE!

Look around you now, and what do you see? Magazines aimed directly at Seniors and their interests, where formerly we were only recognized by the American Association of Retired Persons (AARP). Advertising directed at our age group is creeping into the media—maybe only for Depends and Cardizem CD, but it's a start. There are programs dedicated to the Senior lifestyle in almost every city, Senior sup-

Lizzie's Tips
Ever get a message that says "This disk is locked?" You can't make any changes or trash a file that is on it. Most inconvenient! Don't fret: to unlock a stubborn disk, simply eject the disk and move the toggle in the top left-hand corner to the closed position. You are now free to re-use the disk as you wish!

port groups are sprouting up in churches and medical centers, and special classes for Seniors are offered at most colleges and universities.

STAND UP AND BE COUNTED!

Today, it is becoming nearly impossible to ignore us—research shows that we are the fastest-growing segment of the population. Companies who primarily targeted young families are waking up to the fact that we are out here, and stronger than ever. Now, investment and insurance companies are bidding

Figure 3.6
This celebrity Senior, John Thaw (a.k.a. Inspector Morse), even has a celebrity Web site: The Sub-Orbital Inspector Morse WWW Site.

for our attention and designing portfolios and programs just for us. Isn't it wonderful!

Travel agencies, cruise lines, recreational vehicle manufacturers, and campground owners—not to mention hotels and resorts—have finally taken the blinders from their eyes and realized that we are an important part of their resources and we are in force. I am relishing it!

MOVE IT AND SHAKE IT

Now that we are slowly being acknowledged, it is up to us to carry the ball, keeping abreast of the world around us and flying the banner that reminds the world that physical aging does not have to mean old in spirit. It simply means that we have more years (compute to wisdom) added up than some others.

One way to keep young in spirit is to hang on to our inquisitive natures. We originally came on board with curiosity. Remember Eve, curious about that strange fruit? Look how much she learned by asking questions! The inquiring mind is seldom dull; dangerous, maybe, but never dull.

Other ways to stay young:

- Keep fit with exercise and healthy eating habits
- Try to maintain reasonable energy levels by pacing yourself when life gets full to overflowing
- Hang out with the young
- Keep an open mind—nothing is ever etched in concrete
- Savor the good times; you can always bring out those memories for review and a chuckle or two
- Laugh a lot, even at silly things, especially at yourself

Approach this best part of life with enthusiasm and optimism, enjoying each day as much as you can.

For some with debilitating health problems, or overwhelming responsibilities, this advice may seem patronizing. But personal experience has taught me that an indomitable spirit can keep us out of the doldrums, off the pity pot, and right in the middle of things.

OPEN SESAME

The purchase and avid use of your computer will open up a whole new world to you: first for play, and then even for serious work when you connect to the Internet and the World Wide Web.

With access to the Net, those who have difficulty getting out and about can say goodbye to isolation, and hello to virtual communities of other Seniors with interests just like yours, talking and sharing, offering support, and just having a good old time. For researching, information-gathering, and dipping a bit into the new and unusual keeps those brain cells up to the mark.

What a thrill to find pictures of the old classic car Dad used to drive, or getting connected to a bunch of genealogy freaks who fiendishly search for their links to the past. Want to get involved in a Civil War battle reenactment? You've come to the right place.

For those of you who are still busting through life, not looking back, take up the gauntlet, revel in the adventure, and learn to love staying alive!

We're here world, and we're not going away!

The following Web sites illustrate the many interests of Senior Netizens around the world. They are specifically Senior oriented, and tailored for the things you like to do. Of course, these sites will lead you on a cybertrail to other amazing adventures, so don't stop here. Think of this as your virtual diving board.

SIMPLY SENIOR WEB SITES

AARP—American Association of Retired Persons

http://www.aarp.org/

The grandaddy of Senior resources is personified on this Web page. Its stated mission is to help Seniors develop independent lifestyles with dignity and purpose. Described here are the volunteer and community programs that are available, the benefits to members, and where this group stands on issues and advocacy.

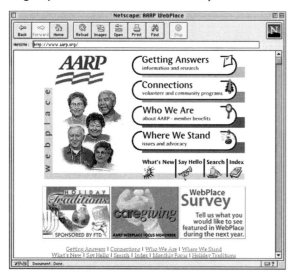

Administration on Aging

http://www.aoa.dhhs.gov/

Coming from the government agency of Health and Human Services, this site is dedicated to contributing information useful to older persons and their families. One feature, the Eldercare Locator, is a repository of information detailing resources for older persons needing special care. The National Aging Information Center, a huge resource of helpful information, can be found here as well.

Blacksburg Electronic Village Seniors Information Page

http://northcoast.com/unlimited/news/ srnews/srnews.html

Seniors are encouraged to represent their special interests and hobbies here. Get your Senior group or program included. Special interests include grandparenting and Senior activities, or check out the member index that includes e-mail addresses.

Calgary Free-Net

http://www.freenet.calgary.ab.ca/populati/ communit/Seniors/sen_menu.html

This access provider answers the call to provide community, provincial, and international information to support 50-plus lifestyles in the Calgary, Alberta area of Canada (but it's a great resource for those outside the region, too). This is a place to share memories and opinions, to explore similar interests, and to communicate with like-minded others. The site provides counseling and support services, and items of general Senior interest.

Charlottesville Senior Surf

http://www.comet.chv.va.us/Seniorpage/

Here you will find links to consumer protection sites, Senior issues, legal resources, and libraries. Put on your apron and link up to the cooking and food sites. Other links include government and health.

Eldercare Web
http://www.ice.net/~kstevens/
ELDERWEB.HTM

Designed to give elderly people, their friends, and family information about health care, living arrangements, and death and dying, the info here could ease the burden of today's caregivers, many of whom may be Seniors themselves. A provider locater is included.

Elderhostel
www.elderhostel.org

Elderhostel, a non-profit educational organization, offers inexpensive, short-term academic programs hosted by educational institutions around the world. You'll live on college and university campuses, in marine biology field stations and environmental study centers, and enjoy the cultural and recreational resources that go with them. Their motto: Studying there is half the fun.

ElderNet
http://www.eldernet.org/

This virtual community of computer-using retired folks who boldly go into the exploration of cyberworlds offers classes and tutoring, all taught by volunteers. ElderNet offers students an opportunity to learn in a friendly atmosphere and at a relaxed pace. There is software and e-mail support.

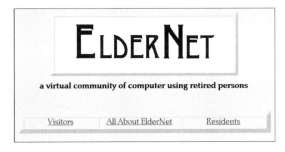

Eugene Free Community Network
http://www.efn.org/

Located in Eugene, Oregon, this is a service of Oregon Public Networking and offers membership to both businesses and individuals, with access to who's online, volunteering info, and Web search.

Fifty Plus R Us
http://shrinvest.com/shr.html

This hip spot offers an opportunity to chat about ideas that concern us all. Speak up about how we can maximize fixed incomes, what will Medicare really pay for, and many other hot topics.

The Florida Department of Elder Affairs
http://fcn.state.fl.us/doea/doea.html

The mission of this department is to maximize opportunities for self-sufficiency and personal independence for the elder population of Florida. This agency acts as an advocate, and coordinates with other state agencies to ensure that services are accessible and responsive. A list of recent legislation is available, along with with health insurance information. Help is provided to those interested in retirement to Florida, and the site links to the Elder Helpline.

Grand Times
http://www.grandtimes.com/

Grand Times is a sprightly publication, designed for active older adults. Articles are timely, entertaining, and sometimes contoversial, with an emphasis on the particular challenges adults face as they grow older. Visitors may want to check out the Senior Friendship Connection to meet new friends.

The Kansas Elder Law Network (KELN)
http://www.ink.org/public/keln/

This network is maintained as a public service to the state and national community of Senior citizens, and claims to be the nation's most comprehensive electronic resource dedicated to elder law. This site is affiliated with the University of Kansas Elder Law Clinic, and is maintained by KU Law Professor Kim Dayton.

Kitsap Computing Seniors
http://www.tscnet.com/kcs/

These optimistic folks have formed a non-profit group to show other Seniors that computing is not as hard as they may have thought, and is certainly not above their abilities. Some members are as many as 94 years young! Even though the membership at this time is spread over the Olympic Peninsula, look to KCS to help your group design its own pilot programs. Contact information is available.

Los Angeles Seniors
http://www.laSeniors.com/

Hosted by the YWCA Intervale Senior Services, this site outlines Intervale meal locations, delivery options, and menus, discusses aging issues and Senior news, and hosts 55 Alive Classes for the mature driver. Job opportunities are also posted.

mag.net online
http://www.vip.awinc.com/magnet/

This online magazine claims it is the more informative online magazine for Seniors. Broken into five distinctive sections, the publication does live up to its boast, including interesting Internet destinations (with tips to enhance your online experience), a Seniors' Symposium so that you can air your interests and experiences, and a spot for the reader to voice comments and feedback to staff. This is a site worth your visit.

Michiana FreeNet
http://michiana.org/

This Free-Net is a community-based service providing local information and Internet service in the St. Joseph and Elkhart counties of Michigan & Indiana, which should be of particular interest to Senior users. There are many links to health sites, local information, a public forum, clubs, and sports.

Mid-Florida Area Agency on Aging
http://Seniors-site.com/

Sponsored by the State of Florida Department of Elder Affairs, this site is directed to Senior residents of that state. It provides information on legal matters, disaster info, special programs and services, plus reference material and an Elder Helpline.

Mrs. McGregor's Mature Citizen
http://biz-comm.com/mcgregor/

This newspaper is published twice a month to serve the mature citizens of Michigan, though its features will be of interest to those outside the state, too. It covers financial, health, and political topics, as well as articles on local affairs. Entertaining and informative, the newspaper hopes to have the entire publication online at a later date. In the meantime, read these excerpts and enjoy!

National Aging Information Center
http://www.ageinfo.org/

The Administration on Aging provides searchable databases for Senior information needs. Forums for discussion of aging issues are available, as well as many publications for download and offline reading. NAIC specialists will also respond to inquiries and provide statistical data and materials, as well as pointers to referral sources.

Nebraska Age Link
http://age1.ndoa.state.ne.us/

The state of Nebraska has provided Seniors with a complete reference to programs and services offered for older adults and their families. These services include care management, nutrition, legal services, and employment referrals. If you live in Nebraska, you will find complete listings of many Senior issues you may have questions about.

Office of Seniors Interests
http://www.osi.wa.gov.au/

Coming to us from Australia, this site provides up-to-date information on aging and on Senior initiatives. The focus is on positive aging, volunteering, and respite care. Other resources are also provided.

SR.News
http://northcoast.com/unlimited/news/
srnews/srnews.html

What a bargain! News and features by and about the Senior community are sponsored by the Humboldt Senior Resource Center, operating in California since 1981. This is the online version of their monthly 20-page newspaper, which currently reaches 7500 subscribers along the north coast.

Selected Sites of Interest
http://www.mbnet.mb.ca/crm/other/
genworld/sources.html

This is a grab bag of sites for Senior citizens. Included are pointers to software and gopher holes, news and magazines, reference and research, as well as the expected links to Gerontology. Seniors will find links to museums, freenets, and specific links to other elder resources on the Web.

Senior.Com
http://www.Senior.com/

Senior.Com states that it is a complete resource for the online Senior user, providing information on lifestyles, travel services, online shopping, legal and financial services, and much, much more. The site comes complete with information on government programs and non-profit organizations of particular interest to oldsters. Participate in online chats on a variety of topics.

Senior Friendly
http://www.Seniorfriendly.com/

This friendly site searches the Internet for items of interest to Seniors and their families. Topics searched are housing options, community resources, government agencies, financial, and medical resources. Delve into this resourceful information bank and learn something about almost any topic on your mind.

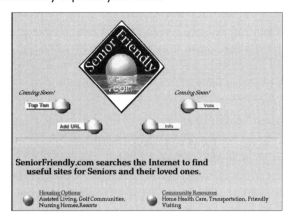

Senior Group Newsletter
http://bcn.boulder.co.us/community/Senior-
citizens/Seniorgroup/center.html

SGN is a monthly newsletter put out entirely by an informal group of Seniors, educators, and others who have an interest in determining how the Net serves the Senior population. The newsletter is mailed to subscribers via e-mail and posted at other sites, such as America Online and SeniorNet. There is no charge to have the newsletter sent to you, and back issues are available.

Senior-Inet
http://www.Senior-inet.com/

The Senior Information Network is a fine source for obtaining information and all sorts of Senior support services across the United States. Categories are concerned with housing, banking, rehabilitation, and other Senior issues. Searches can be made by specific cities.

Senior Internet Project
http://www.rmwest.com/sip/

This pilot project to provide an educational initiative for Seniors is hosted by Mesa County, Colorado. The project aims to give Senior citizens a special opportunity to participate in the technological revolution by acquiring a working knowledge of software tools used on the Internet. Curriculum is broken into three courses of eight two-hour classes.

Senior Japan

http://www.mki.co.jp/Senior/seni.html

This electronic magazine is dedicated to the enrichment of life for all retirees. The publication offers topics on driving safety tips, studying at the University of Japan, introduces Seniors' home pages, and then throws in a dollop of Senior wisdom. In English and Japanese.

Senior Lifestyle

http://www.Senior-lifestyle.com/

This Web version of Senior Lifestyle Magazine, states strongly, "It's fun to be fifty-something...." Coming to you from Northern California, the magazine draws us in with articles on classic cars, recipes, returning to college, and much more of interest to the active Senior.

SeniorNet

www.seniornet.org

This non-profit has Learning Centers all over the United States where volunteer instructors, who are themselves senior, teach older adults how to use computer technology. It also hosts two online sites, one on America Online (keyword: SeniorNet) and another on the Web. Both feature lively message boards.

Senior Times

http://amaltd.com/Seniortimes/

This spirited guide to modern Senior lifestyles comes to the Web from Rhode Island. To accommodate those of us with glasses, the type has been made a bit bigger and easier to read. Image sizes are smaller so that downloads are faster and navigation is easier. You are asked to take a minute to sign in and become a member of the reader advisory board. Articles include portraits of the Senior of the Month and news of gardens, dancing, and electronics.

Senior World

http://www.infi.net/~dthorne/

Seniors in the Roanoke Valley of Virginia can find information on recreation, transportation, and local community services. The aim of this site is to encourage growth and creativity by introducing new ideas and resources to the older population. Other topics include crime prevention techniques and computer clubs.

Seniors' Center

http://bcn.boulder.co.us/community/Seniorcitizens/center.html

Coming from Boulder, Colorado, the Center introduces the reader to local and national resources, links to many Web sites of interest to Seniors, and takes up sports and travel news for your enjoyment.

Seniors Computer Information Project

http://www.mbnet.mb.ca/crm/

SCIP is a world-wide information guide to resources and services aimed at Seniors in Manitoba, Canada. Information is listed by category, geography, features, and selected sites of interest. The site provides a searchable index and a one-minute survey with online results.

Seniors for Seniors

http://www.total.net/~fiftyplus/newsletter.html

This Senior newsletter made its Internet debut in August 1996. Cropping up from the original organization first started in 1985, the group deals exclusively with the needs of Senior citizens. All personnel are Senior volunteers wishing to stay actively involved in worthwhile endeavors. These folks dedicate themselves to other Seniors wishing to maintain an independent lifestyle in their own homes.

Seniors Internet Mall Page

http://www.Seniorsnet.com/mall.htm

This congested mall is chock full of sites from dining to optometry, with much in between to tickle your shopping fancy.

Seniors Internet Resource Center

http://www.Seniorsnet.com/homepage.htm

A service of SeniorsNet (not to be confused with SeniorNet), this complete guide offers guided tours to Africa, Asia, Mexico, Russia, and many other countries. This large listing opens links to earthquake preparedness, food & cooking resources, gardening, home renovations, and anything else you might have on your mind. A must-visit site to keep you up late into the night.

Seniors Online
http://www.Seniorsnet.com/campaign.htm

Come in and meet the winner of the oldest surfer contest. At 91 years old, Bill Heather is still hip. This site was created to encourage Seniors who missed the big technology invasion to become computer literate, stating that anyone who can use a TV remote control can navigate the Internet. The goal is to raise the level of awareness among Seniors and to convince them of the fascination and fun that come as a reward in this friendly technology.

Seniors Online Job Bank
http://www.Seniorsnet.com/jobbank.htm

Recognizing that not all retirees really want to quit working, this job bank provides job listings for those who want to keep their hand in. Take a peek at some online résumés.

Seniors-Site
http://Seniors-site.com/

This lively site is dedicated to providing interesting and unique information to older adults, and also for younger folks who must look after parents, grandparents, or friends. Offered is a free book, "The Second 50 Years," a reference resource for Seniors. Special sections provide information on pets, physical disorders, fun activi-

ties, plus much more on varied topics. This is a huge site with lots of good stuff.

Service Corps of Retired Executives Association (SCORE)
gopher://marvel.loc.gov:70/11/global/econ/biz/federal/sba/sbaprogram/scr

Every hour of every day, over 100 small business owners seek the expertise and assistance of the vast roster of retired experts at SCORE. This site outlines the many areas where SCORE lends its expertise to the development and growth of small businesses. Sponsored by the the U.S. Small Business Administration, SCORE is staffed by dedicated retired volunteers who want your business to succeed as much as you do. Contact information is provided for Seniors wishing to volunteer.

Shepherd's Centers of America
http://www.qni.com/~shepherd/

Shepherd's Centers is an interfaith, non-profit organization that maintains 100 independent centers throughout the United States and Canada. Holding to the philosophy that Senior citizens are not frail, lonely, or dependent, the centers attempt to enrich the later years with opportunities for service to others, self-expression, and meaningful work. Sustaining close friendships and remaining independent are other goals the centers strive to fulfill for oldsters.

Silver Threads
www.freenet.mb.ca/sthreads

Silver Threads is a publication of an informal group of netizens interested in how the Net serves the three-score-plus Internet user, and vice versa. You can read it online or subscribe to the newsletter at:http://bcn.boulder.co.us/communith/senior-citizens/center.html.

Successful Senior
http://www.islandnet.com/~Seniors/Seniors.html

This interesting resource, a magazine published eight times a year in Victoria, B.C., Canada, contains articles on travel, business, health, and finances. Besides regular features and articles on successful Seniors, the magazine offers links to gardening and antiques.

Three Rivers Free-Net
http://trfn.clpgh.org/

For those who live in or near the Pittsburgh area, Three Rivers Free-Net, a community-based computer network appealing to Seniors, provides free access to local and worldwide information. Help for new users is provided, along with a search of the Internet. Take advantage of this opportunity!

Training for Your Needs & Entertainment
http://www.pacificcoast.net/~nexus/train.html

This is 50+ computer training offered by Nexus Informatics. Nexus will create courses to suit your needs, and provide an opportunity for you to get acquainted with the software you need for Windows and Windows 95. Personal training is also available.

United Senior Association
http://www.indy.net/~brandt8/usa.html

This site introduces a non-profit association formed for adult consumers over the age of 50, to encourage commercial discounts and economic advantages for Seniors. Discounts on many retail products and services are offered. A free Sam's club membership is available, as well as economical group insurance plans. Even though the group is based in Indiana, a national ID card is part of the package.

Welcome!
http://www.swcp.com/~bumper/

This inspirational site is devoted to all aspects of life that relate to the promise of living joyfully. If you are concerned with finding fulfillment and contentment in your later years, drop in and get a few tips from Frank Grubbs, who shares a few ideas on how to grow old and be happy.

Chapter 4
A TOUCH OF CLASS

ARCHITECTURE

ART ON THE WEB

Aesthetic appreciation is so much a part of my life that it continually influences my outlook, and often transforms mundane activities into special experiences. Art is everywhere; all you have to do is look for it. The next time you drive to the grocery store, spend a moment noticing the graceful curves of a cornice or the way the sunlight peeps through the leaves of overhanging trees. The next time you sit down to read a magazine, pay attention to the photo composition, the print ads (some are real design triumphs!), and the proportion of white space to photos and text on individual pages. The next time you settle in to surf the Web, notice the way different designers approach this new medium; you'll begin to appreciate good Web design very quickly!

Art appreciation does not require formal study. You only need to make yourself aware of the interplay between the elements of art and design—such as color, light, layout, subject, and vision—to develop a personal aesthetic. Once you've developed and defined your individual predilections, you may well want to pursue formal studies in art history or in a particular medium. But even if you choose to stay with your own determinations of "what you like," your new vision will accompany you everywhere and you, too, will breathe—sometimes in response to a seemingly ordinary object or perception—along with John Keats, "A thing of beauty is a joy forever."

To get you started on the artistic path, I've selected a variety of links that will take you places you may never have been before: to buildings both ancient and new, to paintings both traditional and modern, and to artists...some who follow conventional themes and some who are developing bold new statements with technological tools. It's going to be an adventure.

ARCHITECTURE

Civilizations over the centuries have been identified by their original architecture, from the monolithic monuments of Stonehenge in England, the perfectly proportioned colonnaded examples from ancient Greece, to the remarkably sophisticated and understated building styles of Japan. We know the culture, politics, and lifestyles of these ancient peoples, in part because of the majestic architecture they left behind.

IT'S GREEK TO ME

I am amazed and awed by the monumental examples of architecture created by our forbears, and I have a strong interest in building styles, be it a classical Greek temple or just a warm and well-designed farmhouse in Vermont.

My abiding interest is most likely due to the diverse neighborhood in which I live. Located in the oldest part of the city, I am surrounded by a variety of styles, from Queen Anne Victorian and Painted Ladies, to sober shirtwaists and mammoth foursquares. Our downtown proudly displays many examples of the adorned art-deco buildings built by the WPA in the early thirties, and I am fortunate enough to reside on a city block resembling a college campus, lined with old red brick flats whose sprawling porches are supported by soaring ante-bellum columns, typical of an early Kansas City style.

Most of us are just ordinary folks with no pretensions to being great architects, but if you're like me, you still have an interest in how buildings are made, a curiosity about the construction and period style, and all the adornments and elements that make a special place stand out in our memories, and that continue to fascinate us throughout time.

With that in mind, and the hope that at least some of you share my enthusiasm for architecture, let's get out there and see what's on the Web.

CITY LIGHTS

Almost every major city and country is known by the character of its architecture. Some buildings stand out superbly and become icons for the city they represent. Here are a few sites that represent these memorable buildings.

FARAWAY PLACES

The Acropolis
http://cal022011.student.utwente.nl/
~marsares/

This center of ancient Greece is accepted by some as the root of civilization. This the sacred place where Greeks worshipped their Gods, and art reached an extraordinary level of sophistication.

The Acropolis, for centuries the cultural and religious center of ancient Greece. And according to many the root of civilization. Here the Greeks worshipped their Gods, and here art reached an incredibly high level. Now you have the chance to explore this Holy Rock by yourself....

The Ancient City of Athens
http://www.indiana.edu/~kglowack/Athens/
Athens.html

This is a photographic archive of the architectural remains of this ancient city. Take a tour of the excavated regions and monuments. See where it all began.

Architectural Dublin
http://www.nua.ie/ArchDub/

Sure, and here's the architectural splendor of the Irish capital presented for your viewing pleasure. Tour medieval and 17th century cathedrals and castles, and then move along to the Georgian buildings of the 18th century. The accompanying history notes are like having a per-

sonal tour guide with you along the way, and you'll really enjoy the city planning development section and the notes on street name derivations.

Architecture of the Mediterranean Basin
http://www.ncsa.uiuc.edu/SDG/Experimental/
anu-art-history/architecture.html

This huge collection of images comes mostly from Italy, Sicily, Greece, and Turkey, with a smaller number from France, Spain, and North Africa. It dates from the pre-classical period and stops at about 1820 AD. The greatest emphasis is on classical architecture in Italy, but there are substantial images of medieval structures, as well.

The Barcelona Pavillion
http://archpropplan.auckland.ac.nz/People/
Mat/barcelona/barcelona.html

This renowned masterpiece of modern construction was built in 1929 by Mies van der Rohe as the German Pavillion for the World Exposition held in Barcelona. It is a structure filled with light and reflections. Tours are offered using a QuickTime interface. A little slow to load, but worth it.

Bauhaus: Architecture in Tel Aviv
http://www.interart.co.il/bauhaus/index.html

During the 1930s, Tel Aviv enjoyed a period of intensive development spearheaded by European architects of the modernist movement. This site includes a map of Tel Aviv showing the locations of the most important buildings from this period, along with photographs of 20 of the most typical. The photographs were taken shortly after building construction, so they show the edifices at their best. Expect lots of rounded corners and geometrically precise angles.

Building Canada
http://blackader.library.mcgill.ca/cac/bland/
building/

This site provides a selection of images from the John Bland collection at McGill Univerity. The structures depicted reflect the country's architectural history, both past and present.

Lizzie's Tips
GIF is an acronym for *Graphics Interchange Format*. JPEG stands for *Joint Photographic Experts Group*. Both of these formats are the most widely used for images online, because they can be viewed on multiple platforms using a browser interface, and because they use an efficient compression method to reduce download time. Almost all the photos and graphics you see in your browser window are some form of GIF or JPEG.

The Castles of Wales
http://www.castlewales.com/home.html

I'm a sucker for castles, even though I know they must have been cold and drafty and miserable. I can't help it. The thought of sweeping down those stone staircases and peering through the peepholes as horse-mounted knights galloped off to fight their latest skirmish is one of my most romantic fantasies, so I totally fell in love with this site. Friendly Webmaster Jeff Thomas takes you on an illustrated cybertour of over 170 medieval Welsh castles, and provides lots of lively commentary along the way.

Contemporary Architecture of Hong Kong
http://www.ncsa.uiuc.edu/SDG/Experimental/anu-art-history/hongkong.html

I.M. Pei, the architect who designed the glass pyramid that now graces the courtyard of The Louvre, also designed the Bank of China building in Hong Kong. See images of the edifice at this site, along with a number of others that highlight Hong Kong's emergence as a major contender on the global economic playing field, and its embrace of the 21st century.

Gargoyles Then and Now
http://ils.unc.edu/garg/garghp4.html

Lend an ear to the audio greeting and then read the intro text describing the history and function of these gro-tesque building ornaments. You'll find out about the origin and symbolism of gargoyles and their relation to the medieval mindset. The Cathedral Tour section lets you view some spectacular examples from England and France, or you can tour Duke University's selection of gargoyles. And in case you think these stone fantastics are relics of the distant past, take a look at the work of Walter S. Arnold, a stone carver currently working and selling his creations in Chicago.

Gothic Dreams
http://www.globalnet.net/elore/elore04.html

Explore the magnificent medieval cathedrals of Europe and learn about their history, construction, and architectural peculiarities. From Notre Dame de Paris to Canterbury of England, the images and enlightened text at this site will set your spirits soaring as high as the buttresses. For an added bonus, click on the site's Introduction button to gain access to other excellent offerings from site host Earthlore, including The Ancient Legacy of Celtic Culture, Mythic World, Sacred Animals, and Mysteries, or Lost Histories.

Greek Architecture
http://chs-web.neb.net/usr/katelevy/greek/greek.html

If you're never able to remember the differences between Ionic, Doric, and Corinthian columns, here's your chance to work it all out. These straightforward descriptions and illustrations—mixed with some historical and cultural tidbits—will make you wonder how you ever confused the three styles in the first place.

Florence of the 15th Century
http://www.lib.virginia.edu/dic/colls/arh102/one/one.html

One of the most beautiful cities in Italy, Florence has its own recognizable style. Stroll across the Ponte Vecchio and notice all the details. You're basically on your own here since there are no notes to explain the significance of what you're seeing, but these five images—three from the Baptistry of San Giovanni, one of the Piazza del Duomo, and one "skyline" view of the city—highlight the beauty of the Renaissance architectural style. Click on the thumbnails to view larger images.

Lizzie's Tips
A TIFF is a graphic image stored in a *Tagged-Image File Format*. Though it's primarly used in print production, you'll occasionally run across a TIFF in your Web forays (some image archives include TIFF files), and even if you can't use TIFFs for display in a Web browser, you can display them on your home computer, provided you have a graphics viewer.

AND THERE'S MORE...

The Hadrianic Baths
http://archpropplan.auckland.ac.nz/People/
Bill/hadrians_bath/hadrians_bath.html

Dip your tootsies into this reconstructed model of the baths built by Hadrian, a grand complex of buildings created for Roman indulgence. The site details the reconstruction project—performed entirely via computer modeling—and gives a good historical outline of significant events in the town of Leptis Magna, site of the baths. You'll learn about the photos, texts, and archaeological sources used to research the project, and read descriptions of the materials and statuary that adorned the original structure.

Islamic Architecture in Isfahan
http://www.anglia.ac.uk/~trochford/
isfahan.html

The delicate patterns, rich tracery, and graceful domes characteristic of Islamic architecture are on display in this virtual tour of the city of Isfahan, Iran. Site of buildings dating from the 11th to the 19th centuries, the city contains representative structures from a number of historic architectural styles. Visitors can either hop on the "taxi" for a guided tour, or strike out on their own, armed with the city map available (for free!) at the tourist shop.

Italy in the 15th Century
http://www.lib.virginia.edu/dic/colls/arh102/
eight/eight.html

Some of the most imposing and memorable architecture comes from this period and this country, and this page provides a virtual photo album of representative structures. My favorites are the graceful colonnades of the St. Ambrogio Cloister in Milan (circa 1497-1498), but then the Palazzo Medici Riccardi in Florence is quite lovely, too, and the Arch of Constantine from Rome ... oh, it's too hard to pick a favorite. Take a look for yourself and see if you can recognize the work of these outstanding artisans.

Elsewhere in Italy
http://www.lib.virginia.edu/dic/colls/arh102/
six/six.html

It boggles the mind when thinking of the challenge the architects faced in designing and building Venice. There are many familiar images here, along with slow loading. The good quality of the photos makes it worthwhile.

Karntner Bar
http://archpropplan.auckland.ac.nz/Archivis/
karntner_bar/karntner_bari.html

Before going on with your journey, it's time for a long, cool one at this unusual bar located in Vienna. This building was designed by the famous architect Adolf Loos, and is known as the American Bar. Let's get cozy in the large leather-lined theater boxes, as we watch other patrons stroll down the checkerboard promenade.

More Florence
http://www.lib.virginia.edu/dic/colls/arh102/
four/four.html

Even more architectural marvels from this fabled city are featured here. Palazzos, forums, churches, arches—dating from as early as 42 B.C.E—are arrayed on this page, many with close-ups to highlight the fine architectural details. Feast your eyes.

Lizzie Sez
Leave everything a little better than you found it.

Moscow Architecture
http://mars.uthscsa.edu/Russia/Moscow/

You won't find a lot of images at this site, but you will find some excellent photos of buildings dating from the 13th to the 19th centuries. Several churches and monasteries are represented, along with a few classy town houses and a "hostel" that looks like a palace. There's no explanatory text, so you're on your own except for the name of the site and its construction date, but believe me, these buildings speak for themselves.

Palladio's Italian Villas
http://www.mindspring.com/~gable/

The very word *villa* puts me in mind of sun-drenched white stone, azure skies, crimson flowers cascading over balustrades, and glorious views of the Mediterranean. Let's go! Palladio was a Renaissance architect who designed a number of these glorious palaces, and some of his masterworks survive today in the area around Venice, Italy. This site includes photos of the villas, along with a historical timeline and info about the architect.

Portfolio of Architectural Photos
http://rampages.onramp.net/~blitz/lreens/ruins.html

From the files of professional architectural photographer Louis Reems comes a monthly exhibit of photographs that showcase a particular city. You never know where he'll take you, but I was lucky enough to see Pompeii and some breathtaking photos from Athens. Previous exhibits are archived, though, so you can tag along with this talented photographer on his trips to Thorn in the Netherlands, Kyoto, Paris, and Waxahachie, Texas. (Wait a minute! Waxahachie, Texas?)

Renaissance and Baroque Architecture
http://www.lib.virginia.edu/dic/colls/arh102/index.html

Although this site is a University of Virginia resource for students of its Architectural History 102 class, what do you care? You don't have to worry about getting a grade. Visit the site to enjoy images from architectural masterpieces of the 15th through the 17th centuries in Italy, France, and England.

Seven Wonders of the Ancient World
http://pharos.bu.edu/Egypt/Wonders/

Can you name them? When I was a kid, we had a set of illustrated encyclopedias with a big spread on the seven wonders. My favorite was always the Colossus of Rhodes. The drawing in the encyclopedia showed ships sailing underneath the bronze behemoth's massive legs, and that picture always struck me with awe. A ship sails under the Colossus image at this site, too, so I experienced a pleasant sense of *déja vu* when I visited. Along with our bronze friend, you can also visit the other wonders and enjoy the historical commentary included at the site.

Tracking Hector Guimard
http://www.etca.fr/Users/Sylvain%20Meunier/Guimard/baladepseizeAGL/

This famous French architect and decorator left many examples of his work in Paris subway stations and apartment house. Walk along the Paris streets on this tour and vist the sites. For more information on European Art Nouveau, ask here.

Windsor Castle
http://www.hotelnet.co.uk/windsor/home.htm

Over 900 years ago, William the Conqueror began work on this castle. Today it is an unforgettable sight, and the place where Queen Elizabeth hangs her Home Sweet Home needlepoint sampler and Princess Diana doesn't. Opulent almost to the point of tacky, the frescoed ceilings, ornate furniture (does anybody ever sit on those sofas?), and gilded *everything* attest to the unimaginable wealth of queens (and kings). The photographs at this site, unfortunately, are somewhat muddy and indistinct, but they are enough to give you a good gander at the way the royals live.

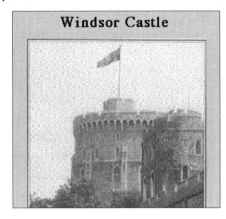

Windsor Castle

CLOSER TO HOME

Architectural Archives of the University of Pennsylvania
http://www.upenn.edu/gsfa/archives/aaupdes.html

For those who have more than a passing interest in the field of architecture, this archive houses a collection of more than 250 designers from the 18th century to the present. Both American and European designers are represented, especially those from the Louis I. Kahn Collection. Kahn was a 20th century American architect, and his drawings, project files, papers, and models are on permanent loan to the University from the Pennsylvania Historical and Museum Commission.

Architecture in America: State Houses to Skyscrapers
http://lcweb2.loc.gov/detroit/archamer.html

The Detroit Publishing Company is the source for these 40 images of government buildings, private residences, and business addresses throughout America. Together, these photos provide a good overview of the types of architectural styles in the New World (the private residences selections run the gamut from shacks to mansions), and the explanatory text, while brief, sets the images within their historical contexts.

Architecture of Atlanta
http://www.gatech.edu/3020/architecture/intro/homepage.html

Some of the most well-known and significant buildings in the city are represented here. Many architectural styles tell the history of this capital of old world charm and new southern lifestyles. No, Scarlett, you are not coming on this tour.

The Architecture of Salem
http://www.star.net/salem/houses.htm

Take a glimpse of the architecture in Old Salem, MA. These homes represent the building period between the 17th and 18th centuries. Beautiful images and colorful descriptions highlight each house and give us a feel of the Republic's early days.

Architecture Slide Library
http://www.mip.berkeley.edu/query_forms/browse_spiro_form.html

If you can't get enough, The University of California at Berkeley has provided an excellent architectural search tool, offering access to slides from the period you name—such as the 19th century—and the style you choose—North American Colonial, for example. You can also search for specific buildings.

Arcosanti
http://www.arcosanti.org/

This 26-year-old project, architected by Italian designer Paoli Soleri, was designed as an answer to suburban sprawl. Built in the Arizona desert, near Phoenix, this natural enviornment creates a pedestrian-oriented city with less pollution and dependency on the automobile, and keeps the countryside close to the urban dweller. There is a complex and creative philosophy at work here, and it looks like fun!

The Big One
http://mat.sapp.auckland.ac.nz/biggie/

Inspired by French nuclear testing, Colin McCahon's "Necessary Protection" series, the Big One, consists of images of a curious shelter to protect you should the ultimate horror of horrors come upon us in the form of a nuclear attack. Stand on a porch and look out toward the court, view the interior, or look down on the power source. Strange, but somehow compelling.

Buffalo's Architecture
http://www.ag.net/nf/nf18.html

Located in Buffalo, New York are many fine examples of the residential work of Frank Lloyd Wright. Just in case you're in the Buffalo area and want to take a look for yourself, the site lists the actual addresses of the homes. I'm not so sure I'd want my address posted on the Web, but then I don't live in a Frank Lloyd Wright. You must check out the Gardener's Cottage of the Martin House. If I'd known gardeners lived this well, I'd have considered a degree in horticulture. Stop in and take a look around.

The Charleston Multimedia Project
http://www.awod.com/ccl/cmh_title_page.html

Charleston's reputation for historic preservation is widely acknowledged, and this Web site showcases the results of their remarkable efforts. The Guide Book takes you on a street-by-street tour of the city's historical areas and contains links to hundreds of images. Articles in the Topics section add to your understanding of the city and its past, with their thematic treatment of historical, architectural, and cultural events and trends. Finally, the Tours section gives you the chance to visit additional forts, historic homes, and public buildings, some of which are not open for public tours.

The Chicago Architecture Imagebase
http://www.uic.edu/~pbhales/imagebas.html

Chicago boasts of its architectural heritage, and images from the Second City are online here to illustrate that the city's pride is well placed. The University of Illinois at Chicago has conveniently categorized its image database so you can browse by architect, by building, or by era.

Current views of the city are also included, along with maps of historic Chicago. I looked, but I couldn't find Mrs. Murphy's cow.

Images of Federal Hill, Lynchburg, Virginia
http://www.inmind.com/people/hughest/fed_pic1.htm

Loriann and Tom Hughes run a bed and breakfast in the Federal Hill area of Lynchburg, Virginia. Not surprisingly, they are fans of the historic area's architecture and use their Web site to share their collection of photographs (63 houses in all) with virtual visitors. Loriann and Tom invite you to take a step back into time and review the architecture of this old neighborhood, read a brief history of the area, and page through information on nearby homes that are currently on the market (you won't believe the low prices on these beauties!). Yes, you'll eventually get to a pitch for their B&B, but if you're in the Lynchburg area, you could probably do much worse than staying in this lovely French Second Empire mansion atop Federal Hill.

The Coral Courts Motel
http://www.cec.wustl.edu/arch/stlouis/coral/History.html

For a last look, visit the Coral Courts Motel in Saint Louis, Missouri. It is a classic example of the streamlined Moderne style and was built in 1941 by Adolf Strubig. Alas, progress has intervened and the Coral Courts may be no more.

The Houses of Key West Home Page
http://members.aol.com/alexc94/hkw/index.html

This site offers images and descriptions of the various architectural styles of 19th century houses in the historic district of Key West, Florida. Notice the wide, cool verandas, the gingerbread architectural details, the pastel colors, and the palm trees. There's no mistaking these inviting residences for anything but tropical homes; they have a style and panache all their own.

Kansas City Architecture
http://cctr.umkc.edu/user/pmichell/kcarch.htm

Would you like to see where I live? Well, unfortunately, my particular house is not on this page of KC images, but a couple of Frank Lloyd Wright-designed homes (and a church) are, along with other lovely buildings, from my city. Some of the photos are too dark, and a bit of explanatory text would certainly enhance the site, but for a quick view of some of KC's architectural treasures, it fits the bill just fine.

McDonald's
http://mirror.syr.edu/image/macdonld/macd1.gif

For a touch of whimsy, check out the oldest McDonald's, located in Downey, California, and still operating. Remember how the golden arches used to extend through and above the building, and the restaurant itself looked like any other milk-shake-and-burger joint? Well, if you don't, you can see it here. But you won't see Ronald. He's off with the Hamburglar.

Preserve and Protect
http://www.preserve.org/

Not only must we build new structures, we must preserve and protect those that are a part of our architectural history. The New York Preservation Society invites historic and preservation organizations across the United States to establish a link on their page. These folks are so serious that they'll even design the Web page and provide the server space. You won't find a lot of resources here yet—a few societies and some events info—but the site includes photographs of some absolutely stunning architectural treasures. I was especially taken with the magnificent homes in the King William Historic District in San Antonio.

Southeastern Architectural Archive
http://www.tulane.edu/~lmiller/SEAAHome.html

Maintained and collected at Tulane's School of Architecture, this archive has records from many important architects working in New Orleans. Its records include 25,000 photographs, surveys and maps of New Orleans, and an architectural reference library. The archive is known for its extensive collections of the architects James Gallier, Sr. (1798-1866), James Gallier, Jr. (1827-1868), and James Freret (1838-1897).

Virtual Library: Architecture
http://www.clr.toronto.edu:1080/VIRTUALLIB/arch.html

For another comprehensive resource on architectural info, try searching here. Topics also include Architectural Landscaping.

Virtual Soma
http://www.hyperion.com/planet9/vrsoma.htm

Planet 9 studios have created a 3D model of the South of Market Street Area (SOMA) in San Francisco, which is fast becoming a haven for Internet and software development companies. You can walk or fly down San Francisco streets, open the doors of SOMA buildings, and take a look inside.

Washington, D.C.
http://rubens.anu.edu.au/imageserve/images/washington/index.htmlr

In the original charter for design and construction of the nation's Capitol building, it was mandated that no structure could be built that was taller. So in Washington, D.C., you'll seldom see buildings higher than two stories. This site hosts a virtual tour of Washington's finest, including federal government structures and the White House—you'll find the architecture and white marble of D.C. both graceful and thrilling.

Welcome to the Gamble House
http://www.bcf.usc.edu/~bosley/gamble.html

This beautiful structure, in the Arts and Crafts style, was designed by Charles and Henry Greene in 1908. The house is located in Pasadena, California, and is owned by the University of Southern California. Take your tour today.

Welcome to Glensheen
http://www.d.umn.edu/glensheen/

Located in Duluth, Minnesota, this stately home was built by Chester Congdon, a self-made millionaire. Completed in 1908, it cost $800,000 to construct. Today, this seven-and-a-half acre estate is priceless. The tour guides you through a 39-room Jacobean-style manor house and details how remarkably it has been preserved.

SOME OF THE GREATS

The Architects
http://design.coda.drexel.edu/students/
clennox/bio.html

This text site features thumbnail sketches of Le Corbusier, Eero Saarinen, and Louis Henry Sullivan, with images of a few of their major accomplishments. Look in the Slideline index for more.

Earth and Cave Architecture
http://www.ping.ch/p.vetsch/

Peter Vetsch of Switzerland is one of the most controversial architects in the world, building minimalist contemporary forms, covered with sod. This site shows two of his cave designs—one a model, one an actual dwelling—and the intro material informs you that "caves and rounded shells emerge without straight angles and corners, but with windings and surprising views. The dissolution of familiar forms allows us to get in touch with the deep, unconscious life forces within us." Well, I'm not sure about those unconscious life forms, but the architectural vision is an interesting one.

Frederick Clifford Gibson
http://www.gibson-design.com/

For a birds-eye view of the contemporary work of Frederick Clifford Gibson, turn to this site, complete with information on current projects and construction.

Kisho Kurokawa
http://www.kisho.co.jp/

This beautiful Web site illustrates the work of contemporary Japanese architect Kisho Kurokawa. Take a tour of his most recent project and jet out to Kuala Lumpur, Malaysia, to see Eco-Media City 2020.

Dave's I.M. Pei Page
http://www.netaxs.com/~dturner/impei.html

Love his work or hate it, you can't deny the influence of this renowned modern architect. A bodybuilder named Dave who lives in a Pei-designed apartment complex in Philadelphia has compiled this page of images of various Pei buildings around the world. Dave's on a crusade to stop the construction of a chain hotel next to his beloved apartment community, and you can read his inflammatory text and keep up with the fray by clicking on the "Location Has Changed" hyperlink. He also has a bone to pick with Microsoft, and you'll have to wade through that diatribe first to get to the Pei stuff.

The Louis Sullivan Page
http://www.geocities.com/CapitolHill/2317/
sullivan.html

Sullivan was one of the chief architects working to rebuild Chicago after the disastrous fire of 1871. This is the guy who bestowed the "form follows function" dictum on the architectural world, and gave us such structures as the Auditorium Building and the Transportation Buildings in Chicago. This page presents an good overview of his life and work, with links to other Sullivan pages on the Web.

Frank Lloyd Wright
http://flw.badgernet.com:2080/

Considered to be the the 20th century's greatest architect, Frank Lloyd Wright designed some of the world's most important buildings, many of which are considered treasures today. For a look at his life and work, keep turning the pages.

ART ON THE WEB

Artists make it, collectors collect it. Some are born with an inspired gift to create, others spend years in training. Great frauds have been perpetrated because of it and millions have been spent on it. Many artists have been taken advantage of because of their talent, and some have been glorified. And in almost every case, art does describe the world in which the artist lives. From the "pictures" she or he creates—whether they be two- or three-dimensional—is left an enduring record of the time, from politics to romance, from social ethos to cultural document.

Vincent Van Gogh was rumored to have said, "An artist is an exhibitionist by profession." And perhaps that is so, as I have a few small renderings of my own hanging about. But I am not a collector, just an admirer, an appreciator; not aspiring to be another undiscovered Grandma Moses, and even with a clearly defined taste for a particular style, just hungry to view it all, from Japan's Hiroshige and his elegant woodblocks, to Andy Warhol's Campbell's soup cans.

I have heard that art, like beauty, is in the eye of the beholder. Let's put that to the test and see what the Web can conjure up for us to behold!

VIRTUAL COLLECTIONS

1925, The Year in Review
http://lonestar.texas.net/~mharden/1925/1925.html

This remarkable exhibit features work from such artists as Kandinsky, Klee, Ernst, Hopper, Picasso, and many more. By choosing the year 1925, the viewer is given an impression that he is actively involved in the art world of that time.

1000 Points of Art
http://members.aol.com/noahnet/art/index.html

Over 1000 artists and galleries can be linked from this site. Consider your field of interest and click away. Sites range from abstract expressionism, to historical and religious art.

A Compendium of Bad Art Form
http://www.power.net/users/janet/alt.art.html

Struck by the unusual poses on the frescoed ceiling of the Sistine Chapel, this Webmaster thought that many appeared to be doing something that they should not be. This site is a humorous, tongue-in-cheek view of art gone bad.

Americans for the Arts
http://www.artsusa.org/

This page announces an important organization dedicated to art and culture. Its aim is to support the arts through private and public resources, to promote leadership development in the arts, and to increase public awareness through education. Sponsoring organization is The American Council For the Arts, who support arts advocacy and education.

AMERICANS FOR THE ARTS

Announcing an important new national organization for organizations and individuals across the United States committed to the arts and culture: Americans for the Arts. ✳ Supporting the arts and culture through private and public resource development, leadership development, public policy development, information services, public awareness and education.

Apparitions
http://jupiter.ucsd.edu/

Apparitions is both a physical space (as in gallery) and a computer-generated virtual environment. A group of artists and programmers collaborated to construct an artistic experience where gallery visitors engage in activities which question what is "real" or "virtual" by interacting with physical objects, exploring ideas on the Web, and moving through a virtual environment via large scale video projections. This may sound pretty bizarre, but the Apparitions exhibit is an interesting look at the new trend toward interactive art.

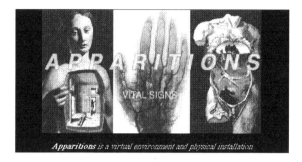

Apparitions is a virtual environment and physical installation

Art Crimes: The Writing on the Wall

http://www.gatech.edu/desoto/graf/Index.Art_Crimes.html

Art that is worth getting arrested for, on the walls, called grafitti, is featured here with sketches of the artists and views of this exciting work. Literally off the streets, this boldly executed art grabs your attention.

ArtSource

http://www.uky.edu/Artsource/artsourcehome.html

Save this site for a day when you have a few unhurried hours to spend in aesthetic pursuits. Mary Molinaro at the University of Kentucky has spent a lot of time compiling this "selective, rather than comprehensive" guide to art and architecture resources on the Net. You'll find links to art libraries and art journals, artists' projects, electronic exhibitions, image collections, museums, events … the list goes on and on. I became totally immersed in this site, linking from one fascinating page to another, and isn't that the most fun way to explore the Net?

The Chagall Windows

http://www.md.huji.ac.il//chagall/chagall.html

Marc Chagall's magnificent stained glass windows in the synagogue of the Hadassah university hospital in Israel depict Jacob's blessings to his sons, the twelve tribes of Israel. The windows are adorned with "floating figures of animals, fish, flowers, and numerous Jewish symbols" in vibrant colors. After you've enjoyed the windows, you can take a virtual Jerusalem tour.

Christus Rex

http://www.christusrex.org/

Talk about your valuable art treasures! This private, non-profit group is dedicated to the "dissemination of information on works of art preserved in churches, cathedrals and monasteries all over the world." You'll find lots of Catholic church and humanitarian information at the top of the page, and toward the middle you'll hit solid gold—literally! How about 325 images from the Sistine Chapel *alone*, and another 596 images from the Vatican museums? Unbelievable riches, but don't stop there. You don't want to miss the Worldwide Tour of Churches exhibit, or any of the other stellar offerings at this incomparable site.

Kenneth Clark on Velaquez' "Las Meninas"

http://lonestar.texas.net/~mharden/meninas.htm

This glorious work is accompanied by an online lecture by the distinguished Kenneth Clark explaining the painting's elements. As you look at the painting, you feel as though you are in the room with its inhabitants, one of the party. Or are you on the outside, looking in? Or is the whole scene a reflection in a mirror? The painting is currently hanging in the Prado at Madrid, and is a marvelous example of the hand (and the mind) often working more quickly than the eye. Pay close attention to details here.

Dali Web

http://www.highwayone.com/dali/daliweb.html

Will any of us ever forget the melting clocks? This is your chance to see them again, along with other Dali works.

Take a wild ride on the Dali Web and test your Dali knowledge. Take the Dali quiz (5000 other people have). You may win a free poster.

The Drum Arts Page
http://206.156.228.3/~kmw/index.html

This is *the* place to go for a look at African art on the Web. Galleries, museums, and individual pages are all included in this relatively short, but representative, list. Jump from here to an unofficial site for the National Museum of African Art, or select the UBP: Art link to access the African art exhibit at the Krannert Art Museum, the interactive African Arts Museum @Harlemm, the AfriNET*Gallery, and the home pages of several contemporary artists. Don't miss Debi's Ordinary People: hand-painted African American folkart figurines. I think Debi's people are anything but ordinary. And she has magnets, too.

The First Impressionist Exhibit, 1874
http://lonestar.texas.net/~mharden/
74nadar.htm

This is a recreation of the first exhibit of the Impressionists, held in Paris in 1874. These artists, rejected by conventional art juries, banded together to show their work to the general public. Represented are Monet, Pissarro, Morisot, Renior, Degas, Sisley, Boudin, and Cezanne. Notes are provided to enrich your pleasure.

Francisco Goya
http://www.imageone.com/goya/goya.html

Eighteenth-century Spanish master Francisco Goya, considered to be the "Father of Modern Art," is the subject of this multipage exhibit. You'll find extensive biographical notes and a good selection of his paintings, including two self-portraits and the bizarre *The Witches' Sabbath*.

Frida Kahlo
http://www.cascade.net/kahlo.html

This Web site devoted to Mexican surrealist painter Frida Kahlo contains biographical information about Kahlo, examples of her work, a sampling of self-portraits (get a load of those eyebrows!), and a link to the Frida Kahlo Commercial Art Gallery.

Roman Rudolph Liedl
http://math1.uibk.ac.at/~liedl/index.engl.html

This site was originally designed by Professor Liedl to prove his theory of the harmony of colors. Along with tutorials on his theory, the Professor offers brilliant color images of the works of famous artists. Thirty paintings are displayed by Paul Cezanne, and many others by Gustave Klimt, Paul Gauguin, Georges Seurat, Auguste Renoir, and several details of paintings done by Michael Betancourt. Downloading these images is slow going, but the reward is great.

Online Art Resources
http://www.msstate.edu/Fineart_Online/art-resources/

This is a directory indexing at least 1000 art resources, including Web sites and mailing lists.

Picasso and Portraiture
http://www.club-internet.fr:80/picasso/
homepage.html

This beautiful exhibit, brought to you by Claude Picasso, the famous artist's son, displays many of Picasso's portrait works. An introduction is provided along with a schedule of coming events.

Tribute Robert Rauschenberg
http://www.electriciti.com/babu/fahrkle/
tribute/Rausch/Rausch.html

The images captured here are in tribute to abstract expressionist Robert Rauschenberg, and are scanned from a collection in New York's Musem of Modern Art, and from the book, *Rauschenberg/Art and Life*, by Mary Lynn Kotz.

Rembrandt
http://lonestar.texas.net/~mharden/
rembrandt/rembrandt.html

This beautiful exhibit allows us to see paintings that, until now, could be seen only in St. Petersburg at the Hermitage. Take the opportunity to revel in the jewel-like colors of this world famous artist.

The Rossetti Archive

http://jefferson.village.virginia.edu/rossetti/rossetti.html

Dante Gabriel Rossetti was a Pre-Raphaelite poet and painter of the mid-19th century, and this archive contains the complete writings and pictures attributed to the enigmatic artist. As a bonus, Web visitors who have the current VRML viewer or plug-in (you can download it here) can visit a virtual reality model of Rossetti's studio, with paintings and drawings on the wall, to scale.

Meyer Shapiro on Cezanne

http://www.connecti.com/~rdarter/schapiro/schapiro.htm

Eight of Cezanne's most familiar works are presented at this site in vividly produced images. Click on each title to read Mr. Shapiro's commentary.

Leo Steinberg: Selections

http://www.connecti.com/~rdarter/steinbrg/steinbrg.htm

Join Leo Steinberg as he invites us to join in his critiques of selected artists and their work. Among these essays are a critique of Formalism, an interview with Jasper Johns regarding the famous work, "Targets," and further essays addressing Picasso and Cubism.

The Surrealism Server

http://pharmdec.wustl.edu/juju/surr/

Although it began as a literary movement in the '20s, the label surrealism is generally associated with its artistic manifestation. This Web site provides background on the movement, images, surrealist games (some great ideas here for your next dinner party!), and the ever-popular Surrealist Compliment Generator. Here's the one I received: "Your fingers staple pine nuts into everything you touch." Great fun!

Vermeer and the Art of Painting

http://lonestar.texas.net/~daldridg/Vermeer/vermeer1.html

This site is an excerpt from the book, Vermeer & the Art of Painting by Andrew K. Wheelock. Many of the Dutch realist's paintings are shown with explanatory text.

World Art Treasures

http://sgwww.epfl.ch/BERGER/

Here's an art site with a slightly different frame (get it?) of reference: create thematic historical art exhibits that attempt to both impart knowledge and create an experience for the viewer. Choose from several "experiences": Pilgrimage to ABYDOS (a 3,000-year-old Egyptian site), Vermeer, Botticelli, the Enchanted Gardens of the Renaissance, and more.

The World of Escher

http://www.texas.net/escher/

M.C. Escher was a Dutch graphic artist, most famous for his spatial illusions, lithography, and geometric patterns. Practically everyone alive is familiar with his work Drawing Hands, and this site contains an Escher art museum packed with works that demonstrate the full range of his incredible genius. If you like what you see, visit the store to order T-shirts, computer accessories, and puzzles adorned with Escher images. Then, when you're finished touring the site, attempt to answer the question posed by the Webmaster on the home page: Was Escher a mathematician or an artist?

World Wide Arts Resources

http://wwar.com/index.html

World Wide Arts Resources is a specialized arts search engine that includes "over 150 categories with over 150,000 pages." You can go to a new and interesting art-related Web creation every day and participate in the site's chat forum to share what you've seen. Galleries, museums, exhibitions, art for sale, art history, festivals, performance art...I could go on, but I'll leave a few surprises for you to discover on your own. What's more, the site is fully searchable.

GALLERIES AND MUSEUMS

African Art: Aesthetics and Meaning
http://www.lib.virginia.edu/dic/exhib/
93.ray.aa/African.html

This impressive online collection from the Bayly Art Museum at the University of Virginia includes examples of masks, headdresses, and statuary primarily from West African societies. Each illustration is accompanied by extensive notes that explain the symbolism and meaning of the piece, and the essays included in the electronic catalog explore the art from an aesthetic—as opposed to a purely cultural—point of view.

@art
http://gertrude.art.uiuc.edu/@art/gallery.html

From the University of Illinois at Urbana-Champaign comes this electronic art gallery curated by faculty members whose "intention is to encourage artists' involvement in the global electronic community, and to provide an electronic viewing space for talented artists of outstanding merit." Both current and past exhibits are archived at this site.

Art Institute of Chicago
http://www.artic.edu/aic/firstpage.html

The patinaed lions that stand as sentinels in front of the Art Institute of Chicago also flank a selection of the museum's artworks on its home page. Unfortunately, the Art Institute is stingy with its online offerings. The exhibition links are to text descriptions only, and the collections information is brief and illustrated by only one representative work. Still, if you're planning a trip to the Windy City, you can get all the important museum info here—including the fact that Tuesday is free admission day.

Art Planet
http://www.artplanet.com/

"Art Planet is a comprehensive on-line fine art directory. It is the place to be when you're looking for art on the Web." With a database of more than 3,200 artists and galleries, you can search by specific artist, medium, style, or century. This is the place to search for links to contemporary artists.

ArtMetal
http://wuarchive.wustl.edu/edu/arts/metal/
ArtMetal.html

A nonprofit group of metalwork artists collaborate to produce this virtual gallery of metal crafts, including jewelry, architectural art (such as windows, doors, and grillwork), and sculpture. Much of this work is incomparably beautiful, and the site also includes metalworking news and ArtMetal Features, an online 'zine with stories and graphics designed to give you a totally new perspective on this ancient art form.

Asian Art Museum of San Francisco
http://sfasian.apple.com/

Although the Asian Art Museum is "the largest museum in the western world devoted to the arts and cultures of Asia," their online offerings consist of a single exhibit—Mongolia: The Legacy of Chinggis Khan—and the requisite location and fee info. Nevertheless, the exhibit is an interesting one with generous historical notes, a selection of images, and QuickTime video clips.

Bas van Reek Art Building
http://www.xs4all.nl/~basvreek/

Artist Bas van Reek has constructed his own virtual gallery on the Web. This site is a lot of fun, sending you down hallways and elevators that take you from floor to floor to view the very original contemporary art displayed here. Accompanied by the funkiest of cartoon characters, you can see works such as *Kiss-1*, *Kiss-2*, *The Family*, and *Kiss-5*. Do you see a theme emerging here? The artist annotates the illustrations with information on the size of the work and the media he used, and advertises silkscreens and originals for sale.

The Brooklyn Museum

http://wwar.com/brooklyn_museum/
index.html

The Brooklyn Museum is "the second largest art museum in the State of New York and one of the largest in the country." Despite the fact that the museum's collection contains over a million and a half items, you won't see too many of those images online. The Brooklyn provides only a few representative images to accompany its gallery descriptions. As a bonus, though, excellent curator's notes are provided for each inline image that place the item in its historical context.

The Dallas Museum of Art

http://www.unt.edu/dfw/dma/www/dma.htm

Founded in 1903, this museum has worked hard to build a diverse and important collection of work both from Europe and America. Many of its holdings include art of Ancient America, Africa, and Indonesia, as well as contemporary art. Step inside to view the works of Monyana, the most important Japanese art exhibit to come to the United States.

The Fine Arts Museum of San Francisco

http://www.famsf.org/index.html

Committed to making their entire collection available online, curators at this museum currently host the largest searchable art image base in the world. You'll find works here from the M.H. de Young Memorial Museum, San Francisco's oldest museum and the largest repository of American paintings on the West Coast; and the California Palace of The Legion of Honor, housing an equally important collection of European masterpieces and large numbers of Rodin sculptures.

The Gallery of Fine Art

http://www.ausart.asn.au/

This gallery, located in East Perth, Australia, exhibits art from outstanding contemporary Australian artists. Each featured artist has a brief bio posted, along with representative samples of work and information on how to purchase. Previous exhibitions are archived, so you can scroll through a selection of paintings, sculpture, ceramics, and objects d'art.

The Glenbow Art Museum

http://www.lexicom.ab.ca/~glenbow/

The Glenbow in Alberta, Canada, houses an extensive collection of contemporary and historical paintings and artifacts. The Native American offerings on exhibit in the Museum of Western Heritage section include fine beaded garments and masks, while the art gallery contains a generous selection of paintings (oils and watercolors) done by 19th century white explorers, along with original Inuit artworks.

The Guggenheim Museum

http://math240.lehman.cuny.edu/gugg/

This truly beautiful site introduces you to an international institution. With three affiliated museums located throughout New York City (and a sister museum in Spain), the Guggenheim intends to promote and encourage an interest in art, and enlighten the public about the nature and spirit of contemporary art. The core collection is built around abstract artists of the 20th century, including Kandinsky, Mondrian, and others, whose paintings expressed breathtaking creativity.

KOMA: Korean American Museum of Art

http://koma.org/

For an absorbing look at the cultural differences between Korean and American societies, visit the Cultural Differences section of the KOMA site. Here you'll learn the surprising (and sometimes unfortunate) meanings of different hand signals, how smiles and gestures are perceived, and the relative importance of privacy. Move on to the gallery area to read historical notes on traditional and contemporary art and view a selection of paintings, including the eerie *Full Moon Landscape*.

The Krannert Art Museum

http://www.art.uiuc.edu/kam/

This museum, located at the University of Illinois at Urbana-Champaign, houses a collection dating back to the fourth millennium B.C.E. Enjoy this electronic sampler from the permanent collection.

Lizzie's Tips

If you are in charge of the membership sign-in sheet for your organization, put your membership list on a spreadsheet program, design it any way you like, and presto: At each meeting, you have every member listed and a place for them to sign in.

Los Angeles County Museum of Art
http://www.lacma.org/

This is the largest art museum west of the Mississippi River, with more than 20,000 square feet of exhibtion space. From prehistory to the present, this impressive display of work appeals to all ages and tastes. If you have an interest in art of the Middle Ages or pre-Columbian art, you will find an ample supply of work to sate your appetite.

The Louvre
http://mistral.culture.fr/louvre//

Indisputably one of the world's greatest museums, The Louvre goes online here to showcase treasures from its seven departments that "represent works of art dating from the birth of the great civilisations of the Méditerranean area until the western civilisation of the Early Middle Ages to the middle of the XIXth century." You won't find all your favorite Louvre artworks online, but the site includes enough images to keep you happily scrolling for hours in awe struck wonder of the geniuses who created these treasures.

Metropolitan Museum of Art
http://www.metmuseum.org/

This famous art museum, located in New York City, is one of the largest and finest museums in the world, containing over two million works of art and spanning 5000 years of world culture. Check the calendar for current exhibits, concerts, and films.

The Minneapolis Institute of Arts
http://www.artsMIA.org

This North American museum, "the most comprehensive fine arts museum in the upper midwest," houses a permanent collection of some 85,000 objects that span a period of 4,000 years. Its Web site offers virtual access to images and descriptions of its permanent collections (textiles, drawings, sculpture, photography, and artworks from every major period), educational programs (both real-time and online), and the museum shop with a wide selection of gifts, postcards, and posters.

Musée des Arts et Métiers
http://www.cnam.fr/museum/index-a.html

From France comes this eclectic art site with loads of fun interactive gizmos and surprises. One warning, though: the Catalogue's about as dry as two-day-old toast because the whole thing's written in French and has no pictures. Go instead to L'Album. Here you'll find photographs of artworks and machines from old-timey days, along with descriptions in … French. Even if you're not a Francophile, you'll still be able to tell what the items are. But here's where the real fun begins: You can download a RealAudio sound file from an 18th-century dulcimer player, or view a QuickTime movie of Foucault's pendulum at the Pantheon. There are more surprises, but you'll have to discover them for yourself.

The Museum of Bad Art
http://www.glyphs.com/moba/

Promise you won't tell anyone, but I actually *like* some of the "bad art" exhibited at the MOBA site. This community-based, private institution in Boston is dedicated to the "collection, preservation, exhibition and celebration of bad art in all its forms and in all its glory." Amusing without being snooty, MOBA challenges our perceptions and forces us to look at art in a whole new way.

National Museum of American Art
http://www.nmaa.si.edu/

From the incomparable Smithsonian comes The National Museum of American Art, the "only museum dedicated to America's art and artists" (better not tell that to the curators at the Whitney). At the museum's multimedia site, visitors can view and read about almost 1,000 pieces of art. The exhibits are updated often, and the site includes general museum information, a calendar of events, and links to the museum's departments and publications.

Nyabinghi's Gallery of African Art
http://www.vgallery.com/art/africa/
gallery.htm

For an interesting browse through contemporary African art offerings, visit the Web site of this New York City gallery. You'll find carved pots from Nigeria, a wooden boat from Senegal, statues from the Congo and Egypt, headdresses from the Ivory Coast, a variety of walking sticks, and many other offerings.

Palmer Museum of Art
http://cac.psu.edu/~mtd120/palmer/

The Palmer Museum of Art is located at Pennsylvania State University, and its Web site features a guided tour of the museum's seven galleries, along with links to representative images. In the Baroque gallery, for example, you can view Trophime Bigot's haunting *The Denial of St. Peter*, with its amazing use of light and dark, and then skip over to the Asian gallery for a look at Bada Sharen's delicate ink drawing *Lotus*. The Palmer also posts a directory of the artists and works represented at the gallery, and an online catalog with 40 images from which you can create your own tour.

The Philadelphia Museum of Art
http://pma.libertynet.org/

The galleries of the Philadelphia Museum of Art hold some real treasures, such as Van Gogh's *Sunflowers*, Picasso's *Three Musicians*, and Cezanne's *Large Bathers*. You can see them all here, along with examples of arms and armor, and art offerings from East Asia and India. Along with the usual museum location and operating hours info, the site also includes a museum store offering a selection of books and posters.

Singapore National Heritage Board
http://www.museum.org.sg/

Three museums for the price of one URL is what you'll find at this spectacular offering from Southeast Asia. Set your mouse to clicking through the Singapore History Mu-

seum, the Asian Civilizations Museum, and the Singapore Art Museum to explore the region's culture and artistic perceptions. Beautiful site design and abundant choices make this a definite stop on your virtual museum tour.

The Tate Gallery
http://illumin.co.uk/turner/tate.html

The Tate Gallery, in London, was founded in 1897 and houses the national collections of British art from the 16th century to the present. Put your feet up, grab a cup of joe, and sit back to enjoy some real history.

The Andy Warhol Museum
http://www.clpgh.org/warhol/

Located in Pittsburgh, Pennsylvania, this museum gives you an opportunity to become well acquainted with one of the most famous, and most influential, artists of our time. Besides its extensive permanent collections, the work of other artists is presented on a regular basis. Bask a bit in Warhol's more than 15 minutes of fame.

The WebMuseum
http://watt.emf.net/louvre/

Bienvenue! from the WebMuseum in Paris, host of a renowned repository of art masterpieces. The Webmaster recommends that new visitors begin with one of the smaller collections, such as the medieval art exhibition or the Cezanne exhibit, that contains *only* 100 artworks. From there you can move on to the Famous Paintings section, the heart of the site, where the artist catalog reads like an art history book "who's who" (Botticelli, Cassatt, Degas, van Gogh, Kandinsky, and many, many more), the images are generous (Kandinsky's link alone contains images of 16 paintings), and the curator's notes are informative and lively. The WebMuseum is an absolutely premiere art site.

Weisman Art Museum
http://hudson.acad.umn.edu/

The Frederick R. Weisman Art Museum, at the University of Minnesota in Minneapolis, presents images from the museum's 13,000-object permanent collection. The site includes a nice selection of images from American artists with interesting curator's notes. Information on exhibitions and current events is listed here as well.

The Whitney Museum of American Art
http://www.echonyc.com/~whitney/
Click on the logo to gain entrance into this sometimes controversial museum located in New York City. Look into the Whitney exhibitions and programs about their extrordinary collection of 20th Century American Art.

welcome to the whitney

Lizzie's Tips
ANNOUNCING YOUR OWN SITE

Have you ever wondered how to promote your own Web site after you have spent so much time designing and developing it?

- Try registering your URL and key search terms with several online search engines and directories, such as Lycos (**http://www. lycos.com**), the Lycos a2z Directory (**http:// a2z.lycos.com**), the Lycos Top Five Percent (**http://www.point.com**), Alta Vista (**http:// www.altavista.com**), and Yahoo (**http:// www.yahoo.com**). Go to their home pages and click on the "submit your URL" or "submit your site" button (each service will have slightly different instructions and submission guidelines, so look carefully for each one's submit area). In some cases, staff at search engine and directory offices will visit your site and gather the data needed to add you to their database, along with a professionally written review. In other cases, your Web site will be added automatically. Sometimes you may need to fill out a form, such as the one Yahoo provides.

- You can also have your site listed with smaller online catalogs, search services, and indexes. A lot of surfers rely on these subject-specific services to select the sites they wish to visit. Search for indexes related to your subject matter using an appropriate search engine, or browse directory listings on Lycos's a2z or Yahoo, which contain indexes and site archives relevant to your topic. For an extensive list of topic-specific catalogs and search engines, you can also visit clnet's meta-search site, search.com (**http://www.search.com**). Once you've found a catalog or index that suits your needs, follow the on-screen guidelines to submit your Web site.

- Announce your site to subject-specific USENET groups. Some groups and mailing lists exist solely to announce new Web sites. If you are an art dealer, for example, use a search engine to look for related keywords such as "rec.art" to find the USENET group you need. Some engines, like Alta Vista, will perform specific newsgroup searches for you. And don't forget to mind your USENET P's and Q's; USENET etiquette frowns on blatant self-promotion or crass advertisement.

- Ask other Webmasters hosting interest-related sites if you can cross-link their site to yours, and if they will host a similar link back to your site.

- Also keep on the lookout for "most popular" lists and sites, "What's New" lists, and "Cool" and "Hot Site of the Day" services. Send them your URL and describe for them what's unique about your site.

NOT LEAST

Last maybe, but certainly not least, is the Web gallery hosted by one of our own SeniorNetters, Jim Rossman. Jim displays his lovely original art in this virtual exhibition space.

Cotntop's Spot on the Web
http://www.fishnet.net/~cotntop/

Jim Rossman, known as Cotntop (cotntop@fishnet.net) shares with us some of his own original paintings in this online gallery. With each painting he gives a brief description that tells a story about each one. Cotntop tells us that he is an older guy with no artistic training, having fun showing that it can be done. With these words of encouragement to other Seniors, Cotntop hopes that others will do as he has done, and jump in to give it a try.

Grandma Moses: *Cazenovia Lake*
http://www.fmhs.cnyric.org/clay/community/ artlang/AL.gif/Moses.html

Here's inspiration for all you weekend artists out there. The incomparable Grandma Moses (Anna Mary Robertson Moses), who lived from 1860 to 1961, was entirely self-taught, and didn't begin her artistic career until she was 78 years old!

Chapter 5
THE WELL OF CIVILIZATION

HISTORY

LITERATURE

A LITTLE HELP FROM YOUR FRIENDS

PHILOSOPHY AND RELIGION

Some people think of civilization as a linear time line, an unbroken procession of people and events that stretches back to the mists of prehistory. This perception acknowledges the influence of earlier generations on succeeding ones, but sees their interaction in terms of a mathematical progression, similar to the process of stacking one building block on top of the other.

I prefer to think of civilization as a well, a life-giving resource, in which all the elements that compose the "water" are mixed together willy-nilly, and depend on each other for their purpose and existence. Wells are not linear; in fact, they are frequently round, and this roundness further symbolizes the continuity and interrelation of the past and the present—inextricable components of our current civilization. To fully appreciate the interrelation of past and present requires a study of both, and the best avenues for such study are history, literature, museums, philosophy, and religion.

HISTORY

When we reach the age of 50, we do tend to look back on our ancestors, think more about the times in which they lived, and become more strongly interested in events that played out then, as well as in our own memories.

Contemplating memories, it is surprising how many historical events have taken place in my own lifetime that I shrugged off, was briefly horrified by, or did not understand. Now, I have a burning desire to delve back into those events, remember them again, get the real truth—I want to steep myself in the history that has been left behind.

Perhaps watching all the wonderful history programs now on television has rekindled my fascination with the Indian wars in the West, and how the Federal Government handled the acquisition of Indian land. It's painful to contemplate the decimation of indigenous populations, and how America relegated the remainder to reservations offering little that would ignite the spirit of any human being.

And then I am struck by the intrigue and excitement of the Oregon Trail, the Gold Rush, the westward settlement of our country, and the fascination we have for pioneer life and wagon trains. Daniel Boone may have been immortalized by Disney, but there is so much more to be learned about the lives of the early settlers, and the contributions they made to our westward movement, often at the terrible expense of those who had laid claims before them.

But painful as this history is, like many other things that are painful, it's best to remember.

REMINISCENCES

I shake in the horror of the Holocaust, so sickened by the incomprehensible brutality that I can barely go on; yet I'm drawn to its hypnotic malevolence because I must know all that I can. Like an addict, I continue to persuade myself to read yet another book—a purge of my own spirit perhaps, or an atonement for others who committed this evil, so I cannot give it up.

> "The reality of the Japanese camps and the impact on individual lives during AND after the war was an eye-opener. I had never considered any of the hardships other than the demoralizing arrests and life in the camps. I was also struck with the realization that most of the racial stereotypes I carry within, rarely hold up when applied to individuals I come in contact with."

So many of my Southern friends and relatives are addicted in much the same way to the history of the Confederacy, and particularly, the War Between the

States. They read everything in print, hoard old maps, and many even participate in re-enactments, just as their counterparts in the Tidewater area do with Revolutionary history and the studies of the colonists.

My own Grandmother's attic was full of old hoop skirts, split pantaloons, and parasols, never thrown away but stored as a harvest for us children on rainy days—we whirled and twirled in a fantasy land of the Old South, never comprehending the hidden injustice and the nightmare of war that was veiled behind the curtsies and the bows.

In Grandmother's home, we were never allowed to mention the "Civil War"—it was the "conflict" between General Sherman and his comrades on the Northern side. Grandmother's mother and relatives had witnessed the horror of the burning of Atlanta, and had shared it all with her when she was a child. Those memories were as vivid to her in 1950 as they must have been to her mother when she lived through them. And the Fourth of July was never acknowledged or celebrated in South Carolina when I grew up there. Fireworks were ignited only on Christmas Eve.

Historical customs and personal memories such as these are probably only left in time's memory bank, as progress moves us in a forward direction. But it is interesting to remember our past, and our histories, that many may otherwise never know.

THE BIG ONE

Most of us creeping into later years contemplate the Wars that have so fragmented our personal histories and families—from the First World War to the Vietnam conflict—and wonder why such a destructive pattern must be a part of our advanced civilization. Our curiosity gets the better of us as we dig for the facts that will make us better understand these monstrous events, and the devastating effects they have had on our lives.

Lizzie Sez

As we move along through this last third of our lives, one thing we have learned is that happiness is not based on money or power, prestige or accomplishments, but on the friends and family that we have grown to love and respect.

AND RECOLLECTIONS

Living in Kansas City as I do, I'm not far away from hearing stories of the pioneers and wagon trains and the journey westward. This city is known as the Gateway to the West, the last jumping-off spot, the final outpost before hitting the rugged trails.

My own old neighborhood was here long before the "City of Kansas" ever sprung up, as this is where the trains were organized and outfitted, where wheels were made, and foodstuffs were stocked before crossing the wide river and going on to the lonely and dangerous prairies. Independence, Missouri, closeby, marked the trails ahead—both the Oregon and the Santa Fe.

AND THEN THERE'S HARRY

Independence is also the home of Harry Truman, one of the Presidents I most admire. His feisty nature and tough-mindedness have stood the test of presidential time. He, himself, added to the legends now told about him, for his sense of humor and sense of what was right was always evident.

Harry S. Truman Presidential Library and Museum
http://sunsite.unc.edu/lia/president/truman.html
The Truman library is the repository of the Presidential and personal papers of "Give 'em hell Harry," and the library's excellent Web site gives you access to all sorts

of Truman-related info. My favorite section is the Trivia Collection that includes a good mix of history and personal details such as the Truman family pets, the man's vital statistics, and some of his inimitable quotes. Photographs throughout the site show the many faces of Harry and his family.

Character Above All: Harry S. Truman
http://web-cr01.pbs.org/newshour/character/essays/truman.html

For a fascinating overview of the man and his work, check out this essay by David McCullough. You'll learn how Truman's experiences in WWI shaped him, and discover interesting details about his upset victory in the 1948 presidential election. Even-handed and studded with hyperlinks to additional info sources (including a brief list of key dates), this essay provides another perspective on the life of this tough, feisty man.

On his desk when he was President he kept two signs. One was a quotation from Mark Twain that said, "Always do right. This will gratify some people and astonish the rest." On the other side of his desk was the best remembered, "The buck stops here."

When I was in college in Washington, D.C., Harry Truman was President, after having reluctantly accepted the vice presidency and succeeding FDR upon his death. I remember how the president tried to foster his daughter Margaret's singing career. After arranging a strongly publicized concert for her debut, he was outraged when the reviewer panned Margaret's voice in such a nasty way that the President's household was much embarrassed, and Margaret completely humiliated. It was a cruel thing to do, but Harry rarely let anything get the better of him, and he soon fired off a letter to the critic. This letter was made public at the time, and caused a wild furor.

The letter went like this:

"I have just read your lousy review buried in the back pages. You sound like a frustrated old man who never made a success, an eight ulcer man on a four ulcer job, and all four ulcers working.

Lizzie's Tips
Scrolling through long documents can be a real bore. If your word processor has a "Go To" command, you can jump to any specific point in your document. If you can't remember where you want to go, use the "Find" command and choose an unusual word that is near the text you want, and whammo, you are there swiftly, no fuss. Beats scrolling for hours on end.

"I have never met you, but if I do you will need a new nose and plenty of beefsteak and perhaps a supporter below. Westbrook Pegler, a guttersnipe, is a gentleman compared to you. You can take that as more of an insult than as a reflection on your ancestry."

Needless to say, Margaret's singing career declined, but the President went down fighting.

Another recollection about Harry Truman has him in an informal discussion with a young man who asked him how to go about getting into politics. "You've already started," replied the former President. "You're spending somebody else's money aren't you?"

In her book, *Souvenir*, Margaret Truman recalled the Christmas of 1955 when the President discovered his wife, Bess, at the fireplace disposing of letters he had written to her over the years. Alarmed and upset by her behavior, he pleaded with her to remember how important these letters would be in later years. "Think of history," he argued. " I *have*," she replied.

Shortly after Mr. Truman was reported to have called a certain politician's speech "a bunch of horse manure," Bess was approached and asked if she would try to persuade the president to tone down his language a little. "You don't know how many years I have worked to tone it down to this!," she answered.

Keeping in mind that all of us have special interests drawn from our pasts and personal experiences, and with so much diversified information available, we can only cover the tip of the iceberg on the Internet. Let's get out there and see what we can find.

"Take NOTHING for granted!!! Everything changes. That's what life is—change, evolution. Forces outside of my control govern my land, house, car, mate, kids…The only thing one can control and be sure of, is what is in one's heart."

BEST HISTORY SITES

A-Bomb WWW Museum
http://www.csi.ad.jp/ABOMB/index.html
Students and faculty of Hiroshima City University constructed this project to provide "accurate information concerning the impact the first atomic bomb had on Hiroshima" and to provide the context for thorough discussion of the topic.

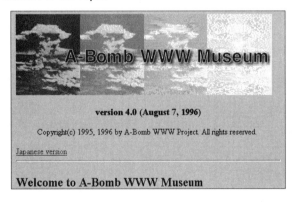

Alcatraz
http://www.nps.gov/alcatraz/
Isolated off the shoreline of San Francisco, California, Alcatraz, home of some of America's most infamous criminals, has a spooky quality that still fascinates us. Look into its lurid past and get all the dirt. Once called "The Rock" and "Hellcatraz," this maximum-security federal penitentiary served a 29-year sentence of its own, allegedly housing the worst society had to offer, yet serving up punishments so severe that the place was eventually investigated and closed. Here visitors can learn more about the prison island's various histories, including its military, Native American, and natural pasts.

The Alexander Palace Time Machine
http://www.travelogix.com/emp/batchison/
The Alexander Palace, located in Tsarskoe Selo outside St. Petersburg, was the home of the last Russian Tsar and his family. This time Machine lets visitors tour its various rooms and treasures, provides floor plans, and introduces its former residents using images and biographies.

The American Antiquarian Society
gopher://mark.mwa.org:70/1
The American Antiquarian Society maintains a research library of American history and culture containing three million books, newspapers, and pamphlets collected since 1812. Visitors can search an online catalog and learn about the society's programs and fellowships.

American and British History Resources on the Internet
http://info.rutgers.edu/rulib/artshum/amhist.html
If you've got the time, this page has the information, much from original documents. Pick your period and find stats, laws, people, maps, and more. From Rutgers University Libraries.

The American Civil War, 1861–1865
http://www.access.digex.net/~bdboyle/cw.html
Visitors can take a long, detailed look at the Civil War here with resources that include a link to the Library of Congress Civil War archive, and various historical preservation groups.

American Civil War Home Page
http://funnelweb.utcc.utk.edu/~hoemann/
cwarhp.html

The American Civil War page, maintained by a University of Tennessee historian, offers links to a wide range of Internet resources about the "War Between the States." Visit here for texts, soldiers' rosters, battle descriptions, links to museums, and more.

American Memories
http://rs6.loc.gov/amhome.html

This collection of primary source material visits American culture and history, and is held by the Library of Congress. Here, visitors can download electronic reproductions contained in the collection, including photographs, sound, manuscripts, and early movies, including some rare footage of President William McKinley at the 1901 Pan-American Exposition.

American South
http://sunsite.unc.edu/doug_m/pages/south/
south.html

Electronic resources for southern regional studies are consolidated at the American South Home Page. Access two major academic centers, the University of North Carolina's Center for the Study of the American South, and the University of Mississippi's Center for the Study of Southern Culture. C'mon all you southern belles and gents; dig in!

Anti-Imperialism in the United States
http://web.syr.edu/~fjzwick/ail98-35.html

Syracuse University provides this document about anti-imperialism in the United States from 1898-1935. Visitors will find a thorough historical background presented, in addition to literature and primary texts on this fascinating movement.

Assyria Online
http://www.cs.toronto.edu/~jatou/

Scratch the surface of thousands of years of history, culture, and literature at Assyria Online. Ancient and modern civilizations are both represented here, dating from the history of Mesopotamian times.

A Brief History of The United States Senate
http://ftp.senate.gov/history/history.html

Everything you ever wanted to know about the history of the Senate (and maybe even some stuff you didn't) is contained in this massive online repository. Find out the age requirement for making your senatorial debut (most of us are well past the minimum), and peruse the laws that govern this august body of folk.

The Brigade of The American Revolution
http://www.brigade.org/

Ever since 1962, the Brigade has been recreating an authentic and broad spectrum of America in the 18th century during the time of the Revolution, from real-time encampments, to actual military tactics and maneuvers. Everything is made as safe as possible. Join in the Revolution along with the Brigade while you hop aboard a virtual time machine.

Britannica's Lives
http://www.eb.com/calendar/calendar.html

Britannica's Lives is a collection of *all* the biographies listed in the current Encyclopedia Britannica. Visitors can enter a birthdate and age range, and Britannica will then provide all the biographies that fit that description. I've been known to spend hours at this site digging up profiles on all sorts of historical figures; and it's a real find for that granchild who's trying to do research for a school paper.

> "Libraries have sure come a long way, haven't they? You can find almost anything you want, or they can get it for you. I wish the nearest library weren't so far from me."

The Canadian Heritage Information Network
http://www.chin.gc.ca/

Find out more about the Great White North at the Canadian Heritage Information Network, with features that include a guide to Canadian museums and galleries, online Canadian cultural and historical exhibits, and information about Canadian publications and courses. In French and English.

Canadian Museum of Civilization: Mystery of the Maya

http://www.cmcc.muse.digital.ca/cgi-bin/
login_display?URI=/membrs/civiliz/maya/
mminteng.html

The Mystery of the Maya features a look at the history of the ancient civilization of Mexico and Guatemala. The page is a joint effort of the Canadian Museum of Civilization and the producers of a new IMAX film on the subject.

California Indian Library Collections

http://www.mip.berkeley.edu/cilc/brochure/
brochure.html

Thousands of texts concerning California's Native American population, both historical and modern, are archived in California's Indian library collections and deposited in California libraries. Here, the collection is introduced, including information about sound recordings, photos, texts of historical value from the collections, and contact info for collections' administrators.

Canadian Heritage Information Network

http://www.chin.gc.ca/

Find out more about the Great White North at the Canadian Heritage Information Network, with features that include a guide to Canadian museums and galleries, online Canadian cultural information, and historical exhibits.

Celebrating 17 Centuries of the City of Split

http://www.st.carnet.hr/split/

Hey, there's a party at Diocletian's! Visitors here can virtually celebrate the 1,700th anniversary of the Roman Emperor Diocletian's palace at Split in Dalmatia. Learn more about the ancient structure and the city that has taken on its unique character.

Concentration Camps: A Factual Report on Crimes Committed Against Humanity

http://zero.tolerance.org/zt/kz.html

Visitors to this page will find a report detailing the medical experiments and other horrors which occurred in Nazi concentration camps during World War II. Attached to the document is a list of witnesses.

The English Renaissance Reenactment Site

http://www.webcom.com/st_mike/

The English were later to enter the Renaissance than the rest of Europe, and King Henry VIII, along with his daughter Elizabeth, were most responsible for England's coming into the era at all. This Web site is devoted to the reenactment of this period, and to sharing information with you on how you can become an active participant in the events. Full of historical information and resources to help you get into the swing of things.

Egyptology Resources

http://www.newton.cam.ac.uk/egypt/

This page, maintained by the Newton Institute at the University of Cambridge in England, provides an abundance of Egypt-related resources. Visitors will find news, history and gossip, announcements of conferences, and exhibitions, along with an Egyptology bulletin board.

Egyptology resources

This page © Nigel Strudwick 1994-96.

This page is set up with the kind assistance of the Newton Institute in the University of

Exploring Ancient World Cultures

http://cedar.evansville.edu/~wcweb/wc101/

Explore the mysteries of eight far-flung cultures in the ancient world in an online classroom which traces the history of cultures that shaped the development of humankind. Follow cultural avenues into essay collections, museums, and other Internet resources at this award-winning site.

First Division Museum at Cantigny
http://www.xnet.com/~fdmuseum/

The Big Red One, the 1st Infantry Division of the U.S. Army, is the focus of the First Division Museum at Cantigny in Wheaton, Ill. This site contains information on Col. Robert R. McCormick, on whose estate the museum sits, as well as information on the museum, the division, exhibits, and more.

Flag of the United States of America
http://www.icss.com/usflag/

Everything you ever wanted to know about the American flag flies proudly at this page. Visit here to learn about the flag's history, evolution, and the attempts to amend the U.S. Constitution with a flag protection rider.

French and Indian War Home Page
http://web.syr.edu/~laroux/

A writer chronicling the 18th century French and Indian War offers research materials on the soldiers, battles, and strategies of the conflict. There's a special emphasis on French soldiers who went to Canada to fight.

Gettysburg Address
http://lcweb.loc.gov/exhibits/G.Address/ga.html

The U.S. Library of Congress maintains this site containing the full text of Abraham Lincoln's 1863 Gettysburg Address. Visitors will find related documents and historical info, too.

The Great Arabian Discovery
http://www.chevron.com/explore/history/arab50/index.html

"The discovery required seven wells, five years, millions of dollars spent during the Great Depression, and a band of dedicated explorers fighting heat and sand in a remote desert. But the payoff was enormous." Read more about the history of Chevron's oil discovery in the Saudi Arabian desert. Sponsored by Chevron Oil. Fascinating reading for all you would-be (and real-life) desert explorers.

Historic Mount Vernon
http://www.mountvernon.org/

Preview the grounds at George Washington's Mount Vernon Estate and gardens at this page, which includes a virtual tour, archaeological details, and pointers to related educational resources.

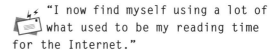
"I now find myself using a lot of what used to be my reading time for the Internet."

Holocaust Internet Sites
http://www.bethel.hampton.k12.va.us/holocaust.html

This comprehensive list of Internet sites provides information on as many aspects of the Holocaust as you could want, including the Anne Frank house and personal memoirs. A few steps away is the Holocaust Museum, site of one of the most moving and informative series of WWII exhibitions in the world.

The Holocaust Memorial
http://wahoo.netrunner.net/~holomem/

Tour the Holocaust Memorial, located in Miami Beach. The sculptures by Kenneth Treister personify the anguish of individuals caught up in Holocaust horror.

Joan's Witch Directory
http://www.ucmb.ulb.ac.be:80/~joan/witches/index.html

If you have an interest in the history of witch hunts, you'll find dozens of links and resources here, spanning from Salem, Mass. to Finland. Included are a topical glossary

and book excerpts describing torture methods that often resulted in "confessions."

Kennedy Assassination Home Page
http://mcadams.posc.mu.edu/home.htm

Whether or not you accept either the "grassy knoll" or the "lone nut" theory, you can learn more about Lee Harvey Oswald and the assassination of President John F. Kennedy at this information-packed page which attempts to deflate rumors of conspiracy surrounding the incident.

Khazaria Info Center
http://acad.bryant.edu/~kbrook/khazaria.html

The medieval Jewish kingdom of Khazaria is the topic of the history, timeline, and quotes featured on this page. A map, an illustration of Turkish runes and links to many topic-related sites are also included.

Medieval Jewish Kingdom of Khazaria, 650-1016

Letters Home From a Soldier in the U. S. Civil War
http://www.ucsc.edu/civil-war-letters/home.html

These letters were written during the Civil War by a private in the 36th Infantry, Iowa Volunteers, to his faithful companion (and future wife) at home. They detail his life as he traveled in Mississippi, Missouri, Iowa, and Arkansas. The site was compiled by the private's great-grandson.

Library of Congress Soviet Archives Exhibit
http://www.ncsa.uiuc.edu/SDG/Experimental/soviet.exhibit/soviet.archive.html

The U.S. Library of Congress presents its Soviet archives exhibit online. Visit here to explore its collection of doc-

uments from the once top-secret archives of the Communist Party's Central Committee.

Macedonia: History and Politics
http://vislab-www.nps.navy.mil/~fapapoul/macedonia/macedon.html

Macedonia: History and Politics, part of a virtual tour of the Peloponnese, presents a comprehensive look at the country from antiquity to modern times. A table of contents and annotated list of links to photographs are provided.

Medieval Resources
http://ebbs.english.vt.edu/medieval/medieval.ebbs.html

For those who take nostalgia to extremes, Medieval Resources offers links to materials devoted to art, literature, and daily life. It also offers links to archives of texts in Old and Middle English, and other European languages.

Muslims in the 19th Century Russian Empire
http://www.uoknor.edu/cybermuslim/russia/rus_home.html

This page, maintained by the CyberMuslim Information Collective, features an exhibit of photography and historical information regarding the Turks and Tatars. Part of an interactive history project, this site's growth depends on the contributions of visitors' ideas and memories.

Operation Desert Storm Debriefing Book
http://www.nd.edu/~aleyden/contents.html

The Operation Desert Storm Debriefing Book, a personal collection of research materials and related links, offers a comprehensive look at the 1990-91 war with Iraq. Visit here for an extensive index of articles covering the politics, logistics, weaponry, and media coverage of the conflict.

National Civil War Association
http://ncwa.org/

You'd never expect to find the National Civil War Association in Northern California. But this group offers re-enactment camps, historic resources to research Confederate and Union forces, and links to other U.S. Civil War sites.

Netherlands Institute for the Near East

http://www.leidenuniv.nl/nino/nino.html

The Netherlands Institute for the Near East in Leiden has long been a center of Oriental studies. Founded in 1939, it produces research and journals on Near East issues. Its home page has information about the institute, its publications and links to related sites.

Northwestern University Library Special Collections: The Siege and Commune of Paris, 1870-1871

http://www.library.nwu.edu/spec/siege/

Northwestern University maintains this searchable collection of links to over 1,200 photographs and images recorded during the Siege and Commune of Paris. The collection is indexed by subject.

Philippine History 101

http://pubweb.acns.nwu.edu/~flip/history.html

Culled from various sources, these colorful recountings of social customs and historical timelines provide an introduction to the history and culture of the Philippine people. Includes photos and details on the islands' occupation by the Spanish and the United States.

Plague and Public Health in Renaissance Europe

http://www.village.virginia.edu/osheim/plaguein.html

Hardly a generation in Europe escaped this deadly pestilence. For two hundred years there was virtually no aspect of society that escaped its devastation. Read how one-half to one-third of Europe's population was destroyed.

Research Institute for the Humanities: History

http://www.arts.cuhk.hk/His.html

The history page from the Research Institute for the Humanities Web site contains links to history servers around the world covering five historical periods: ancient, medieval, renaissance, modern, and World War II. The links are grouped by regions.

Richard III Society

http://www.webcom.com/~blanchrd/gateway.html

The American branch of the Richard III Society offers Web resources for those interested in the interpretations of Richard III, the controversial 15th century English king, and subject of one of Shakespeare's darkest history plays. Here the curious will find publications and discussion topics that include the Battle of Bosworth Field.

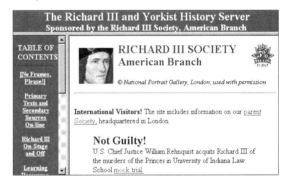

Selected Civil War Photographs

http://rs6.loc.gov/cwphome.html

The U.S. Library of Congress exhibits over 1,000 electronic images in its Selected Civil War Photographs Collection. Portraits of military personnel and battle scene landscapes make up this historic online archive.

Smithsonian Institution

http://www.si.sgi.com/sgistart.htm

"America's Treasure House of Learning," The Smithsonian Institution sponsors this page as a central jump station to its individual museums and resources. Explore the institution's vast array of galleries, research centers, and exhibitions, from historic Americana to aerospace technology and engineering.

Society for Creative Anachronism
http://www.sca.org/

Visit the Current Middle Ages page for an introduction to the Society for Creative Anachronism (SCA), which researches and recreates Middle Age history and culture. Stressing active participation, the SCA stages historical reenactments and role-playing events.

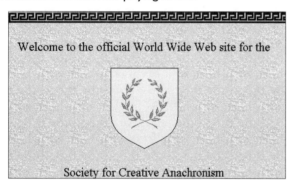

Tito
http://www.fri.uni-lj.si/~tito/tito-eng.html

Presented with a first person perspective, this multimedia "home page" of the deceased Yugoslavian dictator, Tito, offers a collection of recorded speeches, galleries of photos, and other memorabilia from his years in power.

Trinity Atomic Web Site
http://www.envirolink.org/issues/nuketesting/

Visitors here will find information about the Trinity test site, where the United States exploded the first atomic bomb. The page includes photos of high-energy weapons

tested since World War II, and a description of the upcoming commemorative events at the Trinity site.

U.S. Civil War Center
http://www.cwc.lsu.edu/civlink.htm

The U.S. Civil War Center provides an exhaustive array of information on the bloody conflict between North and South. Visitors can check out a wealth of historical information—including maps, diaries, university archives, and much more—or link to hundreds of related sites.

U-Web
http://rvik.ismennt.is/~gummihe/Uboats/u-boats.htm

Learn about the U-boat battles of World War II at this site, which includes information on the unique submersible boats and the men who piloted them. Also available is a bibliography, a glossary, and information on the Sharkhunters, an organization dedicated to submarine history.

Ulster Historical Publications
http://www.gpl.net/users/bradley/

Publications about the history, culture, and heritage of Northern Ireland can be researched at the Ulster Historical Publications home page. The site offers lists of publications that are available by mail order.

United States Holocaust Memorial Museum
http://www.ushmm.org/

The home page of the United States Holocaust Memorial Museum in Washington, D.C., offers information on the center, its research and programs, plus help in planning a visit. Also find online access to the data archive and pointers to sites of related interest.

Vatican Exhibit—Rome Reborn
http://www.ncsa.uiuc.edu/SDG/Experimental/vatican.exhibit/Vatican.exhibit.html

The Library of Congress takes its visitors on a virtual tour of its Vatican Exhibit here. The exhibit includes a close look at the history of the papal city and the arts that flourished within it.

Victorian Web

http://www.stg.brown.edu/projects/
hypertext/landow/victorian/victov.html

At Brown University's Victorian Web, visitors will find a wealth of information about the unique era named after the famed British queen. Aspects here include economics, religion, philosophy, literature, and the visual arts. Gender matters, science, and technology are also covered.

The Viking Home Page

http://control.chalmers.se/vikings/viking.html

The Control Engineering Laboratory at Chalmers University of Technology in Goteborg, Sweden, maintains this site for The Viking Home Page. Visit here to learn about Viking culture and history through an extensive index of internal and related Web links.

Virtual Memorial Hall of the Victims in Nanjing Massacre

http://www.arts.cuhk.hk/NanjingMassacre/
NM.html

Approximately 300,000 people were killed and over 20,000 were reported raped in the December 1937 fall of Nanjing, China to the Japanese Imperial Army. This Virtual Memorial Hall commemorates the victims. It includes photos, videos, and book suggestions.

WWW Virtual Library: History

http://history.cc.ukans.edu/history/WWW_
history_main.html

This segment of the WWW Virtual Library points to a wealth of history resources organized alphabetically, by era, or by region. Visitors can also access historical news-

groups and discussion lists, or get details on topical conferences here.

The World of Mayan Culture

http://www.yucatan.com.mx/mayas/
mapamay.htm

Mayan culture, cuisine, history, travel, and more are addressed in The World of Mayan Culture, available in English and Spanish versions. A link-sensitive map lets visitors explore Mayan regions in Mexico, Belize, Honduras, Guatemala, and El Salvador to learn more about this ancient culture.

World War I, World War II, Easy to Understand Books

http://wally.rit.edu/pubs/guides/easyww1_
2.html

Wallace Library Guides provides us with a list of books that are not so complicated we have to wade through them with shovels (or fall asleep in our chairs). The listings include books on both wars, as well as those specifically devoted to the Holocaust.

World War II Revisited

http://users.visi.net/~cwt/wwii-inf.html

This is the spot to dig up a small retrospective of one of the worst wars in the history of the world, a bit of nostalgia for WW II, the Big One. The site offers photographs from the Signal Corps and the American War Library Photo Collection. A question asks, "Did You Jump With The Weather Parachutists?" Steep yourself in history here.

World War II: The World Remembers

http://192.253.114.31/D-Day/Table_of_
contents.html

The students and faculty of Patch American High School in Vaihingen, a small section of Stuttgart, Germany, have compiled a wealth of info on World War II at this site, including documents from government and military archives, famous speeches, maps, battle plans, and much more.

Worlds of Late Antiquity
http://ccat.sas.upenn.edu/jod/wola.html

This site sweeps the dust off of Mediterranean history and culture dating from 200-700 C.E. Prepared by a University of Pennsylvania faculty member, the site offers history buffs recommended reading lists, searchable databases, scholarly commentary, and online ancient texts, in addition to a class syllabus.

LITERATURE

The last two years of my college days were spent at The University of Mississippi in Oxford, the home town of William Faulkner. The great author of *Absalom, Absalom* and *The Sound and the Fury* could be seen on the street corners visiting with cronies, unpretentious and easily recognized, even from a distance, by his shock of bright white hair, and the kakhi chinos and white shirt sleeves he wore rolled up to the elbows.

William Faulkner on the Web
http://www.mcsr.olemiss.edu/~egjbp/
faulkner/faulkner.html

Literary fans of William Faulkner can explore the author's mythical and actual stomping grounds. The site also includes a trivia page, notes, synopses of the author's works, and resource listings for students of the great southern author.

In addition to his prowess with a pen, the slight Nobel Laureate was one of the last of the great marathon drinkers, and wisely hired a driver to take him on the weekly excursions to his regular bootlegger—Mississippi being totally dry in that day. My brother, George, got lucky, and won the envious position. Many were the sedate trips to the "Ridge" to get some good local "white lightning." Regular whiskey was only available in Memphis, about 80 miles away, so George and Bill junketed up there, too, to lay in a supply of commercial stuff to whet the bard's whistle.

A story goes around that one of the jobs that Faulkner held before establishing himself as a writer was as postmaster of the university post office. When the demands of the job began to interfere with his writing, he wrote this letter to the Postmaster General:

"As long as I live under the capitalistic system, I expect to have my life influenced by the demands of moneyed people. But I will be damned if I propose to be at the beck and call of every itinerant scoundrel who has two cents to invest in a postage stamp.

"This sir, is my resignation."

Later, another story circulated, concerning the time that Faulkner was on a shooting expedition with director Howard Hawkes and actor Clark Gable. Gable turned to the Laureate and asked him who he thought were the five best authors of the day.

Faulkner replied, thoughtfully, "Ernest Hemingway, Willa Cather, Thomas Mann, John Dos Passos, and myself."

Gable replied maliciously, "Oh, do you write for a living?"

"Yes," retorted Faulkner, "and what do *you* do?"

A LITTLE LIGHT READING

"We have so many books in this house, I fear the floors will sink. I don't believe there is a room in our house without a bookcase, and yet they are marching across the floor as I speak, two feet high."

Arthuriana
http://dc.smu.edu/Arthuriana/

"Arthuriana" is a scholarly journal about the legend of King Arthur, published quarterly by the North American branch of the International Arthurian Society. Visitors will find sample articles, subscription information, and related products such as King Arthur T-shirts.

Avalon: Arthurian Heaven

http://reality.sgi.com/employees/chris_
manchester/arthur.html

Travel to the isle of Avalon to learn more about the legend of King Arthur. Links are provided to books, articles, related resources—like the script to the Monty Python version of the story—and an Arthurian study course.

Magellan 3 Star Award Site

Bodleian Library Electronic Texts Gopher

gopher://rsl.ox.ac.uk/11/lib-corn/hunter/
Browse%20Alex/Browse%20by%20Date/
Browse%20by%20Date%3a%201600s

The works of writers such as Blaise Pascal, Thomas Hobbes, and John Milton are featured at this U.K. gopher, which also includes works from John Locke and the first Thanksgiving proclamation from Charlestown, Mass.

Classics Ireland

http://www.ucd.ie/~classics/
ClassicsIreland.html

Classics Ireland, from the University College Dublin, is the online version of a journal published by the Classical Association of Ireland (CAI). On this page find recent volumes with articles relating to the ancient world, its literature, and ideas.

Eighteenth Century Archive Page

http://english-www.hss.cmu.edu/18th/

Part of the English server archive maintained by Carnegie Mellon University, this page provides visitors with an alphabetical list of writings from the 18th century. Visitors can peruse poems, treatises, novels, plays, historical texts, and a whole lot more.

Eighteenth Century Resources: Literature

http://www.english.upenn.edu/~jlynch/18th/

Journey back in time via this Web site, which offers visitors information on the literature of the 1700s. Includes scholarly papers, sound files, and scads of links to 18th-century resources.

Emily Dickinson Page

http://lal.cs.byu.edu/people/black/
dickinson.html

Begun in 1995 after a fruitless Web search for material related to Emily Dickinson, this site has flowered into a repository of points and pointers. Biographical data, online poetry, annotations, summaries, reviews, and references are featured, along with information about the Emily Dickinson International Society.

European Literature Electronic Texts

http://www.lib.virginia.edu/wess/etexts.html

This collection of western European literature is provided by the Western European Specialists Section of the Association of College and Research Libraries. Visit here for fiction and non-fiction titles in a variety of non-English languages.

Ever The Twain Shall Meet

http://www.lm.com/~joseph/mtwain.html

Ever The Twain Shall Meet is a literary reference and resource devoted to Mark Twain. This page has links to some of his works in their electronic entirety, including *The Adventures of Huckleberry Finn* and *Tom Sawyer*.

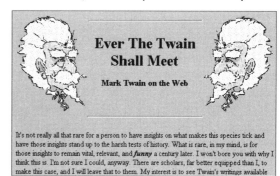

The Hill Monastic Manuscript Library
http://www.csbsju.edu/hmml/

"Fire, flood, theft, war. It only takes a minute to destroy history's greatest ideas." Working since 1965, the Hill Monastic Manuscript Library is one of the world's most comprehensive archives of medieval and renaissance resources. Learn more about the library's microfilm collection, manuscript catalogs, and study centers.

Historical Documents Gopher
gopher://gopher.vt.edu:10010/10/33

Historical documents, philosophical teachings, and literary works by famous authors are on file and ready to download at this gopher hole. Selections range from "The Gettysburg Address" to works from Confucius.

Internet Wiretap Gopher
gopher://wiretap.spies.com/11/Books

Literature buffs can download hundreds of classic and contemporary literary works, from Aesop to Jane Austen, via this gopher.

Lewis Carroll
http://www.students.uiuc.edu/~jbirenba/carroll.html

Devoted to author Lewis Carroll, this page provides information about the author and links to illustrated, electronic texts of his works, including *Alice's Adventures in Wonderland*. Visitors will also find a rotating discussion topic, and a list of organizations devoted to the writer.

The Lindisfarne Gospels
http://portico.bl.uk/access/treasures/lindisfarne.html

A seventh-century manuscript, "written and illuminated in honour of God and St. Cuthbert," and the British Library's gift book and videotape celebrating the artistic treasure, are described at this site. Visitors can read the story of the historic text here.

Literary Kicks
http://www.charm.net/~brooklyn/LitKicks.html

Beat fans will enjoy this site, featuring links to the works of Jack Kerouac, Allen Ginsberg, William S. Burroughs, and other writers from the Beat period. Maintained by an avid reader of the genre, the site provides an in-depth look at the authors who set the 1950s literary community on its ear, and set the stage for the 1960s American cultural revolution.

Literary Resources on the Net
http://www.english.upenn.edu/~jlynch/Lit/

A University of Pennsylvania doctoral candidate maintains this index of links to Web sites "dealing especially with English and American literature." Search by genre, including Classical, Victorian, Renaissance, and 20th century selections. Information about related mailing lists and scholarly publications is included.

Mark Twain on the Philippines
http://web.syr.edu/~fjzwick/twain_ph.html

Mark Twain, who served as a vice president of the Anti-Imperialist League, thought the United States never should have become involved in the internal affairs of the Philippines. Check out this page and find out why; it's filled with Twain's ideas on the subject, as well as a profile of the writer.

The Modern English Collection
http://etext.lib.virginia.edu/modeng.browse.html

The Electronic Text Center at the University of Virginia provides access to this collection of hundreds of complete literary works available for download. Arranged in alphabetical order, selections range from Horatio Alger to Bram Stoker.

The On-line Books Page
http://www.cs.cmu.edu/Web/books.html

Hundreds of hypertext books are available on the Internet, and this index, which includes a search function, will help readers find them.

The Page at Pooh Corner
http://www.public.iastate.edu/~jmilne/
pooh.html

Dedicated to the stories of "Winnie the Pooh" and the "House at Pooh Corner," this unofficial site highlights the misadventures of Pooh, Piglet, Tigger, and all their fictional friends. Includes biographical information on the stories' creators, A.A. Milne and E.H. Shepard.

Pulitzer Prizes
http://www.pulitzer.org/

The Pulitzer Prizes are among the highest awards bestowed upon newspaper reporters, authors, playwrights, and composers in America. Features here include a current list of winners, audio excerpts, full texts of selected news articles, and synopses of honored books.

The Voice of the Shuttle: English Literature
http://humanitas.ucsb.edu/shuttle/
english.html

A professor at the Department of English at the University of California, Santa Barbara, provides this index to a variety of English literature and humanities sites.

Voltaire Foundation
http://www.voltaire.ox.ac.uk/

"Welcome to the Enlightenment!" proclaims this page from the Voltaire Foundation at England's Oxford University. Find publications, images, societies, and more, all related to the great French poet, dramatist, satirist, and historian. In French and English.

Walker Percy
http://sunsite.unc.edu/wpercy/

Southern favorite son Walker Percy is characterized as a "philosophical novelist" by the University of North Carolina archive that collects and presents his work online. Visitors can peruse Percy's papers, fiction, and philosophical treatises here.

FOR YOUR REVIEW

Beatrice
http://www.beatrice.com/contents/

Beatrice, an online monthly magazine, offers a spread of original fiction, essays, book reviews and interviews.

Dogwood Blossom
http://glwarner.samford.edu/haiku.htm

Dogwood Blossom, an electronic haiku journal maintained by a researcher at Samford University in Birmingham, Ala., offers poetry, book reviews, and articles about the Japanese writing form. Includes submission forms and links to other haiku-related sites.

RhetNet: A CyberJournal
http://www.missouri.edu/~rhetnet/

RhetNet is a repository for resources on the Internet of interest to the rhetoric and writing community. It provides articles and essays, Internet conversations and a "general call for participation."

POETRY

There once was a girl name of Hetty
Who cooked a mean pot of spaghetti
It was such a treat
We all wanted to eat
But couldn't keep our forks very steady!

My own offering makes no claim to onomatopoeia, or anything else for that matter. But try your hand and see how you enjoy putting rhyming words together.

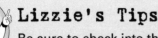

Lizzie's Tips

Be sure to check into the "Poets Press," part of The Arts folder in the SeniorNet Roundtable discussion area. It's chock full of original poetry from bards like us:

http://www.seniornet.org/cgi-bin/We-bX?13 @^4407@.ee6b506

One of the poems that had the greatest impact on me was a rhyme by James Whitcomb Riley from his book, *Riley Child-Rhymes*, written in 1890. It was titled "Little Orphant Annie," and I begged Grandmother to read it to me nearly every night. It has to be read with just the right inflection in order to scare you half to death. We almost wore the poor book to shreds re-reading this particular poem over and over, and I can still recite it today. Of course, this poem would not stand up to the works of Shakespeare or Milton, but it has stood up to its own test of time—and mine.

The Alsop Review

http://www.hooked.net/users/jalsop/

Northern California poet Jaimes Alsop shares his own work and work that inspires him here. Find contemporary poetic offerings, plus a list of links, including pointers to Internet tools, humor, and job search resources.

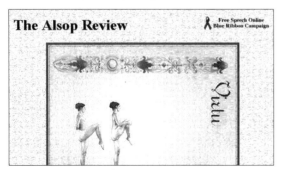

Best Fiction and Poetry from CSUN: 1962-1988

http://www.csun.edu/~hceng029/thebest/bestcontents.html

The Best Fiction and Poetry from California State University, Northridge: 1962-1988, offers an extensive sampling of works during this 25-year span.

British Poetry 1780-1910

http://etext.lib.virginia.edu/britpo.html

With annotated and illustrated texts of notable British poetry, this archive contains guidelines for submissions, and links to the Alderman Library at the University of Virginia and other campus servers.

Cowboy Poetry

http://agricomm.com/agricomm/cp

The spirit of the Old West lives on in Cowboy Poetry, poems and prose that celebrate the uniquely American cowboy mystique. Poems by and about men and women who ride the range bring home the life of the cowboy, and other text spells out current gatherings and projects of interest to modern cowboys.

Haiku for People

http://www.oslonett.no/home/keitoy/haiku.html

Visitors can dabble in the art of haiku, a form of Japanese poetry, at this site. The page contains a history of haiku and some famous examples.

Internet Poetry Archive

http://sunsite.unc.edu/dykki/poetry/home.html

Works of the poets Seamus Heaney, Czeslaw Milosz, and others are electronically reproduced at the Internet Poetry Archive. Find a description of the archive project or access the poetical texts collected here.

Little Orphant Annie

Little Orphant Annie's come to our house
to stay,
An' wash the cups and saucers up, an'
brush the crumbs away,
An' shoo the chickens off the porch, an'
dust the hearth, an' sweep,
An' make the fire, an' bake the bread, an'
earn her board-an-keep;
An' all us other children, when the supper
things is done,
We set around the fire an' has the mostest
fun
A-list-nin' to the witch-tales 'at Annie tells
about,
An' the Gobble-uns 'at gits you
Ef you Don't Watch Out!

Onc't There was a little boy, wouldn't say
his prayers,
So when he went to bed at night, away up
stairs,
His Mammy heerd him holler, an' his
Daddy heerd him bawl,
An' when they turn't the kivvers down, he
wasn't there at all!
An' they seeked him in the rafter-room, an'
cubby-hole, an' press,
An' seeked him up the chimbly-flue, an'
ever'wheres, I guess;
But all they ever found was thist his pants
and rounda-bout:
An' the Gobble-uns'll git you
Ef you Don't Watch Out!

An' one time a little girl 'ud allus laugh an'
grin
An' make fun of ever'one, an all her blood
an' kin;
An' onc't, when they was "company," an'
ole folks was there,
She mocked 'em an' shocked 'em, an' said
she didn't care!
An' thist as she kicked her heels, an' turn't
to run an' hide,
They was two great big Black Things a-
standing by her side,
An' they snatched her through the ceilin'
'fore she knowed what she's about!
An' the Gobble-uns'll git you
Ef you Don't Watch Out!

An' little Orphant Annie says when the
blaze is blue,
An' the lamp-wick sputters, an' the wind
goes *woo-oo!*
An' you hear the crickets quit, an' the
moon is gray,
An' the lightnin'-bugs in dew is all
squenched away,
You better mind yer parents, an' yer
teachers fond an' dear,
An' churish them 'at loves you, an' dry the
orphant's tear,
An he'p the pore an' needy ones 'at
clusters all about,
Er the Gobble-uns'll git you
Ef you Don't Watch Out!

Mark's Poem of the Day
http://www.dataimages.com/poetry/

Maintained by a University of Arizona engineering student, this page offers a daily poem selection. Visit here to read the latest prose and contribute to the collection.

Deborah Sellers' Poetry
http://www.iquest.net/cw/debi/poem.html

Poet Deborah Sellers presents her works, including the award-winning "Life in the Latter Part of the 20th Century," at her home page. It features works in progress and a hotlink to Deborah's favorite Web sites.

A LITTLE HELP FROM YOUR FRIENDS

MUSEUMS

You could say that museums are those huge buildings, taking up city blocks, that harbor the stuff that no one wants to throw away. My attic was like that, until I moved to smaller quarters, and now I have no attic anymore.

But many museums house artifacts that tell of our heritage, some with complete restorations of coal mines and villages, and some with dynamic skeletons of the monster dinosaurs that walked the earth before humans. Colonial Williamsburg, a completely restored Revolutionary village, is in fact a living museum. And many old homes left to municipalities are museums, honoring a time and way of life no longer in vogue. There are science museums to completely mystify those like me, and space museums that will amaze us.

Step out and take in a few of these marvels. Amaze yourself with the fascinating array of materials you are about to see.

Academy of Natural Sciences
http://www.acnatsci.org/

This educational institution and natural history museum, located in Philadelphia, describes its permanent collections—dinosaurs, wildlife dioramas, crystals and gems, endangered species—and its changing exhibits. The museum also offers a number of educational natural science field trips, like archeological digs and exploratory trips to exotic locales, that you might want to consider for your next vacation. The Museum Store is online with a small selection of items, and the bird-eating spider screensaver is a must-see.

Adler Planetarium and Museum
http://astro.uchicago.edu/adler/

The first planetarium in the Western Hemisphere, Chicago's Adler Planetarium and Museum continues its tradition of bringing the universe and its exploration to the widest possible audience. You can preview exhibits and shows, learn about special events and courses, and find links to online resources such as a skywatcher's diary.

Bishop Museum
http://www.bishop.hawaii.org/

Aloha! This Web site, maintained by the Hawaiian state museum of cultural and natural history, includes an ongoing inventory of native and nonnative species of flora and fauna found in the archipelago, a hands-on science display, and links to museum departments.

Canadian Museum of Civilization
http://www.cmcc.muse.digital.ca/cmc/cmceng/welcmeng.html

The Canadian Museum of Civilization has a virtual home with exhibits and features online for members only, but all you have to do is register (for free!) to become a cyber member. Even without registration, you can see images of articles and artifacts in the various collections, such as archaeology, ethnology, folk culture, history, and military history. The museum has also posted some real-time multimedia clips.

The Computer Museum Network
http://www.net.org/

Whoa! Hold on to your interactive hat! If you're a sucker for interesting interactive activities on the Web, visit the Robots Gallery at Boston's Museum of Computing. Not only do you get an introduction to the fascinating field of robotics, you can actually design your own robot online. Next door in the Networks Gallery, you can interact with other online visitors to solve The Networked Puzzle. This site also includes lots of interesting information about computers in general—both past and current— and when you're finished exploring, you can send an on-line postcard to your wired friends.

Exploratorium ExploraNet
http://www.exploratorium.edu/

San Francisco's Exploratorium houses a collection of interactive exhibits for anyone who has even the slightest interest in the sciences. Imaginative and fun, these activities can steer you in the most amazing directions. A recent exhibit, for example, gave Web visitors the chance to dissect a cow's eye. Not everyone's cup of tea, perhaps, but where else could you find such an anatomy lesson? Info about the museum and lots of images are also available online.

Flandrau Science Center
http://www.seds.org/flandrau/

Arizona's Flandrau Science Center intends to "awaken the scientist in us all" with programs that entertain while they educate. This page guides visitors to exhibits and events spanning an astronomical scope of interests. Find astronomy news and a skywatcher's guide, Comet Hale-Bopp info, and descriptions of the center's programs.

Lizzie's Tips

If you've ever thought of replacing your baby monitor with a bigger one, say 17", instead of 14", give it another thought before you chuck the old one away. It's true, you can spread out your work and give relief to your tired eyes when you are working with a larger monitor, but you can use your old monitor to spread things out even further. Keep the clutter on one and the text on the other. If you've already got a good-sized monitor but this idea intrigues you, think of picking up a used grayscale model to use as your spare.

Florida Museum of Natural History
http://www.flmnh.ufl.edu/

The Florida Museum of Natural History at the University of Florida, Gainesville, features more than 10 million animal and fossil specimens, but they're not all online. The museum's Web site includes online exhibits, photo galleries (see actual pictures of alligators!), and educational materials. Anyone planning a snail-watching field trip? Take along the museum's Fieldguide to the Freshwater Snails of Florida and be sure to add the Guide to the Venomous Snakes of Florida—both available here courtesy of the museum.

The Food Museum
http://www.foodmuseum.com/~hughes/first.htm

Now this is my kind of place! Food! What could be more appealing? And speaking of peels, this site evolved from the Potato Museum, a site devoted to the "history and cultural significance of the world's most influential vegetable." The Potato Museum is still online and includes fun, but useless, trivia—like the number of varieties of potatos in the world, and how potato chips rate among the populace as a snack food. After you've explored the potato, move on to the Food News section for a selection of headlines (and links to stories) about comestibles.

From the Food List section, you can learn all you ever wanted to know about persimmons and spinach.

Henry Ford Museum
http://hfm.umd.umich.edu/

The Henry Ford Museum in Greenfield Village is the "nation's largest indoor/outdoor museum," and was founded by the man himself in 1929. The Online Histories section includes the bulk of the online offerings. Look there for the Pic of the Month, an image of an item from the collection, and for the Showroom of Automobile History with its info and images of classic vehicles including the 1896 Quadricycle, the 1908 Model T, and the 1949 Ford. You'll also enjoy a virtual stroll through the J.R. Jones General Store, a local institution since the 1880s, and the profiles of inventors including the Wright Brothers and—of course—Henry Ford.

The Franklin Institute Science Museum
http://sln.fi.edu/

Another excellent interactive museum site (with clever animations) is The Franklin Institute from Philadelphia (named after old Ben himself). At the Franklin you'll be treated to The Heart: An Online Exploration, a multimedia trip through the blood vessels and structures of your ticker. Tips on maintaining a healthy heart and a look at the history of heart science finish off the tour. And no trip to the museum would be complete without a stop at the Ben Franklin exhibit. Along with biographical info and sound files of some of Franklin's most memorable quotes, the exhibit includes a QuickTime movie called Glimpses of the Man. Poor Richard is alive at the Franklin.

Illinois State Museum
http://www.museum.state.il.us/

Have you ever wondered what the American Midwest was like 16,000 years ago? Well, wonder no longer. The Illinois State Museum in Springfield maintains this site with the information you've been seeking, along with news about the museum, its collections, research, and programs. The other online exhibits let you explore the ice age, look at fossils, and learn more about the past.

The Kelsey Museum of Archaeology
http://www.umich.edu/~kelseydb/

The Kelsey Museum is located at the University of Michigan, but you can visit their collections in the dead of winter without having to put on your overcoat. The real fun at this site is the galleries. A collection of images from the Greek and Roman and the Egyptian collections is online, so you can sit and ponder a 3,000-year-old cup from Cyprus or a 2,000-year-old Egyptian funerary portrait. The image collection isn't a big one, but the photos of the artifacts are nicely rendered and show excellent detail.

The Lost Museum of Sciences
http://www.netaxs.com/people/aca3/
ATRIUM.HTM

Pour yourself a cup of java and pull up the chair for some serious cyber browsing through the Lost Museum of Sciences. Jump to more than 300 far-flung museum Web pages in the Hall of Antiquity, the Hall of Physical Science, or the Natural History Rotunda.

Mary Rose Virtual Maritime Museum
http://www.synergy.net/homeport.html

Nautical archaeology buffs will enjoy this online tour of the wreckage of the *Mary Rose*, a warship built in 1510 and sunk in 1545. Discover how the ship was originally operated and recently excavated during your visit to this virtual maritime museum. And the next time you find yourself in Portsmouth, England, stop by to see the old girl in person.

Monterey Bay Aquarium: E-Quarium
http://www.mbayaq.org/

The online offerings from the renowned Monterey Bay Aquarium include an exhibit called Habitats Path, a tour of the local waters from "wave-swept tidepools to the depths of a vast submarine canyon." You'll think twice about going for a dip after you visit the Deadly Beauties exhibit, and read about the bottom-dwelling stonefish and its fatal sting, or the other scary denizens of Davy Jones' Locker, such as sea snakes, cone snails, and warty ghouls. I'll stay on the beach, thank you.

Museo de las Momias
http://www.sirius.com/~dbh/mummies/

Mummies are the featured attraction at the Museo de las Momias of Guanajuato, Mexico, and you can see enough mummy images here to keep you awake for hours (the actual museum has 108 of them). Also included are pictures of the local graveyard, and a lively explanation of the genesis of the museum and its popularity among the locals. But I didn't see a single shot of Boris Karloff.

Museum of Antiquities
http://www.ncl.ac.uk/~nantiq/

If you've ever pictured yourself as a late Stone Age hunter-gatherer, then the Flints and Stones exhibition of the U.K.'s Museum of Antiquities can fuel your fantasy. Follow the shaman as he leads you on a brief illustrated tour of his world. Then meet the archeologist, read more about the era, and take the Food Quiz to see if you could survive under those harsh conditions. Every month, the museum posts a new image of an item from its collection, and previous images are archived so you can gasp over the intricacies of the jewelry and the beauty of the art.

Museum of Radio and Technology
http://www.library.ohiou.edu/MuseumR&T/museum.htm

Remember your family's old radio and your first television set? This museum in Huntington, West Virginia, wants to help you remember by posting photos of items from its collection online. You'll see a variety of vacuum tubes, the RCA Victor dog ("His master's voice"), radios so elaborate that they are room decorations, and TVs with tiny screens. I'll bet the people at the museum are friendly; their helpful Web site includes links to other antique radio sites, directions to the facility, and information about Huntington.

National Air & Space Museum
http://ceps.nasm.edu:2020/NASMpage.html

If you haven't ever been there, this cyber tour of the Smithsonian Institution's National Air & Space Museum will soon have you planning a trip to Washington, D.C. The museum specializes in aeronautics and planetary studies, and includes exhibits ranging from the controversial Enola Gay to NASA spacecraft. This site lets you explore the museum via an interactive map, and includes lots of interesting commentary and photographs.

The National Baseball Hall of Fame and Museum
http://www.enews.com/bas_hall_fame/overview.html

Plan your trip to Cooperstown at this site from the Electronic Newsstand. It provides information on all the basics of the Baseball Hall of Fame, including exhibits, directions, and rates. Online shopping also is available here, but Cracker Jacks are not in the catalog.

National Museum of the American Indian
http://www.si.edu/nmai/

This Smithsonian Institution page doesn't give you a lot of bang for your click, but it does include info about current and past exhibits, some artifact photographs with descriptions, and reviews and ordering info for companion books. If the regrettably meager offerings at this site whet your appetite for more, move on to the page's real value, the list of links to other Native American sites. Via these links you can visit the Oneida and the Sioux, browse a Native American Art Gallery, and access other index sites with links to more, and even more, online Indian presences.

National Museum of Racing and Hall of Fame
http://www.horseworld.com/imh/nmr/nmrmain.html

And they're off! The National Museum of Racing in Saratoga Springs, New York, celebrates the history and excitement of thoroughbred racing in America through its online exhibit that traces the beginning of thoroughbred racing in England to its current incarnation in the racetracks of the United States. Neophytes can bone up on the definition of a thoroughbred, and old-timers can wax poetic over the descriptions of champion horses and their Triple Crown wins. Settle in with a mint julep and you'll almost be able to smell the bluegrass.

National Portrait Gallery

http://www.npg.si.edu/

Pictures? We've got pictures—loads of them. Or at least the National Portrait Gallery does, and they're online here for you to browse. Portraits of all 41 presidents, distinguished Native Americans, and patriots and statesmen from early American history are waiting for your visit, along with brief, but interesting, curators' notes. Be sure to check out the Spotlight: Biography feature, an on-line brochure that presents a different biographical profile each month. Special exhibits are also posted, and the home page collage of changing portraits (how many can you name?) alone is worth the trip.

Natural History Museum

http://www.nhm.ac.uk/

The U.K.'s Natural History Museum brings its "unrivalled collections" and "world-class exhibitions and education" (whew! so much for that British understatement!) to the Web. You can wander through pages devoted to each of the museum's scientific departments (botany, zoology, mineralogy, and more), access a number of its databases, and learn something new at its online exhibits.

Natural History Museum of Los Angeles County

http://www.lam.mus.ca.us/lacmnh/

If you're interested in that whole "life on Mars" thing, you'll want to check out the Mars Rocks online exhibition at the Los Angeles Natural History Museum. Along with descriptions of meteorites from Mars (how do they know?) is a plain-talk discussion of the current scientific theory on whether there are or aren't little green men on the Red Planet. I won't tell you the answer—go check it out for yourself. After your spell with the Martians, you'll want to look at the collection of exotic butterflies and moths, the Petersen Automotive Museum Sampler, and the selection of oceanographic exhibits.

North Carolina Museum of Life and Science

http://ils.unc.edu/NCMLS/ncmls.html

The home page for Durham, North Carolina's Museum of Life and Science features an online illustrated tour of the facility's inside and outside exhibits. Unfortunately there's not much interactivity here, but many pages feature sound clips. You will also find information about the museum, descriptions of its programs and services, and links to related sites.

On-line Exhibitions and Images

http://155.187.10.12/fun/exhibits.html

Save this site for a rainy Saturday afternoon when you don't have any emergencies on the to-do list, and the afternoon movie is one you've already seen three times. This fabulous index includes links to "Internet exhibitions, image archives, illustrated demonstration documents," and more. From Charlotte, the Vermont whale (yes, Vermont!), to the Dead Sea Scrolls, to the River and Rowing Museum, this eclectic compendium truly contains something for everyone.

Perspectives of the Smithsonian: Computer History

http://www.si.edu/resource/tours/comphist/computer.htm

The Smithsonian Institute features the Information Age at this online exhibit of computer history. Visitors here can watch a slide show of the actual exhibit that opened at the Smithsonian in May 1990. Of particular note is the Oral/Video History area that contains transcripts of reminiscences from some of the principal players in the computer revolution, along with bonus sound and video clips.

Pro Football Hall of Fame

http://www.canton-ohio.com/hof/

Fans of the pigskin will get a thrill from the history and biographies posted at the official home page of the museum in Canton, Ohio. The site includes profiles of all 185 "enshrinees" into the Hall of Fame, a timeline of notable events in the history of football, and a history of each pro football team. You can find out, for example, that the Washington Redskins began life in 1932 as the Boston Braves but changed their nickname the next year and actually moved to Washington in 1937. Good thing they moved. The Boston Redskins doesn't have the right ring.

Smithsonian Natural History Museum
http://nmnhwww.si.edu/nmnhweb.html

The pros at the Smithsonian do it again, this time with natural history. A kaleidoscope of online exhibits let you explore subjects as diverse as the planet's oceans and anthropological investigation. Elsewhere, you can wander among the descriptions of the permanent exhibits at the facility. Fascinating stuff.

Stark's Museum of Vacuum Cleaners
http://www.reed.edu/~karl/vacuum/
vacuum.html

I've never thought of my vacuum cleaner as a historical artifact. In fact, I never think about my vacuum cleaner at all if I can help it, but there's actually a vacuum cleaner museum in Portland, Oregon. A part-time janitor and vacuum maintainer at the Stark's Museum of Vacuum Cleaners "smuggled a camera inside" and posts the resulting virtual museum here, which details 100 years of vacuums with pictures and text. Go figure.

University of California Museum of Paleontology
http://ucmp1.berkeley.edu/

Here's an online version of the ultra-impressive Museum of Paleontology at the University of California at Berkeley. You can navigate through their extensive collection of online exhibits using phylogeny, geology, or evolutionary theory as your paradigm. A really snazzy feature of this site is The Subway, a gateway to other science and museum sites on the Web.

Vatican Exhibit Main Hall
http://www.ncsa.uiuc.edu/SDG/Experimental/
vatican.exhibit/exhibit/Main_Hall.html

The U.S. Library of Congress hosts this virtual exhibition that is based on the 1993 real-life exhibit called Rome Reborn: The Vatican Library and Renaissance Culture. The theme of the exhibit is the examination of the Vatican Library as "the intellectual driving force behind the emergence of Rome as a political and scholarly superpower during the Renaissance." Heavy stuff. Explore the various rooms of the exhibit, including Archaeology, Humanism, Mathematics, and Music.

The Robert C. Williams American Museum of Papermaking
http://www.ipst.edu/amp/

Devoted to the fascinating art of papermaking, this museum site includes a virtual tour focusing on the historical, practical, and current uses of paper in society. Even before paper was invented, humans felt the need to write on *something* and used clay, bark, leaves, cloth, wood, and many other materials to record their histories, laws, and transactions. The essay detailing how paper was made in pre-industrial Europe is enough to make you marvel that people didn't go back to writing on bark. But they didn't, and now we have paper mills and recycling—also subjects included at this excellent site.

Williamsburg Online
http://www.williamsburg.com/

The cyber tour of one of America's premiere historical sites leads you via photos and text through the gardens, buildings, sites and sounds, people, and events of Colonial Williamsburg. The Historical Almanac includes materials designed to enhance your understanding of 18th-century American life and—among many other features—includes an exploration of religion, a discussion of the etiquette and presentation in a typical tavern of the era, and profiles of different trades such as blacksmith, brickmaker, and milliner. You can learn more about how early Americans lived from this site than you ever did from Miss Nettles' history class.

The World Wide Web Virtual Library: Museums
http://www.icom.org/vlmp/

The selections I have included in this directory section only scratch the surface of the wonders available on the Web, so I've included this index site from the World Wide Web Virtual Library to aid you in your own cyber explorations. The entire museum world is included here for you to explore: Egypt, Russia, Australia, The Netherlands, Switzerland, Romania, Britain, Germany, Canada, France, Greece, Italy…whew! The list goes on and on, and you can, too—from the comfort of your chair via your trusty machine.

PHILOSOPHY AND RELIGION

I have always had only a passing interest in philosophy—people like Plato and Nietzsche usually put me to sleep.

The most important philosophical lessons in my life came from my father and my grandmother. Father would pontificate from the head of the dining room table. "Every tub must stand on its own bottom," he used to say, a phrase completely meaningless to very young children. But he repeated it throughout our lives at home, attributing it to John Bunyon. Somehow, I am not prepared to accept that.

Over the years, I stored this witticism away, not realizing exactly how I would use this piece of daily philosophy in later years. But I wrote it on the backs of notebooks, chuckled as I shared it with friends, and generally found the humble little saying amusing. Until I was about 55 years old, that is, when I suddenly knew what it meant to me. All along, my father had been preaching self-reliance. And if I did not actually know what it meant then, the phrase did sink in and develop, because I am nothing if not self-reliant. Thanks to my Pop, I have been using these skills all my life.

Grandmother taught me another valuable lesson. She would lean toward me from her dressing table as she was getting ready for the day, her old-fashioned stays demurely covered by a peach-colored oriental dressing gown, to pluck an invisible lint ball from my blouse, or settle an out-of-place hair on my forehead. She was always smiling when she sent me off to school, and every morning before I left she would look lovingly at me at say, "What are you going to do today to make the world a better place to live in?"

What a wonderful way to teach a child to try to be a good citizen, to be kind to her environment, and to put back into her community as much as she is able, replacing what she has taken out for her own use.

Enough of the ethics of my family, and on to the more philosophical area of this chapter. You're on your own!

A SELECTION OF PHILOSOPHY SITES

Analytical Philosophy
http://college.antioch.edu/~smauldin/

Antioch College graduate student Shannon Mauldin features a collection of analytical philosophy links at her personal Web site. Her list includes links to many university philosophy department home pages and to collections of individual philosophers' works. You'll recognize several names here: Marx and Engels, Nietzsche, Hume, and Bertrand Russell. Not the lightest reading, perhaps, but provocative and expansive.

Applied Ethics Resources
http://www.ethics.ubc.ca/papers/
AppliedEthics.html

If you often ponder the thorny problems of ethics in modern-day life (euthanasia, the death penalty, the rights of immigrants), you'll find a wealth of info on this page of links dealing with applied ethics. Categories include business ethics, environmental ethics, media ethics, and others.

Aristotle
http://www.hepth.cornell.edu/~costas/
biographies/aristotle.html

Plato's student and Alexander the Great's teacher, Aristotle emerged as one of the premiere thinkers in the history of Western civilization. This page presents a basic overview of his life, work, and philosophical ideas. During the Middle Ages, Aristotle's writings were considered the sum total of human knowledge and experience. Although his influence has declined, the modern age owes much to his scholarship, and this site will give you a good grounding in Aristotelian thought.

Albert Camus Critical Interpretation Home Page
http://www.wolfenet.com/~willej/indexa.htm

The excellent biographical essay at this site traces the evolution of Camus' theory of the absurd, and existential philosophy, and includes references to numerous works that embodied his ideas and philosophical explorations. Also here are links to essays by Camus and to a number of critical pieces that will help you understand the French philosopher's doctrines.

Chinese Philosophy Page
http://www.monash.edu.au/cc/staff/sas/sab/WWW/index.html

Confucius say: Chinese Philosophy Page has enough links to turn the visitor into an expert on philosophy Chinese-style. Philosophical texts and critical essays relating to Chinese thought, culture, and language are presented, along with basic details about philosophical schools of thought such as Confucianism and Taoism.

Engaged Buddhist Dharma
http://www.maui.com/~lesslie/

Banned in China, the Engaged Buddhist Dharma page features information about human rights abuses and the organizations—such as Amnesty International, Baby Milk Action, the Middle East Children's Alliance—that fight these problems every day. The site also includes world news from a variety of sources (Voice of America, Reuters, the World Tibet News Network), environmental concerns, and links to Buddhist art and writings.

Ereignis: The Heidegger Home Page
http://www.webcom.com/~paf/ereignis.html

Martin Heidegger no longer leaves a paper trail, but an abundance of thought about his writings is posted on the Internet. This page devoted to the German philosopher contains links to Heidegger resources around the Internet including the archive of the Heidegger mailing list.

A Few References to Michel Foucault
http://www.whistler.net/worldtour/homepage/ejournal/foucault.htm

Modern French philosopher Michel Foucault is the subject of this index page that includes links to a handful of Web sites about the controversial thinker. You'll find a bit of philosophical analysis, reviews of the biography written by Didier Eribon, selected quotes, and a list of major works.

Gateless Gate
http://sunsite.unc.edu/zenbin/koan-index.pl

This site hosts a collection of more than 30 philosophical vignettes pertaining to Taoism and Buddhism. Check out classic moral ponderings here, such as "Two Monks Roll Up the Screen" and "This Mind is Buddha."

Hume Archives
http://unix1.utm.edu/departments/phil/hume.html

Peruse electronic texts by and about the Scottish philosopher David Hume at this virtual archive. In addition to Hume's own writings, 18th-century reviews and commentary, biographical info, and the full text of Adam Smith's *Wealth of Nations* are also included.

Internet Services for Philosophers
http://www.phil.ruu.nl/philosophy_services.html

The Internet Services for Philosophers provides a compilation of selected Web sites relevant to the study of philosophy. This catalog includes links to archives, mailing lists, a nice list of philosophical sites, bibliographies, electronic texts, and other resources. If you feel a little mental exercise is in order but you're not sure what to think about, this page will give you plenty of ideas.

Krishnamurti
http://www.well.com/user/jct/

Described on this page as a "spiritual terrorist," Indian philosopher and author U.G. Krishnamurti will, we're promised, overturn "all of our accepted beliefs— God, mind, soul, enlightenment, religion, humanity, heart, love, relationships," and lead us to a "totally different picture of who we are. The result is a grenade in the brain." Intrigued? His book *Mind is a Myth* is available for downloading, as are video clips, transcriptions of conversations with Krishnamurti, and related articles.

The Marx/Engels Archives
http://csf.colorado.edu/psn/marx/

"There's no way to monetarily profit from this project" of posting the Marx/Engels Archives online, the archivist of this site says, but he hopes the material will be pleasurable and enlightening. Despite the communists' unfortunate experiment with putting the anticapitalist philosophy into practice, the works themselves propose a paradigm for an ideal, Utopian society. The texts are accompanied by photos of the two thinkers.

The Nietzsche Page
http://www.usc.edu/dept/annenberg/thomas/nietzsche.html

The Annenberg School of Communications at the University of Southern California maintains this page dedicated to the German philosopher Friedrich Wilhelm Nietzsche. Features include a biography and works bibliography in German and English, links to Nietzsche societies and organizations, and access to selected writings. Now's your chance to see if Nietzsche really is peachy.

No Dogs or Philosophers Allowed
http://www.access.digex.net/~kknisely/philosophy.tv.html

Who says that philosophical inquiry is a lost art? Certainly not the talented staff of *No Dogs or Philosophers Allowed*, an innovative television program that seeks to be the "philosophical agent" of the electronic marketplace of the 21st century and to "inspire graceful and unsettling conversation" from which wisdom can—hopefully—arise. The Web site is an interactive multimedia forum for discussion of the human condition that includes information on NDOPA and where you can tune in to this critically acclaimed show.

Charles S. Peirce Studies
http://www.peirce.org/

You may never have heard of this 19th-century philosopher and scientist, but Charles Peirce was "the first modern experimental psychologist in the Americas" and "the only system-building philosopher in the Americas who has been both competent and productive in logic, in mathematics, and in a wide range of sciences." The site includes hypertexts of Peirce's writings as well as essays explicating his theories.

Plato
http://spruce.evansville.edu/~al22/plato.html

Quick! Who's responsible for the old saying, "Necessity is the mother of invention"? No, it wasn't Shakespeare, but Plato, Greek philosopher extraordinaire. This excellent page includes a biographical overview, a discussion of the Dialogues and Plato's Theory of Forms, and an evaluation of Plato's influence. You can go on from here to other Plato pages, including the full text of *The Republic*, a seminal work on the nature of justice.

The Robot Wisdom Pages
http://www.mcs.net/~jorn/home.html

"Home of the new, conservative-left Responsible Party," Robot Wisdom proposes creating a computer model of the human predicament to help clear the path for a new political paradigm, where "cynical predators" can no longer feed. You may not agree with all the assertions and analyses of the Robot Wisdom pages, but you can't help but nod your head at the site's opening statement: "The world is a mess." You'll find political, philosophical, and social looks at the plan.

Ron's Place
http://www.connect.net/ron/philosophy.html

This personal home page has a great selection of links to overviews of a number of influential philosophers, including Heidegger, Hegel, Sartre, Descartes, and Kant. The approach is basically the *Cliff Notes* down-and-dirty treatment, but you can't beat these profiles for their basic introductory value.

Bertrand Russell Archives at McMaster University
http://www.mcmaster.ca/russdocs/russell.htm

McMaster University in Ontario, Canada is the epicenter for scholarly study of Bertrand Russell, the renowned British philosopher, logician, essayist, and socio/political activist. The University sponsors the online Bertrand Russell Archive, featuring Russell's writings, the Russell Editorial Project, favorite quotations from Russell's works, and much more. Treat yourself to Russell's thoughts on social order ("I found one day in school a boy of medium size ill-treating a smaller boy. I expostulated, but he replied: 'The bigs hit me, so I hit the babies; that's fair.' In these words he epitomized the history of the human race."), skepticism ("I wish to propose for the reader's favourable consideration a doctrine which may, I fear, appear wildly paradoxical and subversive. The doctrine in question is this: that it is undesirable to believe a proposition when there is no ground whatever for supposing it true."), and mathematics ("Mathematics may be defined as the subject where we never know what we are talking about, nor whether what we are saying is true.").

Sean's One-Stop Philosophy Shop
http://www.rpi.edu/~cearls/phil.html

Sean's attempt to "create the ultimate philosophy link list" is a worthy one. Here you'll find university departments, gophers, real-life philosophers, famous works and discussions, various "isms," and more. If you've always wanted to explore nihilism, secularism, and existentialism, this page is a great jumpstation.

Socrates
http://swift.eng.ox.ac.uk/jdr/socrat.html

The philosopher executed for "impiety and corrupting the youth of Athens" is briefly profiled on this overview page. Socrates left no writings of his own, but his profound influence on Western thought and civilization is indisputable. Once you've explored the offerings on this page, link back to the Classical Page for texts and discussions of other classical and medieval philosophers such as Plato, Aristotle, Augustine, and Aquinas.

Lizzie Sez
Learn to be a good listener. Opportunity can knock very softly sometimes.

SpinozaWeb
http://www.stg.brown.edu/~santiago/ SpinozaWeb/

This page bills itself as a resource guide for Spinoza fans around the world, and although you may not be a Spinoza fan yet, the links and resources here just might send you out in search of a classy Spinoza T-shirt to wear on trips to the grocery store. You'll find Book I of *The Ethics* and a handful of links to other Spinoza-related Web pages.

Spoon Collective
http://jefferson.village.virginia.edu/~spoons/

Once you've read and digested a selection of the great philosophical links in this directory, you'll probably want to share your insights, since philosophical inquiry is, after all, very much a societal affair. That's the beauty of this site. Spoon Collective devotes this page to philosophical discussion and archived information. You can discuss such heady topics as the theory of artistic avant-garde, Marxist discourse, Heidegger, or any number of other philosophical ideas from an extensive listing.

Su Tzu's Chinese Philosophy Page
http://mars.superlink.net/user/fsu/philo.html

The Webmaster hopes that searchers into the meaning of life will extend their paradigm beyond the traditional values of Western philosophy, and open their minds to the alternatives offered by the various schools of Chinese philosophy. To that end, he offers a generous collection of links to Chinese philosophy resources on the Web. You'll find electronic texts, as well as centers and institutions offering a variety of general information and instructional teaching.

Theosophical Society

http://ezinfo.ucs.indiana.edu/~mcooke/
mcooke/theosophy.html

Founded in 1875, the Theosophical Society is a world-wide association "dedicated to the uplifting of humanity" through the teaching of universal brotherhood and study of ancient and modern religion, science, and philosophy. This home page provides a brief introduction to the organization and its history, along with snail-mail and telephone contact info for the world headquarters in Pasadena, California.

AND NOW FOR A LOOK AT RELIGION

Anglicans Online

http://www.anglican.org/online/

This is the church where "the songs are singable, the sermon understandable, and you don't need to come in a suit." The site is a gateway that leads to information on Anglican churches throughout the United States, Canada, and worldwide. Visitors can stop by the News Centre for the latest church news events, join discussion groups, or link to resources for biblical study.

The Atheism Web

http://freethought.tamu.edu/news/atheism/

The basic, but comprehensive, Atheism Web contains an introduction to atheism and its arguments, links to its online organizations, and short synopses of atheist books, movies, and other media. The site also includes links to the Usenet newsgroups alt.atheism and soc.atheism.

> "Why can't people say… I don't have the answers as to how the earth began, or why certain things happen, and until an explanation comes along that makes sense, I am perfectly content not to have all the answers?"

The Bible Gateway

http://www.gospelcom.net/bible/

From the Gospel Communications Network comes a searchable virtual Bible in five editions and six languages, including Tagalog. Exegesists can research specific pas-sages or browse entire chapters online. This site should appeal equally to scholars, clergy, and the laity.

Bible Online

http://olt.et.tudelft.nl/fun/bible.html

The chapter and verse of the Bible passage you seek are just a mouse-click away. Visitors will find full text, daily themes, and Bible-related articles from contemporary authors.

Biblical Contradictions

http://www.ugcs.caltech.edu/cgi-bin/
webnews/read/contradictions/0

For everyone who's always scratched his or her head over the apparent contradictions in the Bible, the information at this site may help you resolve some of these issues. The page contains replies to a list of 143 purported contradictions that were originally posted to the newsgroup soc.religion.christian. The helpful Webmaster includes an index to the contradictions for quick reference.

Catholic Resources on the Net

http://www.cs.cmu.edu/Web/People/spok/
catholic.html

Lay Catholic John Mark Ockerbloom has compiled an extensive look at the Catholic church at this home page. Visitors will find explanations of and pointers to Catholic teachings, mass, writings, saints, organizations, and many other topics. The site also includes links to official Catholic pages on the Web.

Christian Classics Ethereal Library

http://ccel.wheaton.edu/

The Christian Classics Ethereal Library presents a searchable online collection that you can browse by author and type. The scope of this collection is breathtaking. Selections include *Summa Theologica* from St. Thomas Aquinas, *Dark Night of the Soul* from St. John of the Cross, John Wesley's *Sermons*, fiction from Dostoevsky, Tolstoy, Chesterton, and MacDonald, and reference works such as the World Wide Study Bible and various Bible dictionaries.

Christian Coalition

http://cc.org/

The Christian Coalition home page provides detailed information on its political agenda, philosophy, and campaigns, and includes scorecards for members of Congress so you can see if your elected officials are voting according to the tenets of the Coalition. News, much of it related to the group's moral stands, is online here and frequently updated, and visitors can also link to other Christian-related sites on the Web.

ChristianAnswers.Net

http://www.christiananswers.net/

Eden Communications provides this extensive site for Christians seeking "biblical answers to important contemporary questions." With over 800 files, this in-depth resource includes questions in categories such as creation/evolution, biblical archaeology, family and marriage, Christian theology, and government social issues. The site also includes news, Christian shopping sites, movie reviews, and Gospel translations.

"Humans seem to not have evolved enough to handle the accretions of civilization. Just as the nuclear bomb does not solve the problems of war, evangelical religion does not solve the question of understanding the nature of society, the universe, and the possibility of God."

CoGweb

http://www.cog.org/cog/

"Wicca, or Witchcraft," we're told at this site, "is an earth religion—a re-linking (re-ligio) with the life-force of nature, both on this planet and in the stars and space beyond." The Covenant of the Goddess Web site explains the activities of the international organization of cooperating, autonomous Wiccan congregations and practitioners. This site offers information on witchcraft and answers to commonly asked questions. It also posts events and offers links to various covens.

Cosmic Web

http://www.sirius.com/~cosmic/welcome.html

Cosmic Web intends to open minds and "awaken souls" with inspirational answers to questions about the world's complexity. You can participate in the daily meditation and read articles about angels, cosmology, healing, indigenous wisdom, and other mind-expanding topics. Learn about the Dreamspell Calendar and its basis in "natural time." OK, so the presentation here is a little new-agey, but it's interesting nonetheless.

Creation Research Society

http://www.iclnet.org/pub/resources/text/crs/crs-home.html

The Creation Research Society is a "professional organization of trained scientists and interested laypersons who are firmly committed to scientific special creation." The Society welcomes members of the Internet community who share its interest in creationism and provides background information, a directory of creationist organizations worldwide, and abstracts and newsletters. The page also includes links to other creationism-oriented pages on the Web.

Daily Wisdom

http://www.gospelcom.net/gf/dw/

Daily Wisdom, provided by the Gospel Communications Network, offers a Christian grain of wisdom each day on the Internet. Visitors can see the daily offering or search a categorized archive of past wisdom. If you like what you see, the site offers a listserv option so you can start each day with a new message, delivered straight to your mailbox.

Dark Zen: The Teachings of Mystical Zen

http://www.teleport.com/~zennist/zennist.html

There's plain Zen, and then there's Dark Zen, that which is "directed towards achieving mystical union with Buddha Mind." Searchers upon this Web path can learn about the study of Dark Zen and find answers to their more mundane questions about the Buddha Mind Institute.

DharmaNet
http://www.dharmanet.org

Presented as a public service by DharmaNet International, this site contains the DharmaNet Electronic Files Archive. The links featured include Buddhist InfoWeb, Buddhist Meditation Retreats and Events, Dharma Newsstand, and the Buddhist e-mail directory.

Dünya: CyberMuslim Information Collective
http://www.uoknor.edu/cybermuslim/

Dünya is a comprehensive resource page for Muslims provided by the CyberMuslim Information Collective. Visitors will find Islamic books, magazines, newspapers, cultural resources, an interactive Qur'aan, and much more here.

Ecole Initiative
http://www.evansville.edu/~ecoleweb/

The Ecole Initiative is an ongoing effort to compile a hypertext encyclopedia of early Christian church history. Chronological listings, a bibliography, documents, and a glossary are here already, along with background information about the project. From the Eleusinian Mysteries to the Holy Grail to pacts with the devil, the documents here provide a scholarly glimpse into the events that shaped the Christian faith.

Episcopal Church
http://www.ai.mit.edu/people/mib/anglican/

Here visitors can find out more about the Episcopal Church through the descriptions of their worship practices and beliefs, online texts, and links to Web sites maintained by Episcopal religious orders. The site also features documents from church officials, as well as resources such as libraries, pictures, mailing lists, and church-oriented links.

Finding God in Cyberspace
http://users.ox.ac.uk/~mikef/durham/gresham.html

An online guide to Internet-based religious information, this site offers links to theological and religious studies libraries, publishers, and more. You'll find pointers to a variety of references on world religions and philosophies, including religious e-texts, journals, and software. Another excellent feature of this site is its links to gateways for biblical studies, mythology, Christianity, Buddhism, Hinduism, and Islam.

"Can you know what you cannot see? I know I hate war, but I have never been in one. I know I love angels, but I have never seen one. I know Prince Charles is a bounder but I don't know Prince Charles and am basing my knowledge on hearsay. I know the sky is blue…but is it? Maybe it's really green and whoever first said it was blue was colorblind and thought he saw blue so we all took his word for it. I know there is a God…but not because someone told me. Since someone I loved and trusted told me, I *believe* there is a God. Since I had a near-death experience, I *know* there is a God."

Firewatch
http://140.190.128.190/merton/merton.html

The Firewatch home page is devoted to the works of Thomas Merton and religious contemplation. The group is affiliated with the Merton Research Consortium, an association of groups, centers, institutes, and organizations interested in the contemplative life. The site includes an e-journal, *Research on the Contemplative Life*, articles and papers on contemplation or mysticism, and a generous list of links to related Web sites.

The Green Pages
http://www.oakgrove.org/GreenPages/

The introductory text to these pages warns that "You will meet many people here who have ways and beliefs different from your own. Please be tolerant." Here are links to resources for pagans, including listings of gatherings, covens, and groups. With your mind wide open to different ideas and belief systems, you can learn a lot from the general information submitted by participating organizations and the links to pagan publications and Web sites.

Guidance Through Bhagavad Gita

http://www.tezcat.com/~bnaik/gita/
guide.html

This introduction to Hinduism from Swami Chinmayananda leads you through a consideration of fundamental topics, including God, peace, mind control, life in the universe, and the nature of the self. Find out how the Bhagavad Gita and Upanishads answer the question, "Who is a happy man?"

Guide to Christian Literature on the Internet

http://www.iclnet.org/pub/resources/
christian-books.html

The Institute for Christian Leadership hosts this guide to Christian literature on the Internet. Visitors will find links to several versions of the Bible, plus church-related news, books, newsletters, essays, articles, and sermons.

Guide to Early Church Documents

http://www.iclnet.org/pub/resources/
christian-history.html

This guide, also provided by the Institute for Christian Leadership, covers early canons and creeds, the writings of the Apostolic Fathers, and other historical works. Visit here for full text of many historically significant biblical passages.

Hare Krishna Home Page

http://www.webcom.com/~ara/

If you've ever wondered about those kids in the airport selling books, here's your chance to find out what they believe. The Hare Krishna page explains the Eastern religion, and offers visitors access to graphics, books, and magazines for more detailed information. If the readings at this site raise your Krishna consciousness, you can seek further enlightenment via Hare Krishna centers (location information is available online) and a free catalog.

International Churches of Christ

http://www.INTLCC.com/

The International Churches of Christ presents its official home page with information about the church, its doctrines, and its mission. Interested visitors and church

Lizzie's Tips
Always buy preformatted floppy disks. You can use them immediately without initializing them. A big timesaver.

members—or disciples—can peruse Kingdom News Net for highlights and features about its news-making disciples.

Jews for Jesus

http://www.jews-for-jesus.org/

Jews for Jesus is a movement within the Jewish community that believes Jesus was the Messiah. Their home page includes an essay on reconciling Judaism with belief in Jesus, access to publications, testifying opportunities, and event schedules.

Judaism and Jewish Resources

http://shamash.org/trb/judaism.html

This gateway to Jewish resources includes information on the state of Israel, Jewish studies, the Holocaust, Yiddish, Jewish learning, communities, and organizations. From news in Hebrew to home pages of Israeli cities to Internet relay chats, this site includes links to Jewish resources worldwide.

Kansas Religion & Philosophy Corner

http://falcon.cc.ukans.edu/~mahyarp/

The Kansas Religion & Philosophy Corner, part of a personal home page, guides visitors through "the deeper meanings of life." Visit here for an index of world religions, cultures, and philosophies. From this platform you can launch yourself into resources as diverse as the All in One Christian Index and the basic daily prayers of Zoroastrians.

LDS Resources Pages

http://www.primenet.com/~kitsonk/
mormon.html

The Angel Moroni stands as a herald on this page of pointers to online resources for members of the Church of Jesus Christ Latter-day Saints. Among the pages you'll find information about the Church, electronic Mormon texts, links to a variety of related Web sites, the Articles of Faith, an Introduction to the LDS Church, and an armload of Book of Mormon resources.

New Heaven, New Earth
http://nen.sedona.net//nhne/

New Heaven, New Earth is a grassroots network that believes the planet is spiraling toward Armageddon; its members aim to "safely pass through whatever changes may come our way and help give birth to a new way of life on our planet." Visitors can get an overview of the network, read prophesies, and join the network's mailing list.

Peregrine Foundation
http://www.matisse.net/~peregrin/index.html

A nonprofit group dedicated to the dissemination of information about "high-demand" religious groups, totalitarian sects, and communes, the Peregrine Foundation offers access to its newsletters and archives via this Web site. This foundation was created in 1992 to assist families and individuals living in or exiting from experimental social groups. The online newsletters make for some interesting reading.

Presbyterian Church (U.S.A.)
http://www.pcusa.org/

The Presbyterian Church in America maintains this site containing religious news and resources. Visit here for an overview of the church, related software archives, online services, and "good, clean religious humor."

Quaker Electronic Archive
http://www.clark.net/pub/quaker/web/archive.html

The Quaker Electronic Archive consists of texts and documents relating to the Society of Friends' theology and everyday life. Newcomers to the faith can find an excellent selection of introductory references including A Guide to Quaker Worship, What Friends Believe, and Friendly Answers to Questions about Quakers. Other selections include journals, discussions of moral issues, and poems and prayers.

Rapture Index
http://www.novia.net/~todd/

The Christian prophecy of the Rapture, found in the Bible's last book of Revelation, states that some time in the future, after a series of signs, believers will be taken bodily into heaven. At the Rapture Index, learn more about this prophecy and read news items and world indicators purported to be signs of its imminence.

Reasons To Believe
http://www.gospelcom.net/rbc/10rsn.home/

For those whose faith needs fortifying, this site offers reasons to believe in the Christian cosmology. It lays out, via Biblical verses and commentary, reasons to believe in the existence of God, the divine foundations of Christianity, and the news about a humble Jewish carpenter who rose from the dead to save us from eternal damnation.

Scamizdat Memorial - Yet Another Scientology Home Page
http://www.well.com/user/jerod23/clam.html

Despite the fact that Scientology is considered trés chic among selected members of the Hollywood crowd, most of the material posted on the Web about Elron Hubbard's belief system is decidedly hostile, and the Scamizdat Memorial page is no exception. Stories of life inside Scientology, a collection of first-person accounts, and general information about Scientology depict the "Church" in an unfavorable light and pull from material that is lurid and sensational.

Selected Works of Martin Luther 1483 - 1546
http://www.iclnet.org/pub/resources/text/wittenberg/wittenberg-luther.html

The Rebel of Wittenberg speaks in his own resounding voice here via his Definitions of Faith ("Faith is a living, bold trust in God's grace, so certain of God's favor that it would risk death a thousand times trusting in it"), his Spiritual Last Will and Testament ("I know Satan very well. If Satan can turn God's Word upside down and pervert the Scriptures, what will he do with my words or the words of others?"), and his Devotional Thoughts ("To have a god means this: You expect to receive all good things from it and turn to it in every time of trouble"). Hymns and prayers, letters, Luther's famous theses, and other writings testify to the man who almost single-handedly ended the European dominance of the Catholic Church.

The Sikhism Home Page
http://www.sikhs.org/

"Sikhism preaches a message of devotion and remembrance of God at all times, truthful living, equality of mankind and denounces superstitions and blind rituals." Learn more about this 500-year-old religion at the Sikhism Home Page, where you can read about the religion's philosophies, browse translations of religious texts, and access Sikh codes of conduct, a glossary, info on ceremonies and saints, and much more.

Torah Fax in Cyberspace
http://www.netaxis.qc.ca/torahfax/

"Torah on the spot for people on the go!" is the motto of this service based in Montreal, Canada. TorahFax began as a way for busy people to learn the Torah via a regular fax delivery. It now offers its services by e-mail, fax, or this daily Web posting.

Unification Home Page
http://www.cais.net/unification/

A member of the Unification Church of the Rev. Sun Myung Moon maintains this page featuring links to Unification resources on the Internet. The church's international works and artistic activities are featured, along with the religion's articles of faith.

United Methodist Church
http://www.netins.net/showcase/umsource/

This unofficial home page for the United Methodist Church includes information on church issues, news, and online conferences. You'll also find links to other churches on the Internet, a Methodist e-mail directory, colleges, seminaries, and specific ministry types.

World Scripture
http://www.silcom.com/~origin/wscon.html

Originally conceived of and commissioned by the Reverend Sun Myung Moon, The World Scripture site is a collaborative effort of religious ministers and scholars worldwide that contains over "4,000 scriptural passages from 268 sacred texts and 55 oral traditions. It is organized in terms of 164 different themes common to all traditions." Maintained by the International Religious Foundation in New York, N.Y., the site provides a comparative anthology of sacred text teachings on such subjects as the ultimate reality, the purpose of life, life beyond death, and sin.

WORLD SCRIPTURE

A Comparative Anthology of Sacred Texts

Dr. Andrew Wilson, Editor
International Religious Foundation, 1991
HTML conversion is now complete through Chapter 9, plus Chapters 17,19 & 20
Archived by Bruce Schuman, United Communities of Spirit

The World Wide Web Virtual Library: Facets of Religion
http://sunfly.ub.uni-freiburg.de/religion/

In true Virtual Library style, Facets of Religion is an exhaustive listing of the major faiths worldwide. It contains general and interreligious information along with related topics and skeptical studies. This is a great site for pursuing your own comparative religion studies; you'll find Sikhism and the Baha'i Faith listed side by side, along with Christianity, Judaism, Taoism, Islam, and several others.

Chapter 6

BANKROLLS AND BUCKS

MONEY IS THE ROOT

INVESTOR WAKE-UP CALL

THE RIGHT STUFF

A FABLE

The last astrology reading I had told me that my finances were a mess! I did not need that reading to tell me, as I already knew that years of procrastination in addressing the state of my finances were culminating in the very mess the horoscope said I was in.

MONEY IS THE ROOT

Growing up in the Victorian family that I drew when I was born may have been part of the problem. Money was never mentioned out loud by anyone!—especially in front of the women and children. As a result, the women in the family never knew what any of the "menfolk" really did, how much they made, where they put their bucks, what the stock market was ("Is that where you buy cows?"), or what goals anyone may have had for becoming financially stable. In the eyes of our husbands and fathers, we were stable already, and it was considered tasteless to discuss it any further.

Money became, to me at least, just an amorphous idea—not real, but a bit of abstract flotsam floating around out there in the ether. There was always enough of the stuff, and nobody ever mentioned it. So, instead of thinking of money as a concrete tool to be used for one's betterment (or even basic survival), I never thought of it at all.

IN THE POT

When I was a young newlywed, an old family friend came to see me to encourage me to put a small portion of my allowance into a mutual fund. He explained how much money would be accrued for me at the end of so many years. I took notice, because it seemed to me that I would be rich if I did exactly as he said. The first month I plopped in $100—at that time, a lot of dough.

By the time the second month's allocation was due, I had completely forgotten the lecture and my dreams of riches, and had gone on to something

Lizzie's Tips

If you are bored with your usual e-mail and want something meatier, don't be afraid to subscribe to a mailing list; they're free. There are two kinds of lists, moderated and unmoderated, with unmoderated being the hands-down favorite. Any message you send to the list will automatically be sent to everyone else on the list. Likewise, any message sent by another will come to you. Moderated lists are screened for relevance before being posted to the entire group. After posting, readers look them over, then respond. It all works in much the same way as a newsgroup, only it happens via your mailbox. If you have online time constraints (your ISP charges you by the hour; you have only one phone line) this can be a nice option—all of your posts and replies can be composed off-line. To find a mailing list that serves your interests (and to learn more about mailing lists in general), browse the offerings at Liszt (**http://www.liszt.com/**), the largest collection of listserv mailing lists on the WWW.

else—something frivolous, no doubt, like buying a new couch, adding to my china…who knows? The bottom line: I never got around to putting another dime into that mutual fund again. The $100 stayed there for years, earning its tiny stipend, and years later, it served as a reminder of my foolishness.

THE COLOR OF MONEY

As time went on and I matured, I did accumulate a 401K for retirement, entirely by accident. The company I was working for at the time offered it, matched my contributions by 6%, and I joined my friends at work in putting a small portion of my salary into this before-tax bonanza. Now, I am awfully

Lizzie Sez

I remember when I took a trip, my mother would make me pin my money to the inside of my brassiere so that it would be safe. Perhaps you don't have to go that far anymore, but it's always a good idea to have a quarter for a phone call, and a ten dollar bill tucked in your sock in case of an emergency.

glad that I did. I have made a friend at Prudential Securities who invests what little I give him. He does not ask me what I want, just tells me what he has done. It is shame and guilt over my early fecklessness, no doubt, that drives me to give him any amount, no matter how small, as money is still a hard concept for me to grasp. John has shared a few rules with me that I will pass on, as they apply to financial planners of any age.

THE RULES OF THE ROAD

Save at least 5% of your income, making a budget and keeping track of any cash that you spend—even if it's for nothing more than a fifty-cent piece of candy. That's the hard part for me. I have never been able to make a budget I could keep! I have learned that you need to make the right kind of budget, starting at ground zero and working your way outward. This is called a "zero-based budget."

Instead of taking your current income and simply subtracting what you spend each week (that's easy enough, eh?), start with zero and add your weekly or monthly expenses one by one, until you have reached the limit that your income will allow. Then make a "spending plan," a simple guideline that you use each week to determine how much you have to spend on necessities (and treats!) *before* you reach for your wallet.

Make a weekly appointment with yourself to review your spending plan, prioritize your upcoming expenses, and plan for the next week. Some people have used envelopes to keep track of their spending, by putting money into specially marked envelopes set aside for expenses, or by recording the amounts of money spent for items in a spending plan on the face of each envelope.

Better still, now that you have a computer, use a simple bookkeeping program—such as Quicken, QuickBooks, or Microsoft Money—that will help you keep your checkbook balanced, and keep you on target with your budget. These programs do most of the hard work for you, and will even reconcile your bank statements, and generate graphs so that you can quickly see how closely you've adhered to your spending and saving plans. Many can track the performance of your investment accounts. If your bank is progressive and has online banking services, you can often use these programs in conjunction with their services to pay your bills and transfer money between accounts.

Some banks and brokerage firms have their own software which you can use to access your account online. Not only can you keep track of all your accounts, stocks, bonds, and mutual funds, but some companies offer a system that enables you to make trades right over your computer. Ask your financial counselor if his or her company has software designed for this purpose.

PLASTIC POCKETS

If you have credit cards, use them *only* if you can pay off the balance each month. That way, you are not caught in the interest trap. Beware the come-on from credit cards advertising low interest rates and no annual fees. It's hard to resist this siren's song, but be sure you look on the back of your application or invitation for the very small print containing

"Important Disclosures." Usually this will reveal that the low rate of interest used for your seduction is only "introductory," will last for only six months, or does not apply unless you transfer balances from other cards.

BANKING AND PERSONAL FINANCE RESOURCES ON THE WWW

AAAdir Directory of World Banks
http://www.upbeat.com/bankweb/index.htm

Banks from Africa, Asia, Australia, Europe, and the Americas are all presented in this searchable directory organized for easy point-and-click access. The section on North America allows users to search for banks by name or state, and features similar search options for locating credit unions.

Bank of America
http://www.bofa.com/

Bank of America, the financial institution begun by an Italian immigrant and established during the 1906 San Francisco earthquake crisis, offers a "money tip of the day," credit cards, special offers on computer checks, home loans, business and corporate banking services, and an interactive way to figure how much you should be saving for retirement.

Bank of Boston
http://www.bkb.com/

Information on personal, corporate, and global banking is online at the Bank of Boston's home page. Visitors can also look into small business banking, explore investment services, or read the latest economic and financial news. Due to a recent merger with BayBank, you might find that the name has changed to BankBoston by the time you visit.

Bank of Montreal
http://www.bmo.com/

Visitors to the Bank of Montreal's home page will find an overview of the bank's services, including current rates, home mortgage information, bank news, and Canadian

Lizzie's Tips
Mac users: To check out your Mac's system configurations, use Apple System Profiler, a freeware utility that gathers, summarizes, and delivers information about your system's hardware and software. Shows you how to troubleshoot problems, and provides a quick and easy way to see which control panels and extensions you are running. You can find out more about this and other Apple utilities at the Apple Support Information page, **http://cgi.info.apple.com/**.

economic forecasts. Small business help and mutual funds information are also available. In English and French.

Bank of the Commonwealth
http://www.pilotonline.com/boc/

Based in Norfolk, Va., Bank of the Commonwealth provides a wide range of commercial banking and financial services to individuals. Visitors to its home page will find financial product descriptions, certificate rates, and customer service resources.

Bank One
http://www.bankone.com/

One of the largest bank groups in the United States, Bank One Corporation operates 59 banks with offices in a dozen states. Stop by for information on loans, credit cards, retirement services, and the other personal financial services offered.

Banking on the WWW
http://www.wiso.gwdg.de/ifbg/banking.html

The Institute of Finance and Banking at Germany's University of Göttingen hosts this repository of Web links relating to money matters. The banking page points to Web sites for banks worldwide, banking guides and information resources, and academic research. Links to IFBG's pages on finance, currency, and stock markets are also featured.

The BankWeb

http://www.bankweb.com/

Access this comprehensive directory to find banks in the United States and abroad that maintain a presence on the Internet. Links to over a half dozen banking associations are also included, along with a rate comparison feature that surveys lending rates across the country.

Bayshore Trust Company

http://www.bayshoretrust.com/

Claiming its place as the "world's first financial institution to offer on-line loan approval on the Internet," Bayshore Trust Company requires visitors to use an SSL (Secure Sockets Layer)-compliant Web browser. Find out more about the browser and Bayshore Trust via this gateway.

Canada Trust Mortgage Co.

http://www.canadatrust.com/

Canada Trust, one of Canada's largest non-bank financial institutions, maintains this site to introduce its personal and corporate investment services. In addition to an extensive index of financial information, visitors will find links to local and national consumer organizations.

Chase Manhattan Bank

http://www.chase.com/

Look into credit cards—including the new Wal Mart MasterCard—loans, and other personal financial services offered by this "brand name" bank. Also find news and commentary on money and other matters of interest to consumers.

Citibank

http://www.citicorp.com/

Citibank, a worldwide banking corporation with branches in more than 40 countries, provides information here on its latest personal and corporate banking services. Use the branch locator to find the Citibank office nearest you.

Commerce Bank

http://www2.yesbank.com/commerce/

Positioning itself as "America's most convenient bank" Commerce Bank, also known as "The YES Bank," offers online banking services for its customers. Look into opening an account online or apply for a loan at this Metro Philadelphia/South Jersey institution.

CoreStates Bank

http://www.corestates.com/

Whether your needs are personal or commercial, Core-States offers a portfolio of products geared to meet your needs. Stop by to see about a loan, to plan for the future, or to get ideas for managing your money. Online tools and news are available to anyone who visits.

Credit Union Home Page

http://www.cu.org/

Maintained by the Florida Credit Union League Inc., a nonprofit association of Florida-based credit unions, this home page shares statistical and consumer information, and explains the credit union philosophy. The site also Includes pointers to individual credit unions' home pages.

Credit Union National Association and Affiliates

http://www.cuna.org/

The Credit Union National Association promotes its industry's unique delivery of financial products. Discover what a credit union is and how to join one, plus find news and consumer financial information.

Crestar: On Finances

http://www.crestar.com/

Sure, money talks. But when it does, can you understand what it's saying? Click on the lucky penny at the On Finances page for financial tips that could help you translate "money talk" into more cash for you. Also find a review of the banking services and rates offered by Crestar Bank.

Currencies and Currency-Exchange
http://www.wiso.gwdg.de/ifbg/currency.html

Before leaving on that trip abroad, visit this currency exchange site hosted by the Institute of Finance and Banking at Germany's University of Göttingen. Visitors can access several exchange rate sites in addition to explanatory information about different currencies.

Federal Deposit Insurance Corporation
http://www.fdic.gov/

Founded in 1933 by the U.S. Congress, the Federal Deposit Insurance Corporation "promotes the safety and soundness" of the nation's banking system. Visit its home page for current assets sales and information on financial institutions across the United States.

First Chicago NBD Corporation
http://www.fcnbd.com/

Insurance, credit cards, and investment services are just a few of the financial services available through First Chicago. Stop by to review the bank's personal, small business, and corporate financial offerings. Also online find an economic forecast and trivia.

First City Bank and Trust
http://www.fcb.abcbank.com/

Link to this "virtual lobby" and check into FCB's home banking options or look over the bank's financial products and services. Other site features include links to personnel, the president's desk, customer service, and the security office.

First Hawaiian Bank
http://www.fhb.com/fhb/

Actor Pat Morita greets visitors to the First Hawaiian Bank page and points out information on the bank's products and services. The latest economic and business news is also featured along with a look at what it's like to work at FHB.

First Union Corp.—The Internet Cyberbank
http://www.firstunion.com/

Based in Charlotte, N.C., First Union National Bank touts itself as "the original Cyberbank" and maintains this site to introduce its Internet-based banking services, both personal and commercial. Visit here for investment reports, economic forecasts, employment opportunities, and online credit applications.

Kingfield Bank
http://www.maine.com/kingfield/

Maine's "first cyberbank," Kingfield Bank maintains this site to provide current rates for loans, CDs, IRAs, savings accounts, and money markets. Visit here for the latest on all the bank's financial packages and a look at other local business sectors.

LawTalk—Business Law and Personal Finance
http://www.law.indiana.edu/law/bizlaw.html

This "talking" index of business law and personal finance information links to audio files on a variety of related topics—everything from bounced checks to investment opportunities. This service is an offering of the School of Law at Indiana University in Bloomington.

Long Island Savings Bank
http://www.lisb.com/

New York's Long Island Savings Bank lets visitors know why they should deposit their cash in the bank's coffers. The argument is bolstered by information on the bank, its parent company, and its menu of financial services.

Mark Twain Banks

http://www.marktwain.com/

Explore the virtual payment system Ecash that allows users to pay real money for purchases over the Internet. Get the FAQs and take the online tutorial. While on-site also look into the Mark Twain Banks' investment opportunities.

Mellon Bank

http://www.mellon.com/

Apply online for a Gold MasterCard, apply for PC Banking, or explore Mellon's banking and investment services. Online financial tools include a mortgage calculator to help estimate monthly house payments.

Merchants National Bank

http://www.bnt.com/~mnb

Based in Aurora, Illinois, Merchants National Bank maintains this site to introduce its consumer and business financial services. Site features include credit and loan information, a corporate profile, and information on branch locations.

Mizrahi Bank

http://www.mizrahi.co.il/

Self-described as the "fourth largest banking group in Israel" and the first to maintain a Web presence, Mizrahi Bank sustains its international presence through a network of branches and subsidiaries which include offices in New York and Los Angeles. Visit this page to learn more about the bank's international services, including tax-free foreign currency accounts, real estate, and investor services. In Hebrew and English.

MyBank Directory

http://www.mybank.com/

Looking for a bank on the Web? Here's a directory of bank home pages sponsored by FiTech Inc. Currently the online directory lists over 600 U.S. banks organized by state. Also find institutions from Africa, Asia, Australia, Canada, the Caribbean, Europe, Mexico, the Middle East, South America, and Central America.

NationsBank

http://www.nationsbank.com/

Curious about PC Banking? Stop in and while on-site, look into NationsBank credit cards and the company's other personal banking services. One of the United States's largest financial service companies, NationsBank offers loans, certain insurance products, and asset management services.

The People's Bank

http://www.peoples.com/

The People's Bank, "the largest independent bank in Connecticut," links visitors with information about its financial services for both consumers and businesses.

Premium Federal Savings Bank

http://www.premium.com/premium/

Based in New Jersey, Premium describes itself as "a leader in branchless banking." Find all the bank's account applications online, a mortgage rate estimation chart to use, a newsletter, current rate quotes, and a hassle-free CD rate comparison service.

Royal Bank of Canada

http://www.royalbank.com/

The Royal Bank of Canada offers details about its personal financial services, business banking, international services, and mutual funds. Visitors will also find corporate news and listings of employment opportunities. Available in English and French.

Security First Network Bank

http://www.sfnb.com/

Self-described as the "world's first Internet bank," SFNB welcomes visitors to its virtual (and only) branch with a

demonstration of its services. Also find general information, an account application, and , for those with business at the bank, account access.

Signet Bank Online
http://www.signet.com/

Checking, savings, money market accounts, payment services, and online quotes are all available through Signet's Online Banking option. Look into these and other financial tools at the Signet Bank home site.

Swiss Banks Directory
http://www.swconsult.ch/chbanks/index.html

Swiss bank accounts have long been favored by discreet customers worldwide because of the tight lips of Swiss bank officials. Netizens hankering for their own Swiss account will find contact information here for hundreds of Swiss banks, as well as links to other pages in peace-loving Switzerland.

U.S. Bank
http://www.usbank.com/

Find concise and creative answers to your money questions, not marble counters and potted palms. It doesn't matter if you "don't speak bank," this site treats you to a little "fun with money" and news you can use to make the most from your assets.

Wells Fargo & Co.
http://www.wellsfargo.com/

Reportedly the second bank on the Internet to offer online banking, this West Coast concern recently merged with First Interstate to increase its holdings, services, and market share. Stop by to review the bank's products and services for your personal finance and small business needs.

INVESTOR WAKE-UP CALL

My favorite stockbroker tells me that, on the whole, 1997 should be a good year for stocks. He believes in holding quality stocks and bonds, does not believe in taking serious risks unless you can (really) afford it,

Lizzie Sez

Measure your success by the hardships you endured, and what you had to give up to get it.

and asserts that holding your good quality portfolio through the long term produces the best returns on your investments. A conservative man, you will say, and he advises me to be conservative, too—except for a wild hare now and then. Unless you are an expert, you can get hurt playing the market. That is, unless you're an aging road hog, and you invested in Harley-Davidson when they made their public offering last year. That stock took off like the bikes it represents, and is flourishing.

HEAPS UPON HEAPS

The economy, along with interest rates and corporate earnings, will continue to do well in the coming year, my expert predicts. Inflation is unlikely to rear its ugly head, as long as commodities remain stable and the price of gold doesn't rise appreciably. Why? Well, in part, when these conditions persist, and the inflation index remains below 3%, the Feds are generally reluctant to raise interest rates.

John says interest rates could even go *down* in 1997, which will make your stock portfolio dance with joy. If that happens, corporate dividends may also increase. And he predicts the economy will not slide into a recession, but should continue to grow at a moderate pace.

So if my friend John the stockbroker is right, things are looking good (but I urge you to consult with your own financial advisor before making *any* investments). Certainly for the investor last year, it was wonderful; for many made from 25%–40% in profits from their investments.

John suggests that, using caution this year, you can do just as well as you did last year. Be safer and more secure by buying stocks in sure things, the carefully researched opportunities where there is little risk.

With all this talk about money, the stock market, and making it big financially, it may be easy to forget that money is merely a means to an end. And that end should be to make your life as enjoyable as you can. So don't get so caught up in your financial security that you forget to enjoy yourself!

And above all, be a smart investor. Read personal finance magazines, talk with friends who invest, and establish a relationship with a financial advisor.

INVESTING AND INVESTMENTS ONLINE

A.G. Edwards

http://www.agedwards.com/

Offering investment services since 1887, A.G. Edwards invites visitors to this virtual center to study, plan, and (hopefully) profit from the features presented. Look into the economic future, read timely news, and explore investment concepts and options. Those ready to talk dollars and cents can check out the branch directory for the nearest office.

American Stock Exchange Market Summary

http://www.amex.com/summary/summary.htm

Investors and those who follow the dealings at the American Stock Exchange can review each day's market activities through this Web service. The site is updated every business day at approximately 6 p.m. Eastern Standard Time.

Charles Schwab & Co.

http://www.schwab.com/

You've seen him on TV, now he's on the Web and ready to broker your trades at a discount. Check into Schwab's online services, open an account, or create a personalized stock watch folder. Trade, research, or explore; Schwab promises Web trading "the way it should be."

eBroker Securities

http://www.ebroker.com/

Home of the $12 trades, eBroker hosts this site to answer questions from curious investors, demo online trading, promote the company's low commission schedule, sign up new investors, and serve current clients' needs. eBroker is owned by All American Brokers of Omaha, Nebraska.

Electronic Share Information Ltd.

http://www.esi.co.uk/

Electronic Share Information Ltd. is a United Kingdom-based company offering free, up-to-the-minute prices and basic information on issues listed on the London Stock Exchange. Visitors can access online trading opportunities and other financial services.

E*Trade

http://www.etrade.com/

Offering its online customers free, unlimited stock quotes, analysis charts, and real-time news, E*Trade also offers one of the lowest per-trade fees going. Stop by the company's site to play the Stock Market Game and demo what it's like to trade online. Plus, look into the other advantages E*Trade offers and see how the company stacks up against Schwab.

Investment Brokerages Guide

http://www.cs.cmu.edu/~jdg/invest_brokers/

U.S., Canadian, European, and Asian brokerage firms are listed and profiled for investors to review. Find full-service, discount, and deep discount brokerage firms and helpful advice on determining which type of firm can best serve your needs. Links point to additional brokerage information offered by the American Association of Individual Investors.

InvestorGuide
http://www.investorguide.com/

Boasting 4,000 links and constantly adding more, here's "your guide to investing on the Web." Find the quality investment information you need (free or at low cost) to make decisions on your money and finances. No matter what your degree of expertise, this site attempts to level the field so the little guy can catch a break.

invest-o-rama
http://www.investorama.com/

Thousands of links, feature articles, a growth stock watch, and an education center only highlight the offerings available through this online investment tool. Need to check a stock quote? No problem. How about a profile of that issue as well?

Legg Mason Investment Center
http://www.leggmason.com/

Receive a free, customized equity portfolio review or asset allocation analysis, and while on-site, access the company's financial planning calculators, stop into the learning center, or review the company's products and investment offerings.

Merrill Lynch
http://www.merrill-lynch.ml.com/

Stop into the Investor Learning Center for investment basics, the Personal Finance Center for an overview of financial issues important to you, and the Financial News & Research Center for the latest market and economic indicators. Information on the company's products and services, seminars, and branch offices are also featured.

Mutual Funds Magazine Online
http://www.mfmag.com/

Published by the Institute for Econometric Research, the *Mutual Funds Magazine* online edition features columns and special reports about mutual funds, retirement planning, mortgage management, and many other financial matters. Includes online and print subscription information.

OLDE Discount Corporation
http://www.oldediscount.com/

A full-service discount brokerage firm, OLDE offers helpful advice, a full line of investment products, and commission savings. Discover how to develop a diversified portfolio, reduce risk, and possibly increase your investment success. And while on-site, check out a few of OLDE's basic investment offerings.

National Discount Brokers Online
http://pawws.com/Broker/Ndb/

Research the who (a wholly owned subsidiary of The Sherwood Group), the what (convenient online trading), and the why (unconditionally guaranteed service with savings off NDB's already low fees) to invest through National Discount Brokers Online. A natural complement of the PAWWS financial network, NDB encourages investors to compare prices using its online calculator.

NCII Online Information Center for Discount Brokerage
http://com.primenet.com/ncii/links.html

The National Council of Individual Investors hosts this interactive review of who's who in the world of discount brokerage. Point and click your way to firms around the world, or look into the NCII's other services and member benefits.

NETworth
http://networth.galt.com/www/home/networth.html

Get stock quotes, research companies, create graphs, review funds and their performance, plus more. You'll find loads of investment talk, tips, and tools to help you chart a course through the investment jungles.

PaineWebber Intelligence Center
http://www.painewebber.com/

Go ahead. Test your Investment I.Q. See how YOU do. And while you're at it, see what kinds of services and products help PaineWebber give its clients the "Edge."

PAWWS Financial Network

http://www.pawws.com/

Advertising itself as "the complete Internet investment resource," PAWWS packages online research and analysis tools, investment guides, publications, account management aids, and discount trading services for the do-it-yourself investor. Log in for a free, no obligation demonstration of PAWWS in action.

Prudential Securities Virtual Branch Office

http://www.prusec.com/

Visit with Prudential Securities' Virtual Financial Advisor for a better understanding of investing and investments. Get current market data, answers to confusing investment questions, and help sorting through life's financial tangles. An overview of the Prudential Securities company and its products is also online for review.

Smith Barney

http://nestegg.iddis.com/smithbarney

Visit with the folks who "make money the old-fashioned way." See if they can't "earn it" for you, too.

Securities & Exchange Commission

http://www.sec.gov/

The U.S. Securities and Exchange Commission, "the investor's advocate," maintains this server featuring SEC news and general information, public statements, policies, and answers to Frequently Asked Questions (FAQ). Links to other federal government sites of interest are featured as well.

Wall Street Research Net

http://www.wsrn.com/

Over 100,000 links point to the information that investors both great and small need to help steer their investment course. Research a company, a stock, the markets, and mutual funds. Also find business news, research publications, and links to brokerage companies.

THE RIGHT STUFF

Make sure you have the right kind of insurance. As we get older, our insurance needs change. We are no longer protecting our children or funding their educations; and perhaps the family home is paid off. Quite possibly, the need for large amounts of life insurance has decreased. Talk to an insurance consultant to make sure that your coverage is appropriate to your current situation.

GLASS SLIPPERS DO BREAK

More rules: Make a will, perhaps draw up a trust agreement with an estate attorney, and have a living will to direct your family in what you wish to be done in case of dire illness; appoint a person to act on it.

Remember Cinderella? She was the favored child of a very wealthy man. He provided her with everything her heart could desire. She had it all while Daddy Dearest was alive. *But, he did not write a will.* And guess what happened to Cinderella? She became a slave to her wicked stepsisters.

Of course, Daddy did not expect to die—no one really does—and even when expected, we certainly can't predict when it will happen. Guess what? There are a lot of Cinderellas running around out there: 70% of Americans die intestate, i.e., *without* a will. Have one drawn up today!

And finally, I guess I don't have to tell you that Medicare isn't the answer to everything (or even to your medical needs, for that matter). Consider adding supplemental health care coverage to your insurance portfolio if you're a Medicare recipient. And even if you're not receiving Medicare benefits, it's best to plan ahead. Many insurance companies and HMOs (Health Management Organizations) now provide comprehensive, affordable Medicare supplement packages; their representatives will be only too happy to discuss your options with you. Make sure you know what your Medicare benefits will (and won't) cover *before* you need them.

INSURANCE-RELATED SITES

Aetna Life and Casualty
http://www.aetna.com/

Stop by this global company's Web home for current information on its life insurance, health and managed care products, and retirement planning services. There's plenty to consider online for anyone considering the future and personal insurance needs.

Aetna Life Insurance Company of Canada
http://www.aetna.ca/

Designed to introduce customers to Aetna and help explain the benefits of life and health insurance, this online newsletter features the latest company updates, news, and views. A comprehensive retirement planning tool assists users in looking ahead, while an interactive question area promises the company "will listen and respond." In English and French.

Allstate Insurance Company
http://www.allstate.com/

Allstate, "the good hands people," maintains this sober home page full of practical insurance and financial-planning advice. Site features include a mortgage rate calculator, tips on saving for college, a health section, a roster of insurance scams, and a video of tornado devastation.

CNA Insurance Companies
http://www.cna.com/

Chicago-based CNA Insurance Companies provides a variety of property and health services for businesses and individuals. Visit CNA's home page to review investor information, product descriptions, and employment opportunities.

Cigna
http://www.cigna.com/

The 45, Cigna group provides health care, insurance, and financial services to more than 10 million people world-

wide. The company's home page provides a primer on individual and group insurance, news from the healthcare front, and financial-planning advice for those young whippersnappers who haven't yet thought about retirement.

Colonial Penn: Auto Insurance
http://www.colonialpenn.com/

Specializing in providing low cost auto insurance to safe drivers over the age of 40, Colonial Penn saves many drivers hundreds of dollars off their insurance premiums. Check into the company's products and services to see if they can save you money.

The Complete Glossary of Insurance Coverage Explanations
http://www.lcgroup.com/explanations/

Hosted by the Lewis-Chester Group, this online dictionary delivers on its promise with easy-to-understand definitions of insurance terms. The terms are alphabetically listed and indexed for quick reference. A link to the company's Insurance and Planning Resource Center offers even more information and answers other questions about insurance.

Farmers Insurance
http://www.farmersinsurance.com/

Auto, boat, home, life, and retirement, Farmers Insurance has policies to cover most things and most events in life. Find easy-to-understand product information, an agent locator, the online *Friendly Exchange Magazine*, advice on what to do when catastrophe strikes, and plenty of information about the company and its business philosophy.

Guardian Insurance
http://www.gre.co.uk/

U.K.-based Guardian Insurance has developed an exclusive PC insurance policy available only to users of the Internet in the U.K. The company also offers domestic, automotive, and healthcare policies.

Insurance Club Home Page
http://www.insuranceclub.co.uk/

The Insurance Club offers a variety of household insurance policies to U.K. residents. Visit the company's home page for a quote on insurance rates, answers to Frequently Asked Questions (FAQ), information on making a claim, and instructions for calculating rebuilding costs.

Insurance Companies & Resources on the Net
http://lattanze.loyola.edu/users/cwebb/insure.html

The Webmaster of this directory has attempted to compile a "one-stop site to find any resources related to insurance on the net." Insurance companies are listed and indexed alphabetically.

Insurance Information Institute
http://www.iii.org/

Sponsored by the property/casualty insurance industry, the Insurance Information Institute offers consumer brochures and reports about auto, homeowners, and business insurance. The institute also staffs the National Insurance Consumer Helpline, a toll-free service offering callers assistance in choosing agents, selecting companies, filing claims, and much more.

Insurance News Network
http://www.insure.com/

The Insurance News Network site features information about the insurance industry, surveys of insurance costs and auto safety, and Standard & Poor's ratings and reports. Links are included to specific insurance information servers and providers.

MetLife Online
http://www.metlife.com/

MetLife, the insurance and financial services company endorsed by Snoopy and his pals, offers a light-hearted and colorful home page that uses the Peanuts gang to provide valuable health and financial advice. Plus, there's a bonus: a tour of the MetLife blimp.

Nationwide Insurance
http://www.nationwide.com/

The Nationwide Insurance home page provides information on the company's auto, fire, life, home, and business insurance policies. Also find links to Nationwide's "fast, fair, and friendly" claims service and its agent locator service.

Northwestern Mutual Life
http://www.northwesternmutual.com/

Learn more about the life insurance corporation that calls itself the "quiet" company. Browse information on the company's life insurance policies and find a state-by-state listing of Northwestern Mutual agents.

Prudential Insurance
http://www.prudential.com

Along with solid information about insurance and retirement planning, the home page for "the Pru" offers a novel feature wherein visitors make career and financial decisions for some "virtual customers," such as Ellen Passad. "Should she continue living with her college roommates? Should she save money by moving back in with her parents? [Oh, heavens no!] Or should she invest her money in a home of her own?" You decide.

Royal Insurance Home Page
http://www.royal-group.co.uk/

Based in the U.K. but with interests worldwide, Royal Insurance promotes its home, motor, and life insurance policies via this corporate home page. Also find information on the company's financial planning services, products for business customers, and a spot of fun as well.

Royal Insurance U.S.
http://www.royal-usa.com/welcome.html

Visit the Royal Insurance company's U.S. Web site to review the types of personal coverage the company offers to its clients in the United States, and to find the Royal independent agent or broker nearest you.

SafeTnet

http://www.safetnet.com/

Find useful answers to troubling questions regarding your personal and business insurance needs. Search by zip code or product line in the "largest" online directory of insurance Web sites, and browse a library of topic-related materials. Quite a safety net indeed!

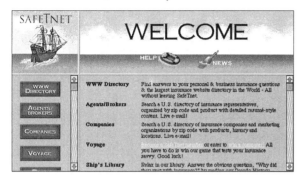

State Farm Insurance

http://www.statefarm.com/

Like a good neighbor, the State Farm home page offers gentle, homey advice about auto, life, health, and home-owner's insurance. Also find hurricane and tornado tips, a safety guide for young drivers, a health quiz, and a corporate salute to America's most innovative school teachers.

Travelers Property & Casualty

http://www.travelers.com/

Those seeking personal lines of insurance will find money-saving tips and interesting facts presented along with insurance coverage explanations that are "almost completely painless." Small business owners can look into the ABCs of protecting their enterprises, plus find news they can use, and valuable safety tips.

UK Insurance Links Directory

http://main.emap.com/insurance-age/link.htm

If it's a "forward looking," U.K.-based insurance company with a Web presence, it's probably listed in and linked to this comprehensive online directory. Companies are listed alphabetically and may be searched using the edit/find option of any typical Web browser.

Lizzie Sez

Never buy anything from a salesperson who is rude or unattentive to you, no matter how much you think you want the item. Find what you want somewhere else where the folks serving you are polite and interested in your business.

A FABLE

Once upon a time, a miser saved every penny he made, burying all his gold in his garden. Once a week he would dig it up and hold it, gaze upon it, and gloat over the large amount he had accrued.

One day, a robber came down the road and stole all the miser's gold. The miser threw a large tantrum, screaming and yelling and disturbing the neighbors so much that they came out to see what had happened.

When they asked the miser what on earth was amiss, he told them about his stolen hoard of gold. One neighbor asked, "Did you ever spend any of it, use it for anything?"

"Of course not," replied the miser, " I only came to look at it and hold it in my hands."

"Then come again and look at the hole where you had it buried," said the neighbor. " It will do you just as much good."

And so, folks, take this fairy tale to heart and get your finances in order. And live happily ever after!

Chapter 7

HOME IS WHERE THE HEART IS

WHAT NOW?

DON'T TRIP OVER THE SILL

NEW ESCAPADES

When the kids grow up and move on—going to college, heading off to the big city, taking a world tour that ends up settling them in a country far away, or just getting married—the house starts to get mighty drafty. You can keep the old rooms empty and ready for visits for a while, but after a few years you to start to wonder, "What better use can I make of this space?," or "Do I really need all this room?" A lot of us start to think about retirement right about this time, and whether we want to remain in the old house that we've called home for so long.

WHAT NOW?

Coupled with the changes in our daily routines as we grow older, comes the question of the "Dear Old Home Place." Some folks have already anticipated that the big old house, cramped when the children were growing up, is just too huge for one or two, and have foraged about for new climes and adventures elsewhere. This can be especially true when you don't live in the sunniest or most climatologically hospitable of places.

When the weather drops to 18 below, and the old furnace starts to make growling noises; the acre-and-a-half lawn that seemed fun when we were forty still needs mowing in the spring—the 6 or 8 rooms to keep clean are looming large, when we never go into more than three—it slowly comes to mind that we might want to make a change in our living arrangements.

"My oldest daughter and husband own a large Victorian home which they occupied for years, and rented out rooms to single people in the area. Well, they started to increase their family and decided to get out of the roommate business. Meanwhile, my other daughter and I moved back to Maine from Florida, and came to live in this house with 5-7 other roommates. I enjoy living here. I have my privacy, but I'm not isolated (no empty nest for me!). These long, cold Maine winters can be pretty lonely, so it's nice to have people around."

SMALLER AND SMALLER

Although I know many who have pursued their dreams of a happy retirement in warm climes, I have stayed in familiar surroundings while reducing myself to smaller quarters. The winters in the midwest can be harsh and uncompromising, but I have so many supports in my community that I am not yet ready to give up familiar shopping and grazing grounds, young friends and familiar streets, just so that I can become a beach bum. It is tempting, however, when November rolls around.

THREE TIMES IS THE CHARM

After three tries at reducing the size of my home, I finally settled on an expansive old cooperative apartment that feels like a townhouse, in an older part of the city. I have only a little lawn to mow, and the co-op takes care of that. I am sheltered in winter from the sleet and snow, and protected from the blistering sun in summer by large wrap-around porches. And it's easy to get the trash out, as I am on the first floor.

Cleaning will always be my bugaboo, but it's manageable now, as I only have to deal with 1000 square feet—all on one floor. And even though I sometimes get behind, I can keep up with it, as long as more fun stuff—like surfing the Net!—doesn't get in the way.

DON'T TRIP OVER THE SILL

All this moving around and changing residences can have its pitfalls. A mistake in this area can be far-reaching, not to mention costly. Drawing from the experiences of my friends and my own mistakes, let me share a few tips with you.

BUYING

When you assess your alternatives to the big old house, you'll find you've got lots of options awaiting you. Some of you will go into a straightforward apartment, others will look at retirement villages and assisted living, and still others will prefer cooperatives and condominiums. Before choosing any of these options, if you're thinking of buying, make sure that you understand the contract language and what it can mean to you—both financially and for peace of mind.

- Be sure you know *where* you want to live. If you are staying in familiar territory, you may have already scoped out areas that seem right for you when you got ready to reduce your living quarters.

- If you want to wander farther afield (especially if you're seeking mild weather), be sure you have researched the area thoroughly, either by reading all you can, checking out a relocation video, or, your best bet, visiting the place several times. Lots of folks have been "snow-birds" for years before making a final move, spending the winters in the hot spots and returning home when the weather warms. This is one sure way to get to know an area, and to make friends who will already be a part of your community when you arrive for the duration.

- Sometimes a friend's recommendation will open new doors to easier living. Ask around.

- If you're planning to live in your RV for extended periods of time while traveling around the countryside, don't sell the homeplace without having a fallback pad. If you're not planning to buy a new spot on *terra firma* right away, rent your old home using a reliable real estate agent, or ask one of the kids to house-sit.

- If you're looking to buy a co-op, be sure that you are protected should any other resident become a major problem; and that the co-op's by-laws state clearly what constitutes a "problem," as well as spelling out the consequences to all residents when problems arise. Check the fiduciary arrangements—are there assessments to owners at any and every whipstitch, and can dues be raised haphazardly? Make sure you understand how the escrow accounts will be handled, and who decides on repairs.

- In a retirement community, if you are buying in, be sure that the contract clearly states what the "Life Care" options are. Will there be a huge increase in dues if you must be moved to a nursing home facility? Is there a skilled nursing facility on the premises for recuperation or rehab so that you will not lose your apartment during recovery? On what basis is it decided that you can no longer manage in your apartment and must go to an off-site facility? Make sure you understand what the community's financial assessments may be for, if any. And know whether escrow dues can be raised willy-nilly.

- "Assisted Living" can pose many of the same questions. At what point is it decided that you are no longer capable of maintaining your lifestyle in an Assisted Living community? Who decides? And where do you go? Many retirement communities offer assisted living as a step down from independent living, and provide skilled nursing and nursing home facilities. Read the contract carefully, and be sure that whatever you choose offers the best and safest options for you.

CHOOSING A LOCATION

City Guide USA
http://cityguide.lycos.com/

The city descriptions at Lycos's City Guide USA were developed to provide an upbeat overview of the place and to highlight its primary attractions. Each of the more than 400 cities in the database is accompanied by a selection of links to government agencies, hot spots, local news sources, sports, weather, pictures, and more. Although some of the information is geared toward potential tourists, the links and descriptions provide a Chamber of Commerce-esque snapshot of each city.

> "I moved from Western Pennsylvania to Winter Park, Florida in 1979 and never looked back. If I ever see snow again, it will be too soon."

USA CityLink
http://usacitylink.com/

Although the intro text to "your link to America's cities" boasts that the site "attracts users wanting to travel or relocate to a United States State or City," the primary thrust here is tourism. The individual city links provide lodging, eating, shopping, and sightseeing info. When you initially link to a state, however, you will find two relocation resources—Rent Net and CityLink's nationwide relocation service for potential home buyers—and a selection of links to state-specific info. For seniors with relocation on the brain, this site's value is primarily as a potentially useful source of state info links.

city.net
http://www.city.net/

If you just want to check out a new city—see what's available in terms of arts and entertainment, restaurants, and regional info—a good place to start is with Excite's city.net. Although the presentation is slanted more toward the tourism, rather than the relocation, angle, you can still find a number of links that will help you get a fuzzy cyberfeel for the area. You won't find any text pieces here, just links. Additionally, this Excite feature includes a Top Cities list and an alphabetical index of the hundreds of worldwide cities in its database. Happy hunting!

How far is it?
http://www.indo.com/distance/

OK, this isn't the most useful site in the world, but it's one of my favorite Web gadgets. You type in the names of two places, and the University of Michigan Geographic Name Server calculates the distance between the two points based on their latitudes and longitudes. Since the server isn't calculating road miles, the results are reported "as the crow flies," but it's enough to give you a general idea of how far your intended destination lies from your current one. You can also view the results graphically; the service provides a map pinpointing the two locations.

Online *Money:* Find Your Best Place
http://pathfinder.com/@@CYlfHwYAwEz
XYO@l/money/best-cities-96/seaindex.htm

Money magazine's well-known Best Place to Live feature is easier to use than ever thanks to this Web presentation. Their database contains information on America's 300 largest metro areas, and you can search for your best place based on any number of 63 quality-of-life factors. Search criteria include categories such as weather, housing, health, crime, transportation, leisure, and arts & culture. If you just want to see how these cities fall out, browse the alphabetical list to see the ratings and click on the city name to see a summary of the *Money* data. This excellent site even includes a cost of living calculator that lets you compare the average costs between two cities.

The Rough Guide
http://www.hotwired.com/rough/

This guide to worldwide cities bills itself as informative, irreverent, and indispensable. Without doubt, this feature from HotWired contains some of the best writing on the Web, and the articles never sound like a rosy PR brochure. Both the best and worst characteristics of states and cities are laid bare, along with the area's historical background. You'll find a lot of tourist information in The Rough Guide, but its frank assessments of cities and states are a nice counterpoint to the sometimes sugary descriptions found in other guides.

U.S. Gazetteer

http://www.census.gov/cgi-bin/gazetteer

Now *this* is cool! The U.S. Gazetteer lets you type in any city in the United States, and the Tiger Map Server returns a map of the area that you can fully customize according to a list of features such as highways, interstate labels, parks, streets, and more. Zoom in and out, download the map, and access the latest census data on population size, zip codes, and demographic data.

RETIREMENT COMMUNITIES AND ASSISTED LIVING OPTIONS ON THE WWW

American Baptist Homes of the West

http://www.retirementlife.com/

Despite its name, ABHOW offers "all-faith" communities throughout the western United States that provide a range of living options: residential living, continued care retirement, assisted living, life residency, and rental living. Explore the meaning of these terms and how best ABHOW can serve your needs.

The Arizona Senior Academy

http://www.al.arizona.edu/academy/
asadesc.html

Imagine a retirement community peopled with professionals not yet ready to retire, where learning and continued personal growth are the norm, and care is something everyone gives and receives. Sound interesting? Then look into the Arizona Senior Academy, a national center for the advancement of learning and creative living. It's only just on the drawing board now, but tomorrow, who knows?

Association of Retirement Resorts International

http://www.retirementresorts.com/

Offering a rich mix of services, amenities, and health care in an "idyllic resort-like setting," retirement resorts support the high quality of their residents' lifestyles. Visit this directory to access links to "The World's Most Beautiful Retirement Communities," including California's Carls-

bad by the Sea, Florida's Shell Point Village, North Carolina's Bermuda Village, and Oregon's Rogue Valley Manor.

Blair Florida

http://www.blairflorida.com/

An award-winning developer of "active adult communities," the Blair Group offers five developments located across central Florida, from Tampa to Daytona Beach. Explore the living options these communities provide, consider answers to Frequently Asked Questions, and find out how to contact the company for further details.

Capital Senior Living, Inc.

http://www.dallas.net/~capital/home.html

A national provider of senior lifestyle accommodations, Capital Senior Living offers independent and assisted living housing options as well as nursing care facilities. Click on the map to locate the company's properties around the United States or link to sample property Web sites.

ElderConnect

http://www.elderconnect.com/ElderCare/
PubHomePage.html

An easy-to-search database, ElderConnect offers information on over 33,000 acute rehabilitation providers, retirement communities, long-term nursing care providers, and home health agencies. Access the listings by location and services provided.

Homestead Housing Center

http://www.winternet.com/~webpage/
homestead.html

Working to offer an independent living alternative for seniors in rural areas of Iowa, Kansas, Minnesota, Missouri,

Nebraska, and Wisconsin, the Homestead Housing Center supports the construction of cooperative apartment buildings designed to meet the needs of older adults. Visit this home page to find out more about the cooperatives and how to become involved.

California Association of Residential Care Homes
http://www.kepnet.com/carch/index.htm

A professional non-profit association of licensed residential care facilities in California, CARCH serves that state's older population by providing free advice and referral services designed to help citizens find the right care facilities for them. Visit CARCH's home page to learn more about independent and assisted living options and to access a searchable directory of member facilities.

Eldercare Web: Living Arrangements
http://www.ice.net/~kstevens/altlivin.htm

This general resource provides a directory of links to Internet sites offering articles and resources as general as "Decisions about Retirement Living" and as specific as HUD's Section 202 Elderly Housing Program. If other site searches have failed you so far, check out this page; it offers some out-of-the-ordinary finds.

Guide to Nursing Homes in Florida
http://wane5.scri.fsu.edu/AHCA/NURSDAT/

An online publication of the Florida Agency for Health Care Administration, this excellent resource aids seniors and their families in considering the option of nursing homes. The guide offers an unbiased, comprehensive directory of Florida's nursing homes and can be searched by keyword or region. The guide may be used online or downloaded for use offline, and is available in a large print format.

Guide to Retirement Living Online
http://www.retirement-living.com/

An outgrowth of the printed "Guide to Retirement Living," this online resource attempts to help users "navigate the senior and caregiving service network." Subject areas covered include retirement housing and health care options, remaining healthy, maintaining independence at home, and practical living.

Life Care Retirement Communities
http://www.tricky.com/lcrc/

With communities in Florida, Kansas, Pennsylvania, and Minnesota, LCRC offers "the country's finest" continuing care centers and retirement homes. Link to each of the nonprofit corporation's eight sites to review the services, amenities, and comforts the communities provide.

New Lifestyles Online
http://www.gothica.com/lifestyles/

Here's a "complete guide for senior living." This directory profiles the retirement communities, nursing centers, and residential care facilities for 26 major metropolitan areas of the United States. Regularly updated, New Lifestyles is available free of charge and a copy may be ordered online.

MetLife Online: Nursing Homes
http://www.metlife.com/Lifeadvi/Brochures/Nursing/nurs-toc.html

Created by the folks at Metropolitan Life Insurance Company as part of their Life Advice series, this online brochure examines the emotional, financial, and practical aspects of using the services of a nursing home. Find out what services to expect, how to compare facilities, and where to look for more in-depth information.

Pringle Development
http://www.pringle.com/pringle/

Offering four distinct planned retirement communities northwest of Orlando, Florida, Pringle promises its buyers the "finest" retirement communities in Florida. Find out what makes Pringle communities different, tour properties, and review the online buyers' guide.

RV-Mobile Home Marketplace (Florida)
http://www.mkpmag.com/

Find information on recreational vehicles and manufactured housing for central Florida's 55 and older retirement communities. Locate sellers, brokers, parks, and communities.

"The past few days have been wonderful down here in Ft. Lauderdale way. The temperature has hovered between 78 and 83 with brilliant sunshine. The "snowbirds" have been swimming all day in the 78 degree water. Us Floridians will go swimming again around Maytime, but we do sit around the pool and watch the "birds" splash and cavort."

The Retirement Net
http://www.retirenet.com/aaa/

Select either the U.S. dream locator and find links to retirement options in each of over half the United States, or choose the international option and see what's available outside the United States. Find retirement communities, resort living, and assisted living options. A directory of "senior friendly" links is also featured.

The Retirement Net: Florida
http://www.retirenet.com/retire/florida/flintro.html

Search for Florida properties and communities offering manufactured homes, site-built homes, waterfront homes, affordable homes, golf course homes, and resort or luxury homes. Also find links to condos and luxury apartments as well as assisted living and continuing care communities.

Robson Communities
http://www.robson.com/

Touting itself as one of the nation's "largest and most successful" builders of communities for active adults, Robson promotes its Arizona developments. Explore Sun Lakes, Pebble Creek, Sunbird, and Saddlebrooke, and order a free copy of the company's brochure.

Senior Resource: Housing Choices
http://www.seniorresource.com/house.htm

To move or not to move; to live alone or not to live alone. These are the questions this growing online resource attempts to help seniors answer. Find discussion, points to ponder, and links to services and facilities offering different levels of care.

Senior Sites
http://www.seniorsites.com/

An online service of the California Association of Homes and Services for the Aging, Senior Sites lists over 5,000 communities across the United States that offer nonprofit housing and services for seniors. Search the listings by state and county, review answers to commonly asked questions about the listings presented, or link to other Web sites exploring topics of related interest.

SeniorFriendly.Com: Housing Options
http://www.seniorfriendly.com/1_1_housing.html

This directory offers pointers specifically selected for their potential interest to seniors. Link to dozens of sites that detail living options, sell properties, or promote lifestyles.

Seniors-Site
http://seniors-site.com/

Explore the housing options available at this site exclusively devoted to seniors issues. Actually there isn't much of anything available yet, but by the time this book reaches you, there should be more under the categories of retirement communities, supportive housing, and the best places to retire.

Western Virginia Retirement Guide
http://www.infi.net/~leisure/retire.html

Review the living arrangements and facilities that are available in Virginia's Roanoke Valley: independent living, independent congregate living, assisted living, and nursing homes. Also read about home health care options, "10 Great Spots for the Good Life," and "Secrets to Golden Years Success."

SELLING

Selling the old place can be a dreadful affair if you're not prepared to think of it in bits and pieces. First, get your mind fixed on the idea that you are moving along (as in "forward"!), and that you will do what it takes to sell the family "mausoleum." Here are some tips to help you make the sale go as smoothly and painlessly as possible.

- Before you list your home, have it cleaned up spic-and-span. Get the kids to help out if you need to, or hire a professional service. If it's anything like my place, you could use the extra help.

- Concentrate on sprucing up two rooms that will definitely help to sell your house. These are often the kitchen and the main bathroom (if you have more than one).

- If the outside entrance is a little dreary, paint it in a fresh, new color that blends with the rest of the exterior. If weather permits, put out pots of blooming flowers—even geraniums will do, but don't be chintzy. The first thing the prospective buyer will see is this inviting welcome.

- Make a run through the kitchen and the closets, the attic, and any other storage place, and decide NOW what you can unload. Unless you truly consider it a treasure, put it in the "to go" pile. Furniture is no exception. Many great but dark pieces of furniture don't make the transition well to sunny climes or smaller apartments—they just hunker there in the dining room and look dark and forboding. Ditto on those old paintings you've been hoarding upstairs. Away with them!

- Have a sale! You can either do this by yourself— and if you've got a lot of stuff, this is a killer, so by all means, get the kids to help—or get a professional to come in. A good service will mark and tag all your items, handle the actual sale, and *you* can go to the movies.

- You've already removed some of the hulking furniture and boxes of stuff at your sale, but if your home is still open to prospective buyers, check each room to make sure it isn't cluttered. If it is, take some things out. Cluttered, overcrowded rooms look smaller than they really are.

- Once again, you have already unloaded a lot of borderline clothes at your sale; but if your closets still look full, take out more clothes so they'll look roomy and spacious.

- Remove at least half of what you keep on your kitchen counters. This is where I really fall down, as everything I use to cook is right up there within reach. But it does look cluttered. And it makes the countertops seem tiny.

- Get a service to clean the outside of your windows while you muddle along cleaning the inside. Sparkling windows are cheerful and inviting.

- If there are leaky faucets and loose knobs about, tighten them up.

- Make sure the porch lights and doorbells are working.

- If your carpets are old, like mine are, have them cleaned and freshened.

LAST MINUTE

Just before the realtor comes with the client to show your house:

- Close the garage door.

- Park Fido with the neighbor while you go shopping.

- Turn on all the lights and open all the curtains, unless you have a particularly ugly wall or fence as your view.

- If you smoke, hide your paraphernalia—ashtrays and stuff.

- Use an air freshener or an electric potpourri with an apple-cinnamon smell. Or better yet, bake an apple pie. The smell of a pie cooking is utterly irresistible.

- Turn off appliances. If you just started the laundry, it will wait for you.

A good rule of thumb is to think like the buyer. The things that would impress you will impress them.

GENERAL REAL ESTATE RESOURCES

Abele Owners' Network
http://www.owners.com/default.htm

Search a national directory of homes for sale by their owners (rather than through realtors). Search by state, price, and amenities. Also find a range of informational resources including insights into real estate law, a glossary of legal terms, and a mortgage calculator.

AllApartments Search
http://www.allapartments.com/aa/

Search through the listings for over 4 million available apartments from every part of the United States and find the one that best suits your lifestyle. Enter a city and state for a general search, a property name to bring up a rental brochure, or an address to access a map of the area.

America's HomeNet & CenterNet
http://www.netprop.com/

Net Properties is a Web publisher whose goal is to provide the most comprehensive real estate information to the industry and general public. Visitors to this site can browse (or list with) residential and commercial real estate "information superstores."

Ask Sherlock
http://accnet.com/cgi-bin/listings.pl

This specialized search engine allows visitors to scan the Internet for property listings and other items related to real estate. Easy-to-follow instructions help the first-time user conduct searches like a pro.

Better Homes and Gardens Real Estate Service
http://bhg-real-estate.com/

Supporting a network of 775 independently owned real estate companies throughout the United States, Canada, and Puerto Rico, this online BH&G directory points users to profiles of current listings, buying strategies, selling strategies, and relocation tips. Also find links to mortgage services and current news of topical interest.

Century 21 Professional Connection
http://www.century21pro.com/

Thinking of relocating anywhere in the United States? Indicate on this national map the state to which you're moving and order a relocation packet for that area. There is a fee for the packet.

Coldwell Banker Online
http://www.coldwellbanker.com/

Whether you're buying or selling, Coldwell Banker offers a wealth of online aid and information. Browse property listings (including luxury, resort, and vacation homes), look into finance options, and locate which of Coldwell Banker's 2,400 offices is closest to where you are or want to be.

CyberHomes
http://www.cyberhomes.com/

Featuring interactive, street-level mapping, CyberHomes allows users to "zoom in" on areas and search for listings by neighborhood—no more driving around! Select a city and begin your search. This map-based tool is easy to use.

Estate Net
http://www.estate.de/

House hunters can access a worldwide real estate database through the Estate Net site. Prospective buyers can view listings by selecting from a world map or check the special offers section for hot properties. The site is based in Germany, but is available in English.

Florida Internet Real Estate Guide
http://www.floridaguide.com/

This real estate information service provides a variety of resources for those looking for a home in Florida. Visit here to link with home-finding services, government and business information, and more. The site's features include a clickable map for honing the home search.

HSH Associates
http://www.hsh.com/

This financial publisher offers a variety of services online, including mortgage and consumer loan information. Aimed at lenders, real estate agents, and consumers, services also include national average mortgage rates, and information on market trends.

HomeBuyer Internet Real Estate Service
http://www.homebuyer.com/

Search a database of properties for sale nationwide by location, price, and amenities. Listings include detailed descriptions of properties and photographs. The site also features a list of buyer's representatives and homeowner tips.

Homebuyer's Fair
http://www.homefair.com/home/

Buying a home, selling a home, hunting for an apartment, and refinancing a home are the topics covered at the Homebuyer's Fair. Play with the salary, mortgage qualification, and moving calculators; visit with the Relocation Wizard; and find out why "what you don't know can cost you thousands of dollars."

HomeOwners Finance Center Loan Calculation Page
http://www.homeowners.com/calculator.html

This simple, yet very useful page, invites users to fill in the form provided with details about the home in question and calculate what the monthly payments will be. As an added feature of this calculator, the payments are divided into principal and interest.

Homes & Land Electronic Magazine
http://www.homes.com/Welcome.html

Homes & Land Publishing Corp. runs an electronic open house here. A real estate information center, this site offers a national database of properties, rentals, and real estate agents. Features also include information on Smart Moves personal relocation software.

HomeScout Search: U.S. and Canada
http://www.homescout.com/

Catch this wave and surf through over 350,000 property listings from over 130 real estate sites on the Web. And that's just to begin. Also find the HomeScout Guide and HomeScout Wizard offering links to over 3,500 sites featuring useful advice on mortgages, home care, and much, much more.

House Buying and Financing
http://www.gsa.gov/staff/pa/cic/housing.htm

Maintained by the General Services Administration's Consumer Information Center, this Web site indexes consumer information for homeowners and home buyers. Visitors can find low-cost pamphlets on buying and financing a house, homeowners' insurance, home improvement, and other topics of related interest.

How much house can you afford?
http://alfredo.wustl.edu/mort/howmuch.cgi

It's a legitimate question, and now you can figure a legitimate answer. Simply fill in this interactive form, hit calculate, and clickety-click, you've got your answer. This free service is thanks to Hugh Chou of the Institute for Biomedical Computing at Washington University.

The International Real Estate Directory
http://www.ired.com/

Self-described as the "single source for independent real estate information on the Web," IRED offers both a comprehensive directory of real estate links and an online e-zine loaded with bits and bytes of interest to sellers and buyers alike. Mirrored in the United States, Europe, and Asia, this interactive search and information tool is truly a global resource.

The Internet Real Estate Network
http://www.iren.com/

Make well-informed and educated choices when it comes to real estate decisions. Here's a host of information of interest to home buyers, sellers, and investors. Among other things, links point to property listings and realty-related service providers.

Internet Yellow Web Pages: Real Estate (Canada)
http://sword.lightspeed.bc.ca/warlight/r-estate.html

The choices are yours. Among other options, select to search the pages by region, type of property, or realtor.

The Mortgage Loan Page
HTTP://LOANPAGE.COM/

Self-described as "the 'True Search' database of mortgage finance," the Mortgage Loan Page boasts the "largest" database of its kind online and the ability to search the listings based on your specific loan needs. Also find a reference desk, a mortgage calculator, and a historical look at interest rate trends.

National Association of Realtors Home Page
http://www.realtor.com/

Realtors can check in here for information on their profession, while Net users looking to buy a home can stop in to access the database featuring thousands of homes for sale. Advice on mortgages, property rights, and taxation is also available online.

Property Line
http://www.vossnet.co.uk/property/index.html

The Property Line home page provides online information about real estate for sale or rent in the United Kingdom, Germany, France, Spain, Portugal, and the United States. Also find links to related financial services and other property resources on the World Wide Web.

The Prudential Real Estate Affiliates
http://www.prudential.com/homeownership/

An international network of independently owned and operated real estate firms, "The Rock" promises the answers for those looking into home ownership. Find information geared for buyers and sellers, as well as those looking into vacation, resort, and retirement living. Tips for relocating and an agent locator service are also online.

RE/MAX Real Estate Network
http://www.remax.com/

Search online for properties, RE/MAX offices, and individual agents around the United States. Look into mortgage options, read topical news about RE/MAX and the real estate market, or review tips for buyers and sellers. There's plenty at this site to do and see for those in the market—whether buyers, sellers, or just browsers.

RealtyGuide

http://www.xmission.com/~realtor1/

RealtyGuide is a collection of pointers to real estate Web sites around the world. Browse the links or search by area for information from international realty companies. You can dream about that retirement villa in Italy, now can't you?

RentNet Online Apartment Guide

http://www.rent.net/

Looking for a new apartment? The task couldn't be easier with RentNet, a free, interactive database representing over a million furnished and unfurnished apartments across the United States and Canada. Each entry comes complete with photographs, floor plans, and location maps.

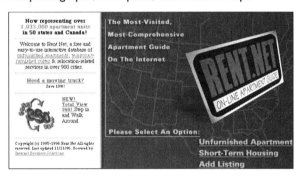

World Real Estate Network

http://www.wren.com/

This free, online search service describes itself as "the future of real estate … today!" WRENet allows users to search residential, commercial, and ranch and land databases. A Directory of Professionals is also online for referrals.

NEW ESCAPADES

With the big move behind you and your immediate life decisions solved, you're ready to go out and get a Ph.D., start your own business, fix up the new house, get a black belt in karate, or…conquer the World!

Hey! Don't forget to take your computer along!

Chapter **8**

ENTREPRENEURIAL YOU

A DILLER, A DOLLAR

LET THE FRESH AIR IN

HOME BODIES

"I retired after 50 years as a doctor. For about six months, I was a little depressed. A doctor who's not a doctor—who the hell is he? It dawned on me—I needed to redefine who I was. I was a poet, and a writer, my wife's husband, a human being—not necessarily in that order.

"What is important is to have a life of the mind. We can't physically go out to the world like we did when we were younger, and now with the computer we can bring it in. This is a tool of communication where you can tap the universe, and have access to as many worlds as you want. Before, I was a member of a small profession. Now, I'm a citizen of the world."

—Dr. Ben Budai, Senior Netizen

Many of us have shared the feelings expressed by Dr. Budai, especially as we near the end of our own work lives. Often the measure of ourselves is made by the work that we do, the "who" that we are in that work environment, and our success within it—not the measure of who we are at home with our families, and what we do outside of that work environment. Some of us identify only with our work, and find that when the end of that chapter in our lives comes, we have limited ourselves severely by boxing our identities into such a small container.

As we come to the time when we must leave the work with which we have so strongly identified, we are faced with many decisions. If we have not faced them earlier, we must decide what in the world we intend to do with the rest of our lives besides poke around and vegetate.

Some folks, who have strong lives outside of work and are deeply involved in satisfying hobbies, find this transition less troublesome. They can begin that landscaping plan they have never had time to do, get a bigger RV and travel more than they were able to when they were younger, attack that stack of old diaries and dig into the family genealogy, drag out the train set and become an engineer, or brush up on writing skills, using them to author training manuals or guidebooks in the fields in which they now have so much expertise.

Yet whenever I hear the word "retire," I conjure up a picture of some frail old gooner in back-flap jammies making his way to bed—for the duration. As long as we are going to use automotive terms to describe the event of permanently leaving a job due to age, why not use "retool"?

It makes more sense to me. For we are far from retiring in our speech, having gotten enough confidence with age to tell it exactly as we see it. We are far from retiring in our actions, as few of us are shy, having learned that we must assert ourselves in a world growing more difficult to live in graciously. I'm getting pretty good at this, speaking out and fighting back. Most of us are not shrinking, unsociable, backward, or withdrawn—all definitions you can find for the word "retire."

A DILLER, A DOLLAR

More and more retirees are looking for ways to generate a little extra income, or start a whole new career. Working in retirement doesn't mean that you have to sit behind a desk all day, or flip burgers at a fast food restaurant. Using a little creativity, you may find a pursuit that tickles your fancy and makes a little money at the same time, or perhaps you'll embark on a strikingly different career. Look what these folks came up with.

Lizzie Sez

When you clean your closets, use the "Three Year Rule": Give to charity all the clothes you haven't worn, or anything else you haven't used, in three years.

I'LL HAVE MINE WITH CATSUP... THIS YEAR

Thirty years ago, my mother, a senior citizen and a math wizard, took a course in preparing tax returns offered by a large company in our town. Once a year she girded her loins, bustled to the tax office, and helped others to get their taxes ready for the good ole IRS. The beauty of this was the lack of permanent commitment. When tax time was done, she was free to pursue her other interests. But once a year for this short period of time she could keep her hand in. If she didn't want to work that year, she simply did not contract to work. It was a perfect job for her: open-ended and short of term.

GIGGLES AND GAGGLES

I also know a gal who has made a name for herself as a clown. After leaving her office job, she threw herself into the one avocation she truly loved. She is now at special events, children's parties, and charity picnics, waltzing around as the entertainment. She calls her own shots, works when she wants to, has built a large following, and is a member of the local Clown Club. Her life is rich and filled with purpose.

Jo Pat Free personifies her last name perfectly. Pat takes jobs if they suit her, looking for those that make her happy, entertain her, or put something back into the community. Money is not her object. Last summer she filled her days driving the local ice-cream truck up and down the residential streets, and enjoyed the laughter of the children who purchased and gobbled down her wares. I wonder what she is up to this year?

THE BELLY OF THE BALL

I read recently of a football coach who at retirement beat feet for overseas, and at 71-years-old still coaches football clinics throughout Europe.

Mildred Riley retired from psychiatric nursing in 1979 and kept busy at home writing historical romances. Her fifth novel was released in May—when she was 78 years old. She and her husband travel around the country gathering material for her books, and she has admitted that writing about all the passionate embraces of her characters while traveling with her husband has added an extra dimension to their retirement years.

One Senior, a school principal, retired and began making art—not the usual kind of thing you think about with watercolors, or oils and brushes, because all of his supplies come from macaroni boxes. Recently, the National Pasta Association featured him and his art as part of a story for a national magazine.

AND PULL OUT A PLUM

And what about David Letterman's mom, Dorothy, who at 75 has authored a cookbook called, *Home Cookin' with Dave's Mom*, an odyssey of comfort recipes, with snaps of the Letterman family and her famous offspring. *Home Cookin'* is a treasury of old favorites. One of Dave's is Fried Baloney Sandwich, and another is a Sour Cherry Pie that she whisks off via overnight delivery to Dave on every birthday.

Lucille, a little whirlwind at 85, still manages the gift shop at a large medical center here. Starting many years ago as a volunteer, she still enjoys getting out and meeting the public, ordering fun things for the shop, and stocking the shelves.

Jack Shurman, retiring after 45 years in magazine publishing, keeps his hand in with a humorous in-

> ### Lizzie Sez
> *If someone offers you a job, even one you think you don't want, go talk to them anyway; you may be slamming the door on opportunity.*

vestment column he writes from home called "Gray Matters." It's a regular feature of the magazine *Successful Retirement*. His column is full of fun and takes up finances from a point of view we can relate to.

FOR SHEER CHUTZPAH

A real success story is the Beardstown Ladies, a group of 15 gals from ages 42 to 88, who formed an investment club in their hometown of Beardstown, Illinois. Meeting weekly, they proved that investing can be fun and amazed their friends and families by outperforming professional money managers, as well as the Standard & Poor 500 Index, getting a 23.4% annual return. These ladies, as a result of their rewarding association, have written two books: *The Beardstown Ladies' Common Sense Investment Guide: How We Beat the Stock Market and How You Can*; and *The Beardstown Ladies' Stitch-in-Time Guide to Growing Your Nest Egg: Step-by-Step Planning for a Comfortable Financial Future*. Now, that's really being entrepreneurial!

BALLOONS AND WHISTLES

A somewhat eccentric but exciting second career was taken up by a 68-year-old grandmother, whose sons gave her a "muscle car" one year for Christmas. In no time this dragster was blowing by drivers in their 20s and 30s, and drove to several World Records in the International Hot Rod Association. At 81, she is still addicted to her souped-up Chevy.

One dedicated fisherman built two stocked ponds to add to his fishing enjoyment when he retired. He soon had the public beating at his door to fish his ponds, and has opened them as a commercial enterprise, letting fisherfolk take their daily catches on a fee-paid basis.

And that is only the tip of the iceberg. So many Seniors are starting fresh, retooling or even continuing their careers. And so can you. All it takes is desire, a little imagination, and the help of the World Wide Web.

BECOMING A POSTRETIREMENT ENTREPRENEUR

BUSINESS-RELATED GOVERNMENT AGENCIES AND SERVICES

FedWorld Information Network Home Page
http://www.fedworld.gov/

Think of FedWorld as a gigantic online library stuffed with government pubs and info. In government-speak, this translates into "a comprehensive central access point for locating and acquiring government information." What's here for the small-business entrepreneur, you ask? Well, my quick search on the keywords *small business* returned 80 hits. That could keep you busy for awhile. Plus, you'll find tax info from the IRS, a link to U.S. Customs, and more official documents than you can shake a stick at.

Service Corps of Retired Executives
http://www.sbaonline.sba.gov/SCORE/

How much would you pay for a one-on-one consultation with a former corporate financial officer to discuss problems you're having with business financing? How about nothing? The Service Corps of Retired Executives (SCORE) is a nationwide group of retired executives and business owners who volunteer their services to help small businesses start strong and continue prosperously. For all you Senior Netters out there, this is an excellent volunteer opportunity to consider.

Small Business Administration Home Page
http://www.sbaonline.sba.gov/

There's no denying that the SBA is in the business of providing information to business. And they've put their warehouse full of pamphlets—covering everything from business plans to taxes—online so you don't even have to take your biggest briefcase down to the regional office to lug all the material home. The easy-to-use interface divides their services into three key areas: starting, financing, and expanding your business. Within each area, find tons of info, including a FAQ, the SBA's famous pamphlets, online workshops, and downloadable shareware. If you still want to visit, a clickable image map shows the locations of the SBA's regional offices.

Small Business Administration Office of Minority Enterprise Devlopment
http://www.sbaonline.sba.gov/MED/

The SBA has established special counseling and assistance programs for minority-owned and -operated businesses. These services are detailed on this page and are accompanied by links to other resources for small and disadvantaged businesses.

Small Business Administration's Office of Women's Business Ownership
http://www.sbaonline.sba.gov/
womeninbusiness/

The government has figured out that female entrepreneurs are a positive economic force and that helping so-called "disadvantaged" women establish and maintain their own businesses works toward ending poverty cycles and welfare dependence. This specialized office of the SBA provides counseling, training, mentoring, and financial assistance programs to help women establish a solid business footing. The site details these programs and includes an excellent (and eye-opening) FAQ.

United States Copyright Office
http://lcweb.loc.gov/copyright/

Don't send off that screenplay until you've registered it with the Copyright Office. Here you'll find definitions and basic info, along with all the filing instructions and downloadable forms (in Adobe Acrobat format). You can also telnet to the Library of Congress Information System (LOCIS) to search the Copyright Office records, request information via fax, and read the latest announcements.

United States Patent and Trademark Office
http://www.uspto.gov/

Isn't technology wonderful? You can actually search the U.S. Patent bibliographic database and download forms from the comfort of your own home. The friendly folks at patents also provide online brochures with basic facts about patents and trademarks, along with a discussion of

intellectual property and U.S. and international legal materials. When you're done, be sure to complete the customer satisfaction report.

GENERAL BUSINESS BOOKS

American Institute of Small Business
http://www.accessil.com/aisb/home.htm

The American Institute of Small Business exists primarily to publish books and other materials related to self-employment and the start-up and maintenance of small business. Their catalog includes some impressive-sounding (but pricey) tomes, videos, and software, covering topics such as business plans, market research, advertising, and home-based businesses.

The Entrepreneur's Bookstore Catalog
http://kwicsys.com/books/

Here's a cheap "bookstore" that caters to all of you who dream of owning and operating your own business. The site advertises "over 600 information-packed" reports that cost only $1 to $2 each. Topics covered include Mail Order (a sample title is "Insider's Know-How To Mail Order Riches"), Direct Response TV ("What Is an Infomercial?"—I've seen enough of them to know the answer to *that* question), and Computers ("There's Gold Inside Your PC!"). The catalog also includes non-business-related pubs concerning health ("Growing Old Gracefully"), how-tos ("How To Get Free Rent"—now that could be useful!), and legal issues ("Entire Interest In Estate Assignment"). I can't vouch for the usefulness of any of these guides, but the range of titles is impressive and the prices are so low that if you order a couple of samples to check them out, you won't put much of a dent in your wallet.

Inc. Business Resources Library
http://199.103.128.199/emgbiznc/cntprovs/
products/incbiz/

Inc. magazine sells books and videos that cover the spectrum of starting, operating, and profiting from your business. You can read a summary and check the table of contents for the offerings in each category—Starting a Business, Business Planning, Time Management, Managing People, and Customer Service—and then order by e-mail, telephone, fax, or regular mail. As a bonus, each category includes some nuggets of free business advice—such as a list of questions to ask yourself before you decide to start a business—so the site is worth a visit even if you're not in the market for business books. Web purchasers get a 20 percent discount.

NetBiz—The Entrepreneur's Bookstore
http://www.hits.net/~netbiz/bookstor.html

With over 1,100 titles of books, reports, software, and CD-ROMs, this online bookstore probably has what you're looking for. And if they don't stock it, they'll find it for you. The catalog is arranged by category (legal kits, taxes, how-to books), and e-mail ordering is available. Click the Freebies button to find out about free software, presentation disks, books, and files.

MAGAZINES, NEWSLETTERS, AND OTHER BUSINESS NEWS SOURCES

Electronic Money Tree
http://www.soos.com/$tree/

This "Netrepreneur's Digest For Small Business and Entrepreneurs" includes a selection of articles for small business owners covering topics such as franchising, taxes, marketing, opportunities, and doing business over the Internet. The 'zine includes a classified ad section and a small business mall. If you like what you see, register for e-mail notification of new issues.

Entrepreneurial Edge Magazine
http://www.edgeonline.com/

This online version of the quarterly print magazine is crammed with useful info for the small business owner

and entrepreneur. Regular feature sections include a marketing and advertising update, management style, sales savvy, finances, global trade…no matter what you're into, this 'zine has a feature to cover it. Past articles are archived (a most excellent feature), and the site includes a number of other value-added links in addition to the magazine. Well worth a lengthy stop.

The Fran Tarkenton Small Business NETwork
http://www.ftsbn.com/

Fran Tarkenton isn't throwing footballs anymore, but he is passing a load of small business information your way via this attractive 'zine format. Find news, a resource center (full of articles and features), company of the week, and a selection of products and services.

Guerrilla Marketing Online
http://www.gmarketing.com/

This weekly Web magazine carries features on marketing for small business owners, entrepreneurs, and professional salespeople. Features like The Weekly Guerrilla and Tales from the Front Line are accompanied by a vendor directory, list of publications for sale, and a fee-based consulting service. There's good information here, but you have to click around a number of guerrilla marketers to find it.

Inc. Online
http://www.inc.com/

One of the big business mags goes online here to provide a virtual reference shelf for the small business owner/entrepreneur. Among other great features, find the current issue of the magazine, along with an archive of over 5,000 past articles. The Virtual Consultant section includes interactive business worksheets developed by successful entrepreneurs that cover all sorts of financial topics. Peer to Peer has eight threaded bulletin boards covering topics from starting a company to networking. And that's not all. Take a look at all the features of this excellent entrepreneurial resource.

Income Opportunities Online
http://www.incomeops.com/

The online edition of the "original small business/home office magazine" includes lists of business and franchise opportunities, along with business links, archived issues, and product reviews.

Internet Scambusters
http://lobos.svr.com/scambusters/

This free e-mail 'zine exposes fraudulent and unethical business offers that are promoted over the Internet. It bills itself as the "zine for entrepreneurs, business owners and marketing folks at small and medium-size businesses, and professionals who are currently using or considering the Internet to promote their products or services." Scambusters exposes bogus claims and provides tips on how to spot a scam. A sample edition is available at the site.

Minority Business Entrepreneur Magazine
http://www.mbemag.com/

This bimonthly publication is "for and about minority and women business owners." You'll have to subscribe to the print version to get the meat; only a few articles are online here, but you can access subscription info at the home page.

NetMarquee
http://nmq.com/FamBizNC/default.htm

NetMarquee is targeted to family-owned businesses and includes hundreds of articles, papers, and other resources to help enhance your business management savvy. The Calendar of Events gives you info on seminars and conferences that you may not want to miss, and you can sign up for a family-business listserv, access news stories about tax and legislative issues, and find articles covering everything from quality management to marketing to venture capital.

The Newsletter Library
http://pub.savvy.com/subject.htm

Collected here in one mega-list is an assortment of free newsletters available online. You don't have to search through countless Web pages to find useful topics; just scroll down the list and check off the titles you'd like to receive via e-mail. The catalog includes a number of business titles—everything from acquisitions to international

marketing to state recycling laws. You'll have to slog through a number of non-business-related titles, but you'll probably see several on the list you'd like to read during your off-hours.

The Something for Nothing Journal
http://www.kauai.net/~kwc2/sfnhompg.htm

This fun 'zine indexes "the best free offers" on the Internet. It's not all business oriented, so you'll find some bizarre stuff (like how to cook a turkey over a fire) mixed in with an eclectic assortment of business opportunities, advice, and free downloads. For example, the June 1996 issue is devoted entirely to Web site promotion, the July 1996 effort is packed with links to free Netscape plug-ins, and the May 1996 page includes links to Bartering for Business and business booklets, sandwiched between the turkey recipe and hiking info.

MISCELLANEOUS RESOURCES ON BUSINESS TOPICS

Advancing Women: Entrepreneur and Small Business
http://www.advancingwomen.com/entrepreneur.phtml

This business start-up advice targeted to women emphasizes the importance of a business plan, discusses the risky nature of all self-employment enterprises, and provides tips for arranging financing, managing effectively, and developing a "system." There's not much new here, but it's nice to have a site written specifically for women.

America's Business Funding Directory
http://www.businessfinance.com/

The Internet's "first business capital search engine" wants to help you find the money to start or expand your business. You'll have to register and answer a bunch of nosy questions about your credit history, projected revenue, and project type, plus write a short summary explaining why you need the money. But if you're willing to entrust all that information to cyberspace, the service promises to return all the funding sources you could ever want. Elsewhere, take advantage of the free Raining Money Workbook to help you create a winning financial proposal.

Answers to Patent, Copyright, and Trademark Questions

http://www.ucc.uconn.edu/~bxb95001/#Intellectualproperty

Here's a first! An attorney specializing in intellectual property and entrepreneurship provides free advice, and he's not even your brother-in-law. For solid definitions (with examples) of what can be copyrighted, trade-marked, and patented, along with a good discussion of "fair use" and the distinction between a trade name and a trademark, visit Breffni Baggot's informative site.

Apple Small Business Home Page

http://www.smallbusiness.apple.com/

Naturally the Apple folks want you to do all your small business computing on a Macintosh, but even if you

 ## Lizzie's Tips

START YOUR OWN!

Starting a business is really not as hard as you might think, and often does not cost a great deal of money.

Here are a few businesses you can set up in your home that require $500 or less:

- Secretarial and Administrative Services: Letters written for small businesses; telephone marketing done for small businesses looking to expand markets; legal documents for sole practitioner attorneys; and more.

- Credit-Repair Service: If you're a good household or business money manager, you can help consumers who have gotten their own budgets into hot water—this can be an especially good business for former bookkeepers and accountants. You would assist in resolving credit disputes, set up payment schedules, and negotiate repayment terms with debt holders.

- Estate Sales: If sales and auctions ring your chimes, this could be for you. After you have attended enough sales to learn pricing and understand how the underlying business works, you can begin soliciting clients of your own. You need to know how to draw up contracts, and you should be fairly knowledgeable about antiques, old furniture, and bric-a-brac. Check your local library (not to mention the Internet) for resources on identifying and understanding the value of collectibles and antiques.

- Meeting Planner: Put together events, meetings, and conventions for businesses. If you've planned a large family's events and activities for years, you're a natural! Must be detail-oriented and imaginative.

- Professional Moving Counselor: I've moved my family so many times, I've lost count. I can out-clean, out-pack, and out-maneuver most professionals, and I can fit an amazing amount of stuff into boxes I didn't even know I had (I can also weed out an awful lot of stuff I thought I needed that I suddenly know I don't want to move). Today, whenever my kids face a big move, who do you think they call first? Consider setting yourself up as a professional moving or relocation consultant. If you've moved a lot with your family (particularly all of you who were formerly with branches of the armed services), you probably know more than you think.

If you put your mind to it, I am sure that many more ideas will come to you: upholstering and refinishing furniture; second-hand sales (a big market these days); alterations; Medicare Supplement sales—just a few that popped into my head without really thinking.

don't, they're still willing to share a tree-full of small business how-tos and networking opportunities. The Small Business Toolbox, with its business-building resources, and Small Talk's newsgroups that focus on issues important to small business owners, can give you new ideas and resources for your entrepreneurial debut.

Assist International
http://www.imex.com/assist.html

You'll have to register (for free) to gain access to this site, but it's worth it to read the ExportFAQ prepared by pros at the Michigan Small Business Development Center at Wayne State University. Fundamental issues covered include: What should I export? How do I find foreign buyers? How do I import? and Do I need a license to export? Another highly touted site feature is ExportFREE, a "listing of over 220 resources for exporters that are free and otherwise inexpensive." Well, I didn't check every offering, but most of the ones I did check were far from free and not what I would call inexpensive. Still, there's useful info here if you're willing to give them your e-mail address.

Basic Guide to Exporting
http://www.maingate.net/us-exports/bge.html

This page is an excellent primer for folks thinking about developing an export business during their retirement years. Here you'll find a general overview of exporting (including the 10 keys to export success), followed by chapters that explain methods of export, how to prepare shipments, making contacts, export regulations, and a host of financial considerations. An excellent reference and introduction.

The Bi-Weekly Raise Money for Your Business without Asking Your Bank Manager Page
http://home.earthlink.net/~fpearce/Craiseho.html

Every two weeks, a new money-making strategy is posted to the list on this page. The site claims that each idea has been used successfully by entrepreneurs and that none is a theoretical shot in the dark. Check them out to see if you can apply any of these ideas to your business.

Lizzie Sez
When beginning a small business venture, don't stress too much about not having enough money for start-up. Sometimes limited funds can be a blessing, not a curse; limitations can give a boost to creative thinking like nothing else can.

BizWomen
http://www.bizwomen.com/index.html

"Bringing business women from all over the world together" is this aim of this site, and its efforts include four mailing lists (career-related discussions, finance and investment, technology, and business), a membership directory, and the opportunity to post a business card, brochure, or catalog at the site.

Business Resource Center
http://www.kciLink.com/brc/

The folks from Khera Communications, Inc., an Internet publishing and consulting service, make a sales pitch here, but they also include a bookshelf full of free business info for both start-ups and established companies. The Getting Started section includes valuable tips on writing a business plan (an absolute must-have, they say), and the Marketing section gives you tips on getting publicity for your business and guidelines on what to include in your capabilities brochure. The Financing Guide covers the money end of things with articles on different types of financing, selling a business, and taking your company public. There's even more to discover at this excellent

compilation of resources, but it would take several pages to describe it all. Check it out for yourself.

Consultant's Corner
http://www.pwgroup.com/ccorner/

Not only does this site sell Web space for you to promote your consulting business, but it also includes some really useful resources, such as an article archive, special offers from consultants advertising at the Web site, a business survival guide containing advice and ideas, and a list of marketing resources.

Consulting
http://www.cob.ohio-state.edu/dept/fin/jobs/consult.htm

Here's a great site to help you explore your potential value as a consultant. Along with no-nonsense advice about the risks (sometimes grueling, often cyclical, work) and requirements (excellent communication and people skills, high degree of expertise, the ability to think on your feet), the site includes links to companies that provide different types of consulting services, along with information on books about the field and pointers to Internet consulting resources.

Consulting Corner
http://www.ccorner.com/

Here's another online consulting directory that wants to list your business in its database for a fee. The prices are higher than those charged by some other directories, but the company includes a comparison table designed to show you that their service surpasses the others. You'll also find tips on topics such as leadership and training, a bulletin board for networking with other consultants, and an Ask the Experts feature.

Cyberpreneur's Guide to the Internet
gopher://una.hh.lib.umich.edu/00/inetdirsstacks/cyberpren%3aschwilk

There's nothing pretty about this text-only page, but it sure delivers the info with a one-two punch. This "guide to selected resources for entrepreneurs on the Internet" includes listservs, newsgroups, gophers, and Web sites, all targeting the specific needs of the cyberpreneur, "one

who operates, organizes, or assume the risks for a business venture, that is related or operated through the global network known as the Internet."

Directory of Freight Forwarding Services
http://forwarders.com/

Here's a directory of air freight, shipping, rail freight, trucking, and specialized transportation carriers, along with info on export documentation, licensing, and letters of credit. Request a quote or additional info online, whether your shipment is within the United States only or to a country outside the States. The easy-to-use interface lets you access companies listed alphabetically by name and by state.

Entrepreneur Information Guide
http://www.magpage.com/~rispoli/index.html

This index to entrepreneurial links includes a library of reference resources (Zip Code Lookup, Home-Based Business Directory), business resources (SalesDoctors Magazine, The Better Business Bureau), entrepreneur business reports (for a fee), mail-order resources (Money-Saving Tips, Directory of Home-Based Income Opportunities), and the Cyberfieds (ads for services and opportunities). Plenty to explore.

Explore India
http://www.exploreindia.com/

Thinking about going into the brass import business? Want information about possible products to export? The Explore India site includes useful information such as the Export Import Trade Flash magazine, the Indian Exporters Yellow Pages, and government information specific to the import-export trade. You'll also find daily and financial news, real estate info, and the Business Bazaar, a list of current opportunities. This is the source for data on doing business with the Indian Subcontinent.

Freelance Online
http://haven.ios.com/~freelans/index1.html

If your background is in the communications field and you are interested in freelance work, stop off at this page. Listings in the directory are free (although small fees are charged for HTML pages and other enhancements), a job bank lists current freelance opportunities, the resource list includes links to excellent editorial and writing sites (including professional organizations), and the message board is a great place to ask questions and obtain feedback from other communications professionals. A fabulous resource for anyone involved in communications-for-hire work.

Global Access to Trade and Technology Server
http://www.gatts.com/

This resource includes information on and links to worldwide conventions and trade shows, customs and tariff rates for several countries, currency exchange rates, transportation and shipping data (including oceanic shipping schedules and railway timetables), world weather, and a host of other practical info sources for the exporter.

Glossary of Export Terms
http://www.ibc-inc.com/glosintl.htm

If you're thinking about going into the export business, you have to know the lingo. Use this site to bone up on the meanings of arcana like arbitrage, C.I.F., and transit shipment. Not all terms are defined, but there's enough here to get you talking like a pro in no time.

Idea Café: The Small Business Channel
http://www.ideacafe.com/

This gathering place of "success tips for entrepreneurs by entrepreneurs" sports colorful, upbeat graphics, and a selection of articles covering topics from finance to how you work. Meet, mingle, and network in the Idea Café's CyberSchmooz lounge, where folks are discussing busi-

ness volunteer opportunities, weird tax deductions, and the first year in business. Lots of fun and lots of value.

Information for Entrepreneurs
http://www.smallbiz.sunycentral.edu/entre.htm

This excellent index provides links under several subject-specific categories to Web sites of interest to entrepreneurs. Business ownership, Internet marketing, small business development centers, manufacturing, legal info, and international trade are just a few of the topics included in the list.

International Business Network
http://www1.usa1.com/~ibnet/index.html

The International Business Network calls itself the "electronic silk road" and in the tradition of open trade routes, indexes information about well over 800 Chambers of Commerce from throughout the world. Chambers exist to promote business in their areas and are a good source of specific demographic info. The G-77 Chambers section lists info on the Chamber organizations in 132 developing countries. Add in the links to trade promotion organizations, trade news, and research tools (like the AP Search Service and the International Law Center) and you've got a great info source.

International Business Resources on the World Wide Web
http://ciber.bus.msu.edu/busres.htm

Michigan State University maintains this über-index of business links. This is definitely a site for an uncluttered afternoon. You'll find reviewed links to over 100 business and news periodicals alone, and that's not even counting the region-specific info (over 200 links), the international trade information and leads (over 50 links), government resources (over 30 links), and mailing lists (over 30 links). And there's even more at this incredible info source.

International Trade Adminstration
http://www.ita.doc.gov/

The ITA's mission is "to encourage, assist, and advocate U.S. exports," and this agency of the U.S. Department of Commerce comes through for exporters with a pile of free info. How about trade leads, reports on a range of overseas industries (including their import statistics), and FAQ? Not enough? Then check out the directories of Federal assistance programs, economic analyses, and cross-cutting export programs like the Advocacy Center, Big Emerging Markets, and American Business Centers overseas. Lots of info here and you can't beat the price.

International Trade Law
http://ananse.irv.uit.no/trade_law/nav/trade.html

The legal-speak on this page may send you scrambling for the yellow pages to track down an international trade attorney for help, but if you have the time, patience, and savvy, you can learn a lot about the laws and practices governing international trade from this page. You'll find the texts of treaties (GATT, NAFTA) and laws covering insurance requirements, dispute settlement conventions, and enforcement practices. Not for the legally impaired, but if you're going to be shipping goods from some far corner of the earth, you need to be aware of the laws that govern the practice.

Internet Business Center
http://tsunami.tig.com/cgi-bin/genobject/ibcindex

Billed as your "one-stop shop for business information on the Internet," the Internet Business Center provides info and links to a wealth of information about developing and promoting business Web sites. Statistics on Internet use and demographics, links to company sites categorized by industry, and links to business forums are just some of the resources at this site.

Inventors Resources & Associations Links
http://iridium.nttc.edu/inventions/inv_links.html

Attention all Rube Goldbergs! Here's the page you've been looking for. From newsletters to legal considerations, from patents to programs, the links on this page address the concerns and hurdles of basement tinkerers who think they've come up with the next Pocket Fisherman. The page links back to the Inventions and Innovations Gateway sponsored by the U.S. Department of Energy.

Learning-Fountain Marketing
http://www.tricky.com/lfm/index.htm

Thinking of putting your small business on the Web? How about this idea? Paul "the soaring" Siegel has developed the concept of "learning fountains." Basically, a learning fountain is a Web site that both sells a product or service and provides intellectual stimulation for its visitors—just like Mr. Siegel's site. What he's selling are a book and seminar presentation. What he's giving away are tips on how to promote your Web site and links to pages that embody his concepts. Siegel also includes a newsletter and the Niche Resource Directory to help you define your audience. Hey, there's definitely something to this learning fountain approach.

Microsoft Small Business Resource
http://www.microsoft.com/smallbiz/

As you'd expect, there are lots of plugs here for Microsoft products, but the site also includes some dandy information for small and at-home business folk, like features aptly named Start, Run, and Grow, the Accounting News Network, and the Small Business Barometer. To see if Bill Gates and his pals have any news for you, take a test run at the Small Business Resource.

National Association for the Self-Employed
http://www.membership.com/nase/

This 15-year-old nationwide organization lobbies hard in D.C. for laws favorable to the self-employed, particularly tax deductions (health insurance, home office), medical savings accounts, and independent contractor status. But NASE is more than a lobbying group; the association also provides a number of benefits, including discounts on a variety of business and personal products and services, a health insurance plan, and access to professional (fee-based) consultants. This well-designed page details all the services and benefits available to members.

National Association of Export Companies
http://www.imex.com/nexco/nexcohom.html

In business since 1965, this nonprofit organization's mission is to "act as the information provider, support clearing house, forum, network, and advocate for the exporter, export service provider, and others who seek to enhance America's trade position by increasing exports." The site includes a global calendar of trade events and a selection of targeted links covering topics such as harbor maintenance and NAFTA. The NEX-connection database, promised to be online soon, will reportedly contain over 4,500 export trade intermediaries such as agents, distributors, and wholesalers. Membership info is available online.

National Black Business Trade Association
http://www.melanet.com/nbbta/

Through its member services and Web site, the NBBTA works to bring together black business people and to "promote Black economic development through entrepreneurship." Here you'll find press releases, business links, and other useful info.

National Fraud Information Center
http://www.fraud.org/

The National Fraud Information Center is a project of the National Consumers League, "America's oldest non-profit consumer organization." This watchdog group maintains reports of fraudulent activities both on and off the Web, so this is a good place to check before you respond to any business offer. A special page for seniors highlights scams directed primarily at us older folks.

Online Small Business Workshop
http://www.sb.gov.bc.ca/smallbus/workshop/workshop.html

The Canada/British Columbia Business Service Centre posts this excellent online workshop to lead would-be entrepreneurs through the process of establishing a business from beginning to end. You'll start by exploring business opportunities, move on to marketing and financing basics, prepare a business plan and cash flow forecast, and then decide what type of legal structure is best for your business. A start-up checklist helps keep you on track.

Procurement Assistance Jumpstation
http://www.fedmarket.com/procinet.html

The U.S. government buys a lot of stuff, and this page can help you find out if you can become a government con-

tractor by providing the whats and the hows. By following the links to acquisition sites, small-, minority-, and women-owned business resources, active federal contracts, the Commerce Business Daily, military specs, and applicable laws, you'll be talking like an in-the-know specialist in no time. The page even includes links to a handful of proposal writing resources.

Sample Business Plan
http://www.kciLink.com/brc/bplan/

Palo Alto Software markets a program called Business Plan Pro, and this site contains a complete sample business plan that they prepared to illustrate the program's capabilities. If you're like me and think that the hardest part of a new writing assignment is developing the darn outline, then you'll really like this site. The outline's already done and you even have sample text to use as a template for each section. Even if you're not interested in buying the program, this page is a wonderful resource. The fine folks at Palo Alto even include downloadable versions of the business plan for both Mac and Windows platforms. Now all you have to worry about is preparing that financial data.

Seaports Infopages
http://www.seaportsinfo.com/

The import-export business depends on shipping and receiving goods via world ports, and here's a page to help you navigate those tricky waters. The Seaports Infopages includes data on shipping lines, industry news, and an industry guide. The Ports Menu isn't the daily blue-plate special at the dock dive, but a list of ports—some with links—from the Americas to the Far East.

Silver Fox Advisors
http://www.silverfox.org/

A selected group of retired business professionals (seniors all) are at your service here to help you grow and nurture your business. The initial consultation is free, and each Silver Fox sets his/her individual fees for consulting services. The site includes advisor profiles and case studies to help you decide if the Silver Foxes would be a good business investment for your endeavor.

Small and Home Based Business Links

http://www.ro.com/small_business/
homebased.html

You'll really like the interface on this index page. Each index heading—reference, franchises, opportunity, news, marketing, and services—is a virtual file drawer. Just click on the drawer and voilá, the annotated links are neatly arrayed on the page for your picking and choosing pleasure. The many good resources and informative descriptions will tempt you to browse, but if you're in a hurry, the site is fully searchable.

Small and home based business info: Small & home based franchises, business opportunities, small business reference material, info to help run & market your small or home based business, small & home based newsgroups, searching tools, services for small business, just about anything related to small & home based business can be found

The Small Business Advisor

http://www.isquare.com/

This site's packed with ads, but it includes a number of good info sources including incorporation offices by state, merchant card accounts, scam alerts, money-saving tips, time-management advice, tax considerations, direct mail … I could go on and on. To keep up with the latest, you can register for the free newsletter.

Small Business Law Center

http://www.courttv.com/legalhelp/business/

Need a confidentiality agreement, a distributorship agreement, or info on copyrights? Visit the Forms and Model Documents section of the Small Business Law Center for these and other legal documents. The site also includes advice on how to select a lawyer and a selection of links to other online small business resources.

Small Business Publicity FAQ

http://www.ibos.com/pub/ibos/prinfo.html

This suggestion-packed FAQ is a quick read, but don't let that fool you. The focus is on generating free publicity for your business by writing snappy press releases with a PR "angle." Learn how to write one and how to compose a pitch letter. Find out if you should schmooze with reporters and if you need a press kit. All this valuable advice and more comes free from Marcia Yudkin, a Boston-area professional writer.

Small Business Resource Center

http://www.webcom.com/seaquest/sbrc/
welcome.html

This site offers free reports on choosing, starting, and running a business, along with a catalog of books, tapes, and courses. The reports cover a number of business possibilities, such as how to start and operate a sports memorabilia shop, a resume service, a consulting service, and more. At the very least, you may find some good ideas here.

Small Office/Home Office (SOHO) Business Guide

http://www.backrest.com/index.html

Here's a one-stop index for business info and products, categorized under five headings: reference, marketing, on-the-Web, graphics, and software. Although several areas are still under construction, this site is already a good resource and promises to be a great one.

STAT_USA/Internet Site Economic, Trade, Business Information

http://www.stat-usa.gov/

The U.S. Department of Commerce offers this fee-based subscription service to folks who need high-powered business info. As a subscriber, you'll receive access to the National Trade Data Bank, "the U.S. Government's most comprehensive source of international trade data and export promotion information." That means you'll be privy to international market research, export opportunities, indexes of foreign and domestic companies, how-to market guides, and reports on the economic and political climates in hundreds of countries. Whew! The National Trade Data Bank is just one of the services included in this package from the Commerce Department. If you want lots of official info, this is definitely the place to check first.

Trade Compass
http://www.tradecompass.com/

Trade news, leads, and a trade library are just some of the free services at this beautifully designed and searchable site. The Marketplace feature includes country-specific info for almost every country in the world. If you need more in-depth services, subscribing to Trade Compass will give you access to live news feeds, a travel service, and a research assistant to help you identify hot business opportunities.

Trade Show Central
http://www.tscentral.com/

Exhibiting at trade shows is a good way to promote your business or service, but it's sometimes hard to locate information on the shows that would provide the most exposure to the best target group. This searchable site indexes over 10,000 shows worldwide. Once you find a show that interests you, you can request additional info. Selected shows are profiled.

University of Michigan Gopher
gopher://una.hh.lib.umich.edu/

The University of Michigan gopher indexes a number of resources for the exporter, including state export resource listings, best market reports for 12 categories, and Eastern European trade leads.

U.S. Exports Directory
http://maingate.net/us-exports.html

Here's "the most comprehensive source of U.S. export data online," with over 14,000 companies in the United States that manufacture goods or services for export. If you're looking for ideas or just want to check out the competition, this database is ready for your search queries—by product, service, company, SIC (Standard Industrial Classification) code, or state.

Vidya's Guide to Advertising on the Internet
http://www.vidya.com/add-lib/

Wow! Talk about a great service! Here's a guide to sites that will give you free ad space (and purchasable ad space). The sponsor is Vidya Media Ventures, a Web development firm, and they also include a generous library of info (demographics, surveys, links) devoted to online advertising.

Website Promoters Resource Center
http://www.wprc.com/

The Website Promoters Resource Center wants to help you design and promote your Web site (for a fee), but they're also giving away a bunch of free advice. If you're thinking about advertising your entrepreneurial effort with a Web site (and why on earth wouldn't you?), take a look at the WebSite Promoters Library, the Idea Chalkboard, and the Links Exchange for lots of do's and don'ts on online marketing.

Women's Business Resource Site
http://www.athenet.net/~ccain/

This page for female entrepreneurs includes a nice mix of advice and links covering the start-up and upkeep of your business. A list of links to women's sites and The Good Ole Girls Network bulletin board distinguish this site as a female domain.

LET THE FRESH AIR IN

Perhaps you are confused about what you want to accomplish, or you have so many interests that you can't narrow them down to just one or two.

One thing you can do to sort out the twisted thoughts is to write down everything you think you want to do, and then systematically eliminate those things that your spouse or children, your brother or cousin, *want* you to do.

JUST FOR YOU

Don't get caught in the trap of making your retirement years over for others. This time is yours! Focus entirely on what you want for yourself. Sound selfish? Well, it is! When you make the discovery that selfish isn't always "bad," you can select those activities that will fullfill *your* desires, instead of doing what you think others want you to do.

WATER YOUR GARDEN AND WATCH IT GROW

Let your creativity flower during this time. So often with the press of life, work, and meeting the needs of family, the basic creativity that we had as youngsters has gone underground. It's time to unbutton and find that most spirited and alive part of yourself again!

Instead of worrying about what you are "going to be" the second time around, write down your thoughts. Here's where your computer comes in! Each morning write three pages. Do it every day.

These "AM thoughts" may wake you up in more ways than one—to the inner voice inside that may be holding you back. If you read over the pages after a week of writing, and you can dectect a whiny, self-pitying voice, then you know that you need to slap yourself around and adjust your attitude. For negative thinking is like wearing a straightjacket, and will certainly put a damper on your enjoyment in retirement.

WORRY WARTS

You might find your pages going like a litany of worry, filled with all the day's preoccupations about what is going on in the trivial side of your life—the stove needs to be fixed, the washer leaks, the trap in the bathroom needs to be adjusted. You need to get over that. This leaves no room for creative self-expression to enter into your life.

Hopefully, you will find that you are writing thoughtful observations about the things that matter to you, about your life, nature, and the people around you. Then you can begin to think about, "What do I want to do with the rest of my life?"

OPPORTUNITIES—SMALL BUSINESSES AND FRANCHISES

BizBuySell
http://www.BizBuySell.com/
The Internet's "largest free database of businesses for sale" invites you to search its listings of established businesses, business opportunities, and franchises. If you don't find what you're looking for, activate the Search 'Bot to monitor new postings and alert you when a business meeting your criteria is listed. The site claims over 1,000 ads, but I didn't have much luck locating bars for sale in Florida or child care opportunities in California. Still, it's a great idea, the database is growing, and it's free.

Business Opportunities Handbook Online
http://www.ezines.com/
This site includes an alphabetical list of business opportunities, but I'm not too sure what you're supposed to make of it. There are no details other than the name of the company and an address. On the other hand, each entry in the List of Featured Business Opportunities includes contact info, a description of the operation, capital requirements, and other information to help you decide if you want to take the next step. The Message Board at this site includes some interesting tidbits, and feature articles cover a variety of entrepreneurial topics. Useful in some ways, but puzzling in others.

Franchise Handbook Online
http://www.franchise1.com/

Ponder the list of featured franchises (food, coffee, maid services, clothing stores, and more), browse the directory of opportunities, catch up on news about the industry, post a query on the message board, and read the "expert" articles—all at this one site devoted to future owners and operators.

FranInfo: A World of Information about Franchising
http://www.frannet.com/

This is a great site for an introduction to franchising. Not only can you read a history of the practice, but you can also take two self-tests to help determine if you're cut out for the franchise game and to help select the type of franchise that best fits your interests. Additional information includes discussions of why to buy a franchise, what to expect, and sources of help.

Internet Business Opportunities and Services
http://www.ibos.com/pub/ibos/busops.html

Here's a short list of business opportunities offered on the Net. From franchises to multilevel marketing, there may be an idea in this list that sets your wheels turning.

International Franchise Association
http://www.entremkt.com/ifa/

There's no doubt that you can make big bucks with the right franchise (just ask your local McDonald's owner), but you can also go broke. Franchises are expensive, but the big advantage of the solid ones is proven, standardized operating procedures that help eliminate the guess-

work and mistakes from day-to-day business operations. If you're in the market for a franchise opportunity, this page includes information on businesses that offer everything from accounting services to weight control. Other links include FAQ, the Women's Franchise Network, and Franchising World, the latest news stories about franchising successes and opportunities.

National Business Exchange Network
http://www.nbe.com/

This service advertises over 5,000 businesses for sale. You can search by state or access the list of relocatable businesses. From art galleries to hockey arenas to watercraft dealerships, you just might find your dream business listed in this huge database. Individual entries include location, sales price, and contact info.

HOME BODIES

What could be more rewarding than working in a virtual office? Just think of getting out of bed a full hour after you would have been, once upon a time, already on your way to the office. Sit down to work in jeans and an old shirt, and never worry about lunch money, or if there is enough gas in the car, or how bad the roads may be in the AM after a severe winter storm.

The money I have saved by basing my office at home is worth counting and thinking about: no more full tanks of gas every week, or wear-and-tear on the car in rush-hour traffic; no more $5-$10 lunches every day; no more worries about clothes that are taking a beating (not to mention their annual replacements).

Working at home is an opportunity to get out from under a dull office routine, leave corporate politics behind, and to call your own shots—from how much you want to work, to when will you start in the AM, and how late into the night you want to drudge on.

Your workload is defined not by office hours, but the time it may take you to meet your deadlines. And take heed: *Working at home is not for everyone*. It requires a lot of self-discipline, and the ability to work autonomously. If there is a lot of work to be done, or if you tend to schedule deadlines close together, your personal life may suffer and your working hours may be long. And if you enjoy the interaction afforded by "water cooler society," your working life could get lonesome.

THE HIGH HURDLES

If you don't mind the solitude, the next biggest hurdle for the home office worker is time management and self-discipline. This need for discipline can often extend to your friends, who may have a problem understanding that you are indeed really working, and cannot visit on the phone at odd hours of the day, or drop everything for spontaneous lunches or shopping expeditions.

It takes time to indoctrinate those close to you. I ultimately purchased a second telephone line with an unlisted number, so that I could still call out while my computer was connected to the Internet via my well-known telephone line. While online, my phone wouldn't ring and disturb me, but instead the calls dumped immediately into a voicemail box which I established with my local telephone company. That voicemail is really important: It takes my messages so that I can return business calls, and it's a sure sign to friends who call me during working hours that I'm indeed busy.

TAKE A BREAK

In the long run, developing a daily ritual is one of the best ways a home office worker can stay on track. When home workers run into trouble, it's generally not because they work too few hours or because they work odd hours, but because they work *too many* hours, averaging about 55 hours a week compared to the office worker's 35-40 hours. It's up to you to take a break so you don't shrivel up and burn out.

Go to the gym early in the morning, *before* you download your e-mail; take a short, brisk walk at lunchtime; in the afternoon, treat yourself to coffee at your favorite joint; or take time out at regular intervals to get up, stretch, and just walk around the house. These breaks may be the only time you mobilize or get out of the house all day.

Business@Home
http://www.gohome.com/

This monthly 'zine includes several departments and features that will interest home workers. The Family Matters section includes articles to help you assess the impact of home work on your family—whether you live with one person or several. Check out Reworking the Way We Work for tips on how to manage your time and become an efficient, self-directed worker. Other sections include Technology, Marketing, Product Reviews, Finance & Taxes, Legal, and more. Well-written articles, timely topics, good advice, and a nice interface make this 'zine a top pick for your monthly reading list.

Your Small Office
http://www.smalloffice.com/

Brought to you by the editors of *Small Business Computing* and *Home Office Computing*, this 'zine includes a number of articles and features about … using computers in your home office. Surprise! Actually, you'll find other info here, including news summaries that have nothing to do with computers, your business horoscope, cartoons, a tech expert section (with buyer's guides, demos, and software picks), advice from the marketing guru, and many more interesting features. Put this one on your bookmarks list. You'll like the 'zine's interface too.

American Association of Home-Based Businesses
http://www.aahbb.org/

This is a nonprofit organization for "those who run a business from their homes." AAHBB prominently states on its home page that the organization does not sell or endorse any business opportunities and the group is not being investigated by the Federal Trade Commission for fraudulent business practices. OK, that's a good start, but unfortunately, they don't tell you who *is* being investigated. Read the list of benefits (discounts, information services, a newsletter) to determine if the $90.00 price tag gives you a good return.

The Home Office Home Page
http://www.bankamerica.com/p-finance/ athome/ho_home.html
Bank of America wants to help you finance your home office setup, and they include info on loans and business credit cards to let you know what kind of financial help may be available. But on top of the plug for their services, the bank includes a number of articles to help you plan and design your workspace, along with some info on the tax advantages.

International Homeworkers Association
http://www.homeworkers.com/
You'll have to examine the benefits of this subscription service carefully to determine if it offers the kinds of information and help you need because it isn't free. One-, two-, five-, and ten-year plans (from $90 to $325) are available. The benefits are graduated, based on the length of your charter membership, but all plans include membership in a shopping service, access to a database of home work opportunities, several reports covering companies that use home workers, and information on becoming a successful home worker. Additional information is available via e-mail.

Chapter 9

YOU'RE NEVER TOO OLD TO LEARN

THE MIND IS A TERRIBLE THING TO WASTE

A BIGGER GAME

Even though we aren't counting birthdays, those insidious signs of aging come creeping across the threshold no matter how hard we try to push them back. The tennis knee flares up, trifocals become an important part of our daily garb, and comfortable walking shoes have replaced the pointy little heels of the past. Instead of flashing through the cleaning chores, we stop intermittently for breaks, to catch our breaths, so stamina is losing its toehold a bit. And I frequently find that on an afternoon or two I have fallen asleep in my chair, an event that would have been unheard of ten years ago.

We can do a few things to stop this inevitable process, such as eating more vegetables and less meat, eating lots of fruit and drinking plenty of water. Don't forget to take your vitamins, such as E and C, and particularly the B's. Add supplements of Beta Carotene, Zinc, Magnesium, and Calcium. And get enough rest and exercise, while curbing your alcohol and caffeine intake.

Try a little Retin-A for wrinkles and to keep your skin soft as a baby's proverbial, and use a good moisturizer to help keep the rest of your skin smooth and moist. I have heard it said that Preparation-H is fabulous to use on your face to keep wrinkles away (honest!). Lena Horne once disclosed this in a "60 Minutes" interview as one of her beauty secrets. If it can do the job for Lena, it can do it for me. The one drawback is that I don't have as much to work with as she does. Some folks rave about Cornhuskers Lotion, an old-timey potion to keep hands and limbs free from harsh drying in the winter. Both these little goodies are available at any drugstore (although you might not find Prep H in the cosmetics department!).

"Into the second month of retirement and we are having a ball! Of course, I have given him my telephone, and my kitchen, and my dust cloth, and my scrub mop; I believe in sharing!"

THE MIND IS A TERRIBLE THING TO WASTE

My own feeling is that along with all the good things we are supposed to do with our diets, exercise, and attitudes, the single most important thing that keeps us young is mental stimulation. Contrary to what many people think, our mental abilities do not have to decline with age. Properly maintained, the brain can be in tip-top condition up to ages of 100 or more.

"I am a member of AARP and a teacher in Boulder, Colorado. I teach English as a Second Language in an elementary school. Most of my students come from all over the world. Last year one of my students did an e-mail penpal exchange with my mother-in-law who also is an AARP member. It was very successful. It encouraged my student to learn how to use the computer. He also got English language practice and had a real purpose for writing. It was also a very positive experience for my mother-in-law. She was looking forward to getting mail, and being a former teacher she had fun thinking of interesting questions, etc., to ask the student. It was a win-win situation."

Researchers no longer believe that brain cells are lost as we age. Look at Albert Einstein, certainly living proof that the brain can be maintained in its highest form, no matter what your age. Researchers have also found that there is no appreciable difference in brain metabolism between healthy older brains and those of healthy young people. Creating and living in a stimulating environment can produce special supporting cells in the brain, called neurons—no matter what your age. And the brain's message-carrying cells can be enhanced at any age.

But to thrive, the brain must be challenged with creativity and exercise.

One of the ways to keep the brain in good form is to develop an inquiring mind, full of curiosity. You can do this at home, with friends, or by embarking on a course of lifelong learning, taking advantage of some of the many educational opportunities now accessible to you via the Internet.

If you're concerned that you've been away from school too long to "get the hang of it again," start doing crossword puzzles and keep your word images strong while rebuilding your vocabulary. Start with the easy ones and move up to the harder ones. Soon you'll be doing *The New York Times* puzzle like a master.

THE GAMES HAVE GOT IT

Another way to keep your mind quick and active is to play games; the logic and problem-solving involved in a good game is a terrific way to prepare for more formal learning environments. Find some bridge players. This is a stimulating game that always changes, and to be a good player, you must have your wits about you. Take lessons in a bridge class and meet some new people while brushing up on your skills. Maybe you prefer other card games or Scrabble. All of these will keep you mentally nimble. Try your hand at jigsaw puzzles, working up to the really difficult ones.

JACK BE NIMBLE

Often it's easy to single out those who have kept their minds active.

I was fortunate the other day to meet a gal who has given much to our community, establishing a really wonderful bookstore in a corner of the Salvation Army Thrift. For twenty years I have wanted to meet her, as I have been buying books of all sorts there for that long. Marian Alshier, now in her sixties, told me that she started volunteering almost as soon as she was married, donating her many talents to the community in a diversity of endeavors. At one point many years ago, she wound up as a volunteer for The Salvation Army.

While working there, she noticed an abundance of really fine books that were donated, but just propped up helter-skelter or left in boxes for patrons to rummage through. She was determined at that point to organize the books so that they could be

Lizzie's Tips

Many retirees can have a lot of trouble when they find themselves at home day after day with little to do. This can be especially difficult for men who are now at home with spouses who have been lifelong "domestic engineers." Husbands can unwittingly disrupt the household unless they have been involved in its activity all along. Some advice:

Before you retire, think of taking up a hobby with your spouse, something that you will both enjoy. And if you are the spouse who has remained outside daily household management, take some time to get familiar with it *before* you find yourself in the way of it. Think of productive ways to participate, and remember: If your wife (or, in some cases, your husband) has been managing the household for two or three decades, she (or he) probably has more than a few good reasons for doing things the way s/he does. Don't try to reinvent the wheel. Women are often better than men at realizing a happy retirement because they have spent their lives perfecting the daily tasks of living. If you're the one coming home to roost, your spouse may have some helpful (and practical) advice for you. Don't be afraid to take it!

> ### *Lizzie Sez*
> *Make the world a better place to live. Volunteer. Those who always have a place to go don't have time to sit around feeling depressed and lonely.*

> ### Lizzie's Tips
> All of us have stories to tell. Take a writing class and learn how to tell them well. You could surprise yourself with how much you know.

easily found by customers, and ultimately bring in more revenue for the charity. Bringing in shelving and tables from outside donations, Marian proceeded to catalog and categorize each book as it came in.

Being a person of method and order with a love of words, Marian maintained her small book area in a cozy, tidy, and well-organized fashion. Tables held special sale books, first editions were kept locked behind glass, and other books could be found by category. Today, Marian is in charge of one of the best secondhand book stores in this large metropolitan area.

Lois Daniel, in her seventies, has kept her mind energized by writing and editing. Some 20 years ago, after teaching a class in writing, she decided to put her lectures into a book with the knowledge that it would reach a wider audience, carrying her message about the importance of telling your family who you are.

This small quality paperback has been reprinted twenty times, and is currently in its fourth edition. *How to Write Your Own Life Story* has reached many people: from individuals just trying their hand at biographical writing, to classrooms all over the country. With families scattered around the globe, and old Aunt Clara too far away to unlock the family stories by the fire, telling your own life story is sometimes the only way that your children will ever know the roots of their heritage. Besides bringing information to her readers, Lois has also added another dimension to their lives. From that first endeavor, Lois began editing a national magazine from an office in her home. She did it all, flogging stories from histo-

rians, unearthing blurry pictures to be restored, editing and layout, right down to the beautiful cover for *The Overland Journal*, the official publication of the Oregon-California Trails Association. And even though the work was unremitting and demanding, Lois survived in good order and still has her youthful outlook on life. Today, she continues to work as a freelance writer.

Anna Dunne, age 70, from Santa Monica, California, has kept a spring in her step by dealing in antiques. Attending auctions every week, she then sells her purchases to waiting customers who depend on her knowledge and expertise to find treasures for them to add to their collections. When not at the auction houses or appraising estates, Anna can be found at a local cafe sipping a cappuccino alongside her standard poodle, Mollie. Keeping abreast of a constantly changing market, making and keeping contact with a growing clientele, and retaining the knowledge of period antiques from many countries, Anna has kept her mind sharp as a tack and her humor as quick and bright as it was when she was young.

A BIGGER GAME

Classes in anything you can think of abound in every community, from informal lessons in flower arranging hosted by a local florist, to full-scale university degrees in both on- and off-campus settings.

At this age we certainly qualify as unconventional students, and can often call our own shots for the classes we wish to take. For example, the University of Mississippi in Oxford offers senior citizens one free class each semester. And many colleges will offer you an option to audit classes, those you wish to take but don't want to complete for a grade.

Or if you want to complete a degree that has languished for years, instead of taking classes at random, you can save time and money by earning a non-traditional degree. At this point does it matter if you don't pursue a traditional course of study? Check with your state's education department, or the admissions offices of local universities or community colleges. You can also check the Web sites listed below, or try these avenues:

- Some schools will award college credits through exams. You could max out as many as 30 credits just by taking a few examinations. That amounts to a whole year of study!

- Many schools will give credit for life experience. If you speak Russian, draw landscape maps, or have managed your own business, for example, you can often apply for credit in these areas.

- Look into traditional correspondence schools. You could get full credit for each course by just passing the final exam.

Two schools that specialize in non-traditional degrees are The University of the State of New York in Albany, 518-464-8500; and Edison State College in Trenton, New Jersey, 609-984-1100. These schools offer courses, administer exams, and award fully accredited degrees to non-traditional students.

If you've always wanted to complete your Master's degree and haven't had the time or money, check out Syracuse University in New York, 315-443-3284. This fine school offers an option in some Masters programs for students to attend three eight-day summer seminars a year apart. Doesn't this sound like fun? A little like your own Elderhostel, which of course is another learning option.

Other schools offering non-traditional Masters programs are:

- Empire State College in New York, 518-587-2100

- California State University in Los Angeles, 310-516-3743

If you're going for the big bang, these two schools offer good non-traditional Ph.D. programs:

- Union Graduate School in Cincinnati, Ohio, 513-861-6400 or 800-486-3116

- Nova University in Fort Lauderdale, Florida, 305-475-7300

The food chain for education is endless, starting with learning to make potholders, to earning a doctoral degree. It all depends on you. The Web sites below should give you some insight into choosing your own direction. You can't start learning too soon.

LEARNING RESOURCES WORLDWIDE

ABZU: Guide to Resources for the Study of the Ancient Near East Available on the Internet

http://www-oi.uchicago.edu/OI/DEPT/RA/ABZU/ABZU.HTML

Compiled by the Oriental Institute in Chicago, this incredible index includes pointers to archaeological sites, museum collections, journals, library catalogs, and book publishers—all dealing with the ancient areas of North Africa and the Middle East. Finding ABZU is like locating a long-buried tomb in the Valley of Kings. The entrance isn't at all imposing, but the treasures inside defy description. The archaeology list alone in the Egyptian index includes links to info about Nubian wall paintings and to several excavations, including those at Abydos and Giza. And that's just one page! From there, go to art, language, papyrology, and more…it's fabulous.

Adult Education & Distance Learner's Resource Center
http://homepages.together.net/~lifelong//dlsites.html
Catch the "shuttle bus" to Online Colleges and Training Institutes for a look at the colleges and universities currently offering courses and degrees through distance learning. All courses and programs listed use varying degrees of online technology; some are available completely online.

Basic Spanish for the Virtual Student
http://www.umr.edu/~amigos/Virtual/
Whether you're planning a trip to Mexico or just want to compliment the chef at your favorite eatery on the sublimity of his chilies rellenos, the 50+ Spanish-language modules at this site will go a long way toward giving you a good background in the lingo.

Bipo & Toni's Spanish School
http://www.qni.com/~mj/bipotoni/bipotoni.html
So once you've finished your virtual Spanish lessons, how about some in-depth instruction in Quito, Ecuador? Bipo & Toni run a total-immersion language school in South America; students receive private lessons and can choose between 20, 25, 30, or 35 lessons per week. You'll stay with specially chosen Ecuadorian families to enhance the cultural exchange and learning environment.

Canadian Universities
http://watserv1.uwaterloo.ca/~credmond/univ.html
This site alphabetically indexes members of the Association of Universities and Colleges of Canada and links visitors to the schools' online resources, if any. Also available here are Canadian university phone books, online news, and links to other universities around the globe. In English and French.

Czech Language and Culture Programs in the Czech Republic
http://www.owlnet.rice.edu/~worm/crlangprog.html
If your ancestral roots lie in Eastern Europe or you've always been fascinated by the city of Prague, this compilation of links to programs in the Czech Republic will set you to dreaming about all you could see and learn there.

Chemeketa Online
http://www.chemek.cc.or.us/chemeketa/onlineed.html
The distance education division of Oregon's Chemeketa Community College offers Internet-based college courses and degree programs. Having proved a success for the past eight years in cultivating a virtual educational environment, the college is currently upgrading its system to offer newer and even better online services.

City University
http://hal.cityu.edu/inroads/welcome.htp
Based in Bellevue, Washington, City University claims the world as its campus and offers its students EDROADS, the Education Resource and Online Academic Degree System. The university's MBA programs are currently available online with other programs soon to follow. Traditional distance learning and weekend courses are also available.

CNU Online
http://cnuonline.cnu.edu/
Christopher Newport University in Newport News, Virginia, offers selected upper- and lower-level online courses in the humanities, mathematics, and the sciences. Currently, the bachelor of science in governmental administration degree can be earned online as well. Other degrees will be available in the future.

College and University Home Pages
http://www.shu.edu/docs/world/schools/univ.html
A volunteer online consultant at MIT provides this directory that offers links to institutions all over the world.

The schools are listed alphabetically and geographically. Links to mirror sites of this resource are also provided to facilitate faster access for users.

CollegeNET
http://www.collegenet.com/cnmain.html

Browse a database of college and university listings or search the entries based on criteria such as location, enrollment, and tuition. Compare schools using the CollegeNET "At-A-Glance" profiles, check into financial aid options, and request more information from colleges online.

Connecting With Nature
http://www.pacificrim.net/~nature/

Psychology and ecology are integrated at Project Nature-Connect. Begin a free e-mail course of personal therapy that focuses on reestablishing a bond with nature to catalyze wellness, spirit, and responsibility. Links emphasize self-help philosophy, counseling, and education.

Commonwealth Open University
http://www.geocities.com/CollegePark/5703/

Offering "non-resident" degree programs for the continuing adult student, COU has no entry qualifications except a desire to learn. Review the online catalog of course offerings (art, humanities, mathematics, and science) and explore whether a virtual learning experience is right for you.

Communication Connections
http://www.widomaker.com/~ldprice/

This extraordinary site was compiled and is maintained by the faculty and students of Gloucester High School in Virginia. Communication Connections is an index of Web sites "dedicated to the study, use, and sheer enjoyment of languages." The site features menus devoted entirely to French, Spanish, Latin/Italian, Japanese, and German resources. Then, under the Multilingual category, you'll find links to general language sites, organizations, and other language indexes.

Community College Gophers
gopher://gopher1.faytech.cc.nc.us/11c%3a/ccgofers

Maintained by the Fayetteville Technical Community College, this gopher site links to the gopher sites at community colleges across the United States. Pointers are sorted and available for browsing by state, although a complete U.S.A. list is available along with a list of links to colleges in Canada.

Community College Web
http://www.mcli.dist.maricopa.edu/cc/

Search alphabetically, geographically, or by college name this extensive database offering pointers to half of the 1,000-plus community colleges in the United States. (The other half apparently don't have Web pages yet.) Also find a collection of information resources of interest to both student and teacher. The CC Web is provided by the Maricopa Center for Learning and Instruction of the Maricopa Community Colleges.

Computer Assisted Learning Center (CALC)
http://www.calcampus.com/

Having served the international adult, college, and high school student since 1986, CALC offers online instruction and courses in all the major subject areas: English, mathematics, science, social studies, computer programming and technology, foreign language, general studies, and business. Courses are designed to offer support for high school study, job skills enhancement, continuing education, and preparation for college credit examination.

Connected Education: Online Courses for College Credit
**http://www.cinti.com/connect-ed/
WELCOME.HTM**

Earn an M.A. in Creative Writing from the United Kingdom's Bath College of Higher Education, an M.A. in Media Studies from New York City's New School for Social Research, or take graduate level courses from Polytechnic University of New York. Opened in 1985, Connect Ed boasts having offered more than 300 graduate and undergraduate classes and serving over 2,000 students from around the world.

CyberED
**http://www.umassd.edu/cybered/
distlearninghome.html**

Hosted by the Division of Continuing Education at the University of Massachusetts at Dartmouth, and the University of Massachusetts at Lowell, CyberEd offers lower-level classes as basic as composition and general chemistry, plus upper-level courses as advanced as literary criticism and human resource management. Both non-credit and for-credit online courses are available.

Digital Campus
http://www.linkmag.com/

Digital Campus is a comprehensive set of links that provides news and information on American colleges and universities. Visitors can link directly to higher education facility Web servers.

Directory of Electronic Text Centers
**http://cethmac.princeton.edu/CETH/
elcenter.html**

Find out where you can read books online. This directory offers pointers to schools and libraries that maintain hypertext archives.

Distance Education Clearinghouse
http://www.uwex.edu:80/disted/home.html

Look into the prospect of participating in distance learning programs in the state of Wisconsin by visiting this information server from the University of Wisconsin-Extension. Among the many items available, find a catalog of distance learning programs and a profile of extended degree programs.

Dun & Bradstreet Online University
http://www.uol.com/dnb/

Another service from one of the biggest names in information services, the D&B Online University is dedicated to providing today's professionals with continuing education programs from leading, accredited institutions around the world.

Ecola's College Locator
http://www.ecola.com/college/

Locate the Web home page for colleges and universities in each of the 50 United States. Search by name or browse by state; the database, which also includes library and alumni pages, contains over 2,500 links and continues to grow.

Educational Courses on the Web
http://lenti.med.umn.edu/~mwd/courses.html

Here's a list of virtual courses offered on the Internet. Visitors can search for courses by category and academic discipline; however, most are related to the sciences.

The Elderhostel Home Page
http://www.elderhostel.org/

Keep expanding your horizons through short, inexpensive programs of study at educational institutions around the globe. Live on college campuses, in field stations, or at study centers—wherever your course work takes you—and enjoy the stimulation of formal-informal study. Check out the Elderhostel catalog to learn more about the programs available and how to sign up.

English 210E: Technical Writing
http://itrc.uwaterloo.ca/~engl210e/

Paul Beam at the University of Waterloo in Waterloo, Ontario, Canada, directs this second-year course in technical writing. The course is conducted on and off campus simultaneously, and offered entirely over the World Wide Web.

English 231: Technical Writing Online

http://fur.rscc.cc.tn.us/TechWrit/
techhome.html

Jennifer Jordan-Henley of Roane State Community College in Tennessee attempts to focus students' attention on the similarities in technical writing for different fields. This online course helps students develop both writing and presentation skills.

English 201: Nonfiction Writing—A Virtual Semester

http://www.idbsu.edu/vcampus/

Chuck Guilford of Boise State University serves as instructor for this writing course. Examine the uses and forms of nonfiction as a means of communication.

The FAMILYHOSTEL Program

http://www.learn.unh.edu/INTERHOSTEL/IH_
FH.html

Designed for parents, grandparents, and schoolagers 8-15 years old, FAMILYHOSTEL offers the family unparalleled 10-day summer learning adventures in foreign countries around the world. Take in the culture, recreate, see sights, and bring home something more valuable than just souvenirs! What a great experience for you and your grandchildren.

Gaelic Languages Information

http://futon.sfsu.edu/~jtm/Gaelic/

There's no denying the lyrical quality of spoken Gaelic, but have you ever seen it in written form? Yow! The words look unpronounceable; they're composed almost entirely of consonants. But don't let all those consonants stop you from learning more about this ancient speech and gaining some insight into your Celtic heritage. The excellent collection of links on this page can point you in the right direction. Along with various language resources, you'll find classes, organizations, online Gaelic texts, and bookstores that carry Irish-language books.

German Studies Trails on the Internet

http://www.uncg.edu/~lixlpurc/german.html

Andreas Lixl-Purcell, Professor of German at the University of North Carolina at Greensboro, has provided this list of links to German resources on the Web. Exercises, teaching tools, and laboratory links will have you reading Goethe in the original in no time.

Global Network Academy

http://www.gnacademy.org:8001/uu-gna/
index.html

Dedicated to providing a comprehensive resource, GNA maintains a database for locating online courses and degree programs available around the world. Listing over 2,000 courses in 25 subject areas, GNA's catalog can be searched by academic subject area or school.

Hebrew: A Living Language

http://www.macom.co.il/hebrew/index.html

Do you know how to say thank you in Hebrew? How about please, or how are you, or see you later? You can learn these words and more by clicking on the Useful Hebrew Words hyperlink on this page. Then click on the word and hear it pronounced. Phrases, question words, numbers, verb conjugations, and more are also included in this basic intro to Hebrew.

History 101: History of Western Civilization

http://www.idbsu.edu/courses/hy101/
index0.htm

Dr. E.L. Skip Knox of Boise State University leads this survey course that traces European history from ancient times to the early modern era. Learn from the ancients why we do what we do today.

History 366: Western Canada Since 1870

http://www.ualberta.ca/~histclas/hist366.htm

Bob Hesketh and Chris Hackett at Canada's University of Alberta lead this exploration of Canadian history.

Interface Technologies Online Training Center

http://www.iftech.com/oltc/

Interface Technologies, Inc. hosts this collection of free, online tutorials developed to help interested users master various computer-related skills. Among other topics, learn Java, C++, and how to develop Web applications. Written for use by anyone with an interest in and a solid understanding of computers.

The INTERHOSTEL Program
http://www.learn.unh.edu/INTERHOSTEL/IH_FH.html

Catering to the adult over 50, INTERHOSTEL organizes two- and three-week learning adventures that explore sights all over the world. Enjoy mini-lectures while you take in the local color and culture of regions you've only read about in books. Request a catalog, select one of over 50 trips, then pack your bags and conquer the world!

International Centre for Distance Learning
http://acacia.open.ac.uk/Online.html

Located at the United Kingdom's Open University, the International Centre for Distance Learning hosts a free database cataloging over 31,000 distance-taught courses from over 900 teaching institutions worldwide. Some courses are basic, others advanced; some online, others not. Easy-to-follow instructions help users search the database which is available via telnet.

Internet College Exchange
http://www.usmall.com/

Need contact information for a school you're interested in attending? Search this database for the names, addresses, and phone numbers of over 5,000 U.S. colleges and universities offering undergraduate, graduate, and/or distance learning programs. E-mail addresses are also available where possible.

JEC Knowledge Online
http://www.jec.edu/

Whether your interests are in earning a degree or just learning something new, Jones Education Company may have a program or product for you. Visit the company's home page to explore its College Connection degree programs, review its TV Program Guide of educational shows, and browse its Knowledge Store of learning products.

Jôyô 96 Japanese Study System Home Page
http://members.aol.com/Joyo96/index96.html

This site promises to be "your passport to mastering written Japanese (Katakana, Hiragana, and the Kanji)." Sounds like a tall order, but think how fun and interesting it will be to learn the delicate calligraphy of Japanese. The lessons are free, although supplemental products are offered for sale.

J.U.I.C.E.—Jewish University in CyberspacE
http://www.wzo.org.il/juice/index.htm

Free online courses covering Jewish theology, social issues, history, and more are available from the J.U.I.C.E. Find a brief description of each course at this site, along with contact information and convening dates.

The Logical World of Etymology
http://www.phoenix.net/~melanie/thelogic.htm

Here's a great introduction to etymology—the study of the origins of words (not bugs). Follow along as your erudite Webmaster looks at Greek affixes, Latin roots, and 13 ways that words are created. Check out the Origin of the Alphabet feature and e-mail a query to find out when your favorite word was born. A good selection of etymology-related links leads you to other resources and additional study.

Metropolitan State College of Denver
http://www.mscd.edu/~options/internet.htm

Select from a variety of 100-level courses including Freshman Composition and introduction theory for statistics, criminal justice, technical writing, and more. Some upper-level classes—including accounting and other business-related subjects—are also available for online study.

MIT Biology Hypertextbook
http://esg-www.mit.edu:8001/esgbio/7001main.html

Learn biology over the Web using this "hypertextbook" developed by the Experimental Study Group at the Massachusetts Institute of Technology. Find instructional text, practice problems, and self-administered quizzes. Virtual students can also contact tutors online.

Mindquest: Online High School Education for Adults

http://www.mindquest.bloomington.k12.mn.us/

You always said you were going to go back and earn your diploma. Now there's no reason not to. Enroll in the "world's first" public high school diploma program that uses the Internet exclusively and earn that degree online, in the comfort of your own home. Go ahead. You can do it.

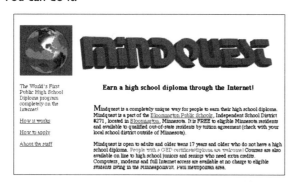

Music Schools

http://stimpy.music.ua.edu/features/addresses.html

Maintained by the University of Alabama School of Music, this online phone book lists music schools found in each of the 50 United States and a few in Canada. Each entry features the school's name, the city and zip code where it's located, and a phone number. Some entries also include street addresses for the schools.

National Extension College

http://www.nec.ac.uk/

Providing distance learning courses that offer full tutor support, this United Kingdom institution brings the college to you. Course offerings range from personal-enhancement to serious study, and cover arts, crafts, disciplines, and trades.

National Outdoor Leadership School

http://www.nols.edu/

The National Outdoor Leadership School is a nonprofit institution—with eight branches in seven countries—dedicated to teaching wilderness-oriented skills and leadership. Visitors to this organizational site can explore the course guide and discover general information about the school. In English and Spanish.

New York Institute of Technology On-Line Campus

http://sunp.nyit.edu/olc/

Through its online curriculum, the New York Institute of Technology awards a bachelor of arts in interdisciplinary studies as well as bachelor of science degrees in business administration, interdisciplinary studies, and behavioral sciences. Students can also apply for credit based on prior learning experiences.

OnLine Education: The Electronic Campus

http://hka.online.edu/newpages/home.htm

Combining cutting-edge technology with first-class courses, OnLine Education helps its student-clients remove the barriers that have kept them from pursuing their formal education. Visit this site to check into the accredited undergraduate and graduate degree programs offered through the company's Electronic Campus.

The Open University (Florida)

http://www.openu.com/

This "virtual university," founded in 1987, concentrates on offering programs to help its students become successful entrepreneurs and self-employed professionals. Using a success-driven and practical approach, the school caters to its students' diverse needs by offering classes through its Graduate School of Business & Entrepreneurship, College of Business & Entrepreneurship, and Center for Business & Professional Development.

The Open University (U.K.)

http://www.open.ac.uk/

Founded in 1969, the United Kingdom's Open University is literally open to any adult in the U.K. or any E.U. member state and has no entry requirements for most of its courses. Visit this site to review information about the school's degree programs and studying via the Internet.

P103 General Psychology Course
http://www.indiana.edu/~iuepsyc/
P103Psyc.html

Whether you register for credit or take it on your own, this intro to psych is taught entirely over the Web. Purchase the textbook at your local bookstore (or from the Indiana University bookstore) and then settle in with the reading assignments and exercises. You'll end up with a good general understanding of basic concepts.

PBS Adult Learning Service Online
http://www.pbs.org/als/

Discover exactly what the Adult Learning Service is and does, and how it fits into the organization of the Public Broadcasting Service. While on-site check into ALS's programs, online forums, and services.

PBS ALSO: College Credit
http://www.pbs.org/college/

Find out how to join the 375,000 people who each year earn college credit from home by taking PBS telecourses. Take a self-quiz, see a telecourse, read what students have to say, then...review the course catalog and go for it!

Peterson's Education Center
http://www.petersons.com/

Provided by Peterson's Guides Inc., one of the premier education information publishers in the United States, this Education Center offers a collection of Web resources for all educational levels. Link areas include K-12, colleges & universities, graduate study, studying abroad, executive education, summer programs, language study, and distance learning.

Simon Fraser University Centre for Distance Education
http://labmac2.cstudies.sfu.ca/

Canada's Simon Fraser University uses this site to spotlight its programs that cater to part-time and nontraditional students. Information about courses, degree programs, and admissions can be found right here.

Spectrum Virtual University
http://pacificnet.net/campus/

Sign up for and participate in free, noncredit online courses that range in diversity from Web page design to personal goal setting to creative writing. Those with special talents are also encouraged to develop new courses to offer.

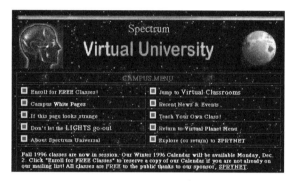

studyabroad.com
http://www.studyabroad.com/

If you've always wanted to have an overseas educational experience, this page will give you lots of choices. It lists thousands of study-abroad programs in more than 100 countries and includes hundreds of links to study-abroad program home pages. From language study in Beijing to history and literature in Ireland, the world is your classroom—limited only by your checkbook and your stamina.

Texas State Technical College's Distance Education Classes
http://surf.tstc.edu/~rpursley/remote.html

Curious about programming languages? Here are a half dozen courses worth looking into. Learn HTML, Java, Perl, and Unix. If you find something you like, you can enroll online.

University Links: Adult Education
http://www-net.com/univ/list/adult.html

Link to over 50 schools, institutes, and universities offering programs and courses geared to the adult student.

Find skill training, studies in various disciplines, and self-enrichment programs.

University of New Orleans— Metropolitan College

http://www.uno.edu/~meco/Welcome.html

The Division of Continuing Education at UNO offers credit and noncredit courses at five off-campus locations as well as the main lakefront campus, telecourses, and International Study Programs. The programs include academic, professional enhancement, leisure, and children's courses.

University of Phoenix Online Campus

http://www.uophx.edu/online/

Arguably one of the most successful online academic programs, UOP's Online Campus offers accredited graduate and undergraduate degrees in business, management, and technology. Certificate programs in strategic management and human resource practices are also available.

University of Tennessee Division of Continuing Studies and Distance Education

http://web.ce.utk.edu/

Promoting lifelong learning, this division at Knoxville's UT campus develops and delivers diverse educational opportunities that include independent studies and community programs.

University of South Carolina— Continuing Education

http://www.midnet.sc.edu/conted/
adulted.htm

Take standard or accelerated classes in the evenings, attend on weekends, or study at home. The flexibility of the University of South Carolina's continuing education program works around a student's busy schedule and offers degrees in more than 400 disciplines from the university's 18 academic colleges.

University Online, Inc.

http://www.uol.com/

Earn academic credits at leading U.S. universities such as George Washington University and Park College. UOL offers students a wide array of online academic programs and courses in business, technology, sciences, language arts, and basic skills.

The University Pages

http://isl-garnet.uah.edu/Universities/

Tour the college and university campuses of the United States. Available in two versions, the pages can be accessed via a map-based interface or a frames-enhanced presentation.

University Without Walls

http://don.skidmore.edu/administration/uww/
Skidmore/index.html

An extension of New York state's Skidmore College, the University Without Walls offers an external degree program for adults. Earn a B.A. or B.S. in a range of disciplines. To find out what makes UWW a "unique experience," apply for acceptance, look into financial aid, and visit with advisors. Stop by this page for directional pointers.

U.S. Universities and Community Colleges

http://www.utexas.edu/world/univ/

Maintained at the University of Texas Web Central, this page offers a direct link to U.S. university and community college home pages. Offering two distinct directories, the page allows users to search both the university and the community college databases either alphabetically or by state.

Virtual Media Lab

http://philae.sas.upenn.edu/

This site contains online teaching materials and resources for academic disciplines such as art history, English, religious studies, and languages. The media lab is sponsored and maintained by the University of Pennsylvania.

Virtual Online University

http://www.athena.edu/

Also known as Athena University, VOU offers liberal arts programs (and courses) presented via a virtual education environment. Advertising its offerings as "Education for the 21st Century," the young university (opened 1995) is currently under consideration for accreditation.

Virtual Seminar in Global Political Economy

http://csf.colorado.edu/gpe/

A unique offering coordinated by Lev Gonick, currently a dean at California State Polytechnic University in Pomona, this upper-division undergraduate/graduate seminar seeks to bring students from around the world together for a directed study in the nuances and gross applications of global political economics.

Western Michigan University Division of Continuing Education

http://www.wmich.edu/conted/

Offering 26 degree and certification programs, and courses for credit through all six of the university's academic colleges, the Division of Continuing Education at Western Michigan University serves its student population via five regional centers located around the state and four offices on the main Kalamazoo campus. Many accelerated weekend-only format courses are available for full academic credit.

World Lecture Hall

http://www.utexas.edu/world/lecture/

This free resource allows users to link to the lecture notes, student projects, and class resources developed for a diverse subject catalog of university courses from across the United States. The home pages for some self-directed and online courses are also featured. A built-in search function affords easy access to the World Lecture Hall's vast stores of data.

WorldWide Classroom

http://www.worldwide.edu:80/

Whether you're in search of university study, adult enrichment, foreign language immersion programs or something other, this compilation of programs may just have what you're looking for. Find intercultural and educational programs from around the globe presented for easy reference by country of origin, program type, and type of school.

World-Wide Web Virtual Library: Education

http://www.csu.edu.au/education/library.html

This searchable, comprehensive list of links points to education resources and sites across the Internet. Links are categorized for quick reference alphabetically, by education level, resource provided, site type, and country.

WWW Resources for French as A Second Language Learning

http://www.uottawa.ca/~weinberg/
french.html

The best way to handle those snooty French waiters at EuroDisney is to talk the talk. If you've always wanted to learn French or just want to brush up on rusty skills, this page from the University of Ottawa is *à votre service*. Not only will you find grammar exercises and an interactive verb conjugator, but also a French-English dictionary, travel phrases, and fables to read *en français*.

Yemen Language Center International Office

http://www.ylcint.com/

If Arabic language and culture appeal to you, take a look at the programs offered by the Yemen Language Center. Full information about the courses of study in the "Land of the Queen of Sheba" and online registration are available at this site. You'll love the background, too; it looks like sand.

ZDNet University

http://www.zdu.com/

Offering computer courses for every level of user, ZDU allows students to learn online at their own pace. Among other areas of interest, learn programming languages and explore how to become a Webmaster.

Chapter 10

GOOFING OFF (OR JUST PLAIN HAVING FUN)

TOMES AND OPUSES—TURN THE PAGE SLOWLY

A LITTLE TOE TAPPING, MAESTRO

COOKING, CRAFTING, AND LIVING

DIGGIN' IN THE DIRT

THE VIRTUAL HOBBYIST

HOLLYWOOD, HERE I COME

THE BLUES YOU CAN USE

OUR BEST FRIENDS

Almost everyone has a passion for something that takes them out of the ordinariness of their daily lives. Some of us are fanatics for model trains, others for stamp collecting, and thousands of us are addicted to photography, cooking, and crafts. Those who garden seem to find a sense of peace and release from stress by digging in the dirt.

Hobbies have historically sustained us in the dark periods of our lives, and some of us have even turned our hobbies into businesses, bringing us both pleasure and income in one lifelong endeavor. The site below will give you an overview of some hobbies that are important to us, and then we'll take up the whole enchilada!

Hobbies
http://www.cs.fsu.edu/projects/group12/
hobbies.html
Visitors will find pages about assorted hobbies from this index. Links send people to sites on amateur radio, aquariums, cooking, home breweries, model railroads, and more. It was created as a class project for a course in navigating the Net at Florida State University.

TOMES AND OPUSES—
TURN THE PAGE SLOWLY

My favorite thing to do is pick up a mystery story and spend a rainy day transported to a foreign land peopled with dangerous spies and spine tingling adventure, or unraveling a bloody murder and getting acquainted with a new hero or heroine. I can no longer go to sleep at night without turning a few pages, and more often than not, I find myself awakened at 3:00 a.m. with the light still on and my glasses lost in the pillow. Books are wonderful companions, slaking our thirst for knowledge and keeping us entertained.

BOOKS ON THE WEB

Alex: A Catalogue of Electronic Texts on the Internet
gopher://rsl.ox.ac.uk/11/lib-corn/hunter
This easy-to-browse gopher server helps visitors find and retrieve full-text documents. The index links to over 700 books and shorter texts from Project Gutenberg, Wiretap, the On-line Book Initiative, the Eric system at Virginia Tech, the English server at Carnegie Mellon, and the online portion of the Oxford Text Archive. Search by author and title.

Amazon.com Books
http://www.amazon.com
Claiming to be "Earth's biggest bookstore," Amazon.com serves up a searchable database of "one million titles," from bestsellers to small presses, from sizzling mysteries to the how-to's of killer Web design—*all* available for order online. As much as I love to browse the shelves of my local bookstore, when it's pouring down rain or three o'clock in the morning and I've just *got* to buy a book, this is my favorite store.

Antiquarian Booksellers' Association of America
http://www.clark.net/pub/rmharris/abaa.html
The Antiquarian Booksellers' Association of America specializes in old, rare books, maps, and prints. Visitors here will find lists of ABAA bookstores, bookfairs, and online catalogs.

Association of American University Presses
http://aaup.pupress.princeton.edu/
The Association of American University Presses (AAUP) is compiling a database of book titles from 100 academic presses and soon expects to offer over 100,000 titles. Visitors can search the database and order books, or link to individual university press pages.

Audio Bookstore @ The Storyteller

http://www.audio-books.com/

Don't have the time to sit down and read a book? Check these virtual bookshelves to see if you can listen to that novel instead. Stop by for news about recent releases, ordering details, or to sample sections of audio books using RealAudio software.

Baen Books

http://www.baen.com/

A small publisher well-known to science fiction and fantasy fans, Baen Books shows off its stuff here. Those who check out the page can read general information about the publisher, preview chapters from upcoming titles, link to author pages, and browse the online catalog.

Banned Books On-line

http://www.cs.cmu.edu/People/spok/banned-books.html

You're mature enough to handle it; read a banned book and see if you can figure out what all the turned up noses, wagging fingers, and withering words were aimed at! You may be surprised by some of the titles on the list such as the Bible, Twain's *Tom Sawyer* and *Huckleberry Finn*, and George Eliot's *Silas Marner*.

Bantam-Doubleday-Dell Online

http://www.bdd.com/

BDD Online features news and press releases from mega-publisher Bantam-Doubleday-Dell. New titles, reviews, and author interviews dot this electronic literary landscape, along with a daily puzzle and horoscope.

Bookport

http://www.bookport.com/welcome/bookport/point/

Link to publishers, online booksellers, and resources for marketing books online. Or, look into the offerings which were chosen by the Webmaster to delight the site's readers. Find recent discoveries, topical reading lists, and literary experiments.

Books @ Random

http://www.randomhouse.com/

Publishing power Random House hosts an online look at its company news and latest literary offerings at this corporate site. Search a catalog of available titles, browse a current list of new releases, or find out how to connect with authors online and elsewhere.

BookWeb

http://www.ambook.org/

Sponsored by the American Booksellers Association, BookWeb offers timely information about books and the venues that sell them. The site's offerings include bookstore directories, book reviews, author information, and the chance to enter a monthly contest.

BookWire

http://www.bookwire.com/

BookWire is an extensive guide to books and book-related resources on the Internet. Visit this site for book reviews, bestseller lists, and an online reading room. Listings of book events and educational resources are also among the wealth of data provided.

CCAT's Public Archive

gopher://ccat.sas.upenn.edu:70/11/Archive/

The Center for Computer Analysis of Texts at the University of Pennsylvania hosts this—one of the largest—collection of online texts. Offerings span the ages from classical texts to modern fiction and poetry. Among the authors featured find Sophocles, Chaucer, Shakespeare, Dickens, and Yeats.

Creating A Celebration of Women Writers

http://www.cs.cmu.edu/People/mmbt/women/celebration.html

Hosted by Mary Mark Ockerbloom, this "special" exhibition points to sites which archive e-text editions of works by women writers. A work in progress, this evolving directory also offers instructions for submitting work to be included.

Cowboy Poetry

http://agricomm.com/agricomm/cp

The spirit of the Old West lives through this offering of poems and prose which celebrate the uniquely American cowboy mystique. Information about Cowboy Poetry events around the country is also corralled for those who've a hankering to attend and lend an ear or a line.

Del Rey Books Home Page

http://www.randomhouse.com/delrey/

A science fiction and fantasy publishing house, Del Rey Books provides an online catalog of its titles, sample chapters, and news of its upcoming publications. The site also includes links to the current featured title, a newsletter, a gallery of covers, and guidelines for submitting unsolicited works.

The Electronic Text Center at the University of Virginia

http://etext.lib.virginia.edu/uvaonline.html

Browse, access, and read (provided you know the language) various texts in English, French, German, Latin, and Japanese. Publicly accessible offerings in English are divided into two collections: Modern and Middle English. Also find British poetry, religious resources, and links to other e-text servers.

The English Server at CMU

http://english.hss.cmu.edu/

A cooperative offering of Carnegie Mellon University's students, faculty and staff, this server has over 21,500 files in the humanities which include art, architecture, drama, fiction, poetry, history, political theory, cultural studies, philosophy, women's studies, and music. Find creative works (novels, short fiction, drama, and poetry), research, articles, historical texts, and much, much more.

Fiction Addiction

http://www.iol.ie/~westrock/fiction/

Readers craving a fix of new titles can turn to the Fiction Addiction page for reviews and recommendations sorted by title, genre, or writer. Mailing lists keep readers current on all featured new material; author interviews feed the hunger for behind-the-scenes information.

Houghton Mifflin

http://www.hmco.com/

Select which division of the publishing house to explore, then link to the School Division, HM Interactive, the Trade and Reference Division, McDougal Littell, or the Riverside Publishing Company. Wander through virtual bookstores, read excerpts of recently published books, link to discussion groups, learn about the authors, and learn about the company wherever your linking leads.

Information SuperLibrary

http://www.mcp.com/index.html

The Information SuperLibrary is the online home of Macmillan Publishing USA, the world's largest producer of computer programming and Internet books, and which also produces popular brand names such as Betty Crocker, Burpee, and Weight Watchers. The site provides access to the MCP catalog, as well as reference tools, downloadable software, and general Internet search tools.

The Internet Book Information Center

http://sunsite.unc.edu/ibic/IBIC-homepage.html

Claiming all rights as "the first book-related 'megasite' on the Web," this "granddaddy" remains a premier resource for book news and views collected or written with the book enthusiast in mind. Linked to "the best information" on the Web, the center points readers to authors and publishers, fiction and poetry, online archives and libraries, reviews, who's whos, and readers' writings, too.

Internet Wiretap

gopher://wiretap.spies.com:70/11/Books

From Twain to Stoker and the CIA to the Bible, this gopher offers a stunning variety of full-text books, stories, and documents online.

John Wiley & Sons

http://www.wiley.com/

John Wiley & Sons publishes books and electronic products for the educational, professional, scientific, technical, and consumer markets. Its home page offers a company profile and history, an online catalog, and ordering information.

Knopf Publishing Group

http://www.randomhouse.com/knopf/
index.html

A division of Random House Publishing, The Knopf Publishing Group posts news and promotes its "many outstanding books and authors" here. Find out what's new and upcoming from the group's five imprints: Alfred A. Knopf, Inc., Pantheon Books, Schocken Books, Vintage Books, and Everyman's Library.

Online Book Initiative

gopher://gopher.std.com/11/obi

Read any good writing lately? If not, then you've not been by this gopher server, where browsers can download works from writers, thinkers, and speakers ranging from Aesop to Martin Luther King, and John Stuart Mill to William Butler Yeats. Offering an extensive collection of freely distributable texts, OBI also provides links to newsletters, libraries, images, and a host of other subject-oriented offerings.

Online Books FAQ

http://www.cs.indiana.edu/metastuff/
bookfaq.html

Visit this site to review a Frequently Asked Questions (FAQ) file "addressing the availability of public domain sources of e-texts." The site also includes links to public domain archive sites.

The On-line Books Page

http://www.cs.cmu.edu/books.html

Search or browse by author or title an index of more than 2,400 English language works available online. Also find a subject listing selection and a listing of new books. This excellent resource is the work of John Mark Ockerbloom and also features a directory of links to general English, foreign language, and specialty e-text repositories.

Prentice Hall

http://www.prenhall.com/

A division of Simon & Schuster, the Prentice Hall publishing company maintains this interactive site allowing visitors to search the company's titles by keyword and subject category. Links to the publisher's FTP site and software library are also featured.

Project Gutenberg

ftp://uiarchive.cso.uiuc.edu/pub/etext/
gutenberg/pg_home.html

Dedicated to serving 99% of the computing public around the world, Project Gutenberg archives "plain vanilla" e-text editions of the world's greatest books and documents for free use and distribution. Search and access the repository by author and title, find out how to become involved in the project, or link to other e-text archives.

Publishers' Catalogues Home Page

http://www.lights.com/publisher/

Publishers' Catalogues Home Page provides a list of links to the home pages of large and small publishing houses from around the world. The list is organized by country, then alphabetically for easy access. Visitors will also find a separate list of international and multinational publishers such as the United Nations, the World Health Organization, and Amnesty International.

ReadersNdex

http://www.readersndex.com/

Promising the "most up-to-date information on your favorite authors and titles," ReadersNdex links to authors' home pages, publishers' sites, and exclusive reviews, articles, and features. Browse a catalog of books by title or subject, or let the auto-browse feature be your guide to the variety of books available.

221B Baker Street: Sherlock Holmes
http://www.cs.cmu.edu/afs/andrew.cmu.edu/usr18/mset/www/holmes.html

Elementary, my dear Watson, this site is not. Rather, it is brimming with a large collection of online Sherlock Holmes books, pictures, and sound files. The site also contains links to a multitude of other Holmes-related Web sites.

Terry's World of AudioBooks
http://www.cuc.edu/~wgts/Audio/audbook.html

Promising "if you can't find it here…you can't find it anywhere," Terry Pogue presents this directory to Web sites with information about audio books. Link to clubs, dealers, publishers, reviews, mailing lists, and more.

W.W. Norton Online
http://www.wwnorton.com/

With offices in New York and London, publisher W.W. Norton now maintains this virtual office to promote its fiction and nonfiction titles. Visitors can click through the company's catalogues, order online, and follow author touring schedules. The page also posts links to its authors' home pages.

The Word
http://www.speakeasy.org/~dbrick/Hot/word.html

The Speakeasy Cafe in Seattle maintains this index pointing to online books and bookstores, journals and magazines, poetry, and reference materials. Also find links to Biblical sites and dozens of literature-related pages.

The Online Writery
http://www.missouri.edu/~wleric/writery.html

Here's a comprehensive resource for writers of most every stripe. Site features include communication sites to contact other writers, marketing information, teachers' resources, links to newsgroups, and writers' home pages.

A LITTLE TOE TAPPING, MAESTRO

"I find younger people are amazed that I can dance somewhat the way they do ... wiggling like Zulus at a pig roast! That ain't too hard to do with a few belts—not for courage, just energy for a few minutes. I find many young women try to "lead" in regular round dancing, but I usually explain in my best Arthur Murray style the finer points. I also find many are interested, too…In dancing, I mean!"

Cajun/Zydeco Music & Dance
http://www.bme.jhu.edu/~jrice/cz.html

Cajun/Zydeco music and dance fans can look for Cajun music venues in their area, or exercise their virtual feet with online dance lessons. The page also posts band schedules, a photo gallery, and links to other spicy dance pages.

Dancers' Archive Gopher Menu
gopher://ftp.std.com/11/nonprofits/dance

The Dancers' Archive gopher provides international listings of dance studios, books, videos, clubs, newsletters, magazines, frequently asked questions (FAQ) files, and more. Visitors will find information on all types of dance here.

Dance Hotlist by Henry Neeman
http://zeus.ncsa.uiuc.edu:8080/~hneeman/dance_hotlist.html

Henry's Dance Hotlist is an extensive list of links for all types and styles of partner dance. Visitors will find organizations and associations offering lessons, classes, and regular dance events for everything from ballroom to swing. Links to newsgroups and general dance resources are also featured.

The Dance Directory

http://www.cyberspace.com/vandehey/
dance.html

From ballet to tango, the Dance Directory surveys the dance resources available on the Web. Link to clubs, companies, or instructional sites via this collection of pointers organized into categories that include ballroom, contra, folk, square, and miscellaneous dances.

Folk Dancing on the WWW

http://ucowww.ucsc.edu/~sla/dance/
dance.html

Steve Allen's index of folk-dancing groups, societies, and resources are organized geographically for easy reference. Also find pointers to general information archives and publications.

Square Dance Resources

http://pages.map.com/~bobl/sdance.htm

Bob Lafleur has compiled this extensive index of square dancing resources. Among the offerings find an alphabetical list of callers, a list of associations and societies, and a list of clubs organized by state.

The U.S. Swing Dance Server

http://www.cs.cornell.edu/Info/People/aswin/
SwingDancing/swing_dancing.html

Swing dancers can practice virtual footwork here. This expansive site includes a library of swing dance steps, a file defining dance terms, and a national events calendar. Plus links lead to clubs, music pages, and much more.

Western Square Dancing

http://suif.stanford.edu/~rfrench/wsd/

Do-si-do and swing your partner at this barnful of square dance information. Find clubs, articles, call lists, software, and the Caller's Corner. Features also include a Guide to Excruciatingly Correct Square Dance Behavior, and Ask the Square Dance Guru.

World-Wide Web Virtual Library: Dance

http://www.artswire.org/Artswire/www/
dance/dance.html

Co-maintained by Arts Wire and DanceUSA, this gateway allows browsers access to the fairly comprehensive dance resources indexed as part of the World-Wide Web Virtual Library. Find links to pages covering all types of dance—from folk to classical forms and everything in between. Submissions are welcome.

COOKING, CRAFTING, AND LIVING

The first person who comes to mind purveying the mastery of cooking and the genius of tasteful crafts is Martha Stewart, the Madonna of modern living who parlayed her talents and personal interests into an empire, and has become a household word.

MARVELOUS MARTHA

Marvelous Martha, doyen of domesticity and wonder woman of Westport, has totally trashed my credibility. Formerly thought of by friends and family as a moderately competent person, holding down as many as three jobs, raising two successful children alone, and keeping an attractive home furnished exclusively from tag sales and thrift stores, I have been brought to my knees by the formidable accomplishments of this overlordess of housewizardy.

It seemed enough to make the one obligatory wreath at Christmas, dust the furniture whether it needed it or not, and occasionally drag out the punch bowl for a draught of "Artillery Punch" with a handful of friends. But in the face of marzipan "Peter Rabbit" cakes, complete with real grass—carefully selected from an untainted portion of the lawn—decorated with miniature gardens of sensitively colored eggplant, cabbages, and tomatoes, tastefully surrounded by white picket fences, my own batches of irregularly made brownies seem puny at best.

A certain admiration for Martha does linger in the haze of my defeatism. For who do you know that has amassed a multimillion dollar fortune by the sweat of their tiny, talented hands? Martha Stewart rose from the ashes of a cruel divorce, and after serving as editor of *House Beautiful* and managing her own catering company, she joined the Time-Warner empire and hit the ground running. Today, besides being veiwed by millions of slack-jawed wannabes on television, Martha produces reams of newspaper columns, writes her own books on entertaining, crafts, and cookery, and stars in her own videos.

SWEET PEAS

On almost every variety of television channel, Martha can be seen sweetly dispensing cooking and gardening tips, and all in lavish detail. On one program, she looked with horror at her sagging sweet peas, and swiftly swung into action weaving ordinary cord into a magnificent macrame trellis to support their tired little heads. On the same program she may whip up 300 tasty meringues, and then design and handpaint personalized invitations for 1000 intimate friends and colleagues to attend the next bash at her country estate.

I greet these performances with a high degree of awe, as Martha's meringues never fall into squishy bundles of goo, and she never dribbles paint on her paper, or knots her cords. How can you find words to criticize one who has become a household word and a cult figure? One whose amazing zeal for perfection leaves the rest of us drooling and slothful in her wake of enthusiam and energy?

IT'S *NOT* A GOOD THING?

There are some, though, who in their smallmindedness, have found fault with the demi-goddess of " It's a Good Thing." Martha made the "Top Ten List" of "Worst Tips for Living" on David Letterman's *Late*

Lizzie Sez

Overnight success usually takes about ten years.

Night show, with suggestions such as, "a heavily sedated pet makes an unusual centerpiece," "spruce up your bathroom with potpourri and a large stack of wrestling magazines," and lastly, "old gym shorts stuffed with cat hair make excellent throw pilllows." Hmmm.

And some folks tire of watching Martha's olympic projects—they claim they would have to have millions of dollars, nothing but free time, and a staff of 100 to achieve the level of perfection that Martha carries off with ease.

Some envious individuals have even called her "Mad Martha," in response to her manic frenzy and probable insomnia, for who would have time to sleep?

MARTHA STEWART DISEASE

We are warned of Martha Stewart Disease, a condition noted by the presence of old shoeboxes and empty tins all over the house that have been decoupaged with old wrapping paper, and doormats made with floral designs from old bottle caps. The disease becomes terminal if you polish every washed lettuce leaf with a clean white cloth until it shines, your hedges are cut to resemble chess pieces, you make your own jello from calves' hooves instead of buying it in the box, and you sleep outside so you don't mess up your perfectly made bed.

For those who rally to her defense, enter the Martha Militia, a hardened group of tough but tasteful women, fighting for fine silverware and valances. The Militia has issued a mission statement, avowing the unfettered mixing of plaids and patterns, the right to build their own porticos, and to paper-mâché anything in sight.

I myself am intimidated by this personification of perfection who glows with outdoorsy health at the age of 54. I am trying on a few projects of my own for size. What do you think of raking the gravel in the driveway into decorative designs, braiding the grass in the front yard, adding little blue barretts on each braid, and making acrylic jewelry from the pigeon droppings left at nearby buildings? Has anyone thought of using belly-button lint for dainty little pin cushions?

DOMESTIC DOMINATION

I am still digging out from under this domestic domination, still trying to regain my self-esteem. But Martha, instead of Living, could you just Live and Let Live? That would be a good thing!

MARTHA NOTWITHSTANDING...

Nothing feels so good as creating good cookery in the kitchen, hearing the sound of the wooden spoon as it thunks against the bowl, or breathing in the heady smell of freshly baked bread. Everyday cares seem to melt away, and your mind is totally absorbed in making the perfect crust, or planning a special meal for the next luncheon, or just making the best and hottest chili imaginable. Everyone can get into the act.

And when you've had enough of domestic wizardry, you can always go out. My favorite part about that? Someone *else* gets stuck washing the dishes!

NETFOOD: COOKING IN AND DINING OUT

American Homebrewers Association
http://www.aob.org/aob/aha.html

The American Homebrewers Association provides members' recipes for beer, information on homebrewing supplies and techniques, and an opportunity for homebrewers to compete against fellow AHA members. Visi-

tors to the association's home page can also learn more about the AHA and how to join.

American Wine on the Web
http://www.2way.com:80/food/wine/

Find vintner profiles, tasting tips, wine country reports and results of wine competitions in *American Wine*, a magazine which explores wine-making in the Americas—from Canada to Chile. The current issue and archive of past issues are featured.

Anderson Valley Brewing Company Beer Links Jumpstation
http://www.avbc.com/avbc/beerlinks.html

Beer drinkers can explore the subtleties of amber, porter, pilsner, and other suds assisted by the links found on this directory of beer-related sites. Part of the Anderson Valley Brewing Company's promotional site, the index points the way to breweries, publications, festivals, homebrewing information, mail order houses, and more.

Beer & Wine Hobby
http://www.eca.com/BeerAndWineHobby.html

Those of you interested in spirits (the drinkable kind) may want to check out this hobby page. These folks are professional consultants and suppliers, and can help with your homebrewing process.

Beertown
http://www.beertown.org/

What can you say about a "town" where floods of suds aren't a disaster, but a celebration? Developed by the Association of Brewers, Beertown offers brew-it-yourselfers and beer lovers a place to call home. Sights to see include Beertown University, city hall, the book store, the newsstand, and the homebrew shop.

The Brewery: Total Homebrewing Info
http://alpha.rollanet.org/

If you've ever toyed with the idea of brewing your own beer, stop by The Brewery first. This page is literally spilling over with the kinds of information you'll need such as recipes, equipment specs, and suppliers. You can also learn how to judge beer, download software, and even find beer clip art.

The Burrito Page
http://www.infobahn.com/pages/rito.html

The Burrito page is a comprehensive and humorous examination of a longtime favorite Mexican food. Visitors will find historical and cultural notes, burrito lore, and an interactive personality profile that judges people according to the types of burritos they like to eat.

The Callahan's Cookbook
http://www.ruhr-uni-bochum.de/callahans/cookbook.html

Here's an international collection of recipes compiled from postings by patrons of the Usenet newsgroup alt.callahans. Recipes range from soup to nuts, serving basic, classic, and exotic dishes.

Cats Meow 3: The Internet Beer Recipe Database
http://alpha.rollanet.org/cm3/CatsMeow3.html

Homebrewers will find an extensive database of beer recipes on tap here, offering beverages ranging from ale and cider to mead, porter, and stout. The site also includes tasting notes, advice for beginners, and a search tool.

The Cheese Page
http://www.zennet.com/cheese/

Literally a definitive page on cheese, this site features a dictionary definition and dozens of GIFs illustrating cheese varieties. Links to cheese pages around the world lead to the Electric Cheese Page, wearable cheese by Foamation Inc., and the Monty Python "Cheese Sketch."

The Chile-Heads Home Page
http://neptune.netimages.com/~chile/

The Chile-Heads home page contains dozens of links and indexes to chile-related information (that's chile peppers, now— you know, the HOT! ones). Explore the Chile Gallery, rummage the archive, and for a really hot time, check out the eats!

The Creole & Cajun Recipe Page
http://www.webcom.com/~gumbo/recipe-page.html

Browsers with Louisiana on the mind will enjoy this page of Creole and Cajun delights. A subset of The Gumbo Pages, it provides information on essential ingredients, complete recipes, and links to Louisiana chefs and restaurants on the Web.

Crockpot Recipes
http://www.cs.cmu.edu/~mjw/recipes/crockpot/crockpot.html

Wait! Don't toss that crockpot into the garage sale pile. Barbecue, meat loaf, and pork chops are among the crockpot recipes featured here (just pop 'em in the pot, and go!), but this index also points to three other collections, one of which is vegetarian.

DineSite U.S.A.
http://www.dinesite.com/

Put down that apron, throw that saucepan aside, and get out of the house! DineSite provides links to thousands of U.S. restaurant descriptions and reviews, all organized by state and city. Visitors can also check out celebrity restaurants, and editors' picks for the "best" restaurants.

Dining Out on the Web
http://www.ird.net/diningout.html

This online index to electronic restaurant guides covers the 50 United States and many international regions, as well. The extensive menu of links is organized geographically for easy reference.

The Electric Cheese Page
http://www.emf.net/~mal/cheese.html

Blue, Swiss, cheddar…find all the cheese anyone could ever want; this page is filled with places to go on the Web to find blocks of compressed milk curds. Just be thankful when you visit the Limburger page that the Internet isn't capable of reproducing smells (yet).

The electronic Gourmet Guide (eGG)
http://www.2way.com/food/egg/index.html

This "Internet e-zine devoted to food and cooking" serves up a smorgasbord of features and columns for chefs and discriminating diners. Includes a link to its sister publication, *American Wine on the Web.*

Eleanor's Kitchen
http://www.columbia.edu/~js322/eleanor/eleanor.html

Here's a collection of hearty treats sure to please any hungry guest. Find authentic Czechoslovakian recipes for about a half dozen dishes, like pork with horseradish, and soup with liver dumplings (er…). The site is hosted by the U.S.-born daughter of Czech and Slovak parents.

Epicurious Food
http://www.epicurious.com/a_home/a00_home/home.html

Your Pavlovian responses may kick in when you look at Epicurious Food. Among other offerings, each day the online service features a menu composed of recipes from *Gourmet* and *Bon Appetit* magazines. A recent menu featured marinated vegetables and rigatoni with shrimp. Yum!

Food Pyramid
http://www.ganesa.com/food/index.html

The timeless wisdom of the Food Pyramid page guides visitors to good nutrition in a world of fatty temptations. This site illustrates and explains the appropriate intake of various food groups to maintain a healthy lifestyle.

The Food Resource
http://www.orst.edu/food-resource/food.html

If you're hungry for food information, The Food Resource page, hosted by ZoeAnn Holmes of Oregon State University, serves a full course of tasty links. Access food-related associations, newsgroups, nutrient analyses, restaurants, recipes, and other resources sure to satisfy.

Fry Cooks on Venus Recipe Index
http://www.cs.ubc.ca/spider/edmonds/recipes/index.html

Part of a personal home page, this index of popular recipes offers complete instructions for making a variety of breakfast dishes, breads, desserts, sauces, and more. Includes recipes for international dishes.

FTP Directory of Recipes
ftp://ftp.cs.ubc.ca/pub/local/RECIPES/

Find recipes for appetizers, entrees, side dishes, and desserts at this culinary FTP archive. Ethnic cooking, meats, breads, soups, and vegetarian dishes are also featured.

Fun Recipes Gopher Menu
gopher://spinaltap.micro.umn.edu/11/fun/Recipes

For the cook who is looking for new inspiration, this gopher server contains recipes for appetizers, drinks, breads, casseroles, pancakes, truffles, and most anything else you can think of to feast upon. A search feature provides easy access to the data.

Galaxy: Recipes—Leisure and Recreation
http://www.einet.net/galaxy/Leisure-and-Recreation/Recipes.html

Chili recipes, chocolate delights, and various to-die-for foods come together on this page from the Tradewave Galaxy Web directory. Whether a vegetarian or a meat eater, everyone will find a tempting something-or-other among this collection of food resources.

The Hop Page
http://www.teleport.com/~gtinseth/

Created for fellow "hopheads," Glenn Tinseth's Hop Page links homebrewers and beer lovers to a variety of information on growing hops and brewing beer. A nice feature here lets guests input information on the beer they are brewing and calculate its expected bitterness.

I Need My Chocolate!
http://www.qrc.com/~sholubek/choco/start.htm

Devoted to chocolate lovers around the globe, this site includes pointers to recipes, chocolate manufacturers, online catalogs, and even chocolate clubs.

Iowa State University's Tasty Insect Recipes
http://www.ent.iastate.edu/Misc/InsectsAsFood.html

To add a twist to the term insect lover, visit here for recipes with bugs in the ingredient list. My favorites: Banana Worm Bread and Chocolate Chirpie Chip Cookies (the crickets provide the chirp). The recipes were compiled by Iowa State's entomology program.

International Food Information Council Foundation
http://ificinfo.health.org/

Curious about those additives in your breakfast cereal and other issues related to food? Check out the IFIC's safety and nutrition information to find out what the heck is going on. Also find links to food-related publications, information for reporters, and a section for educators.

The Internet Epicurean
http://www.epicurean.com

The Internet Epicurean covers the culinary universe from soup to nuts. The site offers menus, recipes, magazines, links to restaurant sites, and an epicurean exchange for articles and cooking tips.

Kitchen Nook
http://www.mmedia.com/becca/recipe.html

Pick up a weekly kitchen tip and recipe sent in by the regular readers of this online kitchen aid. A recent week's taste treat: Buffalo Chicken Lasagna. Now there's a new twist on a familiar theme!

Krispin Komments on Nutrition and Health
http://www.krispin.com/

Digest some essential information about your innards via this page from a clinical nutritionist. Highlights include protein basics, potassium chronicles, and thyroid support.

La Cocina Mexicana
http://mexico.udg.mx/Cocina/menu.html

Browsers with a penchant for Mexican food can download recipes—from sopas to postres—here. The page also offers a brief history of Mexico's cuisine. In English or Spanish.

Les Fromages de France
http://mars.sct.fr/festival/cheeses.html

Les Fromages de France celebrates the cheeses of (you guessed it) France. Camembert, Brie, Valencay, and dozens of other cheeses are described here. Of course, when one discusses cheese, one thinks of bread and wine, and those links are provided, too. In French.

A List of Food and Cooking Sites
http://www.cs.cmu.edu/~mjw/recipes/other-sites.html

Serving links to recipe archives, this page is well-organized for easy reference. Subsections include ethnic food, vegetarian fare, and drinks. Also find pathways to information on restaurants and commercial culinary sites.

Manuela's Recipes
http://he1.uns.tju.edu/recipes/

An Italian-American student at Ithaca College, Manuela presents a collection of mouth-watering Italian recipes that range from antipasti to dolci. Learn how to make risotto, spaghetti alla carbonara, tiramisu, and much, much more.

The Mead Maker's Page
http://www.atd.ucar.edu/homes/cook/mead/mead.html

"If it's good for ancient Druids…it's good enough for me," say the folks behind the Mead Maker's Page. Visit to download recipes for making the ancient drink made with honey, fruit, and yeast.

Medieval/Renaissance Food Home Page
http://www.pbm.com/~lindahl/food.html

Glean table tips and techniques from the Middle Ages and Renaissance periods. Rummage this archive of articles and recipes for forgotten food finds, or just enjoy this look into the epicurean habits in vogue ages ago.

Merrill Shindler's Guide to Eating Pretty Good
http://www.gigaplex.com/food/index.htm

The Foodplex area of the much larger Gigaplex entertainment site, Merrill Shindler's Guide to Eating Pretty Good celebrates food. Shindler lives to eat and serves up tips, tidbits, and humor to food lovers. He also provides a guide to eating, including where to find the best steak in America and how to sniff out good British food in London.

Mimi's Cyber Kitchen
http://www.cyber-kitchen.com/

Mimi's Cyber Kitchen serves up recipes, cooking tips, and food humor for the virtually hungry. Vegetarian, ethnic, kosher, and healthful selections abound, organized for quick and easy reference.

The Mole Page
http://www.slip.net/~bobnemo/mole.html

Get out the chiles, chocolate, and pumpkin seeds for a mole-fest. If you don't know what mole is (pronounced MO-lay), read the description and history here. Then get your pots and pans out to try your hand at over 20 recipes for this Mexican national dish.

Mycelium Welcome
http://www.hcds.net/mushroom/welco.html

This page welcomes visitors into "the fascinating world of mushrooms, fungus and fungi." Webmaster Wayne serves up tips on finding mushrooms in the woods, offers recipes to try in the kitchen, and presents articles to read on- or off-line. Also find book reviews, photos, charts, and much more.

The National Pork Producers Council
http://www.nppc.org/

Pig out on information about the pork industry and the "other" white meat through this official page from the National Pork Producers Council. Among the site's features find cooking ideas and industry news.

The North American Vegetarian Society
http://www.cyberveg.org/navs/

The North American Vegetarian Society is a nonprofit organization dedicated to promoting the benefits of a meatless diet. The organization's Web site offers an overview of the group's efforts and promotes its conferences, booklets, and quarterly magazine, *Vegetarian Voice*.

Pages and Pages of Food
http://www.evansville.net/~wbbebout/food.html

A cook himself, the Webmaster of this page has compiled a select list of sites offering recipes for dishes that range from the exotic (sushi) to the ordinary (Jello). Also find pointers to food-related Usenet newsgroups.

The Pie Page
http://www.teleport.com/~psyched/pie/pie.html

Pastry lovers will just eat up this site devoted to the art of pie baking. Take a step-by-step pie crust making tutorial or dig into yummy recipes for treats like good old-fashioned American apple pie and taffy apple cheesecake pie.

Pit Cooking
http://www.cco.caltech.edu/~salmon/pit.html

The Team Mumu Pit Cooking page teaches visitors "how to tell dinner from a hole in the ground." Find anecdotes and complete instructions for cooking a variety of meats in pits dug into your own back yard.

The Real Cranberry Home Page
http://www.scs.carleton.ca/~palepu/cranberry.html

Maintained by agriculture and information technology consultants Cran Breton Enterprises, this site offers a variety of tips for growing and preparing cranberries. Visitors will find information on cranberry diseases, farming associations, "nearly an exhaustive" collection of recipes, and topic-related links.

rec.food.recipes FTP Index
ftp://ftp.neosoft.com/pub/rec.food.recipes/

An extensive collection of recipes from the rec.food newsgroup is available here. Cooks can download recipes for appetizers, barbecue, beans, grains, vegetables, and meats. The page also includes a section on preserving.

Rolling Your Own Sushi
http://www.rain.org/~hutch/sushi.html

Rolling Your Own Sushi, part of a personal home page, is a virtual cookbook for the Japanese raw fish delicacy. Visit here for everything you need to know to make sushi like a professional chef. Includes special recipes and links to Japan- and sushi-related Web sites.

Shaken Not Stirred
http://www.axionet.com/key/Martinis.html

A toast to the classic martini and everything that goes with it, this swingin' site serves up martini recipes, a trading post for cocktail shakers and other accessories, treasure maps to the last of the great martini emporiums, and links to lounge-lifestyle sites.

The Solar Cooking Archive
http://www.accessone.com/~sbcn/index.htm

The Solar Cooking Archive features links to a host of information about harnessing the sun's energy to cook everything from bread to steak. Site highlights include

Lizzie's Tips

My son sent me the best-ever recipe for a Ramos Gin Fizz:

1 1/2 Oz Gin
1/2 Oz Orange Curacao
3 Oz Half&Half
Juice of 1/2 lemon
2 t sugar
1 egg white
3 drops Orange Flower Water

Put all ingredients in blender with ice and blend until smooth. Top with nutmeg and a slice of lime.
CHEERS!

construction plans for cookers, a gallery of cooker images, and breaking news from the solar cooking grapevine.

Spencer's Beer Page
http://realbeer.com/spencer/

Spencer's Beer Page is designed for the beer lover, particularly the homebrewer. Includes tips from master brewers, recipe files, an abundant supply of reference material, and links to other beer-related pages.

Star Chefs & Cookbook Authors
http://www.starchefs.com/

Dishing up some of the recipes favored by the chefs it profiles, this cooking resource offers insight into preparing delicious meals like the greats. Also find information on culinary careers and an archive of previously featured chefs.

Stuart's Chinese Recipes
http://www-hons-cs.dcs.st-andrews.ac.uk/
~sab/Chinese_Recipes.html

A computer science professor in Scotland, Stuart A. Blair posts his best Chinese food recipes on this popular page. Visitors can browse the current recipe list or add their own recipes to the archive.

Thai Food

http://sunsite.au.ac.th/thailand/thaifood.html

Learn the secrets of preparing and presenting the gastro-nomic delights of Thailand. Find an overview of Thai cooking and ingredients, step-by-step recipes, and tips for serving dishes with style.

Talking About Turkey

http://www.hoptechno.com/book15.htm

This fact-filled tipsheet will negate the need for dialing a turkey hotline come holiday time. Read about how to buy, store, thaw, stuff, and cook a bird. Compiled from a United States Department of Agriculture bulletin.

Tamilian Cuisine

http://www.cba.uh.edu/~bala/tamilnadu/food.html

Learn about the delectable food creations that are part of Tamil cuisine. This page includes an introduction to Tamil foods, as well as complete recipes and cooking instructions.

Texas Foods Recipe Page

http://www.microserve.com/~duane/TexasFoods.html

Fans of Texas cooking can sample recipes for appetizers, main dishes, breads, and desserts here. Includes links to the Chili! Page and a site containing Tex-Mex recipes.

Tokyo Food Page

http://www.twics.com/~robbs/tokyofood.html

Cooks and gourmands who favor Japanese food flavors will enjoy this site devoted to the joys of cooking in the island nation. Visitors can download recipes, brush up on sushi definitions, and browse photographic presenta-tions. A Tokyo restaurant guide is also available. In Japa-nese and English.

The USENET Cookbook

http://www.lysator.liu.se:7500/etexts/recept/main.html

The "pre-main menu" for this online cookbook offers the option to select either metric units or "the US-system"

of measuring units. From there, culinary enthusiasts can go straight to the recipe archives and cook up a mean breeze.

Vegetarian Pages

http://catless.ncl.ac.uk/veg/

The Vegetarian Pages provide a guide to all things vege-tarian on the Web, and in the world. Includes links to news, event announcements, societies, frequently asked questions (FAQ) files, and of course, a worldwide guide to vegetarian restaurants.

Veggies Unite!

http://www.vegweb.com/

Veggies Unite! serves as an online guide to eating a meat-free diet. Visit for recipes ranging from basic beans and rice, to shitake mushrooms and tofu in mushroom sauce. The site also includes a weekly meal planner, a bulletin board, and tips on nutrition.

Webtender: An On-Line Bartender.

http://www.pvv.unit.no/~pallo/webtender/

Impress your friends with bartending know-how gleaned from this electronic mixology reference. A searchable in-dex allows you to pull up the recipes to all your favorite spirited beverages, as well as to a few you probably ha-ven't tried. Includes a "Bartender's Handbook."

Wild Mushrooms

http://www.ijs.si/slo/country/food/gobe/

Visitors to this site can learn how to find, cook, and eat wild mushrooms without experiencing any painful side effects. Created by mushroom enthusiasts in Slovenia, the site walks wanna-be pickers through a hand-in-hand 'shrooming tutorial and provides safety tips to ensure survival.

Wine Lovers' OnLine Searchable Database

http://www.wines.com/magical/search.html

Wine aficionados can prep for wine tastings at this full-bodied, searchable site. Find complete articles on topics like "taste scoring systems and hundreds of other wine terms from abboccato to zymotechnology!"

Wines on the Internet
http://www.wines.com/

Lovers of the grape will appreciate this "cyberspace guide to wine and wineries." Explore "virtual wine country" or check out the "tasting room." Those seeking "unique or exceptional values" can even order selections online.

Wine.Com
http://www.wine.com/

This searchable resource points to what's new, rare, "hot," and up for auction. Also find wine forums, topical features, and shopping opportunities.

World-Wide Sushi Restaurant Reference
http://wwwipd.ira.uka.de/~maraist/Sushi/ sushi-rests-top.html

John Maraist's Sushi Restaurant Reference Page serves up those who serve up raw fish. Find a growing list (and reviews) of establishments around the world who cater to the salt-sea cravings of fresh fish aficionados.

DIGGIN' IN THE DIRT

It's the nation's number one hobby, giving spiritual ease and comfort, relief from stress, and beauty and satisfaction to those who pursue it. Gardening!

"We had a beautiful snow in Kansas yesterday. The trees were covered to the very tops with white frosting. It was a calm and peaceful day. My gardens are outside my upstairs office window. I love to experience the four seasons. Seed catalogs are beginning to come and ideas for next year's plantings are coming to mind. I have a small greenhouse, but heating it doesn't seem too practical at this time. I use it in the early spring. I am thinking that since I have a heating coil, I might be able to grow lettuce under a plastic tent now. Any suggestions?"

GARDENING SITES

AGropolis
http://agcomwww.tamu.edu/agcom/agrotext/ agcommap.html

Stop by this Texas A&M information cyberstop for advice on some of the basics of life: gardening, food and nutrition, family life, environmental responsibility, and taking care of pets and livestock.

American Association of Botanical Gardens and Arboreta
http://192.104.39.4/AABGA/aabga1.html

This professional association for public gardens in North America promotes and supports the horticultural community. Visitors can download images and learn about plant conservation. The association also posts a list of its members and publications.

American Horticultural Society
http://eMall.com/ahs/ahs.html

Turn your thumb green with tips from the American Horticultural Society. Read articles from the society's magazine about growing can't-miss flowers like hoyas and magnolias. Visitors are also invited to join the group by filling out the online membership application.

The Asclepiad Page
http://www.graylab.ac.uk/usr/hodgkiss/ asclep.html

Asclepiads are a family of plants that comprises a large and diverse group of about 2,000 species. View a picture gallery and learn how to cultivate the showy flowers on this page maintained by The International Asclepiad Society. Also find information about the society and its journal, "Asklepios. "

Atlanta Garden Connection
http://www.atlgarden.com/

Here's an information resource for those who fancy they've a green thumb. Learn how to select plants, consult the garden calendar for proper timing, ask "experts" thorny questions, and browse a buyer's directory.

Bonsai on the Web

http://hav.com/bonsai/

Dedicated to enthusiasts who enjoy dwarfing ornamental trees and shrubs for use indoors, this information index points the way to nurseries, suppliers, growers' pages, and species information. Links to a topical mailing list and newsgroup are also featured.

Daylilies Growing Along The Information Highway

http://www.daylilies.com/daylilies/

Browsers are invited to wander among daylilies on this site. Find a collection of daylily photos along with can't-fail instructions for growing the flowers.

Friends of the Daylilies Home Page

http://www.primenet.com/~tjfehr/daylily.html

A group of the American Hemerocallis Society members, the Friends of the Daylilies work to publicize their favorite perennial flower and its culture. Visit this home page to learn more about the daylily and to link to related organizations, publications, and event information.

Gardening & Landscaping

http://www.btw.com/garden.htm

If the smell of sweet soil, the sight of green growth, and the texture of compost fire up your soul, check out this gardening index. Find links to the best garden spots on the Web and a handful of interactive aids such as the Lawn Grass Selector.

GardenNet

http://trine.com/GardenNet/

Self-described as "the premier garden center on the Internet," GardenNet hosts a well-cultivated collection of verdant and flowering sites. Enjoy the wisdom of the Ardent Gardener and fellow green thumbs, pick favorites from among the seeding of magazines, garden shops, and online resources, or find out about travel and floral events.

GardenNet's The Ardent Gardener

http://trine.com/GardenNet/ArdentGardener/

Read issues of the online magazine "Over The Fence," along with book reviews and gardening tips through The Ardent Gardener Web site. If you want to get involved in the gardening talk, jump to the Ardent Gardener Roundtable for discussions of selected topics.

Gardens+Gardening

http://www.cfn.cs.dal.ca/Recreation/Gardening/gg_home.html

Gardens+Gardening explores gardening techniques, various kinds of plants, and environmental issues. Browsers can access a monthly column, plus find answers to frequently asked questions and information about selected plant clubs.

GardenWeb

http://www.gardenweb.com/

GardenWeb provides a bountiful crop of current information and sales of interest to gardeners. Visitors will find features such as online gardening forums, virtual tours of botanical gardens from around the world, contests, and garden variety tips on growing healthy plants.

Home Page for Irises

http://aleph0.clarku.edu/~djoyce/iris/

Gardeners with a penchant for irises will find like minds here. This site contains lists of iris societies, a detailed look at the flower and its needs, images, and links to online articles about the garden beauty.

Horticulture Information Leaflets

http://www.ces.ncsu.edu/hil/

Whether or not you claim to have a green thumb, if you like plants this is a Web site you shouldn't pass by. This vast food and flora information database can help you identify, plant, and nurture your own fruits, vegetable, flowers, foliage, and crops.

Hydroponics! InterUrban WaterFarms Online

http://www.viasub.net/IUWF/index.html

Hydroponics is one way to get those veggies to grow without getting dirt under your fingernails; it's the science of growing plants without soil. InterUrban Water-Farms in Riverside, Calif., gives a detailed look at the technique here. The company provides an online catalog for supplies, too.

The Internet Bonsai Club

http://www.pass.wayne.edu/~dan/bonsai.html

The Internet Bonsai Club is devoted to growing and caring for miniature plants. Visitors can learn the art of bonsai here and post pictures of their plants. The site also includes links to related sites.

Master Gardener Information

http://leviathan.tamu.edu:70/1s/mg

Seasoned and novice gardeners will find useful tips and how-to advice within these Master Gardener files. Browse the data dealing with fruits and nuts, vegetables, flowering plants, grasses, and more. A keyword search tool affords quick reference.

The Orchid House

http://sciserv2.uwaterloo.ca/orchids.html

This vast site succeeds in its aim to provide information for the orchid hobbyist. Offerings include details about artificial lighting, plant nutrition, orchid shows, plus much more about the gorgeous tropical blooms.

Plants by Mail FAQ

http://seidel.ncsa.uiuc.edu/PBM-FAQ/

Read the ins and outs of ordering and receiving plants through the mail. Also find tips on spotting good and bad companies, instructions on how to care for your plants when they arrive, and a list of mail order houses.

The Strawberry Facts Page

http://vanbc.wimsey.com/~jmott/sbfacts/

Strawberry freaks will find the Strawberry Facts Page deliciously informative, offering links to strawberry recipes, growing tips, strawberry art, regional festivals, an area to ask strawberry-flavored questions, and more.

Urban Agriculture Notes by City Farmer

http://www.cityfarmer.org

Urban composting, worm bins, and community gardens take root at the City Farmer's Urban Agriculture Notes site. The voice of a non-profit organization in Vancouver, Canada, the site promotes urban food production and environmental conservation with useful tips, tales, and reports.

The Virtual Garden

http://pathfinder.com/@@GZHyjwcAh1OIPCrl/vg/Welcome/welcome.html

The Virtual Garden's Webmasters say "new gardening information sprouts every few days" here. The site provides tips for garden enthusiasts of all varieties. Visit to browse through magazines, books, and links to botanical gardens and plant societies. The site is maintained by Pathfinder.

World-Wide Web Virtual Library: Gardening

http://www.gardenweb.com/vl/

General, international, and regional U.S. gardening sites only head the list of categories found on this index of gardening links. Also find pointers to plant-specific sites covering everything from bonsai and carnivorous plants to roses and wild flowers, links to plant databases and horticultural sites, and jumps to botanical gardens, museums, and society home pages.

THE VIRTUAL HOBBYIST

Some of us just plain can't sit still by the fire long enough to read a good book—we're desperate to get out of the kitchen, and we just couldn't give a hoot about taking a turn on the dance floor. We'd rather be on the beach flying a kite than digging out peat from beneath our fingernails, or we'd just as soon be engineering a model train as it makes its daily mail run. Ham radio operation? Antiquing? Birding?

Why, there's just no end to the things you can do in your spare time, and there's an equally endless supply of resources on the Web to help you get started.

HOBBIES GALORE

ALL ABOARD!

Aristo-Craft Trains On-line Information Page

http://www.aristocraft.com/aristo

The Aristo-Craft Trains On-line Information Page targets model train hobbyists with news about products and clubs. This is the place to share ideas, get tips from like-minded people, and find new accessories from online catalogs and shops.

Dave Frary's Blue Ribbon Models

http://www1.shore.net/~jdf/tswelcome.html

Alternately known as the Blue Ribbon Models and Track-side Modelers home page, this site acts as a central jump-station for model railroad enthusiasts. Resources include reference books, kits, video tapes, and links to related Web sites.

Grand Central Railway Station of Cyberspace

http://tucson.com/concor/

Con-Cor's Grand Central Railway Station of Cyberspace offers links to hundreds of railroad sites on the Internet worldwide. Find pointers to sites dealing with both model and real trains.

Hotbox Home Page

http://www.cris.com/~felixg/HOTBOX/P1.html

The North Central Region of the National Model Railroaders Association publishes "Hotbox," a journal that focuses on the upper Midwest and includes articles, photos, a calendar of events, and a bulletin board. Visitors can download the journal here.

Interactive Model Railroad

http://rr-vs.informatik.uni-ulm.de/rr/

Watch and operate the interactive model railroad presented online by Germany's University of Ulm. Links to other railroad-related pages are also offered.

Live Steaming

http://mindlink.net/Ron_Stewart/livsteam.html

Devoted to enthusiasts of model engines that use live steam to drive pistons, this page acts as a clearinghouse of resources. Find photos, FAQs, articles, event and club notices, an e-mail directory, products and services, and more.

National Model Railroad Association

http://www.mcs.net:80/~weyand/nmra/

Model railroad enthusiasts will find plenty to play with here. The National Model Railroad Association provides information on membership, convention information, an introduction to special-interest groups, and a look at supplies and collectibles.

San Diego Model Railroad Museum Virtual Tour

http://www.globalinfo.com/noncomm/SDMRM/sdmrm.html

Located in Balboa Park, the San Diego Model Railroad Museum maintains this site for general information. Visit here to learn about its train exhibits, model railroad clubs, and related resources around the United States.

Tried & True Trains

http://www.tttrains.com/

Model train hobbyists will find all they need to complete their models at this resource. Here you'll find how-to articles as well as contact points for world-wide model manufactures. Modelers are also invited to submit their own tips and learned wisdom.

Webville and Hypertext Railroad Company
http://www.he.tdl.com/~colemanc/webville.html

The Webville and Hypertext Railroad Company runs only on the Internet. Use this archive of historical and informational documents to learn about real and model railroads.

ARTING & CRAFTING

Aunt Annie's Craft Page
http://www.auntannie.com/

Aunt Annie dishes up a heapin' helpin' of projects and information for craft lovers, with an emphasis on "learning, creativity, and problem solving." Peruse projects such as making boxes and puppets, join the mailing list, download shareware, exchange ideas, or link to other craft-related pages on the Net.

[Craft Software | Craft Exchange | Craft Project Index]

Aunt Annie's
Craft Page™

Over 50 projects and growing!!!

12/7/96

Aunt Annie's Craft Page is sponsored this month by:

CraftNet Village
http://www.craftnet.org/

Crafters can gather at CraftNet Village to get new ideas and trade tips. Post craft ideas at the project exchange or shop for supplies in the market square. The magazine rack is the place to go for craft-reading pleasure.

CraftWEB Home Page
http://www.craftweb.com/

This unusual project hopes to create an online community where "professional craftspeople" and artisans "meet, share information and promote fine crafts world-wide." Resources here include real-time chat, an FTP site, links to individual artisans, an online gallery, and access to newsletters and related books.

COLLECTING

American Numismatic Association
http://www.money.org/

The American Numismatic Association, a nonprofit organization chartered by the U.S. Congress, is dedicated to the collection and study of coins, paper money, tokens, and medals. This site features information on the association, an online museum and an FTP site with images, radio scripts, software, and more.

Antiques and Collectibles
http://willow.internet-connections.net/web/antiques/

The Antiques and Collectibles site's primary purpose is to provide information and images of antiques to those who are new to collecting. The server deals primarily with items sold at antique shows, auctions, and flea markets.

Clocks and Time
http://glen-ellyn.iit.edu/~clocks/clocks/clocks.html

Visitors to this page will find an index of horology links. From archives, books, and commercial firms, to museums, software, and sundials, the subject receives thorough treatment.

Coin Universe
http://www.coin-universe.com/index.html

Coin collectors will go wild searching for items for their prize collections at Coin Universe. Find classified ads, articles, and information about upcoming coin collecting shows and auctions.

The International Paperweight Society
http://www.armory.com/~larry/ips.html

To the International Paperweight Society, paperweights are not just functional objects, they are objects of art. The IPS site showcases examples of paperweight art and details the history of glass paperweights. The lighter side of the site offers collecting trivia and humor.

Joseph Luft's Philatelic Resources on the Web

http://www.execpc.com/~joeluft/
resource.html

Stamps, in all their color and culture, are the topic of this page. Home pages, shows and societies, world postal authorities, country-specific resources, downloadable images, and commercial traders all are linked here.

Maine Antique Digest

http://www.maineantiquedigest.com/
Welcome.html

The "Maine Antique Digest," a monthly newspaper, provides selected articles from current and past issues. Among the many online resources are auction calendars and catalogs, photos and prices of antiques sold recently, reports of stolen antiques, and much more.

Mobilia Magazine

http://www.mobilia.com/

Catering to fans of automobile collectibles, "Mobilia" magazine's online edition features articles and information about gas-engine mini racers, works of art, and other items related to autos. Collectors of transportation-related toys and art can get their fill using the classified ads offered here.

National Gemstone

http://www.primenet.com/~rgenis/

The National Gemstone home page targets new and veteran gem collectors and dealers with online information sources, price indexes, and forecast newsletters. This site also offers dazzling photographs from the Smithsonian's gem and mineral collection.

Phonecard Collectors

http://www.neosoft.com/internet/paml/
groups.P/phonecard_collectors.html

Just when you thought you'd heard of every possible obsession, here's a page devoted to the collecting of tele-
phone calling cards— wallet-sized debit cards used in phone systems worldwide. This site points visitors to a mailing list and Usenet group for like-minded collectors.

Plastic Princess Page

http://deepthought.armory.com/~zenugirl/
barbie.html

"An online zine for adult collectors of fashion dolls," the Plastic Princess Page provides a variety of collector resources. Visit here for advice on getting started, books and magazine articles, graphics, doll lists, price guides, and a vendors list.

Rockhounds Information Page

http://www.rahul.net/infodyn/rockhounds/
rockhounds.html

Dedicated to rock collectors, this site offers a plethora of links to topical resources and materials. Find mailing lists, software, clubs, commercial sites, articles, images, and sites related to the study of Earth Sciences.

World-Wide Collectors Digest

http://www.wwcd.com/index.html

No matter what their passion, most collectors will find this targeted resource a site to see. Find auctions, classifieds, price guides, clubs, and dealers for most everything from comic books to model trains.

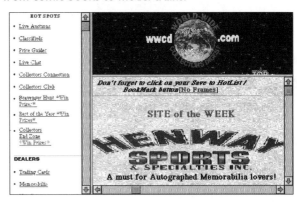

OUR FEATHERED FRIENDS

Birding on the Web
http://compstat.wharton.upenn.edu:8001/
~siler/birding.html

Here's a collection of links for sites of interest to bird watching enthusiasts. Find pointers to the home pages for international birding organizations, answers to frequently asked questions, exhibits, and announcements.

Birdlinks
http://www.phys.rug.nl/mk/people/wpv/
birdlink.html

Birders will find an international companion to their favorite field guide here. This immense site provides extensive links to online resources about birds, including Cornell's bird call site and the National Park Service's species lists. Travelers will find birding tips here, too.

The Bird Web
http://www.abdn.ac.uk/~nhi019/intro.html

The Bird Web indexes news and information about birds and ornithology. Find upcoming conferences, sightings, clubs, lists, newsgroups, articles, collections, and other resources.

FLY ME TO THE MOON

Australian Kite Association Home Page and E-Zine
http://netspace.net.au/~peterbat/index.html

Did an e-mail flamer just tell you to go fly a kite? The Australian Kite Association home page and zine may be the place to get the valuable tips you need. It contains images from kite shows as well as the association's newsletters and calendar of events.

Jason's Kite Site
http://www.latrobe.edu.au/Glenn/KiteSite/
Kites.html

This personal home page archives photos of elaborate flying kites. Also: a link to the Hawaiian Kite FTP site and an explanation and photos of "kite buggying," an unusual

sport which involves hooking a small vehicle to a kite and rolling, brakeless, at high speeds.

GENEALOGY

Everton's Genealogical Helper
http://www.everton.com/

The online edition of Everton's Genealogical Helper is a multimedia offering from the world's largest genealogy magazine. Not an electronic reprint of the paper magazine, this edition is specifically designed for the World Wide Web and employs the varied genealogy resources online.

Genealogy Toolbox
http://genealogy.tbox.com/genealogy.html

The Genealogy Toolbox attempts to provide a comprehensive listing of genealogy links on the Web. Site features include surname and area-specific searches, links to libraries and genealogical groups, plus much more.

Janyce's Root Diggin' Dept.
http://www.janyce.com/gene/rootdig.html

The genealogical resources found here— from reference materials to cemetery locators— are presented to aid those who enjoy digging into the roots of their family tree. Among the resources find regional genealogical information for the United States and beyond, plus tools for finding missing people.

ROOTS-L Home Page
http://www.smartlink.net/~leverich/roots-l.html

A mailing list for people interested in genealogy, ROOTS-L, boasts over 6,500 subscribers and circulates over 100 messages a day. Visitors can subscribe from this page or browse the online library and surname lists.

GREEN EGGS AND ... HAM RADIO?

Amateur Radio Newsline
http://www.acs.ncsu.edu/HamRadio/
News.html

Transcripts of "Amateur Radio NewsLine," an audio program for and about ham radio operators, are published at this site. Articles relating to technology, federal regulations, and world events are presented in an informal format. Find current and past programs.

Amateur Radio Operator
http://www.amateurradio.com/

Amateur Radio Operator, an online magazine for ham radio enthusiasts, offers articles and classified advertisements from around the world. Visit here for news and events information, stolen radio listings, and a chance to participate in its "Hamfest" discussion group.

Boston Amateur Radio Club
http://www.acs.oakland.edu/barc.html

Even for those who don't live there, ham jockeys will find plenty of interest at the Boston Amateur Radio Club's home page. The BARC roster, club journal, and membership information are available, as well as information about amateur radio exams and various conventions.

QSL Information System
http://www-dx.deis.unibo.it/htlzh/

This Web server provides a searchable and updatable database of ham radio operators' callsigns. Includes a link to the University of Arkansas Little Rock's Amateur Radio Club's home page.

HORSEY STUFF

Model Horse Links
http://w3.metronet.com/kira/model-horse/

Add another horse to your stable—model horse, that is. This page links to dealers, shows, and event information, Web magazines, and other resources for the model horse enthusiast.

Racing Memorabilia Pages
http://www.wsnet.com/~sysclp/postcard.html

Horse racing fan Cindy Pierson shows off her collection of track memorabilia, consisting primarily of vintage postcards not likely to be found anywhere else. Like-minded collectors can link to a newsgroup as well as additional resources concerning the sport of kings.

ORIGAMI

Interactive Origami in VRML
http://www.neuro.sfc.keio.ac.jp/~aly/polygon/vrml/ika/

Want to learn origami, the Japanese art of paper folding, but afraid of paper cuts? Check out Interactive Origami in VRML (Virtual Reality Modeling Language), where art-lovers can use VRML technology to create digitized origami art.

The Origami Page
http://www.datt.co.jp/Origami/

Origami enthusiast Joseph Wu maintains this home page containing a wealth of information and graphics about the ancient Japanese art of paper folding. Visit this site to find out how to make different origami forms, see interesting examples, and link to other origami pages on the Web.

Paper Airplanes
http://pchelp.inc.net/paper_ac.htm

The PC Help Group offers step-by-step instructions to quickly turn standard sheets of paper into exotic flying machines. "Click, print, fold and enjoy!"

A STITCH IN TIME

Counted Cross Stitch, Needlework, and Stitchery Page
http://www.wco.com/~kdyer/xstitch.html

Find a diverse collection of links to resources available on the Internet for those interested in decorative stitching. Links point to a newsgroup, documents, supplies, conversion charts, fabric care information, historical/cultural references, activities, and stitching wisdom.

The Online Knitting Magazine
http://www.fearless.net/knit/

Knitters, start your needles! The Online Knitting Magazine contains a wealth of knitting information including patterns, instructions, and subscription information for mailing lists. This truly extensive site also posts a directory to knitting supply stores worldwide and tips on spinning.

Wonderful Stitches
http://www.needlework.com/

Stitchery enthusiasts can download needlepoint and cross-stitch samplers and projects from this page. (New patterns are added monthly.) The page also posts links to related newsgroups and resources on the Internet.

TREASURE ISLAND

International Treasure Hunters Exchange
http://www.treasure.com/

Dreams of discovering buried treasure and the booty of sunken ships awaken in the optimists who visit this page. Check an archive of shipwreck recovery news, read guest editorials, sign up for a free treasure hunting newsletter, or shop in the online mall.

TreasureNet
http://www.treasurenet.com/

TreasureNet should be your first stop for treasure- and gold-hunting resources. Dig into historical photos, information on recovery and preservation, prospecting and archaeology links, plus books, maps, and more.

WOODWORKING

Harry's Woodworking Page
http://hornet.mmg.uci.edu/~hjm/woodworking.html

A woodworker shares his successes— dining tables, pizza paddles, serving spoons, hardwood bowls— through photos and descriptive narratives illustrating how the objects were created. Includes a link to the tip-laden rec.woodworking newsgroup.

W5: WoodWorking on the World Wide Web
http://www.iucf.indiana.edu/~brown/hyplan/wood.html

An extensive directory of resources, this site points the way for cybernauts who enjoy the art and craft of woodworking. Among the featured links find woodturning and carving sites, commercial woodworking pages, and software for woodworkers.

Woodworking at WoodWeb
http://www.woodweb.com/

Learn the finer points of finger joints or how to finesse bends in pieces of ash wood. These and other fine woodworking tips can be found at WoodWeb. This resource includes an online magazine, as well as buying guides and an industry index.

The Woodworking Catalog
http://www.woodworking.com/

A compilation of Web resources of interest and use to woodworkers, the catalog covers subject categories like lumber, hardware, books and plans, finishing supplies, tools, and shops. In addition to the catalog, also find online magazines and forums.

Woodworking Photo Gallery
http://petroglyph.cl.msu.edu/~tigger/WoodWorkPhoto.html

Hobbyists and full-time woodworkers can get a glimpse of works in progress and finished products through this small photo archive. Enjoy images of beds then jump to a more extensive woodworking collection.

HOLLYWOOD, HERE I COME

It's true that a lot of films aren't made in Hollywood anymore. But when I was a little girl, the movies *were* Hollywood, and Hollywood was the movies—it was all one and the same to me. Going to the movies was a major social event, a family outing—how we used to marvel at the grand spectacles and stories on the silver screen! What glamorous lives I imagined the stars led (as I'm sure most of them did). With the specter of WWII clouding almost everything we did, going to the movies was the greatest escape of all—it was the place where I could forget for a few hours that young men and women were dying overseas; where almost everyone was beautiful, and most stories had happy endings; and where your patriotism could be whipped into a veritable frenzy by Hollywood's own particular spin on the war.

Hollywood, and filmmaking, has changed a lot since then—some for the good, and some, I fear, for the worst. But even as movies have grown more violent and explicit, I have to admit that they have probably become more honest, too—not all of them, to be sure, but a good many of them. Films like *Sophie's Choice* and *Schindler's List* make me glad that filmmakers today aren't afraid to tell it like it is (or was); and a small English film called *Wish You Were Here* had me wishing that, when I was a girl, we could have talked as openly about sex as we can today. Even Oliver Stone's near-reckless manipulation of historical fact makes me glad that certain ideas about censorship have eased up somewhat. And like with most other things I do, I prefer to make up my own mind, thank you very much.

MOVIE WEBBING

The Biz: The Entertainment Cybernetwork
http://www.bizmag.com/

News, views, and gossip from this week in music, movies and television are free for the asking at The BIZ, the online entertainment news source. Links to the Reuters/Variety Online Entertainment Report and The Source, an entertainment resource guide, are here as well.

Cinema Sites
http://www.vir.com/VideoFilm/davidaug/Movie_Sites.html

An extensive collection of pointers to online film and television information is maintained here. Topics covered range from film festivals and award updates, to screenwriting and film production resources. The many links here include Hollyweb and Cardiff's Movie Database Browser.

Critics' Roost
http://moviereviews.com/coc-roost.html

Moviereviews.com has gathered a stable of cheeky film critics who render witty reviews of currently showing films. Visitors with their own opinions are invited to link to the main Moviereviews.com site to pen a unique critique.

Disney
http://www.disney.com/

Since Disney does it all, better start at this directory of pointers for links to the many faces of the mouse. Find home video, movies, music, books, television, software, theme parks, and, of course, shopping.

The Dove Foundation
http://www.dove.org/

The goal of the Dove Foundation is to promote "wholesome family entertainment." Visitors can check out the list of movies and videos that fit the Dove bill, and explore the site's various links to family-related resources.

Early Motion Pictures Home Page
http://lcweb2.loc.gov/papr/mpixhome.html

This Library of Congress site provides background information and access to collections of early motion pictures from 1897-1916. Includes detailed descriptions of the collection, and articles on the history and techniques of early filmmakers.

The Envelope Please
http://guide.oscars.org/

The Academy of Motion Picture Arts and Sciences hosts this extensive guide to the Academy Awards. Visitors will find updates on nominees in all Oscar award categories, as well as a historical database of past contenders.

Film and TV Gopher Menu
gopher://riceinfo.rice.edu/11/Subject/FilmTV

Film and TV buffs can browse this repository of video clips and information from Rice University. The gopher site offers archives of experimental film and video, broadcast information resources, and a number of specific subject guides, including the film credits database and the Nielsen TV ratings guide.

Film Festivals on the World Wide Web
http://www.laig.com/law/entlaw/filmfes.htm
This index provides a comprehensive, alphabetical listing of film festivals around the world. Includes links to biggies like the American Film Institute's shindig in Los Angeles and, of course, Cannes. But also find pointers to lesser known festivals— from student expos to Finland's Espoo Cine.

Film Scouts Home Page
http://www.filmscouts.com/
Movie lovers can visit the motion picture feature page for background information on selected films, links to film festivals' pages, and interviews with movie directors.

Film and Television Reviews
http://eng.hss.cmu.edu/filmtv/
Visitors to this page will find a list of selected film and television Web sites. Dozens are listed in alphabetical order by Webmaster— from the Activists Put the Public In Public TV page, to the U.S. Media History site.

Hollywood Network
http://www.hollywoodnetwork.com/
If Hollywood hasn't called yet, why not call Hollywood? Among the entertainment resources collected at this site are talent listings, job opportunities, insider's tips, and directories of services, products, publications, legal information, and merchandise. Also available are an audio library and Hollywood profiles.

Interactive Movie Reviews
http://batech.com/cgi-bin/showmovie
Interactive Movie Reviews lets you be the judge of the best movies in filmdom, instead of "some over-paid pinhead." See how your vote stacks up against other peoples' opinions.

The Internet Movie Database
http://us.imdb.com/welcome.html
Described as "the most comprehensive free source of movie information on the Internet," the Internet Movie Database lives up to its promise. Use the site's search tool or cruise through the detailed index to find anything and everything related to films, filmmaking, and fans.

Left-Wing Films
http://ccme-mac4.bsd.uchicago.edu/DSADocs/Films.html
The Left-Wing Films Web page features a list of films that can be browsed by topics such as environmental and farm struggles, feminism, and sexual freedom. The page is meant to serve as a resource for movie watchers looking for left-wing material from their local video store.

The Lion's Den
http://www.mgmua.com/MGM/index.html
The Lion's Den is the home page for the Metro Goldwyn Mayer/United Artists entertainment conglomerate. Includes information on new motion pictures, television programs, interactive entertainment, and games.

Marquee MovieServer
http://www.marquee.com/
Recent movie reviews and picks of the week are found here. Read about the latest blockbuster or film festival sleeper, check the latest video releases, or read dozens of reviews. Real buffs can also subscribe to the Marquee Magazine for weekly reports through e-mail or fax.

Match Wits With Nicky Facts
http://www.pkbaseline.com/screen/nicky/
Only the best of the best can beat Nicky Facts at this 10-question movie and TV trivia quiz. As for the rest ... Nicky'll "chew you up and spit you out like you was nuthin'."

MCA/Universal Cyberwalk
http://www.univstudios.com/
This mammoth commercial Web site gives the lowdown on Universal Pictures' films and MCA Records' artists. Visitors also can check up on other members of the MCA/Universal corporate family including the Universal Studios Hollywood theme park and Putnam Berkley Online.

Miramax Films
http://www.miramax.com/
Get official Miramax news, preview the studio's latest and upcoming motion picture releases, and take a chance on winning cash and prizes.

Movie Mania

http://www.movievan.com/

What's hot, what's not, and what's coming down the video pike. Stay up-to-date and cutting-edge, chat or discuss current topics, and vote for favorites. There's plenty to do, see, and say when you visit Movie Mania.

The Movie Sounds Page

http://www.moviesounds.com/

"Play it, Sam. Play 'As Time Goes By.'" This and dozens of other sound clips from movies are available for download here. Movie buffs can jump from one film to another in a lineup that ranges from *Casablanca* and *Gone with the Wind* to *Wayne's World*.

Movies.com

http://www.movies.com/

Buena Vista films promotes its latest and soon-to-be released films via this inside report. Link to the home pages of each of the films featured and join in the online fun surrounding each film's premier.

Mr. Showbiz

http://www.MrShowbiz.com/

Visitors to the lively Mr. Showbiz site can read interviews with the stars, download glitzy news and features, search through movie and television reviews, and sniff out the latest gossip.

New Line Cinema

http://www.newline.com/

Movies! Television! Home Video! And New Line Cinema promises even more via this look at what's "new." Shopping anyone?

Paramount Pictures

http://www.paramount.com/homeindex2.html

Explore the motion picture, home video, television, and digital entertainment divisions of this giant in the field of arts and entertainment. While on-site, stop by the studio store for souvenirs.

Sony Pictures Entertainment Movies

http://www.spe.sony.com/Pictures/SonyMovies/

Video clips, audio clips, and other resources on movies from Sony Pictures Entertainment are available here. In addition to current movies, information on older movies and projects in the making are provided.

Sundance Institute

http://www.sundance.org/

The Sundance Institute page contains information about the institute's support of independent filmmaking. Includes information about programs, a calendar of events, links to selected film sites on the Internet, and the Sundance catalog.

Twentieth Century Fox

http://www.fox.com/

Link to this jumpstation for pointers to the Fox TV Network, Fox Interactive, 20th Century Fox Movies, and 20th Century Fox Home Entertainment home pages. Needless to say, there's plenty to see!

Warner Brothers Online

http://www.warnerbros.com/

What'cha after? TV, movies, home video, music, or comics. Warner Brothers does it all and treats its fans to an inside look at the who, what, and when at this "Entertainment Multiplex."

THE BLUES YOU CAN USE

Sitting here one afternoon listening to James Taylor as he rocked the rafters with a wild version of "Steamroller Blues," caroling out "I'm a steamroller, baby, and I want to roll all over you," I thought of Poppa and how he loved the old blues songs and the men (and women) who made them. Poppa was raised in a little town deep in the heart of the Mississippi delta called Moorehead. He was infused with a love of the music that sprung up and flourished there when he was a boy.

He used to tell of the acres of cotton, the back-breaking work at picking time, the harsh delta sun and the cotton fields as far away as the eye could see, claiming that there was a spot where you could stand and turn in all directions and still see the horizon. And in the evenings, tired to the bone after the work was done, sitting on the porches, the old folks would bring out the guitars and harmonicas and sing the songs of their hearts—and their woes—into the delta night.

My grandfather had once owned a small railroad, The Yazoo Delta Railroad,which he lost in the crash of 1898, along with nearly everything else. And Poppa told of W.C. Handy, who worked there, and wrote the song, "The Yellow Dog Blues" in memory of the old train. W.C. Handy wrote many songs that Poppa remembered. "Moorehead Blues" and "Memphis Blues" were only two in a long list.

My mother, on the other hand, hated the old blues songs, primarily because the lyrics were pretty raw, even back then. So Poppa, like a bad kid, would wait until she went shopping. Then he would dig through his huge collection of blues recordings, crank up the Victrola and let loose as loud as it would play. Of course, I was as heavily invested in this activity as he was as we dug through our favorite discs, savored the lyrics and exhuberantly danced the Black Bottom.

We laughed as we sang for it was a magical time, the whole house shaking with low-down and dirty blues, the beat throbbing loudly, the voices weaving in and out soulfully singing, "I've got a long ink pen," and Poppa and me dancing wildly, filled to the brim with the earthy sound of the music we loved. Sadly, it was over too soon as we were always on the lookout for mother, not eager for any lectures when she came back from her shopping expeditions.

Later, living in New York City provided Poppa with a wealth of old record stores to plunder, and on

Lizzie Sez

It's OK to give people a second chance, but think hard before you dole out a third.

Saturday afternoons we would set out for one of his favorite spots to paw through the 78's of the old blues masters. In the 1940s, the blues had not sprung into such general popularity, and Poppa was able to bring home a stash every time he went to the shops, to be carefully hidden for those special days when mother would be gone and we could rock to the funk of the guitar beat, being played in an old roadhouse back on the delta.

All of my life I have been a fan of the blues, and the players who told their stories of pain, loss, and back-breaking work. I'm embarrassed to say that with this rich heritage, I remember few of the old names, and even fewer of the old songs. But when I hear that wild, funky beat I am there, moving to the music, even if only in my mind. " I'm a cement mixer baby, a-burnin' and a-turnin' urn."

Back in the dark ages, when I was a teenager, we were as caught up in the music of our time as much as today's teenagers are in theirs. We danced the jitterbug and swooned over Frankie Sinatra and played Benny Goodman as loud as the old record players would go. Even then, our parents were yelling, "Turn it down!", when all the old 78 platters could do was provide a mild irritation, there being no mega-decibels back then. Saturday nights were often spent by the radio listening to *Your Hit Parade,* featuring the Andrews Sisters' rendition of "The Boogie Woogie Bugle Boy of Company B."

Artie Shaw, June Christie, and Harry James were some of the artists on our Top 10 list, and I still chuckle remembering Spike Jones and the crazy

Lizzie's Tips

It's important to have a support group as you get older. Start expanding your circle today, making sure that some new friends are youger than you are. Their zest for living and energy will energize you.

sounds of the bazooka ripping out such memorable tunes as " In the Fuehrer's Face." Al Jolson had made a comeback, and the Mills Brothers were paddling "Up a Lazy River." And everyone was slightly in love.

We would snap on our "baby doll" pumps, cinch in our waists, and roll out to swing all night to the big band sounds. Your date would pick you up at home in the borrowed family car, go through the agony of a few polite words with the folks, and off you sped to the big dance. And we really did dance—everybody danced with everybody.

There were dense, predatory stag lines lurking all around the walls of the ballroom, and an agile girl could have many partners as she twirled under the spiraling mirrored fragments of light. It was a sweet and romantic time, when guys and their girls actually touched cheek to cheek to the strains of "Blue Moon," while tentatively getting to know each other. A "Big Time Operator" could usually obtain an occasional furtive kiss without the vigilant chaperones taking notice. And as dawn came, the sweet strains of "Good night ladies, 'til we meet tomorrow ... good night ladies, sleep will banish sorrow," would shepherd us reluctantly, arm in arm, to the ranks of waiting Chevrolets for our warriors to take us home.

Today's young girls, at least in my part of town, stomp out of the house to trip the light fantastic in workboots made by "Doc Marten," stuffed with thick black socks wrinkling thickly around their calves. Each dainty arm is wreathed with multicolored tattoos—all the way up to the shoulder. With midriffs exposed and their sweet little belly button rings twinkling in the night, they head out to the nearest bash.

They go out not to listen to romantic music, and not to sway gently to the swing of a lyrical melody in the arms of a favorite beau, but to throb and thrash to the pulsating beat of electric guitars and the shrieking vocals of modern-day alternative rock bands, whose deafening chords reverberate brokenly through the air.

How would you like to wrestle your partner to the ground in a groin-grinding session with Garbage playing their hit tune, "Ugly and Festering," in the background? The Smashing Pumpkins have been wandering around on their Infinite Sadness Tour, a real heartlifter. Bottle Rockets, Mustard Plug, and Contortion Horse are playing wildly all over town. Last, but certainly not least, I hear that Prong and Toenut are packing them in by the hundreds. Never mind the pearls and cashmere, ladies, now you can leap and swoon in your leathers to the pelting beat of The Attack Family, and get down in the mosh pit while gyrating to the blasting thunder of The Crack Babies.

No doubt about it, the romance of my youth appears to be dead in the angst-driven atmosphere of today's rock scene. But nobody seems to be mourning. Who knows? Maybe there's something to all of this; but I'll stick with the tried and true.

MUSIC SITES

A Cappella Web Directory
http://www.casa.org/web_directory.html

This extensive directory can get you started on your search for information about "a cappella" music. Covering both collegiate and professional groups, this well-organized resource contains names, discographies, newsgroups, and ordering options.

Accumulated Accordion Annotations

http://www.cs.cmu.edu/afs/cs/user/phoebe/
mosaic/accordion.html

Check here for a directory to the general and specific information about "squeezeboxes" which is available online. Among the links find cartoons and jokes, buying advice, band and musician pages, and FAQs.

Acoustic Guitar Song Collection

http://www.itsystem.se/culture/guitar/
acoustic.guitar.song.collection.html

This page provides guitar tablatures and musical scores, plus audio and sound files of selected songs by Simon and Garfunkel, Paul Simon, Leonard Cohen, and Serge Gainsbourg. Additional features include links to interviews with the artists and other musical resources.

American Music Network Gopher Menu

gopher://tmn.com/11/Artswire/amn

The Sonneck Society for American Music sponsors the American Music Network gopher server in order to provide browsers access to information pertaining to the appreciation, performance, creation, and study of American music. Visit here to find out more about the society and forthcoming musical events.

Archives of African American Music and Culture

http://www.indiana.edu/~aaamc/index.html

Check out the Archives of African American Music and Culture at Indiana University, for details about exhibitions and events, radio programs, photos, and sound recordings.

Ari Davidow's Klez Picks

http://www.well.com/user/ari/klez/

Resources on klezmer music are collected at this site which says "this generation of klezmer musicians reblends jazz and punk and the spirit of an entire Yiddish revival." Included are reviews, band information, and links to many pages related to klezmer or Jewish music.

Lizzie Sez

Be bold and adventurous. When looking back over your life, you will always regret the things you did not do far more than the things you actually did.

The Bagpipe Web

http://pipes.tico.com/pipes/pipes.html

For experienced pipers and wanna-be blowhards alike, the Bagpipe Web provides a tuneful home. Site features include a calendar of bagpipe festivals, reviews of new bagpipe recordings, links to manufacturers pages, pointers to clubs worldwide, and a classified section for bargain bagpipes. Those with questions should find the answers they seek in the FAQ file.

Barbershop Web Server

http://timc.pop.upenn.edu/

The Barbershop Web Server contains information on barbershop music, recordings, and pointers to online resources. Also find links to Frequently Asked Questions (FAQ), organizations around the world, and sheet music.

BluesNet Home Page

http://dragon.acadiau.ca/~rob/blues/

BluesNet offers itself as "the Internet Blues Resource Center." Blues fans can stop by the center to learn more about various blues performers, see pictures, and link to other topical sites.

CCM Online

http://www.ccmcom.com/

This online edition of "CCM Magazine" provides news, reviews, features, and columns on Christian music. Other features include information on CCM radio and television programming, concert listings, sound files, and pictures.

Ceola's Celtic Music Archive

http://celtic.stanford.edu/ceolas.html

Visitors to Ceola's Celtic Music Archive will find "the largest collection of information on celtic music available online." Areas covered here include background on the music, instruments, and artists, reviews and sound samples, and tour and live music event schedules.

Chinese Music FTP server

ftp://sunsite.unc.edu/pub/multimedia/chinese-music/

Visit this site to download sound files of Chinese music. The files are more or less organized in historical order. Select from all types of music including old and new folk songs, opera and ceremonial music, or pre- and post-liberation songs.

The Choir Links Page

http://www.abc.se/~m9850/

TheChoirLinksPage/

The Web gets vocal through The Choir Links Page. It provides pointers to a long list of choirs with home pages on the Web, including boy's choirs, children's choirs, church choirs, and college choirs.

Christian Music Directory

http://www.ccmusic.org/cmd/

Christian music promoter CCMusic maintains this directory of information on artists, concerts and festivals, radio stations and programs, record labels, studios, and videos. A Frequently Asked Questions (FAQ) file is also provided.

Classical Music on the Net

http://www.einet.net/galaxy/Leisure-and-Recreation/Music/douglas-bell/Index.html

Find links to classical music resources quickly and easily. Search by topic or keyword.

ClassicalNet Home Page

http://www.classical.net/music/

Offering a "point of entry" into a wide sampling of classical music files, this excellent resource links music lovers to composer data, a basic repertoire, a buyer's guide (plus recommendations), reviews, and articles. There's plenty here, but for those who don't find what they're seeking, there are also links to other topical sites, including the home pages of all the ensembles and orchestras with a presence on the Internet.

CultureFinder: The Internet Address for the Performing Arts

http://www.culturefinder.com/index.htm

CultureFinder hosts a wealth of resources for lovers of classical music, dance, opera, and theater. Here browsers can peruse such features as the culture find of the week, news, and interviews, or drop by the online shop and library.

Cybergrass: The Internet Bluegrass Music Magazine

http://www.banjo.com/BG/

Get the latest on traditional music from this electronic publication. Bluegrass festival and society listings, artist profiles, and other reading matter keep fans current. Classified ads connect pickers and other music makers with banjos, mandolins, and fiddles for sale.

Digital Tradition Folk Song Database

http://www.deltablues.com/dbsearch.html

Search this cross-cultural index for folk songs by title, keyword, or tune. The Digital Tradition Folk Song Database catalogs folk music from around the globe and contains over 6,000 songs.

DiscoWeb

http://www.msci.memphis.edu/~ryburnp/discoweb.html

Fans of disco music will enjoy this site which is maintained by Paul Ryburn, the only University of Memphis faculty member with a fully operational disco ball in his office. Visit here for song lists, historical perspectives, newsgroups, merchandise outlets, and many other disco-related resources. Includes a downloadable disco ball graphic.

The Drums and Percussion Page
http://www.cse.ogi.edu/Drum/

The Drums and Percussion Page offers a variety of resources for drummers and percussion enthusiasts. Visit this site for its "groove archive," a message board, links to organizations, and topical sites.

Elvis in Latin: Frequently Asked Questions
http://www.cs.uoregon.edu/~bhelm/misc/elvis.html

For those who thought Elvis Presley and Latin were both dead, think again. Want proof? Check out this site detailing a collection of Presley songs rendered in Latin. Ordering information is available for those who just can't pass up this unusual buy.

Galaxy: Music Index
http://galaxy.einet.net/galaxy/Leisure-and-Recreation/Music.html

From the larger Galaxy index, this page provides a directory to music sites categorized by genre. Also find pointers to dozens of online magazines, collections, and discussion groups.

Global Music Center
http://www.eunet.fi/gmc/

Finland's Global Music Center seeks to promote research, recordings, festivals, and publications relating to world music. Includes links to research projects, recording listings, festival schedules, and other events. In Finnish and English.

Gregorian Chant Home Page
http://www.music.princeton.edu:80/chant_html/

If you're into medieval Christian tunes, you've found your online home here, where an interest in Gregorian chant is shared by Princeton University scholars. Browsers will find a serious and scholarly approach to the genre's history and tradition.

Gyuto Tantric Choir Home Page
http://www.well.com/user/gyuto/

Hear the "transcendentally beautiful" sounds of the Gyuto Tantric Choir at this site, or learn more about this group of Tibetan monks and their centuries-old style of chanting. Guests can also link to information on the dangers posed to the survival of Tibetan culture or to other Buddhist Net sites.

InterJazz: The Internet Jazz Plaza
http://interjazz.com/

Serving as a "global Internet jazz center," InterJazz links visitors to information on clubs, agencies, promoters, festivals, and events. Individual artist's pages are also available, along with live chat, promotions, and more.

Internet Beatles List
http://www.primenet.com/~dhaber/blinks.html

For fans of the British hurricane that hit U.S. shores in the 60s and still keeps things stirred up, this comprehensive list of Beatles-related pages will serve up a virtual feast of Fab Four fact, fun, and fine-tuned musicality. Most pages are hosted by fans who still find magic and mystery in the Beatles' music, and some are posted by commercial concerns. Links also point to newsgroups, FTP sites, and other items of topical interest.

Internet Music Resource Guide
http://www.teleport.com/~celinec/music.shtml

Tune in to all kinds of musically related sites for your listening and viewing pleasure. Find general information sites, band and artists' pages, magazines, and labels. Links also lead to Usenet newsgroups and online music shops.

JAZZ Online
http://www.jazzonln.com/

Calling all jazz enthusiasts! This site offers a cool selection of CD reviews, news stories, radio information, and artist features about that most American of musical genres. Covering everything from Coltrane to the latest players, there's something here to suit most every jazz fan's tastes.

JazzNet

http://www.dnai.com/~lmcohen/

Promoting itself as "your guide to the what's new in Jazz on the Web," JazzNet provides weekly lists and reviews of sites submitted for inclusion in the JazzNet masterlist.

Latin Music On-Line!

http://www.lamusica.com/

Lovers of spicy Latin rhythms should check out this site for a plethora of information about salsa, merengue, rock, Latin jazz, and pop. Here you'll find news, concert information, interviews, reviews, and pointers to related sites.

Library of Congress Music Resources Gopher Menu

gopher://marvel.loc.gov/11/global/arts/music

Those interested in exploring various aspects of the world of music online can begin their search at this general jumpstation. Link to instrument-specific resources, song-lyric databases, and reading rooms.

List of Music Mailing Lists

http://server.berkeley.edu/~ayukawa/lomml.html

Myra Wong hosts this impressive guide to the music-oriented mailing lists available online. Each mailing list exists for the discussion of a specific aspect of the music scene— be it an artist, a group, a genre, or an instrument. Entries in the masterlist of mailing lists include addresses and information for subscribing to each.

Lyrics Page Search Screen

http://archive.uwp.edu/pub/music/lyrics

Just what is that singer grunting or mumbling about? Find out at the Lyrics Page Search Screen, where users can enter song lyric fragments, song titles, or the name of an artist to find a song's lyrics. Guests can also link to other musical sites.

The Music Gopher at Rice University

gopher://riceinfo.rice.edu/11/Subject/Music

This server hosts an extensive collection of music resources. Visitors can access everything from magazines, FTP archives, and catalogs, to gig guides and discographies. Searchable by artist or label.

Musi-Cal

http://concerts.calendar.com/

This site bills itself as "the first online calendar that provides easy access to the most up-to-date worldwide live music information: concerts, festivals, gigs and other musical events." Visitors using this free service simply plug in the name of a performer, an event, or a venue, and submit the request. Other options include searching by date and keyword.

Online Music and Audio References

http://www.art.net/Links/musicref.html

This Art.Net page serves as a gateway to various musicians, bands, and online music services. The page also offers links to record labels, radio stations, and related resources.

Opera on the Web

http://musicinfo.gold.ac.uk/index/opera2.html

There's nothing fancy here, just a simple directory pointing to the Web pages of opera companies around the world. You'll also find links to a few other opera-related pages, including Field Notes of a Rookie Opera Lover, a Basic Opera Dictionary, and Opera Plots Made Easy.

OperaGlass

http://rick.stanford.edu/opera/main.html

OperaGlass explores the many elements of operatic entertainment, offering browsers an inside glimpse of composers, companies, and productions. From this page, fans can obtain synopses, libretti, discographies, profiles, and pictures.

Picture Gallery of Classical Composers

http://spight.physics.unlv.edu/picgalr2.html

Classical music enthusiasts can peruse a gallery of over 1,000 pictures of classical composers organized alphabetically, by nationality, and by time period.

The Plainsong and Mediaeval Music Society
http://www.ncl.ac.uk/~nip2/

Founded in 1888 in Great Britain, this group of scholars, clergy, and musicians is interested in the traditions of music and chant before 1550. On its home page, the society invites new members to join and details its small grant program for musicians.

Ragtime Home Page
http://www.ragtimers.org/~ragtimers/

Ragtime music comes alive on this site through histories, sound clips, and MIDI files. Also find a calendar of current musical events, information about recordings, and answers to frequently asked questions.

The Rat Pack Home Page
http://www.primenet.com/~drbmbay/

The Rat Pack Home Page features a look back at the music and antics of the one-time group of scamps composed of notables like Frank Sinatra, Dean Martin, and Sammy Davis, Jr. The page contains sound clips as well as a dose of hipster history.

Richard Robinson's Tunebook
http://www.leeds.ac.uk/music/Info/RRTuneBk/tunebook.html

Richard's (4th edition) collection of traditional tunes features ethnic ditties from the Scots, Irish, Scandinavian, French, and Balkan tribes, plus a miscellany of other folks. The tunes are indexed by name, country, and type for easy reference. Links to other tunebooks and musical sites add an extra bit of musical fun worth noting.

Tim's Christmas Page
ftp://col.hp.com/html/tbc/Xmas/index.html

How many times have you joined a group of friends in Christmas caroling only to forget the words to the song? Never again. Simply link here for the lyrics to your seasonal favorites.

Tower Lyrics Archive
http://www.ccs.neu.edu/home/tower/lyrics.html

This archive offers pointers to sites containing lyrics from various stage musicals. The works of Andrew Lloyd Webber, Boublil and Schoenberg, and Gilbert and Sullivan are featured among a miscellany of others.

TuneWeb
http://www.ece.ucdavis.edu/~darsie/tunebook.html

This archive of sheet music for traditional tunes is indexed by song type. Categories include reels, jigs, slip jigs, slides, hornpipes, polkas, slow airs, O'Carolan, English country dances, waltzes, marches, American, and miscellaneous tunes. Some audio files are also available for downloading.

Vintage Vaudeville & Ragtime Show
http://www.netrunner.net/~phono/index.htm

Take your seats folks, the show is about to begin. Listen to songs from America's age of vaudeville and learn about the era's biggest stage personalities.

Wolverine Antique Music Society
http://www.teleport.com/~rfrederi/

For those who remember when recorded music came on something other than CDs and cassettes, there is the Wolverine Antique Music Society. Information here includes historical articles, images, and recordings.

World Wide Jazz Web
http://www.xs4all.nl/~centrale/jazz.html

Jazz fans, you've come to the right place for links to all things important in your favorite world of musical entertainment. Musicians, instruments, festivals, and more make up this comprehensive jazz-o-rama.

Worldwide Internet Live Music Archive
http://www.wilma.com/

Say hey to WILMA; she's the "Internet guide to live music," and can tell you most anything you want to know about who's playing what kind of music, where, and when. Just access her Search-O-Matic feature and browse an interactive music database of artists, venues, and concert listings.

World-Wide Web Virtual Library: Classical Music
http://www.gprep.pvt.k12.md.us/classical/

Divided into seven sections, each with its own alphabetical index, the classical music area of the Virtual Library covers biographical information, organizations, online periodicals, general reference materials, reviews and program announcements, computer software, and discussion forums.

World-Wide Web Virtual Library: Music
http://syy.oulu.fi/music/

This outstanding music library features an interactive search system that allows users to specify the type of resources their seeking: academic, commercial, or private; and FTP site, instrument, software, performer, composer, genre, music institution, radio station, record label, e-zine, or shop. Helps users find what they're looking for quickly and efficiently!

OUR BEST FRIENDS

Pets, our faithful companions and friends, our surrogate children, love us unconditionally. And of course, for many of us, they are the most important and fulfilling "hobby" we have.

DOG DAZE

Do you want to live a little longer? Most people would opt for that. Researchers have been gathering data about pet ownership for years, and as a result, we now know that pet owners lead healthier lives than those who do not own pets. People over age 40 who own dogs, for example, have significantly lower blood pressure; 20 percent have lower triglyceride levels, and see their doctors fewer times in a year. All these benefits, just for petting the dog!

> "...and now our dogs are Bubba, the big fun-loving rotty; and Binky, the toy fox terrier that can ride on Bubba's back."

It is easy to understand that a pet, be it only one small goldfish, provides companionship. And those people having responsibility for pets do appear to take better care of themselves. Erika Friedmann, Ph.D., carried her research a bit further by studying 369 heart attack victims. She found that those who owned dogs were far less likely to die within the first year than those who did not own dogs, even though they did not live alone. For one thing, dog owners got more exercise and led more active social lives.

Dogs and other pets have been shown to reduce depression and ease loneliness, especially in Seniors, and to instill a sense of security in people of all ages. Pets can also help reduce the pain associated with loss of a loved one. Seniors with dogs or cats are less likely to experience deterioration in health after a beloved friend or partner has passed away.

"I have had pets most of my life, starting with a Toy Manchester when I was 8 or 9. Currently, I share my home with an 8-year-old Siamese mixed breed cat that was born in my mulch pile by the garden, and a Male Pekingese (approx 18 mos old) that was found sitting in the middle of a busy intersection. What a pair!! Like the cat that started fetching and decided when it was time to quit, this dog will get his toy, bring it onto my lap, and it is either toss it for him or there is no rest. When he gets "tired" he will go to his sleeping pad and go to sleep. Nothing but a visitor arriving at the door will disturb him."

We always had dogs when the children were growing up. Little Impy, a teacup Chihuahua, was hands-down the smartest. Every evening she went around and picked up her toys and put them in her toybox before we retired for the night. As small as she was, she would sit on the edge of the bed protecting her infant charges from rolling off.

Huge Odette, a Russian wolfhound, was the sweetest, most loyal, and certainly the most serene dog we ever had. When she tired of a toddler poking in her ears or rolling all over her, she gently rose to her full height, which was considerable, toppled the toddler gently off her back and silently slipped away. She was truly my friend, protector, and companion, a silent shadow with me always.

But the dog that really stands out in my memory was an old battered Scottie that staggered in through the back gate, all legs broken and terribly ill. At first I tried to ignore him in the hopes that he would disappear. But it didn't take long to realize that this would probably be the last stop he would ever make if I did not come to the rescue.

Fixing a box in the pantry, I gently led him inside and called the vet, who stopped by on his way home from work. Every evening for two weeks, the doctor dropped in to check on his barely surviving patient. And every day we fed the bedraggled Scottie by hand, and watered his dry mouth with a turkey baster. Little by little, the fever dropped and the stubby legs began to heal. The children named him "Scottina Marie," and he was soon following them everywhere on his gnarled little legs, lurching about like a drunken sailor.

It wasn't long before Scottina Marie had established his own routine. Every morning he gathered the children and took them to school, tail wagging, tongue lolling, with a big smile on his face. He had found a purpose in life. When he returned home, he walked down the block to pick up our neighbor, John Taylor, to escort him to the bank where he worked. It was a long run to get back to the schoolyard in time for morning recess, but get there he did. The rest of the morning was free of burdensome responsibilities, so there was time for a hearty meal and a nap.

MAKING ROUNDS

After napping, returning to the bank to pick up John, and frisking about a bit, Scottina Marie was off to his final destination of the day—the neighborhood bar. There he entertained the regulars with his bag of tricks: rolling over, jumping through hoops, and standing up to beg for the generous handfuls of popcorn, peanuts, and praise that he considered his due.

And every evening, just before fixing supper, this grownup homemaker would get in the car, drive to the bar, honk the horn and open the car door for the husky black streak to pile in. Home we would go for supper and a quiet evening with the family.

I look back on those bar stops with amazement—that I actually stopped my daily chores to go to a bar and pick up a dog! But I did it every day of his life!

"I have two male yellow napes (parrots). They're together since they were babies. They are more bonded to each other than to me. One is dominant, the other is submissive, and they both want to breed. They fooled me into thinking they were a pair, but a blood test revealed their true gender. Nothing to worry, the vet told me. Theirs is a substitute behaviour. Well, then it's o.k., I guess."

A MEMBER OF THE FAMILY

It isn't hard to see how strongly a pet can insert himself into your life and become an important member of the family, a character to be reckoned with and a good friend. So for those of you who enjoy the company of a "Best Friend" or a noble companion, remember, too, that the benefits of these faithful pals may help you enjoy a longer, healthier, and more stress-free life.

PET STUFF

Cat Fanciers
http://www.fanciers.com/

If you don't fancy cats, this posting is NOT for you. Feline fans, on the other hand, won't want to miss this fact-filled, kitty-littered corner of the Web. Hosted by a dedicated group of breeders, exhibitors, and other ailurophiles (cat fanciers), the site offers general information about cat care, a breed description database, show news and registries, veterinary resources, and a referral list of over 1,100 breeders of pedigreed cats who've a presence on the Internet.

Lizzie's Tips
LIZZIE'S TIPS FOR DOG OWNERS

- Don't throw that rank, disgusting T-shirt in the wash! Use it to calm your dog when he becomes anxious. If it smells like you, it will reassure him.

- If your dog is bored, chasing his tail, or running around in circles, take an ordinary shinbone and pack the inside of it with peanut butter. Your dog will love the taste and it will be quite a challenge for him to work that sticky stuff out of the inside of the bone. Be sure to check with your vet first before feeding your dog real bones.

- You may be a chocoholic, but never give chocolate to your dog. It acts as a poison to her system when eaten in large quantities.

- You have always been told to eat your carrots, but did you realize that raw carrots can help to keep your dog's teeth clean? Along with regular brushing, eating raw carrots keeps the bacteria around the gums from free floating throughtout his system, and lodging on the heart valve.

- You know what too many beans will do to you. Well, dogs can have flatulence, too, from bolting their food and swallowing too much air. Put a tennis ball into her food bowl and she will have to work harder, thus eating more slowly and hopefully reducing the amount of hot air she ingests.

- When your puppy is teething, give him a frozen rag to ease those swollen gums.

- For fleas: Put a plugged-in nightlight just over the lip of a lasagna pan partly filled with water. Fleas will leap toward the light and drown, poor dears.

Doggy Information on the Web
http://www.bulldog.org/dogs/

Fetch most anything you'd care to know about dogs from the diverse collection of resources compiled, annotated, and presented here. Browse by subject areas including breed clubs, breed pages, breed FAQs, pictures, and publications, or search by keyword.

The Fish Information Service (FINS)
http://www.actwin.com/fish/

Consult this searchable archive for fishy facts and wise ways for dealing with aquarium wonders— be they freshwater, marine, tropical, or temperate. Find chat rooms, vendors, clubs, movies, images, and FAQs, along with gallons of fun and related links.

The Online Book of Parrots
http://www.ub.tu-clausthal.de/p_
welcome.html

Polly want a parrot page? Here's a "virtual encyclopedia" devoted exclusively to Aves of the order Psittaciformes— you know, those tropical and semi-tropical birds characterized by hooked bills, bright plumage, and, in some cases, the ability to mimic human speech. Though the site's focus is not on parrots as pets, it does hold answers of all kinds for parrot owners. And yes, the database is searchable and offers a whole section of photos.

Save-a-Pet On-line
http://pasture.ecn.purdue.edu/~laird/Dogs/
Rescue/

Created by a pet lover for other concerned stewards of the animal kingdom, this index points to organizations which rescue and shelter animals in need. Find canine, feline, and leporine (rabbit) rescue organizations. You can also warm your heart on a few rescue stories, too.

The Virtual Pet Cemetery
http://www.lavamind.com/pet.html

Here lie Touché the turtle, Misty the mutt, Emerson the parakeet, and dozens of other gone but not forgotten pets— all of which have been virtually laid to rest in this cyber-cemetery with fond words and memorable tail tales. Read all the nice things these animals did and meant to the humans they left behind.

Chapter **II**

BIG BROTHER...
WATCHING OVER YOU?

EXECUTIVE BRANCH

SELECTED CABINET AGENCIES

JUDICIAL BRANCH

LEGISLATIVE BRANCH—SENATE AND HOUSE OF REPRESENTATIVES

IN A CLASS BY THEMSELVES—INDEPENDENT FEDERAL AGENCIES

FEDERAL DOCUMENTS AND OTHER INFO SOURCES

STATE AND TRIBAL GOVERNMENT SITES

Most of us today, having lived with years of government intervention, are pretty definite about our growing need to feel more independent of the stranglehold on our personal lives, often enforced by congressional mandate. Myself, I'm a little ambivalent about what the government ought to be doing besides meddling and making laws that make no sense. Some of the time, I can see the need for rules and regs handed down from the federal level, and other times, I don't.

I have very mixed feelings, for example, over the latest welfare reform bill. It is a complicated problem of such long standing, with generations of the underprivileged having lived this way of life, that it seems unlikely that a pen stroke—unaccompanied by any serious discussion of underlying social and economic problems—is going to change much of anything for the better. There are 14 million poor people in America, and two-thirds of them are children. $130 billion was paid out to entitlement programs in 1996. How do you abruptly end that? What do you use as a bridge to another way of life? And what has happened here, in the world's wealthiest society, the one we called "The Great Society"? How can we end the war on poverty without ending poverty itself?

Keeping people on the dole doesn't do much for their confidence and self-esteem, but without extensive job training to provide skills for work opportunities—without an investment in our public schools to help level the educational playing field, regardless of a young person's economic status—how do these people leave the cycle of welfare and make it on their own? And what of other entitlement programs like Head Start? I look at the public schools, financed in part by the Feds and by individual states, and I believe emphatically that I had a far superior education than children get today.

I'm glad that I don't have to solve these problems single-handedly, for I often feel as if I have no sound or practical solutions. So, like others, I am letting the Feds try to solve them.

I can do my part, however—as you can—by staying informed and current about issues surrounding poverty, public education, and, perhaps the keystone to understanding and solving many of our social problems, taxes. Along with understanding taxation (what a task!), comes a willingness to pay

Lizzie's Tips
DEBUNKING THE MYTH

- 75% of families now receiving Aid to Families with Dependent Children (AFDC) did not grow up in welfare homes.

- 38% of these recipients are Caucasian.

- 36% are African American.

- 18% are Hispanic.

- 5.4% of the nation's population received AFDC in 1993.

- 17% of those recipients were African American.

- Welfare payments have sunk by 30% since 1970, not keeping pace with inflation.

- Most people do not enjoy living far below the poverty level or applying for food stamps.

- Most people get assistance for two years or less due to sudden unemployment that devastates the family's living standards.

- The typical welfare mom is 27-years-old with two children, has work experience, and has some other source of income.

- 87% of these women have been assaulted and abused, and 40% were sexually molested as children.

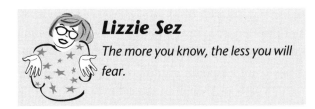

Lizzie Sez

The more you know, the less you will fear.

for certain programs (and not to pay for others), and a desire that we all be assessed according to our abilities to pay (that means *you*, Corporate America!).

And the better informed you are, the better you'll be able to decide, come election time, who is best prepared—and able—to represent your interests at the local, state, and federal levels. The Web sites I've gathered together here will go a long way toward keeping you in the know. Surf to your heart's content—this is still one place where Big Brother *isn't* always watching (er ... except maybe at the CIA's home page!).

EXECUTIVE BRANCH

THE PRESIDENT AND VICE PRESIDENT

White House World Wide Web
http://www.whitehouse.gov/WH/
Welcome.html

Take a virtual tour of the White House, read the official welcomes from the President and Vice President, peek in on their families, and access loads of other government-related info just for citizens, such as the Interactive Citi-

The White House

The Executive Office of the President includes senior policy advisors and offices responsible for the President's correspondence and communications, the Office of the Vice President, the Office of the First Lady, as well as the Office of Mrs. Gore.

zens' Handbook, with more civics information than your eighth-grade textbook.

White House Offices and Agencies
http://www.whitehouse.gov/WH/EOP/html/
EOP_org.html

A number of the agencies you hear about on the news are White House offices, and are not organized under a cabinet department. This page from the White House server lists these offices, and provides hyperlinks to their home pages. Want to know more about the National Security Council, the Office of Management and Budget, or the President's Foreign Intelligence Advisory Board? This page is the place to start.

THE PRESIDENT'S CABINET

United States Department of Agriculture
http://www.usda.gov/

The USDA isn't just responsible for the safety of your food. This federal department is also in charge of administering agricultural price and income support programs, managing the Nation's forests and rangelands, and coordinating Federal assistance to rural areas. Among other interesting features, read about how the Beagle Brigade is an important part of the USDA's agricultural quarantine inspection program (yes, beagles as in dogs—dogs who wear "bright green jackets").

United States Department of Commerce
http://www.doc.gov/

The Department of Commerce page isn't a thrilling stop. There's a minimum of info here and an uninspiring page design. Nevertheless, if you want to learn about the Commerce department's mission to promote American business and trade via the press releases and speeches of its secretary, or if you just want to find out how the department's organized, this is the place to go. Of course, Commerce *is* responsible for the federal budget, so if you want a general background on the process or feel like digging into all the gory details of your tax dollars at work, they've posted plenty of online info for you.

United States Department of Defense
http://www.dtic.dla.mil/defenselink/

DOD, headquartered at the Pentagon, is responsible for the U.S. military forces. Of course, that broad mandate includes the responsibility for *supplying* the military—everything from jets and tanks to MREs (meals ready to eat)—so DOD is a monolithic government contractor and ultimately responsible for those $20 bolts you hear about. Nevertheless, the site includes links to each service branch, along with a history of the department and well-scrubbed updates on world hot spots.

United States Department of Education
http://www.ed.gov/

Despite harrowing stories about the state of public education, the Department of Education adopts an upbeat tone here as it describes all the services available at its Web site. Resources for teachers and researchers, grant and student loan information, program initiatives (Goals 2000, School-to-Work, Safe, Disciplined, and Drug-free Schools), and a page full of programs and services share space with organizational charts, searchable publications, and news briefs.

United States Department of Energy
http://www.doe.gov/

You might not know that one of the missions of the Department of Energy is to provide the leadership necessary "to achieve efficiency in energy use, diversity in energy sources, a more productive and competitive economy, improved environmental quality, and a secure national defense." Wait a minute! Diversity in energy sources? Is that why we fought the Gulf War? National defense? Isn't that another department? Read all about it here.

United States Department of Health and Human Services
http://www.os.dhhs.gov/

The HHS boasts more than 300 programs designed to protect the health of American citizens. Household name agencies under the control of HHS include the Centers for Disease Control and Prevention, the Food and Drug Administration, the Health Care Financing Administration (the Medicare people), and the National Institutes of

Health. HHS awards more grants than any other government agency—around 60,000 grants per year—and the Medicare program is the nation's largest health insurer, processing more than 800 million claims per year. No wonder there's a government bureaucracy; numbers like this require a big staff to move the paper around.

United States Department of Housing and Urban Development
http://www.hud.gov/

HUD has a well-designed home page, giving you the option to select info for citizens or businesses. The citizen area contains facts about buying and renting homes, along with special programs for senior citizens, low-income families, and disabled persons. You'll also find ideas for building strong communities and suggestions for getting involved. On the business side of the fence are funding and contracting opportunities, along with news releases and technical assistance.

United States Department of the Interior
http://www.doi.gov/

Interior has a noble mission: preserve, maintain, and restore federally managed lands, waters, and renewable resources. Find out about the programs they have in place to accomplish this daunting task as they combat the effects of individual litterbugs and corporate polluters. Bureaus under the aegis of Interior include the Bureau of Indian Affairs, the U.S. Fish and Wildlife Service, the National Park Service (my favorite), and the Bureau of Land Management.

PACKING A HEATER

United States Department of Justice
http://www.usdoj.gov/

Justice is the largest law firm in the country, and their site includes loads of legal and law-enforcement info. Want to know about the Freedom of Information Act? Tobacco news? Upcoming seized-assets auctions? Stop off at Justice. You can pretend you're at the post office and look at the mug shots of the FBI's 10 most wanted, current DEA fugitives, and even the U.S. Marshals 15 most wanted fugitives.

While I was perusing the U.S. Department of Justice site, I couldn't help thinking about all the hysteria in these parts just lately about gun control legislation, and the fact that many of the states surrounding mine have relaxed their gun control laws, allowing citizens to carry concealed weapons. Since I live right smack in the corner of a state bordering two others, this is no small thing to me. This means that a private citizen just a few miles away, who formerly had to keep his weapon exposed, can now stuff it away—inside a coat or jacket, in the glove compartment of the car, or in a handbag or briefcase—instead of carrying it out in the open where the weapon can be plainly seen (and I have to admit that even the thought of an average citizen toting a gun in plain view is a bit jarring).

NEW RULES

Some companies that feel affected by the change have come up with startling new rules for their employees. A friend dropped by one afternoon recently, and brought with her the latest memo from a home health care company where she works. This company dispatches those nice little nurses and aides who come to your home to check your medication, change your dressings, and give you a bath.

In bold type, widely spaced, the company demanded that nurses and aides keep their weapons off the premises, defining weapons as, "all firearms, switchblades, butterflies, and all other knives, brass knuckles, and clubs, dangerous chemicals, and explosives..."!

CHECK YOUR BLADE AT THE DOOR

The mental picture of a professional nurse with a switchblade strapped to her thigh, while bending over a patient taking blood pressure, has me somewhat nonplussed. Explosives? Plastique or dynamite? Could you force a few sticks into your brassiere while holding the blasting caps under your tongue? Or a dangerous chemical (how about acid?) wrapped in the gauze from your band-aid box?

I personally have never known anyone who had a habit of transporting brass knuckles around, and I thought that most states had outlawed them years ago. Of course, they would fit in anyone's handbag comfortably without being noticed, ready for immediate use.

And what about clubs? The large club carried about by Alley Oop of ancient comic strip days comes to mind. Where would anyone hide that? As for shotguns and baseball bats, I suppose a pant leg would do for concealment, but that could really hamper you if you should have to make haste.

Should such a law pass in my state, I wonder if I will begin to think that everyone who passes me in the supermarket is carrying a concealed weapon? An afternoon at the movies could be spent in high anxiety, worrying whether half the population of the theater had dynamite stuffed in their pockets.

Used to be I never thought about people going around with explosives and clubs—terrorists, yes, but not plain folks. But now that everyone can conceal their weapons, I wonder where they plan to put them all?

AND NOW FOR SOMETHING COMPLETELY DIFFERENT...

United States Department of Labor
http://www.dol.gov/

The neatest aspect of Labor's Web site is America's Job Bank, an enormous index of sites useful to job hunters. Even though you may not be looking for a job these days, your children might be interested in this excellent resource. The Labor site also includes info on the current minimum wage, and a great online handbook called Protecting Your Pension.

United States Department of State

http://www.state.gov/

If you missed the Secretary of State's latest news conference, you can read a transcript of his or her remarks on current world hot spots at the State Department site. OK, so that's not all that interesting, but the feature on diplomatic history includes some tasty tidbits. For example, did you know that shortly after the presidential election in 1960, then Soviet Chairman Khrushchev sent a message to John Kennedy congratulating him on his victory and expressing the hope that relations between the United States and the Soviet Union "would again follow the line along which they were developing in Franklin Roosevelt's time." Well, that hope wasn't quite realized in the '60s, was it?

United States Department of Transportation

http://www.dot.gov/

I didn't know the Coast Guard was under the administration of the Department of Transportation, did you? I always figured they were a branch of the military (and, in fact, do report to the Pentagon during wartime). After all, the Coast Guard has its own service academy. Well, that just goes to show you that you're never too old to learn. DOT also includes the Federal Aviation Administration, the National Highway Traffic Safety Administration, and the Federal Railroad Administration. This isn't a very exciting page, but I always get a little thrill when I learn something new.

United States Department of the Treasury

http://www.ustreas.gov/

The illustration on Treasury's home page shows the area around the national historic landmark paved with $100 bills. Nice sentiment and meaningful, too, because the Treasury site is easily a $100 page. Here you can take a Web tour of the some of the restored rooms in the landmark building (accompanied by interesting notes) and browse a collection of historic paintings and photographs. Treasury, of course, is in the business of making money—among other things—and they tell you all about their activities at this site.

United States Department of Veterans Affairs

http://www.va.gov/

This is the site you want if you need information about veterans' and dependents' benefits, VA cemeteries, or VA forms (including the SF 180 Request Pertaining to Military Records). The site also includes info on special programs and provides the locations of regional offices and VA medical centers around the country.

SELECTED CABINET AGENCIES

Let's take a look at some of the agencies, bureaus, services, and programs within various cabinet departments. These entries are only a small sample of the bureaucratic tumble in the executive branch. If the agency where your Cousin Bob spent the best 25 years of his life isn't listed here, you can link to it from the cabinet department's home page.

Administration on Aging

http://www.aoa.dhhs.gov/

"Your resource for information on aging" (do we really need to know any more than we do already?) from the Department of Health and Human Services wants to tell you all about The Older Americans Act. This law provides for home- and community-based care, nutritional programs, and various support services. The best feature of this page, however, is the Aging Network Resource Page, a select index of links covering topics from eldercare to financial planning.

Bureau of Engraving and Printing

http://www.ustreas.gov/treasury/bureaus/bep/

The Bureau of Engraving and Printing (a Department of the Treasury office) makes money, postage stamps, identification cards, naturalization certificates, and other security documents. The site includes two videos about legal money-making; I especially like the one called Money Hot off the Press. It reminds me of my basement. (Just kidding!)

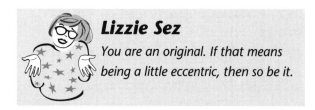

Lizzie Sez

You are an original. If that means being a little eccentric, then so be it.

Bureau of the Public Debt

http://www.ustreas.gov/treasury/bureaus/pubdebt/

The mission of Treasury's Bureau of the Public Debt is to "borrow the money needed to operate the Federal Government and to account for the resulting public debt." I'll bet those people stay busy. To add a sobering note to your day, link to the Bureau's report of the current public debt, reported "to the penny." The number is so large, it took me a few seconds to figure out how to read it.

Federal Bureau of Investigation

http://www.fbi.gov/

The G-men and G-women of the FBI (Department of Justice) cast their agency in a flattering light here with interesting summaries of past cases, fact sheets, and a FAQ. Some of the questions are pretty interesting like, How does the Central Intelligence Agency differ from the FBI? and How much time and money will the FBI spend on a "typical" investigation? You'll also find appeals from the FBI for information on high-profile, in-the-news cases, and, of course, the infamous "Ten Most Wanted Fugitives" list.

Food and Drug Administration

http://www.fda.gov/fdahomepage.html

The FDA (Health and Human Services) has a wonderfully organized home page, with button-style hyperlinks to the various products they control: cosmetics, drugs (human and animal), medical devices, biologics, and foods. These are the folks who make sure that the latest drugs from the pharmaceutical companies don't put you in a coma or burn holes in your stomach, and they include loads of interesting information and insights at this page.

Forest Service Home Page

http://www.fs.fed.us/

The USDA's Forest Service works to protect and manage national forests and grasslands under something called the "multiple-use management concept," so naturally their Web site includes a bunch of tree-related info. One of the best features of this interesting site is the Enjoy the Great Outdoors section. Here you'll find a clickable image map of the United States that identifies national forests, grasslands, and parks. Click on a site for a description of the area and its recreational opportunities, and then access the Campground Reservations page to find out how to reserve your spot in the woods. There's lots more here, including info on volunteer opportunities in national forests.

Health Care Financing Administration

http://www.hcfa.gov/

The Department of Health and Human Services also includes the Health Care Financing Administration, the agency that administers Medicare and Medicaid. This site offers an overview of its mission and its programs—vitally important to so many of us. Statistics, data rates, reports, regulations, laws, manuals, and research results are available for review.

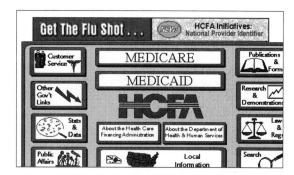

TAXED TO THE MAX

Whenever I think of the Federal Government, the first thing that comes to my paranoid mind is the Internal Revenue Service. It's no wonder that at tax time, a cloud of procrastination filters into my domain and spreads its dark fog all over the place, for finding tax documentation and forms becomes the great challenge of the year. And who wants to look for this stuff anyway?

Internal Revenue Service
http://www.irs.ustreas.gov/prod/

Everybody's favorite government agency (part of the Department of Treasury) wants to communicate with you—in a *positive* way. Their home page is friendly and inviting, and they've gone the extra mile to provide tax info, forms, publications, and tips in a 'zine-type format that doesn't look anything like the pubs you can pick up at the local tax office. But don't be fooled. The IRS is still the IRS. A small-print line on the 'zine's masthead reminds you of the number of days until April 15th.

I am better than I used to be, no longer just throwing papers into a brown paper bag. Now I throw them into drawers: the second drawer of my old Governor Winthrop secretary, the top drawer of the buffet, and an expandable file in the bottom drawer of my home office desk. Would any sane person want to tackle this? But the worry box in my brain keeps spinning, and I must regretfully point my feet and mind in the right direction or the IRS will be knocking at my door. I am told they accept no excuses of the sort I might dream up.

ALL TANGLED UP

Every year I wonder why I save the papers that I do. Many of them have nothing to do with taxes. Some are solicitations I couldn't make up my mind about. Some are book reviews I didn't know what to do with, and still others are just recipes and household debris. But they all have to be sorted through to get to the legitimate papers I need to file my taxes.

I always set up the old battered card table (it gives me a sense of security), lay out the cancelled checks I keep in an old shoebox, make myself comfortable in the worn wing chair facing the TV set (with a wastebasket nearby), and in a flurry of last minute industry, I begin the horrible task of trying to put it all together.

Sally, my accountant, says that I don't do too badly. What does she know? She gets a neatly printed list of deductions coupled with all the correct forms. She has no knowledge of the morass of detritus I have plowed through in order to produce this pristine and professional report. She does have a few pointers, though, to help out, and I thought it only fair to share them with my fellow travelers in disorganization.

Sally says that there are many alternatives for Seniors—places that will prepare your taxes free if you are over 65. Check with your local community centers, banks, hospital senior programs, the ever-present IRS, and any AARP center in your town. Tax Counseling for the Elderly, and Volunteer Income Tax Assistance, offer free preparation advice. For information about a service near you, call 1-800-829-1040. Take advantage of these services if your returns are simple and uncomplicated. Others like myself may feel more secure with a friendly CPA.

Well, next year I'm going to have it all together—with a better filing system, or by using one of those fancy financial software programs that will take care of all this stuff for me. I promise! (And I promise the IRS!)

And speaking of the IRS (that sounds like the opening line of a very bad joke), you'll find more useful information in this selection of nongovernmental tax sites:

1-800-TAX-LAWS
http://www.5010geary.com/

U.S. taxpayers can file federal returns online via this home page for "the largest network of licensed tax professionals." Find a step-by-step set of forms, tax tips and news, and information about the network, including contact numbers.

50 Easily Overlooked Tax Deductions for Individuals

http://www.ey.com/us/tax/50easy.htm

Count them! Here are 50 easy-to-overlook deductions culled from the Tax Guide prepared by the accounting firm Ernst & Young. Have you been claiming the deduction for "fees for safe-deposit boxes that hold investments"? Or how about the deductions for "hearing devices," "contact lenses," and "orthopedic shoes"? No? Well, how about the other 46 deductions listed?

Cyber-Accountant

http://www.cyber-cpa.com/

This online tool was created to help individuals find answers to their tax, financial, and accounting questions, and to find an accountant, CPA, or other financial professional. Search the Cyber-Accountant membership directory to find a qualified professional, or ask the Cyber Accountant your most taxing questions.

Directory of CPA Firms

http://www.cba.bgsu.edu/amis/cpafirms/

Maintained at Bowling Green State University by Dr. David Albrecht, this directory is presented as the "largest directory of CPA firms with Web pages." Link to the Big Six firms, other CPA firms in the United States, and accounting firms around the world. Other options lead to society and association pages, as well as other useful links.

H&R Block

http://www.handrblock.com/tax/index.html

Arguably the largest tax preparation service in the United States, H&R Block claims to have handled one out every seven federal returns filed last year. Visit the company's Web page to find out about the H&R Block Tax Training Course, and how to earn extra income as a qualified tax preparer, or look into the company's tax preparation services for your personal use.

 Lizzie's Tips

DEEDS THAT TRIGGER AUDITS

- Information from banks, investments, or employers that differ from your figures.

- Unusually large deductions. If your deductions are larger than the average in your income group, your return may be flagged. Describe in detail large property losses, dates of long illnesses, or serious accidents.

- Your return shows such large deductions that you have no money left to live on. Whoops!

- Unsupported documentation of large general numbers. How do you explain this?

- Home offices—be sure to keep excellent records.

- Bed and breakfasts—the IRS really scrutinizes this business, so make sure your records are impeccable.

HELP AVOID THE AUDIT BY...

- Answering *all* questions on your return (use "not applicable" rather than leaving blank lines)

- Including all documentation for items you think may be questioned

- Not deducting an item that was disallowed on a previous return

- Completing all schedules that are required

- Sending returns to the right office at the right time

- Not using an inexperienced tax preparer

- Being certain your return has the correct signatures and identifying numbers

Minimizing Your Taxes

http://www.merrill-lynch.ml.com/personal/
taxes/

Explore ways to reduce your tax burden in this section of the Merrill-Lynch Personal Finance Center. Find 96 tips for smart tax planning. Taxes may be inevitable, but there's no reason to overpay.

The Tax Prophet

http://www.taxprophet.com/

Not to be confused with the Tax Wizard, the Tax Prophet presented by Robert L. Sommers offers a FAQ, topical tips, and news worth noting with regard to tax law and tax return preparation. Also find interactive tax applications to help bring various tax issues into focus.

Lizzie's Tips

MORE TAX TIPS FROM SALLY

- Some seniors file tax returns when they don't have to. Be sure to check the filing requirements on the front of your tax booklet that shows income levels for filing. These change every year.

- If you are born on January 1, the IRS gives you credit for your birthday one day early, so that you can take the extra 65+ deduction in the previous year.

- Be sure to itemize interest or dividend income if it is over $400. The IRS will match your return to any 1099 reports of interest and dividends. If there is a discrepancy, your refund could be delayed.

- If the printed label on your tax booklet has the wrong address, use it anyway and write in the correct address after you have scratched out the old one. The IRS can access your tax records more quickly when it has the code number appearing on the pre-printed address label.

- If you should owe taxes, be sure to include your social security number on the check, along with a notation of what the check is for: i.e., the tax form number (e.g., Form 1040) and the tax year for which you owe.

- Record your social security number on each page of your return. If a page separates, it can be easily identified and reattached once it's found.

- State tax refunds may not be taxable if you recieved no tax benefit from the deduction. If you used the standard deduction in the year the taxes were paid, you do not have to include the refund as income this year.

- Only a portion of your social security benefits is taxable. If your income level does not exceed a certain amount, none of it may be taxable.

- If you worked for more than one employer, be sure to claim a credit for any overpaid social security taxes withheld from your wages.

- If you are married, check to see if filing separate returns rather than a joint return is more beneficial.

- Claim the additional standard deductions if you are blind or 65 years or older.

- If you are raising your grandchildren, you may be entitled to an Earned Income Credit. You must care for the child—who cannot be claimed on any other tax return—for more than half the year, and must have earned some income yourself. Ask about the guidelines.

- Keep records of all documents you send to the IRS. Use certified mail for all correspondence. Keep your records in good shape so that things can be found with ease.

Tax Sites Directory

http://www.uni.edu/schmidt/tax.html

Dennis Schmidt, an associate professor of accounting at the University of Northern Iowa, maintains this guide to tax resources on the Internet. Links lead to state and federal tax sites, policy groups, articles, associations, law sites, firms, IRS sites, forms, software, directories, and more.

Tax Tips and Facts

http://www.rak-1.com/

This online newsletter, presented regularly by Roger A. Kahan, a CPA, offers useful tips and topical advice to help prepare for and survive tax time.

Taxing Times 1997

http://www.scubed.com/tax/tax.html

Taxing Times 1997 is "an electronic compendium" of resources offering answers to taxing questions for those who need all the help they can get. Link to this site for information on software, tax newsgroups, preparation tips, and commercial services that can help sort out your money matters at tax time.

TaxSites: Income Tax Information on the Internet

http://www.best.com/~ftmexpat/html/taxsites.html

Organized by content categories, this searchable directory points to government sites, sites prepared by tax professionals, and places offering a variety of topical online resources. Find tax forms, policies, answers to often-asked questions, software, germane articles, newsletters, and much, much more.

Twenty-Five Most Common Tax Preparation Errors

http://www.ey.com/us/tax/25error.htm

Hosted by Ernst & Young, this checklist helps tax return preparers avoid rubbing the IRS the wrong way by making the same stupid mistakes others do. Visitors with an acute fear of the IRS will find some comfort here.

ON WITH THE CABINETS

Joint Chiefs of Staff

http://www.dtic.dla.mil/jcs/index.html

Here's your chance to meet the brass from the Department of Defense: the Chief of Staff, United States Army; the Chief of Naval Operations; the Commandant of the Marine Corps; and the Chief of Staff, United States Air Force. You won't find out any personal tidbits like their favorite foods or TV shows—these bios are all business—but you will find out all about their impressive scholastic and military service records. While you're at the Pentagon, don't forget to stop by and meet the Chairman and Vice Chairman of the Joint Chiefs.

National Oceanic and Atmospheric Administration

http://www.noaa.gov/

Here's one of those bizarre federal anomalies: Why on earth is NOAA a Commerce Department administration? I can't answer that question, but this page includes links to fishery, coastal, and atmospheric ecology programs. Just about anything you can think of that floats (or lives) in water or air is probably included here in one form or another. For example, access info on safe oceanic navigation, satellites, and weather (the National Weather Service is a subagency). To cut to the chase, take a look at the FAQ.

ParkNet: The National Park Service

http://www.nps.gov/

My favorite agency from the Department of the Interior goes online here with a classy page showcasing the wonders of America's national parks. Click on the Info Zone to access background about the service and look into

volunteer opportunities. Move along to the Visit Your Parks feature for all the information you'll ever need about America's national parks. A different park is featured every month, and the site includes info on lesser-known areas and "wild and scenic" riverways. Pack up the RV and get ready to roll.

Veterans Health Administration
http://www.va.gov/vhareorg/vismap.htm

This page from the Department of Veterans Affairs is a clickable image map of the United States showing the locations of the 22 Veterans Integrated Services Network offices. Click on a location to access contact information (names, numbers, addresses), along with hyperlinks to the VA medical centers in the region.

JUDICIAL BRANCH

Decisions of the U.S. Supreme Court
http://www.law.cornell.edu/supct/

Cornell University's Legal Information Institute maintains this comprehensive list of U.S. Supreme Court decisions. Visit here to browse and search by keyword through decisions from 1990 to the present.

FedWorld/FLITE Supreme Court Decisions Home Page
http://www.fedworld.gov/supcourt/index.htm

This archive contains the full text of 7,407 U.S. Supreme Court Decisions dating from 1937 to 1975. The documents are saved as ASCII text files, so you can either read them on your browser's screen or save them to

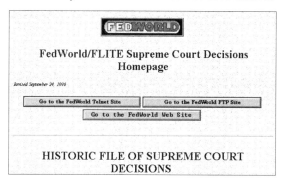

your hard drive. Locate cases via a case name index or perform a keyword search.

Justices of the Supreme Court
http://www.law.cornell.edu/supct/justices/fullcourt.html

This unofficial page is devoted to the nine august individuals who constitute the highest legal authority in the nation and can change lives with the stroke of a pen. Visitors will find photos and biographical information for all current Supreme Court justices. Guess which ones aren't smiling?

United States Federal Judiciary
http://www.uscourts.gov/

This official page, maintained by the Administrative Office of the U.S. Courts, is an information "clearinghouse" from and about the Judicial Branch of the federal government. You won't find any pictures of smiling (or frowning) justices here, but you will find a good introduction to the mysteries of the U.S. Courts in a hypertext document called Understanding the Federal Courts. Press releases, reports, and vacancy lists for judges are about the only other info items in this not-so-generous "clearinghouse."

LEGISLATIVE BRANCH– SENATE AND HOUSE OF REPRESENTATIVES

CapWeb: The Citizen's Guide to Congress
http://www.capweb.net/

This Internet guide to the U.S. Congress includes member lists (by party, name, state, or committee), links to Congressional support agencies and caucuses, e-mail lists, voting records, and links to some nice features on D.C. and its attractions.

Congress.Org
http://policy.net/capweb/Senate/Senate.html

Congress.Org's claim to fame is a search tool that helps you locate the members of your Congressional delegation. Search fields include alphabetic listing, state, and Congressional committees. This excellent locator tool also includes lists of all the House and Senate committees (I was particularly interested in finding out who's on the Permanent Select Committee on Intelligence). Simply select a committee name, click on the search button, and the form returns a list of all the committee members with links to their contact info and a brief bio. When Congress is in session, the Congress.Org home page even includes a daily update on what's happening (or not) in the D.C. halls of power.

THOMAS: Legislative Information on the Internet
http://thomas.loc.gov/home/thomas.html

Named after guess who, this info service from the Library of Congress is an awesome tool that lets you follow the activities in both houses as they make the laws that rule our lives. Find out what's happening in Congress this week, what bills are being considered, and what bills became laws (confused? Click over to the How Our Laws Are Made feature for some background civics info). For each law, find a detailed legislative history (date introduced, date to subcommittee, and on and on and on) and the *actual text* of the law. Similar info is provided for resolutions and bills. Never has politics been so accessible to its citizens. This is a powerful resource, folks, putting the actual day-to-day machinations of government right on your computer screen. Allow yourselves a few moments to be awestruck at the scope and implications, and then use your new power.

U.S. House of Representatives
http://www.house.gov/

This site gives you the official word on what the heck is going on in the House. You'll find legislative updates (bills and resolutions currently on the floor, voting records), schedules, and a membership directory published in three formats (member names listed alphabetically, member names listed by state, and all members listed alphabetically in a complete mailing list format). You'll find this hard to believe, but not all representatives have e-mail addresses. Still, writing your Congressperson has never been easier.

U.S. Senate
http://www.senate.gov/

This server packs in a wealth of U.S. Senate information. Visitors can check out the FAQ, review Senate documents and e-mail lists, or link to the Library of Congress and other government servers. You'll also find general background information about U.S. Senate legislative procedures and the history of the Senate. The virtual tour of the Capitol is a fun diversion, and I particularly liked the Glossary of Senate Terms. You'll sound like the informed citizen that you are if you throw a few of these jargon terms into your next e-mail to Senator Schmoozer.

IN A CLASS BY THEMSELVES— INDEPENDENT FEDERAL AGENCIES

Our government includes a number of independent agencies and commissions that operate outside of the White House and cabinet structure. These agencies are generally created by the enactment of a specific law and exist to perform a rather narrowly targeted function. I've highlighted a few of them for you in the following pages; if you want to see the rest, the White House pages include an excellent roll call at the following URL: **http://www.whitehouse.gov/ WH/Independent_Agencies/html/independent_ links.html**.

Central Intelligence Agency
http://www.odci.gov/cia/

Just as you'd expect, the first thing you read on the CIA home page is a warning and a notification that you're being watched (by whom and from where, I'm not altogether sure—but nobody said Big Bro had to identify his whereabouts). If you tamper with the CIA's page, you'll face criminal prosecution, and by reading the page, you're consenting to government surveillance. Whew! I was ready to back out, but I bravely pressed on (you may re-call that a couple of pranksters hacked into the CIA's site not too long ago, and had a little fun at the government's expense; that may account for the harsh tone of this opening greeting). Inside, the CIA gets a bit friendlier, providing an online tour of its unrestricted areas (actual public tours are not available at spy central, you know) and other nonsensitive-type PR info.

Environmental Protection Agency
http://www.epa.gov/

EPA's not chaining itself to trees or engaging in any other type of radical "green" behavior; instead, this govern-ment agency walks a thin line between ecological protec-tion and the interests of business (read: jobs). EPA calls this approach "reinvention," and defines it as "flexibility in how [improved environmental] results are achieved." The links on this page will help you draw your own con-clusions about what EPA is actually protecting these days.

National Aeronautics and Space Administration
http://www.gsfc.nasa.gov/NASA_
homepage.html

The NASA home page is as fantastic as their missions. There's so much to see and do here, you should definite-ly set aside a significant block of time for exploration of this "space." Images from the Hubble Space Telescope, links to shuttle missions, movies, audio clips, photo-graphs, a FAQ—if it's space-related, it's here.

Peace Corps
http://www.peacecorps.gov/

The Peace Corps sends thousands of volunteers over-seas every year to help interested nations train their own citizens. This page recruits volunteers and donors, and provides a history of the organization, a list of countries it serves, information on "stuff you'll do overseas," and publications. If you thought the Corps was only for new college grads, think again—some folks have volunteered while in their 70s! Think of all the experience you have to offer, and think of the adventures you could have in a new country. Why not?

Social Security Online
http://www.ssa.gov/SSA_Home.html/

Just about everything that used to require a trip to the local Social Security office can now be handled online. Need Personal Earnings and Benefit Estimate Statement, benefit publications, a copy of the Social Security Hand-book? They're here, along with a FAQ, downloadable forms, and more information than you were ever able to pry out of that surly clerk.

United States Postal Service Home Page
http://www.usps.gov/

The Postal Service has opened this "branch office" on the Internet to offer customers information about ZIP codes, stamps, and other USPS products and services. The ZIP+4 lookup feature is one of the handiest Web gizmos going. Rate and delivery guides are included, as well as tips on fraud and how to acquire unclaimed parcels. The site also features a business-oriented section the post-master promises could prove profitable to businesses that depend heavily on the mail.

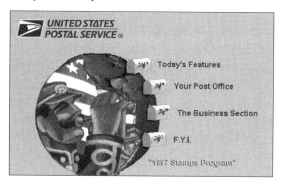

FEDERAL DOCUMENTS AND OTHER INFO SOURCES

Constitution for the United States of America

http://Constitution.by.net/Constitution.html

This excellent online version of the U.S. Constitution includes the original text in a large-print format, annotated with hyperlinks to Constitutional amendments. What this means is that you can first read the original paragraph, section, or the entire article, and then click the amendment link to see how the law has been changed—an excellent example of how to use hyperlinks effectively. An index helps you locate specific subjects quickly, and our beloved (and oft beleaguered) Bill of Rights is also included.

Declaration of Independence

http://www.usia.gov/usa/aboutusa/
deceng.htm

Read the Declaration of Independence again for the first time. You'll be struck by how the elegant phraseology and noble sentiments in the first two paragraphs ring in sharp contrast to the events reported on the evening news. But as you continue through the document that began the Revolutionary War and severed America's colonial ties with Great Britain, you'll see that this country was begun in rabble-rousing fervor, and that we've remained true to the legacy of our founding fathers.

The Federal Bulletin Board

http://fedbbs.access.gpo.gov/

There are enough government documents here to fill a few hundred bulletin boards, and they can all be downloaded for free. Brought to you by the Superintendent of Documents at the Government Printing Office, these files cover the spectrum of government activity: Supreme Court decisions, FDA regulations, IRS forms, Senate voting analyses, State Department background notes, EPA test guidelines, and much more. There's a downloadable user's manual, and the bulletin board includes both Macintosh and Windows source files for the GPO Access service.

FedWorld Information Network Home Page

http://www.fedworld.gov/

Turn on your printer and load it up with paper; you've hit a government document jackpot. The FedWorld FTP site alone has more than 14,000 files, including "information on business, health and safety, and the environment." Tax forms, government reports, the Bacon-Davis Act database (more than 2,000 records with wage information for various jobs), FAA documents, federal jobs, abstracts ... we won't live long enough to read all this stuff.

Government Information Locator Service

http://info.er.usgs.gov/gils/index.html

Think of GILS as a gigantic electronic annotated federal bibliography. All U.S. Federal agencies have been directed to create and maintain GILS records on their information holdings, and to make these records available to the public. GILS records identify federal resources, describe the information in them, and help searchers obtain the actual info. This site includes information on how to use the service, current sites with GILS (not all agencies are online yet), and demos.

GILS Site on GPO Access

http://www.access.gpo.gov/su_docs/gils/
gils.html

GPO maintains GILS records for 25 federal agencies, other records that lead to information sources in all cabinet-level and major independent Federal agencies, and pointer records that link to other U.S. Federal GILS sites (such as DOD, HHS, EPA, and DOI). A search tool helps you narrow your focus, and the helpful hints will turn you into an expert researcher in no time.

The World Factbook 1995

http://www.odci.gov/cia/publications/95fact/

The United States Central Intelligence Agency annually publishes The World Factbook, a very nearly objective profile of the countries that compose our global village. The Factbook offers demographic information, as well as the latest advisories for tourists and diplomats who may be traveling to troubled lands.

STATE AND TRIBAL GOVERNMENT SITES

Here's an alphabetical index to state and tribal government information on the Web. You'll find that the states present their information in a variety of ways. Some state government pages are posted by a state university. Some states include their government data as an integral part of the state's home page (such as Vermont), or have several separate governmental pages branching from the home page (like Connecticut and Delaware). Finally, most states have a separate page devoted solely to governmental activities and issues. Despite these various approaches, you can quickly access the info for your state via the URLs I've provided.

INDIVIDUAL STATE PAGES

Alabama: AlaWeb State Government Page
http://alaweb.asc.edu/govern.html

Alaska: State of Alaska Agency Directory
http://www.state.ak.us/local/akdir.htm

Arizona: State of Arizona World Wide Web
http://www.state.az.us/

Arkansas: Government and Community Relations Home Page
http://apsara.uark.edu/~govinfo/

California: Your California Government
http://www.ca.gov/gov/official.html

Colorado: Colorado Government
http://www.state.co.us/gov_dir/govmenu.html

Connecticut: State of Connecticut Home Page
http://www.state.ct.us/

Delaware: State of Delaware
http://www.state.de.us/

Florida: Florida Government Information Locator Service
http://www.dos.state.fl.us/fgils/

Georgia: Georgia Online Network
http://www.state.ga.us/

Hawai`i: Hawai`i State Government Home Page
http://www.hawaii.gov/

Idaho: Idaho State Government
http://www.state.id.us/governmt.html

Illinois: Statewide Agencies
http://www.state.il.us/home.map?258,85

Indiana: Indiana State Government
http://www.ai.org/state.html

Iowa: Government
http://www.state.ia.us/government/index.html

Kansas: Kansas State Agencies
http://www.tyrell.net/~kdhr/state.html

Kentucky: Alphabetical List of Kentucky State Government Information
http://www.state.ky.us/govtinfo.htm

Louisiana: Info Louisiana
http://www.state.la.us/

Maryland: Maryland State Government
http://www.mdarchives.state.md.us/msa/
mm95_96/html/mdgovt.html

Massachusetts: Massachusetts Access to Government Information Service
http://www.magnet.state.ma.us/

Maine: Maine State Government
http://www.state.me.us/

Michigan: Michigan State Government
http://www.state.me.us/

Minnesota: Minnesota Government Information and Services
http://www.state.mn.us/govtoffice/index.html

Mississippi: State Government Home Pages
http://www.state.ms.us/

Missouri: Missouri State Government Web
http://www.state.mo.us/

Montana: State Government
http://www.mt.gov/gov/gov.htm

Nebraska: Nebraska State Government
http://www.state.ne.us/

Nevada: State of Nevada
http://www.state.nv.us/

New Jersey: State of New Jersey
http://www.state.nj.us/

New Mexico: State of New Mexico Government Information
http://www.state.nm.us/

New York: Citizen's Access to State Government
http://www.state.ny.us/state_acc.html

North Carolina: Agency Info - North Carolina Information Server
http://www.sips.state.nc.us/agency/

North Dakota: North Dakota State Government
http://www.state.nd.us/

Ohio: State of Ohio Government Front Page
http://www.state.oh.us/

Oklahoma: Oklahoma State Government Information Server
http://www.oklaosf.state.ok.us/

Oregon: Oregon Home Page— Government Resources
http://www.state.or.us/governme.htm

Pennsylvania: Pennsylvania State Government
http://www.state.pa.us/govstate.html

Rhode Island: Rhode Island State Government
http://www.doa.state.ri.us/info/

South Carolina: Government in South Carolina
http://www.state.sc.us/gov.html

South Dakota: South Dakota Government Information
http://www.state.sd.us/state/govern.htm

Tennessee: Tennessee—America at Its Best

http://www.state.tn.us/governor/

Texas: State of Texas Government Information

http://www.texas.gov/

Utah: State of Utah Alpha Listing of Agencies

http://web.state.ut.us/alframe.htm

Vermont: Vermont State Home Page

http://www.cit.state.vt.us/

Virginia: Virginia Government

http://www.state.va.us/home/governmt.html

Washington: A Washington State Government Information Guide

http://www.wa.gov/wahome.html

A Washington State Government Information Guide

The *Home Page Washington* pages provide public access to information created by government agencies, while also providing an information resource for public employees. These pages point to a wide variety of Washington information maintained by both public and private organizations. Inclusion in this index does not constitute endorsement in any manner.

West Virginia: West Virginia State Main Page

http://www.state.wv.us/

Wisconsin: Wisconsin Government

http://lcweb.loc.gov/global/state/wi-gov.html

Wyoming: State Government

http://www.state.wy.us/state/government/
text_state_government.html

MULTISTATE RESOURCES

InterLotto—On-Line Lottery Information Service

http://www.interlotto.com/

If Uncle Fred buys Power Ball tickets for you in Wisconsin, Cousin Sylvia plays the lotto for you in Virginia, and you buy your own state's scratch-n-win tickets at the corner convenience store, this is the site for you. All on one neat page are links to the winning numbers from all the state games, along with jackpot sizes.

National Conference of State Legislatures

http://www.ncsl.org/index.htm#sites

The NCSL site includes breaking news on a number of key political issues that affect state governments, including welfare reform, campaign contribution reform, and fiscal considerations. The page is also a convenient jump-station for accessing the legislature in your state and communicating with your elected officials and the NCSL on a variety of issues.

Project Vote Smart: Member Biographical and Contact Information

http://www.vote-smart.org/state/Topics/leg_
biographical.html

This is a slick Web lookup tool. Select your state from the alphabetical listing and then type in your zip code. The search form returns a list of your federal and state elected officials, along with party affiliation, biographical data, and contact information.

State Tax Resources

http://omer.actg.uic.edu/othersites/
stateinfo.html

Planning a move to another state? Find out how much of a bite the tax collector will take at this multistate tax information site.

U.S. State Constitutions

http://www.constitution.org/cons/
usstcons.htm

Not all the states have their constitutions online at this site, but most do. This could make for some pretty sluggish reading, but if you're looking for something in particular, the site is a great resource.

TRIBAL GOVERNMENT SITES

This is by no means an exhaustive list of all the tribal pages available on the Web. For an excellent list of multicultural and tribal/nation sites, check out Native American Cultural Resources on the Internet at **http://hanksville.phast.umass.edu/misc/NAculture.html**, part of Karen Strom's impressive Index of Native American Resources site. Meanwhile, the pages I've highlighted for you provide a good cross-section of Native American governmental organization.

The Cherokee Nation

http://www.powersource.com/powersource/
nation/default.html

The Chickasaw Nation

http://www.chickasaw.com/~cnation/

Choctaw Nation of Oklahoma - Unofficial Home Page

http://www.toners.com/choctaw/
welcome.htm

Citizen Potawatomi Nation

http://www.potawatomi.org/

Confederated Tribes of Siletz Indians (Oregon)

http://ctsi.nsn.us/

Costanoan-Ohlone Indian Canyon Resource (California)

http://www.ucsc.edu/costano/index.html

Delaware Tribe of Indians

http://www.cowboy.net/native/delaware.html

Hawai`i - Independent and Sovereign Nation-State

http://www.aloha.net/nation/hawaii-
nation.html

The Hopi Information Network

http://www.infomagic.com/~abyte/main.html

Lakota Wowapi Oti Kin: Lakota Information Home Page

http://maple.lemoyne.edu/~bucko/lakota.html

Mohawk Nation Council of Chiefs

http://www.slic.com/~mohawkna/home.html

The Navajo Nation

http://crystal.ncc.cc.nm.us/NN/nn.html

Oneida Indian Nation

http://one-web.org/oneida/

Pyramid Lake Paiute Tribe

http://thecity.sfsu.edu/~mandell/plpt.html

Quinault Indian Nation (Washington)

http://www.techline.com/~ghrpc/
quinpage.htm

Sac and Fox Nation
http://www.cowboy.net/native/sacnfox.html

Salt River Pima-Maricopa Indian Community
http://www.saltriver.pima-maricopa.nsn.us/

The Salinan Nation of California
http://www.ucsc.edu/costano/SALINAN1.html

Seminole Tribe of Florida
http://www.gate.net/~semtribe/

United Keetoowah Bank of Cherokee Indians
http://www.uark.edu/depts/comminfo/UKB/
welcome.html

United South and Eastern Tribes
http://oneida-nation.org/uset/uset.htm

United Tribe of Shawnee Indians
http://www.sunflower.org/~hdqrs/

Wiyot Indian Table Bluff Tribe and Community
http://www.ucsc.edu/costano/wiyot1.html

Wyandot Nation of Kansas
http://www.sfo.com/~denglish/wynaks/
wyandot2.html

Chapter 12
TO YOUR HEALTH!

SNARE THE CARE

DOCTOR, DOCTOR!

WELL, WELL, WELL!

BUT WHAT IF I'M REALLY SICK?

MEDICAL CENTERS AND HOSPITALS

PROFESSIONAL HOME CARE, HOSPICE, AND
FAMILY CAREGIVERS

A SELECTION OF MEDICAL REFERENCE
MATERIALS

The health care industry is keeping us on our toes nowadays. What with skyrocketing costs, an increasing reliance upon mystifying tests, and the search for doctors who are personal and sympatico, health care sometimes feels like being lost in a mine field to me.

Thank goodness for the Internet! When I want to know about a symptom I have which isn't getting (to my mind) sufficient attention from my doc, or learn more about an illness, drugs which have been prescribed for me, home-based care, or if I just want to locate a good hospital, the Internet answers my prayers. I am amazed at the sheer volume of information that's available on the Web—information that once seemed elusive, and in many cases, downright out of reach, is now at my fingertips literally.

SNARE THE CARE

Few people would argue that medical science and technology have careened through the 20th century like anything other than a bat on a Harley Davidson. We've developed new vaccines to halt determined viruses as they stampede humanity, nearly annihilating some diseases that once decimated entire populations. Science has designed sophisticated diagnostic tools and surgical procedures. New prescription drugs have been developed to aleviate pain and discomfort in almost every area of disease, from headaches to crippling scoliosis.

Though we may not have an argument with technical advances in medical science, many of us are very discomfited about the current delivery of care, feeling bereft and isolated as we move through a tidal wave of development and into an abyss divested of personal attention. As medical technology has advanced, delivery of care seems to have found its own "Dark Ages."

For many, gone are the days of the personal family physician who knew every nook and cranny of your personal medical history (and who may have even attended your arrival into the world). Instead, we must cope with corporatized medicine and Health Maintenance Organizations (HMOs). But under increasing pressure from health care advocacy groups and concerned physicians, HMOs are responding, albeit slowly, with increasing sympathy and concern to patients's demands. And you can do a lot to improve the care you receive at an HMO:

- Most HMOs ask the primary care physician assigned to you to handle all aspects of your care. If you have a chronic condition that is getting worse, insist on being referred to a specialist.

- Keep a diary of your care and progress while you are enrolled with an HMO. All your medical symptoms and treatment should be carefully recorded. If this seems like a lot of trouble, remember it's for your health. You may need specific documentation to get the referral to a specialist that you need.

- Some HMO plans permit you to change physicians only at specific times, once a quarter or twice a year. Some only allow a change at the beginning of the month, some at the end. Make sure that you understand the provisions in your contract for changing doctors. If you request a change—even if you're unhappy with your care—and your request is not within the proper time frame, you could end up paying significant medical costs yourself.

- You may have to fight hard for a referral to a specialist. In some HMOs, this can be a slow process and can even delay a diagnosis. If you believe that it is urgent for you to see a specialist, and your primary care physician in the HMO disagrees, ask him or her to record in writing why he or she thinks your condition does not warrant the referral. Having to commit an opinion to paper will sometimes cause a change of heart.

- If you should get a specialist referral, make absolutely sure that the physician you have been referred to really specializes in the field you require.

- Be certain that decisions about payment and those about your total health care are clear. If your doctor's decision to do certain tests is based on the HMO policy and not on your health, check other alternatives. If you're unsure about either, *ask.*

- To protect yourself, make sure that any questions or complaints you have about your treatment be made a part of your medical records.

- In every case, before choosing an HMO, read the contract carefully before signing.

Lizzie's Tips

QUESTIONS TO ASK BEFORE JOINING AN HMO

- What constitutes an emergency? If coverage depends on the final diagnosis in the emergency room instead of your own feeling that an emergency existed, you may be denied coverage.

- What hospital may I use? Managed care plans may only cover their member hospitals. Find out what to do if you are out of town.

- Where do I go for after-hours care? Know what the procedures are for treatment after normal working hours or on holidays.

- Who do I call for an emercency procedure, and who can authorize it? Most HMOs require preapproval within time limits for certain emergency procedures or surgeries. Be sure you know the rules, and how to get advance approval if needed.

HMO Locator

http://www.medaccess.com/hmos/s_hmo.htm

"Finding an HMO is easy," this site promises. You can use the form to search by name, city, state, or ZIP. Then, once you receive a list of hits, click on the name of the HMO you're interested in and find contact info, along with a brief summary of services.

Families USA Foundation

http://epn.org/families.html

The Electronic Policy Network houses this Web site, showcasing the efforts of a nonprofit advocacy group calling for affordable health care for Americans. News article reprints, press releases, and other reports address issues like insurance and Medicare.

Health Care Financing Administration

http://www.hcfa.gov/

The Health Care Financing Administration, the agency that administers Medicare and Medicaid, maintains this site to offer an overview of its mission and its programs. Statistics, data rates, reports, regulations, laws, manuals, and research are available for review.

Medicare Rights Center

http://www.wwonline-ny.com/~faylin/ homepage.htm#Homepage

The Medicare Rights Center is a nonprofit organization "dedicated to ensuring the rights of seniors and people with disabilities to quality, affordable health care." Claiming that "Medicare routinely erroneously denies and reduces benefits," this organization helps educate individuals so they understand their benefits and the scope of their medical coverage.

DOCTOR, DOCTOR!

I recall the story of Dr. Ralph Combs, who after graduating from Harvard Medical School, set up practice in a small pioneer town in Kansas in the late 1880s. "Dr. Ralph" visited the sick on horseback, with his supplies and instruments tucked away in saddlebags. Just like the Pony Express, he rode out in blizzards and in blistering heat to bring care and attention to those on his rounds.

Admittedly, his brand of medicine did not approach the sophistication of today, with nuclear scans and MRIs, but he knew everyone in the families he cared for personally, understood their dispositions and predispositions, and the strength of their constitutions. And even when I knew him in his nineties more than 35 years ago, he still dealt his patients a large dollop of humor and kindliness.

IN SEARCH OF THE COUNTRY DOC

When I was in my late 40s and a single mom, I returned to the "homestead" for a while to be near my older relatives. I lived down the road from my Aunt Sara, a committed country doctor from the time she left medical school. Even after rising into a demanding specialty and becoming chairwoman of her department at a nearby teaching hospital, my Aunt Sara continued her good works after hours, making house calls in the little community where she lived— no charge if you were strapped for cash.

She would wake me up in the middle of the night to accompany her on some hair-raising rides over winding dirt roads, to deliver a baby or stitch up a terrible wound, many times to be given only a couple of chickens or a dozen fresh eggs for her trouble. She never refused to go out in any weather and gladly took whatever a patient could give in exchange for care recieved.

Tired after being in the operating room for long hours, she still gave of her time to develop and train volunteers so the county would have a professional rescue squad, even though their first ambulance was only a retired laundry truck called "Maude." Dr. Sara would spend the next 20 years coming home from an exhausting day at the medical center to go out on call with her team. These volunteers gave much more than throwing the patient in the meat

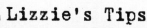

Lizzie's Tips

A simple and effective way to relieve hideous heartburn without having to give up your favorite spicy foods: Lose weight!

wagon and rolling with sirens blaring to the hospital. The squad was proficient in administering IV drugs, checking vital signs, providing cardiac care, and using endotrachial tubes in the field, many years before it became a national standard.

Later, when the county found itself without a coroner and none would apply, Dr. Sara said, "We couldn't get anyone to come, so I decided it would be easier if I did it myself. I became the Medical Examiner."

I am awed when I think of the long years of service gladly given with such humility, concern, and humanity to anyone who needed it.

WHERE IS SUPERDOC?

I am sure that we still have our heroes out there, but as we look to the 21st century, more modern physicians seem to hold exalted stations and are inaccessible to the people that they treat. Modern offices and equipment, cushioned in a brisk, detached and professional atmosphere, seem to be the order of the day. For many, gone is the friendship, concern, and personal involvement of yesteryear.

One day while I was wandering the corridors of a large medical building, I overheard a young doctor explaining to a cohort that if he kept three examining rooms going at once, he could see 35 patients in one day. With such a heavy patient load, combined with hospital rounds, mail, and phone calls, it appeared to me that this Doc had joined the ranks of those that "treat 'em and street 'em," hustling you in, pressing the flesh, and hustling you out as fast as possible.

Lizzie's Tips

CHOOSING A NEW DOC

Some of the best ways to find a new doctor are through friends and professional referral services. Here are some important questions to ask as you consider whether a doc is right for you:

- How long has she/he been in practice?

- What kind of special experience does she/he have?

- How many patients does she/he see a week?

- How many surgeries does she/he perform? What is her/his success rate?

- Ask in advance whether the doctor will spend time getting to know you, answering questions, taking a detailed medical history, explaining any illness you might have, and the medications that you currently take.

- Is the doctor available for emergencies?

- Does she/he live a long way from the hospital?

- How does the call service work?

- What sort of back-up (i.e., type and number of partners) is in place?

- Will the office accept your insurance plan? Can you get help in proscessing claims? Other help in copying and forwarding records?

- What are the billing practices? Does the Doc accept credit cards? Does she/he see both Medicare and Medicaid patients? If she/he refuses to see Medicaid patients, you may want to take your business elsewhere, where there is a higher "humanity quotient."

Once you've chosen your new doctor, stay on your toes:

- Take all medications with you when you go for your first visit to a new doc. If you need refills, ask for them at your first appointment to avoid having the doctor call you back, or scheduling another visit.

- See the same physician on a regularly scheduled basis. Don't be foisted off on a new partner unless you've been consulted first, and you don't mind. Ask how frequently you should return, what the doctor plans to do, and why.

- Ask for drug samples from the office if you're starting on a new med. This can save you quite an investment if you are unable to take the drug due to an adverse reaction. If your doctor doesn't have samples available, ask for two prescriptions: one for just a few pills in case of a reaction, and one for the complete prescription if all goes well.

- Make sure your doctor remains active in your care (accepts on-call duties), and maintains admitting priviliges to the hospital you prefer.

- Make sure you are clear about the goals and priorities decided upon at each visit. Should you lose ten pounds, lower your cholesterol, or work on reducing your blood pressure?

- Always ask if you can be weighed, and have your blood pressure taken.

- Ask for informational pamphlets explaining your condition so that you will have a better understanding of what ails you.

- Communication is a two-way street. If you cannot take a particular medication, inform your doctor. If you are unable to complete a treatment, tell her or him. She/he can't treat you in the dark.

- Don't be afraid to ask about your bill so that you know what everything will cost. If the treatments seem too expensive, ask about alternatives.

In any case, be sure you like your doctor and respect him or her, and that s/he likes and respects you. Will you be treated as a partner in your care, or just another patient? Be sure he or she will be accessible and informative, and that you are comfortable with the office style. You don't need to settle for less!

If you are faced with an abrupt physician who will not take the time to talk to you and rustles you out of the office rudely, or if you must wait six weeks for an appointment, only to wait another hour in the waiting room and yet another in a paper gown, frigidly staring at the walls of a six-by-six examining room, it may be time to make a change.

Medseek
http://www.medseek.com

This comprehensive physician locator lists over 280,000 physicians, their philosophies, and their specialities. 450 hospital links are also provided, all searchable by city and state. This site does not evaluate physician proficiency, but it's a good place to start when you're beginning your quest for a new caregiver.

How to Choose a Doctor and Hospital for Your Treatment
http://www.ccf.org/pc/quality/

The Cleveland Clinic Foundation has prepared this series of consumer guides covering the points you should consider when choosing a doctor for treatment of complicated medical conditions, from brain tumors to ulcerative colitis. Full text is online, but you can order a paper copy free by calling the toll-free number provided at the site.

WELL, WELL, WELL!

The main thing to keep in mind as you consider how best to manage your care, is that you cannot—and you don't have to!—sit passively by today when it comes to your health. You must be an active participant and decision-maker, working with your doctor hand-in-hand, not just taking orders. Remember: You've lived in your body longer than anyone, so you probably know a thing or two about how you feel, and what feels right to you. Don't be afraid to suggest (or try) an "alternative remedy," or one your grandmother used to administer to you as a child that you know has worked for you in the past. Used

carefully and wisely, pure, natural foods and herbs won't hurt you, so why not give them a try? (Keep in mind, however, than anything prepared haphazardly or with little care has the potential to rock your system—consult a good book, some informative online resources like the ones below, or grannie's recipe, *before* you drag out the mortar and pestle.)

Here are a few sites to guide you as you embark on a course of strength and wellness. Take charge of your own health!

Algy's Herb Page
http://www.algy.com/herb/index.html

Self-described as the Web's "most comprehensive archive and index of herb-related information," and "the home of the world's largest seed catalog," Algy's covers both the medicinal and culinary uses of herbs. Also, find books, herb lore, BBSs, and discussion.

The Alternative Medicine Homepage
http:www.pitt.edu/~cbw/altm.html

The Alternative Medicine Homepage, assembled by the Falk Library of the Health Sciences at the University of Pittsburgh, is an excellent index of links to sites that explore the world of unorthodox therapeutic practices such as folk medicine, herbal treatments, faith healing, chiropractic, acupuncture, massage, and music therapy. Long scorned by the medical establishment as mere quackery, alternative medicine practices have slowly begun to shed their back-alley reputation and reach wider acceptance among patients dissatisfied with the assembly line practices at many doctors's offices.

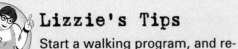

Lizzie's Tips

Start a walking program, and remember: You're in no big hurry. This is lifetime exercise. No stopwatches, no magic, just walking at a comfortable pace for 20 minutes every morning or evening. Chances are, if you're a novice, it will take you that long to walk a mile. Build from there. Forget technique, just get out there. It takes willpower to make walking a habit. If you think it will help, get a dog (there are lots of side benefits to pet ownership, too; see Chapter 10). It's important to stay active.

CHIROWEB

http://www.chiroweb.com/

A chiropractor's delight, CHIROWEB serves up an all-inclusive medley of resources for both medical professionals and patients alike. Drop by the domicile of Dr. Brett for personal answers and info packages such as "a comprehensive history of chiropractic" and "glossary of chiropractic terms," or indulge yourself at the "Feel Better Store." CHIROWEB also helps guests locate the chiropractor nearest them and track down special offers.

Dr. Bil's Cool Medical Site of the Week

http://www.maxface.com/~wcd/cmsotw.html

Dr. Bil's Cool Medical Site of the Week points Web surfers toward interesting sites—some serious, some hilarious, all medically oriented. Includes a link to the home page of this site's creator.

Dr. Bower's Complementary Medicine Home Page

http://galen.med.virginia.edu/~pjb3s/
ComplementaryHomePage.html

Compiled by a medical doctor, this site contains a wealth of information on alternative and complementary medicine. Find out about everything from acupuncture and alternative cancer therapies, to Native American healing

traditions. You can also link to the American Complementary Practice Registry.

Emergency Medical Services Homepage

http://galaxy.tradewave.com/editors/fritz-nordengren/ems.html

Here's information that could save someone's life. At the Emergency Medical Services (EMS) site, find resources ranging from how to recognize an emergency to step-by-step medical emergency instructions to a fun list of links to home pages of medical dramas on television. Once you've exhausted all these possibilities, link to other EMS sites, online medical 'zines, and related emergency organizations.

First Aid Online

http://www.prairienet.org/~cicely/firstaid/

First Aid Online presents instructions for basic first aid, with an emphasis on accidents that occur in the home. Information is provided on shock, poisoning, breathing difficulties, and more. The site also features links to online medical resources.

Food and Drug Administration Center for Food Safety & Applied Nutrition

http://vm.cfsan.fda.gov/

Do your food-handling practices send a hearty "all aboard" to bacteria and invite them to take a ride into your intestinal tract? If you've ever tasted raw cookie dough, eaten a rare hamburger, or chopped the onions on the same board you used to cut up the chicken, you have put yourself at risk of pathogenic infection. The FDA does a fine job of highlighting important safety issues in food selection, storage, preparation, and food-drug interactions.

Food Facts for Older Americans

http://www.aoa.dhhs.gov/aoa/eldractn/
foodfact.html

Onions and garlic help fight cancer. Adequate calcium and potassium help prevent the formation of kidney stones. Two or more drinks per day can cancel the beneficial effects of fruits and vegetables. Find out more about health and nutrition at this fact-packed site from the Administration on Aging.

Free Personal Health Assessment
http://www.youfirst.com/

Yes, you know your lifestyle affects your health, but this free, personal online health assessment can help you zero in on the factors you need to change to feel better and live longer.

GeroWeb
http://www.iog.wayne.edu/GeroWeb.html

This site is the home of the GeroWeb Virtual Library on Aging, a database containing a wealth of information on aging and the general concerns of senior citizens. The site is fully searchable and links to educational facilities, government agencies, organizations, and related archival material. An excellent Seniors' site!

Guide To Women's Health Issues
http://asa.ugl.lib.umich.edu/chdocs/womenhealth/womens_health.html

Links to information on women's emotional, physical, and sexual health are included in this online guide. Topics include body image, stress, nutrition, gynecological exams, and more.

Health & Fitness World Guide
http://www.worldguide.com/Fitness/hf.html

Does an apple a day keep the doctor away? What are the best types of cardiovascular exercise? Find out at the Worldguide: Health & Fitness Forum Welcome Page, where you can link to health and fitness information of all sorts, or check out related software and publications.

Lizzie's Tips

Light, fresh snacks throughout the day can help stave off the hungries and keep your blood sugar at healthy levels between meals. Before reaching into the cookie jar or candy box, consider these alternatives:

- A cup of air-popped popcorn—sprinkle with herbs or nutritional yeast for a healthful taste sensation

- Fresh fruit—the "sugar," or fructose, in fruit doesn't jar your system the way refined sugars can; avoid processed or canned fruit in heavy syrup

- A hot cup of broth-based soup with a few fresh veggies or some tofu thrown in for good measure—vegetable stock or miso, a soybean soup base, is ideal

- Raw veggies with fresh salsa, hummus (a Middle Eastern spread made from chickpeas), or Babaganouj (another Middle Eastern spread, this one made with eggplant)—check with your local health food or specialty store for these delicious spreads, or make them yourself from recipes found in vegetarian or Middle Eastern cookbooks (they're a snap to prepare!)

- A few hearty, baked crackers, such as Wasa or Rykrisp, with a few slices of non-fat cheese—or better yet, choose a cheese alternative made from soybeans, like Tofu Rella or Soya Kaas; these are surprisingly tasty, and much better for you than dairy cheeses

- A slice of pita bread, or a handful of pita "chips," with salsa, hummus, or Babaganouj

- A cup of plain non-fat yogurt, or a type sweetened with fructose or fruit juice instead of sugar (be sure to check the label; you'd be surprised how many things contain unnecessary amounts of sugar!)

- A few rice cakes—they come in a variety of flavors these days; again, be sure to check the label and avoid those which contain sugar

- A cup of hot herb tea—you'd be surprised how well this can fill you up and ease your hunger pangs

HealthGate
http://www.healthgate.com/

HealthGate is *the* Internet source for news and information on health issues. The site boasts of having the "world's largest biomedical database," and you can search it for free. Then take a look at the selection of Healthy Living magazines (Healthy News, Healthy Living, Healthy Woman). Some additional services are available only to paid subscribers, but the amount of free info here makes this site a great health resource.

The Heart: An Online Exploration
http://sln2.fi.edu/biosci/heart.html

Take a guided tour of the human heart, courtesy of the Franklin Institute Science Museum and the Unisys Corporation. Virtual travelers can start with The Heart Preview Gallery, a detailed, hyperlinked introduction to the full exhibit. The preview highlights the interactive activities, images and movies, educational materials, and audio files folded into the virtual tour. Travel on to the table of contents to customize your tour and pick your destinations. Choose from presentations covering healthy hearts, the artery-vein-capillary connection, the oxygen-carbon dioxide tradeoff, and the "fascinating fluid of life."

Homeopathy Home Page
http://www.dungeon.com/~cam/homeo.htm l

The Homeopathy Home Page is a meta-index of homeopathic resources for both practitioners and patients. Access databases, libraries, organizations, and other homeopathy sites. Explore Homeopathy Frequently Asked Questions (FAQ), subscribe to a mailing list, or locate homeopathic practitioners worldwide.

The Integral Yoga Web Site
http://www.webcom.com/~miraura/

Read a general introduction to yoga and browse information about the spiritual path of Integral Yoga through this site. It features biographies of the founders of Integral Yoga along with published works and information about upcoming events around the world.

International Network for Interfaith Health Practices
http://www.interaccess.com/ihpnet/

A joint project of The Interfaith Health Program of the Carter Center (Atlanta, Georgia) and the Congregational Nurse Program of Saint Francis Hospital (Evanston, Illinois), this forum welcomes people of all religions to explore the relationship between spirituality and health. The Network is concerned with "prevention, health promotion, and justice," and supports "many kinds of direct service ministries" for people of all faiths.

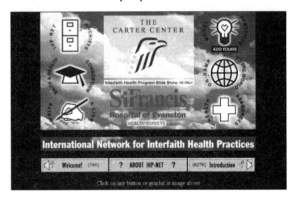

Internet Health Newsgroups and Listserver Groups
http://www.ihr.com/newsgrp.html

Get information on medical issues delivered right to your e-mail box by subscribing to any of the newsgroups or listservs indexed on this page. From aerobics to vegetarianism (with diabetes, general medicine, and several other topics in the middle), this list gives you a lot of choices.

Internet Health Resources
http://www.ihr.com/

With the goal of helping individuals take more personal responsibility for their health care and wellness, this site features pointers to online health information, arranged in alphabetical order by topic. Featured topics range from allergies and attention deficit disorder to vegetarian recipes and women's health. The site also includes lists of state and national health care organizations, relevant publications, and more.

Internet Medical and Health Care Resources

http://www.teleport.com/~amrta/iway.html

The Internet Medical and Health Care Resources page features pointers to health care, nutrition, and alternative medicine resources. From acupuncture to yoga, with the Family Health and Medical Matrix pages in between, these resources cover a wide range of issues.

The Medical College of Wisconsin International Travelers Clinic (ITC)

http://www.intmed.mcw.edu/travel.html

The International Travelers Clinic (ITC) provides a fact-filled tip book covering general info, diseases and immunizations, and environmental hazards. Hot links include the CIA World Factbook and U.S. State Department Travel Warnings. This is a great site for folks planning a vacation abroad.

The Medical Reporter

http://www.dash.com/netro/nwx/tmr / tmr.html

The Medical Reporter's masthead states that this free online journal emphasizes "preventive medicine, primary care, patient advocacy, education and support, as well as topics in sub-specialty medicine of interest to men and women." That's a dauntingly wide scope, but this monthly electronic publication lives up to its promise. Readers will find a combination of reprints and original material covering up-to-the-minute news on a broad spectrum of health issues and recent research findings.

Mind & Body Links and Articles

http://www.stud.unit.no/~olavb/ mindbody.html

Part of a personal home page, this extensive directory of mind and body resources provides links to information about meditation, yoga, vegetarian recipes, psychology, and self-help. There are also instructions for joining the Wellness mailing list.

NicNet: Nicotine and Tobacco Network

http://www.ahsc.arizona.edu/nicnet/

Get the impetus and support to quit that tobacco habit once and for all. From information on tobacco company manipulation to the effects of second-hand smoke on kids, the news and research updates at this site are grim. Nonsmoker wannabes can access a variety of help sheets and support groups.

Nutrition and Senior Citizens

http://seniors-site.com/nutritio/index.html

From meal times to food labels, this site covers just about everything you need to know about good nutrition for the over 50 set. Fiber, salt, water, vitamins, and minerals are all examined separately in terms of their benefits and contribution to overall good health.

Senior Clinic

http://www.drfrank.com/Senior_Clinic.html

Senior Clinic is a syndicated weekly column by Dr. Frank MacInnis that addresses the various health concerns of "post middle-agers." Both current and past columns are online, but if you don't want to read them on your screen, Dr. Frank has compiled his best columns in a book called *The Aging Game* that is for sale at this site.

Wellness Web Senior's Center

http://wellweb.com/seniors/eldershp.htm

This consumer health page prepared just for Seniors includes information on Seniors's health concerns (incontinence, hearing, memory, stroke, and more), government agencies (including Social Security), concerns about aging (living wills and tips for caregivers). This isn't an exhaustive index, but it does cover a number of key issues and will address many of your concerns.

WorldWide Wellness

http://www.doubleclickd.com/ wwwellness.html

Visit the WorldWide Wellness site for resources and information devoted to holistic living. This site features a women's section and contains a directory of holistic health care professionals, health fair conference sched-ules, and a linked index to related alternative health sites.

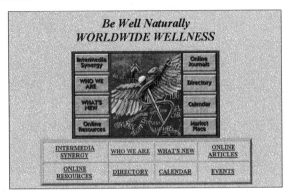

BUT WHAT IF I'M REALLY SICK?

When you start to get forgetful, you really begin to question your overall health and well-being, and you can begin to feel like you are slipping down the slip-pery slopes. Ever stand at the refrigerator and won-der what brought you there? Go down the supermarket aisle and forget what you wanted? Don't despair, your memory may need a tune-up, but you're not ready for the junkyard yet. A balanced diet will help in making sure you get the right min-erals, vitamins, proteins, and amino acids to keep your mind sharp and alert. Yup, the old adage is true: You are indeed what you eat.

Relaxation strengthens memory, too. Try yoga, music, and even chopping firewood. Dreams do wonders for your memory. When you wake up from a vivid dream, immediately write it down. Keep a pen and notebook handy for just this purpose. You'll enjoy reading these dreamscapes later. And of course, we all know that the best remedies for all the signs of aging are exercise, keeping the coffee in the can (instead of in your cup), lowering your blood pressure, and keeping a positive attitude. This is the best recipe I know for staying fit and mentally alert.

Still, sometimes we or those we love can be strick-en by debilitating diseases. From the frustration of Alzheimers to the pain of cancer, it's best to be pre-pared and informed—rather than helpless and afraid—when we find ourselves confronted with a serious illness. The more you know, the better you're able to participate in your treatment, and the better chance you have of recovery.

The Internet is just one place to start. Here are some terrific sites designed to educate and inform.

The Alzheimer Page
http://www.biostat.wustl.edu/alzheim er/
Washington University in St. Louis, Mo., presents a col-lection of Alzheimer's Disease information and links here. Visitors can search and browse the Alzheimer ar-chive, join the mailing list, and link to a variety of aging and dementia sites.

Alzheimer Web
http://werple.mira.net.au/~dhs/ad.html
At this site, researchers and others interested in Alzhe-imer's Disease can link to the Alzheimer's Association, join a discussion group, or subscribe to a mailing list de-voted to advice for caregivers.

Aneurysm Information Project
http://www.columbia.edu/~mdt1/
The Aneurysm Information Project home page presents resources—answers to frequently asked ouestions, pa-pers, a victims' support page, and more—related to ce-rebral and other types of aneurysms. Visitors also can link to related research and reference resources.

Arthritis Information Page
http://www.netshop.net/~nsardy/dancer/ asmp.html
You know it hurts, but do you know why? Here's a com-prehensive guide to the different types of arthritis, along with treatment options and a toll-free number for the Arthritis Self-Management Program.

Ask Noah About: Aging and Alzheimer's Disease
http://www.noah.cuny.edu/aging/aging.html

New York Online Access to Health (NOAH) provides an excellent guide to the aging process at this site, with information about both the physical and psychological changes you can expect, a short list of aging information resources, and a good background on Alzheimer's. Find solid answers to questions about vision and hearing problems, nutrition, sexuality, osteoporosis, high blood pressure, menopause, and a number of other common conditions that accompany gray hair.

Asthma—General Information
http://www.cco.caltech.edu /~wrean/asthma-gen.html

Asthma sufferers looking for treatments for their symptoms and answers to common questions about the condition can check this page, the FAQ for the alt. support.asthma newsgroup. The page creators warn that the FAQ is for discussion only and not meant to be a source of medical advice.

Lizzie's Tips

A FEW TIPS TO DROP AGING IN ITS TRACKS

- Laugh a lot. Don't take yourself, or life, so seriously. Cultivate your sense of the ridiculous.

- Tell yourself how great you are. You may be the only one who will. When you accomplish something that was a challenge for you, congratulate yourself.

- Bag the worrying. Leave it to someone else. It is a profitless occupation and only creates stress. What can you do about it anyway? So why worry about it?

- Ask for spiritual guidance. It is very comforting to know that you are not alone. If you are not a religious person, turn toward what Dr.Deepak Chopra calls the "higher self."

- Live a life of giving to others. Volunteer. People who help others have a significantly lower illness rate, and visit the doctor much less frequently. Find a cause you can believe in and help with service in that area. Make it a habit. Your special talents and abilities may enrich the lives of others as well as your own.

- Cultivate friends. Find a group of sympathetic people, and make good buddies with people of both sexes. Diversity is the spice of life. If you're single, romance may even flourish—you can meet someone most anywhere: on a train, in the park, at the grocery store, in the library.

- Keep a positive outlook. Try to train your negative friends to be more positive, or find new friends. Negativity drags you down, makes you bitter, and contributes to an aging spirit as much as anything. Be realistic and try to make the best of hard times. Quit judging yourself and others. So you can't balance the checkbook, but who else do you know that can make such a wonderful cheesecake? Stop toxic thinking and unload negative thoughts. When you hear your inner voice say, "I'm lousy at...," STOP yourself. Do it enough times and those pesky little negative thoughts will get buried.

Avon's Breast Cancer Awareness Crusade

http://www.pmedia.com/Avon/avon.html

Avon provides facts, links, and phone numbers to various breast cancer resources at this "awareness crusade" site. Visitors can take Avon's "Pledge for Better Breast Health" here and read transcripts of Awareness Online conferences.

Cancer Patient Resources Available Via WWW

http://www.charm.net/~kkdk/

Providing information for cancer patients from a cancer patient is the focus of this page. Dr. Darrel Kilius of Baltimore, a cancer survivor, catalogs links to conventional and alternative treatment resources and provides a comprehensive list of associations, labs, institutes, and documents.

CancerNet Database

http://imsdd.meb.uni-b onn.de/cancernet/cancernet.html

The National Cancer Institute (NCI) provides cancer information for patients. An extensive list of disease topics lets you select an article and then link to a straightforward description of treatment information. You can also browse the current news, databases, clinical trial info, and drug summaries, or link to the NCI home page. The page is available in English and Spanish.

CANSEARCH: A Guide to Cancer Resources

http://www.access.digex. net/~mkragen/cansearch.html

Sponsored by the National Coalition for Cancer Survivorship, this site provides a guided tour of an extensive list of cancer-related resources, including educational sites, research centers, organizations, support groups, and more.

ChronicIllNet

http://www.chronicillnet.org/

ChronicIllNet provides news, research updates, and a compassionate online forum for those who suffer from such chronic illnesses as cancer, AIDS, Gulf War syn-drome, and chronic pain. As a clearinghouse of information, it is equally pertinent to physicians, patients, and the families of the ill.

Communicable Disease Fact Sheets Gopher Menu

gopher://gopher.health.state.ny.us/11/.consumer/.factsheets

This New York State Department of Health gopher contains alphabetized fact sheets on common communicable diseases such as chickenpox and the flu, along with diseases you may never have heard of such as Kawasaki Syndrome and tularemia. Each fact sheet presents a description of the disease, symptoms, methods of communicability, treatment protocols, and prevention techniques.

Crohns Disease Ulcerative Colitis Inflammatory Bowel Disease Pages

http://qurlyjoe.bu.edu/cduchome.html

This site provides an extensive index of medical resources. Visit here for links to FAQ files, medical institutions, clinical trial info, personal histories, patient services, government agencies, commercial health providers, newsgroups, and more.

Diseases/Conditions

http://www.uiuc.edu/departments/mckinley/health-info/dis-cond/dis-cond.html

This index to information on common diseases and conditions includes asthma, high blood pressure, headaches, and even common colds. Part of the McKinley Health Center, the site includes background info such as causes, symptoms, treatment options, prevention, and resources.

Diseases of the Liver

http://cpmcnet.columbia.edu/ dept/gi/disliv.html

Columbia-Presbyterian Medical Center presents an alphabetical list of liver diseases and conditions with links to files, current papers in the field, a multimedia textbook of liver pathology, and other liver-related sites.

Hernia Information Home Page
http://www.demon.co.uk/herniaInfo/

The Hernia Information Home Page, sponsored by the British Hernia Centre in London, explains how hernias develop, defines the different types of hernias, and describes hernia repair techniques, all in straightforward, easy-to-understand language.

Institute for Brain Aging and Dementia
http://maryanne.bio.uci.edu/

The Institute for Brain Aging and Dementia home page provides information about Alzheimer's disease and other senile dementia conditions, along with links to clinical resources. Visitors can jump to the AlzNet discussion group from this site.

Introduction to Skin Cancer
http://www.maui.net/~southsky/introto.html

Maybe that glowing suntan isn't exactly a sign of good health. An Introduction to Skin Cancer helps visitors become acquainted with various kinds of skin cancer as well as ways to avoid becoming a victim.

Johns Hopkins Medical Institution InfoNet: Patient Advocacy Groups
http://infonet.welch.jhu.edu/advo cacy.html

The Johns Hopkins Medical Institution's Information Network provides a huge list of patient advocacy groups with phone numbers and links to home pages if the organization maintains an online presence. These advocacy groups cover a variety of subject areas, and dozens of organizations are listed, such as the Alzheimer's Foundation, the Arthritis Foundation, the Back Pain Hotline, and the American Parkinson Disease Association.

Late Onset Diabetes
http://www.aoa.dhhs.gov/aoa/eldractn/
diabetes.html

Although 13 to 14 million Americans—most of them over 55—have late onset diabetes, almost half don't know it. Find out the symptoms and effects on this fact sheet from the Administration on Aging, and then make the appointment for your annual physical.

Mental Health Net
http://www.cmhc.com/

The "largest, most comprehensive guide to mental health online" features over 4,200 individual resources covering every conceivable aspect of mental health: depression, anxiety, panic, substance abuse, obsessive-compulsive disorder, mood disorders, psychotropic drugs, treatment options, and more.

National Institute of Diabetes and Digestive and Kidney Disease (NIDDK)
http://www.niddk.nih.gov/

The NIDDK of the National Institutes of Health maintains this educational site. Visitors will find information about diabetes and about digestive, endocrine, kidney, nutrition, and urologic disorders. Research and professional info, as well as diverse patient resources, are also featured.

OncoLink, The University of Pennsylvania Cancer Center Resource
http://cancer.med.upenn.edu/

The University of Pennsylvania Cancer Center presents this "first multimedia oncology information resource" on the Net. Visitors will find cancer news and statistics here, as well as information on meetings and access to journals.

The On-Line Allergy Center
http://www.sig.net/~allergy/welcome .html

Many of us have experienced the nasal drips, red eyes, and sneezing, but did you know that hyperactivity, depression, and loss of short-term memory are also allergy symptoms? Dr. Russell Roby of Austin, Texas, knows and has authored this page "to provide helpful allergy tips and information to allergy sufferers worldwide." Dr. Roby explains the allergic reaction so simply and clearly that a child can understand it. Follow along with the good doctor as he enumerates the vexing manifestations of allergies, read his tips for keeping symptoms at bay, and find out how ultraviolet light can eliminate mold spores. The site also boasts three interactive newsgroups devoted to allergy, asthma, and migraine.

The Parkinson's Web
http://neuro-chief-e.mgh.harvard.edu/
parkinsonsweb/main/PDmain.html
This site from Massachusetts General Hospital includes a primer on the disease, signs and symptoms, coping resources, and treatment information.

Phantom Sleep Page (Apnea, Snoring & Other Sleep Problems)
http://www.newtechpub.com/phantom/
Check this site for the causes, symptoms, consequences, and treatment of sleep apnea, a condition characterized by the cessation of breathing during sleep. Browse the FAQ, read the bed-buying tips, explore the wonders of snoring, and link to other sleep disorder sites.

Prostate Cancer Home Page
http://www.cancer.med .umich.edu/prostcan/
prostcan.html
The University of Michigan creates an online information center for news and research related to prostate cancer. From medical articles to drug trials announcements, all aspects of this form of cancer are covered, from the disease itself to current and future treatment options.

The Prostate Cancer InfoLink
http://www.comed.com/Prostate/index .html
Prostate cancer is a high-profile disease, but early detection is complicated by the fact that the disease has no definitive set of symptoms; all the early signs can be caused by other illnesses or normal aging. The Prostate Cancer InfoLink arms its readers with the facts. Written in simple, understandable language, the page carefully lays out the risk factors and symptoms, along with info on screening and early detection.

Quick Information About Cancer for Patients and Their Families
http://asa.ugl.lib.umich.edu/chdocs/cancer/
CANCERGUIDE.HTML
The University of Michigan maintains this index site as a reference for cancer patients and their families. Visit here for resources on the causes and treatment of many forms of cancer, and read testimonials of others battling the disease.

Senior Computer Information Project— Health
http://www.mbnet.mb.ca/crm/health/
index.html
This Canadian site is an excellent health index just for Seniors. Links include specific illnesses, general wellness sites and zines, support organizations and groups, drugs, disabilities, and much more.

The Sleep Medicine Home Page
http://www.cloud9.net/~thorpy/
Snoozing isn't always a soothing balm: Some of us sleep too much, some of us sleep too little, some of us make noises, and some of us have bad dreams. All are accommodated at The Sleep Medicine Home Page, a vast compendium of links to all things drowsy. If it's true that "about 40 million Americans suffer from sleep disorders such as narcolepsy, sleep apnea, restless legs syndrome, and the insomnias," a lot of people out there are dragging through their days. Help is here in the form of information, treatment options, and links to worldwide sleep centers and discussion groups.

Southern California Orthopedic Institute Home Page
http://www.scoi.com/
Southern California Orthopedic Institute's page teaches visitors about sports injuries, orthopedic procedures, and basic anatomy in plain language. Bonuses include Arthritis of the Hip Joint and Arthritis of the Knee Joint, excellent discussions of anatomy, disease, and total joint replacement. And if you want to become intimate with knee surgery, you can even view a QuickTime movie of the inside of a knee here.

USA Fibrositis Association
http://www.w2.com/fibro1.html
This advocacy group for fibromyalgia, also called fibrositis, provides information on the musculoskeletal disease, pertinent contacts and a call to membership.

MEDICAL CENTERS AND HOSPITALS

Toward the end of her life, my grandmother was admitted to Duke University Hospital. The protocol for admission was to have a complete physical examination. This included having blood drawn, an x-ray taken, and, for my grandmother at least, the hideous horror of a gynecological exam. With the family having the benefit of this foreknowledge, I was elected to take her there. Grandmother had birthed seven children in her own bed, and by this time had lived to be 72 years young. Her private parts had remained exclusively her own territory, and I expect they were never fully revealed to a living soul, perhaps not even to her own husband. Imagine how tense the moment, as my grandmother lay back bedecked and draped with hospital sheeting, while waiting for the appearance of the doctor. When he finally arrived and began the loathsome procedure, my handsome, elegant, grande dame of a grandmother squeezed my hand in agony, and together we silently and nobly bore up under the "depravity" of it all.

The doctor was a young resident who, after the examination, bent over grandmother smiling, perhaps to cheer her on. But she turned to him with shocking forcefulness, burning with the indignity she had suffered, and said, "Young man, I hope your mother never finds out what you do for a living!"

These days, an annual trip to the gynecologist is pretty routine (and thank goodness for that!). And whether you're taking your grandmother or youself out for an annual physical, or you're looking for the best research, cancer, or long-term care hospital, you'll want to shop around. These days, the Web makes it that much easier.

M.D. Anderson Cancer Center
http://utmdacc.mda.uth.tmc.edu/

Rated by *U.S. News* as "one of the ten best hospitals in the nation," Houston's M.D. Anderson Cancer Center is one of only 27 comprehensive cancer centers in the country affiliated with the National Cancer Institute. Along with facts about the Center and an online magazine, this site provides information for prospective patients, information on support groups, and links to cancer resources on the Web.

Brigham & Women's Hospital
http://bustoff.bwh.harvard.edu/

Harvard University's Brigham & Women's Hospital puts its divisions and departments online here. Link to home pages for several key departments such as anesthesia, thoracic surgery, and neurosurgery. Explore the hospital's research, education, and treatment resources or link to its gopher to access the hospital's information systems.

Cedars-Sinai Medical Center Home Page
http://www.csmc.edu/

Have you ever noticed how many movie stars go to Cedars-Sinai when they're ailing? This southern California medical facility wants to tell you why. You'll find all sorts of info about the hospital, including the Cedars on Call service, the Senior Care program (a free membership program designed to help Seniors reduce the costs of health care), and the hospital's community health magazine.

Cleveland Clinic Foundation
http://www.ccf.org/

The Cleveland Clinic Foundation gives an overview of its patient care and research activities here. Visitors can request an appointment online and take a virtual tour of the facilities, or follow the latest research issuing from the clinic. The site includes a weekly newsletter.

CPMCnet: Columbia-Presbyterian Medical Center
http://cpmcnet.columbia.edu/

This site serves as the home page for New York City's Columbia-Presbyterian Medical Center. Among other choices, visitors can link to departments and organizations, news and information files, and clinical resource files. The library resources page—under Selected Health Sciences Resources—includes several useful links to sites covering drugs, consumer health, dentistry, alternative medicine, and more.

HospitalWeb

http://neuro-www.mgh.harvard.edu/ hospitalweb.nclk

HospitalWeb is a compilation of links to worldwide hospital Web servers allowing patients, medical researchers, and physicians to access information about specific hospitals. The site also features an interesting medical site of the week, comprehensive medical indexes, and a selected list of medical companies and organizations. A super info site.

The Massachusetts General Hospital WWW Server

http://www.mgh.harvard.edu/

Boston's Massachusetts General Hospital home page features policies and procedures, plus a directory of doctors, staff, and departments. Also find links to databases, library services, and other health-related resources, including a fine selection of pages devoted to consumer health issues, such as HealthWeb from the University of Illinois, and Your Health Daily, an online publication of *The New York Times* that contains daily health news stories.

Mayo Clinic

http://www.mayo.edu/

The world-famous Mayo Clinic goes online here to provide an online tour and comprehensive info about the

medical facility, services for patients, and research activities. Patients traveling to any of Mayo's facilities (in Rochester, Minnesota; Jacksonville, Florida; or Scottsdale, Arizona) will find useful information about local weather, lodging, and travel arrangements. Lots of contact links (appointments, billing, general info) make it easy to find out more.

New England Medical Center

http://www.nemc.org/

The New England Medical Center in Boston serves as both a medical and an educational institution. This page includes an overview of the facility, and information about its many areas of medical expertise. A physician referral guide is also featured.

Sloan-Kettering Institute

http://www.mskcc.org/

The Memorial Sloan-Kettering Cancer Center sponsors this site to provide information about the institution and its services, basic information on cancer prevention and early detection, a physician referral guide, and an overview of ongoing research projects.

U.S. Hospitals on the Web

http://www.usaads.com/CLIENTS/HOSPITAL/ HOSP.HTM

This easy-to-use index to U.S. hospitals with a Web presence is arranged alphabetically by state. Scroll down to your state, find a hospital in the list that interests you, and then just click on the hyperlink to be whisked to the hospital's home page.

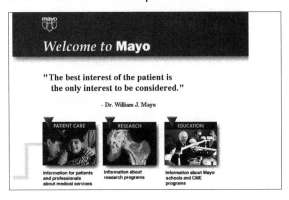

PROFESSIONAL HOME CARE, HOSPICE, AND FAMILY CAREGIVERS

Caregiver's Handbook

http://www.acsu.buffalo.edu/~drstall/hndbk0.html

This valuable online booklet covers common problems in caregiving, the types of help available, support groups, the importance of communication, and taking care of the caregiver.

Caregivers, Caregiving, and Home Care Workers

http://www.aoa.dhhs.gov/aoa/eldractn/caregive.html

From the Administration on Aging of the U.S. Department of Health and Human Services comes this tip sheet for home health caregivers, with such useful advice as how to apply for support services, how to hire additional help, and how to apply for respite care.

Eldercare Web

http://www.elderweb.com/

Although it includes useful information about home care, this wonderful resource isn't just for Seniors who need care and their caregivers; it includes lots of useful advice and links for folks of all ages, covering nutrition, health, legal, and financial concerns.

FAQs about Hospice

http://www.nho.org/ques.htm

Here are answers to many of the questions you may have about hospice care for the terminally ill—covering such topics as financing, pain management, level of medical care, and emotional support. The site includes a toll-free number for the National Hospice Organization helpline.

Home Care/Hospice Industry

http://www.ptct.com/html/industry.html

Here's a good resource for exploring home care options. The site includes two articles about the home care industry and its presence on the Internet, followed by a geographically arranged list of links to specific companies and national listservs. If you're interested in home care, this site provides a good jumpstation to additional information.

How Do You Pick a Home Health Agency?

http://www.homehealthcare.com/pick_art.html

This brief article, posted by a home health care agency, introduces the types of home care companies and offers practical tips for obtaining referrals, along with a list of questions to help consumers evaluate the suitability of a particular service.

Ten Ways to Care for the Caregiver

http://oncolink.upenn.edu/psychosocial/care_caregiver.html

From the University of Pennsylvania's Oncolink site comes this excellent article on how to take care of yourself if you are the primary caregiver for a critically ill family member.

A SELECTION OF MEDICAL REFERENCE MATERIALS

Centers for Disease Control and Prevention

http://www.cdc.gov/

The home page for the CDC includes general information and current news; excellent discussions of diseases, health risks, and injuries; and a link to the CDC Wonder system, a database of CDC reports, guidelines, and public health data. Visitors can also link to any of the 11 CDC internal centers such as Environmental Health, Infectious Diseases, and the National Immunization Program.

HealthWeb
http://www.ghsl.nwu.edu/healthweb/

HealthWeb connects a variety of medical and health science libraries to create a specialized, comprehensive health information resource. The site includes info about the network, listings by subject, descriptions of the member libraries, and search features.

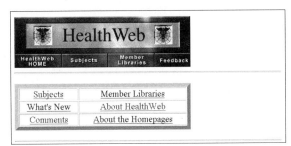

MedWeb: Biomedical Internet Resources
http://www.cc.emory.edu/WHSCL/medweb.html

For sheer volume of information, you can't beat Emory University's MedWeb, a meta-index to medicine, medical science, and health resources on the Internet. What do you want to know today? How to handle suspected health fraud? The source of the name of the Ebola virus? The fat content of fast food restaurant offerings? The answer to just about any medical or health question can be found somewhere in the MedWeb pages.

Multimedia Medical Reference Library
http://www.med-library.com/

The table of contents goes on and on at this searchable site, including everything from AIDS and allergies, to urology and virology. An extensive list of downloadable audio files (.au format) cover medical conditions and safety issues ranging from Addison's disease to blackouts, to taking medication, to yogurt. You'll also find images and movies, hospitals online, and a list of "exceptional sites."

The Virtual Hospital
http://vh.radiology.uiowa.edu/

The multimedia laboratory at the University of Iowa College of Medicine presents The Virtual Hospital, a continuously updated health sciences library. There's loads of information here for health care consumers, including discussions of medical issues classified by organ system, and information about the medical facility itself.

World Wide Drugs
http://community.net/~neils/new.html

Neil Sandow, a Pharm.D., is a person you'd like to see behind the counter at your local drug store. Here's a guy who has all the answers to drug-related questions or knows where to find them. Neil may not compound your prescriptions, but he has made his knowledge accessible by compiling this impressive catalog of pharmaceutical sites. The first entry on the prescription pad is the Rx List, a cross-referenced index of over 4,000 prescription and over-the-counter drugs. Next, take a dose of Martindale's Virtual Pharmacy Center. Martindale's is packed with drug databases, medical dictionaries, online pharmacy journals, and scary facts about drug interactions and reactions. Want more? Check out the World Wide Web Virtual Library Pharmacy. So the next time you want drug facts, don't consult the 1989 Physicians' Desk Reference you picked up at the last library book sale, log on to Neil's site for the best drug sites on the Internet.

Chapter 13
MEET THE MEDIA

ALL FOR ONE AND ONE FOR ALL

MAGAZINES

NEWSPAPERS AND WIRE SERVICES

RADIO AND TELEVISION

When I think of newspapers, magazines, and television, my mind always strays to notions of mass media, and veers off to all the ways we can now communicate. I am faced with so *many* ways to communicate—mail, e-mail, television, phone—and with others trying to communicate *with* me, that I find myself on information-overload much of the time, having little energy to dig for more.

My mailbox is full to overflowing every day with magazines, and offers for newly created newsletters, catalogs, and contest invitations. Many of these magazines I actually read, in bed late at night when I have shut down for the day. I sometimes get some good ideas from them. But they are always recycled (to other people, that is), and the chair in the front room is piled high, waiting for the next unsuspecting visitor to come by so I can unload them. I am riddled with too much guilt to just throw them out, and it seems a shame just to truck them to the recycling center after only one set of eyes has perused their pages.

The newspaper, I am sorry to say, makes it into the house, but many days just gets as far as the recycling bin in the kitchen, because I don't often have time to read it. But it serves other purposes: I sometimes use it for stuffing a box I need to mail. It's good to set wet boots on when coming in from the snow, and it's great for wrapping veggie refuse from the last orgy of cooking (unless you have a compost heap, and then you wouldn't want to mix).

The television often blares away without a viewer sitting in front of it, as I am busy in other parts of the house taking care of more practical things. The evening news is either so gory, or so bland (there never seems to be anything in-between), that you can miss it for days and not feel deprived of anything. And there are so many "all-news" channels nowadays, that it's hard to make a pick. Not to mention "news magazine" formats like *60 Minutes*, taking up breaking news and decoding the issues, investigating

and restating to the point where my brain feels like a whirlagig trying to sort out all the facts.

With the invasion of all these media attempts to communicate with me and bring me the news of the day from all over the globe, my thoughts drift back to a simpler time.

ALL FOR ONE AND ONE FOR ALL

My grandmother's house had one phone—ten bedrooms, eleven residents of all ages, and one wooden crank wall phone, hung in the back hall. All calls were made standing up, because no one talked long enough to need a chair, and the phone was placed so high on the wall there was no other choice. The phonebook, about 1/8 of an inch thick, hung from a nearby string for easy access.

Long distance was an important event. Whoever took the call would shout loudly, "Long distance!," and everyone would gather hurridly from every part of the house to see who on earth was calling. The call took on a circus atmosphere as everyone there had to have a chance to speak to the caller.

To call out, you cranked the handle until you reached "Central," a small woman huddled over a switchboard in a six-by-six room of her home. She also took messages for you, whether you wanted her to or not. And she was one of the main sources of local news and information. While her methods may have raised an eyebrow or two among those seeking the highest standards of journalistic integrity, in those days no one in our community ever questioned her authority, or her accuracy, for that matter.

Later on, when Central was replaced by a still more centralized phone company, and phone lines were wired into every home, the old wall phone was replaced by a standup, stick-like telephone with the ear piece hung in a cradle. Though we lost the pipeline and authority of "News Central," we were still able to keep up with local goings-on, albeit indirectly, by virtue of the party line. At our house, six different homes shared the line, and everyone on the six-party scheme had a different ring, so it was easy to tell when a neighbor was receiving a call. Quite a difference from today's fiber optics and low-cost dialing, not to mention the miracle of e-mail.

Of course, back then there was no television bringing us the news of the day, no stacks upon stacks of magazines and newspapers to contend with, only an old wooden radio reposing in my grandfather's study that could be used only by appointment, and only when he wasn't listening in; and the daily delivery of *The New York Times*, also available from grandfather by appointment (and only *after* he'd completed the crossword puzzle).

These days, to stay current with the news, I welcome the wonder of the Web, where I can pick and choose my headlines and stories carefully, read whatever I want online at my convenience, and feel guilt-free about ignoring the rest. Gradually, I am letting subscriptions lapse for certain magazines I know I can live without, or with which I can keep current online, keeping only those for which the pleasure of page-turning can never be replaced by the computer screen (somehow, I just can't see the value in reading *The New Yorker* anyplace but snuggled deep down under the comforter, or curled up in my favorite wingback chair).

I find it ironic that we have come from such simple beginnings in our world of comunications, to being innundated with information by the airwaves and printing presses of modern times, to finally coming right back to a simpler, more selective way of retrieving the news—simply by virtue of the choices now available via the Internet. I've got to get better organized so that I can handle it all!

MAGAZINES

The American Spectator
http://www.spectator.org/

Its investigative reporting and commentary make this watchdog one of the country's fastest growing publications. Read selected features, including R. Emmett Tyrrell's most recent syndicated column, and the Online Update, refreshed every Tuesday.

The Atlantic Monthly
http://www.theAtlantic.com/atlantic/

Founded in 1857, this monthly has carved itself a niche as a reflector and sometimes deflector of politics, society, arts, and culture. Read the electronic edition of this month's issue, including selections from the ever-evolving Atlantic Unbound journal, or join in the talk via the Post & Riposte Web conferencing system.

Better Homes and Gardens
http://www.betterhomesandgardens.com/

One of America's premier home and garden magazines treats its readers to a preview of upcoming issues, points the way to "favorite spots" on the Internet, and offers a few Web features such as entertainment guides and online shopping.

ComputerLife Online
http://www.zdnet.com/complife/

The family-friendly computing magazine from Ziff-Davis, *ComputerLife* serves up an electronic edition at this site. Find the current issue along with links to other ZD Net sites.

Discover Magazine
http://www.enews.com/magazines/discover/

The popular and lay-friendly science publication, *Discover Magazine* makes its online home at this Web site. Enjoy selected articles from the current issue, an educators' forum, a schedule for TV's Discovery Channel, and an archive of back issues. The editors of the magazine also provide pointers to their favorite science sites.

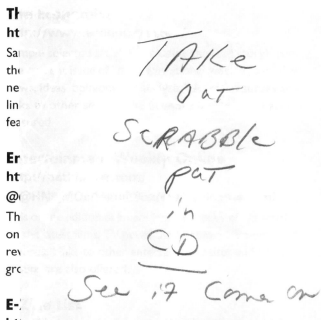

Th
ht
Sa
th
ne
lin
fea

Er
ht
@
Th
on
re
gr

E-
ht
Usually produced by one person or a small cabal, e(lectronic maga)zines, or 'zines for short, generally veer toward the artistic, esoteric, irreverent, bizarre, and beyond. They are an Internet phenomenon in that they are exclusively "electronic" publications. John Labovitz maintains this guide to the more than 1,450 'zines currently online. Browse using the 40 most popular keywords, or try the list of most obscure keywords.

George
http://www.georgemag.com/hfm/index.html
"Not just politics as usual" sums up the publisher's view of this recent entry into the magazine market. Polls, experts via e-mail (congressmen, too!), trivia, and reader forums seem to be the hot highlights of this electronic edition of JFK Jr.'s magazine.

Grand Times Magazine
http://www.grandtimes.com/
"Exclusively for active retirees," this weekly publication offers an entertaining, informative, and sometimes provocative look at life. Read pieces from previous publications as well as the current print edition, find a marketplace of

roducts, browse a travel section, and explore sites worth eeing according to the magazine's editors.

Interactive Week Online
http://www.zdnet.com/intweek/
Browsers can keep up with the latest in interactive technology here. Interactive Week Online covers the telecommunications industry, offering features from the print magazine as well as frequently updated online sections.

Ladies' Home Journal
http://www.lhj.com/
The oldest and one of the most respected women's service magazines comes online with selected articles from the current print issues and standard online features. Link to the latest Journal offerings or browse back issues.

LIFE Magazine
http://pathfinder.com/@@dXV8FgcA3Fjfp7uy/Life/lifehome.html
The quintessential photo-journalism magazine, LIFE brings its unique brand of sightseeing to the Internet. Check out the Picture of the Day, photo essays, and galleries. Plus, take a look at the current magazine's features.

Macworld Magazine Online
http://www.macworld.com/
Taking the global perspective, the online version of Macworld Magazine provides the latest Mac news for the Internet community. Mac fans can visit here to read articles, browse the software library, post a note on the message boards, or loiter in the Technocultural Cafe.

Magazine CyberCentre

http://www.magamall.com/pagetwo.htm

Here's an information center displaying over 1,000 commercial magazines. Browse by title or category, then find the retailer nearest you that carries the publications you desire. Or if you prefer (and one is online), link to the publication's Web site.

Maturity USA

http://www.maturityusa.com/

Available only online, Maturity USA is an e-zine devoted to the concerns of the mature adult, and features stories on social security, health, estate planning, and finances, along with fun travel pieces and news analysis articles.

The MoJo Wire: Mother Jones Interactive

http://www.mojones.com/

The electronic incarnation of the proudly populist *Mother Jones* magazine offers irreverent political commentary and hard-hitting investigative reports.

The Monster (Magazine) List

http://www.enews.com/monster/

Search for your favorite magazines to see if they have a site online. Either enter a keyword, browse the list of all titles, or access publication lists by subject areas that run the gamut from automotive to gourmet and health and medicine to spirituality and religion.

The Nation

http://www.TheNation.com/

Enjoy the digital edition of America's oldest weekly magazine, and one of the country's most respected journals offering opinion on politics, culture, books, and the arts. Enjoy selected articles from the print edition, plus a variety of fixed features including audio excerpts from Radio-Nation, the publication's weekly syndicated radio program.

The New Republic

http://www.enews.com/magazines/tnr/

Those in need of a weekly dose of thought-lines need only stop by this electronic edition of the "weekly journal of opinion." There's plenty of "I think" to go around.

Nest Egg

http://nestegg.iddis.com/index.html

"Nest Egg" keeps an eye on Wall Street. Visitors to this interactive magazine will find news, features, and rumors for the money-minded. Regular attractions include advice on financial planning and links to various Dow Jones publications.

Online Magazines

http://www.physik.unizh.ch/zines.html

An extensive index of online magazines is maintained at this Web site. Magazine categories offered here include news, computers, arts, music, business, and science.

OMNI

http://www.omnimag.com/

Science bordering on fiction, fiction bordering on science, plus a bit of the fantastic and horrible can all be found among the features of this online edition of *OMNI* magazine. Along with the writings, find an art gallery, an arcade, forums, and a bookstore.

Pathfinder

http://pathfinder.com/@@awR5PAcA1Vjfp7uy/welcome/

TIME, LIFE, Money, Fortune, People, and SI Online from *Sports Illustrated* are just a few of the featured attractions at this Time Warner mega-site.

PC Magazine on the Web

http://www.pcmag.com/

A product of Ziff-Davis Publishing Company, *PC Magazine* hosts this Web site offering news, trends, columns, and downloads. Also find Internet highlights, product reviews and announcements, and links to other Ziff-Davis information sites.

People

http://pathfinder.com/people/

People who need *People* will find an electronic version of their favorite "look at me, I'm a celebrity" magazine posted here. Find out who's hot and who's burned out, who's a shooting star and who's shooting stars.

PopSci.com
http://www.popsci.com/

From the editors of *Popular Science* magazine, here's the latest news about the sciences as well as online features that are both fantastic and fun. Regular departments include automotive, computers, science, electronics, and home tech.

Popular Mechanics
http://popularmechanics.com/

The home mechanic's companion for almost 100 years, this monthly has built a loyal following by making new technologies accessible and easy to understand for its readers. Visit this interactive site for automotive, home improvement, and electronic tips and projects, plus a look at the current issue.

Premiere
http://www.premieremag.com/

Visitors can get the latest buzz from Hollywood through the online version of the glitzy yet authoritative *Premiere* magazine. The site includes feature articles, coming attractions, insider gossip, and a detailed look at film magic in the making.

Reader's Digest
http://www.readersdigest.com/

What we've all come to expect from the printed magazine is now available online. Find humor, insight, drama, tips for better living, and a whole lot more. Visit this gateway page to choose from Reader's Digest Interactive, Reader's Digest At Home, or Reader's Digest Shop at Home.

The Saturday Evening Post
http://www.satevepost.org/

Enjoy a gallery of Norman Rockwell illustrations, giggle over a collection of cartoons, and read selected features from the pages of the print publication. You can also shop at the online gift shop and subscribe to the magazine.

Scientific American
http://www.sciam.com/

First published in 1845, the magazine has built a reputation for tracking the key changes in scientific advance-

ment and technology. Find the best of the current issue posted to these pages along with regularly updated electronic features such as Ask the Experts.

Senior Lifestyle
http://www.senior-lifestyle.com/

Find out why "it's fun to be fifty-something." Enjoy articles, classifieds, a calendar of events for seniors in California, and links to "senior-sational" sites.

SI Online from Sports Illustrated
http://pathfinder.com/@@awR5PAcA1Vjfp7uy/si/

News, views, and reviews all find their way to this Web home for *Sports Illustrated* fans and readers. Check the latest scores, find out who's in play and what they're playing at, participate in polls, and even find a chuckle or two.

The Skeptic
http://www.cs.man.ac.uk/skeptic

Published bimonthly in the United Kingdom, *The Skeptic* cocks a suspicious eyebrow toward the pseudo-sciences and claims of the paranormal. Visitors to this page can review the contents of recent issues and find ordering information.

Slate
http://www.slate.com/TOC/current/contents.asp

Is the press soft on the president, should we get soft on God, and has AIDS run its course? These are just a few of the questions tackled in a recent edition of Microsoft's electronic, interactive journal of culture, society, and politics.

Smithsonian Magazine
http://www.smithsonianmag.si.edu/

The official publication of the Smithsonian Institution hosts this online look at its print pages. Check out the current issue, plus find an image gallery, a link to the Smithsonian's Web site, and a pointer to *Air&Space Magazine*.

Southern Living Online

**http://pathfinder.com/
@@HN9jMQcA4lhuZ8bz/sl/**

Southern food, travel, home style, and entertainment come to the Web through the pages of Southern Living Online. Find ideas for adding an air of Southern grace to your life.

Time.com

http://pathfinder.com/time/

Offering a posting of daily news and an electronic edition of this week's *TIME* magazine, Time.com primes its readers for the "hot topic" discussions available in its forums and chat rooms. Multimedia presentations such as photo essays and animated reports also await visitors.

U.S. News & World Report Online

http://www.usnews.com/

The national/international news weekly comes online with highlights from this week's edition, plus fixed features that include a look at colleges and careers, a citizen's toolbox, and a News You Can Use section.

Washington Weekly

http://dolphin.gulf.net/

Claiming to be an alternative to the dreaded and much alluded to "liberal media," this electronic news magazine surveys the week's political events and offers a bracing shot of conservative commentary in its editorial section.

World-Wide Web Virtual Library: Electronic Journals

http://www.edoc.com/ejournal/

Categories of online publications indexed in this directory include academic and reviewed journals, college and university publications, e-mail newsletters, and magazines and newspapers. A keyword search offers quick access if you know what you're looking for.

ZD Net

http://www5.zdnet.com/

ZD Net is the online home of Ziff-Davis, the publisher of technology-based publications such as *MacUser, PC Com-*

puting, and *ComputerLife.* Online versions of these and other Ziff-Davis publications can be found at this site, along with a software library and topical features aimed at assisting users get the most from today's computer technology.

NEWSPAPERS AND WIRE SERVICES

AP Breaking News

http://www.tampatrib.com/ap/breaking.htm

Information junkies can browse breaking news hot off the Associated Press wire. Hosted by Tampa Bay Online, this site allows users to organize and access stories by beat: national, international, sports, and business.

Associated Press: The Wire

http://www.nj.com/apwire/

Get the latest news from the Associated Press. Find U.S., world, business, and sports news presented and indexed for easy accessibility. The Wire is an experimental service of the AP.

ClariNet e.News

http://www.clarinet.com/

ClariNet e.News claims to be the "Net's first and largest electronic newspaper." The fee-based service provides national and international news, technology and financial updates, sports and entertainment features, and stock reports. Visit here for a sample of the service and subscription information.

CReAte Your Own Newspaper (CRAYON)
http://crayon.net/

This site lets you do exactly what the title suggests. Select from a variety of news sources and create the newspaper you've always dreamed of. Finally, you get to be the publisher!

Ecola's Newsstand—Newspapers
http://www.ecola.com/news/press/

This 24-hour virtual newsstand offers browsers the opportunity to access hundreds of electronic publications around the world. Search by location and keyword for newspapers from Alaska to Zambia, or business and consumer magazines from Sri Lanka to Texas.

The Largest Newspaper Index on the Web
http://www.freenet.msp.mn.us/people/trasstw/newspaper.html

Pointing to over 450 local U.S. newspapers with Web sites, this server links readers to small community and capitol city news around the country. The cities with papers online are organized by state. Simply point and click until you reach the news posting desired.

My Virtual Newspaper
http://www.refdesk.com/paper.html

Organized for ease of use, this site serves up the news—social, political, economic, entertainment, scientific and technological—as you like it. Pick and choose from among your favorite news services around the world, plus find a generous dose of features that include weather reports, comics, and crosswords.

The NandO Times
http://www2.nando.net/nt/nando.cgi

This online newspaper offers regional, national, and international stories, updated regularly throughout the day. Features include sections on business, politics, entertainment, science, and technology.

NeWo: News Resource
http://newo.com/news/

Whether searching for your local news or the local news to folks living in some other part of the world, this server delivers the papers available on the Internet. Just click a continent on the map-based interface to begin your search, or if you prefer, access one of the featured news resources presented.

Newspapers Online
http://www.newspapers.com/

Actually this server points the way to much more than just newspapers. Also find publications from the worlds of business and industry, colleges and universities, and religious organizations. There are classified ad and other specialty publications, too.

The Newsroom
http://www.auburn.edu/~vestmon/news.html

No muss, no fuss. Here's a list of links to the selected best Internet sites offering U.S. and world news, business and finance updates, and current affairs stories. Also find features such as lottery information and a collection of resources that include links to a variety of U.S. government pages.

Online Newspapers
http://www.ucc.uconn.edu/~jpa94001/papers.html

Link to the newspapers in each of the 50 United States with an information site on the Internet. Also find pointers to the newspaper sites from 50 other countries as well—from Albania to Uruguay.

PointCast Network
http://www.pointcast.com/

Have all the news you want to know about delivered over the Internet and presented dynamically on your computer screen—free. It works like a screen saver, but replaces flying toasters and the like with news you can use. Visit this home page to find out more about PointCast and download the (yes, free!) software needed to enjoy this innovative service.

Reuters
http://www.reuters.com/reutersnews/
index.html

Stop by the Reuters wire service Web and get right down to "the business of information." Customize your news feed to deliver only the bytes you desire: international, U.S. news, U.S. politics, business, technology, or sports; then find out what's happening in the world where you live.

Taxi's Newspaper List
http://users.deltanet.com/users/taxicat/e_
papers.html

Organized by country, then by state if applicable, here's another directory to the newspapers on the Internet. Over 25 countries are represented. Simply click on the flag of the country of choice to begin a search.

Web News Index
http://recycle.green.ri.cmu.edu/~speck/

Updated every 15 minutes, Web News Index provides an up-to-the-minute searchable index of news (and only news!) articles available on the Web. Stop in here to get the latest on any breaking story.

YOUR QUICK LINK LIST TO FAVORITE U.S. PAPERS ONLINE

Atlanta Journal-Constitution
http://www.ajc.com/

Boston Globe
http://www.globe.com/

Chicago Sun-Times
http://www.suntimes.com

Chicago Tribune
http://www.chicago.tribune.com/

The Christian Science Monitor
http://www.csmonitor.com/

Dallas Morning News
http://www.dallasnews.com/

Detroit News
http://www.detnews.com/

Los Angeles Times
http://www.latimes.com/

Miami Herald
http://www.herald.com/

New York Times
http://www.nytimes.com/

Philadelphia Online (Inquirer & Daily News)
http://www.phillynews.com/

San Francisco's The Gate
http://www.sfgate.com/

Seattle Times
http://www.seatimes.com/

St. Louis' Postnet
http://www.stlnet.com/postnet/

St. Petersburg Times
http://www.sptimes.com/

USA Today
http://www.usatoday.com

The Wall Street Journal
http://update.wsj.com

Washington Post
http://www.washingtonpost.com/

The Washington Times
http://www.washtimes.com/

YOUR QUICK LINK LIST TO OTHER FAVORITE ENGLISH LANGUAGE PAPERS ONLINE

Christchurch Press (New Zealand)
http://www.press.co.nz/

China Daily
http://www.chinadaily.co.cn/

The Hindu (India)
http://www.indiaserver.com/news/thehindu/thehindu.html

The Irish Times
http://www.irish-times.ie/

The Japan Times
http://www.japantimes.co.jp/

The Jerusalem Post
http://www.jpost.co.il/

Johannesburg Star
http://164.88.55.4/online/star/

The Montreal Gazette
http://www.montrealgazette.com/

The Mail & Guardian (South Africa)
http://www.mg.co.za/mg/

The Times of London
http://www.the-times.co.uk/

Sydney Morning Herald
http://www.smh.com.au/

Toronto Globe and Mail
http://www.GlobeAndMail.CA/

Toronto Sun
http://www.canoe.ca/TorontoSun/home.html

The Vancouver Sun
http://www.southam.com/vancouversun/

RADIO AND TELEVISION

ABC
http://www.abctelevision.com/
The ABC television network includes a fun offering in ABC CyberCity, a page of trivia games, a treasure hunt, brain teasers, and a downloadable screensaver. Elsewhere, click into news about the network's programming, including info on local stations (and links when the stations are on line)and previews of upcoming events.

ABC Radio Net
http://www.abcradionet.com/
Did you miss Peter Jennings' newscast tonight? You can listen to it here, along with news on the hour, sports, and weather. Visitors can also pick a city from a clickable image map for links to more localized news and features.

BBC
http://www.bbc.co.uk/
The British Broadcasting Corporation serves as the national broadcasting backbone of the United Kingdom. Find out about the BBC, its television programming, and radio offerings.

CBC
http://www.cbc.ca/
The Canadian Broadcasting Corporation is Canada's public broadcasting service, offering programming in the country's two official languages, French and English. Link to the CBC Web site to find out all about the corporation, its television broadcasts, and radio programming.

CBS News
http://www.cbs.com/news/

Get the latest breaking news, up-to-the-minute and online, from the CBS division that puts on *The CBS Evening News with Dan Rather*.

CBS Radio Networks
http://www.cbsradio.com/

The Forbes Report, CBS News, The Osgood File, and the Mary Matlin Show are only a few of the programs featured on the CBS Radio Networks' home page. Link to information about each of the shows, join the mailing list, or search the station roster to find out where on the radio dial you can tune in the affiliate nearest you.

CineMedia
http://ptd15.afionline.org/CineMedia/

This mega entertainment site hosts over 9,000 links pointing every which-a-way. Among the categories of links, find TV and radio groupings where you can browse or search for sites that pique your interest.

CNBC
http://www.cnbc.com/

Home to some of the cable industry's most opinionated talking financial heads, CNBC not only delivers the daily business news but at night is quite happy to offer general commentary as well. Stop in here for program notes and stock quotes.

CNN Interactive
http://www.cnn.com/

The Cable News Network is all news, all the time. Visit the network's Web home for headline news and features that cover the world in which we live. Find national and international news as well as weather, sports, sci-tech, travel, style, health, finances, politics, and showbiz.

Court TV Law Center
http://www.courttv.com/

The network that televises real life courtroom drama hosts this online center for finding legal advice and aid. A section geared exclusively to seniors' issues is featured along with sections on small business and family law.

General information about the TV network and its programming is also featured.

C-SPAN
http://www.c-span.org/

The channel that literally serves as a government watchdog now serves its viewers with live, online C-SPAN coverage over the Internet. Find out who's currently on and how to link in. Also access a multimedia archive, the cable network's programming schedule, and a variety of topical features such as a guide to Congress and a test to find out if you're a conservative or liberal.

DateLine NBC
http://www.msnbc.com/Onair/nbc/dateline/default.asp

Jane Pauley and Stone Philips host this NBC news magazine covering topics of general newsworthiness and human interest. Visit the show's Web page for followup and support materials concerning the reports that have already been or will soon be aired.

48 Hours
http://www.cbs.com/primetime/48_hours.html

This CBS news program claims to investigate issues indepth to uncover and report the "whole story." Meet the correspondents who help bring the show together, and preview this week's report.

FOX News
http://foxnews.com/

Stay current on national and international affairs with headline news, business, sports, and features presented by the folks at FOX's fledgling news division. Search for a topic of interest or link to specific beats for the latest news. Also find a 24-hour live audio feed.

Frontline Online
http://www2.pbs.org/wgbh/pages/frontline/

PBS's "flagship" public affairs series, *Frontline*, features documentaries that delve into "the thorniest public policy issues." Visit this companion Web site that provides viewer support material related to the documentaries that are aired on the program.

The Guide to Talk Radio Programming

http://www.talkradioguide.com/

Find out who's on talk radio and who's putting them on. This site offers "a complete directory of syndicated talk, news, and sports radio programming." Unfortunately, the listings are not hyperlinked.

Media Online Yellow Pages

http://www.webcom.com/~nlnnet/
yellowp.html

Link to the home pages of local, national, and international television and radio concerns that maintain a presence on the Internet. This searchable, general-industry directory features networks and stations, but also includes trade publications, associations, TV shows and guides, and more.

Meet the Press

http://www.msnbc.com/Onair/nbc/mtp/
Default.asp

The longest-running program in the history of NBC and network television, this grill-em-'til-they're-done interview show serves up "hot topic" segments with today's leaders. Visit the show's Web support page to review this week's show, access special reports, and offer feedback.

The MIT List of Radio Stations on the Internet

http://wmbr.mit.edu/stations/list.html

Search a database of over 2,000 radio stations to find those nearest to you offering the programming you most desire. The list of U.S. stations can be searched/sorted by type (FM or AM), frequency, call sign, state, or format. Also find lists of Canadian, European, and other international stations.

Monitor Radio

http://www.csmonitor.com/

The Christian Science Monitor presents hourly radio newscasts throughout the day that are broadcast over Public Radio International affiliate stations. Find out where to tune in the newscasts, or access today's in-depth programming online.

MSNBC

http://www.msnbc.com/news/default.asp

Fed by the news division at NBC, this collaborative effort with Microsoft Corporation isn't just "any daily news magazine." Visitors can personalize the news this site delivers, choosing what stocks, sports, weather, and types of news they want to see. Other site features include a library of selected NBC news stories and interactive features, plus links to the NBC, CNBC, and MSNBC news program home pages.

National Public Radio

http://www.npr.org/

All Things Considered, *Morning Edition*, and *Talk of the Nation* are only a sampling of the programs broadcast by NPR, the world's first noncommercial, satellite-delivered radio system. Check the full roster of shows, link to their pages, find out more about NPR, and search the directory of member stations for an affiliate near you that carries the programming.

NBC News at Sunrise

http://www.msnbc.com/Onair/Bios/
Sunrise.asp

Offering the day's headline stories, weather, sports and features, this show presents NBC's first shot at the day's big doings. The show's Web site offers little more than a description of the program and an opportunity to meet the anchor and meteorologist.

NET—The Political NewsTalk Network

http://net.fcref.org/

Uncovering Washington intrigue and probing the hot button issues, that's what the 24-hour, talk-it-up, interactive programming of this independent network is all about. Stop by the network's Web home for an insider's look at the NET.

Nightly News with Tom Brokaw

http://www.msnbc.com/Onair/nbc/
nightlynews/default.asp

NBC News' centerpiece program, the *Nightly News* covers the major events in the country and across the globe, plus offers in-depth features of interest to Americans.

Visit this Web site for background on the show and its anchor, reports, transcripts, and resources relevant to the current events covered.

Online Newshour
http://www1.pbs.org/newshour/

The *Newshour* with Jim Lehrer hosts this support site offering news reports, show transcripts, essays, audio files, and viewer forums. Meet Jim Lehrer and his team of PBS reporters, correspondents, and analysts.

PBS
http://www.pbs.org/

If PBS doesn't do it, nobody else will. Host to the *Newshour* with Jim Lehrer, *Firing Line*, *Frontline*, *The McLaughlin Group*, and specials of interest to a broad-based audience, PBS delivers on its promise to serve the public trust. Link to the home pages of its regular shows and special programs, find out more about PBS, or link to your state's affiliate network.

PrimeTime Live
http://www.abctelevision.com/primetime1/ptlive/ptlive.html

Diane Sawyer and Sam Donaldson host this ABC news magazine featuring "hard-hitting" investigative journalism and "compelling" human interest features. Meet the folks behind this show, review some of its past pieces, preview what's to come, and sample a few video and audio highlights.

60 Minutes
http://www.cbs.com/primetime/60_min.html

Considered by most to be U.S. television's premier news magazine, *60 Minutes* has been busting "bad" guys, talking to celebrities, and telling tales of whimsy and woe for almost 30 years. Meet the folks who bring you the stories and find out how to chat with other *60 Minutes* viewers online every Sunday evening after the show.

Talk America Radio Network
http://www.talkamerica.com/

Here's the only national radio network gabbing 24 hours a day, seven days a week. Find out about the network's 40-plus on-air talents and their shows, search out the station nearest you carrying the programming, or link via the Internet to a live audio feed.

The Today Show
http://www.msnbc.com/onair/nbc/today/default.asp

NBC's morning news and general features show has been waking up folks for over 40 years. Visit the show's Web site to take a virtual tour behind the scenes, preview upcoming shows, meet Today's hosts, read show transcripts, and wander down memory lane.

Turning Point
http://www.abctelevision.com/primetime1/turning/turning.html

Rotating anchors such as Barbara Walters, Diane Sawyer, and Forrest Sawyer, this weekly offering from ABC presents hour-long, single-subject reports on issues and events as diverse as the bombing in Oklahoma City and a fight to save an endangered species of African elephant. Stop by the show's promotional Web page to review the show's history, meet its anchors, and preview what's coming on the next broadcast.

20/20
http://www.abctelevision.com/primetime1/
twenty/twenty.html
Hosted by Hugh Downs and Barbara Walters, this ABC
News program is the network's first news magazine. The
show's Web site allows viewers to check out video and
audio highlights, meet the show's cast, and review the
history of the program.

The Weather Channel
http://www.weather.com/
Don't like what the weather is doing outside your window? Check this Web watch to see if there's a change in
the forecast. Those who really like to keep up with the

jet stream can also have customized weather reports
sent to their desktops when they want. Visit this site to
find out how.

World Radio Network
http://town.hall.org/radio/wrn.html
Pick up the audio stream over the Internet or find out
where to tune a conventional radio for the network's 24
hour news and information programming.

Chapter 14

ROADS LESS TRAVELED

WRITTEN IN THE STARS, OR...?

I SEE A TALL, DARK, HANDSOME FUTURE IN YOUR MAN..., ER...

PROVINCES OF THE MIND AND STATES OF CONSCIOUSNESS

SPIRITUAL, MYSTICAL, AND OTHER SOULFUL MATTERS

UFOS, THEIR DRIVERS, AND OTHER MYSTERIOUS CREATURES

As far back as Cro-Magnon scrawling pictures on the walls of caves, humans have been awed by the supernatural, as well as the mystery of the stars. The pharaohs of Egypt plotted the course of their nation using the stars to predict their fates, and believed strongly in an afterworld; early popes cast the wheel of astrology to foretell the future of the church; and English monarchs used this form of divination to keep their edge on the throne.

WRITTEN IN THE STARS, OR ...?

Astrology was studied by the Egyptians, Hindus, Chinese, Estruscans, and the Chaldeans of Babylonia. These are the folks originally credited with the origin of this "science," probably around 3000 BC, when they used astrological forcasts to foretell the seasons and predict the outcome of their crops. The Babylonians presumed that a power within the heavens ruled human life, and that heaven's messages could be read in the stars.

Later in the 4th century BC, the Greeks embraced this science, combining it with their spiritual practice of worshipping many gods, and with the newly emerging science of astronomy.

As astronomy and eventually Christianity gained more credibility, astrology became less acceptable as an exact science, and humanity turned away from practices which seemed supernatural and unempirical—never mind that many Biblical stories are filled with accounts of the mystical and supernatural. As the Christian church gained in authority and power, all practices lacking the official sanction of the church fell into disfavor; and indeed, there have been many periods in our history when those who continued to embrace so-called pagan or supernatural practices were persecuted, even executed. But there are many today who still hold with so-called

supernatural practices, and these sciences and beliefs, inexact though they may be, still have many millions of adherents.

And not all of "bucking the system" is about "science," either—UFO enthusiasts, believers in the paranormal, proponents of conspiracy theories, skeptics—some may call them cranks, but I prefer to think of them as folks who simply choose to walk on roads less frequently traveled by the rest of us. Why not?

CONSPIRACIES, CRIMES, HOAXES, AND INQUIRING MINDS

The B.C. Society for Skeptical Inquiry
http://psg.com/~ted/bcskeptics/index.html

A cluster of critical thinkers in British Columbia, the BC Skeptics (as they like to call themselves) critique and investigate paranormal claims and traditions. The society's home page features topical reports from recent meetings, and articles from issues of the group's newsletter, the *Rational Enquirer*. Those who seek to join the club will also find membership information.

The Bermuda Triangle
http://orion.it.luc.edu/~tgibson/triangle/tri.html

The myths and legends that seem to be the only things to come out of the Bermuda Triangle are taken to task and dispensed with, through a short course of history and geography lessons presented by Bubba, the Salty Dog. Believe it or not.

Committee for the Scientific Investigation of Claims of the Paranormal
http://www.csicop.org/

Organized in 1978 and numbering among its founders some of the biggest names in science (scientists, writers, and academics), CSICOP seeks to investigate unusual phenomena in an effort to offer scientific, rather than fantastic, explanations for the odd occurrences. Read about the group's inquiries into strange matters that range from psychic spying and conspiracy theories, to ghosts and UFOs. A generous sampling of articles from the group's magazine, *Skeptical Inquirer*, is featured.

The "Face on Mars"

http://barsoom.msss.com/education/facepage/face.html

Elaborating on images some believe show an "artificially" shaped, face-like landform on the surface of Mars, Malin Space Science Systems Inc. presents this educational page discussing the raw images that sparked the controversy, and providing a brief lesson on image-processing techniques.

Fair Play

http://rmii.com/~jkelin/fp.html

An investigative magazine purporting to rip the lid off the "lone gunman" theory of the murder of John F. Kennedy, *Fair Play* offers access to its extensive archives of articles, documents, and speculation that buttress the contention that Lee Harvey Oswald was a patsy in a massive conspiracy.

50 Greatest Conspiracies of All Time

http://www.webcom.com/~conspire/

This easy-to-search site delivers on the promise of its title. Get a load of theories on aliens and UFOs, JFK's assassination, and AIDS as a U.S. biological warfare operation. And these are only a few of the conspiracy topics explored. If you suspect it, it's probably covered (or perhaps more to the point, uncovered) here.

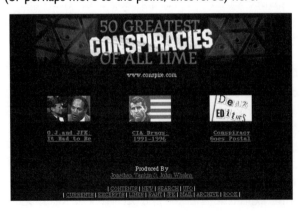

Gonzo Links

http://www.capcon.net/users/lbenedet/

Gonzo Links is your guide to fringe Web sites unlikely to be tampered with by McCarthy's America. Link to sites dealing with conspiracy theories, UFOs, spooks, and paranormal notions that bend the outer limits of "rational" thought.

Hyper-Weirdness by World Wide Web

http://www.physics.wisc.edu/~shalizi/hyper-weird/

Link to the weirdest sites on the Web with this electronic version of popular book *High Weirdness by Mail*. Find surreal sites, wacky religion Webs, conspiracy theories, Elvis worship, and other pages from the freakier sites of the Web.

Internet Crime Archives

http://www.mayhem.net/Crime/archives.html

Offering news, history, and gory details on the grisly work of serial murderers, killer cults, and the like, this archive features unsavory attractions like the "serial killer hit list" and the "digital atrocity exhibition." Not for the squeamish.

Kennedy Assassination Home Page

http://mcadams.posc.mu.edu/home.htm

Whether or not you accept either the "grassy knoll" or the "lone nut" theory, you can learn more about Lee Harvey Oswald and the assassination of President John F. Kennedy at this information-packed site. One aim of the offerings: to deflate the rumors of conspiracy surrounding the incident.

The Kooks Museum

http://www.teleport.com/~dkossy/

Find out where the word "kook" came from and see it applied over and over again to describe the content on display in this public pavilion. A tour of the museum leads from the lobby through the Schizophrenic Wing, the Conspiracy Corridor, the Hall of Hate, the Library of Questionable Scholarship, the Gallery of Gods, and six other exhibit areas.

New Paradigms Project
http://gopher.a-albionic.com:9006/

A virtual library of conspiracy theories, the New Paradigms Project catalogs bibliographic information and links regarding assassination conspiracies, secret societies, and much more.

News of the Weird
http://www.nine.org/notw/latest

The online version of Chuck Shepherd's popular "News of the Weird" newspaper column is a periodic collection of offbeat-but-verified news reports from various publications. The stories tend toward the salacious and verge on the incredible, proving once again that truth is weirder than fiction.

Ovi's World of the Bizarre
http://netmar.com/users/ovigher/ovi.htm

What's considered bizarre? How about the New Zealander who took a radio station hostage just so he could hear Kermit the Frog sing *Rainbow Connection?* Or the mathematician who was so upset when he discovered the textbook he wrote contained an error, he crushed his wife's skull. Want more?

Rajon Institute
http://www.pavilion.co.uk/rajon/

Reports on research into ancient technology, UFOs, mystic arts and pre-Egyptian civilizations occupy the Rajon Institute's site. Visitors are invited to join the organization, send money, and muse upon the mysteries of crop circles, chaos theory, the pyramids, and Stonehenge.

Silo
http://www.xvt.com/users/kevink/silo/silo.html

Explore a relic of the Cold War. Take a virtual tour of an abandoned, decommissioned U.S. missile silo. Your tour directors got busted doing this—crawling down into one of these hazard-filled, man-made chasms is a felony—but you're in "virtually" no danger. And you do have "a right to know!"

The Secret History of the United States 1962-1996
http://w3.one.net/~conspira/Welcome.html

Robert Taylor doesn't buy the official, state-sanctioned version of U.S. history, and instead publishes this online work. He weaves together the darker side of the country's history, quoting from Noam Chomsky, Philip Agee, and others. Leaning heavily on conspiracy theory, he delves into nuclear testing, drugs, and UFOs. Tap into U.S. transgressions organized by year.

SKEPTIC Annotated Bibliography
http://www.public.iastate.edu/~edis/skeptic_biblio.html

Presented through the good graces of the folks who participate in the discussions that thread through the SKEPTIC mailing list, this site provides visitors with an annotated index of resources offering skeptical treatments of fringe science issues such as UFOs, ESP, and paranormal events. Features include links to other Internet resources such as newsgroups and FTP sites. Information for joining the mailing list is also available.

Skeptics Society Web
http://www.skeptic.com/

The Skeptics Society promotes science and critical thinking, and disseminates information on pseudoscience, pseudohistory, and the paranormal. Visit the group's home page to learn more about the society and its work, review a list of skeptical resources on the Internet, or read a sampling of articles and features from the current and back issues of *Skeptic* magazine.

Sources of Skeptical Information on the Internet
http://www.primenet.com/~lippard/skeptical.html

Don't doubt this site offers a fairly comprehensive resource for doubters to use in finding other doubters on the Internet and seeking some shred of "see, I told you so" to further support their doubts. Find magazines, organizations, book distributors, archives, FAQs, and just plain ol' skeptics.

Taos Hum
http://www.eskimo.com:80/~billb/hum/hum.html

Dedicated to the study and discussion of a mysterious, low-frequency noise that allegedly is heard in remote regions of the United States and Great Britain, this site offers a Frequently Asked Questions (FAQ) file and the latest mystery-noise news.

This is True Home Page
http://www2.freecom.com/true/

Some say that truth is stranger than fiction, and Randy Cassingham presents the hard evidence. Stop by for a dose of the weirdest, wackiest news from around the world and find out how to subscribe to free, weekly e-mail updates.

The Unabomber's Manifesto
http://www.panix.com/~clays/Una/index.html

Maybe the Feds bagged the Unabomber, maybe not. But the terrorist's manifesto, "Industrial Society And Its Future," lives on in its full-length, hyperlinked glory here. A table of contents and footnotes are provided.

I SEE A TALL, DARK, HANDSOME FUTURE IN YOUR MAN ..., ER ...

Even though I don't live my life by the horoscope, and I trust in a higher power to look after my interests, I do have my horoscope charted every year, along with monthly progressions, just to see how it all plays out. Who doesn't like to read about themselves?

Astrologers claim that the basic threads of every human being—personality, character, and temperament, and therefore destiny—lie in the stars, and that our futures are dependent upon the sign of the zodiac under which we were born. Planetary positions at the time of our birth are used to chart a horoscope showing the location of the sun, moon, and planets, divided into 12 sections known as planetary "houses." Each house is assigned many meanings that can affect an individual's life, such as marriage, financial security, children, and success in a chosen career.

YOUR HOUSE OR MINE?

The zodiac is an imaginary belt in the heavens that originally included the orbits of the sun and moon, and the five planets—Mercury, Venus, Mars, Jupiter, and Saturn—known to people in ancient times. Each division or house is named for the constellation situated within its limits during the 2nd century BC. These signs are called Aries the Ram, Taurus the Bull, Gemini the Twins, Cancer the Crab, Leo the Lion, Virgo the Virgin, Libra the Balance, Scorpio the Scorpion, Sagittarius the Archer, Capricorn the Goat, Aquarius the Water Bearer, and Pisces the Fishes.

According to astrologers, the house in which your birth falls determines your lifelong characteristics, luck, and chances for success. Romance and relationships with friends and family can be plotted, as well as fields of interest you will develop. There is no area of your life that is not covered.

Interestingly enough, though begun in Babylonia and then taken up by the ancient Greeks, this system has been independently developed by the Chinese and the Aztec Indians.

DEAL THE CARDS!

The Tarot, a deck of 78 cards, has fascinated human beings since the time of the Crusades. Many of us can visualize the gypsy in the caravan, huddled over her cards as she whispers the future. The Tarot was originally a simple card game, and was played all over Europe until it began to be used for fortunetelling.

The deck is somewhat like a modern-day card deck with suits. But instead of suits like hearts, spades, diamonds, and clubs, Tarot decks are divided into cups, wands, swords, and discs (or "pentacles"). And many of the decks used today have beautiful graphics representing the sun, moon, and other phenomena, symbolizing the natural forces that humans must contend with throughout their lives, as well as our own vices and virtues. The trick is in learning how to interpret all these pictures and suits in order to get a "reading" that answers a specific question you want to ask, or provides an overall "prediction" about your future.

TOUGH TAROT

I have a Tarot deck, and years ago, a bunch of us got caught up in learning how to read the cards. It was a tough time for us and we were seeking immediate answers to significant life questions. I was never very good at reading the cards, and I couldn't remember one card from the next, from one week to another. But as long as you don't take it all too seriously, it can be a fascinating, and often very productive, exercise.

If the deck you use is positive and hopeful, it can urge you to keep good thoughts in your head, stay on a positive course, and therefore give a little hope in solving tough questions. The best deck to get is a more contemporary one, with real spiritual overtones and a dose of practical guidance—not the old kind that have harsh, ominous meanings. Any shop dealing in crystals, horoscopes, and the supernatural will be able to tell you about the decks they carry.

There are literally hundreds of astrology, Tarot, and other "fortunetelling" resources on the Web, too. You can find your daily or weekly horoscopes, consult virtually with a professional astrologer, cast the I-Ching, or receive a mini-Tarot reading online. Go ahead ... take a chance!

AdZe MiXXe
http://www.adze.com/

"Astrologist extraordinaire" AdZe MiXXe, hosts this virtual look at the stars. Enjoy astrology news, a zine, celebrity astrology profiles, and more. Visitors can also order MiXXe's books.

Astrology Alive! with Barbara Schermer
http://www.lightworks.com/Astrology/Alive/

A professional astrologer pitches her services and book, but also offers some useful astrology resources and links. Find out about Barbara and professional astrology, discover what an "Astrologer's Cheat Sheet" is, access a consumer's guide, and read a file of articles related to the subject of astrology.

Bantam Doubleday Dell's Daily Horoscopes
http://www.bdd.com/horo1/bddhoro1.cgi/horo1

Will you find romance? Money? Success? See what the stars have in store for you via the daily horoscopes posted by publisher Bantam Doubleday Dell. Other site features include a stock market outlook, a monthly forecast, and a calendar of astrological "get-togethers."

Cosmopolis' High-Tech Horoscopes
http://www.xmission.com/~mustard/cosmo.html

Get a technologically advanced horoscope from Cosmopolis Panopolus, a part-time astrologer and full-time sausage factory fat content manager. Be warned, however; you may not receive the news you desire. A recent horoscope cautioned that Cancers "will discover that you really like country music."

Cyber Stars and Astro Chat
http://www.bubble.com/cybstars/stars.html

John James treats visitors to weekly horoscopes and an online chat forum for those who want to talk about their lives and loves. Visitors will also find a selection of links leading to other astrology and fortunetelling sites.

Esther and Son's Astrological Services
http://www.teleport.com/~esson/

A mother and son astrology team looks to the stars and presents a weekly summary of their findings, along with articles and a look at the moon's cycles. Those interested in private services are welcome to follow the links that lead to the cyber-reading room and resource shop.

I-Ching

http://cad.ucla.edu:8001/iching

I-Ching is an ancient Chinese game for predicting the future. This site offers interpretations, readings, and the historical background of the I-Ching.

I-Tarot

http://manor.york.ac.uk/cgi-bin/cards.sh

The tongue-in-cheek I-Tarot cards are described by the Webmaster as "so mystical that it is in fact dangerous to see the face sides of them." Uh-huh. Access this three-card deal for a text-only look at aspects of your past, present, and future.

Lifestyles International Astrological Foundation

http://www.lifeintl.com/

Find out what's in the stars for you here. Visitors can link to articles and information from astrologers, read celebrity profiles, or find out about the foundation's offer to custom-write astrological profiles for clients or celebrities.

Magic Infinity-ball

http://linex.com/~donham/8ball.html

The Magic Infinity-ball answers questions about love, money, health, or whatever is on your mind. Simply ask a yes or no question to receive prophetic answers such as "outlook not so good" and "it is decidedly so."

Metalog

http://www.astrologer.com:80/

If you're wondering what the stars have to say about your future, perhaps this site will help you find the answers you seek. Access the Metalog Yellow Pages for a country-by-country listing of astrologers, check in with the Astrological Association of Great Britain or the Centre for Psychological Astrology, and find a collection of astrology links worth exploring.

Penny's Skulls of Fate

http://www.dtd.com/skulls/

Visitors to this page are invited to ask a question that can be answered with a yes or no reply. Penny's Skulls of Fate will then divine the answer.

Pray Before the Head of "Bob"

http://www.resort.com/~banshee/Misc/8ball/index.html

Formerly the Ultimate Oracle's Magic 8-Ball site, this page now allows visitors to ask a yes or no question of "Bob," a mystical, multilingual figure much revered by the Church of the Subgenius. Type in questions and see answers in seconds. In English, French, Spanish, Dutch, and Esperanto.

Real Astrology

http://www.realastrology.com/

What is in store for you this week? Check these postings by Rob Brezsny for insights into the days just ahead. Other site features include a collection of topical links, a FAQ file, and a personality test.

RuneCaster

http://crow.acns.nwu.edu:8082/netviking/runecaster/

Why shake your Magic Eight Ball when you can visit RuneCaster? Ask the powers that be to provide life's answers through the rune that appears. For those new to runes, meanings are provided along with some background on the divination system.

TarotWorks

http://ion.apana.org.au/~poisson/tarotworks.html

Choose a server (USA or Australia), then begin bridging the gap between giving and taking your own advice. TarotWorks is a software program that helps users divine the best roads to travel. Find out about the software, sample it, and buy it; or link to sites offering other tarot-related guidance.

Todays Fortune

http://www.earth.com/fortune

To help folks get by, wise words are offered daily at this simple site. A sample of the wisdom available: "The amount of work to be done increases in proportion to the amount of work already completed."

Web-O-Rhythm
http://www.qns.com/html/weborhythm/

Web-O-Rhythm is a personalized, Web-generated bio-rhythm reading. Visitors fill in their birthdays and the month and year for which they want a biorhythm reading, and the program generates a personalized GIF of the results.

World Wide Web Ouija
http://www.math.unh.edu/~black/cgi-bin/ouija.cgi

Visit here to access a modern-day incarnation of a time-honored oracular game. Talk directly to the cyber-spirits and have them respond with answers to life's nagging little questions like, "Does this work?"

The Underground Astrologer
http://www.links.net/astro/

Visit this virtual "house" of the planets to get a grounding in astrology "basix." Learn how the planets act, the roles the signs play, and what it means when a planet is in a house. Links to topical sites are also presented, all to help users plot a course into the future.

The Vedic Astrology Home Page
http://www.fairfield.com/jyotish/index.html

A sister art to Western astrology, Vedic Astrology, also known as Jyotish, not only predicts what will happen in the future but also when to expect it. Visitors can learn about this divination system, get a free sample reading, and find instructions on how to order Jyotish software.

Your Essential Daily Zodiac Forecast
http://stars.metawire.com/

Arguably the granddaddy of online prediction, British astrologer Jonathon Cainer treats browsers to a free daily prognostication. Need Lotto numbers? You can get those for free here, too. The for-a-small-fee services that are available include weekly RealAudio forecasts, personalized astrology charts, and year-ahead horoscopes.

Your Lucky Fortune Cookie
http://hci.ise.vt.edu/~kelso/fortune.html

Presented by John Kelso, this cookie of a site provides visitors with a "fortune" and lucky numbers. The page generates a new fortune and numbers on each visit.

PROVINCES OF THE MIND AND STATES OF CONSCIOUSNESS

Arkuat's Web
http://www.c2.org/~arkuat/

Assembled by a Webmaster who owns up to his desire to become "an immortal superintelligent cloud of intergalactic robot wizards," this smorgasbord of links leads to information about cryptography, Taoism, and the transhuman body. Other site highlights include a discussion of "extropian" principles and politics.

Astral Projection Home Page
http://www.lava.net/~goodin/astral.html

This home page provides links to Internet resources related to astral projection, out-of-body experiences, and lucid dreams. The Astral Library located here supports key-word searches.

Anomalous Cognition
http://macwww.psy.uva.nl/Psychonomie/research/anomal.html

Equal parts academic research and Web oddity, this site explores extrasensory perception, psychokinesis, and related phenomena from a scientific perspective. It also affords the apprentice psychic a chance to test his or her mettle with some Web-based ESP games.

Cosmic Connections
http://iypn.com/cosmic-connections/

Tapping into the cosmic, this site opens the door for visitors to take a walk on the metaphysical side of life. Topic-specific venues provide open discussion and a source of connection for those seeking to affirm and share their own experiences with the supranatural.

Deep Black Magic: Government Research into ESP and Mind Control
http://ourworld.compuserve.com:80/
homepages/T_porter/govtesp.htm

Like something out of the U.S. television hit series *The X-Files*, this site explores reports of the U.S. government messing around with remote viewing and psychokinesis. Based on a paper written in 1994, the information available here lists mind-control experiments and those with whom experiments were conducted.

The Deoxyribonucleic Hyperdimension
http://deoxy.org/deoxy.htm

The contemporary philosophers represented on this page "peer into bits and zones of Chaos," exploring alternate realities and expanded levels of consciousness. Contemplate the writings of Alan Watts, Timothy Leary, Terence McKenna, Robert Anton Wilson, and others.

DreamLink
http://www.iag.net:80/~hutchib/.dream/

Have your dreams interpreted, or learn to translate your own dreams at DreamLink. Visitors can also find tips on controlling and remembering dreams in the Technique a Week department, or participate in the DreamLink roundtable talk sessions.

dreamMosaic
http://www.itp.tsoa.nyu.edu/~windeatr/
dreamMosaic.html

Web dreamers can post their latest mental meanderings at this dream-sharing site. Visitors will find a collection of dreams indexed and cross-referenced for browsing ease and pleasure.

The Dream Page
http://www.cs.washington.edu/homes/raj/
dream.html

Submit a dream for group analysis or join the group and analyze the current batch of dreams posted. Anonymity is expected and respected.

Fight Against Coercive Tactics Network FTP Archive
ftp://ftp.rmii.com/pub2/factnet

F.A.C.T.Net provides this public service, a library of texts offering information about cult activities in the United States and abroad. Background on F.A.C.T.Net is also on file.

Heffter Research Institute
http://www.heffter.org/

Claiming that "psychedelics have the unique ability to transform fundamentally the very functions that we consider uniquely human: the way we think, feel, communicate, and solve problems," The Heffter Research Institute probes subjects related to consciousness and the mind through the refraction of psychedelic experience. Find out what the organization is up to and how to join its mission.

Hypnosis.com
http://www.hypnosis.com/

Sort of a hypnosis mall, this site links visitors to book and tape vendors selling topical materials. Also find a chat room, a forum, information on related educational resources, and a Frequently Asked Questions (FAQ) file.

Hypnotica
http://www.servtech.com/public/hypnotica/

This page presents a primer on the art of self-hypnosis, offering advice on using the process to lose weight, give up smoking, improve concentration, and gain confidence. The site includes a list of offline references.

Koestler Parapsychology Unit
http://moebius.psy.ed.ac.uk/

The Koestler Parapsychology Chair at the University of Edinburgh was established to study ESP and similar phenomena. This page has information about the unit's participants, research, and methodologies, offering a reading list and links to related sites.

Laboratory for Consciousness Studies
http://eeyore.lv-hrc.nevada.edu/~cogno/cogno.html

The Consciousness Research Division at the University of Las Vegas "conducts scientific research on anomalies of human consciousness" with studies on the correlates of mind-matter interaction, extended perceptual capabilities, and physical correlates of mental states. Take a virtual tour of the lab, read descriptions of its mission and research, or participate in its investigation of luck.

Mind Uploading
http://sunsite.unc.edu/jstrout/uploading/MUHomePage.html

Science fiction is fact at the Mind Uploading home page where "the putative future process of copying one's mind from the natural substrate of the brain into an artificial one manufactured by humans" is explored. Subjects include technology, timelines, philosophy, and policy.

MindWarp: The Mind Subpage
http://www.clas.ufl.edu/anthro/noetics/mindwarp.html

Dedicated to all things relating to consciousness, this page points to cyber-pathways leading to alternate states of one kind or another. Read essays, link to gurus, learn about psychic connections, and explore a couple of different models of consciousness.

Moksha Foundation
http://www.moksha.org/

"Dedicated to the liberation of the human spirit," the nonprofit Moksha Foundation describes its study groups, goals, and activities here. Visitors can explore the enlightenment-oriented organization's philosophies based on the teachings of Andrew Cohen.

The Monroe Institute
http://www.monroe-inst.com/

A nonprofit organization based in Lovingston, Virginia, the Monroe Institute fosters the understanding of human consciousness through a variety of methods including out-of-body and other exploratory experiences. Visit the institute's home page for information about its programs and instructional materials.

Telepathy, Research, Parapsychology, Science
http://www.magna.com.au/~rwin/ldhp.html

Members of the World Wide Telepathy Mind Network are a little annoyed that telepathy (communication using only the mind) has gained a reputation as "supernatural." This site runs through the principles of telepathy treated as a pseudoscience.

trancenet.org
http://www.trancenet.org/

A nonprofit publisher of Web sites promoting various "psychological freedoms" serves both the skeptics and believers with "unfiltered information about exploitative psychological techniques and those who use them." Featured Web publications currently include TranceNet, Rama-Llama-Ding-Dong, Moonism, and No Way Out.

Transhumanist Resources
http://www.aleph.se/Trans/

Transhumanism is a philosophy asserting that humankind can surpass its current physical, mental, and social levels. Visit here for information about intelligence amplification, bionics, artificial intelligence, cryonics, and immortality.

SPIRITUAL, MYSTICAL, AND OTHER SOULFUL MATTERS

The Alchemy Web Site
http://www.levity.com/alchemy/index.html

Offering 30 megabytes of alchemy in all its aspects, this introduction to the "art" traces alchemy from its beginnings as a proto-chemistry, to its more modern symbolic, psychological, and mystical incarnations. Features include links to alchemical magazines and groups, along with listings of publishers specializing in alchemical and hermetic books.

Celestia
http://www.celestia.com/alpha/

Providing links to a variety of spiritual- and health-related Web sites, this page points visitors toward Sterling Rose Press, the Spiritual Rights Foundation, and similar resources on the Internet.

Chinmaya Mission
http://www.tezcat.com/~bnaik/chinmiss.html

Visitors will find a religious road map leading to Vedantic truths at the Chinmaya Mission home page. Centers across the world are listed here, along with links to study groups, religious texts, and a biography of founder Swami Chinmayananda.

CoGweb
http://www.cog.org/cog/

The Covenant of the Goddess Web site explains the activities of the international organization of cooperating, autonomous Wiccan congregations and practitioners. This site offers information on witchcraft and answers commonly asked questions. It also posts events and provides links to various covens.

ConsciousNet
http://www.consciousnet.com/

ConsciousNet offers one-stop New Age shopping for products, ideas, and information. Astrology, meditation, and personal healing techniques are among the topics, while online magazines, educational opportunities, retreats, and videos are among the consciousness-raising resources featured.

Current Events and End Times Prophecy
http://www.ionet.net/~wes/

Are these the prophesied "End Times"? Explore the theme at this site which interprets modern trends and how they relate to biblical prophecy. With arguments stemming from political, economic, and moral evidence, the site suggests the end of the world is on its way.

The Dark Side of the Net
http://www.cascade.net/dark.html

The Dark Side of the Net page is a list of gothic, Wiccan, pagan, vampire, occult, and other dark resources available on the Internet. The list also includes IRC channels, mailing lists, FTP sites, newsgroups, gophers, and e-zines.

Earth Portals
http://alive.mcn.org/earthportals/

Earth Portals presents various forms of expression such as new cosmologies, philosophies, social actions, and art forms. Enter any of the five main portal links and take "a journey into new metaphors of consciousness, exploring the mystery of existence through language."

Ethical Spectacle
http://deptserver.me.mtu.edu/~hull/
Random.html

Read the story behind the bumper stickers "Practice Random Acts of Kindness and Senseless Beauty," and share your acts with like-minded souls on this page. If you can't come up with an act of your own, samples are provided. The selfless can also tell others about their good deeds and learn about the growing parallel movement in Russia.

The F.A.C.T.Net 3 Bulletin
http://www.lightlink.com/factnet1/pages/
index.html

The Fight Against Coercive Tactics Network is embroiled in the Scientology controversy on the Net. The Webmasters say that since they began working on this anti-Scientology site, they've been raided by the Church, which took their computer equipment. They explain and call for help and donations here.

The Foundation for Meditation and Spiritual Unfoldment
http://www.cityscape.co.uk/users/ea80/
fisu.htm

The Foundation for Meditation and Spiritual Unfoldment introduces visitors to the teachings of Gururaj Ananda Yogi and promotes the general benefits of meditation.

Seekers of enlightenment and information may submit questions or register for courses online.

The Green Pages
http://www.oakgrove.org/GreenPages/

These pages contain an extensive collection of links to pagan resources, including listings of gatherings, covens, and contacts. Visitors will also find general information submitted by participating organizations along with links to pagan publications and topical Web sites.

Hell: The Online Guide to Satanism
http://webpages.marshall.edu/~allen12/index.html

This page is devoted to providing information about Satanic organizations and belief systems. Links to the Church of Satan, the Temple of Set, and other satanic organizations are provided along with pointers to devilish news and publications.

The Integral Yoga Web Site
http://www.webcom.com/~miraura/

Read a general introduction to yoga and browse information about the spiritual path to which Integral Yoga leads. Site features include biographies of the founders of Integral Yoga, essays, documents, and resources, plus information about upcoming events around the world.

Interlude
http://www.teleport.com/~interlud/

Cybermonks lead this spiritual cyber-retreat, offering poems, prayers, and weekly meditation suggestions to refresh and restore. Visit here for "a few moments of peace, composure and mental expansion." Includes an extensive bibliography of related texts.

Joan's Witch Directory
http://www.ucmb.ulb.ac.be:80/~joan/witches/index.html

If you have an interest in the history of witch hunts, you'll enjoy the dozens of links and resources here, covering activities from Salem, Massachusetts, to Finland. Features include a topical glossary and book excerpts describing torture methods that often resulted in "confessions."

Links to Occult Information
http://www.contrib.andrew.cmu.edu/~shawn/occult/

Shawn Knight hosts this compilation of reviewed and recommended Internet sites dealing with the occult. Link to attractions such as the Pagan Pages, the Onyx Pyramid, and the Trinity College Fortean Society, plus about a dozen more sites.

Look Within: Inspirations of Love
http://www.aimnet.com/~amidaprs/

This site promotes a spiritual book written by an Indian mystic offering to guide readers to a relationship with God. The page offers a glimpse of the book's message, biographies of the author and editor, and quotes that help answer questions such as "Why suffer?" and "What is a miracle?"

The Method of Centering Prayer
http://www.io.com/~lefty/Centering_Prayer.html

Thomas Keating suggests "centering prayer," which to the casual observer resembles meditation, is the best way to open one's consciousness to God. Keating explains the how-tos as well as the thought process behind the prayer method.

Motherheart
http://gnv.fdt.net/~mother/

If "unconditional love nurtures all," Motherheart must be unconditional love. The community-oriented listserv aims to build a nurturing network for members to support and seek support of one another. A list of resources (enjoyed but not endorsed by Motherheart) point to spirituality, health and wholeness, and care-giving links.

Mysticism in the World's Religions
http://www.realtime.net/~rlp/dwp/mystic/

Elements of mysticism in the world's major religions are explored at this Web site. Features include examinations of different aspects of mysticism as they relate to Christians, Jews, Muslims, Buddhists, Taoists, and Hindus.

New Civilization Network Server One
http://www.newciv.org/

Visitors out to change the world will find links to groups aiming to do the same via this server dedicated to "new concepts, inspirations and visions." Explore the New Civilization Network, the Global Ideas Bank, Millennium Matters, and more.

Paper Ships Books & Crystals
http://www.nbn.com/jacob/ship.html

A clearinghouse for information about angels, UFOs, indigenous cultures, personal healing, sacred geometry, and other elements of the mystical brew, this site features reviews, resources, and listings of sightings.

Project Mind Foundation
http://www.webscope.com/project_mind/project_mind.html

The Project Mind Foundation aims "to free the human spirit from the crushing illusion of materialism," and explains its efforts here. Visitors will find an online brochure, essays, and a philosophy that blends spiritualism and science in the hope of ending world suffering.

The Pronoia Page
http://myhouse.com/pronoia/index.html

Giving a familiar whine a positive twist, the proponents of "pronoia" suggest the universe is conspiring to improve your life. Jump to this "pronoia" link list to access happy alternatives to sites that feed paranoia and dull the senses.

Prophe-Zine
http://www.best.com/~ray673/pzhome.shtml

Addressing biblical prophecies and how they may be coming true in modern society, this zine offers extended articles and news briefs about religious and political happenings, technological advances, and other current events that the Webmaster sees as fulfilling the Bible's warnings.

The Rapture Index
http://www.novia.net/~todd/

The Christian prophecy of the Rapture states that sometime in the future, after a series of signs, believers will be taken bodily into heaven. At the Rapture Index, learn more about this prophecy and read news items and world indicators purported to be signs the Rapture is at hand.

The Rosicrucian Fellowship
http://www.cts.com/~rosfshp/index.html

The Rosicrucian Fellowship page outlines the purpose of this organization of Christian mystics. Visitors can view an online magazine archive, read about study courses, or get ordering information for books.

Scientology Gopher
ftp://rtfm.mit.edu/pub/usenet-by group/news.answers/scientology/new-reader-faq

Postings from the alt.religion.scientology newsgroup have been archived here. The site includes a Frequently Asked Questions (FAQ) file and an overview of the Scientology catechism.

Shroud of Turin
http://www.cais.com/npacheco/shroud/turin.html

Get wrapped up in the discussion over whether the Shroud of Turin is indeed the burial cloth of Jesus Christ or an ingenious hoax. This page includes Frequently Asked Questions (FAQ), scientific research, the shroud's history, and links to Catholic resources.

Spirits Evolving
http://www.webcom.com/~spirits/

Seekers in search of sites offering insights and aids for spiritual evolution will appreciate this resource. Among the featured attractions, find a monthly spiritual forecast, energy awareness techniques, help with visualization, relaxation and meditation, and essays offering inspiration.

10 Bulls
http://fas.sfu.ca/cs/people/ResearchStaff/jamie/personal/10_Bulls/Title_Page.html

In the 12th century, Chinese master Kakuan drew pictures of "10 Bulls." As this site asserts, those drawings purely represent the compromises and progressive steps made in the Zen follower's journey toward enlightenment. The illustrations are reproduced here with comments.

The Total Freedom Trap: Scientology, Dianetics and L. Ron Hubbard

http://www.empire.net/~sgorton/co$/atack.html

Scientology critics will find fodder for their attacks on the controversial religion posted at this Web site. Visitors can read up on the historical background of the religion and its founder, or check out critical analyses of its practice and effects.

Voodoo: From Medicine to Zombies

http://www.nando.net/prof/caribe/voodoo.html

Believers and skeptics alike will enjoy a visit here to look into the world of what for many is considered black magic. Prowl this collection of voodoo links for insight into the centuries-old religion and its (not quite so old) followers.

Vodoun (or Voodoo) Information Pages

http://www.vmedia.com/shannon/voodoo/voodoo.html

Angered at the depiction of Voudon in popular media as zombie-producing black magic, this site's author endeavors to present Voudon as a valid religion, explaining how French Catholic and African Yoruban beliefs melded to form the highly ritualistic religion.

The Way

http://www.webcom.com/~way/the-way.html

Read about the New Age spiritual group that subscribes to the belief that Earth's inhabitants are the result of a "seeding" program conducted by a collective of humanoid alien races from the stars. Find out about the Annunaki and what happened when they first met their crop of Earthlings, the Terrans. Enjoy a complete philosophical guide to this group's teachings and beliefs.

The Zen Garden

http://www.nomius.com/~zenyard/zenyard.htm

The subCultureNet from Nomius Eye on the Web sponsors this Zen page. Stories, images, sounds, and enigmatic "koans" that illustrate the Zen worldview (or lack thereof) are featured.

Zonpower from Cyberspace

http://www.neo-tech.com/zonpower/

For those desiring riches, love, and a "god-like" mind and body, the manuscript presented here points the way toward fulfillment. It's a testimonial-backed treatise on illuminati, the "parasitic elite," Earth's anticivilization, and "Neo-Tech Physics."

UFOS, THEIR DRIVERS, AND OTHER MYSTERIOUS CREATURES

Most of my friends and I believe in the supernatural. Some have had "ghostly" experiences, others know of friends who have, and my own daughter swears she once had a close encounter with an alien spacecraft on a lonely country road. One of my friends even had to get a group of "Ghostbusters" in to rid her of a pesky poltergeist.

A good many years ago, some friends of mine purchased a very old house that had been vacant for years. They were thrilled to have made such a good purchase, and were busily renovating when a few strange things began to happen. As they sat in their newly decorated parlor, they would hear strange sounds, and lighted cigarettes would waft lazily across the room. This happened every evening at the same time.

DROP IN ANY TIME

To say that they were unnerved was putting it mildly, as they could not come up with any reasonable explanations for these bizarre occurrences. Eventually, they called the former owner, and established that he too had experienced the same phenomena, and that was why he had sold the house. After eight months they listed their new home, and moved. I think they should have investigated further. There's a terrific story here, just waiting to be told—and by learning the origin of their mysterious, floating cigarettes, they just might have been able to solve the problem. I never kept up with the history of the house after that, but I wonder...?

My own otherworldly experience happened just recently. Some months ago, I lost my mother. She was old and frail and the quality of her life had been poor the last ten years of her life. So I had let go and was not griefstricken, but rather nostalgic, as I thought of the many happy times we had together during her lifetime.

I was washing dishes at the sink in the kitchen, when suddenly I felt my mother standing beside me. She was laughing like she used to when we were doing projects together. Wearing a familiar white blouse and plaid skirt, she stood very close to me. I could see her arms and hands and felt a great sense of warmth and comfort come over me. More and more happy memories have come flooding back since her visit, and I hope she is still around watching out for me.

"I was a working single mother of two. It became necessary for me to get a partime job. I would come home exhausted and my regular job began to suffer. My son became ill and cried each night. I would sit holding him in the rocking chair until he got to sleep, and many nights I didn't get to bed until the sun came up. One night, I was at the end of my tether. I needed sleep badly. I had just dozed off, when he began to fuss again. I waited for a moment, not wanting to leave my warm bed, and when I looked up, and there was mother in her long, flannel night-gown, holding a flashlight so she wouldn't awaken me. She picked up my son and went towards the rocking chair.

"Grateful, I fell back to sleep, getting the best sleep I'd had in a long time. The next morning at breakfast, I thanked my mother profusely. I was so grateful for the help. She looked at me as if I was balmy. She had not heard my son cry, nor did she enter my room!"

The Alberta UFO Research Association (AUFORA)
http://ume.med.ucalgary.ca/~watanabe/ufo.html

The Alberta UFO Research Association presents this home page exploring alien visitations to our humble planet. Visitors will discover the latest UFO news, journals, first-hand accounts of sightings, pictures, a UFOclopedia, and links to related Internet sites.

"Alien Autopsy"—Faked or Fiction?
http://www.trudang.com/autopsy.html#CONTENTS

The title leaves little question concerning the page author's views; however, visitors are welcome to come to their own conclusions regarding the controversial video *Alien Autopsy*. Among the offerings featured, this site provides instructions for making an alien, a list of goofs within the video, a survey of special effects pros' opinions, and autopsy comparisons.

Alien Information
http://www1.tpgi.com.au/users/ron/alien.html

Exploring UFOs and aliens with thought-provoking material that feeds the imagination, this site offers details about the Roswell incident and the U.S. government's High Frequency Active Auroral Research Program. Also find theories from Sheldon Nidle, author of *You Are Becoming A Galactic Human*, an alien archive, and a FAQ.

Area 51: Military Facility, Social Phenomenon and State of Mind
http://www.ufomind.com/area51/

Curious about what is going on in the U.S. government's super-secret Area 51 Research Center? Investigate this UFOMIND database of 749 documents, 310 images, and thousands of links that explore the mysteries of Groom Lake.

Dr. Bruce Cornet, UFO Investigator
http://orion.adp.wisc.edu/bcornet1/

Earth inhabitants may not be alone in the universe, and Dr. Bruce Cornet wants to prove it. Find out more about this lecturer who believes he has hard evidence of UFO activity, and take a good squint at the photographs he took to substantiate his claims.

Galaxy: Unidentified Flying Objects
http://galaxy.einet.net/galaxy/Community/
Parascience/Unidentified-Flying-Objects.html

From the larger Galaxy collection, this index points to resources and information on UFOs. Visitors will find articles and publications, sights and sounds, collections and directories.

Internet UFO Group
http://www.iufog.org/

Experience close encounters of the Internet kind. If you've been abducted, seen lights in the night, or believe Roswell was the biggest cover-up in U.S. history, meet like-minded folks and check the group's links to government secrets and hot new reports.

Nessie on the Net in Scotland!
http://www.scotnet.co.uk/highland/index.html

What's more mad?: the cows or Britain, or the Highland folk who believe in the Loch Ness Monster? For information on bovine psychosis you'll be needin' to look elsewhere, but if you're curious about Nessie, you've come to the right spot. Find an Internet radio station, a live video feed, the Official Loch Monster Fan Club, pictures, text files, and other bytes of local color.

Lizzie Sez
Never apologize for laughter that is too loud, or singing that is too joyful.

Protree UFO Center
http://ufo.protree.com/

Bob Garth hosts this database of UFO files and photos for those convinced, and just curious, about close encounters. Ring! Ring! E.T. calling.

SETI Institute
http://www.metrolink.com/seti/
homepage.html

Scientists engaged in the Search for Extra-Terrestrial Intelligence project publish their research strategies, goals, and findings on the SETI Institute's home page. Link to researchers, investigators, and summaries of their current projects.

SETIQuest
http://www.setiquest.com/

SETIQuest is a magazine that covers scientists' continuing search for extraterrestrial life and intelligence. This promotion for the magazine lists the contents of the current issue, offers a sampling of articles from past issues, and points to topical links of interest to those interested in the world of extraterrestrial research.

UC Berkeley Search for Extraterrestrial Civilizations
http://albert.ssl.berkeley.edu/serendip/

In an attempt to answer the "age-old question `Are we alone?'," SERENDIP (Search for Extraterrestrial Radio Emissions from Nearby Developed Intelligent Populations) attempts to detect radio signals from extraterrestrial civilizations. Visitors to this site can read about research, funding, and results.

UFO & Paranormal & Skeptic Links
http://weikko.tky.hut.fi/ufo.html

If you believe in the extraterrestrial and the paranormal (and even if you don't), you can land on this page for a directory of links to Web sites offering an exploration of the topics advertised in the site's title. A directory of newsgroup links is also featured.

> "We did have a very non-threatening resident in the old farmhouse where I spent my teen years. I always assumed it was formerly male in gender, don't really know why we assumed that. Doors on a non-existent third floor slammed shut or opened; and little things would be moved just to keep you on your toes.
>
> "The most irritating habit was for our resident to insist on turning on the yard light if my sister or I were dawdling even a little after returning from a date. If we didn't promptly get out of the car, on went the very bright light. My mother and dad insisted they were not up and hadn't touched the switch.
>
> "The door slamming came into play if we let our evening chores slide; there was no putting off getting the dishes done or the kitchen put in order, or we would "hear" about it. We moved a photo once that came with the house and it was back in the original spot the next morning. Some people can't deal with change, I guess."

World-Wide Web Virtual Library: Archive X
http://www.crown.net/X/

Archive X contains links to Web pages related to paranormal phenomena. Visitors are invited to submit their own stories of experiences with ghosts—whether prolonged hauntings or single encounters— angels, and channeling.

World-Wide Web Virtual Library: UFOs
http://ernie.bgsu.edu/~jzawodn/ufo/

Walk these electronic aisles and browse the stacks for resources regarding extraterrestrials and their preferred mode of travel, flying saucers. Link to a variety of interesting sites offering UFO-related gold mines like an overhead photo of Area 51, Operation Right to Know, and *The Desert Rat Newsletter*.

Chapter 15

THE WONDERS OF SCIENCE

PROBING THE RED PLANET

ONCE A DUNCE

THE MANY FACETS OF SCIENCE

Mars Attacks! That's the name of a recent sci-fi film illustrating the decimation of our planet by alien beings. I can remember a number of similar films from the past, as well as others that are less diabolical: *Cocoon*, *Star Wars*, and *E.T.*

It couldn't be just a coincidence that the movie release roughly coincided with the announcement that life forms have been discovered on the planet Mars. I have seen pictures of little squiggly things that are portrayed in the media as some form of life, and even though this claim has been challenged, I tend to believe that there have been beings living up there all along. Didn't someone say that there was ice all around? Well, there you have it. Life cannot exist without water. And Mars has water. Therefore it must support—or must have once supported—life.

So, just in case someone's up there thinking about raiding the Earth, I have only one question: Why come down here just to cause trouble? If Martians (or anyone else, for that matter) are up there in some higher developed form, swimming in icy swimming pools and spying on us, don't you think it would be great if they'd use their advanced technology to help us out?

Instead of simply attacking, the Martians could take a little constructive action. The first place they could start is by cleaning up the government on all levels and unloading all the corrupt politicians. They could lend us some power rays to boost the crumbling infrastructure and replace our ravaged environment. If they have special talents in communications, they could share with us.

So here's my invitation: If you've got anything to offer us, Mars, come on down. But can we keep this friendly?

PROBING THE RED PLANET

While we wait to see if Mars responds to my invitation, we can bone up on the Red Planet by blasting off to some of these fascinating sites:

Daily Martian Weather Report
http://nova.stanford.edu/projects/mgs/dmwr.html

Once the Mars Global Surveyor (launched from Cape Canaveral on November 7, 1996) settles into its mapping orbit around Mars, this page will feature a daily weather report for the planet. Although Mars may not be your next vacation destination, it could be fun to see how the climate of the planet changes from day to day. The site also includes background info on the exploration project and links to other interesting Mars sites.

Mars Exploration Program
http://www.jpl.nasa.gov/mars/

"The Martian Chronicle" may sound like the name of a second-rate sci fi movie from the '50s, but in fact is an electronic publication of NASA's Jet Propulsion Laboratory at the California Institute of Technology that provides current news about the Red Planet. Check the September 1996 issue (several back issues are archived) for stories about the earth-shattering announcement that organic compounds were discovered in a Martian meteorite. The site also includes fascinating information on Mars exploration projects such as the Pathfinder spacecraft and the Rover Sojourner that NASA hopes will provide in-depth info about our planetary neighbor.

Mars Images Menu
http://esther.la.asu.edu/asu_tes/TES_Editor/SOLAR_SYST_TOUR/Mars.html

The Smithsonian Institution provides this photo gallery of Mars images and accompanying historical text. Most of the photographs were taken by the Viking and Mariner expeditions of the 1960s and 1970s, and show some amazing features, such as the Valles Marineris, a giant canyon system that would stretch the distance from Los Angeles to New York. I didn't see any squiggly things in the photographs, though.

Viking Mission to Mars

http://nssdc.gsfc.nasa.gov/planetary/
viking.html

In the 1970s, Viking spacecraft 1 & 2 went to Mars and sent back all sorts of information that caused tremendous excitement at NASA and among other astronomy types. This page details the history of the missions and summarizes the data collected by the spacecraft. Images, a FAQ, descriptions of experiments, and lots more goodies are included here.

"We can only divide up our leisure time pie in so many ways. In my case I was bitten by the computer bug less than a year ago. I never imagined I would be so taken with it. As someone who loves information and doing research, it's a natural. Then I stumbled upon SeniorNet and discovered a bright, congenial group of people who I could 'talk' to about almost anything in which I have an interest and develop some new ones should I choose to do so.

"And, talking about trying to explain the appeal to some of our peers—about the Internet in general and SeniorNet in particular—well, there is something about the ability to sit down at a quiet time of my choosing and enter this world. SeniorNet has become another slice of my leisure time pie and many of the people on it feel like my friends and/or interesting people with whom to share ideas.

"The peers of whom I spoke are slowly making their way into the Net. I am the pusher and they are beginning to respond to the drug. I would not be surprised if you get to meet some of them here in the near future. I have started them on e-mail and then some!! Again, having said all those positive things about you people, have I also told you that you're driving me nuts. I have scraps of papers with names of books on them all over my person. How do you get to read so much?"

ONCE A DUNCE

All my life, science and its more specialized cousins, physics, chemistry, astronomy, and mathematics, have always mystified me. In high school, I was an admirable student, falling in the upper third of the class in grade points until I had to take a course in science.

FLUB-A-DUB-DUB

Most of the time I could flounder along and get by, but an algebra course I had as a freshman completely defeated me and I earned the unacceptable grade of "F." My father was understanding, even though he was a genius in the subject, and hired a tutor for me during the summer. He himself, unable to understand any reason why a child with his genes could not cut through the curtain of mystery to full competence in math, did his best, after hours, to confuse me even more.

Poppa was so smart in algebra that he did not know any long cuts, only short cuts to get to the answers, so in agonizing hours of patient repetition, I tried to become friends with "X" and "Y," even though I really did not care what they might equal.

THE BREW OF CHAMPIONS

In my senior year of high school, I found myself with the unfortunate choice of taking either a chemistry or a physics class to complete the hours I needed for graduation. At the time, chemistry looked like the

Lizzie Sez

Learn to recognize the unimportant and inconsequential, then ignore it!

lesser of two evils. Armed with Poppa's tried and true southern recipe, I made a big hit in lab by choosing to build a still and brew moonshine as my lab project. On the last day of class, we cracked it open and had a taste of good ole fashioned home brew.

That was probably the only reason I passed that class, because all the rest of it was a total nightmare of misunderstanding.

WARS WITH THE STARS

When it was time to go to college, unknowingly, I chose a school that was heavily endowed by a donor who was mad about the stars. Part of his endowment was used to build a beautiful planetarium housing a huge telescope on campus, and all students were required to take a class in astronomy before they could qualify for graduation.

Although totally befuddled by azimuths and the like, I managed to struggle to the finish line, but with barely a passing grade. To this day I enjoy stargazing and am fascinated by the stars and the lovely patterns they make in the sky, but have abandoned any ambition I may have had to make it as an astrophysicist.

THEM BONES

Another one of my classes was anatomy. The class for non-science majors was filled, so I was dropped into the class especially designed for nursing students and those in pre-med studies.

We took up the study of a cow eyeball, a fetal pig, and a domestic cat, and were privileged to be able to go to the dank basement and draw out our own animal and eye from the large barrel of formaldehyde that housed them when we were not performing our ghastly surgeries.

Every specimen had a tag to identify it as your very own. And on each day of lab we set about carving up these stinking masses of protoplasm so that we could learn how they were put together. It was

Lizzie's Tips

If you suspect that you have been exposed to a computer virus, either from a corrupted disk or a download from the Internet, any anti-virus utility will remove every trace of the virus from your disks. Launch a clean copy of your anti-virus utility from a locked floppy and check your hard drive, and then run the utility from your hard drive to check other floppies or outboard drives.

also our task to learn every muscle, bone, and nerve fiber in each of these unpleasant lumpy forms.

"If being under the magnifying glass can help, go ahead; I'm not going to stand still, so they will have to move the glass, as I move along."

PULLING THE PLUG

I soon lost my credibility with these very serious students when I carelessly placed my scalpel into the cow's eye while aqueous humor—a dark, gooey, and repulsive fluid—squirted out in force upon my neighbor's good shirt. My cow's eye was out of action for that segment of study and I was thenceforth looked upon with scorn.

While the rest of my peers were studying fruit flies in General Science 101, I was struggling with the humiliation of removing the skin from an embalmed domestic feline. Some folks get all the luck.

Needless to say, I began to practice a sophisticated brand of avoidance whenever a science course was presented as an option for study, only taking the barest minimum needed to complete my coursework for graduation.

Lizzie's Tips

Get used to putting your computer glasses in the same place in your home every day. You won't be like me, searching wildly all over the place when you want to get to the keyboard.

"We have noticed, more and more, especially in SeniorNet, that people new to the world of personal computing are entering into meaningful discussions. The personal computer can bring the reticent out of their shells, and allow the stutterer to speak perfectly and communicate without impediment.

"The computer does provide social intercourse for a multitude of individuals who, without it, would lead a very lonely existence.

"Every piece of communication need not be profound. The simple fact of communicating with another person can be reward enough. We scoff at the banality of some of the posts in this and other forums, but we must consider how important these messages are to those who desperately seek communication with another human being, whatever the subject."

THE MANY FACETS OF SCIENCE

Despite my malfunctioning in the arena of science, I still find the study of stars in outer space a fascinating one, the study of humans and animals in their environments most rewarding, and the history of mammals in prehistory spellbinding. I offer up these Web sites in the hope that you, too, will find them as enthralling as I do. There are no examinations! You will not be graded!

COSMIC WONDERS

Comet Hale-Bopp Home Page
http://newproducts.jpl.nasa.gov/comet/

The comet officially designated C/1995 O1, but more commonly known by the last names of its discoverers, Alan Hale and Thomas Bopp, is the subject of this home page maintained by the NASA Jet Propulsion Laboratories. Comet Hale-Bopp is the farthest comet ever discovered by amateurs, and appeared 1,000 times brighter than Comet Halley did at the same distance. This site treats visitors to news, data, and images of the comet, among other items of interest.

Comet P/Shoemaker-Levy 9 Impact Home Page
http://seds.lpl.arizona.edu/sl9/sl9 .html

View the 1994 Comet P/Shoemaker-Levy 9's collision with Jupiter. This was the first collision of two solar system bodies ever observed, and NASA has reported elsewhere that "the effects of the comet impacts on Jupiter's atmosphere have been simply spectacular and beyond expectations." Visitors to this page will find Frequently Asked Question files, fact sheets, and images of the astronomical event.

Comets and Meteor Showers
http://medicine.wustl.edu/~kronkg/

Gary Kronk's "labor of love" is a brimming compendium of info about comets and meteor showers for experienced and rookie amateur astronomers. You'll find good background primers, reports about upcoming events, and news about how best to see objects approaching earth from the depths of space.

The NASA Homepage
http://www.nasa.gov/

This is where the action is! The home page of the National Aeronautics and Space Administration serves as a guide to NASA's specific online resources, and to general information about the U.S. space program. Geared to the lay visitor more than the research scientist, prepared exhibits, histories, and graphic demonstrations illuminate the role of NASA in the area of space exploration. Check here first for news about the space shuttle, or to view the latest photos from the Hubble Space Telescope.

National Solar Observatory
http://www.sunspot.noao.edu/index.html

The National Solar Observatory is in aptly named Sunspot, New Mexico. The observatory's solar exhibit site provides an overview of general solar information and an image gallery, along with data on flares, prominences, solar activity, and telescopes used in research.

The Nine Planets: A Multimedia Tour of the Solar System
http://seds.lpl.arizona.edu/nineplanets/
nineplanets/nineplanets.html#toc

This spectacular presentation from Bill Arnett (modern-day Renaissance man), hosted by the University of Arizona, provides an "overview of the history, mythology, and current scientific knowledge of each of the planets and moons in our solar system." You'll find interesting text, lots of images, some sound and movie files, and pointers to additional references.

Should We Return to the Moon?
http://www.ari.net/back2moon.html

The National Space Society and ARInternet Corporation sponsor this site, addressing the issue of further missions to the moon. Visit here to weigh the pros and cons, and learn how to add your opinion to the topical forum.

Shuttle-Mir Web
http://shuttle-mir.nasa.gov/

This official page from NASA provides an inside look at the many facets of the Mir Space Station cooperative experiment: the crew, the experiments, the logistics, and the operation. A bonus feature is a collection of videos from docking missions, and a tour of the station guided by America's space hero, Dr. Shannon Lucid. Unbelievable stuff!

Solar System Live
http://www.fourmilab.ch/solar/solar .html

Viewing the entire solar system or perhaps just the inner planets is made possible at the Solar System Live site. Set the time, date, and observing location to track planets, satellites, or asteroids in real time. The site is accessible to amateur stargazers and professional astronomers alike, and includes pointers to public domain astronomy/space software.

The Space Shuttle
http://seds.lpl.arizona.edu/ssa/space.shuttle/
docs/homepage.html

The space shuttle may look like an airplane, but it's a whole lot more, and this site tells you all about it. An imagemap superimposed over a NASA photo of the space shuttle links you to information about external tanks, solid rocket boosters, main engines, the crew cabin, and the cargo bay. A universe of other shuttle-related information is available here as well.

Virtual Trips to Black Holes and Neutron Stars Page
http://cossc.gsfc.nasa.gov/ htmltest/rjn_
bht.html

Astronomy enthusiasts will enjoy this site, featuring virtual trips to astronomical phenomena such as black holes and neutron stars. Links to an assortment of MPEG movies and downloadable MPEG players are available. The site creator says that the movies are scientifically accurate computer animations made with strict adherence to Einstein's General Theory of Relativity, and the descriptions are written so that the curious amateur can understand what's going on.

Welcome to the Planets
http://pds.jpl.nasa.gov/planets/

"Many of the best images from NASA's planetary exploration program" distinguish this cosmic tour of our solar system. Each planetary voyage begins with a profile that includes the largest known surface feature of the planet, followed by a gallery of high-resolution, explicated photographs. The site also includes profiles of some of NASA's most famous data-retrieving spacecraft: *Mariner 10*, *Viking 1 & 2*, *Voyager 1 & 2*, *Magellan*, *Galileo*, *Hubble*, and the incomparable space shuttle.

HELPFUL SITES FOR THE AMATEUR SKY GAZER

The Astronomy Café
http://www2.ari.net/home/odenwald/cafe.html

This site "for the astronomically disadvantaged" is a great intro to the complexities of astrophysics. Dr. Sten Odenwald invites you to "grab a coffee … and have a far-out adventure at the outer frontier of space and time." He has already fielded over 2,200 astronomy questions, and they're all archived and categorized in the Ask an Astronomer section. From the basic to the arcane, these questions and answers cover the entire cosmic spectrum. As a bonus, many of Dr. Odenwald's answers include hyperlinks to sites with additional info. And don't stop once you've finished with the Q&A, because there's lots more to discover on this excellent page.

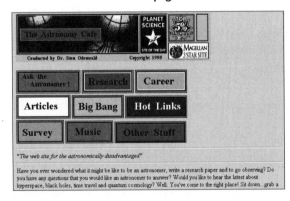

Backyard Astronomy: Choosing Binoculars
http://www.skypub.com/backyard/choosbin.html#top

Alan MacRobert, Associate Editor of *Sky & Telescope* magazine, helps visitors sort through the bewildering array of binoculars on the market today. Find out about power, aperture, focusing, and quality versus price.

Mount Wilson Observatory Online Stargazer Map
http://www.mtwilson.edu/Services/StarMap/

Fill out this online form—specifying date and time, location, and optional parameters—and the folks at California's Mount Wilson Observatory will create a PostScript star map for you. The page also features a What's New section and Frequently Asked Questions.

NASA Space Calendar
http://newproducts.jpl.nasa.gov/calendar/

Maintained by a U.S. National Aeronautics and Space Administration astronomer, the Space Calendar provides information about space-related activities and anniversaries for the coming year. Visit this site to find out about past, present, and future celestial happenings, such as meteor showers, satellite launches, and other events. The site includes over 600 links to related home pages.

On-Line Glossary of Solar-Terrestrial Terms
http://www.ngdc.noaa.gov/stp/GLOSSARY/glossary.html

What is an angstrom? Flux? A penumbra? Beginning astronomers can look up definitions of solar and terrestrial terms in this handy online glossary and learn a bit about the mighty sun in the process.

Sky Online
http://www.skypub.com/

The Sky Publishing Corporation offers a wide variety of astronomy-related books and software. Visit this site to learn more about the company's products and to access its wonderful collection of astronomy pages, including online issues of its magazines, Tips for Backyard Astronomers, and the Comet Page.

ARCHAEOLOGY AND PALEONTOLOGY

ArchNet: The World Wide Web Virtual Library for Archaeology
http://www.lib.uconn.edu/ArchNet/

This popular, comprehensive site is a great guide to the fascinating study of archaeology. Browse the table of contents by subject area or geographical location, link to university departments and projects worldwide, subscribe to newsgroups and listservs, or bone up (get it?) on the scholarly aspects of this branch of science. From a fascinating archaeological tour of the Arctic Circle, to human Chinese fossils, to the ancient civilizations of the Andes, these resources span the globe and put us in touch with the living presence of our evolutionary forebears.

Classics and Mediterranean Archaeology Home Page
http://rome.classics.lsa.umich.edu/welcome.html

This searchable and browseable index from the University of Michigan is a veritable encyclopedia of archaeological sites, museums, atlases, field projects, and university coursework. You'll find features on everything from ancient Roman cooking (ingredients include a thick fig syrup and a salty fish sauce), to pages on Pompeii, to a presentation on the world of the Vikings. Hours of fun.

Dave's Eocene Fossils
http://www.rof.net/wp/rgreg/rgregfos.html

Want to take a look at a 48-million-year-old bug? Here at Dave's collection of fossil images, you'll discover that ancient bugs look a whole lot like the ones flying around in your backyard right now.

Dino Russ's Lair: The Earthnet Info Server
http://128.174.172.76:/isgsroot/dinos/dinos_home.html

Russell Jacobson, the "keeper of the lair," populates his pages with annotated links to dozens of dinosaur and paleontology sites on the Web, including museums, info pages, digs, and dictionaries. If the terrible lizards hold any appeal for you, you'll enjoy the trek through this pre-historic jungle. And for the adventurous, Jacobson includes info about dinosaur dig field programs that you can join (for a price).

Favorite Field Trips
http://www.thomson.com/wadsworth/geo/fieldtrips.html

Here are three fascinating online field trips that take you back into the dim mists of prehistory. Travel central New York state and learn its geographic history, visit a virtual cave, or don your virtual scuba gear for a breathtaking trip through a Jurassic-aged reef.

Honolulu Community College Dinosaur Exhibit
http://www.hcc.hawaii.edu/hccinfo/dinos/dinos.1.html

From Hawaii comes this narrated (.au format) exhibit of dinosaur fossils, including several of your favorites: triceratops, tyrannosaurus rex, stegosaurus, and others.

Material Culture of the Ancient Canaanites, Israelites and Related Peoples
http://staff.feldbeg.brandeis.edu/~jacka/ANEP/ANEP.html

This electronic resource for the University of Pennsylvania course, Introduction to Biblical Archaeology, details materials from "excavations at Beth Shan, Gibeon, Sarepta, and Tell es-Sa'idiyeh as well as Haverford College's excavation at Beth Shemesh." Review articles from the Iron Age through the Persian Period.

A Palaeolithic Cave
http://www.culture.fr/culture/gvp da-en.htm

This site documents the discovery of a network of caves in southern France containing 20,000-year-old paintings depicting a "particularly large and unusual variety of animals (horses, rhinoceros, lions, bison, wild ox, bears, a panther, mammoths, ibex, an owl, etc.) together with symbols, panels filled with dots and both positive and stencilled hands." Link to additional archaeological sites from this page.

Paleontology Without Walls

http://www.ucmp.berkeley.edu/exhibit/exhibits.html

The University of California, Berkeley, Museum of Paleontology presents this wonderful online exhibit that incorporates looks at phylogeny (the "family tree" of life), geological time, and evolutionary thought into the study of fossils, and explains what we can learn from them.

Rabbit in the Moon: Mayan Glyphs and Architecture

http://www.halfmoon.org/

Not only is this site informative, it's fun, too. Learn about ancient Mayan glyphs and try your hand at translating your name. Read about the Mayan diet and their dependence on chilies, the significance of human sacrifice, the classic Mayan concept of beauty, and the use of bees as weapons. Chatty and entertaining, this site is a wonderful example of how scientific discovery can be made accessible to all.

Reeder's Egypt Page

http://www.sirius.com/~reeder/egypt.html

When you think of archaeology, the chances are good that you think of Egypt—the discovery and exploration of the tombs in the Valley of the Kings, and the living monuments of the pyramids. This page looks at various facets of Egyptian archaeology and includes links to other Egyptology pages on the Web.

Scrolls from the Dead Sea: The Ancient Library of Qumran and Modern Scholarship

http://sunsite.unc.edu/expo/deadsea.scrolls.exhibit/intro.html

Examine the Dead Sea Scrolls at an exhibit curated by the U.S. Library of Congress. Delve into the scholarly controversy surrounding the ancient religious texts, or view scroll fragments and other objects comprising the exhibit.

Strange Science: The Rocky Road to Modern Paleontology and Biology

http://www.turnpike.net/~mscott/

Here's an entertaining look at the vagaries of scientific theory through the ages, richly illustrated with clever animations, maps, and drawings. Did you know that the Greek myth of the Cyclops had its origin in the discovery of elephant skulls by ancient sailors? The site features a variety of drawings published in scientific texts, including Otto von Guericke's fantastic rendition of a unicorn (circa 1663), Gesner's sketch of the hydra (circa 1588), and Anathasius Kircher's 1678 dragon.

Three Rivers Petroglyph Site

http://www.viva.com/nm/se.3rivers.html

Archaeology doesn't just happen in Europe, Asia, and Africa; North America has its own archaeological treasures, and this site showcases one of them. The Three Rivers petroglyph site of southeast New Mexico is an outstanding example of prehistoric Native American rock art. Here you can see photos of representative carvings, learn about the history, and find out how to visit the site during your next trip to New Mexico.

GENERAL SCIENCE AND ECOLOGY

Arachnology: The Study of Arachnids

http://dns.ufsia.ac.be/Arachnology/Arachnology.html

What better place to study spiders than crawling on the World Wide Web? This index to courses, info pages, associations, and scientists of the arachnid kind will have you spinning your own educational web in no time.

The Art of Renaissance Science: Galileo and Perspective
http://bang.lanl.gov/video/stv/arshtml/
lanlarstitle.html

This fascinating look at Renaissance science and the ground-breaking physics discoveries made by Galileo (the true laws of accelerated motion and falling bodies, fundamental theory of projectile motion) is well illustrated with numerous drawings and photographs of equipment and locations, as well as videos showing how he conducted some of his experiments. You'll learn other facts about Galileo's work, read about his persecution at the hands of the Inquisition, and find out how Renaissance artists used mathematics.

Australian National Botanic Gardens
http://155.187.10.12/anbg/index.html

Take a virtual tour of the wonders contained in botanical gardens on the other side of the world. The Australian National Botanic Gardens server includes a photo gallery, information on the locations of the gardens, and an interesting piece on the Aboriginal use of indigenous plants.

Biodiversity and Biological Collections WWW Server
http://www.keil.ukans.edu/

Don't be scared off by the note at the top of this page that states the collection is for "systematists and other biologists of the organismic kind." You'll find lots of general-interest info links tucked into its various categories. Want to know about snakes, fish, and other wild creatures? Loads of links will take you to sites of interest.

BioEd: Biology Education Resources
http://www-hpcc.astro.washington.edu/scied/
biology.html

Whether you're looking for a FAQ on the theory of evolution or want to start diving into genetics materials, the BioEd site has what you need. Jump to a zoology site that features an interactive frog dissection, or check out The Visible Human Project.

British Columbia Creature Page
http://clever.net/kerry/creatu re/creature.htm

An index to images, names, and descriptions of the fascinating animals that live in British Columbia's ocean waters is presented here. Among the collected creatures are rockfish, nudibranchs (really!), crabs, sponges, echinoderms, and more.

Carnivorous Plant Database
http://www.hpl.hp.com/bot/cp_home

Meat-eating plants may be the stuff of B-movies shown on late-night TV, but these fascinating specimens actually exist in nature … and not just the Venus fly trap. This site includes a searchable database, FAQ, photos, slide shows, and a plant trading post.

The Chili-Heads Home Page
http://neptune.netimages.com/~chile/

Everything you ever wanted to know—from the purely scientific to the purely fun—is included on the Chili-Heads Home Page. You'll find an answer to the burning question, "What's the hottest pepper?" and a chemistry primer on what makes peppers hot, along with a chili photo gallery, recipes, a mailing list, and growing tips.

Discover Magazine
http://www.enews.com:80/magazine s/
discover/

The popular and lay-friendly science publication *Discover* makes its online home on this Web page that includes selected articles from the current issue, an educators' forum, a schedule for TV's Discovery Channel, and an archive of back issues. The editors of the magazine also provide pointers to their favorite science sites.

The Earth Times
http://earthtimes.org/

This online version of a print-based newsletter—"the leading independent international nonpartisan newspaper on the environment and sustainable development"—is worldwide in scope and covers every conceivable human-made impact on the natural order: surface and subsurface structures, nuclear and chemical "accidents," forest and wildlife depredations, air quality, and more. Read it and weep.

Earthwatch International
http://gaia.earthwatch.org/

Earthwatch International is a nonprofit organization that sponsors scientific field research. It aims to improve human understanding of the planet and our impact on it. Visit for a look at the group and its accomplishments, and to learn about how to join the organization's field research efforts.

The Eco-Source
http://www.podi.com/ecosource/

Do you know what ecotourism is? Well, I didn't either and I'm still a mite fuzzy after reading the info on this page, but basically an ecotourist is a person who learns about the area he/she's traveling to, accepts the culture and customs of the area (displaying none of that "Ugly American" behavior), and does not participate in activities that harm the environment (presumably, African safaris are out). Although this site is really one big sales pitch for products and services (such as travel arrangements to eco-destinations), you can pick up some interesting information, a new perspective, and some interesting ideas here.

Albert Einstein Online
http://www.sas.upenn.edu/~smfriedm/
einstein.html

This site is packed with pointers to Web info about the theory of relativity guy: photographs, biographical info, original works, articles, and more. From the political (Einstein's opinion of Prohibition), to the theoretical (Einstein's relativity texts— whew!), this page introduces you to the scientist who revolutionized twentieth century physics.

Endangered Species: Images and Natural History
http://nceet.snre.umich.edu/EndSpp/
ES.bio.html

This index page leads you to images, maps, and fact sheets about endangered species throughout the world.

Although the northern spotted owl and efforts toward its protection have received most of the attention in recent years, the owl is just one entry on a very long list of mammals, birds, reptiles, fish, insects, and plants that humans and their "progress" are eliminating from the earth. The page includes links to organizations trying to reverse the trend and save the species we still have left.

EnviroLink
http://www.envirolink.org/envirohome.html

Without doubt one of the most beautifully designed pages I've ever seen, the EnviroLink icons feature "ancient artwork from indigenous cultures from around the world, reflecting the rich and diverse heritage of humankind's link to the earth." The site lives up to its promise by providing daily environmental news, a huge virtual library devoted to eco-resources, a "green" marketplace featuring products from earth-friendly companies, and cheeky ratings of sites (called What Soars, What Snores) that the reviewers feel either support or detract from the environmental cause. The site sponsor, EnviroLink Network, is a nonprofit resource for environmental information.

Fermilab Education Office
http://www-ed.fnal.gov/

If you think a quark is related to a Klingon and a lepton is a type of lizard, you've got a lot to learn about nuclear physics. Despair not! The Fermilab Education Office, a division of the Fermi National Accelerator Laboratory outside of Chicago, stands ready with the facts on these smallest of small particles. Fermilab is the home of Tevatron, a gigantic, four-mile ring that sends protons whizzing around at nearly the speed of light. To find out why and explore this subatomic world, start with the Phantastic Physix essay in the QuarkQuest newsletter. It may be targeted to middle school students, but it's written at a perfect level for most non-quarkians. Along with this basic intro to particle physics, you'll also find discussions of high-energy physics and the discovery of the top quark. This crash course may set your head to spinning like the Tevatron, but you'll leave the Fermilab site with a greater appreciation for the most basic particles and forces in nature, not to mention the scientists who probe these mysteries of the universe.

Forensic Entomology

http://www.uio.no/~mostarke/forens_ent/
forensic_entomology.html

One of the wonders of the Web is stumbling across a subject you never even knew existed, like forensic entomology. Entomologists all over the world assist police departments by analyzing the insects present on a dead body to help determine or corroborate the time, place and cause of death. That's right, bugs on dead people. The Webmaster, an entomology student at the University of Oslo, Norway, wants to tell you all about it. He warns off the squeamish, but don't expect gruesome pictures or lurid details; this site avoids sensationalism and concentrates on facts and technique.

Professor Stephen Hawking

http://www.damtp.cam.ac.uk/user/hawking/
home.html

One of the world's most brilliant physics minds—best known for his 1974 discovery that black holes emit radiation—goes online here with reprints of lectures, biographical data, and disability info. Interested folks can read a brief paper (not too technical) about the Big Bang theory.

Herp Pictures, Galleries 1 through 17

http://gto.ncsa.uiuc.edu/pingle to/lobby.html

Lovers of the cold and scaly can check out pretty pictures of frogs, turtles, snakes, and other species that fall under the category of herpetology. Visitors who find the pictures whet their thirst for herpetological knowledge can jump to the author's Herpocultural big links page.

Hydroponic Society of America

http://www.intercom.net/ user/aquaedu/hsa/
index.html

The Hydroponic Society of America gives an organizational overview and solicits memberships here. The page also contains information on growing plants without soil, as well as hydroponic conferences and seminars.

Institute for Global Communications: EcoNet

http://www.igc.apc.org/igc/econet/index.html

The IGC's EcoNet is a comprehensive source of ecological resources, including current news (scan the headlines and link to full-text stories culled from a variety of sources), features on subjects such as frugal living, and action alerts. One distinguishing characteristic of this site is that each news report contains extensive contact information—names, addresses, telephone numbers, and e-mail—so you can make your voice heard in the right offices and offer your support to the causes that interest you.

The Internet Consumer Recycling Guide

http://www.best.com/~dillon/recycle/

If you've never known what those numbers inside the recycle symbol on plastic containers mean, here's your chance to find out. Access loads of recycling facts, find recycling centers in your area, and learn how to reduce the amount of junk mail delivered by your postal carrier. This site is a terrific resource.

Marine Fish Catalog

http://www.actwin.com/fish/species.cg i

The Marine Fish Catalog boasts more than 200 pictures of tropical fish. Visitors can search the entire database, browse pictorial guides to angelfish, butterfly, tangs, and clownfish, and link to a freshwater fish catalog.

Online Environment

http://www.seas.gwu.edu/faculty/sheller2/oe/

This interactive information dissemination service from the Green University project (a collaboration between EPA and George Washington University) features articles, quizzes, and an eco-game to help acquaint you with hot issues in the environmental forum.

Origin of the Celsius Temperature Scale

http://www.bart.nl/~sante/engtemp.html

This single-page presentation explains clearly and simply how astronomer Anders Celsius conceived and tested the temperature scale that is now a scientific standard.

Plate Tectonics—The Cause of Earthquakes

http://www.seismo.unr.edu/ftp/pub/louie/
class/100/plate-tectonics.html

This online tutorial will give you a deeper understanding of the geologic forces that cause earthquakes. Generously illustrated with line drawings, satellite photos, and colorful maps, the site explains basic principles and identifies fault lines throughout the world.

Frank Potter's Science Gems

http://www-sci.lib.uci.edu/SEP/SEP.html

Although it was created to be a resource for students at all levels (kindergarten through graduate school), this marvelous index to science sites on the Web is a real boon to any armchair knowledge questor. Arranged by category, subcategory, and grade level, the index lets you click quickly to your level of understanding and explore the links provided for subjects as diverse as cell biology and quantum mechanics. Bonus links include Martindale's The Reference Desk (a comprehensive index to medical and science sites and other surprises) and Martindale's Health Science Guide.

Raptor Center

http://www.raptor.cvm.umn.edu/

Don't look for the Jurassic Park experience here; the raptors at this Center are predatory birds like eagles, hawks, falcons, and owls. The Raptor Center has treated thousands of sick and injured birds since it was founded in 1972. Although some of these birds sustain natural injuries, many have been shot, poisoned, or injured by contact with human-made structures or equipment. You don't have to be an eco-warrior to appreciate the magnificence of these birds and to be moved by the description of a once-injured bird's release into the skies.

Reduce Garbage—Eliminate Landfills

http://www.geocities.com/RainForest/5002/
index.html

OK, I'll admit that some of these ideas for recycling your garbage are a little extreme (like making a windchime out of old keys!), but many of these suggestions are practical, useful ways to reduce the amount of garbage you throw away or put in the recycle bin. Several of these recommendations will give you great ideas for projects to do with your grandchildren, and craft instructions are included!

Science Hobbyist

http://www.eskimo.com/~billb/

Amateur scientists will find this Web site a hot temptation. It's chock-full of demos and exhibits, "weird science" experiments, and loads of links to science-related resources all over the Web.

Science Made Stupid

http://www.neosoft.com/~kmac/sms/sms.htm

This tongue-in-cheek look at scientific history and theory demonstrates the first law of laughter: a body that chuckles tends to continue chuckling until acted upon by an external force. Warning: do not approach this site with the idea of gaining a theoretical grounding in science and physics. You will, however, find a lot of giggles. One of my favorites is the periodic table of the elements that includes entries such as Velveeta, Jell-o, and Velcro.

Science Online

http://www.aaas.org/science/science .html

Science, a lay-friendly publication of the American Association for the Advancement of Science, maintains this site for news and features, programs and projects, and links to related publications and institutions. You'll have to cough up some bucks for full access, but you can gain partial access by registering (for free).

THE RAPTOR CENTER
at the
UNIVERSITY OF MINNESOTA

WELCOME TO THE RAPTOR CENTER!

The Raptor Center is an international medical facility for birds of prey. Our mission is to preserve biological diversity among raptors and other avian species through medical treatment, scientific investigation, education, and management of wild populations.

Welcome and Thank You for investigating The Raptor Center's world wide web!

INJURED BIRDS: learn what to do and who to contact if you find an injured bird, particularly if the bird needs EMERGENCY care.

Sea World Animal Information Database
http://www.bev.net/education/SeaWorld /
Sponsored by Sea World and Busch Gardens, this info database received the Significant Achievement in Education Award from the American Zoo and Aquarium Association. Kids and grownups alike can access "fast facts about animals," take an animal quiz, send their zoological questions to "Shamu," or learn about building a home aquarium.

Solstice: Sustainable Energy and Development Online!
http://solstice.crest.org/
You don't have to live in the woods without electricity to be earth friendly. Solstice, maintained by the Center for Renewable Energy and Sustainable Technology, provides information and links to resources concerning energy efficiency, renewable energy, and sustainable living technologies. Visitors are encouraged to register and leave comments.

Sustainable Architecture, Building and Culture
http://www.west.net/~prince/
You certainly can't tell it from the new residential developments going up in my city, but earth-friendly, sustainable, and recycled building materials are available, and I'm not talking about living in caves here. Find out the story on rammed earth homes, straw bale construction, and renewable energy resources at this info page, and link to a variety of other ecological resources.

Tsunami!
http://www.geophys.washington.edu/ tsunami/welcome.html
Here's a word that fills coastal dwellers with fear. Visit this site to learn about the physics of tsunami generation and propagation and the impact of tsunamis on humankind.

U.S. Geological Survey Fact Sheets
http://h2o.usgs.gov/public/wid/indexlist.html
The USGS publishes a host of earth science fact sheets covering natural hazards, the environment, and natural resources. A number of them are available online, and this page will point you toward reports—both general and specific—that address various studies undertaken by the USGS.

Virtual Cell
http://ampere.scale.uiuc.edu/~m-lexa/cell/ cell.html
Here's a collection of movies, still images, and text demonstrating how a single plant cell functions. Follow the navigation instructions to learn about chloroplasts and other hard workers within the cell.

Volcano World
http://volcano.und.nodak.edu/
This info-packed site, funded by NASA, includes just about everything you've ever wanted to know about volcanoes and maybe even a few facts you didn't really want to know. Find out about currently active volcanoes, access volcano history, locate volcano parks and monuments, and learn all about terminology and geologic forces in the FAQ.

Web of Life
http://www.envirolink.org/orgs/wqed/
Television station WQED of Pittsburgh presents this page on *Web of Life: Exploring Biodiversity*, a two-hour, public-television special that celebrates the diversity of life on earth. A QuickTime preview is available, along with lots of links, descriptions of scenes, a field guide, and home video info.

WhaleNet
http://whale.wheelock.edu/
A combined project of Wheelock and Simmons Colleges and the U.S. National Science Foundation, WhaleNet is an interdisciplinary effort to foster learning about the natural environment. Visit its home page to find a variety

of fun and informative resources, including whale tracking and marine mammal slide shows.

Windows to the Universe
http://www.windows.umich.edu/

Windows to the Universe contains "loads of information and graphics about the Earth and Space Sciences," including scientific content and supplemental information about the artistic, historical, and cultural connections between science and our lives. Since the project is funded by NASA, information is weighted on the space side, but you'll find some earthbound resources as well.

Wolf Park Home Page
http://tigerden.com/Wolf-park/Wel come.html

Located in Battle Ground, Ind., Wolf Park is a research facility studying the interpack and reproductive behavior of the wolf. Links to the park's educational programs, photo album, and operating information are featured here.

Chapter 16
SHOP 'TIL YOU DROP

THE CART BEFORE THE HORSE

END SHOPPING PAIN

WHEE! IT'S FREE!

ENOUGH ALREADY!

LOTS BETTER THAN THE MALL

Whenever I pull up in front of a mile-wide shopping mall, I shudder and my knees turn to rubber, because I know I will have to walk a million miles to find one small thing that I can only get here. If it weren't for that one mall-only thing, I would be parking directly in front of one of my local merchant's stores and could run quickly in and out, mission accomplished.

I have never been much of a recreational shopper. For me, shopping is something you do to obtain necessities. I spend my leisure time in other pursuits. Hitting the big sales, shoving forward into thousands of deranged shoppers, is not my idea of a good time.

But you can't get around it; shopping is necessary. You need dental floss, candelabra lights, bunion pads—and not all the stuff you need is available in catalogs. Plus, catalogs don't offer the same sales as your local department stores. Sure, you can order sheets through the mail, but you'll miss those fabulous white sale prices. There's really no choice but to shop for the best deals!

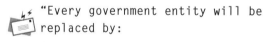 "Every government entity will be replaced by:

1. A computer
2. A rottweiler
3. One politician

The computer will make the decisions, the politician will feed the rottweiler, and the rottweiler will keep the politician away from the computer."

THE CART BEFORE THE HORSE

My friend, Edie, faced with storming some of the enormous mega-stores, found the perfect solution. First you must picture Edie: She's a very large woman, dresses lavishly in fashionably flowing clothes, is addicted to enormous, classy hats, and has a diabolical sense of humor accompanied by a maniacal laugh.

Edie began wearing extravagant hats and carrying a cane because she discovered that these props gave her a decided advantage. She noticed that without them, the maître d' would sit her at a tiny restaurant table close to the kitchen. With hat and cane, however, she was ceremoniously placed at a better table. No doubt, she was a person of importance or at least waiting for one. Now she never goes anywhere without her accoutrements and advises all women over 50 to do the same. They get results!

PILING DOWN THE AISLE

Edie discovered on one of her shopping forays that many large independent stores like Wal-Mart and Sam's Club provide small motorized carts for their customers who have disabilities, or who just don't want to take the long hike through the bewildering aisles of towering merchandise, preferring instead to whip to the aisle of choice and then head out for "Dodge."

Edie's not disabled, but she did like the idea of sitting while she shopped. So on her first attempt at cart shopping, Edie—wearing hat and carrying cane—shoved herself and her large purse into the first awaiting cart, turned on the power, and sped wildly down the first aisle. She knew at once that her cart was completely out of control. Laughing joyfully, she took down the toilet paper display on her first turn, left a tower of ladies' purses on the floor at the second turn, and proceeded to kitchen wares at the speed of light. She had neglected to get instructions on steering and didn't know the locations of the fast and slow controls on the cart.

"What you do is you take last year's income, divide it by your 1986 income, multiply by your age, add

```
your social security number, subtract
your phone number, multiply by the megs
remaining on your hard drive, and then
subtract the number of times you have
lied about your age. If the answer is
a plus, you get to vote."
```

With the manager bearing down on her none too cheerfully, she managed to pull her cart to the curb, right by the shoes. Smiling at him beatifically, she found "slow" and proceeded at a dignified, if wobbly pace, to hardware.

Now that she is an expert and skillful cart driver, she has proposed all-Senior rallying tournaments down the aisles of various colossal stores, with the store awarding prizes to Seniors who can run the course through the maze of shopping aisles in the best time. We still laugh hysterically when we remember her first outing in the cart at Wal-Mart.

END SHOPPING PAIN

For those of you who, like me, prefer yard sales, catalogs, and thrift stores to staggering down the never-ending courtyards of the newest mall—this chapter is for you. Everything you can imagine is sold on the Net, including automobiles!

HELLO!, NOAH

This past spring our street was visited with a horrific flood when the ancient sewers collapsed in the middle of a torrential rain. The rising waters took out several cars. One of them was my old 1983 Nissan Maxima, a stick shift with 198,000 miles. It could not be salvaged. It was time to face up to the fact that I would not flame out with my "Ruby" (a distant cousin to Ruby Perl), 'cause she was no more.

KEEP 'EM ROLLIN'

Knowing my adverse affect on automobile salesmen, I preferred to avoid the confusion of the myriad models of autos reposing on any lot you could name, along with the pressurized car salesmen hyping their wares. What's an old gal to do? Turn to the Web, of course!

The automobile sales sites are many and very informative. You can do a lot of comparative shopping in the comfort of your own home.

A SHOPPER'S DREAM

I had already decided that I would replace the old Maxima with another, because I'd had a long and comfortable association with my beloved Ruby. I also knew exactly what I wanted to pay for the car. In my Web searching, I came across local dealer sites that listed many of their cars and prices.

Finding some listings that were close to my original ideas, I called the dealership, spoke to the salesman, narrowed the choices down to one, and asked that he drive the car to my home.

That afternoon, he drove the car over and after a test drive and inspection at my garage, I bought it, at *my* price: a beautiful 1989 Nissan Maxima, fully loaded, with 60,000 miles on its odometer and in perfect condition.

HASSLE-FREE

No days of driving from dealership to dealership surveying the confusing array of models and brands. No haggling over price with different salesmen. Buying this car was easier than buying a tube of toothpaste!

To get you started on the road to buying your own new (or used) car, here are a few auto sites on the Web with pointers to dealers, pricing services, auto reviews, and even parts.

All Things Automotive Directory

http://www.webcom.com/~autodir/

The All Things Automotive Directory is essentially a huge index to, well, all things automotive on the Web. You'll find links to classic car sites, manufacturers, parts sites, dealers, auto clubs, and even news and chat rooms. Once you finish cruising the features, move along to the classifieds that contain—the site says—listings of over 16,000 vehicles for sale.

Auto-By-Tel

http://www.autobytel.com/

Web surfers who'd rather be driving can buy or lease a new car or truck online from Auto-By-Tel. The company claims to offer the lowest prices for the purchaser's area.

The Automobile Buyers' Network

http://www.dmssoft.com/

Kick tires online at the Automobile Buyers' Network. Visitors can peruse classified listings complete with color photos, or link directly to a list of dealers via this service.

Automobiles2

http://www.w2.com/pacepub.html

Pace Publications pitches its automotive price and buying guides at this site, a segment of the World Square online mall. Visitors will find prices and ordering information for such items as new- and used-car buying guides, and the *Auto Price Almanac*, a magazine published seven times a year that includes dealer's cost and the manufacturer's suggested list price for all new American and foreign cars, trucks, vans, and 4x4s.

AutoNetwork

http://www.autonetwork.com/

Take some of the mystery out of buying a car at Auto-Network. Visit its Interactive Purchasing Agent site for preferred service and updated price listings that they say will get you the best deal possible on a new or used automobile.

AutoRow

http://www.autorow.com/

You'll like the animation and the easy-to-use interface at this site. Click on the showroom icon to visit manufacturers' sites and select your brand new Alfa Romeo or Bentley (okay, or the Chevrolet, Ford, or Oldsmobile you've been considering). Locate a dealer, access car news and info, or browse the classifieds and the listings for preowned cars.

AutoWeb Interactive

http://www.autoweb.com/

The slogan at AutoWeb Interactive is "Your Car, Right Now!" This Cupertino, Calif.-based online guide for car buyers offers detailed information and listings from dealers around the United States. Visit here to check deals on new or used cars.

Cars @Cost

http://www.webcom.com/~carscost/
welcome.html

This "revolutionary auto buying organization" likens itself to an HMO for new car buyers. The organization says that it can find you a new car at factory invoice prices through its nationwide network of dealers. There's a price for the service of course, but they claim to be able to save you thousands. Check the FAQ for complete information about how the service works and how much it costs.

DealerNet: The Source for New Car Information

http://www.dealernet.com/

With its "virtual showroom," DealerNet wants to sell you not only a car, but a car dealer. Use this site to search for a nearby dealer or a car with your specifications. Visitors can also flip through auto reviews, download a copy of a confidential credit application, or check on prices for parts.

WHEE! IT'S FREE!

Better even than sales and thrift stores, the best stuff of all is free stuff. And the Web has many sites with offerings that will cost you nothing at all. You could make a hobby of this, sending for everything in the blessed world and never having a single free minute to examine boredom. Try it out and see what it's about.

> For the ultimate in freeloading: A panda sauntered into the saloon, sat down at the bar and told the bartender "Give me a sandwich and a beer." Now, the bartender had seen a lot of strange characters out west, and knew it was important to keep his cool, so he just replied, "Sure enough, stranger," and slapped a ham sandwich and a cold frosty one in front of the bear. The panda, having obviously been on the trail for some time, gulped down the sandwich and washed it down with the beer. He then deftly pulled his six-shooter, drew a bead on the piano player, and plugged him squarely between the eyes. The bartender was dumbfounded as he watched the bear return his gun to his holster and walk out the front door. "Hey, you! What the hell is going on here?," shouted the bartender as he ran after the bear. The panda stopped and turned slowly in his tracks. "Well, what did you expect?" he said.
>
> "Well, I sure didn't expect you to shoot the piano player. Good help is hard to find. Besides, you still owe me for lunch."

"I'm a PANDA. Look it up," replied the bear before continuing on his way. The bartender was too upset and nervous to rile such an unpredictable sort, so he picked up his unabridged from the shelf, and flipped through it for the entry for "panda." "Damn," he muttered as he read the entry. He realized that there was not a thing he could do. There it was, in black and white, written by an authority no less than Noah Webster himself: "pan-da *n*. A large bear-like animal of the mountains of China and Tibet, with distinctive white and black markings. Eats shoots and leaves."

STUFF FOR FREE

AJ's Free Stuff Page
http://pilot.msu.edu/~gavinand/homefree.htm
Link to sites offering freebies in exchange for information. Sites feature computer software, apparel, music, and more.

ClickIn
http://www.Clickin.com/
Participate in surveys and possibly win a free phone card.

CraftNet Village
http://www.craftnet.org/prime/freestf2.htm
Here's a guide to some free stuff and other "great offers" for crafts enthusiasts.

Cuervo Gold
http://www.cuervo.com/blender/blender.html
Play the game and maybe win a Cuervo Gold T-shirt.

FlossNet, Inc.
http://www2.southwind.net/~fni/floss5.html
Order a free sample of Quik Floss.

Free Lunch
http://www.pebbs.com/megabites/
freestuff.html

Who say's there's no such thing as a free lunch? Here's "The Free $tuff Directory."

Free Stuff Galore
http://www.pathcom.com/~camwildo/
free.htm

Fill out surveys and vie for cash and prizes.

FreeWay
http://www.vivanet.com/~woodj/money-mart/
freeway/freeway.html

There's "something free at every stop!" Find samples, services, contests, CD-ROMs, magazines, catalogs, and much more!

Kool Ties
http://www.kooltie.com/

Register for a free Kool Tie.

Leanin' Tree Greeting Cards
http://www.leanintree.com/cgi-bin/leanintree/
get

Get a free sample greeting card and a coupon for $2 off your next purchase from the company's catalog of products.

L'eggs Women's In.Site
http://www.leggs.com/

Play the games, join the club, win prizes, receive coupons, and more.

Next to Nothing
http://www.winternet.com/~julie/ntn.html

Updated weekly, this page is dedicated to the art of getting something for nothing. Links to previous postings are also available.

Revlon Cosmetics
http://204.71.0.61:80/revlon/freestuff/

Care for some free lipstick samples?

Savor the Garlic Gourmet Spices
http://www.galaxymall.com/spices/garlic.html

Sample the seasonings free. Try mesquite, lemon pepper, or Cajun-bayou-flavored garlic powder.

Scavengers Quest
http://www.aracnet.com/~crow/sq/

Offering "the best of the best of what is free," this site directs users to all manner of free offers on the Web. Dozens of offers are featured.

Solar Gear Sun Care
http://www.solargear.com/

Print the retail coupon redeemable with purchases at stores, or order sunscreen online and enjoy a buy-one-get-one-free offer.

SuccessTEAM Online
http://www.4success.com/

Get a free "Connections" travel and leisure membership for trying the company's long distance service. Contests, too.

3M Active Strips Flexible Bandages
http://www.mmm.com:80/profile/ads/leg.html

Find out how to get a free sample of this new bandage.

Lizzie's Tips

When you move or copy files directly into a new window on your Mac, they will fall into the same disorderly heap as they were in their prior location. Place each file on the window's title bar, release the mouse, and voilà! they will be arranged in an orderly manner. Use for general housekeeping. If you want to organize files in a folder, use the "Select All" command, move the files to the title bar, release the mouse, and your files will be sorted alphabetically.

3M Office Survey and Product Sample
http://www.3m.com/market/omc/forms/
omcndjar.html
Fill in the form for information and samples when available.

Tabitha's Freebies
http://www.freestuff.pair.com/
Find links to sites offering freebies, plus pointers to contest pages, too.

Volition
http://www.volition.com/
Free stuff, free e-mail, and contests, too. Discover who's giving what away and where.

Weblynx Forum
http://weblynx.com.au/win.htm
Participate in the forums and be eligible for fabulous prizes.

The Weekly Freebie Compilation
http://www.nb.net/~sxm/free/freebie.html
The title of the page makes the promise, and the page's contents deliver—weekly!

ENOUGH ALREADY!

Don't relax! Buying may be only the first part of the shopping experience. After the purchase, you may have to deal with the customer service department. And that can be a nightmare in its own right.

VOICE MAIL FROM HELL

Murphy's Law informs the service industries today, and the public is no longer being accommodated with the fairness and friendliness of yesteryear. Instead, the smiling customer service representative has been replaced with "voice mail," making it nearly impossible to speak to a real person. Instead, you are told by a recording to punch in the proper keys and leave your message in "voice mail boxes." If you are finally put through to a real live customer service person, with today's change in attitudes and lack of training, your scenario could read like this.

"The computer and the Internet are extremely important to society in the matter of gathering information, if nothing else.

"Yesterday, if students wanted a piece of information found in a book at the library, here is what they used to do. They went to the library, removed the book from the shelf, and immediately made that information UNAVAILABLE to any one else who wanted it.

"Today, if students want a piece of information, they can find it on the Internet, and so can everyone else at the same time."

BE A BULLDOG

Kathy G. recently purchased an expensive couch from a prominent local furniture dealer. Since the couch was not available as a floor model, it had to be paid for up-front before the store would place the order. Delivery was to be in approximately six weeks.

At the end of the seventh week, Kathy called customer service and politely asked about her order, only to be told that the order had never been made and was still sitting on the desk of a representative who had quit a few weeks earlier.

"What do I do now?" she asked.

"You can reorder," she was told.

"Reorder!" she replied, "I'm afraid of doing that! Just return the check to me and I will get the couch somewhere else."

"After you come in to fill out the check return forms, it will take three weeks before we can process your check to be sent back to you," she was told.

Asking to speak to the next higher up, Kathy reached a young man who asked her impertinently, "What do you expect ME to do about this?"

"Well, son, you work for this company and you are the supervisor directly responsible for the team that let this order slip through the cracks! Let me speak to YOUR supervisor!" But he was gone for the day.

Not intimidated by all this rudeness, Kathy persevered, calling the Better Business Bureau and a well-publicized service at a local TV station that exposes incompetent or illegal behavior by local companies who may be exploiting the public.

Leaving this latest information—that she had reported the company's error, and subsequent failure to satisfy her, with both the BBB and a local TV reporter—on the voice mail service of the very Top Manager, Kathy felt at least some small amount of satisfaction.

On the Sunday following, the very Top Manager called to tell her that her check would be returned to her in the next company mail drop.

The moral of this story is to remain undeterred by rudeness and bad service. Assert yourself, use every avenue you can think of to get results, insist on proper treatment, and boycott stores that don't treat customers like royalty (or at least human beings).

LOTS BETTER THAN THE MALL

You don't have to drive, park, or walk to get to these stores. The Web has everything from the biggest mall to the smallest specialty store. The array of goods and services is staggering. Leap in here and explore the opportunities. You're bound to have fun.

MAJOR RETAILERS AND CATALOGERS

Bloomingdale's
http://www.bloomingdales.com/
Browse the shops, shop the sales, or use the search service to find exactly what you're looking for. It's "Bloomie's" on the Web!

Current
http://cybermart.com/bin/sct22/current/v2/
catalog/catalog/index2.html
The catalog retailer that built a name in the stationery, greeting card, and novelty gift market welcomes shoppers to its online catalog, featuring much the same merchandise found in its print catalog. Browse and buy from a wide selection of decorations, calendars, cards, stamps, labels, and other paper goods.

Dillard's Online
http://www.azstarnet.com/dillards/
A favorite anchor store for malls in 23 states, Dillard Department Stores hosts this look at featured merchandise and gift ideas. Also find a bridal guide and employee recipes.

Federated Department Stores
http://www.federated-fds.com/
Parent company of such shopping institutions as Macy's East and West, Bloomingdale's, and Rich's, FDS posts a corporate profile, as well as shopping opportunities, on its home page. Link to the corporation's online store sites, check into stock options, and see what else is "hot" and happening.

Lizzie Sez

Buy whatever the kids in your neighborhood are selling on card tables set up in their front yards—no matter what it is.

Fingerhut Online
http://www.fingerhut.com/

Selling brand names and private-label merchandise through its catalogs, Fingerhut now presents customer opportunities via the Web. Order a catalog online right now, but soon find other features and customer services available.

JCPenney
http://www.jcpenney.com/

From the malls of America straight into cyberspace, here's one of the United States's major department stores offering secure online shopping to its customers, plus a full range of special features like online coupons and value-enhanced offers.

Kmart
http://www.kmart.com/

Back from the brink, this retail giant owes much of its renewed popularity to supremely popular pitchwomen, Rosie O'Donnell and Penny Marshal. Find the weekly sale circular, a virtual tour of the "new" Kmart, recent store news, and information about the Kmart credit card.

Lands' End
http://www.landsend.com/

Order online, check out the overstocks, and browse the other Internet offerings of the direct marketing company with the two-word guarantee: "Guaranteed. Period." Women's, men's, and children's clothes are the specialty, but seasonal gift items are also featured.

Lillian Vernon
http://www.lillianvernon.com/

Online and in-line with its pricing strategies, Lillian Vernon now brings to the Web the value-shopping that has been available via the company's direct mail offerings for over 45 years. Find toys, office items, household gadgets, sports gear, and gift ideas galore.

L.L. Bean
http://www.llbean.com/

The cataloger from Maine that made dressing warmly "fashionable," now hosts this online look at its products and services. Order catalogs or shop online to order the clothing and other products that made L.L. Bean a household word.

Macy's
http://www.macys.com/

Whether you want to know more about the retailer's annual Thanksgiving Day parade, find the location of the store nearest you, or shop online, Macy's can accommodate your wishes. For the holidays, extra help is added online, such as the MBA Personal Shopping Service and a look at the Top 40 Gifts.

Marshall Field's
http://www.shop-at.com/marshallfields/

One of the first stores to use the merchandising strategy of arranging "fashionable" window displays to feature its wares, Chicago-based Marshall Field's presents its latest window into what's in store for customers. Keep an eye on fashion while you enjoy online shopping and ordering.

Neiman Marcus
http://www.neimanmarcus.com/

Those who find it fashionable to shop "The Legend" can stay in touch with the world of fashion via the trendsetting giant's home page. Information on customer programs, store locations, and company news is featured.

Nordstrom Personal Touch America
http://www.nordstrom-pta.com/

Find out how to shop via e-mail at "one of the United States' leading fashion specialty stores." While on-site, also check into what's new at Nordstrom and read a profile of this shopper's favorite.

Pier 1
http://www.pier1.com/

Stop in here for an overview and history of the chain store that has built its reputation and customer following by presenting the best and most unique import products from over 40 different countries. Also find out what is currently on sale, locate the store nearest you, or check out the bridal registry.

¥ ¥ ¥ ¥ Pier 1 Announces Record Sales ¥ ¥ ¥ ¥

Sam's Club Online
http://www.samsclub.com/

The "warehouse sales" division of the Wal-Mart discount chain presents news and views its customers can use to get even more value from their membership in the club. Read the monthly newsletter, *Buy-Line*, check into great values, and yes, shop! Those who are not already members can look into and sign up for club membership online.

Sears
http://www.sears.com/

Come see the virtual side of Sears! Find out about the company, including its products and services, locate the outlet nearest you, and link to online customer services such as an e-mail reminder service.

The Sharper Image Catalog
http://www.sharperimage.com/

Cool gadgets, whatcha-ma-call-its, and curiosities have helped make The Sharper Image a fun catalog and store to shop. Now the "Image"-conscious can shop via the Web, and find a whole new kind of catalog filled with neat stuff to browse and buy. Be sure to check out the Internet-only specials.

Spiegel
http://www.spiegel.com/

Shop "the most extraordinary catalog of the Web," plus find online features that teach and entertain. Those curious about what trends are ahead can also access a fashion preview for the coming season.

Target
http://www.targetstores.com/

Promoting its general merchandise stores by promoting the products and customer services it offers, Target presents some special online features such as the Lullaby Club, for new mothers and mothers-to-be (are you listening grandparents?). Also find an opportunity to sample new music releases available at the stores, a company profile, and a store locator service.

The Ultimate Outlet
http://www.ultimate-outlet.com

Get a great deal on Spiegel merchandise at the cataloger's online "clearance" site. Women's, men's, and home fashions are marked down to move.

Wal-Mart
http://www.wal-mart.com/

Why fight the traffic snarl around and inside the stores when you can now shop online? Okay, so not everything is available online right now, but the big ticket (and medium ticket) stuff is. Can household cleaners be far behind?

ONLINE SHOPPING MALLS AND CATALOG SHOPPING OUTLETS

All-Internet Shopping Directory
http://www.webcom.com/~tbrown/

Here are the selected "best" shopping sites on the Web, compiled into one, easy-to-use directory. Find hundreds of sites organized by category and selling everything from art books to videos. Travel agents and other service providers are also featured.

American Shopping Mall
http://www.greenearth.com/

Bloomingdale's, Definitive Audio, and the California Wine Club are only a few of the stores offering "luxury online affluent shopping" in this virtual mall. Stores are organized into categories such as antiques, apparel, food and wine, golf, home and furniture, unique gifts, and travel.

Avante Garde
http://www.infoanalytic.com/index.html

Think of it as "a virtual marketplace" where products and professional services can be found. Find most anything from gifts and specialty items to technology and travel services.

The Best Mall Online
http://www.the-best-mall-online.com/

Don't take the mall's name for it; go see if indeed this is the best shopping site on the Internet. While on-site you can shop JCPenney, Circuit City, Wickes Store, and about a half dozen other retailers.

Catalog Live!
http://cataloglive.com/

If "upscale" is part of your criteria for making shopping selections, this outlet may be the virtual shopping site for you. Thornberry's Select, Hansen Caviar Company, and Flowers USA are only a sampling of the catalogs and shops that are online and open for business.

Catalog Select
http://pathfinder.com/
@@PNQXIQcAd19VTsPS/CatalogSelect/

Here's a one-stop opportunity to have some of the biggest catalogers in the country send you their latest catalog free. Order one or order them all. The catalogs are organized by type.

Cyberspace Wholesale Marketplace
http://www.halcyon.com/rlucas/
Welcome.html

Anyone looking for a deal won't mind the little extra required to shop the businesses listed here. You'll find that none (or few) have Web pages, only addresses and phone numbers you can call or write. The discounters listed offer all manner of products.

The Dream Shop
http://www.dreamshop.com/

Find some of the biggest names in shopping, online and ready to serve you with a cyber-smile. Enjoy Saks Fifth Avenue, Eddie Bauer, Williams-Sonoma, The Sharper Image, Spiegel, and about a dozen other retailers of one type or another.

Galaxy Mall
http://www.galaxymall.com/

Like most malls, Galaxy's directory of shopping groups stores by category; however, unlike most malls, Galaxy's categories include education, religious, and medical sites. Enjoy hundreds of shopping and service outlets, secure online ordering, and a classified ads bulletin board.

iMALL
http://www.imall.com/

Advertised as "the largest retail Web site," this mall fronts over 750 stores. Be sure to shop what the mall considers its "premium" stores, check out the deals of the day, and don't forget to watch for monthly and special features.

Internet Liquidators, Inc.
http://www.internetliquidators.com/

Shop via the live "Dutch action" auction where the prices go down, not up. Or, link to the discount mall. A schedule of what's going up for bid will help auction participants, and a directory aids those in the mall.

Mall of Malls
http://www.westcomm.com/westpg10.html

Get "malled" here and you may not survive if you try that shop 'til you drop thing! Find an alphabetical list of pointers to cybermalls from around the world. The roster includes sites of most every size, caliber, and theme.

malls.com
http://malls.com/

Promising one-stop resources, this index offers two search tools. A directory organized by products points to stores, and a set of radio buttons locates malls by size, theme, and location. The mall list can also be reviewed alphabetically.

MegaMall
http://infotique.lm.com/cgi-bin/
phpl.cgi?megamall.html

The MegaMall Tower may not actually be a 50-story skyscraper, but this mall has enough tenants to fill a building that size. Search by department, keyword, or store name. While on-site, be sure to watch for freebies, specials, and contests.

NetMall
http://www.netmall.com/

Businesses can add pages to this site free; perhaps that's why some of the big names have links here. Find L'eggs, Spiegel, Sara Lee, Encyclopedia Britannica, and AT&T.

123 Shop
http://www.123shop.com/

Nothing too fancy here. Simply choose a product category, pull up a directory of links, and you're off on a spree. Choose from books, flowers, software, food, wine, travel, and music.

Park Avenue
http://www.avenue.com/park.html

They say that if you've got to ask, you can't afford it. This shopping area was modeled after renowned shopping districts like Fifth Avenue and Michigan Avenue. Shop merchants like Spiegel, Horchow, The Bombay Company, and The Sharper Image.

ShopInternet: Malls and Catalogs
http://www.ro.com/ShopInternet/malls.html

No mystery here, just a directory of online malls and mail order company home pages. Find a broad mix of retailers, from Access Cottage Industries to the Spiegel catalog.

The Shopper
http://www.shoppingdirect.com/

Claiming its place as "your number one shopping starting point," this site welcomes visitors to search or browse its database of 850 online malls and shops. Listings include reviews of each site, and shopping tips are available.

The Virtual Emporium
http://www.vemporium.com/

Devoted to online shopping, this site delivers the "selected best" of the thousands of shopping sites available on the Web. Presented by category, the shopping sites can also be listed and searched alphabetically.

Web Warehouse
http://webwarehouse.com/

About what you'd expect: lots and lots of "big name" shopping links organized by category. Something you might not expect: the featured products are current, trendy, and a nice welcome feature to this virtual directory to the likes of J. Crew, Lands' End, Clinique, Louis Vuitton Paris, and many more.

SPECIALTY SHOPS

Absolutely Fresh Flowers
http://www.cts.com/~flowers/

At Absolutely Fresh Flowers, shoppers can have arrangements of multicolored miniature carnations shipped via Federal Express from the southern California grower to any location within the United States. Electronic orders are accepted.

Amazon.com Books!
http://www.amazon.com/exec/obidos/subst/
index2.html/2020-8800495-371974

You've see the banner ads for this mammoth online bookstore all over the Web; now's your chance to visit in person. Browse their catalog of over one million titles, register for their notification service, or write a great book review and win $100 worth of books. The fun never stops at Amazon.com.

America's Shirt Catalog
http://www.cottonshirt.com/

This site sells men's shirts and ties at, they claim, savings of 45 to 60 percent. These are dress shirts of broadcloth, oxford cloth, and pima cotton in a variety of colors with prices that don't exceed $30.00. Worth a look.

Antiquarian Booksellers' Association of America Booknet
http://www.clark.net/pub/rmharris/abaa.html

If you're searching for a rare or antiquarian book, map, or print, you might find it in this site's database of online

Check out the sites below for more information.

CyberCash
http://www.cybercash.com/

Found something you want to buy online? Visit Cyber-Cash to learn about its "secure purchase" services for consumers and merchants on the World Wide Web.

First Virtual Internet Payment System
http://www.fv.com/html/fv_main.html

Working toward becoming the Internet's answer to secure financial transactions, First Virtual offers registration at this site for its "virtual accounts." With this service, users can buy or sell without passing credit card numbers through cyberspace.

NetBank
http://www.teleport.com/~netcash/

Software Agents, Inc. maintains this site to introduce its NetBank NetCash system, offering "easy, natural and secure" cash transactions over the Internet. Visitors will find service descriptions and cash standards, plus security updates.

 Lizzie's Tips

PAYING FOR YOUR PURCHASES

If you're concerned about the security of your credit card purchases online, don't be. These days, sending your credit card account number across the wires of the Net is probably safer than handing over the plastic card to an unknown wait- or salesperson. Security and privacy is pretty much ensured by sophisticated "encryption," a method of coding your order and credit card information so that only the intended recipient can access it. Sound impossible? It's not really—your access to pay TV stations, like HBO, works on the same principle to "scramble" signals and decode them, but only for those who have the right little black boxes (and who have paid their bills!).

At some shopping—and even some banking—sites, you can also make payments and transfers directly from bank accounts you specify (or establish specifically for virtual purchases), in much the same way as you now can use your bank ATM or debit cards to pay for goods and services at retail outlets.

booksellers and catalogs. I located a first edition of Charles Dickens's *A Christmas Carol* for a mere $9,000 (the description says it's worth $15,000), but decided to buy the paperback instead.

Archie McPhee
http://www.halcyon.com/mcphee/

Archie McPhee boasts a broad selection of popular cultural artifacts available for sale online. Visitors can browse this eclectic collection of objects, ranging from rubber chickens to voodoo dolls and bizarre candy.

Auntie Q's Antiques & Collectibles
http://www.teleport.com/~auntyq/

Auntie Q's Antiques & Collectibles lets you browse an online catalog of gifts and books, complete with ordering information. Find out what's "new" among the "old" in a weekly special offering.

Cabot Creamery
http://www.cabotcheese.com/cabot/index.htm

I always thought cheddar came from Wisconsin (and it does), but here's a dairy in Vermont that touts its "award-winning" cheddar. The prices are quite reasonable, and the gift packages sound wonderful (cheese, maple syrup, special mustards—yum!). Bonus: The site has an embedded sound file that moos like a cow when you link back to the home page.

Celtic Cultures
http://www.sover.net/~celtic/

This online market specializes in Celtic goods, offering books, clothing, jewelry, and more for electronic purchase. The page also features links to other Celtic sites on the Internet.

Chic Paris
http://www.inetbiz.com/chic/

The Chic Paris site is an online fashion catalog and shopping site for selected Paris fashions, with browsing and search features, instructions on ordering, and that all-important return policy.

Chile Today—Hot Tamale
http://emall.com/Chile/Chile1.html

Chile Today—Hot Tamale is a company offering personal gift memberships for monthly deliveries of chile or hot sauces. Visitors to this site can obtain ordering info, read a variety of factoids about chile, or browse numerous chile and hot sauce recipes.

The Chocolate Lovers' Page
http://bc.emanon.net/chocolate/

The Chocolate Lovers' Page presents a comprehensive list of shops and companies that sell chocolate on the Internet, as well as links to recipes and other chocolate goodies.

Chosen Reflections
http://www.primenet.com/~magazin

Commemorate a birthday with a magazine printed on the date of the recipient's birth. Chosen Reflections serves up information on over 1,000 available magazines for collectors or gift givers. Order magazines or browse a catalog of available products.

Clambake Celebrations, Inc.
http://www.netplaza.com/plaza/strfrnts/1004/storepg1.html

In the mood for fresh lobster, clams, or mussels? You can have them tomorrow—guaranteed fresh and delivered to your door. (The seaweed is free.)

The Classic Angler
http://www.gorp.com/bamboo.htm

The Classic Angler provides information and products for tackle collectors and fly fisherfolk alike. The Fly Fishing Mini-Mall link takes anglers shopping for everything, from modern fly reels to specialty products for rod builders.

Classique Structure
http://www.netaxs.com/~vlad/cs

Need a gargoyle? How about a cherub? The Pennsylvania-based Classique Structure sells gift items and home furnishings over the Internet. Online ordering is available.

Cobra Golf
http://www.cobragolf.com/

"Become a believer" with Cobra Golf's oversized woods and irons in both men's and women's models. The Cobra home page also features a Pro Shop Locator and a chance to win a free driver.

The Cowboy Trail
http://www.cowboytrail.com/

If you want to dress like John Wayne or just need a new outfit for Saturday's square dance, you might find what you're looking for at this purveyor of Western wear. Besides the sartorial offerings, the site includes loads of cowboy lore and info.

Dakota Engraving
http://www.getnet.com/engrave

Put your name, e-mail address, or whatever you choose on miniature license plates at Dakota Engraving. Other services include sports logos and cartoons. Bicycle plates and license-plate frames are also available.

The Dragonfly Toy Company
http://www.magic.mb.ca/~dragon/

The Dragonfly Toy Company offers products for children with special needs, including musical instruments, puzzles, board games, and books. Dragonfly also provides a search service for any product that they don't stock.

Earrings by Lisa!
http://mmink.cts.com/mmink/kiosks/earrings/earrings.html

If your earlobes are full of empty holes, or if you just can't get enough of bangles, French hooks, hoops, and studs, stop by Earrings by Lisa! to find handmade bobs for your lobes. Visitors can browse images of the earrings and reserve them online. Payment is made through the mail. Sorry, no virtual piercing available (yet).

Energy Efficient Environments
http://www.mcs.net/~energy/home.html

Energy Efficient Environments, Inc. is a retailer of "environmentally friendly" products. Visitors are invited to browse the company's online catalogs of cleaners, energy-saving goods, and household items.

Faucet Outlet Online
http://www.faucet.com/faucet/

This is the online pipeline to kitchen and bathroom faucets. Faucet Outlet makes its catalog of faucets and other plumbing accessories, complete with prices, available at this site, along with information on plumbing basics and tips on choosing a faucet.

FlowersUSA
http://flowersusa.com/flowers2.html

Sure, FlowersUSA offers a huge selection of plants and flower arrangements, but they also carry a full line of fruit and gourmet baskets, candy, balloons, and other gifts. Same-day service is available for U.S. deliveries, and the company offers an online reminder service.

FolkArt & Craft Exchange
http://www.folkart.com/

The FolkArt & Craft Exchange, a service of Sunnyvale, Calif.-based arts promoter Latitude International, provides a forum for buying and selling hand-made crafts by indigenous peoples throughout the world.

Gallery of American Artisans
http://www.usa.net/gallery/
The Gallery of American Artisans offers a collection of hand-crafted gifts and accessories. The site includes an electronic catalog, ordering information, and artisans' bios.

Grapes
http://www.grapes-wineline.com/
This site for "America's Top Rated Wine Selection Specialists" showcases different wine regions of the world, and includes features such as wine finds of the month, a gift service, and monthly specials.

Indian River Gift Fruit Company
http://www.giftfruit.com/
Shop here for citrus from Florida—grapefruit, oranges, tangelos—flowers, and meats (ham and turkey). The wide variety of gift possibilities include no-frills packs, baskets, and fruit clubs.

Jan's Custom Knits
http://www.puffin.com/puffin
If you've got a hankering to give your new grandchild a personalized baby blanket but you can't knit, you might consider this option. Order a custom-made blanket (or other item) at this site and let your children think you made it yourself. Many designs are available in a variety of languages.

Khazana - India Arts Online
http://khazana.com/
Khazana, a Minneapolis, Minn.-based retailer of collectibles from India and Nepal, maintains this site containing general information abouts its wares and services. Visit here to view its wide range of handmade ornaments, statues, and more.

Kosher Express
http://www.marketnet.com/mktnet/kosher
Stumped for the holiday feast? The Matzah Market offers a range of kosher culinary delights, including recipes for the essential kugel, potato knish, and mandelbrot. You can fax in an order for bagels, kishka mix, or gefilte fish selected from the online catalog.

Lamp Technology, Inc.
http://www.webscope.com/lamptech/info.html
Lamp Technology, Inc., located in Bohemia, N.Y., offers over 10,000 types of light bulbs at discounted prices, with product and pricing information, interesting facts about lighting, and an order/catalog request form.

The Master's Collection
http://www.joes.com/masters/index.html
If you've always wanted your own Degas, Pollock, Monet, or Van Gogh, but can't afford the multimillion dollar price tags, check out The Master's Collection. This firm offers framed oil replicas on canvas that they claim are "virtually indistinguishable from an original oil painting." Take a leisurely browse through the catalog or check the artist listing to find, among dozens of other offerings, a copy of Van Gogh's *Sunflowers* for under $500.

Michigan Marketing Association Earthy Delights Home Page
http://earthy.com/index.htm
The Michigan Marketing Association (MMA) distributes specialty produce to restaurants, clubs, hotels, and the "adventurous gourmet." Sample MMA's top-shelf products, including hot chiles and Southwest cuisine, baby vegetables, edible flowers, and purple sticky rice.

Mighty Dog Designs
http://sashimi.wwa.com/~notime/mdd/mddhome.html
Mighty Dog Designs (self-proclaimed "cyber.outfitters") of Anderson, S.C. supplies vibrant images and information on its T-shirts and coffee mugs. Great designs announce to the world that you're wired to the Net. An online ordering form is included.

Native American Art Gallery, Ltd.
http://www.info1.com:80/NAAG/
Here's a source for unusual gifts such as spirit masks, drums, Kachina dolls, flutes, and other items hand-crafted by Native American artisans. As a bonus, the site includes biographical info about the artists, and paragraphs explaining the history and symbolism of each item.

Naturally Yours

http://www.america.com/mall/store/
naturally.html

Based in Daytona Beach, Fla., Naturally Yours promotes health and better eating through its varied selections of natural organic grains, berries, sprouts, and uncooked honey. Visit this electronic storefront to shop or link to pages offering recipes, health guides, and more.

Online Sports

http://www.onlinesports.com/

Online Sports is a collection of sports-related products and services available via the Internet, including links to various sports resources on the Web, and the Online Sports business center.

Pacific Coast

http://www.pacificcoast.com/

The Seattle-based Pacific Coast company offers a full line of high-quality goose down products (pillows, comforters, feather beds) for comfortable sleeping. Sweet dreams are just ahead.

Rayco Tennis Shop

http://www.cts.com/~tennisa1

Ray's Tennis Shop specializes in volume closeout merchandise. Visitors here can browse its online catalog and order via e-mail, fax, phone, or snail mail.

Sophisticated Shirts

http://www.a1.com/shirt/t shirt.html

This online shop sells "artistic" T-shirts and sweatshirts (Einstein, Shakespeare, Julius Caesar, and many more). Visit their promotional site for shirt previews and ordering information.

Spice Merchant

http://emall.com/Spice/Spice1.html

Cooks and spice specialists can harvest those hard-to-find spices at this online source. Find Chinese condiments, Thai and Indonesian specialties, and Indian spices and teas. Order online.

Virtual Vineyards

http://www.virtualvin.com/

Virtual Vineyards gives advice on how to buy the gourmet foods and fine wines recommended by renowned wine expert, Peter Granoff. Visit this site to use Peter's trademarked tasting chart and to order food and wine selections online.

White Rabbit Toys

http://www.toystore.com/

The "Internet's first full service, specialty toy store" specializes in high-quality, international toys that "help children to create, learn, imagine, and explore." A good site to check when you need a birthday gift for your grandchild.

Chapter 17

CITIZENRY AND COMMUNITY, ISSUES AND AFFAIRS

WHAT'S WRONG WITH THIS PICTURE?

UNCLE SAM WANTS YOU!

BACK TO BASICS

WHAT'S THE ANSWER?

HOT-BUTTON ISSUES

MAKING YOUR VOICE HEARD AND
YOUR EFFORTS COUNT

Maybe it's because we have been marinating in the pot of life a little longer, steeping and learning a little more than the average bear, but I find that Seniors in my acquaintance, as well as those posting to Senior-Net, seem to hold very strong views on important issues of the day and are very well informed about them. It could be that we have more time to ruminate about things that affect our larger community, or we have witnessed experiments in justice that have not worked. Whatever the reason, none of us minds telling it like it is ... and emphatically!

> "What do you think would happen if a specific TV or news station, such as ABC/NBC/CBS, or even better, CNN, would get several thousand letters or faxes from the senior citizens? Do you think they would assign someone to investigate it? The key here would be that on a given signal, all of the letters, etc., would have to be sent within a short period of time to the same location.
>
> "WHAT A FIRE THAT WOULD START, PARTICULARLY IF IT INVOLVED A SINGLE ISSUE THAT ALL OF US ADDRESSED AT THE SAME TIME.
>
> "I don't know of any other way to start a clamor over a subject than to get the press involved."

WHAT'S WRONG WITH THIS PICTURE?

The divisive issues facing this country and our communities are myriad; the arguments are shrill and emotions are at a fever pitch. We have become a nation of Greedy Guts. But underneath all this hollering and screaming, it seems to me that most of the hoopla is caused by two types of people: those who are afraid of losing a piece of the pie (corporate lobbying, the whole capital gains roller coaster, middle-

Lizzie Sez
Don't expect other people to take your advice and ignore your example.

class endowments, welfare, the militia movement), and those who want to legislate other people's morality (abortion, gay issues, criminal justice).

This country was founded by rebels, and no one will uphold our privilege (notice I did not say right) to protest any louder than I will. But we've reached the point that the competing voices of our protesting citizens have stalled the government. We've splintered into so many special interest self-interests that essentially no one is satisfied by the compromises, and our government just limps along—placating some here, some there, but doing little for the overall common good.

UNCLE SAM WANTS YOU!

Remember that? The common good? Remember what it was like during the War? Can you remember any time since then when this country has been as united toward a common goal? As a country, we were willing to make sacrifices. Here in the States, virtually everyone did his or her part to conserve, ration, and equip the military. Most of our men were overseas—voluntarily. Talk about patriotism. Talk about unity.

But let's not forget the price. War is a horrible thing: People DIE, lives are destroyed, and in the midst of war, the distinctions between the "good guys" and the "bad guys" become blurred and indistinguishable, like so much smoke on the battlefield.

No, war is not the answer, but it is a useful metaphor. Our country is experiencing a civil war of sorts right now that will not end until its citizens realize that their competing claims, their clamoring for preferences, and their hate-filled rhetoric are destroying any progress toward the common good. No one is willing to make sacrifices anymore.

"You are so correct. Everything is becoming a "right" to anyone who thinks he should have something. I pulled the Bill of Rights down on the Internet and read it carefully. The rights are very specific. There's no "right" to medical care but many claim there is. Nor to dental care, nor a good haircut or a good manicure.

"Quoted: "...one has the right to become head of corporation." Nonsense. If that's true, we have hundreds of millions of people being deprived of their right. There aren't enough corporations to go around. One may find the "opportunity" to become head of a corporation but it certainly isn't a right.

"I think I'll go exercise my right to a scotch and water before dinner."

BACK TO BASICS

So what is the common good? I contend that the definition of the common good is right there in the Declaration of Independence, in a sentence so well worn that it has become a cliché: "We hold these truths to be self-evident, that all men are created equal, that they are endowed by their Creator with certain unalienable rights, that among these are life, liberty and the pursuit of happiness."

So what do these words mean for us on the brink of the twenty-first century? As I see it, the issues basically come down to two:

- Ensuring equality under the law for all. And if equality can only be gained through affirmative action programs, then so be it.

  Let me tell you a little story about affirmative action. When my daughter began working in the early '70s, she discovered that even though she was a full-time salaried employee, pregnancy benefits were not available to her under the company's medical plan. None of the women who worked at that company (and most of the employees were women) was covered. The wives of the MEN who worked there, however, were covered for pregnancy. My daughter and several other women lobbied for an extension of the benefits several times. Each attempt met with failure because, as the financial officer explained, "It's too expensive." The company refused voluntary compliance. Guess what it took to get equal benefits for the female employees? Yep, government action.

- Ensuring each citizen the right to live as he or she pleases, as long as the lifestyle choice hurts no one else.

  Here's where we start to tangle with the ultra-right, who claim that the moral fabric of this country has unraveled. Their solution is to legislate everything from school prayer, to abortion, to the treatment of gays and lesbians. Maybe the country's morality is in tatters, but I don't think it's because kids aren't mumbling rote "Our Fathers" along with the Pledge of Allegiance every morning before school starts, nor do I think it's because gay people want to get married. Nope, the moral crisis in this country can be traced to one cause: a near-complete lack of personal and corporate responsibility.

  Corporate irresponsibility is the reason our movie and television screens are filled with unspeakable violence. Personal irresponsibility is the reason there's even a market for these shows and the reason children are allowed to watch them. Want more examples? Corporate irresponsibility is the reason our environment is close to destruction. Personal irresponsibility is the reason our children are out of control, our divorce rates are sky-high, and our streets are unsafe.

I could go on in this vein until my voice gives out, but you get the picture. The fallacy of the ultra-right is that they have confused morality with responsibility. Can you legislate private morality? No, I don't think so, nor does the Constitution give you the right. Can you legislate responsibility? To a limited degree, yes, as in environmental protection laws, but the ground gets really shaky beyond that point, because then you're moving into sacrosanct areas such as censorship and individual liberties.

Our Bill of Rights gives us a lot of room; the problem is that too many people push the envelope way beyond the limits of the common good, and then loudly proclaim their "right" to carry concealed weapons, their "right" to produce blood-soaked television shows, their "right" as white Americans to march through a black neighborhood wearing sheets over their faces. Each of these actions may be a "right," folks, but that doesn't mean that they're right.

WHAT'S THE ANSWER?

I believe that most of us will agree that nothing good comes from hate. Screaming at one another across the sidewalk, across the Internet, or in community meetings, accomplishes nothing. The first answer is to purge ourselves of hatred.

The second answer is to adopt a live-and-let-live attitude. We should learn the other side's point of view and accept the fact that we're not all going to agree. And most important, we should avoid trying to shove our attitudes and beliefs down each other's throats. Let's save our rhetoric and resistance for the times when the other side attempts to *directly* influence our lives by their legislative manipulations.

And finally, let's make a difference when we can. This chapter is filled with pointers to positive groups of many types that are working on real problems and

Lizzie's Tips

Computers are supposed to make our lives easier, but sometimes they can make us crazy. If your screen freezes, what do you do besides tear out your hair?

- Check your keyboard and mouse cables. If they are loose your screen will appear to freeze.

- Force your program to quit. If you have not saved your material, you will lose it. Mac users should press Option, Command, and Escape all at the same time.

- Perform a warm start using Control, Option, and Restart. If you have not saved your work, you will lose it.

- Turn off the machine as a last resort after all else has failed. If you have persistent freezes, you may have to call an expert or perform more complicated troubleshooting tasks.

attempting to find solutions to environmental messes, poverty, inequality, and government ineptitude. Let's get involved, but let's pursue a positive course that works toward the common—rather than the individual—good.

"How about becoming an Ombudsman? This is a program under the "Council on Aging," and every state has one. Ombudsmen are volunteer advocates for nursing home residents. After taking training (about 34 hours), the Ombudsmen are certified and assigned to a nursing home in their area. Takes about 2 to 4 hours a week, depending. You don't have to be a nurse or in the medical profession to be an Ombudsman. All you need is the time and compassion."

HOT-BUTTON ISSUES

SOMETHING BORROWED, SOMETHING BLUE

One of the most controversial issues of the moment is the legislative clamor over same-sex marriage. On March 6, 1996, the Missouri Senate Civil and Criminal Jurisprudence Committee voted to pass Senate Bill 895, outlawing same-sex marriages. As of this writing, the bill had not yet reached the senate floor for a vote. Yet at about the same time, San Francisco decided to recognize same-sex "domestic partnerships" as legal, and hundreds of homosexual couples rushed to tie the knot in a group ceremony, graciously presided over by the city's controversial Mayor Willie Brown.

Meanwhile, in September 1996, the U.S. Senate passed the anti-gay Defense of Marriage Act (DOMA). The following December, the First Circuit Court in Hawaii awarded gays and lesbians a preliminary victory in that state by ruling that same-sex marriage would be recognized under the state's constitution, unless a "compelling state interest" in discrimination was established in a lower court. This issue will continue to be played out in the Hawaiian courts and is being closely followed by gay activist groups.

I sit here, an old timer, in an eccentric inner-city neighborhood populated by artists, writers, and young professionals—many of whom are gay—and wonder what all the fuss is about.

Most of my gay friends have lived in stable relationships for many years. They are productive, good people, and solid citizens. They provide goods and services to the local economy and contribute beauty and immense creativity to this community. What of them, who cannot find any instrument to protect their relationships from legal vandalism? Many lose their homes and possessions to insensitive and greedy families when a partner dies because they are not protected as heterosexual partners are. Nothing is more heart-wrenching than to witness avaricious relatives swarming into the home, relieving the grieving partner of all he once owned, including a place to sleep.

To help this issue along, I have come up with my own solution: Let's try "parriage" instead.

Forget about the word marriage altogether. The way to protect any gay union is to negotiate a formal, legal partnership just as many businesses do. This partnership would be recognized as a legal entity, binding and protective of both partners' assets. All properties, money, furnishings, and personal belongings would fall within the jurisdiction of the legal partnership, and would therefore be safe from invading relatives. What do you think about that?

To give you a window into the problems and discrimination faced by gays and lesbians in this country, click over to these sites:

Civil Rights or Special Rights?
http://www.cnn.com/US/9605/21/gay.reax/index.html
Although this 1996 news story concerns the Supreme Court's decision to strike down the Colorado amendment to ban discrimination laws aimed at protecting homosexuals, it effectively encapsulates the two opposing points of view and reflects a much wider constituency than simply the voters in Colorado. The site includes links to related sites and invites feedback.

Gay & Lesbian Alliance Against Defamation (GLAAD)
http://www.glaad.org/glaad/
Billed as the "Lesbian and Gay News Bureau" and a national multimedia watchdog organization, this site is a good source of info on current issues facing the gay and lesbian population, including same-sex marriage and unflattering or stereotypical portrayals in the media. Even-

handed and professional, this site avoids inflammatory rhetoric and instead focuses on clear, fact-based presentations of news stories and action alerts.

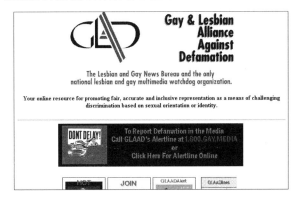

Partners Task Force for Gay and Lesbian Couples
http://www.buddybuddy.com/

This site provides one of the best, most comprehensive looks at the issue of same-sex marriage. Links include both personal essays on the subject and excerpts from the Defense of Marriage Act arguments from the *Congressional Record*. Read John Kerry's argument that "this debate is fundamentally ugly, and it is fundamentally political, and it is fundamentally flawed," and Ted Kennedy's assertion that "This bill is designed to divide Americans." Legal updates, information resources, and background provide a good basis for understanding the fundamental issues at stake for gay couples.

> "When are we going to take our country back? We certainly sit back and let the radicals have their say and many times they change things. (Not necessarily for the better, either.) We are too dignified to scream and holler over the injustices we suffer. Isn't it time we show a little leg?"

CAPITAL PUNISHMENT

I was leafing through *Interview* magazine a few months ago, and a colorful advertising supplement stopped me in my tracks with the electrifying statement, "If there were a public execution, would you

KEEP SAFE

Older folks are often at a higher risk for crime, but there are steps you can take to help keep safe. To start, check out the Rate Your Risk pages at http://www.nashville.net/~police/risk/. Written by a police lieutenant in Nashville, this site provides threat assessment tests that will help you determine your chances of becoming a crime victim. The site includes links to a multimedia violence reduction game, self-defense tips, and other crime prevention pages.

go watch it?" The next page blared, "What would you wear?" And the next page continued, "Use your head."

Would you go?

The death penalty has always stimulated vociferous debate, and the prevailing attitudes change as the political climate changes. Most people hold an unshakable opinion on this issue.

Many proponents of capital punishment are motivated by fear (and the hope that harsh punishment will act as a deterrent to violent crime) or by feelings of vengeance and retribution (the families of murder victims). The opponents of capital punishment point out the inherent moral conflict in murder (state-sanctioned or not) and the very real possibility that innocent people may be put to death.

There's no question that senseless crime is rampant. There's no question that the criminal justice and prison systems in this country are riddled with loopholes and inequalities. But think of crime and the justice system as shards of broken glass on a trail. The death penalty is a band-aid, an after-the-fact—and largely ineffectual—attempt to stop the bleeding. Our country's problems of violence and the criminal justice system require pro-action, not reaction. To keep from cutting our feet, we have to pick the glass up off the trail before we step on it.

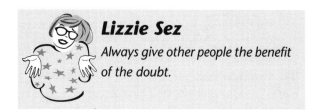

Lizzie Sez
Always give other people the benefit of the doubt.

OUR CHILDREN ARE AT RISK

The causes of most violent crime are tied up in issues of personal responsibility and social disenfranchisement. These problems seem to defy solution. Children are abused or neglected and are denied (through poverty, indifference, and lack of education) a chance to participate in the mainstream. Our comfortable, middle-class lives are as foreign and as unimaginable to them as theirs are to us. These children grow up, grow angry, and grow violent.

Other than individual intervention programs such as Head Start, Foster Grandparents, Big Brothers and Sisters, and others, these children have no safety net. And many children get no help at all.

NOT EXACTLY A CHAIN GANG, BUT ...

Our social problems may defy solution, but the criminal justice system—particularly the prisons—is a good candidate for wholesale reform. We hear a lot about prisoners' rights these days, and I certainly don't think that prisoners should be tortured or starved, but I do think that crime should carry a stiff price. How about making prisons self-sustaining? Every inmate should be required to work toward the up-keep and maintenance of the facility, to produce food, and to make goods for sale. These products can be sold, along with any excess food, to obtain operating money for the facility. Every prisoner serves his or her full sentence and every prisoner has a choice: work or don't eat. You can think of this plan as an extended form of community service. No tax money would be spent on prisons. If the prisoners can't make it, grow it, or buy it, they can't have it. How about my solution as an alternative to lethal injection?

WHAT OTHERS ARE SAYING

I found far more anti-capital punishment sites on the Web than pro, but here are some pointers to what others think about the death penalty.

Abolition Now!
http://www.abolition-now.com/

The goal of Abolition Now! is to abolish capital punishment. To that end, the site includes a number of facts and figures, arguments against the practice, state listings, case stories of inmates who were executed despite evidence of their innocence, and stomach-turning descriptions of executions that didn't go exactly as planned.

Capital Punishment: The Death Penalty
http://web.canlink.com/ocrt/
execute.htm#forcp

This interesting site presents text from both Hebrew and Christian scriptures (the Old and New Testaments) relevant to the death penalty. People on both sides of the argument can find justification here, but the summary section detailing reasons for and against capital punishment is weighted on the anti side.

Justice Against Crime Talking
http://users.deltanet.com/users/ghc/

There's no denying the anguish of this family over the murder of their daughter, and the appeal at this site is a two-pronged argument for both capital punishment and swift justice. Most of the focus is on California issues, but you'll find contact information for a number of national "pro-justice" organizations.

THE COMMUNICATIONS DECENCY ACT

The Communications Decency Act of 1995 was introduced by Sen. Jim Exon (D-NE) and included in the larger telecommunications deregulation bill (S.652) that was passed into law in February 1996. A firestorm of protest has surrounded this attempt to censor the Internet, and the ACLU led a successful suit (brought by a total of 27 plaintiffs) against its provisions. In June 1996, a federal court in Pennsylvania granted an injunction against the law, pronouncing it unconstitutional and a violation of First Amendment rights. On December 6, 1966, the United States Supreme Court agreed to hear the government's appeal, and the case is expected to appear on the docket sometime in spring 1997.

So what's so bad about this bill that merely wants to protect minors from offensive and obscene material on the Internet? Well, everything.

First, the CDA is censorship. And censorship, no matter what its purported lofty goal, is unhealthy. It provides too much power over what we can see and know to too few. The founders of this country considered free speech such an important right that they made it the first amendment. Not the third or the tenth, but the *first*. Any thinking person who reads the law can recognize the Constitutional conflict just as readily as those three federal judges in Pennsylvania.

Second, the CDA is an attempt to legislate private morality. But *whose* private morality? Who decides, exactly, what we should be able to see? The right? The left? The lobby with the most money? Are you willing to surrender your personal judgment to politics?

Third, the CDA is a poorly written law that effectively establishes different standards for material posted on the Internet than for printed materials such as newspapers, magazines, and books. Under the terms of the law, posting information on breast cancer and abortion could be considered a punishable violation. A short story containing a four-letter word, although acceptable in a magazine or journal, could be grounds for prosecution under the CDA if the story is posted on the Internet.

We all know that obscene, violent, and tasteless sites exist in cyberspace. But the issue comes down to the same old watchwords: personal responsibility. I haven't the slightest interest in pornography, bomb recipes, or government subversion, so none of these sites has ever been displayed on my computer screen. We can each make our own choices.

And as far as children are concerned, where are their parents? Either the parents can supervise their kids' surfing (now there's a novel idea!) or use any number of highly effective software packages designed to lock out offensive material.

Here are a number of sites that reflect both sides of the CDA argument. Use them to become more informed about this latest challenge to the First Amendment, and to make up your own mind about the suitability of this governmental censorship attempt.

Computer Pornography Questions and Answers
http://www.townhall.com/townhall/FRC/infocus/if95k4pn.html
The Family Research Council comes out in favor of the CDA at this site, maintaining essentially that parents are not technologically savvy enough to protect their children from offensive material. According to this site, "They [the ACLU and other "ideological groups"] fight virtually any legislative restriction on materials distributed on-line, and want to dump all responsibility for action into the laps of parents, many of whom are far less technologically capable than their children."

Electronic Frontier Foundation
http://www.eff.org/
This group stays on top of several cutting issues including censorship, privacy, encryption, and copyright. The links to censorship-related sites include pointers to bulletins from the Citizens Internet Empowerment Coalition, a leading opponent of the law.

June 12, 1996 Decision in ACLU vs. Reno
http://www.eff.org/Alerts/HTML/960612_aclu_v_reno_decision.html
Here's the text of the Pennsylvania decision in which three federal judges granted a preliminary injunction against the law and declared its provisions unconstitutional.

Law and Order Comes to Cyberspace

http://web.mit.edu/afs/athena/org/t/
techreview/www/articles/oct95/Diamond.html

This fascinating article, written in 1995 by Edwin Diamond and Stephen Bates, covers several key issues and discusses test cases related to censorship, accountability, and copyright on the Internet.

Senator J.J. Exon's Letter to the *Washington Post*

http://www.eff.org/pub/Censorship/Exon_bill/
s314_hr1004_95_exon_post.letter

The senator who introduced the CDA defends his actions and his bill in this letter to the *Post*.

Speak Freely, Act Responsibly

http://www.pageturners.com/CDA/

A CDA supporter posts his argument at this site, along with ideas for implementation designed to placate folks on both sides of the issue.

Telecommunications Act of 1996 (S.652)

http://thomas.loc.gov/cgi-bin/query/
z?c104:s.652.enr:

Don't take everybody else's word for it; read the law yourself. Here's the full text courtesy of the Library of Congress site, THOMAS. Look for the CDA in Title V.

Voters Telecommunications Watch

http://www.vtw.org/

This nonprofit watchdog organization that follows telecommunications and civil liberties legislation roundly denounced the Communications Decency Act. The site includes files that provide insight into the act, a lobbying guide, and organizing tips.

MAKING YOUR VOICE HEARD AND YOUR EFFORTS COUNT

As I promised earlier in this chapter, I've identified a number of positive-focus organizations that could use your help in their efforts. I have intentionally left out groups with any kind of exclusionary focus, so you won't find the white supremacists here. That's not to say that the groups I've included don't have a political agenda; many do. But their work is geared more toward positive change than disenfranchisement and hatred.

> "When I retired, I decided that I would 'Give Back.' I belong to the Salvation Army Women's Auxiliary; this group of women raises funds to support the programs of the Salvation Army. More volunteers are needed. I have really enjoyed working with all the women in the Auxiliary. It's fun and makes a real contribution to those who need it most."

No matter if your interests lie with social issues, environmental depredation, or legislative debacles, you'll find an organization (or two or three) in this directory that can help you make a difference.

ANIMAL RIGHTS

Animal Rights Resource Site

http://envirolink.org/arrs/index.html

Here's a great site to help you understand the many facets of animal rights. Along with a general FAQ, you'll find a position paper and FAQ on vegetarianism, a leather alternatives FAQ, and a manual of animal rights. Journals, essays, photos, news briefs, and other resources help this organization make its compelling case.

Defenders of Wildlife

http://www.defenders.org/

Defenders of Wildlife led the charge to return the wolf to Yellowstone. The organization also fights to keep the Endangered Species Act intact and champions other wildlife issues. Visitors to this home page can become keyboard activists by reading action alerts and firing off e-mail to officials.

Farm Animal Reform Movement
http://envirolink.org/arrs/farm/index.htm

The Farm Animal Reform Movement (FARM) is a national organization that promotes plant-based eating and farm-animal rights through grassroots campaigns throughout the United States. Visit their page to learn about their mission, history, and programs; to find out how to get involved; and to link to a number of related sites.

Welcome To FARM

FARM (Farm Animal Reform Movement) campaigns for the rights of farmed animals, promotes wholesome plant-based eating, and encourages environmental consciousness. FARM conducts five national programs, including the Great American Meatout

PETA Online—People for the Ethical Treatment of Animals
http://www.envirolink.org/arrs/peta/

You may not agree with their methods—and there's no doubt that these people are *extreme*—but PETA has certainly brought the plight of misused, tortured, and sacrificed animals into the bright, cold light of national scrutiny. This page has loads of animal info, fact sheets, action alerts, and practical suggestions you can use to help animals.

Save-a-Pet Online
http://pasture.ecn.purdue.edu/~laird/Dogs/Rescue/

Save-a-Pet Online, a page at the Purdue Dogs site, provides a list of online dog, cat, and bunny rescue organizations, along with heart-warming stories about saved animals.

CHILD ADVOCACY

Big Brothers Big Sisters of America
http://www.bbbsa.org/

"For over 90 years, a caring adult in the life of a child" explains the simple concept behind Big Brothers Big Sisters. A landmark study in the early '90s showed that Little

Brothers and Little Sisters were 46 percent less likely to begin using illegal drugs, 27 percent less likely to begin using alcohol, and 53 percent less likely to skip school. Who can argue with success rates like these? Find out how to become involved and make a significant difference in the life of a child.

Children Now
http://www. childrennow.org

This national advocacy organization peppers its site with startling facts about children in America. For example, in 1993, 15.8 million children lived below the federal poverty level and experienced hunger; in 1992, 43.2 per 1,000 children (4 percent) were reported as abused or neglected. To find out what you can do to reverse this trend, check out the excellent site feature called There are Hundreds of Ways to Help America's Children: How to Help in Your Community, and learn other ways to become a child advocate.

Children's Defense Fund
http://www.tmn.com/cdf/index.html

The Children's Defense Fund pays "particular attention to the needs of poor, minority, and disabled children." Their stated goal is "to educate the nation about the needs of children and encourage preventive investment in children before they get sick, drop out of school, suffer family breakdown, or get into trouble." Focus issues include the programs of Healthy Start, Head Start, Safe Start, and others. Find out how you can "stand for children everyday" by following the Fund's suggestions for 10 Things You Can Do to Help Children.

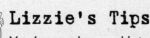

Lizzie's Tips

You've sunk a wad into a 28,800 modem and now the technology has produced 33,600 modems. Don't gnash your teeth. Maybe you can upgrade your modem with software. The U.S. Robotics Winmodem, for example, can be upgraded. Contact the manufacturer of your modem or check the company's Web site.

Children's Protection and Advocacy Coalition

http://www.geocities.com/CapitolHill/3581/

The focus of this organization is on providing better protection for children who have been victims of sexual abuse. Action alerts, background info, and suggestions for becoming involved in the advocacy movement are detailed at this site.

KidsPeace

http://www.kidspeace.org/main.html

KidsPeace is dedicated to "creating opportunities for kids in crisis to become kids who overcome." This goal is pursued through medical, intervention, and educational programs on campuses and in communities throughout the United States. Learn more about their mission and objectives at this informational site.

National Committee to Prevent Child Abuse

http://www.childabuse.org/

Learn about the advocacy efforts and the prevention and education programs sponsored by this nationwide organization and learn how to become involved in the fight against child abuse.

United Children's Fund

http://www.cais.com/childfund/

One of the programs sponsored by the United Children's Fund is Rescue America, an entrepreneurial program for teenagers (much like Junior Achievement) that

emphasizes a "can-do" spirit and job creation. Find out more about the program, how to help establish a network in your own community, and how to nominate your grandchild or an at-risk child for the program.

CIVIL LIBERTIES AND CIVIC RESPONSIBILITY

American Civil Liberties Union Freedom Network

http://www.aclu.org/

The actions of the ACLU may sometimes make you madder than a hornet's nest, but there's no disputing the fact that this Bill of Rights watchdog is "the nation's foremost advocate of individual rights"—and they mean *everybody's* individual rights, whether you agree or not. Nonpartisan and nonprofit, the ACLU, since 1920, has taken cases on hot-button issues that run the gamut from free speech for neo-Nazis to affirmative action for minorities. Learn more about threats to your rights and how to become a "card-carrying member of the ACLU."

Citizens Against Government Waste

http://www.govt-waste.org/

This organization claims to have over 600,000 members united in the common cause of identifying and eliminating wasteful practices in government. This site includes research resources, a "pork" watch for the upcoming legislative session, and membership info.

Electronic Privacy Information Center

http://epic.org/

The Electronic Privacy Information Center is a public interest research center in Washington, D.C., established to address the issues of civil liberties relating to national ID cards, medical record privacy, and the sale of consumer data. The site includes a link to Privacy International.

League of Women Voters of the United States

http://www.lwv.org/~lwvus/

Education and information are the two hallmarks of the nonpartisan (but definitely not nonpolitical) League of Women Voters who encourage all Americans to participate in their government. The League provides a number of tools to help each voter become more informed and a summary of their legislative priorities.

National Civic League
http://www.ncl.org/ncl/

"Creating communities that work for everyone" is the aim of the National Civic League. Founded by Theodore Roosevelt, the nonprofit outlines its initiatives to revitalize communities and posts a list of its publications, which include "Model City Charter" and "Measuring City Hall Performance."

Public Citizen
http://www.essential.org/orgs/public_citizen/

The stated purpose of this group—founded by consumer advocate Ralph Nader—is to "fight for safer drugs and medical devices, cleaner and safer energy sources, a cleaner environment, and a more open and democratic government." A summary page lists Public Citizen's most significant successes over the past 25 years. Their lobbying efforts have included the push for labels warning of Reye's Syndrome on aspirin, support of the campaign finance bill, and efforts toward the ban on silicone gel breast implants. Concerned citizens are invited to join.

Vote Smart Web
http://www.vote-smart.org/

This nonprofit "one-stop shopping center for political information" provides fact-based, nonpartisan info on voting records, candidate biographies, election results, and more. Read about the organization, access its databases, and learn how to become a member.

THE ENVIRONMENT

Creating Land Trusts: Help Conserve Our Land and Natural Resources
http://www.possibility.com/LandTrust/

Quietly and without fanfare, some 900 land trusts have protected—forever—nearly 3 million acres of land in America. This page explains how to form a land trust and details a trust's basic preservation tools: conservation easements and land donations.

Environmental Working Group
http://www.ewg.org/

The Environmental Working Group researches a wide range of environmental issues. Visit here for scientific, political, and economic looks at farming, pesticides, drinking water, and much more.

Friends of the Earth Home Page
http://www.foe.co.uk/

The Friends of the Earth is an environmental group that aims to alert the public about known chemical releases. Visitors can gather information and view maps of chemical release sites, learn about the group's worldwide chapters, and join Friends of the Earth here.

Friends of the Environment
http://www.fef.ca/

Canada's Friends of the Environment Foundation funds community environmental projects across the country. Visit here for an overview of the foundation, application guidelines, and online press releases.

Greenpeace International
http://www.greenpeace.org/

Greenpeace is an organization devoted to identifying, confronting, and proposing solutions to global environmental problems. Visitors to the group's home page will find membership information, descriptions of current campaigns, and a searchable index of Greenpeace articles and publications.

National Parks and Conservation Association
http://www.npca.org/home/npca/

The National Parks and Conservation Association is a private, nonprofit watchdog of the nation's parks. Visitors here will learn about the association's park preservation and maintenance efforts at both the grassroots and national levels.

The Natural Resources Defense Council
http://www.nrdc.org

The Natural Resources Defense Council fights for the environment in the courts and the halls of Congress. It dispenses environmental news, opinion, and mobilization information here, where browsers can keep up with the current status of the clean air campaign, pending legislation, and other issues. The site also includes a list of NRDC's books and magazines and information on how to become a member.

The Nature Conservancy
http://www.tnc.org/

The Nature Conservancy bills itself as "Nature's real estate agent." This group preserves habitats and species "by buying the lands and waters they need to survive": over 1,500 nature preserves (9.5 million acres protected since 1953; 1.3 million acres managed by the Conservancy) in the United States alone. Learn how the Conservancy identifies land for purchase, watch a video of the group's beginning, or learn how you can get involved with this worthwhile environmental watchdog.

OceanVoice International
http://www.conveyor.com/oceanvoice.html

The Canada-based conservation and environmental organization Ocean Voice International promotes harmony between people, marine life, and the environment. This site includes background about the organization, its history, and its mission, as well as information on how to get involved.

Sierra Club
http://www.sierraclub.org/

Since 1892 the Sierra Club has worked to protect "America's vast natural heritage" for current and succeeding generations. Their efforts include legislative initiatives, educational programs, local chapters, outings, and more. Visit their home page for the rest of the story.

HUMANITARIAN ORGANIZATIONS

Amnesty International
http://www.io.org/amnesty/

This high-profile human rights activist organization highlights rights violations and abuses by prominently featuring new cases in the Stop Press section. The Campaigns area explains the organization's various efforts to expose and stop human rights abuses. Visit this site to become a member of AI or to contribute to the organization's current campaigns.

The Carter Center
http://www.emory.edu/CARTER_ CENTER/ homepage.htm

The home page of Jimmy and Rosalynn Carter's progressive public policy institute offers an overview of the center's efforts in fighting disease, hunger, poverty, and oppression worldwide. Access details of the African

Governance Program, a child survival and development task force, and the Carters' much-publicized urban revitalization initiatives.

Food For The Hungry: Virtual Learning Center
http://www.fh.org/

Hunger-relief programs worldwide are described on the Arizona-based charity Food for the Hungry home page. Also here are links to famine statistics and information on how to sponsor a child in the Third World.

Habitat for Humanity
http://www.habitat.org/

Habitat is dedicated to eliminating poverty housing and homelessness. Since 1976, volunteers worldwide have built or renovated more than 50,000 homes that were sold to low-income families and financed with interest-free mortgages. Use this site to find a Habitat affiliate in your area and join the fight against substandard housing.

International Committee of the Red Cross
http://www.icrc.ch/

If there's a war or natural disaster anywhere in the world, you know the Red Cross will be there to provide medical care, relief services, and protection for at-risk civilian populations. Find out how the ICRC is financed, learn the scope of its humanitarian activities, check into volunteer opportunities, and discover how families are reunited by the Central Tracking Agency.

National Coalition for the Homeless
http://www2.ari.net/home/nch/

The story of one family's descent into homelessness—through no fault of their own—and their subsequent mauling at the hands of government aid organizations will wrench your heart. Visit this page to really learn about homelessness and find out how to become involved. The page includes a directory of state and national housing advocacy organizations.

PeaceNet
http://www.peacenet.apc.org/peacenet/

PeaceNet is a resource dedicated to peace, social justice, human rights, and the struggle against racism. The organization's home page explains its goals and posts news items about current world problems. Also find listings of related organizations like Amnesty International and the Center for Third World Organizing.

The Salvation Army International Headquarters
http://www.salvationarmy.org/

Founded in London in 1865, the Salvation Army has spread worldwide and continues its humanitarian work of housing the homeless, feeding the hungry, and assisting the elderly, along with its many other worthwhile programs. This site includes a brief history, organizational info, and program descriptions.

VISTA Home Page
http://libertynet.org/~zelson/vweb.h tml

Volunteers in Service to America (VISTA) is to America what the Peace Corps is to the developing world. If you want to get involved and actually make a one-on-one difference, VISTA may be your answer. Visitors here will learn about its volunteer programs that help the country's urban and rural poor. The site also includes news, local chapter listings, and links to other service-related resources.

SPECIFICALLY FOR SENIORS

AARP—American Association of Retired Persons
http://www.aarp.org/

The stated mission of the granddaddy of senior resources is to help seniors develop independent lifestyles with dignity and purpose. This page describes its volunteer and community programs, the benefits available to members, and its positions on issues and advocacy.

CARP—Canadian Association of Retired Persons

http://www.fifty-plus.net/

CARP is Canada's over-50 advocacy group dedicated to protecting the rights of its members, providing information on lifestyle choices and political issues, and obtaining discounts and special offers for members.

Environmental Alliance for Senior Involvement

http://www.easi.org/

EASI provides the "springboard by which senior citizens can become active, positive participants in determining the sustainability of their communities, their nation and their world." The site includes background on the organization, a newsletter, invitation to membership, and a number of pointers to environmental info on the Web.

National Senior Service Corps

http://www.cns.gov/senior.html

The federal Americorps program has a special division just for senior volunteers. The program include Foster Grandparents, Senior Companions, and Retired and Senior Volunteers. Foster Grandparents serve as mentors, tutors, and caregivers for children with special needs and work in schools, hospitals, and youth centers. Talk about a great way to fill up your extra time! Over half a million seniors devote time to these worthwhile programs. Find out how you can contribute.

Shepherd's Centers of America

http://www.qni.com/~shepherd/

Shepherd's Centers is an interfaith, nonprofit organization that maintains 100 independent centers throughout the United States and Canada. Holding to the philosophy that senior citizens are not frail, lonely, or dependent, the centers attempt to enrich the later years with opportunities for service to others, self-expression, and meaningful work. Sustaining close friendships and remaining independent are other goals the centers strive to fulfill for seniors.

Shepherd's Centers of America

Shepherd's Centers of America (SCA) is an interfaith, not-for-profit umbrella organization that coordinates nearly 100 independent Shepherd's Centers throughout the United States and Canada.

Shepherd's Centers reject the myth that senior citizens are frail, lonely and dependent, sliding down the hill to the end of life. People of all faiths work together in Shepherd's Centers to help older adults sustain and celebrate life. The primary purpose of a Shepherd's Center is to enrich the later years with opportunities for service to others, self-expression, meaningful work, and close friendships. An equally important goal is to help older adults remain independent in their own living situation as long as they choose.

Each center is planned and developed by the people who use it. At a typical center, you might see people learning foreign languages, studying local history, practicing tai chi or learning how to use a computer. Outside, in the neighborhood, you might find Shepherd's Center volunteers delivering meals, repairing houses and giving care-givers much-needed relief. And the people doing all of these things are older adults themselves.

United Seniors Association

http://www.unitedseniors.org/

This lobbying group for seniors describes itself as "the leading group for seniors who want to stop the 'raid' of the Social Security Trust Funds, cut taxes, and protect their Social Security and Medicare Benefits." The group details its lobbying efforts at this site and encourages membership by offering a number of benefits including discount long distance, prescription savings, and travel discounts.

Chapter 18

TAKE ME OUT TO THE BALL GAME

COUCH POTATOES AU GRATIN

GERONIMO!

THE SPORT OF KINGS

OLDER AND BOLDER

GENERAL SPORTS AND GAMBLING SITES

THE GAMING ARCADE

Many youngsters perceive us oldsters as little more than couch potatoes when it comes to sports participation. In my case, they are more right than wrong, as I spend too much time behind the computer and have so little discipline that I have belonged to a spa for eight months and have not gone to work out even once.

COUCH POTATOES AU GRATIN

This was not always so, however, as I was a great netwoman in varsity volleyball, loved to swim, and played golf and tennis until my knees cried "uncle." How I got into this vegetative state is beyond me.

My friend Maxine, age 85, still goes to her aerobics class three times a week religiously, and Virginia, at 68, swims five times a week without fail. She also walks one mile a day—even if there's snow on the ground! Lois, at 75, trains on the machines at her spa everyday. I am merely contemplating taking up a bit of yoga one day when I get around to it.

These women are an inspiration, and we all know that exercising will keep our hearts healthy and our bones strong. But somehow it is easier for me to watch sports these days than to be an active participant.

GERONIMO!

I am *really* ashamed of myself when I read about stouthearted 60-year-olds who skydive. Skydiving is the sport in which you hurl your body out of a moving plane and fall at about 120 miles an hour toward the ground 10,000 feet below.

The United States Parachute Association maintains that the sport is safe because modern equipment is high-tech, jumpsuits are designed by computers to adjust the freefall, and the new square canopies allow skydivers to hit the ground with the shock equivalent of stepping off a curb. However,

TAKING OFF FOR THE WILD BLUE YONDER

Here's contact information for the U.S. Parachute Association and the Skydivers Over Sixty club:

U.S. Parachute Association
1440 Duke Street
Alexandria, VA 22314
Telephone: 703-836-3495

Skydivers Over Sixty
3350 St. Francis Place
Long Beach, CA 90805
Telephone: 310-633-1226

you are warned to pay close attention and be in pretty fair physical condition before starting out.

According to the national director of the United States Parachute Association, 10 percent of its 32,000 members are seniors. In fact, a special group exists that caters exclusively to the mature skydiver. Skydivers Over Sixty (SOS) started in 1992 and now has 100 members from all over the world.

THE SPORT OF KINGS

My father was an accomplished horseman who appeared in many shows and exhibitions. When I was young, we both rode, preferring to hurtle over fences than gallop through the park. For many years, no matter where we were, we took in every horsey event we could find. I have witnessed steeple-chasing in Warrenton (the heart of Virginia's horse country), thrilled to jumpers vaulting over fences in Japan, been on the sidelines for the polo games in West Palm Beach, and enjoyed the flat racing in almost every city that has a track.

So my love of horse racing and horse sports goes back a long way. But even if you know nothing about horses or races, you can still have a pleasurable time

Lizzie's Tips

If you use Microsoft Word 6.0 and want to make samples of the fonts you have installed, choose Open from your File menu and navigate to the Macros folder. Open the file called Word 6.0 Macros, choose Macro from the Tools menu, and select FontSampleGenerator from the list. Choose the font size and character set you wish to be displayed. The Macro will display a font sampler document for you to view.

at the track these days. Most larger tracks are equipped with attractive boxes, excellent restaurants and bars, and comfortable seats.

If you are an admirer of horseflesh, there is no greater thrill than to watch these powerful animals pound into the home stretch on race day. Even if you don't place a bet, the air of excitement that surrounds the ritual of racing carries throughout the stands and will give you a lift. The track is a great place to spend the afternoon or evening; the good food, the anticipation, and the overall atmosphere will have you smiling and rooting for horses with bizarre names before you even know it. And it's *really* fun if you win!

THE HANDICAP

To see the race from start to finish, choose seats on the top floor of the track situated in the middle near the finish line, or watch the action from the restaurant. Most track restaurants are laid out for full-track viewing.

Lizzie Sez

Always have something beautiful nearby, even if it's just a daisy in a jelly jar.

Take plenty of tipping dollars with you. It is an old custom to tip the maître d' at least a fiver for a decent table; a bigger tip gets an even better table. Some tracks let the ushers seat patrons in boxes that are not being used by their owners that day. But you should know that boxes are essentially purchased from the usher for the right tip. Figure on slipping him at least $10.

If you are not an expert and are just visiting the track for a fun day, don't burden yourself by trying to figure out the statistics found in the *Daily Racing Form*, the track addict's bible. Just sit back and enjoy the horses, the jockeys, and the colorful atmosphere. You can pick up racing tips from the track program which usually costs about $2. The program includes information on the horses running that day, along with a rundown on how they performed in their last races, and will give you a little advice from the track handicapper.

The track handicapper will broadcast tips 15 minutes before the start of each race and will make a lively pitch for each horse. Listen also to the televised reports from trainers that provide information on horses that have never run before. The trainer reports include breeding info and can be very informative. Track tout sheets offer a few picks for each race as well. You can even visit the paddock area to watch the horses being paraded. Seeing the horses up close like this really helps you pick a favorite, even if your choice is based on a factor that has nothing to do with its ability to run, like the horse's colors. All these activities add to the exciting atmosphere of horse racing.

PLACE YOUR BETS!

No question, you will have more fun if you pick a few horses and make a few bets, even if they are small. Laying your money down at the betting window really puts you in the middle of the action and is much more exciting than passive participation. If you start attending often, you may want to delve into "The Sheets," which sell at most tracks for about $25. These sheets tell the horse's racing history and make it easier to spot a trend in his racing performance.

Whatever you do, decide how you want to place your bets before you approach the betting window. Don't expect the person taking bets to explain the system to you and don't wait until you're at the window to decide if you want to bet on *King Joseph* to win, place, or show! All bets must be placed within an allotted time limit before the next race starts. If you dawdle, the anxious people behind you will be pounding on you to hurry! At the window, call out your bet loudly, stating clearly the race number, the amount of your bet, and whether you are betting for win, place, or show. Give the number of the horse on the program, not his name or post position.

Just think, you could be a winner and begin another addiction! If you do win, be sure that you collect your winnings from the cashier and make sure the entire payoff is all there. Track cashiers count money in an unusual fashion; they start with the smallest bills instead of the largest. For example, $67 will be counted out with two one dollar bills first, followed by a five, then a ten, and finally a fifty. If you are in a hurry, you could leave some of your winnings at the window.

Now that you have a vague idea of how things work at most tracks, get out there and join the happy throng! Here are a few sites to get you started.

American Quarter Horse Association On-Line
http://www.aqha.com/

Based in Amarillo, Texas, the American Quarter Horse Association presents a page full of information about the horse's "colorful history." The site gallops from online racing and performance publications to show schedules and AQHA rules. Also find the quarter horse museum here.

LIZZIE'S EXPLANATION OF BETTING TERMS

Win—Horse comes in first.
Place—Horse comes in second or first.
Show—Horse comes in third, second, or first.
Exacta—Two horses come in first and second in that order.
Quinella—Two horses come in first and second in either order.
Trifecta—Three horses come in first, second, and third in that order.
Trifecta Box—Six bets are made for horses to finish first, second, and third in any order.
Exacta Box—Two bets are made for any two horses that come in first and second.
Daily Double—Horses are winners of two successive races.

Beat the Bookie
http://www.theborg.demon.co.uk/

The Beat the Bookie page is a "source of free methods and systems, as well as a few tips for the day" that the site creator says are "aimed at the novice punter." First read the Golden Rules of Punting (#1 is willpower) and then check out the strategies.

Cyber Horse
http://www.internetmc.com/cyberhorse/

Cyber Horse bills itself as "your #1 source for horse handicapping." Registration and fees are required, but the site includes daily handicaps for several tracks. Take a look at the previous week's info to help you decide if this site has what you're looking for.

Running Horse
http://www.webcom.com/~alauck/index.html

The Running Horse home page is a compilation of resources "of interest to horse lovers in general, and particularly those that love to watch horses go fast." Links include the latest U.S. race horse standings, the Texas Thoroughbred Association, and a variety of thoroughbred racing directories.

Lizzie's Tips

Even light exercise will reduce the risk of strokes. People who walk 20 minutes a day three times a week are 60 percent less likely to suffer a stroke than couch potatoes.

Thoroughbred Horse Racing

http://www.iglou.com/zamboni/horse.html

Zamboni provides this extensive collection of links to sites concerned with thoroughbred horse racing. Divided into topical areas such as handicapping, race tracks, and general racing information, bettors and spectators alike can find the answers to their questions via the links on this page.

OLDER AND BOLDER

Although the term *senior sports* is often considered an oxymoron by younger iron men and women, many seniors are physically involved in a number of less-than-sedentary activities. And even those of us who don't run marathons, golf three times a week, or play beach volleyball, are passionate spectators.

Let's take a look at what some SeniorNetters do for exercise and the sports they are crazy about watching.

BASEBALL

We've all got our favorite baseball team and our favorite players. Baseball truly is the American pastime, and many of us have nostalgic memories of attending games with our fathers back in the old days. To find out what's happening in baseball these days, check out some of these home-run sites.

Baseball Yellow Pages

http://www.tdl.com/~chuckn/mlb.html

Link to official Major League Baseball team home pages. Also find unofficial team pages, a grouping of college baseball links, and a Web search tool.

The Baseball Server

http://www.nando.net/SportServer/baseball/

Fans of America's pastime can spend hours exploring the Baseball Server. An online World Series guide, current baseball news, previews and updates of games for all divisions, statistics, standings, and transactions are just a few of the resources available (sweeter than a box of Crackerjack).

Instant Baseball

http://www.instantsports.com/baseball.html

A service of Instant Sports Inc., this server provides near-live animated renditions of major-league games. Look at what's happening today or what happened yesterday, review the standings and statistics, or check out schedules.

John Skilton's Baseball Links

http://www.pc-professor.com/baseball/

Major league, minor league, college, amateur, semi-pro, youth, even international baseball ... this comprehensive index points the way to play in all the parks. Find stats, scores, schedules, stadiums, merchandise, publications, newsgroups, and more.

MLB@BAT

http://www.majorleaguebaseball.com/

Major League Baseball's @BAT follows league play from the opening day through the postseason. With this site's news and notes, box scores and statistics, and even a photo gallery, if you can't get to the park, you don't have to miss the game.

The National Baseball Hall of Fame and Museum

http://www.enews.com/bas_hall_fame/overview.html

Those who can't get to Cooperstown can now make a virtual visit to the birthplace of baseball. Take an overview tour of the National Baseball Museum, review who's in the Hall of Fame, and enjoy other online features such as shopping. Those who may be going to Cooperstown will also find plenty of information to help plan a successful trip.

BASKETBALL

"I love basketball, all of the teams, but of course Chicago Bulls w/Michael, and Scottie are my team!"

No matter if your interests lie with the college crowd or the professionals, these two Web sites can point you toward the goal.

College Hoops
http://www.onlysports.com/bball/
Rankings, schedules, news, and game results are among the resources available at this comprehensive index of college basketball sites. Links are also provided to conferences, individual teams, rules changes, and recruiting information.

NBA.com
http://www.nba.com/
Here's the official page of the National Basketball Association. Find news, standings, statistics, rosters, schedules, and merchandise. Among the site's features, NBA Theater offers highlight videos and Fan Fare provides interaction with players and announcers.

BOWLING

One of my friend's grandsons cherishes a 1950s bowling shirt he found in a local thrift store. He only wears it on special occasions. That's the way lots of devoted bowlers feel about their shirts and their sport. If you're one of them, take a look at some of the fun sites the Web keeps out of the gutter.

Bowling Page
http://www.rpi.edu/~miller3/bowling.html
Schedules and results from the men's and women's professional bowling tours in the United States are featured on the Bowling Page. Site highlights also include national and regional events, as well as links to other resources such as the Bowling Hall of Achievement.

Professional Bowlers Association
http://www.pba.org/
Bowlers and bowling fans will find information from and about the PBA Tour, including tournament results and schedules. The site also offers message boards and online chats with bowling pros.

Tenpin World
http://www.shef.ac.uk/uni/union/susoc/sutbc/index.html
Bruce Hartley posts what he describes as "the definitive guide to bowling on the Web"—tenpin being what the British call bowling. Find sport news, reference materials, results, event calendars, and information on organizations around the world.

CLIMBING AND SPELUNKING

OK, I'll admit that rock climbing and cave exploring aren't for everyone. (I think my feet are way too big for climbing up a rock face.) But let me tell you a little story about an experience I had not too long ago. I had the chance to attend one of those outdoor team building-character building programs. You know, the ones where you're supposed to develop your self-confidence and learn to work with other people? Anyway, some of the activities were a little ridiculous (like all of us trying how to fit on top of a stump), but some of the activities were great. The one I liked the best was rappelling.

First you have to step into and strap on this apparatus that fits around your waist and hips, don a crash (!) helmet, and let the people who know what they're doing (you hope) string a bunch of ropes through the hooks on your apparatus. Then comes the fun part. Holding onto the rope for dear life, you lower yourself over the side of a cliff and start walking or bounding down.

I thought I'd be paralyzed with fear, but I wasn't. It was one of the biggest rushes of my life. Jealous? Check out some of these sites for other rock-related activities.

The Cave Page

http://rschp2.anu.edu.au:8080/cave/cave.html

The Cave Page provides links to cave exploration sites around the globe. Features here include notes on techniques, a cave rescue guide, a cave songbook, a cookbook, plus other useful resources.

Climbing Archive!

http://www.dtek.chalmers.se/Climbing/

Rock and mountain climbing enthusiasts will enjoy the Climbing Archive, featuring articles and resources related to the popular outdoor sport. Visit here to view guidebooks, link with equipment providers, learn new climbing techniques, and more.

The Climbing Dictionary

http://www.fm.bs.dlr.de/misc/climbing/climbing_dict.html

This site contains an alphabetized list of English language climbing terms and definitions. Within each entry are translations in German, French, Dutch, Italian, Spanish, and Swedish.

Rappelling

http://petzl.com/petzl/english/dir/rappel.html

European climbing equipment maker Petzl sponsors this instructional page on rappelling and includes it as part of its online product catalog. A diagram of the proper apparatus, explanation of terms, and tips on safety will help you know what to expect *before* you find yourself hanging over that cliff face. The site also includes info on climbing, caving, and canyoning.

CYCLING

They say that once you learn to ride a bike you never forget. Well, you might not forget *how* to ride, but maintaining your balance can sometimes be a problem. Nevertheless, for seniors whose knees start screaming after a walk or run, cycling is a good alternative because it places far less stress on those aging joints. A brisk ride can give you a perfectly adequate aerobic workout, and it's fun (especially when you go fast)! These Web sites are all devoted to cycling and its many aspects.

Bicycles FAQ

http://www.cis.ohio-state.edu/hypertext/faq/usenet/bicycles-faq/top.html

From the technical (common torque values) to the practical (avoiding dogs), this archive of Usenet FAQ files provides a variety of bicycling information. It includes a FAQ on mountain biking.

Cyber Cyclery: Internet Bicycling Resource

http://cyclery.com/

Visitors to Cyber Cyclery can check out *Cycling Times* magazine (among many other publications), join in chats, or link to almost any cycling-related club, company, product, or event with a presence on the Internet. Users also can post bicycling events to the page.

The Cyberider Cycling WWW Site

http://blueridge.infomkt.ibm.com/bikes/

A hub site for cycling enthusiasts, Cyberider Cycling links visitors to an amazing amount of information. Learn the best places to ride, check out cycling news and newsgroup postings, download bike images, or link to other Web cycling sites.

cycling.org

http://www.cycling.org/

A sister site to Cyber Cyclery, this resource features a database of over 200 cycling-related mailing lists and a directory of more than 400 cycling clubs from around the world. Get in touch with fellow enthusiasts and discuss the local, regional, and global cycling issues that interest you most.

The Stolen Bike Registry
http://www.nashville.net/cycling/stolen.html

This interactive site features a registry for bike owners to document ownership of their bikes. The site also includes a list of bikes that have been reported stolen.

The Unicycle Page
http://www.unicycling.org/

OK, sue me. I included this one just for fun. The site is a comprehensive roundup of facts and tips on the sport of unicycling. Learn how to ride (yeah, right!) and what kind of 'cycle to buy. Site features also include a "trading post" for buying and selling.

The Virtual Breakaway
http://www.eskimo.com/~cycling/
breakaway.html

Cycling links from across the Internet can be reached through the Virtual Breakaway page. It features pointers to racing schedules and results, cycling newsgroups, biking magazines, enthusiasts' pages, and e-zines.

WWW Bicycle Lane
http://www.cs.purdue.edu/homes/dole/
bikelane.html

A personal collection of bicycling-related Internet resources, The World Wide Web Bicycle Lane offers an extensive index of news, publications, and commercial sites. Find links to cycling clubs, bike shops, trade publications, online discussion groups, and more.

FOOTBALL

Ah, football: the crashing of helmets, the grinding of flesh, the long pass. Throughout the winter, Saturdays go to college ball, Sundays and Monday nights to pro. Some of us just can't get enough. The Web has plenty for the gridiron fanatic. Search for your favorite team or visit one of these sites.

SENIORNET ROUNDTABLE

A young boy was caught in the middle of a custody fight between his mother and his father. The judge asked him whether he wanted to live with his mother.

"No, sir" he replied. "She beats me."

"Then you want to live with your father?" the judge asked.

"No, sir, he beats me."

"Well, how about with your grandparents?"

"No, sir, they beat me, too."

"Well then, who do you want to live with?" asked the puzzled judge.

The boy replied, "With the Giants. THEY never beat ANYBODY!"

The Football Server
http://www2.nando.net/SportServer/football/

Nando presents the latest news from the National Football League and NCAA Division I colleges around the United States.

NFL.com
http://www.nfl.com/

Visit the National Football League's home page for the latest news headlines, statistics, and information from U.S. professional football. A kids' page, merchandise, and keyword search are also available.

Two Minute Warning
http://www.dtd.com/tmw/

Think you know all there is to know about football? Try your luck at Two Minute Warning, the NFL Trivia Game where visitors can enter monthly contests for prizes. Links to other interactive games from the MindSports team at Downtown Digital are also available.

"If I lived somewhere that I couldn't watch pro football, I'd move!! :-)"

USA Football Center Online
http://cybergsi.com/foot2.htm

USA Football Center is an extensive resource for fans of college and professional football. Fans can tune in for scores, betting lines, predictions, articles, and player profiles.

GOLF

"Have you ever played a round of golf? It takes considerable talent and self-control to play well. But even if you don't play well, to spend a day walking in beautiful surroundings, well, that ain't so bad."

You want golf? The Web's got golf! Check out this assortment of hole-in-one sites (no greens fees required!).

Golf FAQ
http://dunkin.princeton.edu/.golf/faq/golf-faq.html

Frequently Asked Questions from the newsgroup rec.sport.golf and the GOLF-L mailing list are posted at this Web site. This FAQ includes information on golfing resources, equipment, handicaps, and other topical subjects.

Golf Scorecard Archives
http://golf.traveller.com/golf/scorecards/

Scorecards from golf courses such as the Pebble Beach Golf Links in California, the Pinehurst-Plantation in North Carolina, the Inverness Club in Ohio, and dozens more around the world are collected in this archive. The images are arranged by state and country.

"You're right about golf being a tough game. Just when you think you've got everything figured out,

something else goes wrong. Keeps you humble."

InterGolf
http://www.golf.com/travel/packages/InterGolf/

At this site featuring golf-oriented travel packages, golf nuts can make plans to take their swings around the globe. Stop by for information on the Tour of the Month and read about custom packages that take golfers to several courses in scenic regions.

The Virtual Golfer
http://www.golfball.com/

Check out course reviews or shop for a new nine iron at this golf-intensive site. Duffers will find tips to improve their game, professional golfing news, a chat room, and an online golfing magazine. The Canada-based site also details destination resorts.

HOCKEY

Not long ago, hockey was a regional sport. Only northern teams played this game—in places where the lakes froze in the winter. Not any more! Professional hockey is such a hot sport these days, it threatens to melt the very ice it's played on. Teams have spread all over the country—even into Deep South states like Louisiana, Alabama, and Florida where the lakes *never* freeze. Fans rave about the excitement, the action, and the fact that televised games just don't do the sport justice. Well, I'm still skeptical, but millions of fans can't be wrong. That barometer of popular culture, the Web, has laced on its virtual skates and presents a number of hockey-related resources. Here are a few.

Hockey Links On The Web
http://www.liglobal.com/sports/hockey.html

Hockey lovers, get your virtual gear on and take a spin around this generous directory of hot spots. Among the dozens of links presented are separate listings for the home pages on every NHL team.

Liam Maguire's NHL Hockey Trivia
http://infoweb.magi.com/~liam/hockey.html

Ice hockey fans can test their knowledge at this personal home page which runs weekly trivia contests. The author's hockey trivia book and links to other hockey resources are also available.

National Hockey League Players' Association
http://www.nhlpa.com/

Hockey fans can get sports news and views right from the puck's mouth at this official Web site for the members of the National Hockey League Players' Association. Meet the player of the day, take the trivia test, pick up stats and other facts, or listen to audio sound bites from the pros.

NHL Pages
http://www.wpi.edu/~defronzo/

From standings, statistics, and schedules to injuries, rosters, and rules, this unofficial National Hockey League site has it all. Included here is a listing of team pages, unofficial and official, for every NHL franchise.

NHL Wreckroom
http://amadeus.ccs.queensu.ca/Hockey/Hockey.html

One of the main attractions at this fan site is an image collection of National Hockey League players arranged by team. Other features include standings, statistics, schedules, and rumors.

Professional Hockey Server
http://maxwell.uhh.hawaii.edu/hockey/hockey.html

A Canadian-gone-Hawaiian maintains this fan page devoted to the National Hockey League. Visitors can take in statistics, schedules, team standings, and lots of action photos at this site or link to a handful of other hockey-related sites.

WWW Hockey Guide
http://www.hockeyguide.com/

The World Wide Web Hockey Guide nets information for its visitors on National Hockey League schedules, statistics, and awards. The site includes over 1,000 links to home pages devoted to specific NHL teams, a roundup of the Web's best hockey sites, and information on playing Small World interactive, rotisserie-style hockey.

MARTIAL ARTS

No longer just the province of Chuck Norris wannabes, martial arts training has entered the mainstream. The disciplined forms appeal to many people, and their motivation in taking classes is not to learn to split a board in half, but to enjoy enhanced health benefits and spiritual well-being. Lots of Web sites contain info on the various types of martial arts training available. Check these out.

Martial Arts Resource Site
http://www.floor6.com/MARS/MARS.html

This Web document presents an organized collection of links to martial arts-related Internet sites. The extensive list itemizes literature, histories, biographies, and glossaries available in hypertext form. Also find archives of newsletters, mailing list postings, and FAQ files.

Rico's Martial Arts Page
http://www.update.uu.se/~rico/martial_arts/

Does aikido take longer to master than other martial arts? Find out that fact and most anything else you could ever want to know about the martial arts. In addition to aikido, this page has resources on jujitsu, judo, and karate.

WWW Martial Arts Resources Page
http://www.middlebury.edu/~jswan/martial.arts/ma.html

This enthusiast's page boasts over 700 links related to martial arts resources on the Web. Featured topics in the index include self defense, judo, karate, Japanese sword arts, and aikido.

RUNNING, WALKING, AND HIKING

"I am 69 years old and enjoy running 5K for good health. I practice physical fitness 6 days a week at the local YMCA. My exercise consists of the following: A. 45 minutes on the stairmaster. B. 15 minutes on the bicycle. C. 60 minutes on the treadmill. D. 5 minutes on weight lifting."

Lots of seniors run 5K and longer races. Lots more run a few miles every day to keep in shape. Even more do that "walking thing," in the mall, around the neighborhood, or down a scenic trail. If your knees can take the pounding, these sites can help speed you on your way.

Dead Runners Society
http://storm.cadcam.iupui.edu/drs/drs.html

The Dead Runners Society is a listserv discussion group for folks who love running. At its Web site, browsers will find instructions on joining the mailing list, forum and publication archives, and links to all things afoot.

Dr. Pribut's Running Injuries Page
http://www.clark.net/pub/pribut/spsport.html

Dr. Stephen Pribut offers this site dedicated to running injuries and what you can do about them. Visitors can peruse a wide selection of information including shoe-buying tips, tips on avoiding injuries, basic biomechanics, sports physiology, track records, and links to related Web sites.

Hiking and Walking Homepage
http://www.teleport.com/~walking/hiking.htm

Looking for a place to hike? This is a good place to find it. In addition to listings of hiking areas, information on vacations and walking tours is available as well. Plus, there are plenty of other resources including links to organizations, newsgroups, and a chat page.

The Running Page
http://sunsite.unc.edu/drears/running/running.html

Want to find out if there is a marathon next month in Sweden? A pit stop at The Running Page will provide information on upcoming races worldwide. Also find listings of running clubs and race results.

Volksmarch and Walking Index
http://www.teleport.com/~walking/

The Volksmarch and Walking Index is provided by the American Volkssport Association in support of its "whole different kind of walk." Along with information on Volksmarch events and clubs, visitors will also find links to resources of interest to individuals who walk for fitness, enjoyment, and sport.

WebRunner Running Page
http://www.catalog.com/webrun/running/running.html

The WebRunner Running Page is an online guide to race and fitness running, with an emphasis on the southeastern United States. Visit here for race updates and schedules, links to running clubs, downloadable software, and more.

SKIING

Few sports are as thrilling as snow skiing. Here are some excellent Web sites to help veterans plan their next trip or give rookies an idea of what they're missing.

"I started skiing when I was 50 and really got hooked. Most of the winter I ski at Okemo or Killington. There are many areas that provide free skiing for 70+ members. In previous years I have skied in Europe and Canada. This leaves me only a couple of places to go before I pack it in, New Zealand and Chile/Argentina."

Alpine World

http://www.alpworld.com/sno/mag.html

The world of "alpine sports, fitness, travel, and environment" comes to the Web through this online magazine. If the site's graphics—complete with animation—aren't enough to satisfy visitors, then the resort guide and ski reports from around the globe should be.

Ski America

http://www.skiamerica.com/biz/skiamerica/

Ski America's Web site offers ski resort information, slope condition reports, travel assistance, ski-related humor, and commercial services. Site features also include information on a free subscription to *Ski America* magazine.

Telemarque

http://www2.telemarque.com/teleski/

Skiing takes the Web by storm through the Telemarque Web page. The site features "online resources for free-heel skiers" such as the North American Telemark Organization and a selection of articles submitted by site users.

World Skiing

http://wwwmbb.cs.colorado.edu/~mcbryan/bb/ski/ski.html

The World Skiing page reports on weather and slope conditions around the world. Select a region and choose a preferred style, Alpine or Nordic. The site returns an index of report items listed alphabetically.

SOCCER

You may not be one of those "soccer moms" (or dads) that the candidates were blathering about during the last presidential election, but you may be a soccer grandparent. If you're mystified by this game that has only recently become a popular alternative to football among the school-age set, check out these sites for some inside information. Your grandkids will be amazed at your soccer savvy.

International Soccer Server

http://dmiwww.cs.tut.fi/riku/soccer.html

Fans of European soccer (or what they call "football") will find the stats and scores from their favorite teams and can contribute to the site with their own fanatical ravings.

Nando Soccer Features

http://www.nando.net/newsroom/sports/oth/1995/oth/soc/feat/soc.html

The Soccer Features section of the handy Nando Times Sports Server contains an enormous collection of information about the world's most popular sport. You'll find British, French, German, Italian, and Spanish standings as well as NCAA men's and women's soccer updates.

National Professional Soccer League

http://www.students.uiuc.edu/~mitzel/npsl.html

Fans of U.S. indoor soccer can follow the National Professional Soccer League on this unofficial page. The site contains news, game statistics, historical information, and links to team home pages.

The RSSSF Archive

http://info.risc.uni-linz.ac.at:70/0h/misc-info/rsssf/archive.html

From the home page of the Rec.Sport.Soccer Statistics Foundation, this area houses lots of soccer statistics. But then, what else would you expect? These archives contain scores, standings, rankings, and trivia from soccer leagues and competitions worldwide.

Soccer Information

http://www.marwin.ch/sport/fb/index.e.html

For soccer information from around the globe, this is the place to start. The site includes pointers—grouped by country—to sites posting standings, club information, and competition news. In English and German.

TENNIS

I see lots of seniors taking beginner tennis lessons at our community recreation center. You don't really have to be a good player to have a great time playing this game (as long as you're playing another beginner). Many of the seniors I know bought their first rackets second-hand at the thrift store so they could minimize the up-front investment, figuring that they could drop serious cash on an expensive racket later if they decided they liked the sport enough. I know one guy, however, who still plays with his second-hand racket, even though he devotes three mornings a week to the sport and is now well beyond beginner status.

Besides your local rec center, many apartment complexes and retirement communities have tennis courts, so finding a place to play usually isn't a problem. Bend your elbow into these tennis-related sites on the Web.

Tennis Server Home Page
http://www.tennisserver.com/

The World Wide Web Tennis Server features original writing from *Tennis Magazine* contributor David Higdon, news from the pro circuit, and the player tip of the month. Visitors can also check out the tennis rules page and find answers to FAQ about the game.

Tennis Web
http://www.tennisw.com/tweb/

Tennis anyone? This Web site contains a "comprehensive" list of links to tennis-related resources on the Internet, including camps, schools, newsgroups, clubs, resorts, tournaments, and FAQ.

Tennis Worldwide
http://www.tennisw.com

Home to *Tennis Worldwide* magazine and a Web page devoted to junior tennis, this site also offers amusements such as contests and a fantasy tennis league. Classified ads and the site's Tennis Mall point visitors toward a smashing array of equipment and services.

VEHICULAR SPORTS

Besides being an almost indispensable tool of modern life, cars hold a fascination for us all—especially when they go fast. And how about motorcycles? How many times have you seen a caravan of seniors on their big Harleys cruising down the highway and wished you could join them? Let's take a look now at some Web sites devoted to autos, auto racing, and motorcycles.

American Racing Scene
http://www.racecar.com/

NASCAR and Indy Car fans can turn to the American Racing Scene for the latest standings and happenings. Dig into photographs and articles about racing personalities and a calendar of events.

Matt's Solar Car Page
http://www-lips.ece.utexas.edu/~delayman/solar.html

Matt's Solar Car Page offers a variety of information about environmentally friendly auto development and the international solar car racing circuit. Visitors will find articles, graphics, and scheduled race postings.

Motorcycle Online
http://www.motorcycle.com/motorcycle.html

"The world's largest and most-read digital motorcycle magazine," is how the editors of *Motorcycle World* describe their publication. Regular features include daily news, bike and product reviews, mechanical advice, and letters to the editor.

Motorsport News International
http://www.motorsport.com/Index.html

Motorsport News International serves as an online source for news, race results, and feature articles on motor sports of all levels—from Indy cars to regional midget races. Site features include a searchable archive of articles and links to related Web, FTP, and Usenet newsgroup sites.

RaceZine

http://www.primenet.com/~bobwest/
index.html

RaceZine shifts into high gear by offering visitors images, trivia, sound bites, and news about auto racing. The site includes links to Sandman's MotorSports page and other online racing resources.

Sports Car Club of America

http://www.wizvax.net/rwelty/scca/

This unofficial collection of links points to sites relevant to the Sports Car Club of America (SCCA) and sports racing. An abbreviated index is provided for quick reference.

Tracks Around the World

http://www.bath.ac.uk/~py3dlg/tracks.html

Automotive racetrack information from around the world is organized here by country and continent. Click on one of the listed countries to get track locations and contact information.

WATER SPORTS

The water just naturally lends itself to sports activities: fishing, boating, swimming, diving. Here are some fun sites to give you ideas or help you actually make the limit during your next fishing trip. I've included lots of scuba sites for you real adventurers.

American Canoe Association

http://www.aca-paddler.org/

The American Canoe Association posts resources for canoeing enthusiasts of all skill levels. Visitors can check out current news items, competition results, and trip information. *The American Canoeist* newsletter, *Paddler Magazine*, a photo gallery, and an online store are also featured.

The Anadromous Page

http://www.peak.org/~robertr/fishing.html

A Greek word, anadromous means "running upward." And at this site, the fishing resources are constantly on the rise. Find regional and local fishing reports from around the world along with tips, techniques, and recipes, all contributed by volunteers.

Anadromous: from the Greek *anadromous* meaning "running upward"

Anglers Online

http://www.inetmkt.com/fishpage/index.html

Anglers Online provides everything a fisherman could want. Hook into classified ads, current fishing reports, online equipment catalogs, outfitter and guide listings, even a fish photo archive. Also enjoy a variety of categorized pointers to Web fishing holes.

Fly Fishing Database and FAQ Home Page

http://www.geo.mtu.edu/~jsuchosk/fish/ff-faq/masterIndex.html

Fly fishing enthusiasts can peruse a collection of databases and FAQ here. This site's resources cover most every aspect of the sport and are offered courtesy of the fly fishing mailing list and the Usenet group rec.outdoors. fishing.news.

MarineNet

http://www.gsn.com/

Pointing the way to "recreational watersports communities on the Internet," MarineNet floats a boatload of links related to watercraft, scuba diving, sailing, fishing, and other moist diversions. Find classifieds, manufacturers' sites, calendars of events, clubs, schools, and more.

PADI World Wide Web Site

http://www.padi.com/

The Professional Association of Diving Instructors presents information on its courses in scuba, snorkeling, and open-water diving at this home page. Visitors can also check out PADI products and a travel network.

Sailing Page
http://community.bellcore.com/mbr/sailing-page.html

Mark Rosenstein's page is a must for sailing fanatics. Visitors will discover tons of Net resources, with subjects ranging from maritime museums to learn-to-sail opportunities, and from tall ships to sailing clubs.

SailNet
http://www.sailnet.com/

SailNet features The Sailing Directory, a listing of sailing-related commercial sites that include builders, magazines, and marinas. Other resources available here include weather reports and software archives.

Scuba FAQ
http://www.cis.ohio-state.edu/hypertext/faq/usenet/scuba-faq/faq.html

Visit this site to review the FAQ file from rec.scuba, a newsgroup created for the discussion of scuba, snorkeling, and other underwater activities. Questions generally focus on safety, equipment, and certification.

Scuba.Net
http://www.scuba.net/

Divers can gather information on dive sites, weather conditions, dive shops, and instructors around the United States. Also featured here is information on scuba mailing lists and links to other scuba sites.

Underwater Sports World
http://www.uwsports.ycg.com/

Self-described as "the premiere interactive resource for divers," Underwater Sports World posts the current issue of its interactive magazine on this page. Also find an archive of back issues, a virtual dive shop, forums, a bulletin board, industry listings, and much more.

World-Wide Web Virtual Library: Sportsfishing
http://wmi.cais.com/www/sportfsh/index.html

Charter fishing businesses, magazines, associations, fishing guides, and fan home pages can be reached via this directory. Whether you prefer fresh or saltwater fishing, there's bait here that's sure to get you to bite.

SPORTS MISCELLANY

Here are a few additional sports sites that don't really fit into any of the other categories, but I just couldn't resist putting them in. You may find one of your favorites in this list.

Badminton
http://mid1.external.hp.com/stanb/badminton.html

The Badminton page dishes up a wealth of information for those who enjoy watching shuttlecocks and the players who bat them back and forth. Read background information on the game, check out current events and tournaments, or link to organizations and other badminton-related Web sites.

CricInfo
http://www.cricket.org:8000/

Here's the "home of cricket on the Internet." CricInfo provides up-to-date information on the sport, including news, scores, statistics, player profiles, and league standings for British and international cricket circuit.

Hunter
http://www.wolfe.net/~hunter/

Among the resources at this hunting page from Bill Hunter (do you think that's his real name?) are essays on hunting and a hunting trophy room. Visitors can also learn about hunting equipment and link to other hunting sites including pro-hunting and anti-hunting discussion pages.

RugbyInfo
http://rugby.phys.uidaho.edu/rugby.html

Video clips of rugby action are among the many resources at the RugbyInfo page. This comprehensive listing of rugby links also includes the basics and rules of the game, coaching information, and trivia.

Volleyball WorldWide

http://www.volleyball.org/

Whether you're interested in beginner or professional, national or international volleyball, the links are here to point you to the information you desire. The offerings include an extensive index of playing rules and instructional materials.

Weight Training Page

http://www.cs.unc.edu/~wilsonk/weights.html

Weightlifting enthusiasts will enjoy this personal home page featuring a variety of weight training and fitness resources. Visit here for links to professional and amateur associations, fitness clubs, and nutrition publications.

WWW Snooker Home Page

http://www.ifi.uio.no/~hermunda/Snooker/

What do you call a person who plays snooker? No, not a snookie—just a snooker player. Learn about snooker, a variation of pool, at this home page featuring the rules of the game as well as information on top players and tournaments.

GENERAL SPORTS AND GAMBLING SITES

ESPNET SportsZone

http://espnet.sportszone.com/

The NFL, college football, NBA, college basketball, NHL, baseball, soccer, and other sports are the focus at this Web site. Get the latest news and highlights, scores and schedules, plus standings and statistics for your favorite teams and their arch rivals.

America's Sports Headquarters

http://www.sport-hq.com/

Use this dedicated search tool to find the "great sports sites" on the Web—no matter if they're spectator sports, outdoor adventure sports, or recreational sports. After one visit you'll know why the site is described as "the Web's sports directory."

GambleNet

http://www.gamblenet.com/

Put your money where your mouse is at this wagering site. Interactive Gaming & Communications Corp. plans to erect a virtual casino here, but until the slots start spinning gamblers must content themselves by placing bets with the online sports book.

Great Outdoor Recreation Pages

http://www.gorp.com/default.htm

Bringing the great outdoors onto a computer screen is no easy task, but GORP does it. With resources on everything from biking and backpacking to rafting and hang gliding to birding and boating, GORP covers it all. Anyone planning an outing, whether locally or some distance from home, will find plenty to ponder posted to this truly "great" outdoor recreation resource.

The Sports Network

http://www.sportsnetwork.com/home.html

Live scoreboards, news headlines, and the sportsbook are online for athletic contests from around the sports world. Find football, baseball, basketball, soccer, auto racing, horse racing, boxing, tennis, and golf.

Stadiums and Arenas

http://www.wwcd.com/stadiums.html

Why go to the stadium when World-Wide Collectors Digest brings the stadium to the Web? All professional stadiums and arenas in North America are listed at this site, with information such as address, phone number, and capacity; most also have photos. Some racetracks and college stadiums are also included.

Vegas.Com Sports Central

http://www.vegas.com/sports/sports.html

Get handicapper news and information, link to an online sports bookie, or get the odds for the event you're interested in. A page on boxing also offers news and views from the ring.

World Wide Web of Sports

http://www.tns.lcs.mit.edu/cgi-bin/sports

Here's a massive resource for folks with a massive desire for sports information. Find resources organized by individual sport, spanning everything from archery to wrestling. Enjoy photos, video clips, game schedules, and home pages. There's also a section devoted to sporting publications such as *Sports Illustrated*.

World Wide Web of Sports		
Custom Page	Submit A Link	Sports Search
Archery	Athletic Games	Aussie Rules
Badminton	Ballooning	Baseball
Basketball	Billiards	Boomerang
Bowling	Boxing	Cheerleading/Music
Chess and Checkers	Climbing	Commercial Sites
Cricket	Croquet	Curling
Cycling	Dancing	Darts
Equestrian	Fencing	Field Hockey
Fishing	Fitness	Footbag
Football	Frisbee	Golf
Gymnastics	Hand Ball	Hang Gliding

THE GAMING ARCADE

Besides their addiction to outside and team sports, Seniors, like anyone else, are just as addicted to parlor and computer games. The Web is loaded with games of all types that you can download or play online. Computer gaming is perfect for those times when your human partners are unavailable, and for when you want to learn the rudiments of a new game.

Some of these games, like solitaire, can keep you at your terminal for hours past the time you planned, ignoring family, friends, and undone chores. Just one more round! You can even get up a bridge game online. And for those who like arcade games, there's plenty of shoot 'em up options out there.

ONLINE PARLOR GAMES

For barrels of fun and excitement, test a few of these sites and keep your hand in.

Araneum's Cyber Poker

http://www.araneum.dk/poker/indexuk.html

Anyone with a standard Web browser can play and enjoy this video 5-card draw poker simulation game. Players begin with a $5,000 credit in play money and try to build from there. Jacks or better are needed to win; nothing is wild. Registration is only required for those who want to be ranked among the other players.

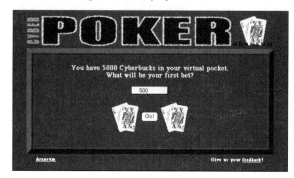

Backgammon Frequently Asked Questions

http://www.cybercom.net/~damish/backgammon/bg-faq.html

Edited by Mark Damish, this FAQ has been compiled to answer the questions most often posed by new visitors to the Usenet newsgroup rec.games.backgammon. Section headings include Essentials; Electronic Backgammon: vs Other Humans; Electronic Backgammon: vs Machine; Resources; and Miscellaneous. Beginning with the basic rules of play, the FAQ then explores the world of online and computer-based gaming. A list of topical books and newsletters is also included, as is a review of other games that can be played on the backgammon board.

Backgammon Galore!

http://www.io.org/~takeith/bg/main.html

Learn the game rules, review the terminology of play, and read about "doubling" strategies for winning big at backgammon. Related articles and annotated matches are also online for further study. Those eager to play online and who have a Java-capable browser can access an on-site game and play the computer. Others may want to follow the pointer to information about FIBS, the First Internet Backgammon Server.

Battleship—Interactive Web Game

http://godfather.ifs.univie.ac.at:8080/~apo01/

This interactive version of Battleship allows players to set the game parameters. Those unfamiliar with how the game is played can refer to a brief overview of the rules and game objectives. For curious browsers more interested in how the game works than how it's played, the computer code is available as well.

Bingo Zone

http://www.bingozone.com/

Play Bingo live, on the Web, through any browser, up to 24 hours a day, and win $5, $10, or $20 cash jackpots. Play is free, but all players must register before logging into a game. Eight types of games are featured; online help assists newcomers in getting settled. You must have a valid e-mail address to register.

Black Jack on the World Wide Web

http://www.web-source.com/blackjack/

Most anyone with a Web browser can belly up to this virtual gaming table and try their hand at blackjack. This online version was created with care to ensure that no "special technology" is needed to enjoy it. Folks fuzzy about the rules of play will find online help, and anyone eager to leave a comment for the dealer is encouraged to do so. Play is for points, so don't expect to win any jackpots, but the best players appear on the Top 10 list.

Chinook

http://web.cs.ualberta.ca/~chinook/

Hosted by the Department of Computing Science at Canada's University of Alberta, this site treats players to an online checkers challenge. Visitors can test their game skills against a world championship checkers program developed as a by-product of research into gaming strategies. Those more interested in boning up for future play can view the endgame database and review world championship matches. Or if you need a little inspiration, visit the WWW Wall of Honor or International Checker Hall of Fame. Other pointers lead to free checker software, commercial programs, and related items for sale.

ChessLive!

http://oasi.shiny.it/chess/index.html

As the site's title suggests, visitors can play chess live on the Web with this Java applet hosted by Francesco Bosia. Play features include the ability to privately chat with opponents during games and to suspend play and resume at a later date. An automatic rating system lets players know where they stand, a chat area lets bolder players issue public challenges, and the spectators' gallery affords lurkers dynamic viewing of all games in play. If you've got the plug-in, this site's jumping!

Chess Space

http://www.chess-space.com/

From archives to Usenet, if it's on the Internet and involves the game of chess, there's probably a pointer to it from here. With over 700 links organized into obvious, easy-to-understand categories, this directory serves as a superior resource for chess players of every level. Find FAQs, organizations, online gaming sites, playing strategies, publications, even links to the home pages of masters and novices around the world. For anyone serious about the game of chess, this site is a must see.

Connect Four

http://www.dbai.tuwien.ac.at/cgi-bin/rusch_
four/aanqdcbk/large/

Peter Wansch and Klaus Johannes Rusch host this browser-friendly Connect Four game. Select text mode, small graphics, or large graphics. Rules of the game are close at hand, the skill level is adjustable, and simple directions help players begin the game quickly. Play is against the computer.

Crossword Puzzles

http://www.primate.wisc.edu/people/hamel/
cp.html

Ray Hamel has compiled and hosts this extensive directory of crossword resources available online. Featured links lead to tournament information, organizations, puzzle generators, and sites offering puzzle play. There's plenty to do and see.

DominoNet

http://neon.ingenia.com/dominet/

Replete with its own theme song and a movie, this multimedia adventure into the world of dominoes offers something of interest for the novice and master gamer alike. Learn the essentials of play, become familiar with the correct use of terms, and gain insights into the strategies of play. Links lead to newsgroups, a search utility, and the DominoNet FTP site.

Envoy: A Beginners Guide to Diplomacy

http://www.pegasus.oz.au/~cjallen/envoy.htm

Chris Allen hosts this introduction to the game where honesty isn't always the best policy. Read a general overview of Diplomacy, review rules and strategies, and find out how to get started playing via e-mail. Information on face-to-face tournaments is also online, along with links to other players' home pages and game resources. For anyone curious enough to learn the playful nuances of international negotiation, here's an excellent place to begin.

Ferret Frenzy

http://www.delphi.co.uk/delphi/interactive/ferrets/intro.html

Everyone starts with an even stake but only those with an eye keen enough to pick the winners get ahead. Place bets and watch the field of ferrets race down the track. Races begin with regularity and a new race is probably starting right now. But be warned: for ferret races, these are kind of slow!

FIBS - Backgammon on the Internet

http://www.cybercom.net/~damish/backgammon/mike_quinn/fibs.htm

Compiled by Mike Quinn, this unofficial page provides a general guide to playing backgammon via telnet connection with the First Internet Backgammon Server (FIBS). Find out exactly what FIBS is and how to connect, download a list of FIBS commands, and look into improving the enjoyment factor of online play by downloading and setting up a graphical browser.

Great Bridge Links

http://www.cbf.ca/GBL.html

The title tells it all! These are great bridge links and there are loads of them, too. No matter what you're after, you'll find direction here. Pointers link to organizations, magazines and newsletters, online play, software sites, players' bridge pages, archives, newsgroups, and mailing lists. There is even a bridge shopping mall. The page is well organized and maintained by Jude Goodwin-Hanson.

Happy Puppy

http://happypuppy.com/games/link/index.html

Old dogs with an interest in learning new tricks—or at least the newest computer games—should pay a visit to this mega-site offering free demos and downloads of game software. Search to seek or browse until you're blue; the site is easy to navigate despite its size. If a game is not here, it's probably not available or just not worth the disk space. Find everything from action adventure games to puzzles and simulations.

Internet Chess Library

http://caissa.onenet.net/chess/

Offering visitors a wide variety of fact and fancy, the Internet Chess Library caters to the interests of true chess enthusiasts. Browse the FAQ (parts 1 and 2) from the Usenet newsgroup rec.games.chess for answers to all manner of questions detailing what's what in the world of chess, online and off. Study the games databases that archive the winning moves of masters and champions. Review the ratings information to learn how the different systems work and read profiles of who's where in the standings. Or, stop by the art gallery for a look at some exceptional boards, gaming pieces, and chess celebrities.

Internet Gaming Zone: Bridge

http://igz2.microsoft.com/bridge.html

Play bridge against others or practice against the computer at Microsoft's Internet Gaming Zone. Play is free, but users must download the necessary software. Visit this page for the details on playing bridge or link back to the Zone's home page for information on the other card and gaming options available.

The Internet Mahjong Meta-Server

http://www.math.princeton.edu/~ztfeng/mj_servers.html

Play mahjong online, in real time, against real opponents from around the world using this Java applet by Thomas Zuwei Feng. Links to sites running the game are featured, along with a list of players who frequent each site. Also find links to other mahjong pages and the mahjong mailing list. For those interested, the source code for this applet is available. A Java-enabled browser is required.

Jackpot

http://www.cs.umu.se/cgi-bin/scripts/jackpot

At this basic slot machine interface, play for points, for laughs, or for want of anything better to do. A basic Web browser is all that's required to play.

The Jackpot

http://www.initiative.com/

Classic Media hosts this live slot machine where players can win payouts of real U.S. cash. From all indications, play is free and prizes come from the site sponsors. Check for restrictions that may apply.

JavaGammon

http://www-leland.stanford.edu/~leesmith/JavaGammon.html

Backgammon players with Java-capable browsers can test their skills against other players via this interactive game. To start, players must load the applet and board image, then wait to be paired with an opponent. Players are matched on a first-come, first-served basis. If no challenger connects, waiting players can open another window on their browser and play themselves.

Letter R.I.P

http://www.dtd.com/rip/

Here's a graphically gruesome spin on an old favorite. It's hangman all right, but rather than building a stick figure to twist from the gallows, missed letters mean Zeppie the Zombie loses a limb. The words are a cut above on the difficulty scale ... all the worse for Zeppie!

Mahjong: The Chinese Game of Four Winds

http://www.cs.utk.edu/~clay/mahjongg/

Clay Breshears hosts this tutorial explaining the tile game mahjong. Find descriptions of the tiles and instructions for starting, playing, and winning a hand. Scoring and playing a full game are also covered. A list of books on the game and links to other mahjong sites on the Web are also featured.

NET-Scrabble

http://elf.udw.ac.za/~scrabble/

Gamers! Play Scrabble in public or in private on this server that requires nothing more than a Web browser to play. Though this is not a real-time game server, play can go quickly if opponents are so inclined. An automatic e-mail notice alerts players when it's their turn to play. Be sure to read the Hints and Tips section of the Rules and Information; knowledge is the key to winning and having a good game. By the way, lurkers are welcome.

The rec.puzzles Archive

http://einstein.et.tudelft.nl/~arlet/puzzles/index.html

This site should be the first stop and could be the last for anyone looking for puzzles. Compiled from the Usenet newsgroup rec.puzzles, this archive organizes puzzles (and their solutions!) by subject category and points the way. Find things like language equations and probability puzzles, as well as trivia, riddles, and games. A link to the rec.puzzles FAQ is also featured.

Scrabble FAQ

http://www.teleport.com/~stevena/scrabble/faq.html

More than simply an FAQ, this directory points to a host of Scrabble and crossword game-related resources on the Internet. Look into rules for Scrabble tournament play in North America and around the world, find out when and where tournaments are taking place, and check to see if a Scrabble club is close enough to join. New words accepted by the official Scrabble monitors, articles of interest, and player ratings are also featured. Those interested in play-by-mail games can find out how to become involved, while computer versions of the game are also covered, including shareware versions available via FTP.

SlotMania
http://slots.inetwave.com/

Offering a simulated Las Vegas-type experience, this server features a variety of slots and uses Java, HTML, and VRML enhancements for better display and action. Credited play requires registration.

The Track: Home of Server-Push Horseracing
http://www.boston.com/sports/thetrack/cgi-bin/horse_race.cgi

Racing sports fans begin with a $500 virtual stake from which they can place bets on server-push horse races. The server tracks a player's wins and losses and players can watch the virtual race. Compete for a spot among the Top Ten winners. Registration is required for "accounting" purposes.

Undernet Poker
http://www.atlantic.net/~phod/

Which is the best IRC poker server on the Internet? That's up to individual players to decide, but this server's following is certain they're in the right place. Find out the who, what, when, and where to judge for yourself, or visit the Vault of Glittering Prizes to see why Undernet Poker players, and casual passers-by, think this server is something special.

Universal Access Inc. Blackjack Server
http://blackjack1.ua.com/welcome.mhtml

Start with $1,000 play money and see how much you have left at the end of play. Standard rules apply (and are available for review). Players can choose the regular blackjack option (which shows play information as the game progresses) or professional blackjack (which only shows card images). Nothing fancy in the way of a Web browser is needed, just point, click, and play with most any model. Registration is requested, but not required.

WebCube
http://info.gte.com/gtel/fun/cube/cube.html

Here's a Web version of the Rubik's Cube that most any browser can handle. Created by Steve Belczyk, WebCube is composed of 27 colored cubes; players manipulate the cube to get the colors to line up. Easy-to-follow instructions help the newcomer get acquainted with the game.

The Web Go Page Index
http://ltiwww.epfl.ch/~warkent/go/golinks.html

If Go resources are your goal, go here. This gigantic resource links to players' home pages, products, books, articles, tournament announcements, news, and general information including FAQs, rules, and game collections. Also find links to playing on the Internet via telnet and Java applets, pointers to worldwide associations and clubs, and FTP sites. Compiled and hosted by Ken Warkentyne, the index is well-organized and easy to use.

WebSlots
http://pandarus.usc.edu/ken-bin/slot2.pl?instruct=start

Sporting a "new improved" design, this server starts players with $500 in play money. Bet $1 to $5 per spin. Before leaving, players can deposit winnings in the DigitalVegas Bank.

WebSpades
http://okapi.dws.acs.cmu.edu/fred/webspades.html#anchor224676

Play a rousing game of spades in real time against others around the globe. Online instructions for joining a game and rules for playing spades help make newcomers feel right at home. A Java-capable browser is required.

Web Yahtzee

http://www.cs.fsu.edu/~kalter/yahtzee.html

Bill Kalter offers Yahtzee players their choice: play the
Java version, the frames version, the graphics version, or
the text-only version. So no matter what type of browser you have, you can play here. Better know a little something about the game upon arrival however. There's little
in the way of game instruction.

Chapter 19

RAMBLING, TOURING, AND TREKKING

ON THE ROAD AGAIN

A FEW FREEBIES (OR NEARLY FREEBIES)

DESTINATION: FUN, ADVENTURE, ROMANCE... WHATEVER

THIS AIN'T NO STAGECOACH

The world has certainly grown smaller. We no longer have to pack up the pots and pans in the back of the family prairie schooner and trudge the tortuous miles for days, weeks, or months to get where we're going. Today we can call our favorite travel agent, hop a jet to Aruba, and be there in an afternoon. And even if we don't choose to fly, modern roads can help us get places faster than ever before. High-speed travel has opened up all kinds of possibilities, and lots of folks are on the move, exploring every corner of North America as well as exotic climes that used to be merely the stuff of legends.

Thousands of families head out on their annual family vacations to revel in the sun on the beaches, or lay back in luxurious comfort at famous resorts. Others rough it a bit by camping in national parks, but many of them drive late-model vans or RVs equipped with every comfort. The lure of the interstate beckons to many as it ribbons along its thousands of miles, transporting vacationers to their fantasy leisure pleasures.

But who could ever forget the vacations of the old days—and the old days weren't all that long ago—that we took with our families?

ON THE ROAD AGAIN

How different our own family vacations were back in the 1940s after World War II. Poppa would decide one steamy summer morning that we would drive to Mississippi from New York City to see the home folks, and that we would leave before dawn the next day. This announcement would whip everyone into a frenzy of packing and planning.

At three the next morning, we would be summmoned from our beds, still in pajamas, and we would crawl, clutching our pillows, into the old navy blue Packard that Poppa loved. This hulking car with its enormous tires would be our home on the

Lizzie Sez

Pay attention to the details!

road for longer than any human being should be expected to endure.

The trips were long, but I remember them fondly. The plump, padded back seat was comfortable and large enough for both my brother and me to stretch our small bodies in sleep, or play as we rolled along the dusty roads. Mother packed shoe boxes, carefully tied with string, that were filled with fried chicken and homemade biscuits, bacon sandwiches, and other edible delights.

BURMA SHAVE

We played games for hours to relieve the boredom of the road. Poppa didn't participate in our merry games. He never seemed to need any relief from his driving. He gripped the wheel fiercely, his face hawk-like as he concentrated on the road ahead.

One of our favorite games was collecting license plates. The object was to spot plates from every state in the union. Billboard alphabet was another game that helped us pass the time. We'd start with the first letter in the alphabet and add letters from billboards we passed. The challenge of this game was finding seldom-used letters like Q and Z. But the best part of the drive was spotting those little red Burma Shave signs and reading their clever limericks out loud.

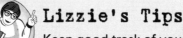

Lizzie's Tips

Keep good track of your own frequent flyer miles. No one else will be as accurate as you are. A computer program called "Max Miles" can help.

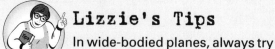

Lizzie's Tips

In wide-bodied planes, always try to get a seat in the center section of the plane. The middle seats in that section are the last to be filled. If you are a frequent flyer, ask for the preferred seating section. Middle seats there are held until the last minute.

NO-MAN'S LAND

Poppa didn't use maps. He preferred to wing along on his instincts. As a result, we frequently found ourselves lost on lonely, rutted roads out in the middle of no-man's land. When he got lost, Poppa would grow extremely irritable, and we would grow extremely quiet. All Burma Shave sightings from that point would be read quietly to ourselves. After an interminable ramble around muddy and infrequently traveled byways, he would eventually find his way out of the maze at about the point where he had first entered, and would announce in a happy voice, "Wasn't that a wonderful opportunity to see the scenery?"

In the blistering summer heat, for those of us sweating into the back seat's wool upholstery, that long detour was far from wonderful, but we never dared say so. Poppa prided himself on never having to ask for directions, so we often found ourselves on the scenic route to nowhere.

THE FACILITIES

Mayonnaise jars were an important part of our traveling equipment, because Poppa was reluctant to stop anywhere for anything. And even if he had been more sympathetic to our calls of nature, rest rooms were few and far between. If you did find a rest room in those days, it was a formidable testimony to the lowest state of personal hygiene.

Any mention of bathroom needs offended Poppa's delicate sensibilities, so we gingerly—if grudgingly—put the jars to use. Success required a high degree of hand and eye coordination. Even though the rest rooms were bad, we preferred them over the mayonnaise jar and were always thrilled when Poppa actually agreed to stop.

IT WAS A FUNNEL STORY

I'll never forget the landmark day—the start of yet another trip—when Poppa showed us the newest feature of the dignified Packard. He had drilled a large hole in the floorboard between the front and back seats. Brandishing a large tin funnel, he announced to his bug-eyed backseat passengers the end of the mayonnaise jar routine and the beginning of the funnel regime.

For years after, Poppa boasted of the success of his funnel innovation and its superiority over the mayonnaise jar. He claimed that before the installation

Lizzie's Tips

If you are visiting in Europe, expect a lot more cigarette smoke than you find in the States. Call restaurants in advance to see if they have a smoke-free section and make a reservation.

Lizzie's Tips

Flight crew bags are just the thing for the everyday traveler. They hold enough clothes for three days and can fit right under a coach seat, so you don't have to check your luggage. Be sure to buy the right size and make certain that breakable parts (such as handles) can be replaced.

Lizzie's Tips

When you book a flight, always tell your travel agent to order a special meal even though you have no medical need. Special meals are prepared to order and you will eat fresher and better prepared food than you would otherwise.

of the funnel, he could only travel 250 miserable and interrupted miles a day. With the funnel, he could make as many as 400 miles!

To this day, I wonder how Poppa drove obsessively for so many hours with no sleep, no picnicking, and no sightseeing stops. The only sights we saw were roadside signs beckoning us to "Dave's Reptile Gardens" or "Polly's Alligator Farm," but of course we never got to stop (even though we were dying to) and gape at the snakes and gators. No, Poppa drove on relentlessly, his chin thrust stubbornly outward, his eyes focused on the road ahead, and his fingers clenched on the steering wheel. Our trips were adventures, all right, for all of us.

OVER HILL, OVER DALE

Although our trips had their drawbacks, I'm not sure they were as bad as the one Maxine and Jack Collister took back in the thirties. Maxine and Jack were young and adventurous and piled into an old Whippet touring car with the idea of making their way from Kansas City, Missouri to Santa Fe, New Mexico.

Their first mistake was picking a bad time of year to go. It was extremely hot, with the temperatures hovering at the 100-degree mark, even at night. Their second mistake was trying to drive that distance in a Whippet. The Whippet was a rough rider with open sides and a convertible top, and its maximum cruising speed was about 45 miles an hour.

Since the sun beat down at temperatures of over 110 degrees during the day, Maxine and Jack slept by day and traveled by night. Each day when the sun rose high enough to make travel miserable, they'd stop and sleep on a quilt in a shaded spot in a farmer's field until the sun went down. At night they covered the miles through the Kansas prairie. The roads were scorching due to the heat of the day, and flat tires became a familiar enemy, with one exploding about every 100 miles. The tires had tubes that had to be removed and patched right there on the road. Poppa would have been a basket case if he had been on that trip.

But travel is a lot more comfortable these days, and we are on the roads, in the skies, and on the oceans like never before.

A FEW FREEBIES (OR NEARLY FREEBIES)

Although you can spend a small (or large) fortune on a vacation, good planning and research can save you a bundle. You don't have to be a millionaire to have a good time on your travels, and there are some really great travel opportunities out there for those of us who are flexible enough to take advantage of them.

MOVE OVER KATHY LEE!

Believe it or not, a cruise aboard a luxury liner can be free. Cruise lines are always looking for people to

---

PASSPORT TIPS

- Have a secure place to carry your passport so it can't be 'picked' from your purse or pocket.
- Don't let unauthorized people handle your passport.
- Photocopy all data pages, including the front and back covers.
- Have two passport pictures made instead of one in case you lose your passport. Taking this precaution will save time if you have to replace your passport.
- Carry your extra picture and photocopied passport separately from your real passport.

---

give speeches and seminars for the other folks on board. If you qualify as a guest speaker, your trip is free. And once you gain a reputation, they'll be calling you for trip after trip. Think of all the buffet table ice sculptures you'll see!

Many retired people guest lecture on exotic voyages. Hot topics are self-enrichment, fashion, time management, relaxation techniques, investing, and subjects related to retirement. If you're interested in cashing in on this ticket to ride, it is vital to keep up on trends and to be flexible enough that you can sail on a day's notice.

If you have an interest in being a cruise lecturer, assess you skills and past experience, choose your topics and develop your presentations, arrange to give some lectures for local groups, and then create a snappy resume. Sell your skills and appeal to the cruise line of your choice via letter and credentials and hope for the best.

YOUR CALL!

Another way to enjoy a nearly free vacation is to organize a tour of your own or to act as a group leader for a travel agency. Contact your local travel agencies to see if they use group leaders or would be interested in beginning such a program. In some cases, you might have to guarantee that a certain number of people will take the tour. If so, rush out and sign up all your friends and relatives. Everybody can have a ball!

YOU CAN TAKE IT WITH YOU

The very best travel bargain is to work as a travel courier, and 60 courier companies use members of the general public to carry documents and packages abroad. A flight to the Orient can cost as little as $200. The downside is that you will have to give up your luggage allotment and travel only with carry-on luggage, and you'll have to follow a specific timetable set by the courier company, usually between seven and ten days.

To find out more about this unique travel opportunity, you can do it the old fashioned way by writing to the International Association of Air Travel Couriers, Box 1349, Lake Worth, Florida 33460; or you can do it the new-fashioned way and visit their Web site at http://www.courier.org/. Another good site to check is the Air Courier Association at http://www.aircourier.org/. Their mission is to "assure that there will be an adequate number of freelance couriers to fill 40,000 round-trip flights from the US each year." Yep, you read it right—40,000 flights. At lease one of them probably has your name on it.

ROLL WITH IT!

Another bargain travel experience is to cruise by freighter, an old mode of sea travel that you seldom hear about today. These cruises are rarely advertised, and many travel agencies don't know much about them, but freighter cruises are making a comeback and are perfect for folks who like the sea but don't like the large cruise ships that carry hundreds of passengers.

Lizzie's Tips

When you are traveling in Europe, pay your bills by credit card whenever you can and obtain local currency by using your bank ATM card. The rate of exchange is better.

About 100 traditional freighters ply the open seas. They carry from four to twelve additional passengers aside from the crew. These ships are not the tramp steamers of old, but thoroughly modern and well-designed ships. All cargo is containerized and the ships are equipped with every modern technological convenience.

The folks who travel by freighter usually want to get away from all the hustle and bustle and the "Vegas" atmosphere of the busy cruise lines. The freighters have no activity directors, no aerobics classes, no dress codes, and very few people. Freighter travel is a real getaway that offers a relaxed atmosphere and the opportunity to see the world at your own pace. A well-planned trip can cost as little as $100 per day.

Expect comfortable accommodations, television, exercise rooms, and laundry facilities. Tasty food with the ship's officers is plentiful and nutritious. Check to see if you need to BYOB or if the ship offers steward service. Most lines require passengers over 65 to provide a certificate of good health, and all travelers must receive any required immunizations.

Most freighter cruises take from 30 to 90 days, so freighters are not a good choice for short hops. Also, you had better love the sea, because you'll be out there awhile. But if you're a seafaring, independent spirit who can make your own entertainment, you will love the solitude of these comfortably outfitted vessels.

Lizzie Sez

Every now and again, take the scenic route!

For tips about freighter trips, call Ford's Freighter Travel Guide at 818-701-7414 for a $24 subscription. Additionally, some travel agents on the Web advertise freighter trips.

DESTINATION: FUN, ADVENTURE, ROMANCE... WHATEVER

No matter what type of trip you envision, the Web is waiting to answer your questions, suggest options, direct you to resources, and make your reservations. Talk about a travel agent deluxe! We'll take a look at some of the fabulous travel sites available in cyberspace. I'll bet you've never even considered some of the wonderful trips you'll learn about from these stellar resources.

GENERAL TRAVEL SITES

You'll be able to find just about all the information, tips, and suggestions you could ever want in these general travel sites.

American Passport Express
http://www.americanpassport.com/
This commercial passport expediting service posts all the information you'll need to obtain or renew your U.S. passport, including requirements, FAQ, a nationwide list of passport offices by state, and downloadable passport forms. And if you're flying to Europe next week but just remembered that your passport expired two years ago, you might want to check into their expediting services.

Lonely Planet Online
http://www.lonelyplanet.com/

Lonely Planet publishes practical travel guides for the budget-minded wayfarer. You won't get all the info from their guides at this site, but you will get extensive online brochures about destinations all over the world. Let's say you've always wanted to go to Peru. It's here, and you can learn that a cheap room runs $5 U.S. and a hotel room goes for $10 to $15. Descriptive paragraphs provide an overview of the country, info on climate, sightseeing, offbeat activities, and more. This is a super site for gleaning all that background information that helps make your trip enjoyable.

Microsoft Expedia Travel Service
http://expedia.msn.com/home10.hts?

Want vacation ideas, recommendations from travelers, maps, and an illustrated guidebook to over 250 locations worldwide? Check out Microsoft Expedia, a travel agent extraordinaire. Check room availability online, take a look at the local weather, join a travel forum, or just click through the interesting features and services.

On-Call Vacations
http://www.on-call.com/^5769728678996576/home/index.html

Travelers aged 55 or over who are members of United Airlines' Silver Wings Plus program can join this travel club and enjoy "great savings on cruise, hotel and resort vacations."

rec.travel Library
http://www.solutions.net/rec-travel/

Travel the world for information before packing your bags with the help of the Usenet newsgroup rec.travel archive. The site includes links to places to go, with contact information for travel agents and accommodations and tips from other travelers. You'll find all sorts of useful features here, from how to pack to currency exchange rates to driving tips. A super resource.

The Rough Guide
http://www.hotwired.com/rough/

HotWired's travel service, The Rough Guide, tells it like it is for destinations across the world. The even reporting highlights the location's ups and downs (and we all know that no place is perfect, no matter what its rep) and provides recommendations for lodging, eating, seeing, and touring. Seasoned travelers are invited to share their experiences. A welcome change from the chamber of commerce text of many travel sites, the excellent writing in the Rough Guide features is entertaining even if you're *not* planning a trip.

Time Out
http://www.timeout.co.uk/

Time Out Net provides city guides and arts and entertainment listings for international hot spots. Here you'll find features about Berlin, London, Madrid, New York City, Paris, San Francisco, and other world-class cities. Access is free, but users must register.

Tourism Offices Worldwide Directory
http://www.mbnet.mb.ca/lucas/travel/

Visitors to this page can search a database of over 1,200 entries to locate tourism offices throughout the world. Type in Bulgaria, for example, and the search engine will return info on two offices—one of them in the States—that will help you plan the Balkan vacation you've always longed for.

Travel & Entertainment Network
http://www.ten-io.com/

The Travel and Entertainment Network is a trunkload of information for travelers. The site includes products and services available online, free demonstration software, and the TEN-10 database that you can use to quickly locate lodgings information from Marriotts to hostels, links to all the big cruise companies, and some fabulous destinations you may never have considered.

Travel Source
http://www.travelsource.com/

Wow! Talk about your specialized vacations! Travel Source indexes links to vacation packages for interests you never knew you had: golfing, diving, trekking, boating, sea kayaking, ecotours, wine tours ... you name it! There's even a section called Senior Leisure. I could happily spend the next several years going on these trips.

📧 "I read yesterday that the majority of mosquito bites are on the ankles and mosquitoes are attracted to the smell of feet!?! I don't have smelly feet— but if I DO go to Africa, I will definitely take socks, socks, and more socks!"

Travel Weekly
http://www.traveler.net/two/

I don't have enough space to adequately describe all the great travel info crammed into this frequently updated site, so you'll have to discover some surprises on your own. For starters, click on the U.S. Sites link to find travel info for almost every state and the Virgin Islands. Then I was intrigued by the heading Theme Travel, but was a little disappointed to discover that it didn't have anything to do with costumes or masks. But it sounds fun anyway. The links in the theme section point to different *types* of vacations—adventure, diving, golfing, honeymooning, skiing, and the enigmatic miscellaneous. Turns out the miscellaneous category includes learning trips and genealogical tracking journeys. There's lots more here; travel through its pages and see.

TravelASSIST
http://travelassist.com/

Don't you just love small, intimate inns and B&Bs? TravelASSIST offers a grab bag of online travel info, including a directory of more than 750 inns, small hotels, and bed and breakfasts, along with descriptions of travel-related products and services. How about the CrossTrails Bed & Breakfast in the Blue Ridge area of southwest Virginia or the Hearthstone Inn in Colorado Springs? They're here, along with many more listings, and all are hyperlinked to descriptions, room rates, and contact info. And it's not just the United States. The register includes selected listings from Europe, the Caribbean, Canada, and Central America. Le Chateau de Livet sur Authou in France looks like a great choice. Check it out.

TravelGram—Bargain Discounts
http://news.travelgram.com/travelgram/

Updated daily, this site brings you news on the latest discounts in airfare, hotels, travel packages, and more. Subscribe to TravelGram and have the news delivered directly to your PC.

ISLAND DESTINATIONS

Who can resist the siren call of the islands? Think white sand, rum drinks, sparkling waters, rum drinks, first-class treatment, and rum drinks. Sounds pretty good, especially when piles of sooty snow line every curb and your fingers are so cold you can barely pick up the newspaper from the front lawn. Visit these sites for descriptions and photos that will warm your heart. To warm the rest of you, you'll have to go there.

Bali: The Online Travel Guide
http://werple.mira.net.au/~wreid/bali_ p1a.html

The Bali Online Travel Guide promises a complete view of the Indonesian island from off the beaten tourist track. Visitors to this site can find cheap accommodations, cultural attractions, and a gourmet restaurant guide.

"Bali was expensive with all costs already in US$. Round of golf was $160 including cart, club rental $25 and tip to caddy $20 for 2 players. Still cheaper then Japan where you are talking $300-400 for green fees and caddy.

"Played a round of golf in Bali at Bali Golf & Country Club next to Hilton. I've never seen sand traps so huge, like small lakes."

Big Island of Hawaii

http://bookweb.cwis.uci.edu:8042/Books/ Moon/moon.html

The Big Island of Hawaii is a hypertext travel guide leading tourists on a cyberpath through the history, culture, and landscape of the Big Island. Visitors will find background information, maps, photos, and audio files.

Caribbean On-Line

http://www.caribbean-on-line.com/ welcome.html

No matter where you're thinking of going in the Caribbean—Aruba, Curaçao, St. Maarten, the Dominican Republic, Antigua—you'll find pages devoted to each island at this site, along with info on shopping, sleeping, and sipping. Oh, and don't forget the maps and weather updates.

Jamaica!

http://www.jamaicatravel.com/

This official site from the Jamaican Tourist Board invites you to visit the "island that's like no other island on

earth." The delights of Jamaica are laid before you like a platter heaped with exotic fruits. You'll want to taste them for yourself.

NetWeb Bermuda

http://www.bermuda.com/

NetWeb Bermuda is crammed with travel info for the potential tourist. You'll learn, for example, that the Bermuda dollar equals the U.S. dollar and that American money is graciously accepted everywhere (I'll bet!). You should also know that Bermudans get downright testy if you don't start a conversation with a pleasant greeting such as "Good afternoon." The site includes even more indispensable travel tips and a link to the Bermuda Central Reservation Service that includes all manner of accommodations under its roof (cottages, guest houses, private clubs, and hotels).

United States Virgin Islands

http://www.usvi.net/

This Web site offers information on the United States Virgin Islands: St. Croix, St. Thomas, and St. John. Can't you just hear those palm trees rustling in the sea breeze? The site provides an extensive guide to shopping, island hot spots, travel agency information, and weather updates.

The Webfoot's Guide to the British Virgin Islands

http://www.webfoot.com/travel/guides/bvi/ bvi.html

The Webfoot's Guide to the British Virgin Islands contains everything you need to know before launching off to visit this tropical paradise. Check out travel advisories, temperature, and precipitation at different times of the year, currency exchange rates, sailing charters, and diving sites.

NORTH AMERICAN DESTINATIONS

From Canada to Mexico, and including all points in between, North America is a vacation wonderland. You probably don't even know about all the attractions waiting for you just down the road or right around the corner, but these sites will help you locate them in a jiffy.

Appalachian Trail Home Page
http://www.fred.net/kathy/at.html

You're never too old to do the AT. I recently saw a show on television that profiled a group of through-hikers— folks who do the whole thing—and a senior couple was included in the group. The Appalachian Trail stretches from the mountains of Maine to Georgia. This guide offers extensive resources on its more than 2,000 miles. Visit here to learn about the footpath and find maps, hiking tips, news and much more.

City Guide
http://cityguide.lycos.com/

City Guide USA from Lycos profiles more than 400 cities across the United States and includes links to hot spots, news sources, weather info, sports, photographs, and more (over 7,500 links in all) to help you get a feel for your destination. A value-added bonus is the SuperPages feature for each city that provides listings from the yellow pages covering transportation, lodgings, restaurants and bars, and attractions. This combination of city profile, hand-picked links, and phone book listings makes City Guide USA an excellent trip planning resource.

city.net
http://www.city.net/countries/united_states/

Excite's city.net is another type of city guide service that indexes its city-specific links in categories such as city info, news and media, travel, and weather. Predictably, larger cities have far more links than the smaller ones, so you'll find that the coverage of cities varies significantly. Nevertheless, the links are good jumpstations to info about a specific area, and the city.net interface is easy to use.

Connections: A Southern Golf & Vacation Guide
http://www.aesir.com/Welcome.html

Well, the name of this site is a little misleading since it only includes the extreme southeastern portion of the United States from the Outer Banks in North Carolina to Fort Lauderdale. Nevertheless, if you're interested in a golf game (or two or three) at one of the premiere clubs in this area (Hilton Head anyone?), then this site is a good jumpstation to information, resorts and accom-modations listings, rental companies, and other tourism resources.

Discover Canada Online
http://www.discovercanada.com/

Promising to provide "the best of Canada on the Internet," this site won't disappoint you. Trip suggestions (along with accommodation info) are conveniently classified into summer adventure and winter adventure sections, and the site includes descriptions of several one-price travel packages. Vancouver, Calgary, Quebec City, Montreal—the treasures of Canada are on display for you at this comprehensive site.

Freetime Guide
http://www.ftguide.com/default.html

This searchable database bills itself as "your #1 source for events and attractions in the USA" and claims to have information for almost 2,700 cities. A few test searches I did came up empty, but then I learned the trick. Keep your initial search broad by only specifying a month and a state. Then, if you get too many hits, refine your search by specifying a week, city, or keyword. This is a nifty database that can clue you in to events like the Victorian Garden Party at Cypress Gardens (Florida) and the Hinsdale (Illinois) Fine Arts Festival. Both these events occur in June, though, so you'll have to choose.

> "The drive up the Okanogan valley in Washington and lower BC is one of the most beautiful drives in the world. Big Horn sheep grazing along the side of the road, grey wolves (not coy-

otes, I know the difference), lots of black bears and Majestic Mountains."

Grand Canyon Official Tourism Page
http://www.thecanyon.com/

Everyone should see the Grand Canyon, and the photos and tour descriptions at this official site will have you packing your bags before you even log off. Whether you choose the north rim or the south, summer or winter, this site provides maps and loads of info on accommodations, special trips, weather, and more.

Mexico Travel
http://www.mexconnect.com/mex_/
mextravel.html

From Mayan ruins to modern cities, Mexico has something for every traveler. Access info about what our southern neighbor offers in terms of activities and sights, and think about planning your next trip to coincide with the butterfly migration.

Walt Disney World
http://www.travelweb.com/thisco/wdw/
wdwhome/wdw.html

Find out what Mickey and his pals are up to in central Florida. Maintained by the Walt Disney Company, this home page includes information on the Magic Kingdom, Epcot, and Disney-MGM Studios. Visitors can get the inside info on tickets, events, and reservations. And for those still in the planning stages, check out the numerous package deals detailed at the site.

Werner's "Not Disney" Theme Parks, Fairs, and Amusement Parks
http://www.mcs.net/~werner/parklinks.html

If you want to do the roller coaster/amusement park thing but just can't face the Disney crowd, take a look at the alternatives indexed on this page. From Knott's Berry Farm to Cedar Point in Sandusky, Ohio (home of twelve coasters), you'll find lots of choices from parks all over the United States.

Yahoo—Regional: U.S. States
http://www.yahoo.com/Regional/U_S__
States/

It would be hard to get more comprehensive information that that provided in the Yahoo links to the individual states. Tennessee alone has over 2,500 sites and Texas weighs in with a whopping 10,235. Don't let these numbers daunt you, though. Yahoo has cleverly arranged these links under descriptive subcategories like travel, entertainment, and recreation and sports, so you can find what you're looking for fast.

WHERE IN THE WORLD?

By no means comprehensive, the links in this section are just a hint of what's available out there in the world beyond our borders. If you don't see your dream spot listed here, check the general travel sites indexed earlier (most of them contain exhaustive info about overseas travel) or do your own keyword search.

Austria: City.Net Index
http://www.city.net/countries/austria/

Excite's City.Net information service maintains this site for its extensive Austria resource index. Visitors will find links to national, regional, and local organizations, culture and language guides, tourist information, and much more.

Australian Alpine Information Service
http://www.adfa.oz.au/aais/

The Australian Alpine Information Service maintains this site featuring an interactive guide to the snowfield resorts in Australia and New Zealand. The pages also offer a photo archive, a listing of clubs and associations, short stories, and links to other related Web-based resources.

Costa Rica Photo Travel Journal
http://swissnet.ai.mit.edu/cr/

Take a look at "the canopy," the community of wildlife and plants living in the treetops of the Costa Rica rainforest. These images and a detailed guide to visiting the Central American country are provided here by a fellow traveler.

Data Wales Country Guide
http://www.data-wales.co.uk/

Data Wales maintains this site for a detailed guide to resources in the British principality. Visitors will find information on local tourism, including recommendations on the best accommodations and sightseeing destinations (castles and abbeys, anyone?). The site is fully searchable and includes links to general United Kingdom-related sites.

Finnish Travel Reservations
http://www.webtravel.fi

Tourism information service provider WebTravel maintains this site for its Finland resource index. Visitors will find updated reservation listings from travel, accommodations, local events, ski resorts, and other related services.

Frau Richardson's Pictorial German Homepage
http://ibis.ups.edu/homepage/Richards/
RICHARDS.HTM

This photo archive shows many of the top sightseeing attractions (most of them architectural) in Berlin, Munich, Marburg, Bremen, and Regensburg. All you get are the photos, but this site is a wonderful way to preview the architectural treasures of Germany.

In Italy Online
http://www.initaly.com/

This Webzine is updated monthly and is compiled by American writers who have lived for 20 years or more in Italy. The site is a great source for info on places to see, lifestyles, cooking tours, villa rentals, and travel bargains.

Plus, the authors include "loads of practical information for the traveler."

Irish Country Holidays
http://www.humming-bird.co.uk/clients/ICC/
index.html

You'll want to be wearin' the green when you click onto this site offering Irish country cottage vacations and caravan holidays. Order the brochure online.

Japan National Tourist Organization
http://www.jnto.go.jp/

The Japan National Tourist Organization maintains this informational site for news and travel updates in the East Asian country. Visitors will also find national and local maps, budget travel tips, and suggested itineraries.

The London Guide
http://www.cs.ucl.ac.uk/misc/uk/london.html

Look honey! Big Ben! Parliament! The London Guide, an unofficial guide to visiting the British capital city, offers links to hotel, entertainment, and travel resources.

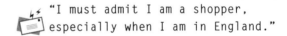 "I must admit I am a shopper, especially when I am in England."

Morocco Guided Tour
http://maghreb.net/morocco/

Take off for the north African coast with this online guided tour of Morocco. Sample local culture and cuisine, read about Moroccan history, and find a wealth of travel and tourism information.

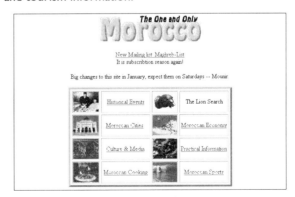

Online Scotland

http://www.ibmpcug.co.uk/~ecs/

After a hearty Highland welcome, click on shopping info, travel tips, a business information exchange, and accommodations assistance—and that's only a partial list of offerings online at this site. Who knows? You could be the one to finally take the definitive photo of the Loch Ness monster.

Paris Page

http://www.paris.org/parisF.html

Whether you're planning a real or virtual trip to the French capital, you'll enjoy a visit to the Paris Pages. "Clique" here for information and graphics covering tourism, entertainment, cultural exhibits, shopping, and many other Parisian resources. In French and English.

Tour in China

http://www.ihep.ac.cn/tour/china_tour.html

Talk about your exotic vacation! Travel to the Tour in China home page to take a virtual trip through Asia's "middle country" and each of its provinces. The site also includes a link to the Hong Kong online guide and a map of China.

The Trans-Siberian Railroad

http://www.ego.net/tlogue/xsib/

Some friends of mine who traveled to Russia a few years ago came home with this advice, "Take your own toilet paper." The only reference to toilet paper I found at this site is the comment that "Traveler's checks don't even make good toilet paper." Nevertheless, this travelogue details an exotic journey—"the greatest rail journey on the planet"—that most of us will only read about. For those of you who are thinking about going, the site includes great tips on how to prepare and what to expect.

Travel 2 Indonesia

http://www.travel2indonesia.com/

Maintained by an Indonesian expatriate in the United States, this guide to the Southeast Asian archipelago (the largest in the world) offers a variety of cultural, geographic, and tourist resources. Among the vital info you'll learn here is that the "moisture-laden" west monsoon occurs from December to March. To keep dry, plan your trip during the east monsoon from June to September.

Turkey Travel Guide

http://www.metu.edu.tr/~melih/ turkeyhome.html

Ankara. Istanbul. The very names of Turkish cities have a mysterious cachet. And this travel guide promises to provide "all you may need to know traveling Turkey." From maps to manners, the factual and cultural resources at this site can help you prepare for the trip of a lifetime. You can even ski there, and the site includes information on the ski centers in Turkey.

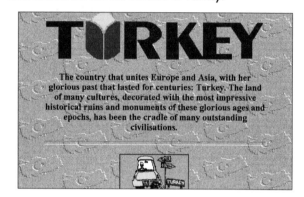

The Webfoot's Guide to Spain

http://www.webfoot.com/travel/guides/spain/ spain.html

The Webfoot's Guide to Spain provides the prospective traveler with the basic facts of that sunny land, including a cultural overview, maps, currency exchange rates, the latest weather, and excerpts from the handy CIA Factbook on the potential trouble spots for ill-prepared travelers.

THIS AIN'T NO STAGECOACH

Bob and Doris have been addicted to camping out for over 30 years, ever since their kids were small. They started out with one of those small pop-up campers they dragged behind the car. The pop-up had its limitations—especially with three children and two adults scrunched inside. Even worse, sometimes the top refused to pop and everyone ended up sleeping on the ground. Cooking arrangements were primitive as well, and many *meals* ended up on the ground. So, over the years, Bob began to upgrade. And boy, did he upgrade!

Now retired, Bob and Doris land-cruise the United States in a totally modern behemoth over 40 feet long, complete with shower, real kitchen, TV, and stabilizers to keep the whole thing upright. The family car and boat trail along behind while this computerized, customized coach tells Bob if a vehicle is behind him and when he can pass. Bob even has his own personal computer on board. While Bob steers them toward Sedona, Doris prepares dinner in the microwave.

For a full six months every year, these RV adventure hounds trip to their favorite campgrounds and renew the friendships they've made over the years with other RVers.

A whole subculture of retirees is doing the RV thing and loving every minute of it. It's an RV world! Let's follow these guys awhile and see where they go.

LIVIN' ON THE ROAD

These pointers will give you plenty of information about the RV lifestyle, suggest destinations, and link you to like-minded travelers. Many RVers choose to do their own thing; they hit the road and let the adventure unfold. But for those of you who don't like to drive and prefer a preplanned trip with a specific itinerary, a number of tour operators conduct RV excursions. The trip options are as unlimited as your imagination. How about the Branson Music Festival, Biltmore at Christmas, or a leisurely jaunt through Gatlinburg and the Smokies? Agency personnel handle all the arrangements, provide the vehicle, and do all the driving—all you have to do is sit back and enjoy the trip. To find agencies that specialize in these trips, search for RV tour operators on the Web.

For those of you who want to blaze your own trail, these sites will help keep you on the right path.

Campground Directory
http://www.holipub.com/camping/director.htm

The Campground Directory bills itself as "the most comprehensive campground directory on the Internet," and it very well may be with its database of over 10,000 campgrounds (no, I didn't count them). You can search by state or zip code to find contact and location information, along with a summary of the campground's amenities. The interface isn't the greatest, but a nice feature of this site is the online classifieds where you might be able to pick up a good deal on a used RV.

Campgrounds.Net Directory
http://www.campgrounds.net/

This site claims to be "the Internet's BEST Campground directory," with over 9,500 campgrounds listed in its database. The interface is easier on the eyes than the Campground Directory's, but less basic info is provided here. You'll get location and contact info, but no amenities summary (unless the campground has a home page and the directory includes a hyperlink). One excellent feature of this page, however, is the RV Advice section, where the service manager for an RV shop answers questions about all aspects of RV sales, ownership, and maintenance. There's loads of great info here, covering topics from buying a used vehicles to how to operate the air conditioner.

Good Sam Club
http://www.tl.com/roads/goodsam/roads_club_goodsam.html

This RV club claims to have 900,000 members and invites you to become member 900,001. The club looks like a great deal. They offer a free 30-day trial membership and if you decide you want to stay in, you'll pay only $25 for 13 months. Club benefits include a trailer full of discounts (parts, campground fees, fuel, insurance, and lots more) and a backpack full of freebies (trip routing, mail forwarding, a magazine, and more). Plus, Good Sam members can participate in "Samboree" rallies, cross-country caravans, and special Good Sam Tours and cruises around the world.

Happy Campers
http://www.hcampers.com/

This directory lists and maps 1,100+ campgrounds and dozens of attractions in the southwestern United States and Mexico. Don't expect too much detail other than the location, number of camping sites, and availability of sewer and electric, but attractions in the area are sometimes listed with hyperlinks and the site includes a good feature on obtaining health care in Mexico.

Internet RV and Camping Guide
http://www.rvzone.com/

This page is a good index to RV and camping-related links on the Internet. The listing includes newsgroups, campground directories, individual campgrounds, commercial sites (sales and rentals), tourist info, and more.

National Park Service Home Page
http://www.nps.gov/

Before loading up the RV for Yosemite or other national parks, contact this electronic visitor center for maps, weather, and camping fees. The site includes a list of all national parks and an overview of the Park Service's work to "preserve America's heritage."

Park Search
http://www.llbean.com/parksearch/

Outdoor outfitter L.L. Bean brings this excellent database of parks and outdoor activities to the Web. Well-written summaries and details of activities and facilities complement the listings of nearly 1,500 outdoor areas. The 2,000 photos give you a preview of what you'll see when you get there.

Recreational Vehicles and Motorhome Living
http://www.pitre.com/rv1.html

This index to RV-related sites includes over 100 links to newsgroups, info sources, road condition phone numbers, magazines, and weather updates. You'll also find a glossary of RV terms, a route-planning tool, and an interesting travel diary posted by the site creator.

RV and Camping FAQ
http://www.kiz.com/campnet/html/journal/rvfaq.htm

Whether you're just starting to think about life on the road or have already logged a few thousand miles on the odometer, you'll find useful information at this FAQ. From definitions of the different types of RVs to battery recommendations, the Q&A here cover many issues specific to RV travel and camping. A site bonus is the list of related sites pointing to dealers, newsgroups, supplies, and more.

RV Online
http://www.rv-online.com/

Folks in the market for a used motorhome, 5th wheel, or trailer might want to check this site from "America's premiere RV marketplace." Sellers post descriptions, prices, and photos of their vehicles, along with contact information. Potential buyers contact the seller directly. Listings can be sorted by price, location, or size to help you find the deal of a lifetime fast.

RVers Online
http://www.pacificrim.net/~tgonser/RV.html

All you wired RVers will love this page. Tom & Stephanie Gonser, seasoned RV travelers and Web devotees, have designed their site for the new breed of RVer. They include info on modem-friendly RV parks, a directory of RV-related links, a great list of RV articles (covering destinations, lifestyle, technical issues, and "full-timing"), and reviews of top parks from both the authors and their readers.

Chapter 20

UP CLOSE AND PERSONAL

LIZZIE'S TIPS FOR LONG DISTANCE GRANDPARENTING

IN THE MOOD

JUST AWAY

A CAPPELLA

I thought that as you got older, things were supposed to be easier. But for me, the world spins faster, and "easier" seems to have passed me by. I have learned a lot, though, as the years of my tangled life have unwound. I've learned that planning is better than winging it, financial security beats poverty any day, and being assertive in the face of real stupidity is far better than taking it on the chin.

The most important thing I have learned as my skein has unraveled is that friends and family count for more than anything. As we get older, relationships seem harder to make and harder to keep. Friends who have nurtured us and supported us through all the ups and downs of life, and who have been there when times were rocky and the ride was rough, may have passed on and left us to see things through. Making new friends in this wildly whirling world can be complicated because there is no history. Building one takes time.

"To be completely honest, 3 out of 9 of my grandchildren are selfish boors."

Relations even in the immediate family can wither, especially if your children and relatives live thousands of miles away and the only bridge is long distance calls and perhaps a yearly visit. Divorce, up to 50 percent in this country, has separated us even more, scattering husbands, wives, and grandchildren in all directions. Keeping relationships with friends and family fresh and meaningful takes special thoughtfulness and a lot of energy.

From a distance it's hard for our scattered relatives to see us as the family rock or pillar of wisdom, major supporter, or best friend. About all we can do is stand back and watch as our younger family members, strewn all over the landscape, struggle with their life problems as we did years ago with ours. But

we are not there to help. How do you ship chicken soup by FedEx?

Sometimes, the ones to suffer the most are the grandchildren who don't have the refuge of the comfortable, nonjudgmental arms of grandmas and grandpas. Grandparents can be more user friendly and relaxed than parents because dealing with children is different when you're one step removed. Grandparenting isn't like raising your own children. The heavy focus on discipline eases.

"Since I am unfortunate enough to have all 3 of my grandchildren 9 hours away in New Jersey, and only get to see them once or twice a year, I trust their parents are raising them right. Good bad or indifferent, I would love to have them near me. Be thankful today, on Thanksgiving, that yours are near enough to know what they are really like."

LIZZIE'S TIPS FOR LONG DISTANCE GRANDPARENTING

But what if your grandchildren are so far away they seem like strangers? Well, few of us are lucky enough to have our grandchildren nearby, but a little effort and a few tricks can keep those long-distance kids near at heart. It takes a bit of energy and creativity, but it can be fun.

- Be sure they have a picture of you in their rooms. I know you hate to have your picture taken; so do I. A trip to the dentist is more welcome. But a new picture every year keeps your image out front, friendly, and familiar. Send pics of pets. A picture of your beloved dog or cat will help keep you in their minds, too.

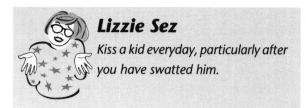

Lizzie Sez

Kiss a kid everyday, particularly after you have swatted him.

- Try your hand at a little artwork. Even the dullest of us can grind out something lively, even if it's in crayon, to send to the littlest ones. Maybe you can graduate to water colors. Remember those paint boxes from the dime store? Experiment with painting a scene of you in the kitchen or garden and send it along. You *could* get good at this.

- Almost all of us have tape recorders and some of us can remember the old stories we were told by our own grandmothers. If you can't remember any, get some children's books from the library and read from those, or make up your own stories about the silly things your dog does. Make a habit of sending tapes that tell about what happened this week at your place. These tapes will keep any age child, up to adult, much closer to you than silence. The tapes you send will be eagerly anticipated. Make it a habit.

- The art of letter writing has about died, I know, but cards are cheap enough that you can send them regularly. Include a short note to let those kids know you are thinking about them. Inside you can put riddles and puzzles, word games, and code words you both have made up. Keep the letters interesting and lively. Don't dwell on your latest case of warts.

- Many of us have video cameras. How about granddad producing an ongoing soap opera about his doings? Kids of any age, including your own adult ones, would be excited to receive this kind of movie. And what a great way to keep close.

- Send a box of old clothes for dress-up. Even some of grandpa's stuff will be fun for boys of the right age. You might even suggest a title of a play in which they could use these clothes, with items specifically named for each part. Kids love to put on amateur theatricals.

- If you have a hobby, share it with your grandkids. Even flowers can be shared. Send a catalog, ask the child to pick out the seeds or plants he/she wants, and see that the child gets them with planting instructions. Then you can share some of your expertise and encouragement. Stamps, coins, and baseball cards are also easy to share.

- If you have a grandchild who is an eager sports fan, make small bets on the games you are both interested in. A wager makes for more excitement. And the kids absolutely love to win.

- Boxes of unusual recycled stuff delight the kids on the receiving end. Almost every thrift shop has bags of yarn, old cards, and other items that any child can use for craft activities. This idea is especially good for a pre-Christmas gift. Your grandchild could make his/her own gifts or tree ornaments.

- With the computer coming of age, almost everyone can get on the Internet, so send e-mail directly to the kiddies frequently. Answer promptly and lovingly.

"I fully realize that all grandchildren (including my own) are wonderful, selfless, future Nobel prize winners, but it is time for us grandparents to get real. If any of us were subjected, like today's children, to the overindulgence to their slightest whims and their avalanches of expensive electronic devices and the psychobabble of their parents re: self-esteem, we, too, would be overstimulated, bored, and jaded—rather than the flawless, wise, and complete individuals we old timers are. Right?"

CLEAN UP YOUR ACT!

If your grandkids do live at a distance and you are expecting an imminent visit, put your own life on hold while they are there and dedicate the time exclusively to them. Plan age-appropriate activities. Little ones love visits to parks and playgrounds. Older children may enjoy a day on the golf course or a mega-shopping trip to the mall. Use your head when you plan the time.

Give your house the once over and put up treasures and breakables. Put poisons away and keep your medications out of reach. Even the most manageable children are curious, and your unfamiliar house is an uncharted sea of new discoveries and unexpected hiding places. Don't leave any dangerous or breakable treasures around for them to find.

BAG THE NAG

Whatever you do, don't criticize the way they have been brought up, their manners and deportment, their sloppiness, or their inability to perform certain tasks. If a disciplinary problem arises, stay friendly and firm. You don't have to give in, but don't lose your cool, either. Never criticize their parents!

Expect your entire household to be disrupted, your routine to be demolished, and everything to be messy. Ignore it! The visit will last only a short time and a little mess is not the end of the world. You can dig out after they've gone home. Take their visit as an opportunity to pass on your heritage, your values, your unique expertise. Mix that up with some old family stories, and a few things you can teach, like managing and investing money. Why not? Did you ever know an 11-year-old boy who was not fixated with money?

Lizzie's Tips

Here are some actions you should take if you are anticipating a visit from small children:

- Tuck lamp cords behind furniture so they are not accessible.

- Cover electrical outlets with safety plates.

- Install collapsible gates to keep dangerous areas shut off.

- Put away any items that can be swallowed.

- Buy or borrow high chairs and cribs, diapers and wipes, car seats, and other necessities before the children arrive. This will ease the pain a great deal and make your visit much more enjoyable.

- Have their favorite foods on hand.

- Create a place where they can play and do projects. Have some quiet projects planned and the materials available to make it happen.

- Plan some excursions—a trip to the zoo or a children's play.

- Make sure they have a time and a place to burn off some of that energy.

- Don't overschedule activities.

- Fill a toybox with different kinds of toys.

- Be flexible; plans change and kids get sick. Have a backup babysitter just in case, so you and the other children won't be disappointed.

- Get a medical emergency release form from their parents so that you can have your grandchildren treated if necessary.

ON THE WAVELENGTH

Friends of mine whose grandchildren live nearby have established their own unique rituals, special to them and the children. Virginia, 71 and an artist, is visited by her twin 5-year-old granddaughters one Saturday every month. For this day, Virginia organizes projects appropriate to their age. Most of these activities have to do with her own skill as a painter and art teacher and her knowledge and appreciation of art. These are lucky little girls to have such an opportunity to learn about grandma and what she does. Everyone has fun on these special Saturdays.

"There is no love greater than that for our grandchildren. Bores? Hell no!!! I can have adult conversations with them. They can reason pretty well. We were never that smart when we were their ages. The world is much more advanced today and they learn about computers even in Kindergarten. We just bought Disney discs for the computer that teach the ABCs. That's for the 3 yr. old. Our children live within an hour from us. Yes, we realize how lucky we are. We see our grandchildren a few times a month."

Toni, 71, a tireless volunteer and expert cook, designs and directs programs for nursing homes all over the city. Her grandchildren benefit from her skills and from her commitment to carrying on a tradition she learned as a child from her grandparents. Toni designs special holiday programs for her grandchildren to perform. She includes a part for every child and supplies scripts and music appropriate for each holiday. The performances are totally charming. Toni's grandchildren will remember these events all their lives and hopefully will pass the tradition down to their own children.

THE SLIPPERY SIDE

There is a downside to this sweetness and light, however. Many grandparents rarely get to see their grandchildren, due to messy divorces and the animosity of the custodial parent. Check your state laws. Almost all states make grandparent visitation a right, granted by the court. If you cannot make headway with the parents for visitation, seek legal help.

"My children and my children's children all still address men and women as "yes, sir" and "yes, ma'am" no matter where they are. A very close and loving family, thoughtful and thankful to God. Spoiled? If compared to the difference in the way we were reared without all the materialistic diffusion and temptation I guess they are spoiled, but not selfish and never boorish. We laugh, play jokes on one another, sing, and always say a prayer for our good health and many, many blessings. And we have not been without deep sorrow or a need for forgiveness...giving and receiving."

NUCLEAR GRANDPARENTING

About three million grandparents are acting as surrogate parents in today's changing world. If you find yourself in this spot, either because of parental abuse or abandonment, you may want to seek legal help so that you can obtain permanent custody. An order of permanent custody provides stability for the child and legal protection for you. However, you must provide a very convincing argument to persuade the court that awarding custody to you is in the child's best interests. Grandparents could be awarded custody just for the stable environment they can provide.

AN OSCAR WINNER

My own grandmother was the most important person in my life. We were separated by great distances for long periods of time, yet I always remained close to her. Every week of her life I received a long newsy letter from her, and she frequently sent books she hoped I would read or stuffed dolls she had made. One large stuffed doll she sent came with hidden pockets brimming with candy. It was a poignant moment for me when I gave this beloved ragdoll to my own daughter to hug in her sleep.

For awhile, my grandmother even sent cakes. These were gorgeous layer cakes, iced and placed on a 78 rpm record, packed in a box, and shipped by the post office. They always remained completely intact.

Through this intimate contact with my grandmother, I learned things that my parents rarely had time to share: a deep love of classical music and opera; how to cook and paint; but most of all, how to be a truly nonjudgmental, loyal friend, interested in the welfare of others.

PARENTING, GRANDPARENTING, AND GREAT-GRANDPARENTING

Even if you live far away, you can be a positive force in your grandchildren's lives. Don't sit back and wait for your children to bring the grandchildren to you. They may mistake your reticence for disinterest. Instead, show how vitally interested you are in your grandchildren and do everything you can to establish a connection with them.

I don't know many couples who wouldn't jump at the chance to have grandma and grandpa take the kids for a weekend. All you have to do is ask. If you start early, you and your grandchildren can develop a wonderful relationship that will last the rest of your life.

The Web has a variety of sites with super tips for grandparents. You can always turn here for advice and fresh ideas.

Ask Great-Granny
http://www.mbnet.mb.ca/crm/granny/granny.html

Her common sense, degree in psychology, and experience in journalism recommend this mother of six, grandmother of 14, and great-grandmother of two. Great-Granny responds to reader questions and offers advice for coping with generational divides.

Family.Com
http://family.com/

Affiliated with over 100 parenting magazines, this zine and archive posts articles dealing with issues most on the minds of parents—from caring for a child with special needs to grandparents as proxy parents. Articles are written to be reassuring and offer practical suggestions for nurturing children and maintaining a healthy family life.

Family Relations
http://www.personal.psu.edu/faculty/n/x/nxd10/family3.htm

Here's a collection of articles that offers insight into most aspects of family relationships, including the impact grandparents can have on their grandchildren. An index of links to sites offering other topical information is also included.

Grandloving: Grandparenting with Activities and Long-Distance Fun
http://world.std.com/~jcarlson/senior/

Defy the miles that separate you and a loved grandchild with the ideas and suggestions found on this practical and timely site hosted by Sue Johnson and Julie Carlson. The pair have authored a book on the subject, *Grandloving: Making Memories with Your Grandchildren.*

Grandparent E-mail Pen Pals
http://iquest.com/~jsm/moms/grand.html

Young parents and children come here to find the wisdom that comes with aging. Seniors come here to share that wisdom. Read the profiles to find a pen pal or post your own profile.

Grandparent Times

http://www.uconnect.com/cga/

Stop in here to find ideas for making your grandparenting experience all it can be. Join the online discussion to share your ideas or harvest the suggestions of others.

The Multimedia Grandma

http://www.hometown.on.ca/mmgram/

Marguerite Oberle Thomas posts tips and tales that long-distance, multimedia grandparents can use to help nurture and provide support for their grandchildren despite the intervening miles. Those with ideas and experiences to contribute are encouraged to do so.

The Multimedia Grandma

You are visitor number **BUSY** since 5 June 1996.

Meet the Long Distance Multimedia Grandma

ParentsPlace.com

http://www.parentsplace.com/

Here's an online index of parenting resources on the Internet. Visitors can read articles and books, chat with other parents, or perform a keyword search of the ParentsPlace databases. Links to a variety of parenting centers and related businesses are also available.

IN THE MOOD

There's no question that family relationships take thought and energy to sustain. But probably the most ticklish relationships to foster are those with the opposite sex, especially after 60.

TIE THE KNOT TIGHTER

If you are married, retirement gives you more time to beef up what may be a tired relationship. Start making your relationship a priority. Schedule dates

---

WAYS TO KEEP *YOUR* LOVE ALIVE

- Be the first to admit you were wrong.
- Always praise a job well done.
- Don't forget to ask his/her opinion.
- Remember the "P" word, please.
- Always say thank you.
- Never forget you are "WE."

for lunch or dinner, and make more time for each other with the extra time you now have. Quit bagging your feelings. It's time to let it all hang out by saying clearly and without anger what bothers you. Your partner cannot read your mind, no matter how many years you may have been together.

MAGIC FINGERS

For many years, old friends of mine, well into their eighties, made a beeline to a well-known sleazy motel where they would spend every Saturday afternoon, watching cheap porn movies, lolling on the vibrating bed, and keeping their love alive. They were so frail that we used to worry about them driving out there and getting home safely. But nothing could discourage these outings, and they looked forward to them as much as if they were teenagers. I'm happy to report that they lived well into their nineties and died with their boots on.

Think up little surprises: unexpected theater tickets, flowers, or a wild and woolly weekend. Women's lib has opened the floodgates for women to have creative ideas as well as the guys. Whatever you do, keep the flame burning. It's a whole lot more fun.

TWO HEARTS BEATING AS ONE

On the other hand, if you are single and anxious to meet a prospective partner, you have several options.

The hard part is getting started on the dating process again. But retirement offers great opportunities to be more active than ever before. Not shackled with a 9 to 5 job, it's easier to get out and go places, stay out late and sleep in, go where you want when you want, and best of all, most family responsibilities are already taken care of. You're free as a bird!

Once you decide to reenter the dating game, one thing you can try is placing ads in the personal columns. Compose your ads thoughtfully and select discriminating magazines or papers. Keep in mind the type of folks who will be reading that publication. You don't want "Chain Saw Charlie" (or Charlene) answering your ad for a date.

Another good place to hang out to meet new people is SeniorNet. I have been told that romance has flourished in the chat rooms and that six weddings have been announced. But SeniorNet is such a wonderful resource that whether or not you meet a life partner may become irrelevant, because you'll get so involved and have so much fun.

Of course, you can meet people anywhere: at church, the laundromat, grocery store, or just walking in the mall. But, today, with the new popularity of the coffee houses, I think I would hang out in one of those, sipping cappuccino. Even the book stores have coffee, so you can browse for both a book and a kook (or a cook!).

There are some drawbacks to dating after you have been widowed for over 20 years. First, your friends will hate you. The strong relationships you have built that incorporate their routines will be changed. They will be jealous of the time you spend with someone outside the widow (or widower) group. Your kids will probably feel uncomfortable with your dating, since you will be throwing a real role reversal on them. Lastly, you may be terrified that this new friendship may lead to sex. After 20 years or more of being single, you're entitled. But

Lizzie's Tips

Dr. Ruth says modern research has validated that people can be sexually active until the age of 99, and advocates "dating rooms" in retirement and nursing homes. Sounds like a plan, Stan.

what's the rush? Take your time; wait until you're ready. Your new friend may have the same feelings of inadequacy.

Join a group, take a class, learn to dance. Savor the richness of life. You won't meet anyone by staying at home and just thinking about it. And while you're looking, you might as well do something interesting!

RELATIONSHIPS SITES

People meet people on the Internet every day. Lots of sites focus on making new friends; others deal strictly in romance. Join in the fun at some of these sites.

Adopt-A-Grandparent
http://www.soulzone.com/soulzone/
commzone/agp/index.html
The Mountain Light Center of Taos, New Mexico created and maintains this program to aid Native American elders. Read the story of AGP and find out how everyday people are finding cross-cultural and cross-generational relationships through the program.

Christian Dating Service International
http://www.christiandating.org/
The nondenominational Christian Dating Service provides a network of eligible Christian singles by city. Its goal is to promote marriage and build Christian families worldwide.

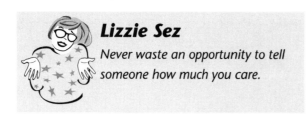

Lizzie Sez

Never waste an opportunity to tell someone how much you care.

Cupid's Personals

http://www.cupidnet.com/cupid/bureau1/

Individuals can seek same and opposite sex dates through these online personals. Read the ads, find a match, then call the 1-900 number and leave a message. Costs nothing to browse or to place an ad.

CyberPals

http://www.mbnet.mb.ca/crm/cyberpal/index.html

The Seniors Computer Information Project of Manitoba, Canada hosts this electronic twist on the idea of making friends via the post. Stop by to find a CyberPal, or register yourself so others can find you and begin a correspondence via e-mail. The rolls include folks (seniors and juniors) from all over North America and around the world.

Cyrano Server

http://www.nando.net/toys/cyrano.html

"Shy and unimaginative" lovers are invited to let the Cyrano Server write form-based love letters for the objects of their unarticulated desires. Electronic dumping is also offered.

E-mail Pen Pals

http://www.retire.net/penpal/

Sponsored by Retire.Net, this electronic pen pal program welcomes participants of all ages. Browse the current listings by keyword to find someone with similar interests as your own or add your profile to the roster and encourage others to write to you.

P.S. I Love You International

http://www.psiloveyou.com/

Here's the '90s version of mail-order brides. This site features a roster of international female clients that includes images and brief descriptions. Visitors who like what they see can order videos to find out more.

Scott's Chat Room Index

http://members.tripod.com/~ScottRichie/Chat

Here's one-stop shopping for those who like to chat online. This directory points to all, or almost all, the chat opportunities available on the Internet. Search by keyword for sites with particular topics or browse the full list.

Senior Chit-Chat

http://shrinvest.com/chat.html

Hosted by the Fifty Plus R Us site, Chit-Chat Central allows users to connect with one another online and discuss current events, memories of the past, or whatever else comes to mind.

Senior.Com SNN Chat Area

http://www.senior.com/chat2.html

Only registered users may enter the chat area, but once inside you'll find dozens of topical and non-topical places where you can mingle and move around. It's like an online cocktail party—but you have to BYOB.

SeniorNet RoundTables

http://www.seniornet.org/cgi-bin/WebX?14@^78@/

Introduce yourself and join any of over 100 discussions on topics ranging from art to travel. Don't be shy. Everyone here is friendly and eager to hear from you.

Single Search
http://nsns.com/single-search

This international matchmaking network uses a computer for compatibility matching and is operated by a marriage counselor. The site's features include background information on the network's services and membership, a classifieds section, and a singles mall.

WebPersonals
http://www.webpersonals.com/

Here's a semi-moderated, free, online service for people seeking love and companionship. Browsers can submit personal advertisements or search the WebPersonals for that special someone.

The Wedding Source
http://www.pep.com/pep/tws/tws.html

Visit this site for a "global network of wedding related topics and information, giving you what you want, when you want it." From simple advice to total event planning, the Wedding Source covers the bases.

JUST AWAY

One of the saddest facts of life is that all relationships eventually must end. The two Ds—death and divorce—change our lives irrevocably, and the resulting grief and loss can practically consume us. For those who have been in long relationships and have been left behind, and for those who have lost loving friends or family, take heart and join with others who share the same pain. Jonathan Swift once said, "It is impossible that anything so natural, so necessary, and so universal as death should ever have been designed by providence as an evil to mankind." S. Hall Young wrote, "No laggard steps, no faltering, no shirking / Let me die, working! / My soul undimmed, alert, no question blinking / Let me die thinking! / The wine of life, the cup of mirth quaffing / Let me die laughing!"

GRIEF AND TRAUMA SUPPORT SERVICES

Only time dulls the pain of grief, but a number of support groups exist to help you make your way through the darkness. Many of these groups have a presence on the Web and can put you in touch with chat rooms, newsgroups, and professionals who want to hear your story and help you work through the loneliness and pain.

The Bereavement Education Center
http://bereavement.org/#MGR

The resources at this site cover many aspects of grief and bereavement: self-help, outreach, helping children cope, funerals, helping a dying friend, and suicide. The site also features the Men's Grief Resource, a non-moderated online private forum where men can share their concerns, beliefs, wounds, questions, and insights.

Christians in Recovery
http://www.goshen.net/cir/

Through mutual sharing and dependence on the 12 Steps and the Bible, this group assists those who are in recovery and provides information "for anyone who DESIRES to recover from abuse, family dysfunction, depression, anxiety, grief or addictions of alcohol, drugs, food, pornography etc."

Death, Dying, and Grief Resources
http://www.cyberspy.com/~webster/death.html

Find help coping with your personal loss or seek support in helping someone you love cope with loss. This master index points to everything from general grief and healing resources to online memorials and remembrances. Newsgroups and listservs are also included.

Divorce Online
http://www.divorce online.com/index.html

Divorce Online, a service for people considering or in the midst of divorce, outlines basic legal facts and tips for surviving a divorce, psychologically and financially. Visitors here will also find an online directory to lawyers, therapists, and financial planners.

FuneralNet

http://www.funeralnet.com/

Leading the resources hosted at this site is a comprehensive guide to U.S. funeral homes with a presence on the Internet. You'll also find a guide to information about funerals, cremation, and cemeteries, a guide to U.S. veteran death benefits, and the FuneralNet classifieds.

Grief and Loss Resource Center

http://www.kanservu.ca/~fairchild/grief/grief.html

This huge index to grief-related sites includes resources to help you cope with death and with other sources of grief such as trauma and stress, moving, and divorce. Comprehensive and tasteful.

Pen-Parents, Inc.

http://pages.prodigy.com/NV/fgck08a/PenParents.html

This international nonprofit seeks to help bereaved parents and grandparents through the grieving process by matching them with others whose circumstances are similar. The idea is that by communicating with one another the bereaved can help themselves by offering mutual support and encouragement.

The Pets Grief Support Page & Candle Ceremony

http://ourworld.compuserve.com/homepages/edwilliams/

Those mourning the loss of a beloved pet or anyone upset over a pet's illness can find sympathy and support from the pet lovers who congregate at this site. Join the weekly Monday Candle Ceremony, read words of comfort, post a tribute to your pet, link to support groups and sites found on the Internet, or seek and find phone numbers to call for counseling and other grief management services.

Widow Net

http://www.fortnet.org/~goshorn/

For both women and men, Widow Net provides resources to help you cope with the overwhelming grief of losing your life partner. You'll find a list of bereavement support groups, FAQ, bulletin boards, and ways to share your experiences with others. Along with emotional support, the site also provides practical help in the form of death benefit information and a pointer to the Federal Trade Commission's consumer guide to funerals.

WorldWide Cemetery

http://www.cemetery.org/

Open to all religious faiths, this virtual final resting place allows family and friends to erect monuments to the memory of their loved ones who have gone before. Visitors to the cemetery can view the memorials and leave flowers. For some, creating virtual memorials helps them move through the grieving process.

A CAPPELLA

The Swedes have an old proverb: "Those who wish to sing will always find a song." Let's get on with it and mingle with the singers and the songs and find the ones we wish to sing ourselves.

SENIORS' HOME PAGES AND PROFILES

Lots of active seniors have posted home pages on the Web. You'll enjoy meeting them.

The AirShow BBS

http://www.pig.net/~stearman/airshow/

Carol and Ron Rex proclaim "BiPlanes are Better!" then proceed to prove the point with a multimedia presentation on the "Golden Age of Aviation"—the period between the World Wars.

Akio's Interesting Things In My Travels
http://pweb.aix.or.jp/~akio-ya/

Akio Yakata treats visitors to photographs and notes illustrating the beautiful and inspiring places he has visited while traveling outside his native Japan.

Aubrey & Ann Roberts
http://www1.pcsvcs.com/~annrob/

Aubrey lends his name and talent to a band of senior musicians, "Aubrey Roberts and the Good Ole Boys," that plays the seniors' functions around Jackson, Miss. Ann likes to fish for bream and bass in the pond on their five acres.

Basic Applied Ethics
http://www.escape.ca/~nyaki/

Nicholas J. Yakimishyn, Ph.D., presents his essays concerning "applied and effective ethics of morality," or what is more commonly known as the greatest commandment: "Love thy neighbor."

Bellwether One
http://www.mindspring.com/~hfuberto/

H.F. Uberto of Marietta, Ga., publishes this "interactive political action publication intended to support U.S. citizens in participating in politics on an issues basis." The idea is to connect citizens to useful historical and current information resources.

Beyond the Veil
http://www.artnet.net/~dgoble/

Diane Goble, a "near-death experiencer," writes about her brush with the eternal and answers questions "most people are afraid to ask." Links also lead to discussion areas dedicated to death and dying, legal information, counseling services, and other topical resources.

Bill Grego
http://www.purplenet.net/~william/index.html

He runs an automotive repair shop for something to do; perhaps it's just too hard to completely retire from the fast-paced world of auto racing. Bill also likes to fish and boat in the waters around his home in Orlando.

Bob LaFara's Pages: Index
http://www.in.net/~rlafara/

He holds advanced degrees in astronomy and engineering, but computing has been his profession. A shareware author since 1989, Bob points visitors to a page that profiles his products. Visitors will also find links to his daughters' pages, one of whom is Aunt Annie of the Aunt Annie's Craft Page featured in chapter 10.

Bonnie Best
http://www.infopoint.com/people/best/

Bonnie runs a communications consulting firm that helps businesses and the individuals who run them define and achieve their goals.

Carole's Nature Page
http://edge.edge.net/~franklin/CJPage.html

Carole Franklin treats her visitors to a look at living in Tennessee and some wildlife photos. A link to Kody the Smoky Mountain Black Bear's home page is also provided for the kids.

"Chai"
http://members.tripod.com/~rebah/shalom.html

Bea likes Betty Boop, music boxes, and poetry. She also likes to chat. Follow Bea to several of her favorite chat sites including Senior Chat and Hawaii Chat Universe.

Charlie's Home Page
http://www.cyberspc.mb.ca/~rainec/

A native of Manitoba, Canada, now living in that province's capital city, Winnipeg, Charles M. Raine posts a portrait of his life along with links to a few of his favorite haunts in cyberspace.

Dennis Smith—Retiree-at-Large
http://www.islandnet.com/~densmith/denhome.html

Stop in here for greetings from Victoria, Vancouver Island, British Columbia, Canada, and to find out what London-born Dennis does now that he has retired from business and the military.

Edwina Marie Elliott

http://206.217.20.5/cgi-bin/
WebX?135@^78@37@.ee6b8fc

Mother to six, grandmother to eight, Edwina lives in Missouri with her husband of 38 years, Bob. She loves playing with genealogy software, and lists CNN Interactive, the Smithsonian Museum, and Great Seniors Sites among her favorite URLs to visit online.

Elizabeth A. Kaspar

http://206.217.20.5/cgi-bin/
WebX?135@^78@9861@.ee6b4d5

A retired university professor, Elizabeth is the Roving Restaurant Reviewer for the online zine "Grape Expectations." She's also a pilot and, of course, loves to travel.

Gary Thomas Moore

http://206.217.20.5/cgi-bin/
WebX?135@^2934@6122@.ee6b316

This computer guy says he's "GoingToPot." Perhaps we should ask his wife of 26 years or his two adult children about that.

Goldngal, The Cyberspace Granny

http://www.fyi.net/~goldngal/goldn2.htm

Her computer was a 50th anniversary gift from her Goldnguy. A mother of three, grandmother of two, and great-grandmother of one, this seventy-something native of Pittsburgh shares her personal story and points visitors to a few of her favorite sites.

Hal Fritts

http://www.ltrr.arizona.edu/people/hal/
hal1.html

Meet a guy who made a living counting tree rings. Actually, he's a retired professor from the University of Arizona's Laboratory of Tree-Ring Research. Married with two children and three grandchildren, Hal is eager to share his interest in trees.

Herbert Harari

http://www.ccnet.com/~herbca/

Dedicating his home page to all those out there who love jazz, blues, boogie, stride, and country music, this retired college professor offers midi music files his visitors can download.

The Holmespage

http://www.magicnet.net/~wholme/

Bill and Kowanda Holmes met in a chat room at Senior-Com. Stop by the couple's home page to see the happy newlyweds, meet their family, and read their delightful story.

Jackie Brown

http://www.seniornet.org/cgi-bin/
WebX?135@@5176@.ee6c846

This mother of five and grandmother of eleven lives with Ernie, her husband of 50 years, in the house they built on the family farm in Tennessee.

James Kirk-White

http://onlink1.onlink.net/~krkwyt/

He's also known as the Duke of URL and GentleBen, or at least he has pages posted under these monikers. Other postings include a midi page, a hobbies page, and a variety of "theme" pages. This directory points the way to them all.

Jim Olson

http://206.217.20.5/cgi-bin/
WebX?135@^2934@87@.ee6b7c3

An outdoor enthusiast from Wisconsin, Jim has retired from teaching to write, travel, and enjoy life. Some of his favorite URIs include the Sierra Club, the Nature Conservancy, and the Elderhostel home page.

Joan Grimes
http://206.217.20.5/cgi-bin/
WebX?135@^2934@49@.ee6b7c3

A retired teacher living in Alabama with her husband, Joan posts a brief biography and links to some of the "interesting" sites she likes to visit online.

John R. Dye
http://www.cco.net/johnrd/

Also known as Olympia's "Old Geezer," this retired senior posts a clickable map of his home town, a brief personal biography, and links to some of his favorite sites, including the Senior RoundTable at SeniorNet.

Keith R. Bradley's Home Page
http://www.mbnet.mb.ca/~kbradley/

Setting an example for seniors, Keith posts "mostly personal stuff" with the hope of encouraging others to post pages detailing their histories and achievements. Keith is affiliated with the Seniors Computer Information System, a project of Creative Retirement Manitoba.

Lady Unicorn5
http://members.wbs.net/homepages/l/a/d/
ladyunicorn5.html

Barbara Rice's handle suggests the depth of her 42-year devotion to her husband Marvin who is known as Unicorn5. Her hobbies include chatting online, reading, and sewing.

Laurie Jenkinson
http://www.ruralnet.net.au/~jenki/laurie.html

Anyone wondering about the land down under can take a tour of Australia hosted by this resident of Leitchville, North Victoria. Among the online resources, find a glossary of Aussie terms, the story of Vegemite, and a currency converter.

L.J. Klein
http://pw1.netcom.com/~ljklein1/athome.html

A father to five, and soon-to-be grandfather to just as many, L.J. hails from the Kentucky hills where he works at his hobbies (he built his own computer) and whatever "clinic" type medical jobs he can find. Some of his favorite links include CNN Interactive, Ziff-Davis, and Discovery OnLine.

Louise See's Family
http://www.wtco.net/~mlsee/index.html

Louise posts a photographic introduction to her family. A mother of two grown boys, Louise is also a grandmother.

Maggie G. Severns
http://206.217.20.5/cgi-bin/
WebX?135@^78@9289@.ee6d570

Married 46 years to Red, Maggie is the mother of three, grandmother of six, and great-grandmother of two, and resides in a town that is consistently rated as one of the "safest" places in the United States to live.

My Graphics Page
http://www.trader.com/users/9675/3462/

Glen Curtis posts graphics and pointers to some of his favorite sites. Along with places like the White House, also find links to other seniors and friends online.

The Old Guy @ Home
http://www.mbnet.mb.ca/~kyletomi/

See what The Old Guy does behind closed doors, read his musings and meanderings, or pick and click links to sites of wonder. Born in Scotland (he wasn't The Old Guy then), Tom Kyle lives in Canada with his wife, children, and grandchildren.

Pat & John's Prose and Poetry
http://www.net-gate.com/~patmci/

Read what the Muse had to say to New Jerseyites Pat and John McIntyre. Actually, this site offers more in the way of a "who we are and what we do."

Pooh-Bear-6

http://members.wbs.net/homepages/p/o/o/
poohbear6.html

Darlene Bryant loves bible jokes and invites contributions to her growing collection of knee-slappers. "What is the first recorded case of constipation? It's in the Book of Kings where it says David sat on the throne for forty years."

Philip Grosset

http://subnet.virtual-pc.com/gr468626/

A retired United Kingdom TV executive profiles his passions and pursuits, plus recommends links he likes and thinks others will, too. Fifty Plus, a section of interest to retired folks in the U.K., is also featured.

Rambler66

http://htp.com/gharris/rambler.html

Gil Harris has taken his handle from his favorite set of wheels. See a picture of the car, link to some of Gil's favorite sites, and find out what this semi-retired New Yorker does for fun when he's not hugging the person sitting next to him, his wife Maddalen.

Rhea Coleman & Burt Vose

http://www.lascruces.com/~tuneriw/

The author of *Gutsy's Luck*, Rhea is the mother of four and describes herself as an "all around good egg!" Burt is a total cyber-junkie and ham radio enthusiast.

R.N. Wahner, DiSc

http://www.execpc.com/~wahner/

R. N. Wahner, a widower and retired writer living in Wisconsin, profiles his life and times. Links to favorite Web sites point to NASA, PBS Online, and the WebMuseum.

Rosaleen Diana (Leslie) Dickson

http://www.flora.org/books/personal.html

A published author, a master's degree candidate, and a newsgroup moderator (among other pursuits) who hails from Canada, this mother of nine, grandmother of 14, and great-grandmother of three illustrates for visitors

what her opening quote means: "For this life there is no rehearsal; just the main performance."

Senior Frolic

http://www.geocities.com/Heartland/4474/

These sites weren't chosen because they will make you healthy, wealthy, and wise, but you may pick up a thing or two. The directory includes two dozen categories offering a mix of interests from Americana to words.

Seniors Corner

http://www.trader.com/users/9675/5981/

A senior living in Indianapolis, Donna has collected a group of links she finds useful and feels can be useful to other seniors. She also hosts a directory of seniors online and posts a few pictures of herself and her children.

smprfi IN

http://members.wbs.net/homepages/s/m/p/
smprfiin.html

Ed Herzog waves the American flag and points visitors to many of his cyber-friends. Married and living in Jasper, Ind., Ed considers his home page "always under construction and never complete."

Spudlix

http://www2.coastalnet.com/~cn3468/
index.html

Find out how Richard Boyd came by the name Spudlix, meet a few of his friends, and link to some of his favorite sites. Also play cards, chat, and generally enjoy the hospitality of a guy who describes himself as a "teller of tall tales and resident magician."

The Telson Spur: A Way Station for Snark Hunters
http://www.islandnet.com/~pjhughes/homepage.html

Phil Hughes hunts for the fantastic "snark" composed of space, time, and evolution, and invites all to sign on for the voyage. Onboard the Telson Spur, find an eclectic cargo of academic and scientific resources ideal for "exploring the lee shores of the imagination."

Tom & Pat's Home Page
http://oz.plymouth.edu/~tos/home.html

Born in Germany and now living in New Hampshire, Tom Schlesinger retired after serving 21 years in U.S. Army Intelligence and then retired again after teaching 27 years at Plymouth State College. Pat Schlesinger is president of the Pemigewasset River Council.

Unicorn5
http://members.wbs.net/homepages/u/n/i/unicorn5.html

Father of three, grandfather of five, Marvin Rice lives with his wife near one of the happiest-sounding towns in Texas, Smiley. Retired from the field of aviation, Marvin is regularly bled (apparently they still do that!) to compensate for an overabundance of iron in his system. Not surprisingly, one of the links on his hotlist leads to the Iron Overload Diseases Association.

The Wild, Wacky World of Marty Z—Senior Citizen
http://www.he.net/~martyz/martyz.html

Marty Zucker has been there and done that. Visitors can share his thoughts on what has gone before and what is to come as he looks at '60s poetry, religion, politics, and the stock market. Marty also takes his hat off to a few friends and favorite people including the Amazing Traveling Lady who helps folks take trips—"people who otherwise couldn't."

Appendix A

TIPS FOR USING LYCOS TO SEARCH THE WEB

To search the Lycos catalog, just enter one or more words (better known as a "search query") in the text entry box on the Lycos home page or search results page. Next, press the Enter key (or click the Go Get It button). Lycos will display the results. If you need to customize or refine your search, however, Lycos provides an easy way for you to "fine-tune" your search.

The Customize Your Search form is a tool that Lycos provides to make searching its index easy for you to do. It's especially helpful if you need to do any of the following:

- Make your search wider or narrower

- Have the search match ALL words in a query rather than ANY single word (which is the default setting)

- Search for special variations of a given term (for example, to search for several possible spellings of a word AND some other word)

Most of the time you won't need to use this search form at all if you only want to perform "wide" searches of the Web. However, Lycos gives you other Search options, which you can change if you want to search for different types of information, such as pictures, sounds, and sites that have been categorized by subject.

You can also "refine" your search by making it more narrow or wide. You can have the search match ALL words in your query rather than the default ANY word. You can also search for a number of terms which are DIFFERENT from the number you entered (for example, to search for several possible spellings of a word AND some other word).

The search form gives you two ways to control your search: *Search Options* and *Display Options*. You'll notice that both Search Options and Display Options are pull-down menus. Simply click the down-arrow in each of these pull-down menus and look at the selections that are available.

USING SEARCH OPTIONS TO SET TERMS TO MATCH (BOOLEAN)

You might wonder why you can't do Boolean searches on Lycos. You might also want to know what exactly a *Boolean search* is. Boolean searches are those queries that let you search the Web for very specific combinations of words. For example, you might want to see all instances of peanut and butter together, but only where they appear without jelly.

Although you can't perform true Boolean searches on Lycos, you can come very close by using the Search Options features. Just keep these simple guidelines in mind:

- AND searches are possible by selecting the match all terms (AND) option and then entering whatever words you want in the search box. In the above example, you'd simply enter peanut butter.

- NOT searches are a bit trickier. You may currently prepend (that is, begin) a term with a hyphen to make it a negative indicator, like this: -jelly. This will only reduce the score for sites containing the word jelly, not remove them entirely. The good news is that the first set of results you get will most likely give you what you want: peanut butter without jelly.

By default, Lycos will find all documents matching any word you type in your query (except for certain words like "a" and "the" which are generally not meaningful in a search). If you type "jeep cherokee" as your query, Lycos will find all documents containing either "jeep" OR "cherokee." This is the match any term (OR) Search Option, and is what you get when you type a query into the form on the home page, or if you select the match any term (OR) option on the Customize Your Search form.

Sometimes you might want to find only documents that match ALL the words in your query. This is the match all terms (AND) option. Try it on the form and then see what Lycos returns for "jeep cherokee" when you use the "OR" option and when you use the "AND" option.

SYMBOLS YOU CAN'T USE IN YOUR SEARCHES

You can't use + in search terms. A common instance of this is the term C++, which gets stripped down to c. Unfortunately, this leaves a single letter which, being shorter than three characters, is ignored. This behavior can be annoying, but Lycos is in the process of choosing the best solution to solve it (and related problems) without affecting the speed and performance of conducting searches. For now we suggest you search for related terms: Instead of C++, for instance, you might try programming languages. Hopefully, Lycos will fix this soon.

You also cannot search for numbers. The current version of Lycos strips out all numbers at the beginning of words. This causes problems if you search for 3DO, 4AD Records, or any other letter-number combination.

The problem is that numbers are a whole different breed of cat from letters. Lycos is trying to teach its retrieval engine to determine for itself which sequences of letters are words and which are not; once they do, you'll be able to make these searches.

SYMBOLS YOU CAN USE IN YOUR SEARCHES

At the present time, you can use the following symbols in your search queries:

- (-) As we mentioned earlier, you can use the - symbol to help narrow down your search. For example, to search for bank, but without river turning up in the search, you would type bank -river in your search query. This is similar to the NOT Boolean search term.

- (.) Use a period at the end of the keyword to limit it with no expansions. Bank. will bring up only results with the keyword "bank" and ignore expansions like "bankers" and "banking."

- ($) Put this symbol after the keyword to make the search engine expand it. The search term "gard$" will bring up results like "garden" and "gardenias." This feature is great if you don't know how to spell a word, or if you aren't sure what you're looking for.

LIMITING YOUR SEARCH TO A SPECIFIED NUMBER OF TERMS

You might also be wondering why you need "match 2 terms," "match 3 terms," and so on. These options give you more flexibility in your search. Suppose you wanted to find references to Sarajevo and Yugoslavia. But you're not sure whether Sarajevo is spelled "Sarajevo" or "Sarayevo." So you enter your query "Sarajevo Sarayevo Yugoslavia." To get the best results, you can use the Search Options.

You can't use match all terms (AND) because that would give you only documents which contain both spellings of "Sarajevo" AND Yugoslavia, and there probably aren't any of those. You could use match any terms (OR), because that would return all documents that contain any of these three terms, but you would also get lots of documents you don't want in the list.

Here's what you do: Enter "Sarajevo Sarayevo Yugoslavia" as your query, and choose match 2 terms. This selection will match at least two terms in each document. Since it's quite unlikely Sarajevo will be spelled two different ways in the same document, the results returned will have references to BOTH one of the two spellings of Sarajevo AND Yugoslavia.

USING THE SEARCH OPTIONS TO SET THE SELECTIVITY OF THE SEARCH

You can change the Search Options to adjust the selectivity of the Lycos search engine. When set to "loose match," you will get more documents, but they will tend to be less relevant to the query you've made. Often, particularly when you are beginning a search and wish to cast the widest possible net, this is exactly what you want.

If you want the Lycos search engine to be more selective, change the Search Option from loose match to "strong match." Lycos will return only documents which have a very high relevance to your query. If you are on a slow dial-up connection, setting the selectivity to "strong match" can save you time by reducing the number of irrelevant hits downloaded to you.

You should try out the effect of changing various selectivity settings on the form. Try some searches with various selectivity settings to get a feel for how it affects your results.

SETTING THE DISPLAY OF THE RESULTS PAGE SIZE

Lycos always gives you all the results or "hits" matching your query, even if there are hundreds or thousands of documents. If the number of hits is large, however, Lycos does not display them all at once, so you don't need to wait a long time for the whole page to come to you. By default, Lycos displays 10 hits on each results page. Once you've looked at those 10, you click on the "Next 10 hits" link at the bottom of the page to get the next 10 hits, and so on until all the hits are displayed.

To change the default from 10 hits displayed on each page, you can set the number in the Display Options pull-down menu. Simply choose another value from 10 to 40 results per page.

SETTING THE AMOUNT OF RESULTS DETAIL YOU WANT DISPLAYED

You can also control the amount of information you want Lycos to display about each result. There are three levels of detail you can choose from:

- Standard (the default)

- Detailed (all information displayed)

- Summary (the minimum amount of information is displayed)

INTERPRETING THE RESULTS OF A SEARCH

The percentage numbers are simply Lycos's way of showing you how close it thinks each site will match what you're looking for, based on the words you asked Lycos to search for.

When the Lycos search engine compares each page to your query, it gives higher scores to pages that contain the words as you typed them in. It also looks for pages that mention these words early on, rather than far down in some sub-section of the site. The page with the combination most like the words you typed in is ranked at the top and assigned the number 1.000. Other sites are ranked below and assigned numbers based on how much or how little they resemble your search terms.

This means that if you asked for Hungarian goulash, then a site titled The Hungarian Goulash Recipe Page will end up above sites that mention Carpathian goulash, salad, and Hungarian bread, or some less precise combination.

The percentages are in no way a rating of how good Lycos thinks any page is. They're simply a tool to help you narrow down your choices.

Appendix B
USING THE CD-ROM

The CD-ROM that's packaged with this book includes software for you to use. The software will not only allow you to explore the Internet and search the Web, but will also allow you to view a fully hyperlinked HTML version of the printed book, also contained on the CD-ROM. Before you can use the software, you will need to install it on the hard drive of your computer. This is a simple procedure that will take only a few minutes.

WHAT'S ON THE CD-ROM?

The CD-ROM includes the following software and other items that can be installed on your computer:

- Microsoft Internet Explorer Web browser for PCs and Macs
- Earthlink Internet connection software for PCs and Macs
- A fully hyperlinked HTML version of the book for PCs and Macs, which you can view using your Web browser

VIEWING THE HYPERLINKED HTML VERSION OF THE BOOK

The CD-ROM contains the fully hyperlinked text of the book, which lists thousands of Web sites and Internet addresses, including live links to SeniorNet and Lycos, the search engine. Although you can use the CD and view the HTML book version without a live Internet connection, every section of the CD allows you to select an Internet address and instantly connect to the actual site. To connect directly to these Web sites, however, you'll need an Internet connection.

USING THE CD-ROM

To view the hyperlinked version of the book, you will need to use a Web browser. Simply follow the steps below.

RUNNING MOST WEB BROWSERS (INCLUDING NETSCAPE NAVIGATOR)

1 Place the CD-ROM in your CD-ROM drive.
2 Launch your Web browser.
3 Choose Open File from the File menu.
4 Select your CD-ROM drive. For PC users, this is usually drive D. Mac users, this is on your desktop.
5 Open the file named Welcome.htm.

RUNNING MICROSOFT INTERNET EXPLORER

1 Place the CD-ROM in your CD-ROM drive.
2 Launch Internet Explorer.

3   Choose Open from the File menu.

4   Click the Browse button.

5   Select your CD-ROM drive. For PC users, this is usually drive D. Mac users, this is on your desktop.

6   Open the file named Welcome.htm.

7   Click on OK.

INSTALLING WEB BROWSER SOFTWARE

If you do not have a Web browser currently installed on your computer, we have included Microsoft's Internet Explorer on this CD. The steps for installing Internet Explorer are described below.

RECOMMENDED PC SYSTEM

- 486 Processor (Pentium Processor preferred)

- Windows OS (3.x or 95)

- 8MB of RAM (16MB preferred)

- 8MB free space on your hard drive (15MB preferred)

- 2x CD-ROM drive (4x recommended)

MACINTOSH SYSTEM REQUIREMENTS

- Apple Macintosh or Power Macintosh (or clone) running System 7.0.1 or later

- 8MB of RAM (16MB preferred)

- 8MB of free space on your hard drive (16MB preferred)

- 2x CD-ROM drive (4x preferred)

INSTALLING INTERNET EXPLORER

INTERNET EXPLORER VERSION 3.01 FOR WINDOWS 95

You must be using Microsoft Windows 95 to run Microsoft Internet Explorer 3.01. Locate the IE-Win95 folder in the MS-IE directory on the CD.

Double-click on the IE301M95.EXE file. Follow the instructions that appear on your screen to complete the installation.

INTERNET EXPLORER VERSION 2.1 FOR WINDOWS 3.1

You must be using Microsoft Windows 3.1 to run Microsoft Internet Explorer 2.1. Locate the IE_WIN31 folder in the MS-IE directory on the CD.

Double-click on the DLMINI21.EXE file. Follow the instructions that appear on your screen to complete the installation.

INTERNET EXPLORER VERSION 2.0 FOR THE MACINTOSH

Double-click the Internet Explorer installer icon, located in the MS Internet Explorer Folder, to install. Follow the prompts that appear on your screen to complete the installation.

Note: Eudora Light is an Internet Mail client application that is included in Microsoft Internet Explorer 2.0 for the Macintosh. Documentation for Eudora Light is not included. To download the Eudora Light Manual separately, visit the Microsoft Internet Explorer Web site at: http://www.microsoft.com/ie/iedl.htm#mac.

INSTALLING EARTHLINK INTERNET CONNECTION SOFTWARE (FOR MACS AND PCS)

To install Earthlink as your Internet service provider, follow these steps:

FOR PC'S

1 From the Earthlink Folder on the CD-ROM open the Win31 or Win95 directory (depending on your system).

2 Run the Setup.exe file appropriate for your system and follow the onscreen setup instructions.

FOR THE MAC

1 From the Earthlink Folder on the CD double-click on the TotalAccess Installer.

2 Follow the onscreen instructions to load Earthlink as your Internet Service Provider.

Credits

A Bomb WWW Museum page. Used with permission.

Age of Reason page. Used with permission.

Acropolis page. Used with permission.

Algy's Herb Page. Use with permission.

Alien Information page. Used with permission.

All Things Automotive Directory page. Used with permission.

The Alsop Review page. Used with permission.

American Civil War page. Used with permission.

Americans for the Arts page. Used with permission.

The Anadromous page. Used with permission.

Apparitions page. Used with permission.

Araneum's Cyber Poker page. Used with permission.

Architecture of Salem page. Used with permission.

Art Crimes: The Writing on the Wall page. Used with permission.

Association of Retirement Resorts International page. Used with permission.

The Astronomy Café page. Used with permission.

Aunt Annie's Craft Page. Used with permission.

Avalon: Arthurian Heaven page. Used with permission.

BankWeb page. Used with permission.

Bas van Reek Art Building page. Used with permission.

The Best Mall Online page. Used with permission.

BookWeb page. Used with permission.

Business Resource Center page. Used with permission.

The Cave Page. Used with permission.

CenterNet page. Used with permission.

Charlottesville Senior Surf page. Used with permission.

Chile Today–Hot Tamale page. Used with permission.

CollegeNet page. Used with permission.

Comets and Meteor Showers page. Used with permission.

Computer-Related Stress page. Used with permission.

Cotntop page. Used with permission.

Creating Land Trusts page. Used with permission.

CultureFinder page. Used with permission.

Cyberian Outpost page. Used with permission.

CyberPals page. Used with permission.

Discover Canada Online page. Used with permission.

Egyptology Resources page. Used with permission.

Entrepreneurial Edge Online page. Used with permission.

E*Trade page. Used with permission.

Ever The Twain Shall Meet page. Used with permission.

Exploratorium ExploraNet. © 1996 The Exploratorium. Used by permission.

Farm Animal Reform Movement page. Used with permission.

Federal Deposit Insurance Corporation page. Used with permission.

FedWorld page. Used with permission.

50 Greatest Conspiracies of All Time page. Used with permission.

Fifty Plus R Us page. Used with permission.

Floral Design Newsletter page. Used with permission.

Free Lunch page. Used with permission.

Gay & Lesbian Alliance Against Defamation (GLAAD) page. Used with permission.

Goldngal, The Cyberspace Granny page. Used with permission.

Grand Times Magazine page. Used with permission.

Happy Campers page. Used with permission.

Health Care Financing Administration page. Used with permission.

HealthWeb page. Approval for use granted by HealthWeb.

Homes & Land page. Used with permission.

Index

1-800-TAX-LAWS **217**

10 Bulls **276**

1000 Points of Art **68**

123 Shop **309**

1925, The Year in Review **68**

20/20 **263**

221B Baker Street: Sherlock Holmes **177**

3M Active Strips Flexible Bandages **303**

3M Office Survey and Product Sample **304**

48 Hours **260**

50 Easily Overlooked Tax Deductions for
Individuals **218**

50 Greatest Conspiracies of All Time **266**

60 Minutes **262**

A

A Cappella Web Directory **200**

A. G. Edwards **120**

AAAdir Directory of World Banks **115**

AARP—American Association of Retired Persons **329**

ABC **259**

ABC Radio Net **259**

Abele Owners' Network **134**

Abolition Now! **322**

A-Bomb WWW Museum **82**

Absolutely Fresh Flowers **310**

ABZU: Guide to Resources for the Study of the Ancient
Near East Available on the Internet **162**

Academy of Natural Sciences **96**

Accumulated Accordion Annotations **201**

Acoustic Guitar Song Collection **201**

Acropolis **60**

Adler Planetarium and Museum **96**

Administration on Aging **215**

Adobe Systems **11**

Adopt-A-Grandparent **377**

Adult Education & Distance Learner's Resource
Center **163**

Advancing Women: Entrepreneur and Small
Business **144**

AdZe MiXXe **269**

Aetna Life and Casualty **123**

Aetna Life Insurance Company of Canada **123**

African Art: Aesthetics and Meaning **72**

AGropolis **187**

AirShow BBS **380**

AJ's Free Stuff Page **302**

Akio's Interesting Things In My Travels **381**

Alabama **40**

Alabama: AlaWeb State Government Page **225**

Alaska: State of Alaska Agency Directory **225**

Albert Camus Critical Interpretation Home Page **103**

Albert Einstein Online **292**

Alberta UFO Research Association (AUFORA) **278**

Alcatraz **82**

Alchemy Web Site **273**

Alex: A Catalogue of Electronic Texts on the Internet **173**

Alexander Palace Time Machine **82**

Algy's Herb Page **235**

"Alien Autopsy"—Faked or Fiction? **278**

Alien Information **278**

All Things Automotive Directory **301**

AllApartments Search **134**

All-Internet Shopping Directory **308**

Allstate Insurance Company **123**

Alpine World **343**

Alsop Review **94**

Alternative Medicine Homepage **235**

Alzheimer Page **240**

Alzheimer Web **240**

Amateur Radio Newsline **193**

Amateur Radio Operator **194**

Amazon.com Books **173**

America Online **17**

American and British History Resources on the Internet **82**

American Antiquarian Society **82**

American Association of Botanical Gardens and Arboreta **187**

American Association of Home-Based Businesses **155**

American Baptist Homes of the West **130**

American Canoe Association **345**

American Civil Liberties Union Freedom Network **326**

American Civil War, 1861–1865 **82**

American Civil War Home Page **83**

American Homebrewers Association **180**

American Horticultural Society **187**

American Institute of Small Business **142**

American Memories **83**

American Music Network Gopher Menu **201**

American Numismatic Association **191**

American Passport Express **359**

American Quarter Horse Association On-Line **335**

American Racing Scene **344**

American Shopping Mall **308**

American South **83**

American Spectator **252**

American Stock Exchange Market Summary **120**

American Wine on the Web **180**

Americans for the Arts **68**

America's Business Funding Directory **144**

America's HomeNet & CenterNet **134**

America's Shirt Catalog **310**

America's Sports Headquarters **347**

Amnesty International **328**

Anadromous Page **345**

Analytical Philosophy **102**

Ancient City of Athens **60**

Anderson Valley Brewing Company Beer Links Jumpstation **180**

Andy Warhol Museum **75**

Aneurysm Information Project **240**

Anglers Online **345**

Anglicans Online **106**

Animal Rights Resource Site **324**

Anomalous Cognition **271**

Anonymizer **33**

ANS CO+RE Systems Inc. **18**

Answers to Patent, Copyright, and Trademark Questions **145**

Anti-Imperialism in the United States **83**

Antiquarian Booksellers' Association of America **173**

Antiquarian Booksellers' Association of America Booknet **310**

Antiques and Collectibles **191**

AP Breaking News **256**

Appalachian Trail Home Page **363**

Apparitions **68**

Apple **33**

Apple Small Business Home Page **145**

Applied Ethics Resources **102**

Arachnology: The Study of Arachnids **290**

Araneum's Cyber Poker **348**

Archie McPhee **311**

Architects **67**

Architectural Archives of the University of Pennsylvania **64**

Architectural Dublin **60**

Architecture in America: State Houses to Skyscrapers **64**

Architecture of Atlanta **64**

Architecture of Salem **64**

Architecture of the Mediterranean Basin **60**

Architecture Slide Library **64**

Archives of African American Music and Culture **201**

ArchNet: The World Wide Web Virtual Library for Archaeology **289**

Arcosanti **64**

Area 51: Military Facility, Social Phenomenon and State of Mind **279**

Ari Davidow's Klez Picks **201**

Aristo-Craft Trains On-line Information Page **190**

Aristotle **102**

Arizona Senior Academy **130**

Arizona: State of Arizona World Wide Web **225**

Arkansas: Government and Community Relations Home Page **225**

Arkuat's Web **271**

@art **72**

Art Crimes: The Writing on the Wall **69**

Art Institute of Chicago **72**

Art of Renaissance Science: Galileo and Perspective **291**

Art Planet **72**

Arthritis Information Page **240**

Arthuriana **90**

ArtMetal **72**

ArtSource **69**

Asclepiad Page **187**

Asian Art Museum of San Francisco **72**

Ask Great-Granny **375**

Ask Noah About: Aging and Alzheimer's Disease **241**

Ask Sherlock **134**

Assist International **146**

Associated Press: The Wire **256**

Association of American University Presses **173**

Association of Retirement Resorts International **130**

Assyria Online **83**

Asthma—General Information **241**

Astral Projection Home Page **271**

Astrology Alive! with Barbara Schermer **269**

Astronomy Café **288**

Atheism Web **106**

Atlanta Garden Connection **187**

Atlanta Journal-Constitution **258**

Atlantic Monthly **252**

Aubrey & Ann Roberts **381**

Audio Bookstore @ The Storyteller **174**

Aunt Annie's Craft Page **191**

Auntie Q's Antiques & Collectibles **311**

Australian Alpine Information Service **364**

Australian Kite Association Home Page and E-Zine **193**

Australian National Botanic Gardens **291**

Austria: City.Net Index **364**

Auto-By-Tel **301**

Automobile Buyers' Network **301**

Automobiles2 **301**

AutoNetwork **301**

AutoRow **301**

AutoWeb Interactive **301**

Avalon: Arthurian Heaven **91**

Avante Garde **308**

Avon's Breast Cancer Awareness Crusade **242**

B

B. C. Society for Skeptical Inquiry **265**

Backgammon Frequently Asked Questions **348**

Backgammon Galore! **348**

Backyard Astronomy: Choosing Binoculars **288**

Badminton **346**

Baen Books **174**

Bagpipe Web **201**

Bali: The Online Travel Guide **361**

Bank of America **115**

Bank of Boston **115**

Bank of the Commonwealth **115**

Bank of Montreal **115**

Bank One **115**

Banking on the WWW **115**

BankWeb **116**

Banned Books On-line **174**

Bantam-Doubleday-Dell Online **174**

Bantam Doubleday Dell's Daily Horoscopes **269**

Barbershop Web Server **201**

Barcelona Pavillion **60**

Bas van Reek Art Building **72**

Baseball Server **336**

Baseball Yellow Pages **336**

Basic Applied Ethics **381**

Basic Guide to Exporting **146**

Basic Spanish for the Virtual Student **163**

Battleship—Interactive Web Game **349**

Bauhaus: Architecture in Tel Aviv **60**

Bayshore Trust Company **116**

BBC **259**

BBN Planet **18**

Beat the Bookie **335**

Beatrice **93**

Beaucoup Search Engines **32**

Beer & Wine Hobby **180**

Beertown **180**

Bellwether One **381**

Bereavement Education Center **379**

Bermuda Triangle **265**

Bertrand Russell Archives at McMaster University **105**

Best Fiction and Poetry from CSUN: 1962-1988 **94**

Best Mall Online **308**

Better Homes and Gardens **252**

Better Homes and Gardens Real Estate Service **134**

Beyond the Veil **381**

Bible Gateway **106**

Bible Online **106**

Biblical Contradictions **106**

Bicycles FAQ **338**

Big Brothers Big Sisters of America **325**

Big Island of Hawaii **362**

Big One **65**

Bill Grego **381**

Bingo Zone **349**

Biodiversity and Biological Collections WWW Server **291**

BioEd: Biology Education Resources **291**

Bipo & Toni's Spanish School **163**

Bird Web **193**

Birding on the Web **193**

Birdlinks **193**

Bishop Museum **96**

Bi-Weekly Raise Money for Your Business without Asking Your Bank Manager Page **146**

Biz: The Entertainment Cybernetwork **196**

BizBuySell **153**

BizWomen **146**

Black Jack on the World Wide Web **349**

Blacksburg Electronic Village Seniors Information Page **50**

Blair Florida **130**

Bloomingdale's **305**

BluesNet Home Page **201**

Bob LaFara's Pages: Index **381**

Bodleian Library Electronic Texts Gopher **91**

Bonnie Best **381**

Bonsai on the Web **188**

Bookport **174**

Books @ Random **174**

BookWeb **174**

BookWire **174**

Boston Amateur Radio Club **194**

Boston Globe **258**

Bowling Page **337**

Brewery: Total Homebrewing Info **180**

Brief History of The United States Senate **83**

Brigade of The American Revolution **83**

Brigham & Women's Hospital **245**

Britannica's Lives **83**

British Columbia Creature Page **291**

British Poetry 1780-1910 **94**

Brooklyn Museum **73**

Buffalo's Architecture **65**

Building Canada **60**

Bureau of Engraving and Printing **215**

Bureau of the Public Debt **216**

Burrito Page **181**

Business@Home **155**

Business Opportunities Handbook Online **153**

Business Resource Center **146**

C

Cabot Creamery **311**

Cajun/Zydeco Music & Dance **177**

Calgary Free-Net **50**

California **40**

California Association of Residential Care Homes **131**

California Indian Library Collections **84**

California: Your California Government **225**

Callahan's Cookbook **181**

Campground Directory **367**

Campgrounds.Net Directory **367**

Canada Trust Mortgage Co. **116**

Canadian Heritage Information Network **83**

Canadian Museum of Civilization **96**

Canadian Museum of Civilization: Mystery of Maya **84**

Canadian Universities **163**

Cancer Patient Resources Available Via WWW **242**

CancerNet Database **242**

CANSEARCH: A Guide to Cancer Resources **242**

Capital Punishment: The Death Penalty **322**

Capital Senior Living, Inc. **130**

CapWeb: The Citizen's Guide to Congress **221**

Caregivers, Caregiving, and Home Care Workers **247**

Caregiver's Handbook **247**

Caribbean On-Line **362**

Carnivorous Plant Database **291**

Carole's Nature Page **381**

CARP—Canadian Association of Retired Persons **330**

Cars @Cost **301**

Carter Center **328**

Castles of Wales **61**

Cat Fanciers **208**

Catalog Live! **308**

Catalog Select **308**

Catholic Resources on the Net **106**

Cats Meow 3: The Internet Beer Recipe Database **181**

Cave Page **338**

CBC **259**

CBS News **260**

CBS Radio Networks **260**

CCAT's Public Archive **174**

CCM Online **201**

Cedars-Sinai Medical Center Home Page **245**

Celebrating 17 Centuries of the City of Split **84**

Celestia **274**

Celtic Cultures **311**

Centers for Disease Control and Prevention **247**

Central Intelligence Agency **222**

Century 21 Professional Connection **134**

Ceola's Celtic Music Archive **201**

CERFnet **18**

"Chai" **381**

Chagall Windows **69**

Channel 1 BBS **29**

Character Above All: Harry S. Truman **81**

Charles S. Peirce Studies **104**

Charles Schwab & Co. **120**

Charleston Multimedia Project **65**

Charlie's Home Page **381**

Charlottesville Senior Surf **50**

Chase Manhattan Bank **116**

Cheese Page **181**

Chemeketa Online **163**

Cherokee Nation **228**

Chess Space **349**

ChessLive! **349**

Chic Paris **311**

Chicago Architecture Imagebase **65**

Chicago Sun-Times **258**

Chicago Tribune **258**

Chickasaw Nation **228**

Children Now **325**

Children's Defense Fund **325**

Children's Protection and Advocacy Coalition **326**

Chile Today—Hot Tamale **311**

Chili-Heads Home Page **291**

China Daily **259**

Chinese Music FTP server **202**

Chinese Philosophy Page **103**

Chinmaya Mission **274**

Chinook **349**

CHIROWEB **236**

Chocolate Lovers' Page **311**

Choctaw Nation of Oklahoma—Unofficial Home Page **228**

Choir Links Page **202**

Chosen Reflections **311**

Christchurch Press (New Zealand) **259**

Christian Classics Ethereal Library **106**

Christian Coalition **107**

Christian Dating Service International **377**

Christian Music Directory **202**

Christian Science Monitor **258**

ChristianAnswers.Net **107**

Christians in Recovery **379**

Christus Rex **69**

ChronicIllNet **242**

Cigna **123**

Cinema Sites **196**

CineMedia **260**

Citibank **116**

Citizen Potawatomi Nation **228**

Citizens Against Government Waste **326**

City Guide **363**

City Guide USA **129**

City University **163**

city.net **129**

Civil Rights or Special Rights? **320**

Clambake Celebrations, Inc. **311**

ClariNet e.News **256**

Classic Angler **312**

Classical Music on the Net **202**

ClassicalNet Home Page **202**

Classics Ireland **91**

Classics and Mediterranean Archaeology Home Page **289**

Classique Structure **312**

Cleveland Clinic Foundation **245**

ClickIn **302**

Climbing Archive! **338**

Climbing Dictionary **338**

Clocks and Time **191**

Club Mac **7**

CNA Insurance Companies **123**

CNBC **260**

CNN Interactive **260**

CNS, Inc **18**

CNU Online **163**

Cobra Golf **312**

CoGweb **107**

Coin Universe **191**

Coldwell Banker Online **135**

College Hoops **337**

College and University Home Pages **163**

CollegeNET **164**

Colonial Penn: Auto Insurance **123**

Colorado: Colorado Government **225**

Comet Hale-Bopp Home Page **286**

Comet P/Shoemaker-Levy 9 Impact Home Page **286**

Comets and Meteor Showers **286**

Commerce Bank **116**

CommerceNet Directories of Products & Services **18**

Committee for the Scientific Investigation of Claims of the Paranormal **265**

Commonwealth Open University **164**

Communicable Disease Fact Sheets Gopher Menu **242**

Communication Connections **164**

Community College Gophers **164**

Community College Web **164**

Compendium of Bad Art Form **68**

Complete Glossary of Insurance Coverage Explanations **123**

CompuServe **17**

Computer Assisted Learning Center (CALC) **164**

Computer Museum Network **97**

Computer Pornography Questions and Answers **323**

Computer Related Stress **47**

ComputerLife Online **252**

Concentration Camps: A Factual Report on Crimes Committed Against Humanity **84**

Confederated Tribes of Siletz Indians (Oregon) **228**

Congress.Org **222**

Connect Four **349**

Connected Education: Online Courses for College Credit **165**

Connecticut **40**

Connecticut: State of Connecticut Home Page **225**

Connecting With Nature **164**

Connections: A Southern Golf & Vacation Guide **363**

ConsciousNet **274**

Constitution for the United States of America **224**

Consultant's Corner **147**

Consulting **147**

Consulting Corner **147**

Contemporary Architecture of Hong Kong **61**

Coral Courts Motel **65**

CoreStates Bank **116**

Cosmic Connections **271**

Cosmic Web **107**

Cosmopolis' High-Tech Horoscopes **269**

Costa Rica Photo Travel Journal **365**

Costanoan-Ohlone Indian Canyon Resource (California) **228**

Cotntop's Spot on the Web **77**

Counted Cross Stitch, Needlework, and Stitchery Page **194**

Court TV Law Center **260**

Cowboy Poetry **175**

Cowboy Trail **312**

CPMCnet: Columbia-Presbyterian Medical Center **245**

CraftNet Village **191**

CraftWEB Home Page **191**

CReAte Your Own Newspaper (CRAYON) **257**

Creating A Celebration of Women Writers **175**

Creating Land Trusts: Help Conserve Our Land and Natural Resources **327**

Creation Research Society **107**

Credit Union Home Page **116**

Credit Union National Association and Affiliates **116**

Creole & Cajun Recipe Page **181**

Crestar: On Finances **116**

CricInfo **346**

Critics' Roost **196**

CRL Network Services **19**

Crockpot Recipes **181**

Crohns Disease Ulcerative Colitis Inflammatory Bowel Disease Pages **242**

Crossword Puzzles **349**

C-SPAN **260**

Cuervo Gold **302**

CultureFinder: The Internet Address for the Performing Arts **202**

Cupid's Personals **378**

Currencies and Currency-Exchange **117**

Current **305**

Current Events and End Times Prophecy **274**

Cyber Cyclery: Internet Bicycling Resource **338**

Cyber Horse **335**

Cyber Stars and Astro Chat **269**

Cyber-Accountant **218**

CyberCash **310**

CyberED **165**

Cybergrass: The Internet Bluegrass Music Magazine **202**

CyberHomes **135**

Cyberian Outpost **10**

Cyberider Cycling WWW Site **338**

CyberPals **378**

Cyberpreneur's Guide to the Internet **147**

Cyberspace Wholesale Marketplace **308**

cycling.org **338**

Cyrano Server **378**

Czech Language and Culture Programs in the Czech Republic **163**

D

Daily Martian Weather Report **283**

Daily Wisdom **107**

Dakota Engraving **312**

Dali Web **69**

Dallas Morning News **258**

Dallas Museum of Art **73**

Dance Directory **178**

Dance Hotlist by Henry Neeman **177**

Dancers' Archive Gopher Menu **177**

Dark Side of the Net **274**

Dark Zen: The Teachings of Mystical Zen **107**

Data Wales Country Guide **365**

DateLine NBC **260**

Dave Frary's Blue Ribbon Models **190**

Dave's Eocene Fossils **289**

Dave's I.M. Pei Page **67**

Daylilies Growing Along The Information Highway **188**

Dead Runners Society **342**

DealerNet: The Source for New Car Information **301**

Death, Dying, and Grief Resources **379**

Deborah Sellers' Poetry **96**

Decisions of the U.S. Supreme Court **221**

Declaration of Independence **224**

Deep Black Magic: Government Research into ESP and Mind Control **272**

Defenders of Wildlife **324**

Del Rey Books Home Page **175**

Delaware Tribe of Indians **228**

Delaware: State of Delaware **225**

Dennis Smith—Retiree-at-Large **381**

Deoxyribonucleic Hyperdimension **272**

Detroit News **258**

DharmaNet **108**

Digital Campus **165**

Digital Tradition Folk Song Database **202**

Dillard's Online **305**

DineSite U.S.A. **181**

Dining Out on the Web **181**

Dino Russ's Lair: The Earthnet Info Server **289**

Directory of CPA Firms **218**

Directory of Electronic Text Centers **165**

Directory of Freight Forwarding Services **147**

Directware **7**

Discover Canada Online **363**

Discover Magazine **291**

DiscoWeb **202**

Diseases of the Liver **242**

Diseases/Conditions **242**

Disney **196**

Distance Education Clearinghouse **165**

Divorce Online **379**

Doggy Information on the Web **209**

Dogwood Blossom **93**

DominoNet **350**

Dove Foundation **196**

Dr. Bil's Cool Medical Site of the Week **236**

Dr. Bower's Complementary Medicine Home Page **236**

Dr. Bruce Cornet, UFO Investigator **279**

Dr. Pribut's Running Injuries Page **342**

Dragonfly Toy Company **312**

Dream Page **272**

Dream Shop **308**

DreamLink **272**

dreamMosaic **272**

Drum Arts Page **70**

Drums and Percussion Page **203**

Dun & Bradstreet Online University **165**

Dünya: CyberMuslim Information Collective **108**

E

Early Motion Pictures Home Page **196**

Earrings by Lisa! **312**

Earth and Cave Architecture **67**

Earth Portals **274**

Earth Times **291**

EarthLink Network **19**

Earthwatch International **292**

eBroker Securities **120**

Ecola's College Locator **165**

Ecola's Newsstand—Newspapers **257**

Ecole Initiative **108**

Economist **253**

Eco-Source **292**

Educational Courses on the Web **165**

Edwina Marie Elliott **382**

Egyptology Resources **84**

Eighteenth Century Archive Page **91**

Eighteenth Century Resources: Literature **91**

Eldercare Web **247**

Eldercare Web: Living Arrangements **131**

ElderConnect **130**

Elderhostel Home Page **165**

ElderNet **51**

Eleanor's Kitchen **182**

Electric Cheese Page **181**

Electronic Frontier Foundation **323**

electronic Gourmet Guide (eGG) **182**

Electronic Money Tree **143**

Electronic Privacy Information Center **326**

Electronic Share Information Ltd. **120**

Electronic Text Center at the University of Virginia **175**

Elizabeth A. Kaspar **382**

Elsewhere in Italy **62**

Elvis in Latin: Frequently Asked Questions **203**

E-mail Pen Pals **378**

Emergency Medical Services Homepage **236**

Emily Dickinson Page **91**

Endangered Species: Images and Natural History **292**

Energy Efficient Environments **312**

Engaged Buddhist Dharma **103**

English 201: Nonfiction Writing—A Virtual Semester **166**

English 210E: Technical Writing **165**

English 231: Technical Writing Online **166**

English Renaissance Reenactment Site **84**

English Server at CMU **175**

Entertainment Weekly Online **253**

Entrepreneur Information Guide **147**

Entrepreneurial Edge Magazine **143**

Entrepreneur's Bookstore Catalog **142**

Envelope Please **196**

EnviroLink **292**

Environmental Alliance for Senior Involvement **330**

Environmental Protection Agency **223**

Environmental Working Group **327**

Envoy: A Beginners Guide to Diplomacy **350**

Epicurious Food **182**

Episcopal Church **108**

Ereignis: The Heidegger Home Page **103**

ESPNET SportsZone **347**

Estate Net **135**

Esther and Son's Astrological Services **269**

Ethical Spectacle **274**

E*Trade **120**

Eudora **11**

Eugene Free Community Network **51**

European Literature Electronic Texts **91**

Ever The Twain Shall Meet **91**

Everton's Genealogical Helper **193**

Exploratorium ExploraNet **97**

Explore India **147**

Exploring Ancient World Cultures **84**

E-Zine List **253**

F

"Face on Mars" **266**

F.A.C.T.Net 3 Bulletin **274**

Fair Play **266**

Families USA Foundation **232**

Family Relations **375**

Family.Com **375**

FAMILYHOSTEL Program **166**

FAQs about Hospice **247**

Farm Animal Reform Movement **325**

Farmers Insurance **123**

Faucet Outlet Online **312**

Favorite Field Trips **289**

Federal Bulletin Board **224**

Federal Bureau of Investigation **216**

Federal Deposit Insurance Corporation **117**

Federated Department Stores **305**

FedWorld Information Network Home Page **141**

FedWorld/FLITE Supreme Court Decisions Home Page **221**

Fermilab Education Office **292**

Ferret Frenzy **350**

A Few References to Michel Foucault **103**

FIBS—Backgammon on the Internet **350**

Fiction Addiction **175**

Fifty Plus R Us **51**

Fight Against Coercive Tactics Network FTP Archive **272**

Film Festivals on the World Wide Web **197**

Film Scouts Home Page **197**

Film and Television Reviews **197**

Film and TV Gopher Menu **196**

Finding God in Cyberspace **108**

Fine Arts Museum of San Francisco **73**

Fingerhut Online **306**

Finnish Travel Reservations **365**

Firewatch **108**

First Aid Online **236**

First Chicago NBD Corporation **117**

First City Bank and Trust **117**

First Division Museum at Cantigny **85**

First Hawaiian Bank **117**

First Impressionist Exhibit, 1874 **70**

First Union Corp.—The Internet Cyberbank **117**

First Virtual Internet Payment System **310**

Fish Information Service (FINS) **209**

Flag of the United States of America **85**

Flandrau Science Center **97**

Flightpath Communications **19**

Floral Design Newsletter **47**

Florence of the 15th Century **61**

Florida **40**

Florida Department of Elder Affairs **51**

Florida: Florida Government Information Locator Service **225**

Florida Internet Real Estate Guide **135**

Florida Museum of Natural History **97**

FlossNet, Inc. **302**

FlowersUSA **312**

Fly Fishing Database and FAQ Home Page **345**

Folk Dancing on the WWW **178**

FolkArt & Craft Exchange **312**

Food and Drug Administration **216**

Food and Drug Administration Center for Food Safety & Applied Nutrition **236**

Food Facts for Older Americans **236**

Food For The Hungry: Virtual Learning Center **329**

Food Museum **97**

Food Pyramid **182**

Food Resource **182**

Football Server **339**

Forensic Entomology **293**

Forest Service Home Page **216**

Foundation for Meditation and Spiritual Unfoldment **274**

FOX News **260**

Fran Tarkenton Small Business NETwork **143**

Franchise Handbook Online **154**

Francisco Goya **70**

FranInfo: A World of Information about Franchising **154**

Frank Lloyd Wright **67**

Frank Potter's Science Gems **294**

Franklin Institute Science Museum **98**

Frau Richardson's Pictorial German Homepage **365**

Frederick Clifford Gibson **67**

Free Lunch **303**

Free Personal Health Assessment **237**

Free Stuff Galore **303**

Freelance Online **147**

FreeMark Communications **19**

Freetime Guide **363**

FreeWay **303**

French and Indian War Home Page **85**

Frida Kahlo **70**

Friends of the Daylilies Home Page **188**

Friends of the Earth Home Page **327**

Friends of the Environment **327**

Frontline Online **260**

Fry Cooks on Venus Recipe Index **182**

FTP Directory of Recipes **182**

Fun Recipes Gopher Menu **182**

FuneralNet **380**

G

Gaelic Languages Information 166

Galaxy Mall 308

Galaxy: Music Index 203

Galaxy: Recipes—Leisure and Recreation 182

Galaxy: Unidentified Flying Objects 279

Gallery of American Artisans 313

Gallery of Fine Art 73

GambleNet 347

Gardening & Landscaping 188

GardenNet 188

GardenNet's The Ardent Gardener 188

Gardens+Gardening 188

GardenWeb 188

Gargoyles Then and Now 61

Gary Thomas Moore 382

Gateless Gate 103

Gay & Lesbian Alliance Against Defamation (GLAAD) 320

Genealogy Toolbox 193

George 253

Georgia 40

Georgia: Georgia Online Network 225

German Studies Trails on the Internet 166

GeroWeb 237

GES Internet 19

Gettysburg Address 85

GILS Site on GPO Access 224

Glenbow Art Museum 73

Global Access to Trade and Technology Server 148

Global Music Center 203

Global Network Academy 166

Glossary of Export Terms 148

Glossary of Internet Terms 30

Goldngal, The Cyberspace Granny 382

Golf FAQ 340

Golf Scorecard Archives 340

Gonzo Links 266

Good Sam Club 367

Gothic Dreams 61

Government Information Locator Service 224

Grand Canyon Official Tourism Page 364

Grand Central Railway Station of Cyberspace 190

Grand Times 51

Grand Times Magazine 253

Grandloving: Grandparenting with Activities and Long-Distance Fun 375

Grandma Moses: Cazenovia Lake 77

Grandparent E-mail Pen Pals 375

Grandparent Times 376

Grapes 313

Great Arabian Discovery 85

Great Bridge Links 350

Great Outdoor Recreation Pages 347

Greek Architecture 61

Green Pages 275

Greenpeace International 328

Gregorian Chant Home Page 203

Grief and Loss Resource Center 380

Guardian Insurance 123

Guerrilla Marketing Online 143

Guggenheim Museum 73

Guidance Through Bhagavad Gita 109

Guide to Christian Literature on the Internet 109

Guide to Early Church Documents 109

Guide to Network Resource Tools 25

Guide to Nursing Homes in Florida 131

Guide to Retirement Living Online 131

Guide to Slip and PPP 24

Guide to Talk Radio Programming 261

Guide To Women's Health Issues 237

Gyuto Tantric Choir Home Page 203

H

H&R Block **218**

Habitat for Humanity **329**

Hadrianic Baths **62**

Haiku for People **94**

Hal Fritts **382**

Happy Campers **368**

Happy Puppy **350**

Hare Krishna Home Page **109**

Harry S. Truman Presidential Library and Museum **80**

Harry's Woodworking Page **195**

Hawaii **40**

Hawai`i - Independent and Sovereign Nation-State **228**

Hawai`i: Hawai`i State Government Home Page **225**

Health Care Financing Administration **216**

Health & Fitness World Guide **237**

HealthGate **238**

HealthWeb **248**

Heart: An Online Exploration **238**

Hebrew: A Living Language **166**

Heffter Research Institute **272**

Hell: The Online Guide to Satanism **275**

Henry Ford Museum **98**

Herbert Harari **382**

Herbert's Midi Music Page **47**

Hernia Information Home Page **243**

Herp Pictures, Galleries 1 through 17 **293**

Hiking and Walking Homepage **342**

Hill Monastic Manuscript Library **92**

Hindu (India) **259**

Historic Mount Vernon **85**

Historical Documents Gopher **92**

History 101: History of Western Civilization **166**

History 366: Western Canada Since 1870 **166**

HMO Locator **232**

Hobbies **173**

Hockey Links On The Web **340**

Hollywood Network **197**

Holmespage **382**

Holocaust Internet Sites **85**

Holocaust Memorial **85**

Home Care/Hospice Industry **247**

Home Office Home Page **156**

Home Page for Irises **188**

HomeBuyer Internet Real Estate Service **135**

Homebuyer's Fair **135**

Homeopathy Home Page **238**

HomeOwners Finance Center Loan Calculation Page **135**

Homes & Land Electronic Magazine **135**

HomeScout Search: U.S. and Canada **135**

Homestead Housing Center **130**

Honolulu Community College Dinosaur Exhibit **289**

Hop Page **182**

Hopi Information Network **228**

Horticulture Information Leaflets **188**

HospitalWeb **246**

Hotbox Home Page **190**

HotJava **12**

Houghton Mifflin **175**

House Buying and Financing **136**

Houses of Key West Home Page **65**

How to Choose a Doctor and Hospital for Your Treatment **235**

How Do You Pick a Home Health Agency? **247**

How far is it? **129**

How much house can you afford? **136**

HSH Associates **135**

Hume Archives **103**

Hunter **346**

Hydroponic Society of America **293**

Hydroponics! InterUrban WaterFarms Online **189**

Hyper-Weirdness by World Wide Web **266**

Hypnosis.com **272**

Hypnotica **272**

I

I Need My Chocolate! **183**

IBM Internet Connection **19**

I-Ching **270**

Idaho: Idaho State Government **225**

Idea Café: The Small Business Channel **148**

IDG Books Worldwide **10**

I-Link **19**

Illinois **40**

Illinois State Museum **98**

Illinois: Statewide Agencies **225**

Images of Federal Hill, Lynchburg, Virginia **65**

iMALL **309**

In Italy Online **365**

Inc. Business Resources Library **142**

Inc. Online **143**

Income Opportunities Online **143**

Indian River Gift Fruit Company **313**

Indiana **40**

Indiana: Indiana State Government **225**

InfiNet **19**

INFO.Net **19**

Information for Entrepreneurs **148**

Information SuperLibrary **175**

Instant Baseball **336**

Institute for Brain Aging and Dementia **243**

Institute for Global Communications: EcoNet **293**

Insurance Club Home Page **123**

Insurance Companies & Resources on the Net **124**

Insurance Information Institute **124**

Insurance News Network **124**

Integral Yoga Web Site **275**

Interactive Model Railroad **190**

Interactive Movie Reviews **197**

Interactive Origami in VRML **194**

Interactive Week Online **253**

Intercon: Internet Information and Resources **19**

Interface Technologies Online Training Center **166**

InterGolf **340**

INTERHOSTEL Program **167**

InterJazz: The Internet Jazz Plaza **203**

InterLotto—On-Line Lottery Information Service **227**

Interlude **275**

Internal Revenue Service **217**

International Business Network **148**

International Business Resources on the World Wide Web **148**

International Centre for Distance Learning **167**

International Churches of Christ **109**

International Committee of the Red Cross **329**

International Food Information Council Foundation **183**

International Franchise Association **154**

International Homeworkers Association **156**

International Network for Interfaith Health Practices **238**

International Paperweight Society **191**

International Real Estate Directory **136**

International Soccer Server **343**

International Trade Adminstration **148**

International Trade Law **149**

International Treasure Hunters Exchange **195**

Internet Access Providers List **25**

Internet Beatles List **203**

Internet Bonsai Club **189**

Internet Book Information Center **175**

Internet Business Center **149**

Internet Business Opportunities and Services **154**

Internet Chess Library **350**

Internet Classroom **30**

Internet College Exchange **167**

Internet Consumer Recycling Guide **293**

Internet Crime Archives **266**

Internet Epicurean **183**

Internet Explorer **33**

Internet Gaming Zone: Bridge **350**

Internet Health Newsgroups and Listserver Groups **238**

Internet Health Resources **238**

Internet Liquidators, Inc. **309**

Internet Mahjong Meta-Server **351**

Internet Medical and Health Care Resources **239**

Internet Movie Database **197**

Internet Music Resource Guide **203**

Internet Phone **12**

Internet Poetry Archive **94**

Internet Real Estate Network **136**

Internet RV and Camping Guide **368**

Internet Scambusters **144**

Internet Services for Philosophers **103**

Internet Sleuth **32**

Internet UFO Group **279**

Internet White Pages **26**

Internet Wiretap **176**

Internet Wiretap Gopher **92**

Internet Yellow Web Pages: Real Estate (Canada) **136**

Introduction to PC Hardware **7**

Introduction to Skin Cancer **243**

Inventors Resources & Associations Links **149**

Investment Brokerages Guide **120**

invest-o-rama **121**

InvestorGuide **121**

Iowa: Government **225**

Iowa State University's Tasty Insect Recipes **183**

Irish Country Holidays **365**

Irish Times **259**

Islamic Architecture in Isfahan **62**

Italy in the 15th Century **62**

I-Tarot **270**

J

Jackie Brown **382**

Jackpot **351**

Jamaica! **362**

James Kirk-White **382**

Jan's Custom Knits **313**

Janyce's Root Diggin' Dept. **193**

Japan National Tourist Organization **365**

Japan Times **259**

Jason's Kite Site **193**

JavaGammon **351**

JAZZ Online **203**

JazzNet **204**

JCPenney **306**

JEC Knowledge Online **167**

Jerusalem Post **259**

Jews for Jesus **109**

Jim Olson **382**

Joan Grimes **383**

Joan's Witch Directory **275**

Johannesburg Star **259**

John R. Dye **383**

John R Dye's Home Page **47**

John Skilton's Baseball Links **336**

John Wiley & Sons **176**

Johns Hopkins Medical Institution InfoNet: Patient Advocacy Groups **243**

Joint Chiefs of Staff **220**

Joseph Luft's Philatelic Resources on the Web **192**

Jôyô 96 Japanese Study System Home Page **167**

Judaism and Jewish Resources **109**

J.U.I.C.E.—Jewish University in CyberspacE **167**

June 12, 1996 Decision in ACLU vs. Reno **323**

Justice Against Crime Talking **322**

Justices of the Supreme Court **221**

K

Kansas **40**

Kansas City Architecture **66**

Kansas Elder Law Network (KELN) **52**

Kansas: Kansas State Agencies **225**

Kansas Religion & Philosophy Corner **109**

Karntner Bar **62**

Keith R. Bradley's Home Page **383**

Kelsey Museum of Archaeology **98**

Kennedy Assassination Home Page **266**

Kenneth Clark on Velaquez' "Las Meninas" **69**

Kentucky **40**

Kentucky: Alphabetical List of Kentucky State Government Information **225**

Khazana - India Arts Online **313**

Khazaria Info Center **86**

KidsPeace **326**

Kingfield Bank **117**

Kisho Kurokawa **67**

Kitchen Nook **183**

Kitsap Computing Seniors **52**

Kmart **306**

Knopf Publishing Group **176**

Koestler Parapsychology Unit **273**

KOMA: Korean American Museum of Art **73**

Kooks Museum **266**

Kool Ties **303**

Kosher Express **313**

Krannert Art Museum **73**

Krishnamurti **103**

Krispin Komments on Nutrition and Health **183**

L

L. J. Klein **383**

L. L. Bean **306**

La Cocina Mexicana **183**

Laboratory for Consciousness Studies **273**

Ladies' Home Journal **253**

Lady Unicorn5 **383**

Lakota Wowapi Oti Kin: Lakota Information Home Page **228**

Lamp Technology, Inc. **313**

Lands' End **306**

Largest Newspaper Index on the Web **257**

Late Onset Diabetes **243**

Latin Music On-Line! **204**

Laurie Jenkinson **383**

Law and Order Comes to Cyberspace **324**

LawTalk—Business Law and Personal Finance **117**

LDS iAmerica **19**

LDS Resources Pages **109**

League of Women Voters of the United States **326**

Leanin' Tree Greeting Cards **303**

Learning-Fountain Marketing **149**

Left-Wing Films **197**

Legg Mason Investment Center **121**

L'eggs Women's In.Site **303**

Leo Steinberg: Selections **71**

Les Fromages de France **183**

Letter R.I.P **351**

Letters Home From a Soldier in the U. S. Civil War **86**

Lewis Carroll **92**

Liam Maguire's NHL Hockey Trivia **341**

Library of Congress **24**

Library of Congress Music Resources Gopher Menu **204**

Library of Congress Soviet Archives Exhibit **86**

Life Care Retirement Communities **131**

LIFE Magazine **253**

Lifestyles International Astrological Foundation **270**

Lillian Vernon **306**

Lindisfarne Gospels **92**

Links to Occult Information **275**

Lion's Den **197**

List of Food and Cooking Sites **183**

List of Music Mailing Lists **204**

Literary Kicks **92**

Literary Resources on the Net **92**

Live Steaming **190**

Logical World of Etymology **167**

London Guide **365**

Lonely Planet Online **360**

Long Island Savings Bank **117**

Look Within: Inspirations of Love **275**

Los Angeles County Museum of Art **74**

Los Angeles Seniors **52**

Los Angeles Times **258**

Lost Museum of Sciences **98**

Louis Sullivan Page **67**

Louise See's Family **383**

Louisiana **40**

Louisiana: Info Louisiana **225**

Louvre **74**

Lycos Press **11**

Lyrics Page Search Screen **204**

M

M. D. Anderson Cancer Center **245**

Mac OS Software and Hardware Guide **10**

Macedonia: History and Politics **86**

Macintosh Tips and First Aid **7**

MacLinq **11**

MacUser **7**

MacWarehouse **7**

Macworld **7**

Macworld Magazine Online **253**

Macy's **306**

Magazine CyberCentre **254**

Maggie G. Severns **383**

Magic Infinity-ball **270**

mag.net online **52**

Mahjong: The Chinese Game of Four Winds **351**

Mail & Guardian (South Africa) **259**

Maine Antique Digest **192**

Maine: Maine State Government **226**

Mall of Malls **309**

malls.com **309**

Manuela's Recipes **183**

Marine Fish Catalog **293**

MarineNet **345**

Mark Twain Banks **118**

Mark Twain on the Philippines **92**

Mark's Poem of the Day **96**

Marquee MovieServer **197**

Mars Exploration Program **283**

Mars Images Menu **283**

Marshall Field's **306**

Martial Arts Resource Site **341**

Marx/Engels Archives **104**

Mary Rose Virtual Maritime Museum **98**

Maryland **40**

Maryland: Maryland State Government **226**

Massachusetts General Hospital WWW Server **246**

Massachusetts: Massachusetts Access to Government Information Service **226**

Master Gardener Information **189**

Master's Collection **313**

Match Wits With Nicky Facts **197**

Material Culture of the Ancient Canaanites, Israelites and Related Peoples **289**

Matt's Solar Car Page **344**

Maturity USA **254**

Mayo Clinic **246**

MCA/Universal Cyberwalk **197**

McDonald's **66**

MCI **20**

Mead Maker's Page **183**

Media Online Yellow Pages **261**

Medical College of Wisconsin International Travelers Clinic (ITC) **239**

Medical Reporter **239**

Medicare Rights Center **232**

Medieval Resources **86**

Medieval/Renaissance Food Home Page **184**

Medseek **235**

MedWeb: Biomedical Internet Resources **248**

Meet the Press **261**

MegaMall **309**

Mellon Bank **118**

Mental Health Net **243**

Merchants National Bank **118**

Merrill Lynch **121**

Merrill Shindler's Guide to Eating Pretty Good **184**

Metalog **270**

Method of Centering Prayer **275**

MetLife Online **124**

MetLife Online: Nursing Homes **131**

Metropolitan Museum of Art **74**

Metropolitan State College of Denver **167**

Mexico Travel **364**

Meyer Shapiro on Cezanne **71**

Miami Herald **258**

Michiana FreeNet **52**

Michigan Marketing Association Earthy Delights Home Page **313**

Michigan: Michigan State Government **226**

Microsoft **33**

Microsoft Expedia Travel Service **360**

Microsoft Small Business Resource **149**

Mid-Florida Area Agency on Aging **52**

Mighty Dog Designs **313**

Mimi's Cyber Kitchen **184**

Mind & Body Links and Articles **239**

Mind Uploading **273**

Mindquest: Online High School Education for Adults **168**

MindWarp: The Mind Subpage **273**

Minimizing Your Taxes **219**

Minneapolis Institute of Arts **74**

Minnesota **41**

Minnesota: Minnesota Government Information and Services **226**

Minority Business Entrepreneur Magazine **144**

Miramax Films **197**

Mississippi: State Government Home Pages **226**

Missouri **41**

Missouri: Missouri State Government Web **226**

MIT Biology Hypertextbook **167**

MIT List of Radio Stations on the Internet **261**

Mizrahi Bank **118**

MLB@BAT **336**

Mobilia Magazine **192**

Model Horse Links **194**

Modern English Collection **92**

Mohawk Nation Council of Chiefs **228**

MoJo Wire: Mother Jones Interactive **254**

Moksha Foundation **273**

Mole Page **184**

Monitor Radio **261**

Monroe Institute **273**

Monster (Magazine) List **254**

Montana: State Government **226**

Monterey Bay Aquarium: E-Quarium **98**

Montreal Gazette **259**

More Florence **62**

Morocco Guided Tour **365**

Mortgage Loan Page **136**

Moscow Architecture **63**

Motherheart **275**

Motorcycle Online **344**

Motorsport News International **344**

Mount Wilson Observatory Online Stargazer Map **288**

Movie Mania **198**

Movie Sounds Page **198**

Movies.com **198**

Mr. Showbiz **198**

Mrs. McGregor's Mature Citizen **52**

MSN **20**

MSNBC **261**

Multimedia Grandma **376**

Multimedia Medical Reference Library **248**

Musée des Arts et Métiers **74**

Museo de las Momias **99**

Museum of Antiquities **99**

Museum of Bad Art **74**

Museum of Radio and Technology **99**

Music Gopher at Rice University **204**

Music Schools **168**

Musi-Cal **204**

Muslims in the 19th Century Russian Empire **86**

Mutual Funds Magazine Online **121**

My Graphics Page **383**

My Virtual Newspaper **257**

MyBank Directory **118**

Mycelium Welcome **184**

Mysticism in the World's Religions **275**

N

Nando Soccer Features **343**

NandO Times **257**

NASA Homepage **287**

NASA Space Calendar **288**

Nation **254**

National Aeronautics and Space Administration **223**

National Aging Information Center **52**

National Air & Space Museum **99**

National Association of Export Companies **149**

National Association of Realtors Home Page **13**

National Association for the Self-Employed **149**

National Baseball Hall of Fame and Museum **99**

National Black Business Trade Association **150**

National Business Exchange Network **154**

National Civic League **327**

National Civil War Association **86**

National Coalition for the Homeless **329**

National Committee to Prevent Child Abuse **326**

National Conference of State Legislatures **227**

National Discount Brokers Online **121**

National Extension College **168**

National Fraud Information Center **150**

National Gemstone **192**

National Hockey League Players' Association **341**

National Institute of Diabetes and Digestive and Kidney Disease (NIDDK) **243**

National Model Railroad Association **190**

National Museum of American Art **74**

National Museum of the American Indian **99**

National Museum of Racing and Hall of Fame **99**

National Oceanic and Atmospheric Administration **220**

National Outdoor Leadership School **168**

National Park Service Home Page **368**

National Parks and Conservation Association **328**

National Pork Producers Council **184**

National Portrait Gallery **100**

National Professional Soccer League **343**

National Public Radio **261**

National Senior Service Corps **330**

National Solar Observatory **287**

NationsBank **118**

Nationwide Insurance **124**

Native American Art Gallery, Ltd. **313**

Natural History Museum **100**

Natural History Museum of Los Angeles County **100**

Natural Resources Defense Council **328**

Naturally Yours **314**

Nature Conservancy **328**

Navajo Nation **228**

NBA.com **337**

NBC News at Sunrise **261**

NCII Online Information Center for Discount Brokerage **121**

Nebraska **41**

Nebraska Age Link **52**

Nebraska: Nebraska State Government **226**

Neiman Marcus **306**

Nessie on the Net in Scotland! **279**

Nest Egg **254**

Net Search Directory **32**

NetBank **310**

NetBiz—The Entrepreneur's Bookstore **143**

NETCOM **20**

Netherlands Institute for the Near East **87**

NetMall **309**

NetMarquee **144**

Netscape **33**

NET-Scrabble **351**

NET—The Political NewsTalk Network **261**

NetWeb Bermuda **362**

Network-USA's ISP Catalog **20**

NETworth **121**

Nevada **41**

Nevada: State of Nevada **226**

New Civilization Network Server One **276**

New England Medical Center **246**

New Heaven, New Earth **110**

New Jersey **41**

New Jersey: State of New Jersey **226**

New Lifestyles Online **131**

New Line Cinema **198**

New Mexico: State of New Mexico Government Information **226**

New Paradigms Project **267**

New Republic **254**

New York **41**

New York: Citizen's Access to State Government **226**

New York Institute of Technology On-Line Campus **168**

New York Times **258**

NeWo: News Resource **257**

News of the Weird **267**

Newsletter Library **144**

Newspapers Online **257**

Newsroom **257**

Next to Nothing **303**

NFIC MultiHost Server **20**

NFL.com **339**

NHL Pages **341**

NHL Wreckroom **341**

NicNet: Nicotine and Tobacco Network **239**

Nietzsche Page **104**

Nightly News with Tom Brokaw **261**

Nine Planets: A Multimedia Tour of the Solar System **287**

No Dogs or Philosophers Allowed **104**

Nordstrom Personal Touch America **307**

North American Vegetarian Society **184**

North Carolina **41**

North Carolina: Agency Info - North Carolina Information Server **226**

North Carolina Museum of Life and Science **100**

North Dakota: North Dakota State Government **226**

Northwestern Mutual Life **124**

Northwestern University Library Special Collections: The Siege and Commune of Paris, 1870-1871 **87**

Nutrition and Senior Citizens **239**

Nyabinghi's Gallery of African Art **75**

O

OceanVoice International **328**

Office of Seniors Interests **53**

Ohio **41**

Ohio: State of Ohio Government Front Page **226**

Oklahoma **41**

Oklahoma: Oklahoma State Government Information Server **226**

Old Guy @ Home **383**

OLDE Discount Corporation **121**

OMNI **254**

On-Call Vacations **360**

OncoLink, The University of Pennsylvania Cancer Center Resource **243**

Oneida Indian Nation **228**

On-Line Allergy Center **243**

Online Art Resources **70**

Online Book Initiative **176**

Online Book of Parrots **209**

Online Books FAQ **176**

On-line Books Page **176**

OnLine Education: The Electronic Campus **168**

Online Environment **293**

On-line Exhibitions and Images **100**

On-Line Glossary of Solar-Terrestrial Terms **288**

Online Knitting Magazine **194**

Online Magazines **254**

Online Money: Find Your Best Place **129**

Online Music and Audio References **204**

Online Newshour **262**

Online Newspapers **257**

Online Scotland **366**

Online Small Business Workshop **150**

Online Sports **314**

Online Writery **177**

Open University (Florida) **168**

Open University (U.K.) **168**

Opera on the Web **204**

OperaGlass **204**

Operation Desert Storm Debriefing Book **86**

Orchid House **189**

Oregon **41**

Oregon: Oregon Home Page—Government Resources **226**

Origami Page **194**

Origin of the Celsius Temperature Scale **293**

Ovi's World of the Bizarre **267**

P

P103 General Psychology Course **169**

Pacific Coast **314**

PADI World Wide Web Site **345**

Page at Pooh Corner **93**

Pages and Pages of Food **184**

PaineWebber Intelligence Center **121**

Palaeolithic Cave **289**

Paleontology Without Walls **290**

Palladio's Italian Villas **63**

Palmer Museum of Art **75**

Paper Airplanes **194**

Paper Ships Books & Crystals **276**

Paramount Pictures **198**

ParentsPlace.com **376**

Paris Page **366**

Park Avenue **309**

Park Search **368**

Parkinson's Web **244**

ParkNet: The National Park Service **220**

Partners Task Force for Gay and Lesbian Couples **321**

Pat & John's Prose and Poetry **383**

Pat Scott's Irish Recipe Page **47**

Pathfinder **254**

PAWWS Financial Network **122**

PBS **262**

PBS Adult Learning Service Online **169**

PBS ALSO: College Credit **169**

PC Magazine **6**

PC Magazine on the Web **254**

Peace Corps **223**

PeaceNet **329**

Peachpit Press **11**

Pennsylvania **41**

Pennsylvania: Pennsylvania State Government **226**

Penny's Skulls of Fate **270**

Pen-Parents, Inc. **380**

People **254**

People's Bank **118**

Peregrine Foundation **110**

Perspectives of the Smithsonian: Computer History **100**

PETA Online—People for the Ethical Treatment of Animals **325**

Peterson's Education Center **169**

Pets Grief Support Page & Candle Ceremony **380**

Phantom Sleep Page (Apnea, Snoring & Other Sleep Problems) **244**

Philadelphia Museum of Art **75**

Philadelphia Online (Inquirer & Daily News) **258**

Philip Grosset **384**

Philippine History **101 87**

Phonecard Collectors **192**

Picasso and Portraiture **70**

Picture Gallery of Classical Composers **204**

Pie Page **184**

Pier 1 **307**

Pilot Network Services Inc. **20**

Pit Cooking **184**

Plague and Public Health in Renaissance Europe **87**

Plainsong and Mediaeval Music Society **205**

Planet Earth **30**

Plants by Mail FAQ **189**

Plastic Princess Page **192**

Plate Tectonics—The Cause of Earthquakes **294**

Plato **104**

PointCast Network **257**

Pooh-Bear-6 **384**

PopSci.com **255**

Popular Mechanics **255**

Portfolio of Architectural Photos **63**

Power Computing **7**

Pray Before the Head of "Bob" **270**

Premiere **255**

Premium Federal Savings Bank **118**

Prentice Hall **176**

Presbyterian Church (U.S.A.) **110**

Preserve and Protect **66**

Primenet **25**

PrimeTime Live **262**

Pringle Development **131**

Pro Football Hall of Fame **100**

Procurement Assistance Jumpstation **150**

Prodigy **17**

Professional Bowlers Association **337**

Professional Hockey Server **341**

Professor Stephen Hawking **293**

Project Gutenberg **176**

Project Mind Foundation **276**

Project Vote Smart: Member Biographical and Contact Information **227**

Pronet Global Interactive Business Centre **20**

Pronoia Page **276**

Property Line **136**

Prophe-Zine **276**

Prostate Cancer Home Page **244**

Prostate Cancer InfoLink **244**

Protree UFO Center **279**

Prudential Insurance **124**

Prudential Real Estate Affiliates **136**

Prudential Securities Virtual Branch Office **122**

P. S. I Love You International **378**

PSINet **20**

Public Citizen **327**

Publishers' Catalogues Home Page **176**

Pulitzer Prizes **93**

Pyramid Lake Paiute Tribe **228**

Q

QSL Information System **194**

Quaker Electronic Archive **110**

Quantum Net **30**

Quick Information About Cancer for Patients and Their Families **244**

Quinault Indian Nation (Washington) **228**

R

R. N. Wahner, DiSc **384**

Rabbit in the Moon: Mayan Glyphs and Architecture **290**

RaceZine **345**

Racing Memorabilia Pages **194**

Ragtime Home Page **205**

Rajon Institute **267**

Rambler66 **384**

Random Access **20**

Rappelling **338**

Raptor Center **294**

Rapture Index **276**

Rat Pack Home Page **205**

Rayco Tennis Shop **314**

Reader's Digest **255**

ReadersNdex **176**

Real Astrology **270**

Real Cranberry Home Page **184**

RealAudio **12**

Real/Time Communications **20**

RealtyGuide **137**

Reasons To Believe **110**

rec.food.recipes FTP Index **185**

rec.puzzles Archive **351**

rec.travel Library **360**

Recreational Vehicles and Motorhome Living **368**

Reduce Garbage—Eliminate Landfills **294**

Reeder's Egypt Page **290**

RE/MAX Real Estate Network **136**

Rembrandt **70**

Renaissance and Baroque Architecture **63**

RentNet Online Apartment Guide **137**

Res-Links **33**

Research Institute for the Humanities: History **87**

Retirement Net **132**

Retirement Net: Florida **132**

Reuters **258**

Revlon Cosmetics **303**

Rhea Coleman & Burt Vose **384**

RhetNet: A CyberJournal **93**

Rhode Island: Rhode Island State Government **226**

Richard Robinson's Tunebook **205**

Richard III Society **87**

Rico's Martial Arts Page **341**

Robert C. Williams American Museum of Papermaking **101**

Robot Wisdom Pages **104**

Robson Communities **132**

Rockhounds Information Page **192**

Rockpile BBS **30**

Rolling Your Own Sushi **185**

Roman Rudolph Liedl **70**

Ron's Place **104**

ROOTS-L Home Page **193**

Rosaleen Diana (Leslie) Dickson **384**

Rosicrucian Fellowship **276**

Rossetti Archive **71**

Rough Guide **360**

Royal Bank of Canada **118**

Royal Insurance Home Page **124**

Royal Insurance U.S. **124**

RSSSF Archive **343**

RugbyInfo **346**

RuneCaster **270**

Running Horse **335**

Running Page **342**

RV and Camping FAQ **368**

RV Online **368**

RVers Online **368**

RV-Mobile Home Marketplace (Florida) **131**

S

Sac and Fox Nation **229**

SafeTnet **125**

Sailing Page **346**

SailNet **346**

Salinan Nation of California **229**

Salt River Pima-Maricopa Indian Community **229**

Salvation Army International Headquarters **329**

Sam's Club Online **307**

Sample Business Plan **150**

San Diego Model Railroad Museum Virtual Tour **190**

San Francisco's The Gate **258**

Saturday Evening Post **255**

Save-a-Pet On-line **209**

Savor the Garlic Gourmet Spices **303**

Scamizdat Memorial—Yet Another Scientology Home Page **110**

Scavengers Quest **303**

Science Hobbyist **294**

Science Made Stupid **294**

Science Online **294**

Scientific American **255**

Scientology Gopher **276**

Scott's Chat Room Index **378**

Scrabble FAQ **351**

Scrolls from the Dead Sea: The Ancient Library of Qumran and Modern Scholarship **290**

Scuba FAQ **346**

Scuba.Net **346**

Sea World Animal Information Database **295**

Sean's One-Stop Philosophy Shop **105**

Seaports Infopages **150**

search.com **32**

Sears **307**

Seattle Times **258**

Secret History of the United States 1962-1996 **267**

Securities & Exchange Commission **122**

Security First Network Bank **118**

Selected Civil War Photographs **87**

Selected Sites of Interest **53**

Selected Works of Martin Luther 1483–1546 **110**

Seminole Tribe of Florida **229**

Senator J.J. Exon's Letter to the Washington Post **324**

Senior Chit-Chat **378**

Senior Clinic **239**

Senior Computer Information Project—Health **244**

Senior Friendly **53**

Senior Frolic **384**

Senior Group Newsletter **53**

Senior Internet Project **53**

Senior Japan **54**

Senior Lifestyle **255**

Senior Resource: Housing Choices **132**

Senior Sites **132**

Senior Times **54**

Senior World **54**

Senior.Com **53**

Senior.Com SNN Chat Area **378**

SeniorFriendly.Com: Housing Options **132**

Senior-Inet **53**

SeniorNet **43**

SeniorNet RoundTables **378**

Seniors' Center **54**

Seniors Computer Information Project **54**

Seniors Corner **384**

Seniors Internet Mall Page **54**

Seniors Internet Resource Center **54**

Seniors Online **55**

Seniors Online Job Bank **55**

Seniors for Seniors **54**

Seniors-Site **55**

Service Corps of Retired Executives **141**

Service Corps of Retired Executives Association (SCORE) **55**

SETI Institute **279**

SETIQuest **279**

Seven Wonders of the Ancient World **63**

Shaken Not Stirred **185**

Shareware.Com **34**

Sharper Image Catalog **307**

Shepherd's Centers of America **55**

Sherlock and the Search **32**

ShopInternet: Malls and Catalogs **309**

Shopper **309**

Should We Return to the Moon? **287**

Shroud of Turin **276**

Shuttle-Mir Web **287**

SI Online from Sports Illustrated **255**

Sierra Club **328**

Signet Bank Online **119**

Sikhism Home Page **111**

Silo **267**

Silver Fox Advisors **150**

Silver Threads **55**

Simon Fraser University Centre for Distance Education **169**

Singapore National Heritage Board **75**

Single Search **379**

Skeptic **255**

SKEPTIC Annotated Bibliography **267**

Skeptics Society Web **267**

Ski America **343**

Sky Online **288**

Slate **255**

Sleep Medicine Home Page **244**

Sloan-Kettering Institute **246**

SlotMania **352**

Small Business Administration Home Page **141**

Small Business Administration Office of Minority Enterprise Devlopment **142**

Small Business Administration's Office of Women's Business Ownership **142**

Small Business Advisor **151**

Small Business Law Center **151**

Small Business Publicity FAQ **151**

Small Business Resource Center **151**

Small and Home Based Business Links **151**

Small Office/Home Office (SOHO) Business Guide **151**

Smith Barney **122**

Smithsonian Institution **87**

Smithsonian Magazine **255**

Smithsonian Natural History Museum **101**

smprfi IN **384**

So Much Software, So Little Time **33**

Soccer Information **343**

Social Security Online **223**

Society for Creative Anachronism **88**

Socrates **105**

Solar Cooking Archive **185**

Solar Gear Sun Care **303**

Solar System Live **287**

Solstice: Sustainable Energy and Development Online! **295**

Something for Nothing Journal **144**

Sony Pictures Entertainment Movies **198**

Sophisticated Shirts **314**

Sorcery BBS **30**

Source Internet Services, North America **20**

Sources of Skeptical Information on the Internet **267**

South Carolina: Government in South Carolina **226**

South Dakota: South Dakota Government Information **226**

Southeastern Architectural Archive **66**

Southern California Orthopedic Institute Home Page **244**

Southern Living Online **256**

Space Shuttle **287**

Speak Freely, Act Responsibly **324**

Spectrum Virtual University **169**

Spencer's Beer Page **185**

Spice Merchant **314**

Spiegel **307**

SpinozaWeb **105**

Spirits Evolving **276**

Spoon Collective **105**

Sports Car Club of America **345**

Sports Network **347**

SprintLink **21**

Spudlix **384**

Square Dance Resources **178**

SR.News **53**

St. Louis' Postnet **258**

St. Petersburg Times **258**

Stadiums and Arenas **347**

Star Chefs & Cookbook Authors **185**

Stark's Museum of Vacuum Cleaners **101**

State Farm Insurance **125**

State Tax Resources **227**

STAT_USA/Internet Site Economic, Trade, Business Information **151**

Stolen Bike Registry **339**

Strange Science: The Rocky Road to Modern Paleontology and Biology **290**

Strawberry Facts Page **189**

Stuart's Chinese Recipes **185**

studyabroad.com **169**

Su Tzu's Chinese Philosophy Page **105**

Successful Senior **55**

SuccessTEAM Online **303**

Sundance Institute **198**

Surrealism Server **71**

Sustainable Architecture, Building and Culture **295**

Swiss Banks Directory **119**

Sydney Morning Herald **259**

T

Tabitha's Freebies **304**

Talk America Radio Network **262**

Talking About Turkey **186**

Tamilian Cuisine **186**

Taos Hum **268**

Target **307**

TarotWorks **270**

Tate Gallery **75**

Tax Prophet **219**

Tax Sites Directory **220**

Tax Tips and Facts **220**

Taxing Times 1997 **220**

Taxi's Newspaper List **258**

TaxSites: Income Tax Information on the Internet **220**

Telecommunications Act of 1996 (S.652) **324**

Telemarque **343**

Telepathy, Research, Parapsychology, Science **273**

Telson Spur: A Way Station for Snark Hunters **385**

Ten Ways to Care for the Caregiver **247**

Tennessee **41**

Tennessee: Tennessee—America at Its Best **227**

Tennis Server Home Page **344**

Tennis Web **344**

Tennis Worldwide **344**

Tenpin World **337**

Terry's World of AudioBooks **177**

Texas **41**

Texas Foods Recipe Page **186**

Texas State Technical College's Distance Education Classes **169**

Texas: State of Texas Government Information **227**

Thai Food **186**

Theosophical Society **106**

This is True Home Page **268**

THOMAS: Legislative Information on the Internet **222**

Thoroughbred Horse Racing **336**

Three Rivers Free-Net **56**

Three Rivers Petroglyph Site **290**

Time Out **360**

Time.com **256**

Times of London **259**

Tim's Christmas Page **205**

Tito **88**

Today Show **262**

Todays Fortune **270**

Tokyo Food Page **186**

Tom & Pat's Home Page **385**

Top 5% of All Web Sites **32**

Torah Fax in Cyberspace **111**

Toronto Globe and Mail **259**

Toronto Sun **259**

Total Freedom Trap: Scientology, Dianetics and L. Ron Hubbard **277**

Tour in China **366**

Tourism Offices Worldwide Directory **360**

Tower Lyrics Archive **205**

Track: Home of Server-Push Horseracing **352**

Tracking Hector Guimard **63**

Tracks Around the World **345**

Trade Compass **152**

Trade Show Central **152**

Training for Your Needs & Entertainment **56**

trancenet.org **273**

Transhumanist Resources **273**

Trans-Siberian Railroad **366**

Travel & Entertainment Network **360**

Travel 2 Indonesia **366**

Travel Source **360**

Travel Weekly **361**

TravelASSIST **361**

Travelers Property & Casualty **125**

TravelGram—Bargain Discounts **361**

TreasureNet **195**

Tribute Robert Rauschenberg **70**

Tried & True Trains **190**

Trinity Atomic Web Site **88**

Tsunami! **295**

TuneWeb **205**

Turkey Travel Guide **366**

Turning Point **262**

Twentieth Century Fox **198**

Twenty-Five Most Common Tax Preparation Errors **220**

Two Minute Warning **339**

U

U. S. Bank **119**

U. S. Civil War Center **88**

U. S. Exports Directory **152**

U. S. Gazetteer **130**

U. S. Geological Survey Fact Sheets **295**

U. S. Hospitals on the Web **246**

U. S. House of Representatives **222**

U. S. Internet **21**

U. S. Internet Service Providers List **21**

U. S. News & World Report Online **256**

U. S. Senate **222**

U. S. State Constitutions **228**

U. S. Swing Dance Server **178**

U. S. Universities and Community Colleges **170**

UC Berkeley Search for Extraterrestrial Civilizations **279**

UFO & Paranormal & Skeptic Links **280**

UK Insurance Links Directory **125**

Ulster Historical Publications **88**

Ultimate Outlet **307**

Unabomber's Manifesto **268**

Underground Astrologer **271**

Undernet Poker **352**

Underwater Sports World **346**

Unicorn5 **385**

Unicycle Page **339**

Unification Home Page **111**

United Children's Fund **326**

United Keetoowah Bank of Cherokee Indians **229**

United Methodist Church **111**

United Nations **24**

United Senior Association **56**

United South and Eastern Tribes **229**

United States Copyright Office **142**

United States Department of Agriculture **212**

United States Department of Commerce **212**

United States Department of Defense **213**

United States Department of Education **213**

United States Department of Energy **213**

United States Department of Health and Human Services **213**

United States Department of Housing and Urban Development **213**

United States Department of the Interior **213**

United States Department of Justice **213**

United States Department of Labor **214**

United States Department of State **215**

United States Department of Transportation **215**

United States Department of the Treasury **215**

United States Department of Veterans Affairs **215**

United States Federal Judiciary **221**

United States Holocaust Memorial Museum **88**

United States Patent and Trademark Office **142**

United States Postal Service Home Page **223**

United States Virgin Islands **362**

United Tribe of Shawnee Indians **229**

Universal Access Inc. Blackjack Server **352**

University Links: Adult Education **169**

University of California Museum of Paleontology **101**

University of Michigan Gopher **152**

University of Minnesota **24**

University of New Orleans—Metropolitan College **170**

University Online, Inc. **170**

University Pages **170**

University of Phoenix Online Campus **170**

University of South Carolina—Continuing Education **170**

University of Tennessee Division of Continuing Studies and Distance Education **170**

University Without Walls **170**

Unnamed List of Access Providers **25**

Urban Agriculture Notes by City Farmer **189**

USA CityLink **129**

USA Fibrositis Association **244**

USA Football Center Online **340**

USA Today **258**

USA.NET **21**

USENET Cookbook **186**

Utah: State of Utah Alpha Listing of Agencies **227**

UUNET Technologies **21**

U-Web **88**

V

Vancouver Sun **259**

Vatican Exhibit Main Hall **101**

Vatican Exhibit—Rome Reborn **88**

Vedic Astrology Home Page **271**

Vegas.Com Sports Central **347**

Vegetarian Pages **186**

Veggies Unite! **186**

Vermeer and the Art of Painting **71**

Vermont **41**

Vermont: Vermont State Home Page **227**

Veterans Health Administration **221**

Victorian Web **89**

Vidya's Guide to Advertising on the Internet **152**

Viking Home Page **89**

Viking Mission to Mars **284**

Vintage Vaudeville & Ragtime Show **205**

Virginia **41**

Virginia: Virginia Government **227**

Virtual Breakaway **339**

Virtual Cell **295**

Virtual Emporium **309**

Virtual Garden **189**

Virtual Golfer **340**

Virtual Hospital **248**

Virtual Library **33**

Virtual Media Lab **170**

Virtual Memorial Hall of the Victims in Nanjing Massacre **89**

Virtual Online University **171**

Virtual Pet Cemetery **209**

Virtual Seminar in Global Political Economy **171**

Virtual Soma **66**

Virtual Trips to Black Holes and Neutron Stars Page **287**

Virtual Vineyards **314**

VISTA Home Page **329**

Vodoun (or Voodoo) Information Pages **277**

Voice of the Shuttle: English Literature **93**

Volcano World **295**

Volition **304**

Volksmarch and Walking Index **342**

Volleyball WorldWide **347**

Voltaire Foundation **93**

Voodoo: From Medicine to Zombies **277**

Vote Smart Web **327**

Voters Telecommunications Watch **324**

W

W. W. Norton Online **177**

W5: WoodWorking on the World Wide Web **195**

Wal-Mart **307**

Walker Percy **93**

Wall Street Journal **258**

Wall Street Research Net **122**

Walt Disney World **364**

Warner Brothers Online **198**

Washington **41**

Washington D. C. **41**

Washington, D. C. **66**

Washington Post **258**

Washington Times **258**

Washington: A Washington State Government Information Guide **227**

Washington Weekly **256**

Waterfalls Online **47**

Way **277**

Weather Channel **263**

Web Go Page Index **352**

Web of Life **295**

Web News Index **258**

Web Warehouse **309**

Web Yahtzee **353**

WebCube **352**

Webfoot's Guide to the British Virgin Islands **362**

Webfoot's Guide to Spain **366**

Weblynx Forum **304**

WebMuseum **75**

Web-O-Rhythm **271**

WebPersonals **379**

Webreference.com **33**

WebRunner Running Page **342**

Website Promoters Resource Center **152**

WebSlots **352**

Webspace **12**

WebSpades **352**

Webtender: An On-Line Bartender. **186**

Webville and Hypertext Railroad Company **191**

Wedding Source **379**

Weekly Freebie Compilation **304**

Weight Training Page **347**

Weisman Art Museum **75**

Welcome to Delphi Internet **25**

Welcome to the Gamble House **66**

Welcome to Glensheen **67**

Welcome to the Planets **287**

Welcome! **56**

Wellness Web Senior's Center **239**

Wells Fargo & Co. **119**

Werner's "Not Disney" Theme Parks, Fairs, and Amusement Parks **364**

West Coast Online Inc. **21**

West Virginia: West Virginia State Main Page **227**

Western Michigan University Division of Continuing Education **171**

Western Square Dancing **178**

Western Virginia Retirement Guide **133**

WhaleNet **295**

White House Offices and Agencies **212**

White House World Wide Web **212**

White Rabbit Toys **314**

Whitney Museum of American Art **76**

Widow Net **380**

Wild Mushrooms **186**

Wild, Wacky World of Marty Z—Senior Citizen **385**

William Faulkner on the Web **90**

Williamsburg Online **101**

Windows News and Reviews **10**

Windows to the Universe **296**

Windsor Castle **63**

Wine Lovers' OnLine Searchable Database **186**

Wine.Com **187**

Wines on the Internet **187**

WinNET Communications Inc. **21**

Wisconsin **41**

Wisconsin: Wisconsin Government **227**

Wiyot Indian Table Bluff Tribe and Community **229**

Wolf Park Home Page **296**

Wolverine Antique Music Society **205**

Women's Business Resource Site **152**

Wonderful Stitches **195**

Woodworking Catalog **195**

Woodworking Photo Gallery **195**

Woodworking at WoodWeb **195**

Word **177**

World Art Treasures **71**

World of Escher **71**

World Factbook 1995 **224**

World Health Organization **24**

World Lecture Hall **171**

World of Mayan Culture **89**

World Radio Network **263**

World Real Estate Network **137**

World Scripture **111**

World Skiing **343**

World War I, World War II, Easy to Understand Books **89**

World War II Revisited **89**

World War II: The World Remembers **89**

World Wide Arts Resources **71**

World Wide Drugs **248**

World Wide Jazz Web **206**

World Wide Web of Sports **348**

World Wide Web Ouija **271**

World Wide Web Virtual Library: Facets of Religion **111**

World Wide Web Virtual Library: Museums **101**

Worlds of Late Antiquity **90**

WorldWide Cemetery **380**

WorldWide Classroom **171**

World-Wide Collectors Digest **192**

Worldwide Internet Live Music Archive **206**

World-Wide Sushi Restaurant Reference **187**

World-Wide Web Virtual Library: Architecture **66**

World-Wide Web Virtual Library: Archive X **280**

World-Wide Web Virtual Library: Classical Music **206**

World-Wide Web Virtual Library: Dance **178**

World-Wide Web Virtual Library: Education **171**

World-Wide Web Virtual Library: Electronic Journals **256**

World-Wide Web Virtual Library: Gardening **189**

World-Wide Web Virtual Library: Music **206**

World-Wide Web Virtual Library: Sportsfishing **346**

World-Wide Web Virtual Library: UFOs **280**

WorldWide Wellness **239**

Worldwide Yellow Pages **26**

WWW Bicycle Lane **339**

WWW Hockey Guide **341**

WWW Martial Arts Resources Page **341**

WWW Resources for French as A Second Language Learning **171**

WWW Snooker Home Page **347**

WWW Virtual Library: History **89**

Wyandot Nation of Kansas **229**

Wyoming: State Government **227**

Y

Yahoo—Regional: U.S. States **364**

Yemen Language Center International Office **171**

Your Essential Daily Zodiac Forecast **271**

Your Lucky Fortune Cookie **271**

Your Small Office **155**

Z

ZD Net **256**

ZDNet University **171**

Zen Garden **277**

Ziff/Davis Press **10**

Zonpower from Cyberspace **277**